Climbing and Hiking in the Wind River Mountains

Third edition

Joe Kelsey

FALCONGUIDES

GUILFORD, CONNECTICUT
HELENA, MONTANA
AN IMPRINT OF **ROWMAN & LITTLEFIELD**

FalconGuides is an imprint of Rowman & Littlefield.
Falcon, FalconGuides, and Outfit Your Mind are registered trademarks of Rowman & Littlefield.

Photos by Joe Kelsey
Maps: Alena Joy Pearce © Rowman & Littlefield
Topos: Sue Murray © Rowman & Littlefield

Disributed by NATIONAL BOOK NETWORK

Library of Congress Cataloging-in-Publication Data

Kelsey, Joe, 1938–
  Climbing and hiking in the Wind River Mountains / Joe Kelsey. — Third edition.
    pages cm
  Includes index.
  ISBN 978-0-7627-8078-5
  1. Mountaineering—Wyoming—Wind River Range—Guidebooks. 2. Hiking—Wyoming—Wind River Range—Guidebooks. 3. Wind River Range (Wyo.)—Guidebooks. I. Title.
  GV199.42.W82W565 2013
  796.52209787'6–dc23
                                                                                    2013012493

Printed in the United States of America

WARNING:

Climbing is a sport where you may be seriously injured or die. Read this before you use this book.

This guidebook is a compilation of unverified information gathered from many different climbers. The author cannot ensure the accuracy of any of the information in this book, including the topos and route descriptions, the difficulty ratings, and the protection ratings. These may be incorrect or misleading, as ratings of climbing difficulty and danger are always subjective and depend on the physical characteristics (for example, height), experience, technical ability, confidence, and physical fitness of the climber who supplied the rating. Additionally, climbers who achieve first ascents sometimes underrate the difficulty or danger of the climbing route. Therefore, be warned that you must exercise your own judgment on where a climbing route goes, its difficulty, and your ability to safely protect yourself from the risks of rock climbing. Examples of some of these risks are: falling due to technical difficulty or due to natural hazards such as holds breaking, falling rock, climbing equipment dropped by other climbers, hazards of weather and lightning, your own equipment failure, and failure or absence of fixed protection.

You should not depend on any information gleaned from this book for your personal safety; your safety depends on your own good judgment, based on experience and a realistic assessment of your climbing ability. If you have any doubt as to your ability to safely climb a route described in this book, do not attempt it.

The following are some ways to make your use of this book safer:

1. Consultation: You should consult with other climbers about the difficulty and danger of a particular climb prior to attempting it. Most local climbers are glad to give advice on routes in their area; we suggest that you contact locals to confirm ratings and safety of particular routes and to obtain first-hand information about a route chosen from this book.

2. Instruction: Most climbing areas have local climbing instructors and guides available. We recommend that you engage an instructor or guide to learn safety techniques and to become familiar with the routes and hazards of the areas described in this book. Even after you are proficient in climbing safely, occasional use of a guide is a safe way to raise your climbing standard and learn advanced techniques.

3. Fixed Protection: Some of the routes in this book may use bolts and pitons that are permanently placed in the rock. Because of variances in the manner of placement, weathering, metal fatigue, the quality of the metal used, and many other factors, these fixed protection pieces should always be considered suspect and should always be backed up by equipment that you place yourself. Never depend on a single piece of fixed protection for your safety, because you never can tell whether it will hold weight. In some cases, fixed protection may have been removed or is now missing. However, climbers should not always add new pieces of protection unless existing protection is faulty. Existing protection can be tested by an experienced climber and its strength determined. Climbers are strongly encouraged not to add bolts and drilled pitons to a route. They need to climb the route in the style of the first ascent party (or better) or choose a route within their ability—a route to which they do not have to add additional fixed anchors.

Be aware of the following specific potential hazards that could arise in using this book:

1. Incorrect Descriptions of Routes: If you climb a route and you have a doubt as to where it goes, you should not continue unless you are sure that you can go that way safely. Route descriptions and topos in this book could be inaccurate or misleading.

2. Incorrect Difficulty Rating: A route might be more difficult than the rating indicates. Do not be lulled into a false sense of security by the difficulty rating.

3. Incorrect Protection Rating: If you climb a route and you are unable to arrange adequate protection from the risk of falling through the use of fixed pitons or bolts and by placing your own protection devices, do not assume that there is adequate protection available higher just because the route protection rating indicates the route does not have an X or an R rating. Every route is potentially an X (a fall may be deadly), due to the inherent hazards of climbing—including, for example, failure or absence of fixed protection, your own equipment's failure, or improper use of climbing equipment.

There are no warranties, whether expressed or implied, that this guidebook is accurate or that the information contained in it is reliable. There are no warranties of fitness for a particular purpose or that this guide is merchantable. Your use of this book indicates your assumption of the risk that it may contain errors and is an acknowledgment of your own sole responsibility for your climbing safety.

Contents

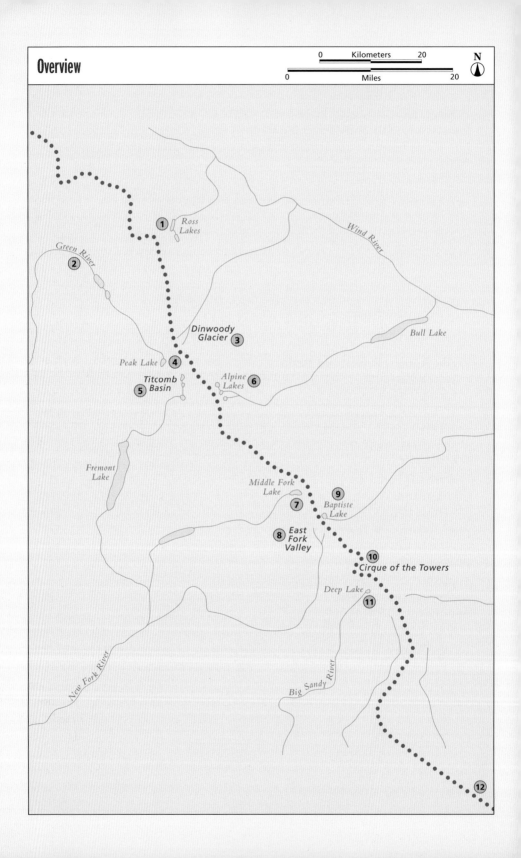

Kilometers

Miles

N

Ross Lakes ①

Wind River

Green River ②

Bull Lake

Dinwoody Glacier ③

Peak Lake ④

Titcomb Basin ⑤

Alpine Lakes ⑥

Fremont Lake

Middle Fork Lake ⑦

⑨

Baptiste Lake

East Fork Valley ⑧

⑩

Cirque of the Towers

Deep Lake

⑪

New Fork River

Big Sandy River

⑫

Preface

In the late seventies, to gather information for the first edition of this guidebook, I wrote letters, affixing a 15 cent stamp and enclosing a stamped, self-addressed envelope. I treasure as keepsakes the fat envelopes returned by the likes of Fred Beckey and Finis Mitchell. I was in Jackson Hole, as were many climbers I needed info from, and would visit them, equipped with a notebook, a six-pack, and a box of slides. By the time I was gathering info for the second edition, in the early nineties, there was an innovation called e-mail, and the six-packs were no longer necessary. For this third edition e-mail remains the most important communication tool, but there are also even more sophisticated devices. Websites, notably mountainproject.com, are devoted to the reporting of new routes. And there is Google Earth. A route was reported in the *American Alpine Journal* with an accompanying photo, but I couldn't correlate it with anything on a topographic map. So I launched myself in Google Earth and soared around till I found a perfect match, the indisputable evidence being background peaks. I could imagine the day when a guidebook writer could appear authoritative without leaving his desk.

But not to worry: I haven't given up the actual mountains. I continue to spend as much of each summer as I can wandering the Wind Rivers, and my experience isn't all that different from what it was during the seventies. Pingora may not offer the thrill of discovery that it did in 1969, but I may have been as thrilled to discover, a year ago, a valley, within sight of Pingora and within a few hundred feet of the trail, that I hadn't known existed. And just last year I needed information from an old friend who has resisted electronic mail. I contacted him by a letter with a 44-cent stamp.

While the list of people to whom I am grateful has grown too long for individual acknowledgments, the length of the list is a vivid reminder that in our community I am a mere scribe, less an authority than a collector of information. All you contributors should think of this as your book too. And beyond contributors, I'm even more grateful to the people I've shared good times and bad with in the Wind Rivers, and in a way the golden retrievers—these days Julia and Katy—I share the trails with and who get more from a backcountry adventure than those of us who rely on books and maps.

I particularly thank John Burbidge, Julie Marsh, and Ann Seifert at FalconGuides for bringing a twentieth-century guidebook into the twenty-first century and converting my collection of personal notes, e-mail exchanges, online posts, and Baby Brownie snapshots into a coherent, hopefully useful guide. I will admit having been concerned that the additional photography would diminish everyone's chance for adventure. Then I had two thoughts: that the photos should stir your imagination and suggest possibilities, and that the photos cover only a tiny fraction of the range.

When I was compiling the first edition, geologist David Love explained that everything he or I wrote was a work in progress. Now, twenty-two years and two editions later, I'm still involved in a work in progress. I haven't even given up the dream that somewhere, at the head of some valley I have yet to discover, stands another Pingora, another Wolf's Head.

The Wind River Mountains are supposed by the Indians to be the home of the spirits, and they believe a person can see the spirit land, or the land they will occupy after death, from the top of them. They are fond of describing the beauties of this land, and the enjoyments and pleasures they will find therein: fresh and pure streams; wide prairies covered with grass and flowers, and abounding in deer; beautiful squaws to wait upon them; horses, always ready and never tired, to take part in the chase; new lodges supplied with every comfort, and provisions and meat so plentiful that they will never again suffer the pangs of hunger.

They believe that when a good Indian dies, he falls into a beautiful stream of bright, fresh water, and is carried to the pleasant grounds I have described. When an old man is dying he finds himself near the top of a high hill on the Wind River Mountains, and, as the breath leaves his body, he reaches the top of it, and there, in front of him, the whole magnificent landscape of eternity is spread out, and the Sun-Father is there to receive him and to do everything in his power to make him happy.

—*Col. Albert G. Brackett*
"The Shoshonis, or Snake Indians, Their Religion, Superstitions, and Manners"
Annual Report, Smithsonian Institution, 1879

Bald Mountain Basin

Introduction to the Wind River Mountains

Eighteen million acres of northwestern Wyoming and adjacent slivers of Idaho and Montana constitute a vast, mountainous ecosystem—the Greater Yellowstone, the largest reasonably intact ecosystem left in the Lower 48 or in any temperate climate on earth. Nearly all the plant and animal species that existed here before the European conquest of the continent remain, if not in their earlier abundance, and are able to migrate between components of the ecosystem. While the forests, mountains, lakes, rivers, and meadows within the boundaries of Yellowstone National Park constitute the core of this system, the Greater Yellowstone also includes several surrounding mountain ranges, including the Tetons, Gros Ventres, Beartooths, Absarokas, Wyoming Range, and Wind River Mountains. The Wind Rivers, a southeastern outlier, protruding into the high plains that stretch across eastern and southern Wyoming, contain all but a few of the highest peaks of the Greater Yellowstone.

In the late 1700s French trappers ascending the Missouri learned from Indians of a major tributary that crosses present-day Montana. This river, the Yellowstone, has a tributary named the Bighorn, which flows from a canyon in northern Wyoming. Upstream from the canyon the river changes both direction and name. Becoming the Wind River (a translation of the Crow Indian name), it flows southeast parallel to a mountain chain that was thus named the Wind River Mountains.

Most of the crest of the Wind River Mountains forms a section of the Continental Divide, separating the Wind River's Atlantic-bound drainage from tributaries of the Green River, which flows across the plains of southern Wyoming to join the Colorado in Utah's canyonlands. However, at the range's southeastern end, the Continental Divide splits from the crest. An area west of the crest is drained by the Sweetwater River, which, rounding the range's southern tip, flows east to the Platte and hence the Missouri. A small section of the Wind Rivers' northwest corner drains to the Snake River and eventually the Columbia.

The Wind Rivers' crest runs northwest-southeast, so the range has northeast and southwest sides—inconvenient when trying to give concise directions. To improve readability this guide often considers the crest to run north-south, with a west (Green River) side and an east (Wind River) side.

Geologically and by definition the Wind Rivers extend from South Pass northwest as far as Togwotee Pass. However, the non-alpine expanse from Union Pass to Togwotee Pass is of interest to few hikers and fewer climbers, so this guide treats Union Pass as the range's northwest terminus.

Climbing

The Wind Rivers, being composed of rock well suited to climbing and with peaks as high as 13,000 feet that enjoy relatively sunny skies, might seem a likely range for mountaineering to reach its fullest development. Yet as Chris Jones puts it in

1

Climbing in North America, "The Wind Rivers have a history of their own, but . . . they have contributed little to the development of North American climbing." The above-average weather perhaps retarded the progress of Wind River climbing. A dry climate kept Wyoming unpopulated, and the lack of snow prevented the mountains from resembling the Alps, where the sport's styles and aesthetics originated.

When American rock climbing came of age, and climbers brought to the high country their newly developed skills and techniques from Yosemite, the Colorado and Utah foothills, and the Shawangunks, they created splendid routes in the Wind Rivers. However, rock climbing continued to extend its limits, not in remote areas like the Wind Rivers, but where other aspects of life were more convenient. Solitude and scenery count for little when technical significance is assessed, and remoteness is now measured relative to Tierra del Fuego and the Tien Shan.

If the Wind Rivers offer little to fame-seekers, they offer less to someone out to impress the workaday world. Pingora is not a household byword; you'll gain more adulation by climbing the Grand Teton. Nevertheless, many of America's best-known climbers have touched Wind River rock. The first ascent list includes the names Ellingwood, Henderson, Underhill, Petzoldt, Stettner, Kraus, Steck, Beckey, Chouinard, Kor, Pratt, Robbins, and Lowe.

When a journal carries the account of a climb, you learn something about the styles, tools, and attitudes prevalent in the area. At crowded crags you may feel pressure to conform, to play the game. But Wind River climbing is largely ignored by journals, purists, and officialdom. You can climb for days without encountering fellow climbers. You are constrained only to climb in a style that you find satisfying, that requires no more gear than you can pack, that does not get you into a predicament you cannot get yourself out of, and does not damage the land. This freedom may partly explain the range's attraction to climbers who have already made a name in the climbing world.

A guidebook, fortunately, cannot dictate climbing style. The mountains' characteristics—size, rock, weather, and remoteness—and their history do. Unavoidably, however, an author describes routes according to his experience, aesthetics, and whims. I've tried to minimize imposing myself by adapting my writing to what I perceive to be the Wind Rivers and their traditions.

Wind River climbers have traditionally taken pride in self-reliance. Most prefer the pleasures of solving routefinding dilemmas to the efficiency of guidebook recipes. This book's primary purpose is to help you enjoy the mountains; keeping you on route is secondary. Assuming you would rather know *what* to climb than *how* to climb it, I make an effort to characterize a route, even when details are sparse. And details often suggest a route's flavor more than they ensure success. When the book is working properly, details lead you to more adventure than you would find on your own.

Pingora, Northeast Face

Read the description or study the photo while studying a route from below. If the reading is sufficient to get you up the climb, leave the book behind; we will both have succeeded. Once on a route, respect your own judgment; you are there, looking at and touching the rock. Instructions are phrased as commands ("traverse left") for the sake of brevity and because of my faith that climbers are anarchists who will freely ignore imperatives. In particular, instructions to use aid indicate only that I or the first ascent team did—not that you should.

Photos are intended to give a sense of a route, not to prevent you from straying. When I have a choice of photos, I tend to select a distant view that shows a route's setting over a close-up on which you can identify ledges and cracks. You'll find it difficult to stand 3 feet from a wall and try to see the rock as a camera did from a mile away. Moreover, some route lines are drawn more precisely than others. Nontechnical routes are deliberately drawn imprecisely.

While this guide tries to promote the spirit of adventure, many climbers learn to follow a route by referring to a topo. I've therefore included topos of some popular routes. I hope they help you get up some climbs, but I also hope you study the actual rock, and, if a way other than the topo's makes more sense to you, you try your way. And I hope the climb gives you the confidence to then try routes that are not so fully documented.

Stating guidebook philosophy is easier than applying it to 900 routes. I've learned about routes by climbing them twenty times, and I've learned about routes by finding a nearly illegible note in a tobacco tin/summit register. Many routes have had only one ascent. Most haven't been climbed enough that a well-defined topo line can be drawn to represent them.

Writers of ascent accounts determine not only the accuracy of the information but also the amount of information. Some reports itemize hardware requirements; others don't. I suspect some accounts here of extraneous detail, but if I don't personally know a route, I'm reluctant to edit out detail. A surprising number of summit registers describe otherwise unreported routes. Sometimes the detail is extravagant and presumably quite accurate, though typically the entry includes only a compass direction, a few names, and a date.

The only information about certain routes is what Orrin and Lorraine Bonney included in *Guide to the Wyoming Mountains and Wilderness Areas*. Since I choose not to be responsible for the accuracy of their information, I haven't used their guide for details, but for completeness I do mention the routes.

This guide is without a doubt incomplete. Wind River climbers are more casual about reporting exploits than climbers in most areas. The fact that a ridge or face—or even a peak—isn't mentioned here doesn't mean it hasn't been climbed (though if you climb it, I encourage you to report your climb).

A note about topos: Topos of other climbing areas typically indicate the type of climbing: "thin hands," "stem," "layback," etc. The scarcity of such notation on topos here doesn't reflect stinginess in providing information but rather a characteristic of

Wind River cracks that to me enhances climbing. A crack here seldom stays uniform long enough for you to use one technique repetitively. Move by move you must decide whether to jam, stem, layback, or face climb, so a topo can't endorse a single technique.

Pitch lengths pose a dilemma. Most routes described here were first climbed—and climbed by me, if I've climbed them—with 50-meter (165-foot) ropes. You are probably climbing with a 60-meter (200-foot) or even a 70-meter (230-foot) rope and can stretch pitches beyond what a topo or route description indicates. However, some savvy veterans have found that nearly all Wind River routes can comfortably be climbed with 50-meter ropes, thus reducing weight and rope-handling. In fact, a few recent first ascents of hard routes have been accomplished with 50-meter ropes. So climb with whatever length rope you are comfortable and use mountain sense when deciding where to belay. If you need guidance, assume that a route first climbed in 1961 was climbed with a 50-meter rope. If a route was first climbed in the twenty-first century, it was probably climbed with a 60-meter rope or longer. (First ascenders who believe that 70-meter ropes are essential generally make a point of reporting such, and I make a point of relaying such information.)

The arrangement of route descriptions, with some arguably subsidiary summits treated as separate peaks and others lumped with the main summit, isn't determined by rigorous topographic criteria. Rather the aim is to make this book readable, and one criterion is whether climbers generally consider a subsidiary summit to be a destination, even if topographically insignificant, or a satellite to be crossed en route to a less ambiguous summit. Wolf's Head, topographically a minor summit of Bollinger Peak, is a separate peak in this book.

A majority of Wind River formations have a walk-up way to the top (and walk-down descent route), and such routes should be obvious from the guidebook and/or by looking at the formation. Descent routes are described only when I feel they need to be. When there is more than one descent route, I often give pros and cons of each.

Two important rock climbing areas near the range's south end—Sinks Canyon and Wild Iris—aren't included in this guide. Greg Collins and Vance White, who know these areas intimately, feature them in *Lander Rock*. Wesley Gooch's *Rock Climbing Jackson Hole & Pinedale, Wyoming* is a day-climbing guide to the range's western foothills.

First ascent data is relegated to the back of the book. History is thus recorded, but without you stumbling over names while locating the start of a route.

Safety

Experienced climbers respect high, remote mountains and are wary even of the Wind Rivers' comparatively solid rock, benign weather, and crevasse-free glaciers. However, many climbers learn the sport on low, densely populated crags where routes are well-defined by bolts and chalk, difficulties precisely assessed by numerous ascents, holds well-tested, and rescues quick. Some aspects of mountaineering safety are worth mentioning.

Few environments offer as much freedom as mountains such as the Wind Rivers—or affect you so immediately and drastically with the consequences of what you do. A climber in the Wind Rivers must be self-reliant. Any accident is more serious when you're in a remote area, so you should be more cautious, climb somewhat easier routes perhaps, or not run it out as far. If a route is longer than those you're familiar with, pay extra attention to routefinding, weather, and time. I often take an extra rope I wouldn't carry on a comparable Yosemite route. However, a heavier pack doesn't necessarily translate to increased safety, and you must balance a piece of equipment's potential usefulness with its potential for slowing you down.

Most Wind River climbing accidents are attributable to three phenomena: loose rock, lightning, and the slipperiness of snow and ice. My closest calls have involved holds breaking and electricity. Overall the rock is as solid as mountain rock gets, but any rock that is unclimbed or seldom climbed (especially rock subjected to freezing water) isn't entirely trustworthy. Be especially skeptical of flakes that look too good to be true.

During summer the Wind Rivers seldom experience multiday storms that suppress all desire to climb. More typical are days that begin with clear skies that turn into thunderstorms. About the only way to predict such activity is to suspect that if a storm occurs at a certain time one day, another one is more likely to hit about the same time the next day. To minimize exposure to electrical storms, begin early, move efficiently, and don't forget to watch the sky. If a storm does catch you, try not to be perched on a lightning rod. (Ten percent or more of teams on Wolf's Head's *East Ridge* experience electricity; at least one fatality and two nonfatal direct hits have occurred.)

The lack of snow and ice in the Wind Rivers is a cause of accidents on snow and ice. Unless you're in the Dinwoody Glacier or Titcomb Basin areas, you're unlikely to carry an ice axe, but the infrequent snow and ice you encounter is nevertheless slippery.

Be wary of fixed pitons. Most were placed years ago, and few of us now carry hammers with which to properly test (and, if necessary, re-drive) them. Test rappel pitons as best you can—with stones, large hexes, shafts of cams—and be completely satisfied before trusting them. Perhaps back them up with an additional, temporary anchor while the first person rappels. Be similarly careful with rappel webbing. The nylon deteriorates, especially in sunlight, and the fact that it held the previous rappeller at some unknown time in the past doesn't guarantee that it will hold you.

Wind River rescues are directed by the sheriffs of Sublette and Fremont Counties. However, when a technical rescue is required, they immediately call local mountain-rescue groups. In my experience these locals are highly competent, but if a rescue requires extraordinary expertise, they in turn call Grand Teton rangers. Victims are billed for such expenses as helicopter time and horse rental.

Don't comb the backcountry looking for a ranger; backcountry rangers are sparse these days. During summer, though, you may find a ranger at Green River Lakes, Elkhart Park, or Big Sandy Opening, or just below at Dutch Joe Guard Station but are better off calling from a cell phone, if you have one, or borrowing one, though coverage is spotty. The higher you are, the better your chances. For example, phones work from the tops of Gannett and Camel's Hump, marginally from Pingora, and from just the right places near Jackass Pass. You won't get through from the Big Sandy Opening trailhead, but if you drive a few miles out, to the lower end of the meadow, your chances are good. Wherever you call from, call 911.

Equipment

This book strives to keep the adventure in climbing. However, I don't believe carrying unnecessary equipment enhances the adventure, so I try to make suggestions when information is available, and needs aren't obvious.

Many equipment considerations apply throughout the range. The nubbly granite gives cracks an irregular texture especially well-suited for nuts. Most cracks are 1 inch or less wide; in the absence of further information, carry a rack that emphasizes stoppers. I normally don't carry pieces for cracks wider than 3 inches unless I expect to need them. In this guide I make a point of mentioning the need for big pieces—when I have that information. Likewise the use of pitons has become so rare that I mention their need—almost always on a big wall—again, when I have that information.

While you probably won't carry a hammer if you don't carry pitons, you should know that, despite being high mountains bounded by arid plains, many Wind River cracks are surprisingly vegetated, especially on unclimbed or seldom-climbed routes. One solution is a light hammer with a curved pick for gardening, but an extra nut tool for the leader is usually adequate.

Bolts don't require as intense a discussion as they might in a lowland guide. Most climbers take pride in the Wind Rivers' wilderness aura. Perhaps more importantly, a power drill (in addition to being illegal) means a heavier pack than most are willing to shoulder, and extensive hand-drilling requires more time than most are willing to squander, especially as there is little incentive to place bolts that the mainstream will deem at best superfluous, at worst intrusive. You could place a line of bolts in the middle of nowhere, and, so no one would take offense, not publicize your feat, but other than self-gratification, you would accomplish little. Most routes follow vertical crack systems, and bolts that appear near cracks are likely to disappear—quietly, without letters to an editor. Within the past twenty years rappel bolts have now and then appeared, near cracks, where a newer route intersected a popular existing route, presumably to spare climbers the indignity of following easier rock to the summit and the standard descent route. The bolts, which had the feel of a mannered stylistic statement, akin to wearing your cap backward, suffered frontier justice.

It is also worth considering that "fixed anchors"—mainly meaning bolts—in wilderness areas has been a sensitive issue with the Forest Service. Promiscuous bolting, while not at present illegal, could give the Forest Service cause to revisit the issue. Climbers' organizations such as The Access Fund have been working with the Forest Service to come up with a policy regarding climbing in Wilderness that we all can live with. The following are among the main points of the proposed policy, at least in its present draft version: Climbing that does not rely on fixed anchors should be the norm. Fixed anchors are appropriate where necessary for rappelling when no other safe means of descent are available. Extensive bolt placement is inappropriate in Wilderness. And, of course, motorized drills and chipping and gluing holds are prohibited.

It appears to me that this agreement reflects the attitude of an overwhelming majority of Wind River climbers, perhaps more than at almost any other climbing venue. A minuscule number of climbers visiting the Wind Rivers carry a bolt kit. For most of us, it actually enhances the sport's dignity to have to trudge across a formation's upper slopes to locate a feasible descent, rather than simply turning around at the end of difficulties and sliding down ropes directly to our approach shoes.

Nevertheless, I can imagine a bolted face route so well conceived and executed that many of us who try to balance climbing values with wilderness values would want to climb it. Just be sure you carry out such a project without losing either a sense of the sport's dignity or a reverence for the rock.

Perhaps we should concoct our own definition of wilderness: a place where we are free to place bolts but refrain because of our sense of wilderness.

You'll need an ice axe on routes done from the northern glaciers, but you can climb a majority of Wind River routes and descend from most peaks without one. Ice axes are seldom useful in the range's southern half. You should be able to determine the need for an axe from maps and route descriptions.

You won't need heavy mountaineering boots to keep your feet dry, except for snow and ice climbing or very early in summer. Light hiking shoes, even running shoes, are sufficient to get you into the mountains. You may want to carry comfortable shoes up long routes to avoid a long descent in climbing shoes.

Rating Difficulty

Routes (and pitches) are rated according to the system developed in the Alps a century ago and adapted by the Sierra Club during the 1930s. A route is assigned to a class from 1 to 6. Class 1 is hiking; class 2, scrambling in rougher terrain in which, according to the traditional definition, "proper footgear is advised." Class 3 climbing requires handholds but not a rope, while class 4 indicates a rope for belays but no protection between belays. Class 5 is free climbing where the leader places protection between belays, and class 6 entails direct aid.

Fifth-class ratings are made more precise (except when information isn't available) by the decimal system devised at Tahquitz Rock during the 1950s and now prevalent throughout America. According to this system the easiest 5th-class route is rated 5.0, and 5.1, 5.2, etc. are progressively more difficult. The system stretches the definition of decimal by rating the hardest climbs 5.10, 5.11, 5.12, etc. A climb's rating may be further refined by a + or – (e.g., 5.9+) or, for climbs of 5.10 or higher, a letter from a to d (5.10a being the easiest 5.10, 5.10d the hardest).

If a route involves artificial aid of any sort (except rappelling, which is mentioned separately), the aid's difficulty is indicated by an A followed by a number. A1 once indicated the easiest aid, but A0 is now used for trivial aid (e.g., clipping a bolt). At the scale's upper end, rating nuances try to distinguish merely difficult from dangerous, but no Wind River aid merits a rating of more than A4.

The Winds Rivers aren't an ice climbing arena, so I mostly use a simple system, analogous to the classes of rock climbing, to rate snow/ice routes. Snow 2 indicates you don't need an ice axe, Snow 3 that you need an axe but not a rope, Snow/Ice 4 that you need a rope and a belay but no protection between belays, and Snow/Ice 5 that you're likely to place protection—either in ice or nearby rock—between belays. Most of the 5th-class ice routes in the Wind Rivers are WI2 or WI3 (WI meaning seasonal water ice).

In addition a Roman numeral grade assesses the overall effort, expertise, and commitment a route requires. The grade takes into account the time required, the sum of difficulties, and whatever intangibles affect a route's seriousness. A Grade I may be 2nd-class scrambling, or have one 5.8 pitch but otherwise be scrambling and take only a few hours. A Grade IV generally involves moderate or hard 5th-class climbing and takes a competent team most of a day. A Grade V traditionally requires more than a day, while a VI typically takes at least two days and involves either difficult free and aid or extensive, extremely difficult free climbing.

The above suggests that attaching numbers to routes is a scientific process. However, ratings don't so much measure the physical properties of rock as they do humanity's interaction with it, so scientific objectivity isn't possible.

Ratings aren't applied uniformly in different parts of the country, and the Wind Rivers attract climbers from the East, Midwest, Wyoming, Colorado, Utah, California, and the Northwest. For this reason alone, inconsistency is inevitable. Also there is a suspicion among us elders that the decimal system has been softening. I've tried to stick to the original standards without being overly severe.

Moreover, while consensus ratings evolve for popular routes, many Wind River routes have had but one ascent. I suspect certain climbers of overrating or underrating climbs, but if someone submits an account to a journal or website or sends me a description, I owe him/her the courtesy of accepting the rating until I do the route myself.

The archaic definition of 2nd class, with its "proper footgear," implies you can climb a 1st-class route with anything (or nothing) on your feet, which is probably true for the few routes rated 1st class.

In the 1980 guidebook I gave 2nd class a whimsical definition, thinking it was safely buried in the introduction where no one would read it: "I will confess distinguishing between class 2 and 3 . . . according to my golden retrievers' ability to do a route." Ironically, this turned out to be the book's most-quoted passage. I should have known that on rainy days, tent-bound climbers read anything. (I've been questioned for tying dogs below Pingora's south shoulder, because "the guy who wrote the guide says reaching the shoulder is 3rd class, and dogs can only do class 2.")

I abandoned this apparently "scientific" distinction, between 2nd and 3rd class for two reasons: Now that I purposely gather guidebook data, I consciously note my use of handholds; and, having now roamed the hills for forty years with the beasts, one first as a four-month-old puppy and eventually a veteran of fifteen Wind River summers, I've seen a range of abilities, including the ability to reach Pingora's south shoulder (but not descend from it). Much 2nd and 3rd class involves blocks and boulders, and boulders too big for a dog don't necessarily make a route 3rd class.

Except for situations of extreme youth, age, disability, or weather, you shouldn't need a rope in 3rd-class terrain. The distinction between 3rd and 4th class is less a matter of difficulty than exposure. On such 3rd-class routes as Fremont Peak's and Warbonnet's, short slabs and chimneys require a bit of footwork and technique, but a slip wouldn't drop you more than a few feet.

The concept of 4th class—a leader facing falls of up to 400 feet while followers climb with a tight rope—has long been enigmatic. Fourth class makes sense only when one member of a team is markedly more competent than another—for instance, on a guided climb. A guide myself, I use 4th class as a signal to fellow guides to bring a rope for a generic client.

Many obscure routes haven't been climbed, that I know of, since the advent of the decimal system. When accounts of such ascents mention pitons, I simply describe the route as 5th class and don't try to be more precise.

Most of us are aware that Roman numeral grades are inherently subjective and vague. However, whether a route is a IV or a V is an important factor in deciding whether to haul bivouac gear, and we'd like a more precise distinction than an early definition of Grade V that said, "like IV, but limited to experts." The guidebook's rating, though, can't decide for you. The 1981 *American Alpine Journal (AAJ)* reported a Wind River first ascent done in a day and rated V. Another report included a complaint that the guidebook, by rating a route a V, burdened the party with bivouac gear on a one-day climb. Guidebooks can indicate how long a first ascent took (and by whom and in what year), but when you should be prepared for a night on a mountain wall must remain one of the critical decisions that no one can make for you.

Recommended Routes

Most climbers care at least as much about a route's quality as about its difficulty. During the 1970s, when we had to evaluate a route's desirability by looking at it, the Cirque of the Towers offered several dozen routes. After the publication of Steve Roper and Allen Steck's *Fifty Classic Climbs of North America* in 1979, the list dwindled to Wolf's Head's *East Ridge* and Pingora's *Northeast Face.* Gannett Peak, as Wyoming's highest, also attracted inordinate attention, but other worthy routes were virtually ignored.

George Bell Jr. revealed the secret to *Fifty Classic Climbs* in the 1989 *Ascent,* at the end of a piece titled "Fifty Crowded Classics": "[returning to] the Winds, I was amazed as we completed climb after climb, all beautiful lines on excellent rock and of

Wolf's Head, East Ridge

remarkably similar nature to the two Classics just across the way. It brought home a point that I had not realized on my first trip to the Winds: that in any area containing one of the Fifty, numerous other climbs of comparable quality lay nearby."

The status of classic should result from a consensus of many climbers who have done a climb. In the Wind Rivers such a consensus isn't generally possible; in the mountains climbers are too concentrated to check out many potential classics and, away from the mountains, too dispersed to compare notes. The bane of recommended route lists is the euphoria expressed by first ascenders but no one else.

Therefore, the list below reflects my personal favorites—and not much more. I've done most of the routes but have included a few spoken highly of by at least two teams who did not make the first ascent. There are undoubtedly modern, hard routes that deserve a place on the list, but they haven't been climbed enough to establish them as classics. Asterisks mark my special favorites.

Gannett Peak, Gooseneck Glacier Route (I 4th) Dinwoody Glacier ★

Glover Peak, East Ridge (I 2nd) Peak Lake

Mount Arrowhead, South Face Left (III 5.8) Peak Lake

Mount Arrowhead, South Face Right (II 5.7) Peak Lake

Stroud Peak, Southeast Ridge (I 2nd) Peak Lake

Henderson Peak, North Ridge (II 4th) Titcomb Basin ★

Mount Helen, Tower 1 Gully (IV WI 3+) Titcomb Basin

Mount Helen, Tower Ridge (III 5.7) Titcomb Basin

Mount Sacagawea, West Face Right (III 5.9) Titcomb Basin

Fremont Peak, Five-Finger Couloir (II Snow 4) Titcomb Basin

Fremont Peak, West Face Dihedral (IV 5.9 A1) Titcomb Basin

Jackson Peak, North Face, Right Couloir (III Ice 5) Titcomb Basin

Ellingwood Peak, North Arête (III 5.6) Titcomb Basin ★

Prairie Falcon Peak, Southeast Face (III 5.8) Middle Fork Lake

Ambush Peak, North Buttress Center (IV 5.10d) East Fork Valley

Midsummer Dome, South Face Center (III 5.9+) East Fork Valley

Musembeah Peak, West Buttress (IV 5.8 or 5.10a) Baptiste Lake ★

Bollinger Peak, West Pillar (IV 5.10 A0) Cirque of the Towers

Wolf's Head, East Ridge (III 5.6) Cirque of the Towers ★

Pingora Peak, South Buttress (II 5.6 or 5.8) Cirque of the Towers ★

Pingora Peak, East Face Cracks (III 5.7) Cirque of the Towers

Pingora Peak, Northeast Face (IV 5.8) Cirque of the Towers ★

Pingora Peak, Southwest Face Right (III 5.8/5.9) Cirque of the Towers

Overhanging Tower via Ridge Tower (II 5.3) Cirque of the Towers

Shark's Nose, Northwest Buttress (II 5.6) Cirque of the Towers

Shark's Nose, Southwest Face (III 5.8) Cirque of the Towers ★

Shark's Nose, North Face Right (III 5.8) Cirque of the Towers ★

Warbonnet Peak, Black Elk (IV 5.11a) Cirque of the Towers

Mitchell Peak, Ecclesiastes (IV 5.9) Cirque of the Towers

Dog Tooth Peak, A-Frame Buttress (IV 5.9) Cirque of the Towers
Haystack Mountain, North Face (II 5.6) Deep Lake
Haystack Mountain, West Face, Major Dihedral (IV 5.10d) Deep Lake
Haystack Mountain, West Face, Minor Dihedral (III/IV 5.9) Deep Lake ★
Haystack Mountain, West Face, Central Corner (III 5.9) Deep Lake ★
Haystack Mountain, West Face, Southern Wall Center (IV 5.10c) Deep Lake ★
Haystack Mountain, East Pillar (IV 5.9) Deep Lake
Steeple Peak, North Ridge (III 5.8) Deep Lake ★
Lost Temple Spire, Southwest Arête (IV 5.10a) Deep Lake ★
Temple Peak, Northwest Ridge (II 5.3) Deep Lake

Hiking

The nature of the Wind Rivers suggests combining a climbing and hiking guide within one cover. The range is extensive enough, with a complex enough trail system, that climbers need directions for hiking from their car to the base of a peak. Hikers, on the other hand, are often tempted to scramble to summits. In the Wind Rivers climbers and hikers are often indistinguishable.

Scenic Pass

This isn't a beginner's hiking manual. You aren't admonished to eat a warm break-fast or carry extra socks. Nevertheless, while the Wind Rivers demand a certain level of common sense and self-reliance (and some tolerance for wind, mosquitoes, and wet feet), they can be an ideal place for someone with limited experience to learn to wander through mountainous terrain.

Historically the trail system hasn't been a system. It's been trails cleared and marked by the Forest Service; trails shown on maps (even Forest Service maps) but not maintained; old roads closed to vehicles; and paths that evolved because they were useful to climbers, hikers, anglers, hunters, geologists, Indians, trappers, elk, bighorns, sheepherders, and/or seekers of solitude.

The Forest Service doesn't maintain all these roads, trails, and paths for two reasons: Their management plan designates large chunks of wilderness as trailless areas ("with no perceptible evidence of past human use"), and their budget doesn't allow it. They must decide which trails they can realistically afford to maintain. The Wind Rivers' west side has about 600 miles of trail, the Bridger-Teton National Forest estimates that they should schedule 250 miles a year for maintenance, and as of a few years ago, they were funded to maintain 150 to 190.

If the Forest Service includes a trail in its system, you can expect signposts at junctions and blazes or cairns where the trail is obscure or ambiguous. The Forest Service theoretically clears fallen trees yearly, so you shouldn't have to detour deadfall (and deepen the detour till it becomes more visible than the trail). However, popular trails—Big Sandy—for example, get priority, and maintenance crews get to less-traveled trails only when time—and funding—allow.

To paraphrase Forest Service policy: If you stay on maintained trails, you shouldn't have to be able to read a map; if you can't read maps, you shouldn't leave maintained trails. If you can read a map, the Wind Rivers offer unsurpassed country for unfet-tered roaming, and you should feel free to leave the government-sanctioned. How-ever, guidebooks and maps pointing people beyond maintained trails have caused backcountry rangers and Forest Service offices to be besieged with complaints from the recently lost or befuddled. To help keep your trail expectations realistic, this book tries to clearly distinguish maintained trails from what the Forest Service terms "user-developed" and "bootleg" trails. Whether or not a map indicates a trail, be handy at reading maps and keep a map handy. Don't expect signposts at junctions involving unmaintained trails; the Forest Service has removed signs that imply the existence of non-system trails.

There is no official trail system on the Wind River Reservation, and signposts are few. Any maintenance is done by horse packers, who keep the trails they use in shape for their needs.

This guide also mentions cross-country routes. The term *route* refers to a way between points A and B that is too vague to be represented by a line on a map. The route may be locally well defined, as at a feasible stream crossing or a notch in a ridge, but typically it is as broad as the valley it ascends or the plateau it crosses. The distinction between unmaintained trails and cross-country routes is fuzzy, and the Wind Rivers present a spectrum of intermediate situations. In general, though, if a map shows a trail, a trail presumably once existed but was allowed to go to seed. It is worth looking for its track, and you may as well walk on it. But when following a trailless route, don't look for a path and, if you come upon something path-like, don't follow it.

If a trail is maintained, try to stay on it, though I can't insist you rigorously stay on a trail that consists of mudwater-filled horses' hoofprints. If a track is beginning to develop through use in an area you believe should be trailless, walk elsewhere to keep the track from deepening. Those who study land use honestly disagree about intermediate situations, in terms of when you should stay in a trail's main track and when you should avoid a developing track.

The route over 11,400-foot Texas Pass, from Lonesome Lake to Shadow Lake, illustrates contrasting situations. South of the pass is gently rising tundra, where scattered snowpatches linger in pockets. The most efficient route varies with the amount of snow. With sparse signs of human traffic and the Cirque of the Tower's hubbub far below, it seems a good place to not create a trail. North of Texas Pass, though, the

South Fork Little Wind River

talus is a bit steep and unstable for backpacking, and switchbacks formed as hikers repeatedly found the soundest footing. I can't see that the self-sacrifice of avoiding those switchbacks would improve anyone's experience of wilderness. And avoiding the unsanctioned but easily followed path that has evolved along the shores of Barren and Billy's Lakes below would only create duplicate tracks.

Since guidelines are vague, keep in mind the ideal of minimum impact and rely on your instincts and goodwill toward the land. I offer an addendum, though: Don't build cairns. Maintained trails shouldn't need them, and off-trail jaunts shouldn't display such conspicuous signs of human passage. Don't even try to resurrect abandoned trails by reconstructing cairns. If you find cairns along otherwise ill-defined routes, you should feel a righteous urge to scatter the stones, especially in places designated trailless.

You needn't limit your travels to trails and routes mentioned in this book. Other than the mountains and larger streams, the Wind Rivers present few barriers. Much terrain near and above treeline is meadow. You can traverse the large glaciers—with a few precautions—and even follow sections of the Continental Divide for miles.

On trail or off, pay heed to stream crossings. In terrain that, for mountains, is notably friendly to hikers, many streams stand out as obstacles. Especially during June and July, some require you to scout for a way across or engage in annoying wading; others are dangerous or even impossible to cross. Bridges are few, and, according to the Bridger Wilderness Action Plan, "bridges will be built . . . only where no safe opportunities exist to cross a steam during periods of normal water flow." I would characterize stream crossings more precisely were it possible, but streams change during each summer and from year to year.

The Wind Rivers offer splendid opportunities for starting from a trailhead, hiking in a loop, and returning to the trailhead several days (or weeks) later by a different trail. The possibilities are endless, and much of the pleasure for most groups seems to be in concocting such a venture on their own, immersing themselves in maps during winter and spring planning sessions.

If you need ideas for off-trail jaunts, check out Nancy Pallister's *Beyond Trails in the Wind River Mountains of Wyoming*. Don't overlook the CD that comes with it.

Special mention should be made of the Highline and Fremont Trails, which enable you to hike from Green River Lakes to Big Sandy Opening, or vice versa, paralleling the crest on its west side. Traversing relatively open, lake-filled country near treeline, you are never quite in the mountains, but you can make easy excursions to such exemplars of mountain scenery as Island Lake, Middle Fork Lake, and Shadow Lake. From Green River Lakes as far as Pole Creek, the Highline is unambiguous. From Pole Creek to Big Sandy Opening, though, there are two trails, and maps' labeling of one or the other as the Highline has been inconsistent. According to the most recent maps, the trail nearest the mountains is the Fremont Trail; the one to the west is the Highline (see the Middle Fork Lake chapter for more in-depth discussion), but

Near Fremont Crossing

combining the northern Highline with the more rugged, scenic, and recommended Fremont Trail makes more sense. From Green River Lakes to Big Sandy Opening, including the Fremont Trail, is 65 miles; following the maps' Highline the entire way is 72 miles.

Of less interest is the Lowline Trail, which parallels the Highline but in lower country to the west, typically at trailhead elevations. This book mentions the Lowline and other trails that crisscross the low country only when they coincide with trails useful for getting into the mountains.

A classic way to cross the range involves the Glacier Trail from Trail Lake Ranch to Dinwoody Glacier, the glacier to Bonney Pass, a descent to Titcomb Basin, and a hike out to Elkhart Park on the Indian Pass, Seneca Lake, and Pole Creek thoroughfare. You pass under the range's seven highest summits, some of which you may want to detour up. Of note are the ecological differences, not only between different elevations but also between the range's east and west sides.

Maps

The maps in this guide should give an overview of an area and help you decide how to reach it, but the book is meant to be used in conjunction with topographic maps. Maps are so useful for both on- and off-trail travel that with them you hardly need this guide, except perhaps for an overview of the trail network. The book takes place names (with a few quibbles) and elevations directly from topographic maps. It locates peaks and passes using distances and directions on these maps, and refers to unnamed features by their official elevations (e.g., Peak 12,846).

The range is covered by US Geological Survey 7.5-minute quadrangles, with a scale of about 2.5 inches to a mile. Contour lines mark 40-foot intervals. The majority of the USGS sheets were published in 1968 or 1981, recently enough to show most trails accurately. (Much of the South Pass area, however, is covered by 1953 maps that are somewhat dated.) You can find topographic maps in stores in Jackson, Pinedale, Dubois, and Lander.

Earthwalk Press and Beartooth Publishing both publish two pairs of topographic maps of the Wind Rivers (a map on each side of a sheet) using USGS data. One pair from each publisher covers the northern half (this guide's first six chapters), the other the southern half (the last six chapters). Earthwalk's scale is 1:48,000; the contour interval is 40 feet. Beartooth's scale is 1:50,000; the contour interval is 50 feet. The Earthwalk maps are more generous in showing unmaintained and abandoned trails (Bridger Lakes, Hay Pass) and rely on this guidebook for names not given on USGS maps. The Beartooth maps are limited to USGS nomenclature, and "unofficial, secondary trails . . . are not shown, as their routes have not been surveyed and their continued existence cannot be guaranteed." The areas covered are not quite the same, especially at the range's southeast end. Earthwalk's coverage extends southeast only through the area covered by the 7.5-minute Sweetwater Gap quad (to Stough Creek Basin), while Beartooth's coverage extends to WY 28. Earthwalk, on the other hand, extends a bit farther north than Beartooth, though this matters for only a few features, such as Whiskey Mountain. Beartooth gives trail mileages between junctions, to a tenth of a mile.

Unless you are writing a guidebook and squinting through a magnifier counting contour lines, these smaller-scale maps work well. In fact, the detail on 7.5-minute maps—and the need to juxtapose several for a hike of any length—makes it easy to lose sight of the forest because of the trees. Earthwalk's and Beartooth's scales make it easier to see how to get from Trailhead A to Lake B.

Bridger-Teton National Forest publishes a Bridger Wilderness map (though, with the range's northwest-southeast slant, it can't help but cover area east of the Divide also). The scale is 1:63,360, with a contour interval of 50 meters. Trails not part of the official system are not shown, and nomenclature is limited to the USGS's.

USGS Topo Index

USGS Topographic Map Index (7.5-Minute Quadrangles)

1   Union Peak
2   Simpson Lake
3   Torrey Lake
4   Big Sheep Mountain
5   Green River Lakes
6   Downs Mountain
7   Ink Wells
8   Hays Park
9   Kendall Mountain
10   Squaretop Mountain
11   Gannett Peak
12   Fremont Peak North
13   Bob Lakes
14   New Fork Lakes
15   Fremont Lake North
16   Bridger Lakes
17   Fremont Peak South
18   Alpine Lake
19   Paradise Basin
20   St. Lawrence Basin
21   Fremont Lake South
22   Fayette Lake
23   Horseshoe Lake
24   Halls Mountain
25   Roberts Mountain
26   Washakie Park
27   Moccasin Lake
28   Boulder Lake
29   Scab Creek
30   Raid Lake
31   Mount Bonneville
32   Lizard Head Peak
33   Dickinson Park
34   Big Sandy Opening
35   Temple Peak
36   Sweetwater Gap
37   Cony Mountain
38   Fossil Hill
39   Jensen Meadows
40   Sweetwater Needles
41   Christina Lake
42   Louis Lake

Living in Wilderness

A friend, camped at Shadow Lake, watched a fellow circle the lake from a camp-site on the other side and take a soap bath near my friend's camp. To my friend's protest the bather replied, "Don't you know you're supposed to treat your water?" You wonder, of course, why this person circled the lake to bathe, and whether he considered the effect of soapy water on fish (they don't like it). But there's a deeper question: Why did he hike 11 miles to Shadow Lake if its water quality didn't matter to him?

The Wind Rivers are largely protected from abuse by not affording anyone the opportunity to gain riches or fame or a stage on which to demonstrate gymnastic prowess or fashionable sportswear. There isn't much reason to make the effort required to visit the Wind Rivers unless you believe in something—something encompassed, however imprecisely, by the term *wilderness*. If you believe in the concept of wilderness and you're in the Wind Rivers, you must believe that humanity can find a legitimate niche in wilderness.

We go to experience wildness, and we want the mountains to remain wild. Back-country climbers and hikers, except for a very small minority, try to take excellent care of the Wind Rivers. Nearly all environmental damage is caused by people who won't be reading this guidebook. Furthermore, I believe most of us have become more conscious of our impact and are doing better than ever. The 1980 first edition used noodles on lake bottoms as an example of thoughtlessness, but I now rarely see lacustrine pasta.

Nevertheless, despite the good intentions of most, there are two reasons for concern. One is that first-time visitors may be drawn by the concept of pristine wilderness but without an eye for what is pristine. If you're coming from Yosemite's Camp 4 or the Grand Teton's Lower Saddle, the Cirque of the Towers may look untrammeled. A second reason for concern is the cumulative impact of a succession of well-meaning campers doing little things wrong.

Several years ago the Forest Service began taking a more active interest in the quality of Wilderness areas. On the one hand they more prominently display the rules, on maps and trailhead signboards, indicating how many feet from this you can do that. But then backcountry rangers much prefer to teach you to do something properly than to issue a citation. They also prefer that you use common sense and follow the spirit of the rules, rather than merely being familiar with legalistic details. As a believer in that approach, rather than restating formal regulations here, I supplement rules with personal observations.

Campsites

The obvious place to camp when you arrive at a lake is between the trail and the lake. However, there your camp is most conspicuous to everyone else. Camp on the side of the trail away from the lake or walk partway around the lake, then back from it.

Camping in the Cirque of the Towers

Or don't camp at a lake. Forest Service signs, this book's chapter titles, the column in trail registers where we indicate a destination, and our way of telling friends our plans ("We're going to Pyramid Lake this summer") all predispose us to drop our packs near a lake. You may be able to find a campsite that offers everything a lakeside site does, but with more privacy, near a creek far from standing water.

Once you locate a site, your goal should be to leave the site looking as if you'd never camped there. To do so takes an eye, work (ironically), and creativity.

Your campsite would be better off without being improved, especially if you are improving it by moving rocks—to balance a stove, hold tent stakes down, build a windbreak, or remove the Murphy's Law stone that would gouge your hip at an otherwise perfect tent site. There is increasing evidence that ripping stones from the ground is among the more destructive of mankind's bad habits. Moving inanimate objects may seem trivial compared to destroying living things, but over the years it leads to significant soil erosion. (Compare the Lower Saddle to less popular sites in the Tetons.)

At one time it was considered the sign of a savvy camper to dig a trench around his tent. Fortunately, trenches have gone the way of trenching tools and piton hammers, because trenches survive for eons in fragile soil. However, it now too often seems obligatory to heap rocks on each tent stake, or worse, build windbreaks. After all, Wind is in the range's name (though the name refers to the sound of the river, and the Wind Rivers are no windier than other ranges of the American West). At least, before resorting to architecture, first determine if the turf is perfect for unanchored stakes, which it usually is—not too soft and not impenetrable gravel. And do you really need a windbreak, or is it merely an autonomous response acquired from photos of base camps on Baltoro Glacier moraines? Rendering tent-stake rock heaps and windbreaks unnecessary usually involve no more than care in picking a tent site.

Campfires

Other than trails, campfire rings are the most prevalent sign of humanity in the Wind Rivers. I've encountered not only fire rings several hundred feet above treeline, but also stacks of firewood brought by who-knows-what beast of burden. Although in the more arcadian past, the woodsman's code of honor inspired us to leave wood for other weary wayfarers, we must reconsider our altruism in light of present realities.

A fire ring is a reasonably benign form of human intrusion, but two other aspects of campfires aren't: depletion of wood and trash left in fire rings. Most climbing base camps and backpacking sojourns are situated between 10,000 and 10,500 feet—that is, near treeline. In this zone the soil's nutrient content is a limiting factor in sustaining plant life, and fires destroy nutrients that would otherwise recycle from decaying wood. And, soil considerations aside, there isn't enough wood near popular campsites for everyone to be able to burn as much as they might want to. Fires near Island Lake or in the Cirque of the Towers are unconscionable.

The Bridger Wilderness map color-codes no-campfire zones, and some trailhead signboards specify where you may and may not have fires, but even where fires are permitted, build one only if there is an abundance of wood. (In much of the low country the accumulation of deadfall is such that the issue isn't the squandering of a precious resource but preventing a massive conflagration. In 2008 a neglected campfire near New Fork Lakes eventually spread nearly to Trapper Lake, 8 miles away.) When you are really wet and cold, or if your stove malfunctions, you can indulge in a small fire with a clearer conscience and some wood. If you do have a fire, use an existing fire ring if available. If not, build your fire on bedrock if possible. Don't build a fire directly on grass; first pile rocks or sand on the grass. Before you leave a campsite, scatter fire-ring stones and charcoal.

Burning trash doesn't significantly lighten your load for the trip out, unless you leave everything that doesn't burn with the ashes. Most Wind River backpacking litter consists of charred aluminum and partially melted plastic left in fire pits. Burn

Pingora from a Cirque of the Towers camp

trash more than 5 minutes before you leave a campsite, so the remains won't be too hot to pack when you're ready to leave—or too wet if you cool them by dousing.

Stone windbreaks, a prominent landscape element in upper Titcomb Basin, are equivalent to fire rings as human artifacts, though they usually lack the charred aluminum.

Water

Take seriously the Forest Service's admonition to suspect all water of containing giardia and campylobacter organisms. The water is probably not polluted, but it's not worth taking a chance. There are three methods for treating water: chemical, filter-pump, and boiling. Chemicals tastier than iodine have become available, while filter-pumps have become lighter and more reliable. Boiling, of course, requires extra fuel.

But don't suffer dehydration because you're afraid of the water. Dehydration can be a serious debilitation in the mountains, while giardia (the symptoms of which typically appear a week or two later) can be treated when you return to civilization.

Restrooms

A puzzling number of people deposit "human waste" (as the regulations call it) in places that would otherwise make good campsites. Among the questions to ask yourself when searching for just the right place to answer nature's call is "Would someone else camp here?"

Most of us were trained early in life to close the bathroom door but weren't taught to avoid contaminating a water supply. Consequently some seek privacy by ducking into creek drainages. You must avoid early toilet training lessons and go far from lakes and streams; dig a hole (an ice axe is useful, as is a light trowel) or visit a boulder field; burn your paper or carry it out.

Bears

Once upon a time folklore insisted there were no bears in the Wind Rivers. Black bears took advantage of this misconception, most notably in the Cirque of the Towers and at Big Sandy Lake. Marmots and other small mammals also took advantage, because climbers would blithely leave food in their tents. The bear problem was alleviated when the Forest Service began aggressively educating climbers, even at one point posting a ranger at Big Sandy Opening.

Hanging food above bears' reach prevents a chain of unhappy consequences: You needn't leave the mountains early, hungry; campers who come after you needn't deal with ursines who thought enough of your freeze-dried chicken tetrazzini to return for seconds; and when autumn comes and pickings become slim in the Cirque, the bears don't become pests at outposts of civilization bordering the mountains, where they may encounter frontier justice. Where trees are scarce, as in the Cirque, boulders are an option for keeping food from bears, but be warned that during their heyday, bears were credited with working out problems as hard as 5.6 to get at food bags.

Grizzly bears have for a long time been preying on cattle near Togwotee Pass and were occasionally reported at Green River Lakes, so it was not surprising

when griz recently became regular visitors to Green River Lakes and are sporadically rumored to be elsewhere in the range, especially along the eastern fringes. I
am reluctant to specify places where you will not encounter grizzlies. You surely
are aware that pepper spray is a more effective defense than Second Amendment–
type armaments.

Horses

Shoshones traveled through the range on horse. Benjamin Bonneville and John
C. Fremont reached the mountains by horse. Trails for pack trains were built using
horses. Horses still serve a valid purpose, enabling people to visit the Wind Rivers
who otherwise, for one reason or another, would not be able to. Nevertheless, horse
users should be aware that they now constitute a small minority of backcountry travelers, that hoofs tear up trails far more than boots do, and that meadows above treeline,
such as in Titcomb Basin, don't quickly recover from off-trail horse travel. Local com-
mercial outfitters share climbers' and hikers' affection for the mountains (they aren't
there for the decadent lifestyle or the big bucks) and have as much at stake as anyone
in sustaining the land. From what I've seen, unscrupulous horse-inflicted damage has
been caused by amateurs. If you use horses, do so with humility and responsibility.

Sheep

During the early 1900s the range was overrun by over 100,000 sheep per year, more
than the land can tolerate. While Forest Service controls and industry economics have
reduced this number to roughly 10,000, limited to the Bridger Wilderness between
Mount Baldy and Big Sandy Opening, your camp can still be overrun by sheep when
you're expecting solitude.

It's not in Forest Service regulations, but sheepherders have been subject to different rules than the rest of us because rangers don't have the means to enforce the rules
against herders. You may be camping properly on one side of a lake, while across the
lake sheepherders shit near the shore, build bonfires at noon, and leave a heap of tin
cans when they move on.

The existence of these parallel universes requires you to be philosophical. Don't take
it out on the land; don't leave trash, rationalizing that yours is less than theirs. If you are
inspired to complain to the Forest Service, great, but keep in mind that the 1964 Wilderness Act authorizes grazing, which the Forest Service can't prohibit per se.

In the past, however, I've had two complaints about the Forest Service's management of grazing. One was that they appeared timid about making sheep people abide
by Wilderness regulations. In theory the Forest Service schedules sheep bands for specific areas during specific time periods. In practice it seemed sheep people felt free to
ignore the schedules. My second complaint was that it was hard, if not impossible, to
get Forest Service personnel to divulge these schedules. It was tempting to infer that
embarrassment about the lack of control led to this reticence. However, signs have
been appearing on the Big Sandy Opening trailhead bulletin board proclaiming the
sheep's whereabouts, so perhaps my cause for complaint is a thing of the past.

Cattle graze the fringes of the range, but in number and destructiveness they are unimportant compared to sheep. The occasional mavericks that startle me when I think I've left civilization seem more comical than inappropriate.

Regulation

Depending on your vision of wildness, you may consider the Forest Service's efforts to preserve designated Wilderness a threat in itself. Most backcountry rangers blend in well with the landscape, but it is possible to feel that uniformed personnel telling you how to preserve the appearance of Wilderness (capital W) destroys the spirit of wilderness (small w). The 1993 draft of the Bridger Wilderness Action Plan contained the ominous suggestion that if backpackers don't stop camping in lakeside meadows, then boulders and shrubs should be transplanted at "obvious tent sites."

Many of us wouldn't consider such artificial landscaping to be wilderness. Whoever made this shortsighted proposal forgot that the best protection against abuse of the land is our reverence for it, that our reverence is for what is real, and that deliberately confusing what is natural with what is regulatory will destroy our spiritual relationship with more than the meadows being rearranged. No CAMPING signs would be preferable to cosmetic wilderness. (Not all visitors, apparently, equate wild with natural. Groups have complained to the Forest Service that "the bears are ruining our wilderness experience.")

The way to preserve wilderness is with your own spirit, not by having a ranger precede you and, however politely, require other campers to move their tents out of sight so it looks like you're in wild country. Do your best to keep the Wind Rivers wild.

Humanity

Surveys produce ambiguous data regarding wilderness visitors' feelings about other visitors. Many of us automatically express a desire for solitude and fewer "trail encounters" and "campsite encounters," but we belie our responses by pausing to chat with passersby on the trail and inviting neighboring campers for tea.

I suspect that most of us enjoy encountering people who seem to belong in the backcountry and dislike meeting people who don't. I never think of the trail as crowded when I pass hikers who smile and exchange pleasantries, but when I pass hikers who stare sullenly ahead, pretending I don't exist, the land seems overrun.

I believe that complaints about crowding are largely complaints about lack of community and that, when we set foot in the wilderness, we have an obligation not only to become part of the natural environment but part of the human community as well. This involves acts more social and less mundane than such housekeeping chores as packing out trash, and less obvious and entangling than rescuing a stricken stranger, but it is far easier to fit in with people in the mountains than in civilization. Perhaps one attraction of wilderness is that we can interact more naturally there than in cities.

Seasons and Weather

Mountain weather has never been very predictable, but it seems that what is called global warming would be more accurately termed global weirding, with weather patterns becoming more erratic. Nevertheless, a few observations:

A climatologist estimates that the Wind Rivers receive 40 to 50 inches of precipitation a year. (Pinedale, at 7,180 feet in the Green River basin, averages 9.1 inches; Dubois, at 6,917 feet in the Wind River valley, 9.4 inches; Lander, down the valley at 5,563 feet, 13.6 inches.)

While no data are available on the distribution of precipitation, climbers—and motorists on US 191—note that the high peaks around Dinwoody Glacier and Titcomb Basin attract a disproportionate share of storms. The range's southern tip is drier than the mountains to the north, though perhaps windier.

June is northwestern Wyoming's wettest month. While the snowpack varies markedly from one year to another, you can usually expect snowpatches on lower trails, continuous snow cover above 11,000 feet, and soggy campsites.

Most people visit the Wind Rivers during July and August, with the mountains being most crowded in early August. Days are longer in July and flowers at their best,

June

Late September

but mosquitoes also reach their peak. Streams are higher during early July, and certain crossings can present a significant obstacle.

Most summer weather comes from the southwest, and some precipitation—as rain, snow, or sleet—occurs during half or more of the days of summer. In the past you could declare with some confidence that afternoon thunderstorms typified July, while a few storms during August would last for two or three days, including a traditional end-of-August storm. However, such a pattern was more apparent then than now. Ice climbs usually become icy in late August, though in some years not until September.

Lightning is a more frequent summer hazard than is cold. Temperatures during July and August rarely drop much below freezing; an exceptionally hot day may be in the high 80s.

Toward the end of August, a thin layer of ice forms on the edges of lakes overnight. In September the layer becomes thicker, and frosty mornings inhibit early departures from camp. Nevertheless, September can be a fine month. Flowers are gone, but so are mosquitoes and people. Many Septembers have been memorable for long stretches of warm, sunny days, though you must be ready to be driven from the mountains by a serious storm. Good weather may continue into October, though it isn't a month for ambitious projects or trips planned far in advance. Snow that falls in October may not melt before winter, so you should be prepared to leave through a foot or more of it.

Access is a major obstacle to winter mountaineering. The paved road to Elkhart Park is plowed to White Pine Ski Area, 3 miles from the summer trailhead, but other west-side roads are closed. Snowfall is often light on the east side, in which event you can drive to summer trailheads. But if the snowline is above the trailhead, you may have to carry your skis some distance. The best approach to the southern Wind Rivers is the Middle Fork Trail, which begins just above Sinks Canyon, near Lander. If you travel through the Wind Rivers during winter or early spring, you should be able to recognize and deal with avalanche conditions.

Names

The most eccentric name on maps of the Wind River Mountains may be the name of the range itself; by naming earth for water and water for air, it combines three of the Greek's basic elements. It is a poetic name but causes confusion. "We're going to the Wind Rivers" puzzles the uninitiated, who ask, "How many rivers are there?" or "Are you climbing or rafting?"

While the range's name won't perplex backpackers, other nomenclatural quirks will. Worst is the multiplicity of North Forks, South Forks, East Forks, and Middle Forks. (West Forks are conspicuously absent.) You can ascend the South Fork of the Little Wind River to its headwaters and go west over Washakie Pass to the East Fork River (the east fork of the New Fork River, which is a fork of the Green). Going north from the East Fork's head, you reach the South Fork (of Boulder Creek). Continuing north past Middle Fork Lake, you can cross Photo Pass to another South Fork—Bull Lake Creek's—and work back south to the North Fork of the Little Wind River. A compass doesn't help.

Also confusing is the duplication of names. The Wind Rivers abound in clichés: Baldys, Cathedrals, Roaring Forks, Boulder Creeks, Clear Lakes and Bear Lakes, Lost Lakes and Hidden Lakes, Deep Lakes and Long Lakes (one less than 0.25 mile long). If you're going to Haystack and wonder why the trail to Clear Lake begins 80 miles away at Green River Lakes, check the index for other Clear Lakes. If you plan to camp at one of the Alpine Lakes below the Brown Cliffs, don't use the Alpine Lake quad, which refers to a different lake. Beware of three Indian Passes within 8 miles of one another. There are even two Squaretops.

Regarding the quaint custom of naming peaks for animal anatomy—Bear's Ears, Lizard Head, Camel's Hump, Shark's Nose—realize that the shape reminded someone only from a particular vantage point. Don't look for lizards, sharks, and wolves from Lonesome Lake.

The names used to identify peaks and passes in the headings for route descriptions depend on how topographic maps identify them. When peaks and passes (and lakes) are named on USGS maps, and therefore on Earthwalk and Beartooth maps, I don't feel obliged to further identify them.

Fremont Peak is named and given a precise elevation on its USGS quad, and the heading **Fremont Peak** (13,745) should suffice.

Turret Peak is named on maps, but its elevation is not explicitly given, thus the heading **Turret Peak** (13,600+). The highest contour line represents 13,600 feet. With contour intervals being 40 feet, we only know that Turret's elevation is between 13,600 and 13,640 feet.

Bollinger Peak has been named by climbers but not named on the Lizard Head Peak quad, though its elevation is given. This guide identifies it as **Bollinger Peak** (12,232), but to further help identify it, the text locates it in relation to a feature that is named on maps—that is, as being 0.2 mile north of Wolf's Head.

Other peaks are named neither by climbers nor on maps, though maps give their elevations. Such unnamed peaks are designated by their elevation, for instance, **Peak 11,246.** Again the text locates unnamed peaks in relation to named features—in this case Peak 11,246 as being 1.1 miles northwest of Porcupine Pass. When maps give a peak neither name nor precise elevation, I make an extra effort to identify it.

It isn't necessary to pronounce names correctly to have a fulfilling Wind River trip. Nevertheless, you may be curious about some less obvious names:

Absaroka	ab-SOR-uh-kuh
Arapaho	uh-RAP-uh-ho
Dubois	DU-boys
Gros Ventre	GRO-vont
Oeneis	EE-nee-us
Pingora	pin-GOR-uh
Popo Agie	po-PO-zha
Sacagawea	SACK-uh-juh-WE-uh
Shoshone	sho-SHO-nee
Stough	STO
Togwotee	TOE-guh-tee
Washakie	WASH-uh-kee

Management

The Wind Rivers west of the crest are situated in Bridger-Teton National Forest's Bridger Wilderness. The northern and southern thirds of the east slope are, respectively, in the Fitzpatrick Wilderness and Popo Agie Wilderness of Shoshone National Forest. The central section of the east side is part of the Wind River Reservation, administered by the Shoshone and Arapaho tribes.

The 1964 Wilderness Act specifies that Wilderness Areas, which Congress estab-lishes, "be administered for the use and enjoyment of the American people in such manner as will leave them unimpaired for future use and enjoyment as wilderness, and so as to provide for the protection of these areas [and] the preservation of their wilderness character." The Wilderness Act prohibits or restricts certain activities. Motorized vehicles and equipment—snowmobiles, aircraft, motorboats, chain saws, and bolt guns—can only be used in emergencies. Airdrops are prohibited. Permanent buildings are illegal.

Establishing such noble intentions as law required compromise. The Wilderness Act specifies that livestock grazing, "where established," be allowed to continue "subject to such reasonable regulations as are deemed necessary by the Secretary of Agriculture."

The mountains on the reservation are wilderness with a lowercase w. To fish, camp, hike, boat, or picnic there, you must obtain a fishing permit. Permits are avail-able for a day, a week, or a season; the cost is less for Wyoming residents than nonresi-dents and senior citizens get a break. Permits are sold at the Tribal Fish & Game office at Fort Washakie and at various stores in Dubois, Crowheart, Lander, and Pinedale. The Cold Springs Road, which gives access to the closest trailhead to Gannett Peak, is on the reservation and is closed to the public. You must use transportation provided by a designated outfitter. For more information on backcountry travel on the reserva-tion, contact Fish & Game Department, Shoshone and Arapaho Tribes, Box 217, Fort Washakie, WY 82514 or (307) 332-7207.

Organization of This Guide

This book divides the range into twelve sections, progressing from northwest to southeast, with a chapter devoted to each (see the overview map with the table of contents). Divisions are made according to the valleys, lakes, and glaciers from which climbers approach the peaks, with some consideration also given to the type of climbing the section offers. The Deep Lake section, for instance, is a small area with a high concentration of rock climbs, while Alpine Lakes is a catchall section that includes extensive areas on both sides of the Divide that are of more interest to hikers and wanderers than to climbers.

An awkward feature of this arrangement is the fact that you can climb certain peaks, such as Divide summits between Dinwoody Glacier and Titcomb Basin, from either side. All routes on such peaks are described in one chapter. For example, routes on both the Dinwoody and Titcomb sides of Mount Woodrow Wilson are included in the Dinwoody Glacier chapter.

You needn't be a mystic to see that the Wind Rivers are an integral whole, not twelve sections. The divisions are meant to help make the geography comprehensible, not to confine you to one valley, nor are chapter titles meant to suggest the Wind Riv-ers have only twelve lakes and valleys with suitable campsites. Some sections include good camp locations miles apart. Baptiste Lake area peaks loom above Baptiste, Grave, Valentine, Washakie, and Cathedral Lakes. Other lakes lie between peaks of two sections—Jean Lakes, south of Peak Lake and west of Titcomb Basin, for example.

Within chapters, peaks are arranged along main crests, with excursions along spurs. The routes on a peak are arranged counterclockwise as seen from above (a map view) or from left to right when viewed from the ground, beginning with the peak's original route, easiest route, or usual descent route—typically one and the same.

Trails, passes, and climbing routes on peaks are also divided among the twelve sections. When a trail extends from one section to another, part is described in each appropriate chapter. The mileage listed for the hiking routes is one-way.

Geology

If climbers distilled Wind River geology into one word, that word would be *granite*. Granite—igneous rock crystallizing from molten magma below the earth's surface—suggests antiquity, and Wind River granite, which crystallized 2.5 billion years ago, has existed through more than half of the earth's 4.6 billion years.

However, the rocks around and into which the melt flowed are even older. In the range's undramatic midsection, a band extends west from Hall's Lake through Medina Mountain to Lake Victor; some of the rock there has existed within the earth's crust for 3.4 billion years. Moreover, dikes cut through other segments of this band but not the 3.4 billion-year-old rock, implying that the dikes existed before 3.4 billion years ago and that the segments they cut preceded the dikes. Recent tests indicate that crystals in the older rock have been present in the crust for 3.8 billion years, which briefly (even in human time) gave Medina Mountain claim to the oldest rock found on earth.

It is believed that the earth's crust took half a billion years or more to form, so although slightly older rock has turned up in Greenland, Antarctica, and the Northwest Territories, the existence of rock much older is unlikely. The small age differences are less important than the hope that these nearly contemporaneous rocks can offer a glimpse into the initial formation of continents. The Wind Rivers are part of a very old block that includes most of Wyoming and extends to the Beartooths in Montana, the Black Hills in South Dakota, the Wasatch in Utah, and the City of Rocks in Idaho.

Most of the rock in this ancient band, indeed most of the Wind Rivers' northern half, is gneiss. Gneiss is metamorphic rock, which doesn't crystallize from melt but forms when existing rock—in this case probably sedimentary, but perhaps also granite and volcanics—is subjected to such high temperatures and pressures (miles below the surface) that it softens, flows plastically, and changes mineralogically.

Gneiss contains the same minerals as granite, but its layered texture distinguishes it from granite. Light-colored bands rich in quartz and feldspar and dark bands, mainly biotite and hornblende, reflect rock texture prior to metamorphosis, not the homogeneous melt from which granite forms. The layers are often deformed into complex swirls, suggesting a history of repeated compressions over time.

The distinction between igneous and metamorphic rock is clearer in textbooks than underfoot in the Wind Rivers. Sometimes rock only partially melts. Intruding magma doesn't simply solidify as granite next to existing gneiss but melts nearby rock, further metamorphosing and deforming it by heat, pressure, and chemical reaction. Magma flows into cracks; gneissic chunks drop into the granitic soup before the melt crystallizes. The resulting mixture of gneiss and granite, called migmatite, is more prevalent in the Wind Rivers than is pure granite. Medina Mountain's 3.8 billion-year-old crystals occur in migmatite.

Migmatite depicts its history graphically. In the ice cream–concoction swirls of Titcomb Basin's floor you can visualize heat softening rock so that it folded without breaking, like chocolate in a pack on a warm day, then deforming again when compressed in a different way. Fuzzy boundaries between gneiss and granite indicate their chemical effects on one another. Geologists have described Wind River migmatite as "alternating dark and light stripes, swirling around in complex patterns," "layers . . . stretched and separated by flowage into lenses, wisps, and streaks," "soupy," "swirly and chaotic." Different geologic maps have characterized the same rock as gneiss, granite, and migmatite.

Climbers tend toward homogeneous rock, be it granite, basalt, or limestone, and suspect rock that reveals structure. However, the Wind Rivers' most conspicuous walls, on Helen, Sacagawea, and Fremont—and Squaretop, Arrowhead, Ellingwood, Bonneville, and Musembeah—consist of migmatite hardly inferior to Pingora granite.

Granodiorite and Granite

Gneiss and migmatite were the rocks intruded by the magma that became granite, but first, 2.6 billion years ago, they were invaded by magma that crystallized as granodiorite.

Igneous rocks are classified according to their proportions of various minerals. Granite's predominant minerals are light-colored quartz and feldspar, with lesser amounts of the dark minerals biotite and hornblende. (Belay-ledge mineralogists can identify feldspar by its tendency to break along planes—best seen when reflecting—and to weather to chalky white. Quartz fractures in curves and remains glassy. Biotite, or black mica, is the brownish-black mineral you can flake with a fingernail, while hornblende forms greenish-black rods.)

Granodiorite contains more of the dark minerals than granite; patches of it contrast with lighter granite on such walls as Pingora's north face. Most rock south of Temple Peak and much of the Middle Fork Lake and Baptiste Lake areas is granodiorite. Less resilient than granite, it tends to be brittle when crumpled by mountain-creating forces. Climbers have returned from the north face of Mount Hooker, the range's preeminent wall, complaining about the quality of its darker rock.

A hundred million years after the intrusion of granodiorite, the future Wind River core was invaded by the melt that became the Cirque of the Towers, the Deep Lake peaks, Midsummer Dome, New Fork Canyon, and much of the terrain east of the Divide from Ross Lakes to Dinwoody Creek. In the past this granitic rock (and Yosemite's) was correctly called quartz monzonite; its proportions of various feldspars differed from granite's, though a belayer can't see the difference. However, geologists have redefined the terms, broadening granite's domain and shrinking quartz monzonite's. The Cirque of the Towers is now considered granite, though you may encounter the term quartz monzonite in older writings.

The rate at which a melt cools determines the size of the resulting crystals. Lava, for example, cools quickly, forming fine-grained rock. The nubbly texture of Wind River granite indicates an origin deep in the earth's crust. Of particular interest to climbers in search of holds are very large feldspar crystals, called phenocrysts, and veins of large granitic crystals, or pegmatite, which cut across various types of rock.

As an array of interlocked crystals, granite tends to be stronger than layered rock and rock consisting of cemented particles. With its massive texture it typically fractures in long cracks.

Not many years ago geologists only cared that granite crystallized from magma. Now they examine granitic rocks, speculating about the origins of the magmas. It seems probable that the magma that became Wind River granite derived partly from material in the earth's mantle and partly from recycled crust, as magma is produced when an oceanic plate collides with a continental plate, forcing the oceanic plate down toward the mantle, where its leading edge melts beneath the overriding continent.

More Recent Rock

During the 2.5 billion years since the granite intruded, little has happened to the Wind Rivers' core. The only events that geologists can detect occurred sporadically from 2 to 1.2 billion years ago, when molten rock flowed into vertical fissures. This melt crystallized as feldspar and the dark mineral pyroxene, and the resulting dark diabase dikes, some as wide as 150 feet, are conspicuous in many Wyoming ranges. One extends northeast for more than 8 miles through Ambush, Tower, and Musembeah Peaks. Another, which crosses Goat Flat and Downs Mountain, can be traced for 30 miles.

Since diabase tends to be more brittle than granite or gneiss, most dikes weather more rapidly than the surrounding rock. Consequently dikes typically form chimneys in walls, notches where they cross ridges. Wide dikes show the relation of cooling rate to crystal size. Near their edges, which cooled quickly, the rock is finer grained than toward the slower-cooling center.

During this period, for all anyone knows, the block that eventually became the Wind Rivers may have risen as mountains, which then wore away. But 600 million years ago western Wyoming was a gentle plain that drained west to a sea that covered parts of Idaho, Utah, Nevada, and southern California. Then western Wyoming subsided, and the sea advanced eastward over the land, depositing sand beaches. Continuing to advance, it deposited mud and, later, carbonates on top of the sand. Subsequent compression compacted these sediments into sedimentary rock (sand as sandstone, mud as shale, carbonates as limestone and dolomite) that covered the gneiss, granite, and migmatite.

Geologists can see the sea's advance and subsequent fluctuations in the sedimentary layers that are now exposed. These layers form the upper parts of Big Sheep Mountain and other peaks west of Green River Lakes; White Rock, south of Green River Lakes; and the tilted strata of Horse Ridge and other long east-flank ridges. Using fossils to help assign ages, geologists have determined that these strata were deposited from 600 million to 250 million years ago (roughly from the time life evolved enough to leave fossils until the appearance of dinosaurs). Between 250 million and 90 million years ago, seas continued to periodically submerge western Wyoming, but the sediments they deposited have either been removed by erosion or buried beneath more recent deposits.

Uplift

The event that exposed rock billions of years old occurred within the past 100 million years, an event known as the Laramide Revolution. Horizontal compression had been crumpling the earth's crust to the west and, like a wave, this disturbance progressed eastward. Where the crust bowed upward, mountains formed; where it bowed down, valleys formed.

Ninety million years ago the crystalline core of the Wind Rivers lay beneath sediments that were just emerging from the sea. The Laramide Revolution bent the rock up as an arch. An asymmetrical arch, leaning southwest, it began to overturn and eventually reached its breaking point.

The rock fractured along fault planes, dipping northeast at a low angle. Sliding on these fault planes, the Wind River block was lifted up and thrust southwestward. Relative to the Wind River and Green River basins, the block rose more than 50,000 feet, one of the greatest vertical movements known. During the Laramide Revolution's 40 million years, the block inched southwest for about 15 miles.

The main Wind River fault lies under the range's southwest flank, several miles from the crest, in bedrock buried under debris shed by the mountains since Laramide times. However, two subsidiary faults cut through exposed bedrock and give vivid evidence of thrust-faulting. One crosses the mouth of New Fork Canyon; the other parallels Slide Creek, a section of Elbow Creek, and the Green River from Three Forks to Beaver Parks. In places these faults are made obvious by granite and migmatite (formed far below the surface at least 2.5 billion years ago) overlying sandstone and limestone (deposited offshore 300 million years ago). You can see granite above younger sedimentary rock as you hike toward New Fork Canyon and migmatite thrust over sedimentary rock in the walls of Flat Top Mountain above the confluence of Slide and Clear Creeks.

Asymmetrical arching, accentuated by overthrusting, produced a range with an asymmetrical cross section. On the southwest side much of the sedimentary rock that covered the crystalline core was buried, while on the northwest side the strata were left tilted in long, gentle slopes. As a result of tilting and overthrusting, the high peaks are more conspicuous from the west than the east.

The concept of plate tectonics has so transformed geology that we expect mountains to be explained in terms of colliding continents, of ocean floors recycled under continental edges. However, the much-studied Rockies have resisted plate tectonic explanation as stubbornly as any large piece of the planet. Geologists reconstruct the past by observing the present and see nothing happening quite like the Laramide Revolution. The enigma involves a plate that disappeared, though it once lay under much of the Pacific Ocean. About 200 million years ago (as North America and Europe separated and the Atlantic Ocean opened), North America drifted west, overriding this Farallon Plate. Descending plates typically melt, providing magma that crystallizes below the surface as granite, as well as lava that surfaces via volcanoes. The subducting Farallon Plate generated the magma that became the granite that eventually rose as the Sierra Nevada—until 80 million years ago.

Between 80 million and 40 million years ago, the Farallon Plate didn't melt, as subducting plates typically do. During this period the Rockies rose—also atypically—1,000 miles from a plate boundary. Efforts to explain the Rockies have focused on this coincidence of anomalous events, but explanations have been speculative. Perhaps the Farallon Plate didn't dive as deeply as most descending plates. If not, perhaps its rock was unusually buoyant. Maybe it was more buoyant because of light rock it acquired during its trek under the Pacific. Answers to the riddle of the Rockies' rise could come from as far away as the mid-Pacific floor.

Erosion

When the Laramide Revolution raised the Wind River block 10 miles relative to adjacent valleys, it didn't create mountains 50,000 feet high. Even during uplifts streams were eroding rock and carrying sediments to adjacent valleys. Indeed, since a steep gradient increases a stream's erosive power, the size and distribution of sediments provide information about the Wind Rivers' rise.

Stream erosion soon stripped sedimentary rock from most of the block, exposing underlying granitic and gneissic rocks. As erosion lowered the mountains, the valleys accumulated the sediments removed from the mountains. Before renewed faulting occurred, erosion had time to reduce the ancestral Wind Rivers to a gently rolling plain and fill the valleys to their level. The Absarokas, Beartooths, Big Horns, Medicine Bows, and Granite Mountains suffered similar fates; 90 percent of Wyoming was one vast plain, with a few rounded hills protruding here and there. The ranges' crystalline cores still existed, but they had been buried.

Streams flowed across the plain following courses unaffected by the buried mountains. The Wind River, which had flowed east from Riverton to the Sweetwater, instead crossed the buried Owl Creek Mountains into Bighorn Basin. The Sweetwater cut back over the buried south end of the Wind Rivers, moving the Continental Divide west and,

Goat Flat

in effect, creating the Oregon Trail. Another river carried volcanic sediments from the Absarokas across the buried Wind Rivers.

One idiosyncratic aspect of the Wind Rivers is vast expanses of flat terrain at elevations as high as 13,000 feet. While you can locate high places on most topographic maps by the darkness of clustered contour lines, Wind River maps are whitest where they represent such elevated surfaces as Ram Flat, Goat Flat, Horse Ridge, and, to the south, the Continental Divide from Mitchell Peak to Wind River Peak. Less extensive flats suffice for the summits of such massifs as Squaretop (the emblematic Wind River formation), Jackson Peak, Mount Hooker, and Lizard Head. A subtler feature of the range is a terrace west of the crest at elevations ranging from 10,000 to 10,500 feet, 6 to 8 miles broad, that extends from the range's north end south to Big Sandy Opening. These plateaus, flat summits, and terrace were once parts of a continuous surface. Although now properly called an erosion surface, it was once termed a peneplain (and *peneplain* is a more memorable term).

Big Sheep Mountain provides evidence that the surface formed after the Laramide Revolution. Big Sheep, west of Green River Lakes, consists of sedimentary beds that were deposited horizontally but are now tilted. The summit is a horizontal surface that bevels the tilted strata; therefore tilting must have preceded beveling.

The Wind River erosion surface, or peneplain, has been worn away at its edges but is otherwise singularly immune to erosion. Frost shatters the bedrock into blocks, but streams cannot transport the rock across such flat terrain—streams, moreover, too near their headwaters to have much velocity. The frost-shattered, angular blocks accumulate in fields of felsenmeer or seas of rock. Scientists chose an erosion surface at the Wind Rivers' north end, where rock has been exposed virtually since the Laramide Revolution, for a study of the long-term effect of cosmic radiation on rock.

Post-Laramide Uplift

The extent of the skyline plateau and the west-side terrace signifies a long period when the crust was stable enough that erosion outpaced any uplift. The crest's elevation above the terrace indicates uplift after the stable period, with current studies producing evidence for an uplift between 30 and 23 million years ago.

Between the intrusion of granite and the deposition of the sediments 600 million years ago, the block had been shattered by faults. These faults were planes of weakness, and mountain-building forces refractured the block along these old planes.

Sorting post-Laramide uplift from Laramide uplift has involved geography that, on the one hand, is subtle enough that geologists had overlooked it and, on the other hand, is an important factor in our travels. The crest's northwest-southeast trend stands out on a Wyoming map, but we talk of climbing the west faces of Fremont and Haystack, and the east face of Ambush. We cross the Divide at Dinwoody and Jackass Passes by following fault lines that intersect, rather than exactly parallel, the Divide. The Laramide thrust fault and the range's crest trend northwest-southeast, but valleys leading to Dinwoody, Hay, Photo, and Jackass Passes, the upper Green River, and the fault zone followed past Dad's and Marm's Lakes, are aligned north-northwest to south-southeast. The pressures that caused the uplift of 30 to 23 million years ago acted in a different direction from Laramide forces, and it was along the north-northwest/south-southeast faults that the more recent uplift occurred, elevating the crest not only above the treeline terrace but higher than other Wyoming mountains.

Evidence for an uplift 30 to 23 million years ago comes from sediments west of the Wind Rivers' south end. Farther north equivalent sediments are buried under younger debris, but the range's southern end has sagged into the Green River basin, preserving the older deposits from burial. Their granitic composition indicates an origin as Wind River rock; their coarse pebbliness indicates transportation by swift streams.

The crest's rise seems not to have been geometrically simple. Geologists imagine "blocks jostled upward." These geologists did provide one detail, discovered by analyzing samples taken from a series of elevations on Temple Peak, at 12,972 feet the second highest summit in the southern half of the range, and Independent Mountain (11,653), 3 miles southwest of Temple. Dating rock by its thermal history, they found a correspondence between Temple rock and Independent rock, which is 1,000 to 1,500 meters lower. That is, the study implies that since Laramide time, Temple has risen on the order of 4,000 feet relative to Independent.

During the past 10 million years, the Wind River block—terrace as well as crest—has been exhumed, as have other Wyoming mountains. From the Green River valley you see the erosion surface as the terrace, standing a few thousand feet above the valley, and above it, the Divide with its plateaus. You also see canyons cut into the terrace and cirques cut into the crest.

The elevation of the range gave new life to previously sluggish streams, and these streams carried away much of the debris that accumulated during burial. The rejuvenated streams eroded most vigorously toward the bottom of their gradients, flattening their lower reaches first and developing concave profiles, steeper near the head than downstream. Pauses during uplift gave the streams time to deepen the canyons of the Green River, New Fork River, Pine Creek, and Fremont Creek. Creeks also began carving the valleys back toward the Divide—the valleys of the North Popo Agie, the Big Sandy, and the East Fork—which have become popular base camp sites.

A notable number of Wind River streams flow not with the general slope of the land but at a right angle to it, parallel to the crest. These streams occupy old faults, zones of shattered, easily eroded rock. Stream erosion further accentuates these lines of weakness, though some creeks that flow through such zones are disproportionately tiny for their valleys. In many fault zones streams flow in diametrically opposite directions from a pass. Trail Creek flows north from Green River Pass; Pine Creek flows south.

Northwest-southeast fault zones have influenced the trail system, making travel parallel to the crest easier than in most ranges. The Highline follows such a zone past Dad's and Marm's Lakes. You have the impression of following a drainage, though you are actually traveling against the grain.

However, not all fault zones are parallel. Such L-shaped lakes as Big Sandy mark the junction of fault zones. Island Lake lies at the intersection of a fault zone that includes Titcomb Basin, Dinwoody Pass, and Dinwoody Glacier with one that passes through Jean Lakes.

Ice Ages

As recently as a million years ago, the Wind Rivers lacked their present ruggedness. They were high but gentle-sloped hills, as Downs Mountain and Wind River Peak remain. Streams had created valleys approximately where streams flow today, but the valleys were narrower, with V-shaped cross sections. Fremont Lake, Bull Lake, the Green River Lakes, and the other large foothill lakes didn't exist, nor did Lonesome Lake, Peak Lake, Shadow Lake, or the Titcomb Lakes. Then the climate changed.

Several times, for periods of thousands of years, temperatures averaged a few degrees below normal. During each cool period, ice spread from the North Pole. While polar ice sheets didn't reach as far south as Wyoming, separate ice caps covered such ranges as the Wind Rivers. Glaciers flowed from ice caps down valleys and spilled onto the plains; one extended 50 miles down the Green River valley to an elevation of 7,700 feet, nearly to the site of the present-day US 189/191 junction. It was 7 miles wide at the Big Bend. Valley glaciers coalesced on the 10,000-foot terrace from Boulder Canyon to Big Sandy Opening, forming an ice sheet 1,000 feet thick.

Signs of glaciation, which are everywhere, are of two types: erosion and deposition. A glacier's rock-sculpting power is greatest where its ice is thickest. As a result it deepens and widens canyons into a characteristic U-shaped cross section: steep walls, level floor. At the canyons' heads glaciers carve semicircular bowls, or cirques. Where cirques in opposite sides of a ridge intersect, a narrow, jagged crest results. The Cirque of the Towers is but one of dozens of Wind River cirques, and Wolf's Head's east ridge just one example of a jagged crest. Classic cirques lie above Peak Lake and at the heads of Titcomb Basin and the East Fork Valley. Mounts Woodrow Wilson and Bonneville and the Divide from Block Tower past Shark's Nose and Overhanging Tower to Wolf's Head, represent back-to-back cirques.

Ice carries the rock scoured from cirques as it creeps downhill. This debris increases erosion, gouging depressions in the bedrock of cirque floors. When the ice retreats, these depressions become lakes. When ice can't strip bedrock, it may nevertheless polish, scratch, or groove it, marks that are good indicators of the geographic extent of glaciation. Geologists determined the depth of glaciation in the Green River's canyon by noting horizontal scratches at the base of Squaretop, marks that must be glacial, since stream-worn grooves descend fall lines. Near Deep Lake the sparsely fractured bedrock resisted glacial erosion (and resists vegetation), and examples of polishing and scratching abound. The valley is separated from Rapid and Miller Lakes by a typical glacial formation called a roche moutonnée, for its supposed resemblance to a sheep. This ridge was resistant enough that glaciers were forced to flow over and around it, rounding and smoothing the up-valley end and plucking blocks from the down-valley end, to leave a steep face broken by ledges. Pingora and Midsummer Dome also stood in the path of glaciers and survived.

Between the two Green River Lakes, Clear Creek joins the main river from the east, Porcupine Creek from the west. When a glacier occupied the Green's canyon, smaller glaciers joined it from these tributary valleys. With less erosive power, the tributaries didn't sculpt as deeply; their retreat left the upper Clear and Porcupine Creeks in hanging valleys far above the Green. The waterfalls by which these creeks drop to the main canyon are thus legacies of glaciation.

The sculpting of cirque headwalls, creation of hanging valleys, and gouging of lakes is cumulative from one glacial episode to another; you can't use cirques and lakes to distinguish or enumerate glacial episodes. Geologists, though, can decipher much from the chaotically heaped boulders of a moraine—curving ridges of rubble formed where glaciers melt and deposit the debris carried from their upper reaches. Moraines distinguish episodes, for each glacial advance deposits terminal moraines at its farthest descent down a valley.

Early in the twentieth century, geologists had no way to correlate the sequences of moraines found in the Rocky Mountains with continental glaciations (ice ages), so they used a Rocky Mountain terminology. Eliot Blackwelder, working in the Wind River region, identified three episodes of Rocky Mountain glaciation and named them for the locales where he found moraines that typified an advance.

Blackwelder named the oldest (since dated at 200,000 years ago) the Buffalo glaciation, for the Buffalo Fork of the Snake River, which flows from Togwotee Pass into Jackson Hole. He named an advance of 80,000 to 35,000 years ago the Bull Lake glaciation; moraines near Bull Lake represent deposition during that period. He defined moraines "near each of the large lakes near Pinedale" as specimens of a glacial advance that peaked 18,000 years ago: the Pinedale glaciation. The terms Buffalo, Bull Lake, and Pinedale were applied throughout the Rockies and are still in use today.

Each glacial advance was less extensive than its predecessors. Buffalo moraines are farther from the mountains than Bull Lake moraines, which are down-valley from Pinedale moraines. (This chronological progression signifies only that a glacial advance obliterates evidence of earlier glaciation. If a major advance follows a minor advance, the earlier episode is unlikely to be detected.)

Only faint traces of Buffalo glaciation have been found on the Wind Rivers' fringes, but the rubble piles of Bull Lake moraines are notable near the community of Boulder, where the road to Big Sandy Opening leaves US 191, and along the Big Sandy road. Toward the southern end of the range, Pinedale moraines occur from 8 to 10 miles downstream from cirque headwalls, at elevations ranging from 8,500 to 9,500 feet—for example, at Big Sandy Opening. Perhaps the best place to see Pinedale moraines is on the road from Pinedale to Elkhart Park, which climbs a massive morainal ridge and gives you a sense of the enormous scale of ice-age glaciation.

By the end of the Pinedale glaciation, the Wind Rivers had been carved into their present form. The last ice age was followed by a warming trend. During the period from 7,500 to 5,000 years ago, known as the Altithermal or Climatic Optimum, glaciers may have completely disappeared from the range. (The glaciers that exist today aren't remnants of the ice ages but of more recent minor advances.)

The Altithermal was followed, 5,000 to 3,000 years ago, by renewed glaciation at higher elevations, an episode that in the Rockies was called the Temple Lake advance. Below Temple Peak's north face lies a small remnant glacier, glacial deposits, and moraine-dammed Temple Lake. When the moraine that inspired the name turned out to represent a Pinedale re-advance before the Altithermal, the Temple Lake glaciation was less ambiguously renamed Indian Basin for moraines below Ellingwood Glacier. At the time of the Indian Basin advance, people were living near the confluence of the Big Sandy River and Little Sandy Creek.

Another minor glacial advance occurred from 100 CE to 1,000 CE. Its name, Audubon, comes from Colorado, not from the Wind Rivers. Audubon deposits occur at 11,000 feet in upper Titcomb Basin.

A final set of moraines, just below existing glaciers, represent the Gannett Peak advance of 100 to 300 years ago. Geologists date such recent deposits by the lack of soil and vegetation and by the near lack of lichen. Climbers can date moraines by their instability; since the blocks haven't had time to settle, young moraines can be treacherous to cross.

Historical evidence also documents the Gannett Peak advance. When Fremont camped below 7,000 feet by the East Fork River on August 9, 1842, water froze at night. In Indian and Titcomb Basins, Fremont found quantities of snow and ice that would surprise visitors to these valleys during recent Augusts. He described an August 15 snow line of about 12,000 feet, which is now typical for June or early July.

Glaciers survive in high cirques, typically terminating at 11,000 to 11,500 feet; twenty-four are named on topographic maps. Most are in the northern section of the range, where elevations are higher, and most lie east of the Divide, presumably because the prevailing west wind clears the west slopes and blows snow over the Divide. The same wind was presumably also responsible for the gentle west slopes of the western-most peaks: the Dragon Head-Pronghorn ridge, the Raid-Geikie ridge, Watch Tower and Pylon on the Cirque of the Towers rim, and Temple Peak. While their east faces have been ice-sculpted into near-vertical walls, all are accessible by scrambling on their windward sides.

Between many of the existing glaciers and their highest terminal moraines sit small ponds indicative of recent glacial retreats—retreats with alarming climatic implications. A study of Knife Point Glacier from 1986 to 1995 found the glacier's terminus had retreated 360 feet; comparison with 1963 aerial photos indicated a retreat of 1,100 feet. Comparison with 1922 photos suggested a loss of depth of 300 feet, a decrease of mass of two-thirds. A 2012 study indicated a 46 percent loss of area since 1966.

Lakes and Streams

Generally, though, lakes are the most ephemeral alpine feature, recent creations that will vanish relatively quickly. Their demise is brought about by inlet streams, which bring in silt and sand. When the water enters a lake and stops moving, it deposits this sediment, building a delta. (From Pingora the cloudy water brought by Lonesome Lake's inlet streams is especially visible.) The speed of delta formation is apparent when you compare Lower Green River Lake on the 1906 and 1968 topographic maps. On the 1906 map Clear Creek flows directly into Lower Green River Lake. But with Clear Creek and the Green River building a delta, the creek now flows into the river a few hundred yards above the inlet.

Eventually a lake fills up with sediments, which acquire vegetation and evolve into a meadow. Along Dinwoody Creek you can envision a vanished chain of lakes, transformed into meadows by a stream that must transport the range's heaviest load of sediments.

Streams flowing through meadows give rise to another ephemeral phenomenon: meanders, curves of uncanny sinuosity, regularity, and symmetry. Meanders elicit curios-ity because we expect water to simply flow downhill. Streams only meander through nearly level terrain, where water is both flowing and held back; it is in a sense backed up. Once a meander begins, water on the outside of the curve, moving faster and erod-ing more powerfully, accentuates the curve, while slower-moving water on the curve's inside drops sediment, often creating a sandbar. However, floodwaters tend to straighten a stream, stranding meanders as oxbow lakes.

On September 6, 2003, an outfitter camped in Downs Fork Meadow, where the Downs Fork joins Dinwoody Creek, noticed the Downs Fork rising. By the time he moved his tents to higher ground, the water was a foot deep. The deluge continued for four days, covering the meadow with 5 feet of water. From an airplane the source of the flood was traced to what had been an unnamed 0.3-mile-long lake sitting at 12,200 feet at the head of Grasshopper Creek and the base of Pedestal Peak. An estimated 650 million gallons drained down Grasshopper Creek to the Downs Fork. This event was newsworthy, but the news account explained that similar events happen often, geologically.

While most of the Wind Rivers' countless lakes owe their existence to glaciation, a different agent is responsible for many ponds at the range's lower elevations. These ponds are impounded by dams of mud and sticks, their ends chewed to the shape of pencil tips. These dams are the work of beavers, the animals that first brought white men to the Wind Rivers.

History

Meriwether Lewis and William Clark, returning down the Missouri River in 1806 after crossing the continent, met two trappers on their way upstream. The trappers wanted a guide, someone who had been upriver, so one of Lewis and Clark's men, John Colter, though he hadn't seen civilization in two years, returned to the mountains. When he came down the Missouri the next year, Colter again encountered trappers who persuaded him to guide them upstream.

From his new companions' post at the confluence of the Missouri and Bighorn, Colter continued south and west. The only documentation of his journey has been what could be seen on a map William Clark drew after Colter visited him in St. Louis in 1814, which allowed fanciful conjectures. Moreover for some years after Colter's trip his report of "hidden fires, smoking pits, noxious streams, and the all-pervading smell of brimstone" on the upper Yellowstone hardly enhanced his credibility. However, recent scanning techniques have enabled scholars to detect faded lines and notations on Clark's map and trace Colter's wanderings more confidently. These rediscovered lines indicate that from the east edge of the Absarokas, he crossed between them and the Owl Creek Mountains, reaching the Wind River near the site of Dubois. He then followed the Wind River up to Brooks Lake and proceeded north, east of the Divide, to Yellowstone Lake.

Colter may thus have been the first white man to see the Wind Rivers, but such distinctions are slippery; most known explorers were preceded by unknown trappers and wanderers. And of course no white man was the first person to see the Wind Rivers. The Lewis and Clark expedition included an interpreter, who was accompanied by a young Shoshone woman named Sacagawea, whose people had inhabited the mountains for several centuries.

The Shoshones had migrated northeast from the Great Basin around 1500. They were designated in sign language by a wiggly gesture—perhaps because they wove lodges from grass rather than constructing tepees from skins—and thus became known to whites as the Snakes. During the early 1800s Shoshones occupied the Green River basin southwest of the Wind Rivers.

Across the range, in the Wind River valley, lived the Absarokas, or Crows, a tribe that had migrated west from the Missouri. The Shoshones got on well with whites, and the Crows might have, too, had they not been so skillful at stealing horses.

Bison were the basis of Plains Indian life, the main source of food, clothing, and housing. Indians migrated in search of bison, tribes from west of the mountains traveling east in summer. This annual migration brought Shoshones and Crows into contact—and conflict—with Blackfeet and Gros Ventres from north of the Yellowstone, Sioux and Cheyennes from the Black Hills, and Arapahos of eastern Colorado.

Shoshones adopted Plains culture, but their relatives, the Sheepeaters or Mountain Shoshones, settled in the mountains—in the Big Horns, Wind Rivers, Absarokas, Tetons, and Yellowstone high country. Their staple foods were bighorn sheep, elk, and deer, rather than bison, though whitebark pine nuts were a surprisingly important part of their diet, and in the mountains they found dogs more useful than horses for hunting and dragging their travois. Sheepeaters spent summers in high alpine meadows; archaeologists have recently been uncovering artifacts from as many as twenty-five summer habitations, notably in the vicinity of Whiskey Mountain and Burro Flat, some as high as 11,500 feet and as old as 6,000 years. Their flakes and arrowheads turn up on game routes through passes. They also funneled game by long wooden fences, remnants of which have been found high in the Wind Rivers. Sheepeaters' trade specialties were clothing and bows; on the Plains their ram's-horn bows were worth five to ten ponies.

House pits more than 4,000 years old have been excavated in the Green River basin. On the plains where the Big Sandy River and Little Sandy Creek meet, 7,000- to 9,000-year-old knives, scrapers, and Yuma-type points have been found. Someone, or his prey, dropped a Yuma point at an 11,000-foot lake in the northern Wind Rivers.

The retreat of the last continental ice sheet apparently opened an ice-free corridor east of the Rockies 15,000 to 12,000 years ago. Nomadic tribes, having recently crossed from Asia to Alaska, spread through North America and may have discovered South Pass in their early days on the continent.

South Pass

In 1811 John Jacob Astor sent an expedition, led by Wilson Price Hunt, to establish a fur post at the mouth of the Columbia. It was the next expedition after Lewis and Clark to cross the continent. On the Missouri River three trappers, John Hoback, Jacob Reznor, and Edward Robinson, returning east after several years in the mountains, were convinced to join the expedition as guides.

Hunt had planned to follow Lewis and Clark's route, but his guides persuaded him to avoid hostile Blackfeet on the Missouri by taking a route through the mountains.

The Astorians passed the Big Horns, followed the Wind River to its head, crossed Union Pass to the Green, descended the Snake tributary now named for Hoback, and continued to Oregon.

In June 1812 Robert Stuart, who had sailed to Oregon, led an Astor party east with the first dispatches from the Pacific post. In eastern Idaho Crows ran off Stuart's horses, and the destitute Astorians crossed Teton Pass on foot to Jackson Hole. Shoshones told them of South Pass, and Stuart led his men to the Green River valley. They had been without food for a week when someone proposed the grim casting of lots so often featured in tales of starving men. Stuart cocked his gun and vetoed the lottery. The next day they killed a solitary decrepit bison.

Stuart's party continued southeast along the west edge of the "Spanish River Mountains" (the Wind Rivers), encountering Shoshones who had lost all but one old horse to the Crows. The Astorians traded for the horse and, strapping meat to its back, continued. Warned by the Shoshones of Crows camped in South Pass, the white men skirted somewhat south but reached the Sweetwater, which they descended to the North Platte and civilization.

The Astorians, more intent on avoiding Crows than in pathfinding, didn't recognize South Pass's significance. Astoria was abandoned during the War of 1812, and South Pass was forgotten. The "effective discoverers" of South Pass were led by Jedediah Smith, after Lewis and Clark the West's greatest explorer.

In February 1822 William Ashley placed an ad in the *Missouri Gazette* that began, "To Enterprising Young Men: The subscriber wishes to engage One Hundred Men, to ascend the river Missouri to its source, there to be employed for one, two or three years. For particulars. . . ." Jim Clyman, one of the few literates attracted by the ad, later wrote, "A description of our crew I cannt give but Falstafs Battalion was genteel in comparison." But the ad and another the following year brought to the mountains Smith, Clyman, Jim Bridger, Thomas Fitzpatrick, David Jackson, William Sublette, and others destined for roles in western history.

Early fur entrepreneurs established outposts to which Indians brought furs, but Ashley had his own men do the trapping. While their predecessors had ascended the Missouri by keelboat, Ashley's men rode overland on horse. Thus was born the mountain man, setting traps in icy streams, loaded Hawken across his lap, wary eyes scanning a distant horizon for game and Indians.

Trapping required exploration, and Smith in particular was on the lookout for new streams. During the winter of 1823–24 he and a party that included Fitzpatrick, Clyman, and Sublette reached the Wind River. The Crows reported plentiful beaver on the other side of the range, so in February 1824 the trappers tried to cross Union Pass, only to be turned back by snow. They returned to the Crows, where, according to Clyman, "I spread out a buffalo Robe and covered it with sand, and made . . . heaps to represent the different mountains. . . . From our sand map . . . [we] finally got the idea that we could go to Green River, called by them Seeds-ka-day."

This primitive map sent Clyman and his companions up the Popo Agie and around the south end of the Wind Rivers. Clyman and Sublette nearly froze while hunting, and when the party reached the Sweetwater, the men spent the night keeping their blankets from blowing away. In the morning the wind was still too strong for a fire. They waited behind a clump of willows that day and the next night, but the wind didn't let up. The following morning they shot a "mountain sheep" (which might have been either a bighorn or a pronghorn) but again couldn't start a fire. The wind finally died enough to allow a fire, and the men spent the second night broiling meat. The next day, during a heavy snow, they moved camp to an aspen grove, where they stayed for several weeks.

When game ran out in mid-March, Smith and his men resumed their journey, though confronted by a continual ground blizzard. By the sixth day they were desperate, having not eaten for four days, when Sublette and Clyman shot a bison. Again they couldn't light a fire, but they were hungry enough to eat the meat uncooked. Needing unfrozen water they moved on, but couldn't find a stream that day.

When the explorers reached the Little Sandy, according to Clyman, the thirsty men "went immediately to cutting the ice with their Tomahawks caled out frose to the bottom." But Clyman shot a pistol into a hole, and water came spurting up. Eventually Smith's party reached the Green, the valley of which within a few years was the heartland of a thriving fur business.

South Pass is not an alpine notch; it is a 12-mile stretch between streams, one flowing to the Atlantic, the other to the Pacific. Fremont, the pass's first surveyor, had trouble locating the actual Divide. "We were obliged to watch very closely to find the place at which we had reached the culminating point." He mused on using "pass" to describe a feature that "in no manner resembles the places to which the term is commonly applied—nothing of the gorge-like character and winding ascents of the Allegheny passes in America, nothing of the Great St. Bernard and Simplon passes in Europe." A modern traveler, despite a marked highway turnoff, may be equally skeptical. But its lack of topographic drama gave South Pass a dramatic place in western history, history that began with Smith's cold, thirsty party crossing South Pass unwittingly.

Rendezvous

In a move that further revolutionized the fur trade, Ashley didn't require his men to bring furs back to St. Louis or come east to resupply. Instead each spring he sent a pack train west with traps, powder, coffee, sugar, and what was called whiskey (raw alcohol to which ginger, molasses, or tobacco was added for flavor) to a location decided upon the previous summer. The pack train returned east with a year's harvest of fur. The first Rendezvous was held in 1824 on the Green River. Seven subsequent Rendezvous were held near the Green, two on the Popo Agie, the others at sites farther from the Wind Rivers.

A Rendezvous, which lasted three weeks, was more than an exchange of furs for supplies; it was the social event of the Rocky Mountains. Trapping was a solitary profession, and trappers—independents as well as company men—came not only to trade but to renew friendships, hear news from the States, and enjoy themselves. Shoshones, Flatheads, and Nez Perces also attended, erecting hundreds of tepees over the prairie, adding to the revelry with dancing, chanting, showing horses, and engaging in mock battles.

If there was a teetotaler present, he dispensed the whiskey, which had been diluted with Green River water. As the trappers became drunker, the alcohol was further diluted. A drunken trapper was disinclined to quibble about prices and soon spent his year's furs on whiskey, supplies, and the ribbons and needles necessary to catch the eye of an Indian lass—whether for a short-term or long-term relationship. When the whiskey kegs were empty, the trappers rode off for another lonely, vulnerable fall and spring in cold, swift streams, another winter of boredom in a sheltered valley, perhaps near the confluence of the Wind River and the Popo Agie.

No one became rich from actually trapping. Ashley, seeing that the money was in financing and supplying, sold out to Smith, Jackson, and Sublette. Four years later they in turn sold to a group that included Bridger and Fitzpatrick, who in 1834 were forced to merge with the more powerful American Fur Company, with trading posts on the upper Missouri.

Benjamin Bonneville

In 1831 Benjamin Bonneville took a two-year leave from the US Army, ostensibly to try the fur trade near South Pass. Because he did so poorly in the fur business and spent so much time exploring, historians suspect that the government had actually sent Bonneville to collect information beyond its frontiers (South Pass at the time being the point where the United States, Mexico, and British Oregon converged).

Bonneville's travels come to us from Washington Irving's *Adventures of Captain Bonneville,* compiled from a manuscript the captain wrote after returning east. Irving's biography, while giving a vivid sense of the West, has frustrated scholars—including those trying to identify the first Wind River peak to be climbed—with geographic inaccuracies.

In 1832 Bonneville built a post west of present-day Pinedale. Skeptical mountain men christened it Fort Nonsense. That August, learning that the upper Green was windy in winter, Bonneville headed up the Green, crossing the Wind Rivers apparently by Union Pass and eventually wintering in Idaho. He returned for the 1833 Rendezvous, which took place near his fort. In late July he cached supplies and crossed South Pass to trap along tributaries of the Bighorn. However, the Blackfeet so depleted his trappers of traps that Bonneville decided to return with three or four of his men (Irving's count varies) to Fort Nonsense to resupply. To avoid the indirect route through South Pass, they attempted to cross the Wind Rivers.

"The mountains were lofty, with snowy peaks and craggy sides," according to Irving. "It was hoped, however, that some practicable defile might be found." Bonneville first tried a branch of the Popo Agie but was turned back. However, the men recalled seeing a slope that appeared to rise continuously to "the snowy region." This slope, though, took Bonneville only to "the brink of a deep and precipitous ravine, from the bottom of which rose a second slope, similar to the one . . . just ascended." He descended into this ravine and ascended the second slope, only to find that what had seemed a continuous slope "was shagged by frightful precipices, and seamed with longitudinal chasms, deep and dangerous."

Nevertheless, after two days—and a night spent in a "wild dell"—the trappers found themselves in "the heart of this mountainous and awful solitude," though Irving also places them at "two bright and beautiful little lakes, set like mirrors in the midst of stern and rocky heights, and surrounded by grassy meadows, inexpressibly refreshing to the eye."

Leaving two men with the horses, the captain and one or two companions set out among the "huge crags of granite piled one upon another, and beetling like battlements far above them," still hoping to discover a route through the range. Choosing from the "gigantic peaks . . . towering far into the snowy regions of the atmosphere" the summit that appeared highest, these first white men known to have penetrated the Wind Rivers began to climb. The climbing was difficult enough that they were "frequently obliged to clamber on hands and knees, with their guns slung upon their backs" and "exhausted with fatigue . . . threw themselves upon the snow, and took handfuls of it to allay their parching thirst." But, according to Bonneville's biographer, "the pride of man is never more obstinate than when climbing mountains."

Here Irving interjects an anticlimax: "At one place they even stripped off their coats and hung them upon the bushes." This and cooling breezes seemed to reinvigorate the men, for "springing with new ardor to their task," they soon stood on a summit. "Here a scene burst upon the view of Captain Bonneville, that for a time astonished and overwhelmed him with its immensity. He stood, in fact, upon that dividing ridge which Indians regard as the crest of the world"—presumably, though not necessarily, the Continental Divide.

In order to "give some idea of its collective grandeur," Irving gives a "simple enumeration of . . . features . . . of this vast panorama." The sight included the Sweetwater, "pursuing its tranquil way through the rugged regions of the Black Hills"; the Wind River, which "forced [its] way through the range of Horn Mountains"; "glimpses of the upper streams of the Yellowstone"; "some of the sources of the . . . Columbia, flowing . . . past those towering landmarks, the Three Tetons, and pouring down into the great lava plain"; and "almost at the captain's feet, the Green River . . . dashing northward over crag and precipice . . . and tumbling into the plain, where, expanding into an ample river, it circled away to the south." Bonneville estimated the peak's elevation as 25,000 feet.

The identity of the peak climbed by Bonneville has long been a matter of speculation. Of the two sets of clues Irving provides—details of the route into the mountains and the "enumeration of features" seen from the summit—the latter has proved more distraction than help. From many northern Wind River peaks and even a few southern ones you can see the Tetons, but from none can you see lava plains beyond (in Idaho) nor Yellowstone headwaters, even with an "atmosphere . . . so pure that objects were discernible at an astonishing distance." From no summit can you see both the Sweetwater and the Green's Big Bend (which Bonneville presumably noted the year before when crossing Union Pass).

Nevertheless, Irving's details of the geography encountered by Bonneville while entering the mountains and approaching his peak enable us to narrow the possibilities to a few candidates, one being Wind River Peak. While correlations with Irving's geography do not prove that Bonneville climbed it, details match at enough points to make Wind River Peak a plausible conjecture—far more plausible than all but a few other peaks.

According to this conjecture, the branch of the Popo Agie is the South Fork of the Little Wind River. The slope that Bonneville's men hoped would take them to the "snowy region" is approximately that up which the present Dickinson Park Road switchbacks. If Wind River Peak was his peak, the "wild dell" may well have been Dickinson Park. Whether it is or not, this conjecture has them crossing Dickinson Park, rounding Dishpan Butte, and descending to the North Popo Agie, reaching it below Sanford Park. Continuing south they would have left the North Popo Agie about where today's Pinto Park Trail does. The bright and beautiful lakes would be in the Deep Creek Lakes vicinity, perhaps the Echo Lakes. Krumholz growing as high as 11,000 feet on the peak's east slopes could have provided a coat rack.

Moreover, Wind River Peak could more easily be mistaken for the high point of the Rockies than other candidates in the southern Wind Rivers. Nevertheless, in 1924 someone proposed that Bonneville's peak was Mount Chauvenet, which we know as an obscure 12,250-foot peak unmistakably east of the Divide and within sight of obviously higher peaks. However, a friend of mine explored the open slopes presumably ascended by Bonneville between the Little Wind River and the North Popo Agie. He feels the proposed Wind River Peak itinerary is too contrived, that the 1833 explorers would have simply continued up onto the Bear's Ears plateau and summited Chauvenet.

However, on the map produced by the Hayden Survey of 1877–78, the name of surveyor Louis Chauvenet is attached to the peak we know as Lizard Head, at 12,842 feet the highest summit in the Cirque of the Towers area. While the description of Bonneville's approach provides no particular evidence for his having climbed Lizard Head, and trying to identify his summit is futile, we can at least imagine him contemplating the array of Warbonnet, Shark's Nose, and Pingora standing between him and his destination.

Sir William Drummond Stewart

The first white man to think of the Wind Rivers primarily in terms of recreation appeared in 1833. Sir William Drummond Stewart was a Scot who had served as a captain under Wellington at Waterloo. An older brother inherited the family barony, and Stewart, between jobs, arrived in St. Louis in spring 1833. He fell in with the firm of Sublette and Campbell, which outfitted trappers, and traveled with Robert Campbell to Rendezvous, held that year on the Green. Stewart apparently spent the winter of

1833–34 in the West, perhaps with Jim Bridger on the Green. The summer of 1834 found him again at Rendezvous, and he returned to the West each summer until 1839.

With fast horses brought from St. Louis, Stewart often won the wild races at Rendezvous. Although he had a wife back in Scotland, one senses little passion—he had sailed for America two years after marrying and didn't return for seven years. There are indications that the handsome captain (played by Clark Gable in *Across the Wide Missouri*) was a favorite of the Indian ladies.

Stewart's military training made him useful in country where Indians might run off unguarded horses. He stood night guard, and, as one who could enforce military discipline, took charge during skirmishes. He won the respect of a tough bunch, as Kit Carson wrote, "for his liberality and many good qualities," the liberality presumably involving the liquor he brought west.

Beaver fur was most valuable when taken in spring or fall. During the summer a trapper relaxed. After a Rendezvous Stewart would invite his friends to one of the large lakes on the Wind Rivers' west slope (Fremont and New Fork are two for which we have evidence) for a week or two of fishing and hunting.

In 1837 Stewart, perhaps sensing that a way of life was ending or that his days in the West were numbered, brought the young painter Alfred Jacob Miller to Rendezvous, which was again held on the Green. (On the Sweetwater the artist was absorbed in a painting when his head was suddenly grabbed from behind and forced down. The captain was teaching him to be alert for Indians.) Toward the end of Rendezvous, Stewart took Miller and some mountain men up to Fremont Lake (once Stewart's Lake). Miller's notes mention casks of brandy and port and also trout that "were unsophisticated and bit immediately we placed the bait near their mouths in the clear water." There Miller sketched the earliest surviving illustrations of the Wind Rivers.

Stewart's brother died in 1838. In 1839 he returned to Scotland, Sir William, Baronet of Grandtully, but didn't completely leave the Wind Rivers behind. He brought his hunting guide, Clement, as a valet/gamekeeper and wrote to William Sublette requesting bison. Stewart's estate included Birnam Wood, which must have seemed as strange with buffalo roaming as it did marching toward Macbeth. Miller converted his watercolor sketches to oils, which took their place in the castle alongside Caravaggio, Corregio, Raphael, and Da Vinci.

The Oregon Trail

The last Rendezvous took place in 1838. By 1840 beaver hats were out of fashion, and Wyoming was trapped out. Some mountain men returned to the States to farm, but others had the mountains in their blood. Their one resource was intimate knowledge of a vast country that had hardly been mapped.

In 1836 Eliza Spalding and Narcissa Whitman became the first white women to cross South Pass. With their husbands they had been sent as missionaries to the Flatheads and Nez Perces and had traveled as far as the Green River Rendezvous with the year's pack train. Eliza was shocked by Rendezvous, Narcissa delighted. Marcus Whitman, a physician, won the trappers' admiration by removing a Blackfoot arrowhead from Jim Bridger's shoulder.

Missionaries' reports from Oregon soon had middle-class families leaving eastern farms for the promise of a better life out west, and during the next two decades thousands of emigrants, their worldly possessions in covered wagons pulled by cattle or oxen, followed a route that mountain men had pioneered. Veteran trappers found employment guiding emigrant parties. Wagon trains formed in western Missouri, headed overland to the South Platte, then crossed to the North Platte. The country became increasingly bizarre and alarming: grass sparser, water more alkaline, storms more violent, Indians more menacing. Even the vastness of the sky and treeless prairie were menacing. Animals weakened, loads lightened; the Oregon Trail was strewn with bones and furniture. Fort Laramie in eastern Wyoming was the first building in 600 miles. There the emigrants could resupply, repair, recuperate, and learn about the wilder, ruggeder terrain ahead. The Oregon Trail then continued up the North Platte to the Sweetwater, which it followed to South Pass.

On the prairie, progress of 15 to 20 miles a day was common, but on the Sweetwater emigrants, lowering wagons into gullies by rope and double-teaming oxen to haul them out the other side, often had to be content with a mile a day. To be trapped by winter in the mountains, as the Donner party was in the Sierra in 1846–47, was a source of constant anxiety.

At Devil's Gate the Wind Rivers came into view, and for several days parties approached Wind River Peak's otherworldly snow dome. Beyond South Pass the original Oregon Trail followed the Little Sandy and Big Sandy down to the Green. Later shortcuts (such as a well-used variant that crossed the Big Sandy at the site of the present road from Boulder to Big Sandy Opening) passed nearer the Wind Rivers, though the distance between streams and springs meant that a party was in danger of not reaching water by dark. The various versions of the Oregon Trail converged at Fort Hall, near present-day Pocatello, where the routes to Oregon and California diverged.

John C. Fremont

In 1842 an obscure young lieutenant of topographical engineers, his reputation at the time based upon his elopement with a senator's daughter, took a steamboat up the Missouri. Also aboard was a practitioner of an obscure profession—Rocky Mountain trapper—and thus John C. Fremont met Kit Carson. The US Army was sending Fremont west to survey the wagon road (not yet called the Oregon Trail) to South Pass. Carson had tried returning to civilization after sixteen years in the West, but after a few days in St. Louis he became, according to his autobiography, "tired of the settlements" and realized he preferred the mountains.

Carson told Fremont "that I had been some time in the mountains and thought I could guide him to any point he would wish to go. He replied that he would make inquiry regarding my qualifications." Apparently the references were favorable. Fremont, who later ran for president as "The Pathfinder," hired Carson as scout, adding him to a party of other experienced trappers.

Fremont's Peak, Island Lake

Carson was orphaned at a young age. An 1826 *Missouri Intelligencer* ad signaled the start of his career in the West:

> *Notice is hereby given to all persons, That Christopher Carson, a boy about 16 years old, small of his age, but thick-set; light hair, ran away from the subscriber, living in Franklin, Howard Country, Missouri, to whom he had been bound to learn the sad-dler's trade, on or about the first of September last. He is supposed to have made his way to the upper part of the state. All persons are notified not to harbor, support, or assist said boy under the penalty of the law. One cent reward will be given to any person who will bring back the said boy.*

Fremont's cartographer and artist was Charles Preuss, an impoverished German immigrant. Preuss, though, never let his gratitude for the job stand between him and his disdain for the West and the man who dragged him through it. His cynical, whining diary, published as *Exploring with Fremont,* is the perfect foil to Fremont's rosy *Report of the Exploring Expedition to the Rocky Mountains in the Year 1842.* Some of Preuss's entries are pointedly terse: "Murky weather, melancholy mood." On other days he discourses more freely: "For breakfast, yesterday's dish was warmed up; it did not taste excellent"; "Had a remarkably bad night. . . . The others lay safely under their [mosquito] nets; mine had been forgotten because of Fremont's negligence." Fremont provoked Preuss's longest commentaries, as when Carson got too far ahead:

This and other small troubles and annoyances had gotten on Fremont's nerves, which is not all surprising with a childishly passionate man like him. In consequence he decided to let this be the end of the expedition and go straightway back to the Sweet Water. . . . He imparted the news to me last night, and who was happier than I? I gladly agreed to all his reasons, whether good or bad.

Preuss sensed "a certain tension, not only between Fremont and myself, but also between me and the rest of the people. Only, of course, because I want to be smarter than the others."

Here is Preuss approaching the Wind Rivers:

Whoever has seen Switzerland and expects something similar here is bound for a great disappointment. An American [Bonneville] has measured them to be as high as 25,000 feet. I'll be hanged if they are half as high, yea, if they are 8,000 feet high. A little snow on their peaks; that is all, as far as I can see now, that distinguishes them from other high mountains.

I am reminded of the day when I walked from Liestal to Solethurn. When I came around a corner of rocks, I saw in front of me the entire range of the Alps from Mont Blanc to the Alps of Tirol. If I compare that view with the one I see today, it is as though I were to turn my eyes from the face of a lovely girl to the wrinkled face of an old woman.

It must be added that Preuss was a brave man who handled himself well in emergencies and that he produced the first competent maps of the West, resisting the temptation to incorporate the hearsay that plagued most early maps.

Fremont's assignment was to explore as far west as South Pass, but his mountain veterans were of the opinion—without the benefit during previous trips of transit or barometer—that the Wind Rivers included the highest peak in the Rockies. According to Fremont, the height of this peak "had been a theme of constant discussion." There was, therefore, enthusiasm for getting a barometer to the top.

Fremont led his entourage along the west flank of the range, camping one night on the East Fork River, the next night by Boulder Lake. With fifteen men on mules, he headed toward the high peaks. They passed through a complicated topography of hills, crooked streams, and many lakes. Evening found them in a small valley "smoothly carpeted with a soft grass, and scattered over with groups of flowers," presumably Monument Creek's valley. At a pass at the head of Monument Creek, the Titcomb Basin peaks suddenly came into view: "a gigantic disorder of enormous masses, and a savage sublimity of naked rock, in wonderful contrast with innumerable green spots of a rich floral beauty, shut up in their stern recesses." The going beyond was rocky, so three men stayed with the mules while the others proceeded on foot. Fremont Peak looks deceptively close from the pass above Monument Creek. It appeared so close to Fremont and his men that, expecting to climb it and return that day, they took little clothing and no food—except Preuss: "Only I, a more experienced mountaineer, stuck a piece of dried buffalo meat in my pocket."

They descended to Little Seneca Lake. The next few miles are frustrating for a modern backpacker, who may find slight consolation in recognizing the route in Fremont's century-and-a-half-old description:

> *The first ridge hid a succession of others; and when with great fatigue and difficulty we had climbed up five hundred feet, it was but to make an equal descent on the other side. . . . We clambered on, always expecting, with every ridge that we crossed, to reach the foot of the peaks, and always disappointed, until . . . pretty well worn out, we reached the shore of a little lake, in which there was a rocky island.*

Thus the name Island Lake, the only name Fremont left in the Wind Rivers and one of the few he left anywhere. (Golden Gate was another.) The men made what camp their scant provisions allowed on a bluff overlooking Island Lake, near the falls that drop from Titcomb Basin.

Before Island Lake, according to Preuss, "the leader, Carson, walked too fast. This caused some exchange of words. Fremont got excited, as usual. . . . Fremont developed a headache. . . ." Although altitude's effects weren't then well known, Fremont's own notes also suggest that the leader suffered from altitude more than most.

The wind and cold of the dinnerless, blanketless bivouac didn't improve Fremont's condition, and as for Preuss, "as always, the best spots were already taken . . . and I can truthfully say that I did not sleep a single minute." Both mention being grateful for daybreak, though the day, August 14, was hardly a success. The party evidently approached their objective via Indian Basin, then scattered in search of a feasible route. Fremont became progressively sicker and eventually could go no farther. Two French Canadians became ill and lay down on rocks. Preuss, trying to cross snow, slipped and fell a few hundred feet into rocks, where he "turned a couple of somersets" but survived with minor bruises. Nevertheless, Carson climbed the peak to the right of their objective, to see if he could cross to the main peak. He could not, and did not deem the ascent worth mention in his autobiography, but he evidently climbed 13,517-foot Jackson Peak—the second reported ascent of a peak in the Wind Rivers, even if its identification is speculative.

Some of the men had gone back for mules, blankets, and food, and the second night at Island Lake was more comfortable than the first. Fremont, planning to leave the mountains in the morning, sent Carson out ahead at dawn. But the remaining men—Fremont, Preuss, Basil Lajeunesse, Clement Lambert, Johnny Janisse, and de Coteau (or Descoteaux)—felt well enough for another try at their peak and headed up "a defile of the most rugged mountains known." The defile was probably

Titcomb Basin, though it could have been Indian Basin. In either they would have been "riding along the huge wall which forms the central summits of the chain . . . terminating 2,000 to 3,000 feet above . . . in a serrated line of broken, jagged cones" and encountered "three small lakes of a green color, each of perhaps a thousand yards in diameter."

The six made a point of taking their time and resting when tired. Halfway up, Fremont changed from thick-soled moccasins to a thinner pair, "as now the use of our toes became necessary to a further advance." Fremont's route is today rated class 3. Nevertheless, he describes ascending a crack by jamming hands and feet. Upon reaching the crest he "sprang upon the summit, and another step would have precipitated me into an immense snow field five hundred feet below"—Upper Fremont Glacier.

The victorious climbers rammed a pole into a crevice, attached the American flag, and admired the setting:

> *Around us, the whole scene had one main striking feature, which was that of terrible convulsion. Parallel to its length, the ridge was split into chasms and fissures; between which rose the thin lofty walls, terminated with slender minarets and columns. A stillness the most profound and a terrible solitude forced themselves constantly on the mind as the great features of the place. Here, on the summit . . . the stillness was absolute, unbroken by any sound, and the solitude complete.*

Fremont's barometer indicated an elevation of 13,570 feet—remarkably close to the 13,745 feet on current maps. Preuss guessed in his diary that the barometer readings "will probably correspond to almost 10,000 feet."

Preuss did not keep his diary for several days but caught up after the climb, his entries suggesting he was as anxious as the others to reach the top and pleased with the climb. His one complaint is that Fremont did not give him time to make measurements on top and that "when the time comes for me to make my map in Washington, he will more than regret this unwise haste."

Fremont's wife, Jessie, polished his journals for publication, adding much in the way of flair, but these may have been his own reflections as he left the summit:

> *We had accomplished an object of laudable ambition, and beyond the strict order of our instructions. We had climbed the loftiest peak of the Rocky mountains, and looked down upon the snow a thousand feet below, and, standing where never human foot had stood before, felt the exultation of first explorers.*

Washakie

The mountain men needed to distinguish Indian friends from enemies and to fight those enemies in equal numbers, with similar weapons. Neither emigrants nor the US Army, which appeared in the area around 1850 to guard the Oregon Trail, needed these abilities. Emigrants did not need Indians for business or in-laws and were frightened by all natives; soldiers were better armed. It was railroads, settlers, miners, and the disruption of bison herds that led to atrocities later in the century. The Union Pacific reached Cheyenne in 1867, and the following year South Pass's gulches and hillsides were torn up by 2,000 new arrivals in search of gold. The gold rush soon fizzled, but other strikes, notably in the Black Hills, brought whites into conflict with the region's tribes. Hostilities on the plains to the east resulted in Indians settling in the out-of-the-way Wind River valley.

The Shoshones were blessed with a great leader through most of the nineteenth century. This man, Washakie, foresaw the country's future and sought a home that would be out of the whites' way. The Shoshones fought the Crows for the Wind River valley from 1856 to 1859, until, in the Battle of Crowheart Butte, the Shoshones finally prevailed. (According to legend, the battle reached a stalemate on the third day, so Washakie and the Crow chief resolved it in single combat.)

At a council involving government agents and several tribes held in 1868 at Fort Bridger, Washakie requested the Wind River valley. Whites, glad to have natives away from the railroad being extended across southern Wyoming, signed a treaty establishing the Wind River Reservation. Sheepeaters later joined the Shoshones. Their last chief, Togwotee, achieved fame for guiding Chester Allen Arthur during his trip to Yellowstone.

In 1864 the Arapahos left Colorado to join the Sioux after Colorado militia massacred 500 Arapahos and Cheyennes, mostly women and children, at Sand Creek. After the 1876 Battle of Little Big Horn, when these tribes wiped out an entire unit led by the US Army's most renowned Indian fighter, Lt. Col. George Armstrong Custer, the army set out to kill all hostiles or herd them onto reservations. Starving, the Arapahos came to Washakie to ask for shelter. Washakie agreed to let them stay the winter. When spring came, the US government realized that by keeping the Arapahos on the reservation, they could dispose of them without further land grants. Today the reservation is shared by 2,500 Shoshones and 5,000 Arapahos.

Surveyors

In 1870 Americans knew little about the interior West, but government survey parties were filling in the map. As they mapped, these surveys studied geology, biology, archaeology, and ethnography according to the whims of their leaders—John Wesley Powell, Clarence King, George M. Wheeler, and Ferdinand Vandeveer Hayden. With domains only vaguely identified and their efforts barely coordinated, the leaders often acted more like entrepreneurs than scientists, scrambling through Washington to increase their territories and funding. Art attracted Congress's attention, so the surveys competed not only for turf but for artists, the best being painter Thomas Moran, photographer William Henry Jackson, and a sketcher of topography and geology far superior to modern rock-route topo artists, William Henry Holmes.

The energetic Hayden wandered unsystematically through Colorado and Wyoming, investigating whatever interested him. The summer of 1877 found Hayden's men in the Wind Rivers. A. D. Wilson led a survey party that left South Pass in late June, climbed Wind River and West Atlantic Peaks (another party climbed Atlantic Peak), then continued northwest, "keeping near the foot of the great granite plateau which here flanks the range." After passing "beautiful glacial lakes which lay embedded between those great moraines," Wilson, with Ernest Ingersoll and Harry Yount (who held the important position of hunter), "started for the point I then took to be Fremont's Peak." Setting out in early morning, they reached the summit by 9 a.m., only to find themselves on an insignificant peak; their description fits 11,857-foot Mount Baldy suspiciously well. Their consolation was a view of their intended objective, 8 miles north, but deep snow led Wilson to postpone his assault on what he believed to be the range's highest peak.

Wilson returned to the Wind Rivers in 1878, later in the summer than his visit of 1877 and bringing Jackson and Holmes to depict the landscape. This time they found Fremont Peak, and on August 7 a group that included Wilson, Jackson, Holmes, and Hayden climbed it. In an era when glaciers greatly interested scientists, they were delighted to find glaciers on the flanks of Wind River and Fremont Peaks—according to Hayden, the "first known to exist east of the Pacific coast."

A Holmes sketch catches a triangulation team at work on Fremont's summit, with (according to its caption) a "snow capped peak north of Fremont's" visible in the background. Wilson's report, though, gives no hint that the surveyors found this snowcapped peak to be higher. The surveyors were establishing a triangulation network across the West, and it was more important to them to sight lines to Wind River Peak and the Grand Teton than to an unknown nearby promontory. By 1905–06, when that snowcapped peak was determined to be nearly 60 feet higher than Fremont, the four surveys had been consolidated as the US Geological Survey, its chief geographer being Henry Gannett.

Mountaineers

In the early twentieth century climbers began to visit the Wind Rivers for sport, and Gannett Peak was climbed by Arthur Tate and Floyd Stahlnaker in 1922. Between 1924 and 1926 Colorado parties that included Albert Ellingwood climbed Warren, Turret, Helen, Sacagawea, Fremont, Knife Point, and the peak we call Ellingwood. Mount Woodrow Wilson was climbed from Dinwoody Glacier in 1924 and from Titcomb Basin in 1930. In 1929 New Englanders Kenneth Henderson and Robert Underhill, sometimes with Henry Hall, made first ascents of Doublet and the Sphinx and established new routes on Turret, Warren, and Gannett.

During the 1930s the lower summits on Titcomb Basin's west side and around Peak Lake—Split, the Twins, American Legion, Arrowhead, Sulphur, and Henderson among them—were first visited, some by Henderson and Underhill, others by Paul Petzoldt. A series of articles published by Henderson in *Appalachia* during the 1930s served as the first guidebook to the Wind Rivers.

In 1945 and 1946, Hans Kraus visited Dinwoody Glacier and Titcomb Basin, and, while his predecessors limited themselves to easy 5th-class routes, Kraus established routes as hard as 5.7. Demonstrating an eye for an elegant line, he climbed the east buttress of Gannett, the northwest buttress of Warren, the Sphinx's southwest ridge, Les Dames Anglaises, Woodrow Wilson's south face, and Helen's Tower Ridge.

Ellingwood wrote in 1930 that "the main attractions of the Wind River range lie between Knife Point Mountain and the North Gannett Glacier." He, Henderson, Underhill, and Kraus, bringing the alpine tradition of glaciers and high summits, climbed only from Dinwoody Glacier, Titcomb Basin, and Peak Lake. But locals had long been clambering throughout the range. In 1906 young Finis Mitchell and his family arrived by mule-drawn wagon near the range's west slope. Three years later, while hunting with his father, the boy climbed New Fork Lookout Point. In 1930 Mitchell started a fishing camp, over the years planting trout in hundreds of lakes. By Henderson and Underhill's time, his list of summits included Washakie, Big Sandy, East Temple, Nystrom, the Warriors, Watch Tower, and the peak since given his name—southern peaks unknown to the out-of-state alpinists. Mitchell was continuing to ramble through the Wind Rivers eighty years after his initial climb.

The North Popo Agie flows from terrain that was unknown to the climbing world when Orrin Bonney and Frank and Notsie Garnick followed it to its source in 1940. From Lonesome Lake they climbed Lizard Head—the highest nearby peak—and a tower beyond the lake. The following year Bonney returned to climb a peak that had defeated him the year before. In an *Appalachia* article he called the tower Pingora, the 1941 peak Warbonnet, and the basin they enclose the Cirque of the Towers. Eight years later much of the range was still unknown when George Bell, Denny Fox, and Joe Sargeant traveled its length. Climbing whatever caught their fancy, they paused at Shadow Lake, behind the Cirque from the perspective of Lonesome Lake, and made first ascents of Wolf's Head and Shark's Nose. Additional Cirque pioneering was carried out by Midwestern outing clubs; the Wisconsin Hoofers (in 1951), the Chicago Mountaineering Club (in 1953), and the Iowa Mountaineers (in 1958) visited virtually every summit accessible from Lonesome Lake.

Overhanging Tower was first climbed in 1948, an event reported in the *American Alpine Journal* by Fred Beckey. He next reported a Wind River route in 1961, and for forty years thereafter his accounts of Wind River ascents were an annual *AAJ* feature. Beckey's routes surmount the high (Gannett, Fremont, Helen), the conspicuous (Squaretop, Bonneville, Temple), the popular (Wolf's Head, Pingora, Haystack), and the best of the obscure (Spider, Arrowhead, Musembeah). His 1960 achievements included routes on Squaretop, with Layton Kor, and Shark's Nose, with Ken Weeks and Yvon Chouinard. Kor and Chouinard were bringing to the mountains a more expansive vision of what climbing could be, acquired from experiences on walls bigger than anything in the Wind Rivers. In 1964 Yosemite climbers Royal Robbins, Dick McCracken, and Charlie Raymond spent three and a half days ascending Mount Hooker's 1,800-foot north face. During the next decade hard climbing concentrated in the granitic south: the Cirque, Haystack, and the East Fork Valley.

During the 1970s climbers looked again at the less Yosemite-like north, and most of the notable routes of the 1970s ascended such alpine peaks as Fremont, Helen, and Sulphur. In 1971 Ray Jacquot and Bill Lindberg climbed the 1,500-foot ice finger of Tower Gully on Mount Helen, which became the range's classic ice climb.

It is inevitably harder to make sense of recent history than to see the patterns in long-ago events. When I read recent journal and online accounts, receive e-mails, or, as in the old days, simply talk with climbers, I learn of climbers doing harder routes in familiar places (Wolf's Head, Warbonnet); studying maps for obscure places (Lost Eagle Pinnacle, Continental Towers); looking at previously overlooked minor formations (Kendall Candle, Not Notch Pinnacle), routes that fill gaps between existing lines (Ambush, Hooker), routes that are merely worthy, not historic (Arrowhead, Musembeah North), and first free ascents of existing aid routes (Lost Temple). When I encounter humanity in the mountains, I am also impressed by the variety—climbers hiking faster than I ever did, carrying packs heavier than I ever did, families with kids on their first outing, recluses wandering the least accessible, least documented valleys and plateaus, average climbers maximizing short vacations by focusing on certified classics. I encounter people fishing, photographing, studying wildlife, walking from Mexico to Canada. If there is a pattern, it is increasing diversity.

Access and Trailheads

Highways parallel the Wind River crest on both sides: US 191 (coinciding with US 189 part of the way) in the Green River basin to the southwest and US 26/287 in the Wind River valley to the northeast. These roads are connected by WY 28, which crosses South Pass at the range's southeast end.

You reach trailheads, which the Forest Service calls Wilderness Entrances, by turning from highways onto roads that are typically unpaved. The Forest Service is good about placing signs at key junctions on roads to popular Wilderness Entrances, but since a missing sign can send you astray, access roads are described here. Trailheads that entail four-wheel-drive roads, cross private property closed to the public, or aren't generally useful are omitted. Numbers in parentheses are trailhead elevations.

Union Pass Road

At one time reaching the Wind River valley from the upper Green River via Union Pass was a motoring adventure that involved careful map-reading to avoid washed-out, pot-holed jeep tracks, but logging has, for better or worse, led to road improvements.

The Union Pass Road leaves the Green River Road just past Whiskey Grove Campground, 28 miles from US 191. It intersects US 26/287 by the Wind River 10 miles from Dubois and 21 miles from Togwotee Pass.

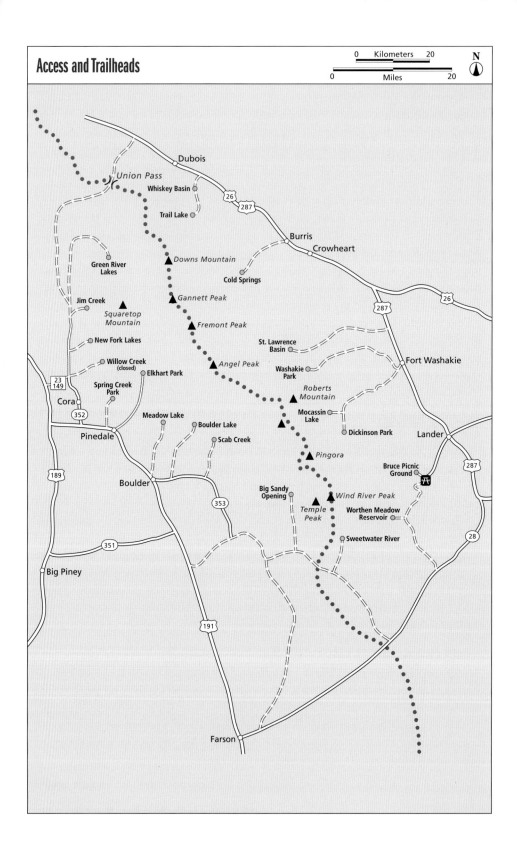

0 — Kilometers — 20

0 — Miles — 20

N

Union Pass
Dubois
Whiskey Basin
26
287
Trail Lake
Burris
Crowheart
Green River Lakes
Downs Mountain
Cold Springs
287
26
Jim Creek
Squaretop Mountain
Gannett Peak
New Fork Lakes
Fremont Peak
St. Lawrence Basin
Willow Creek (closed)
Elkhart Park
Angel Peak
Washakie Park
Fort Washakie
23 149
Spring Creek Park
Roberts Mountain
Cora
352
Meadow Lake
Mocassin Lake
Lander
Pinedale
Boulder Lake
Dickinson Park
287
Scab Creek
Bruce Picnic Ground
189
Pingora
Boulder
Big Sandy Opening
Wind River Peak
28
353
Temple Peak
Worthen Meadow Reservoir
351
Sweetwater River
Big Piney
191
Farson

Green River Lakes (8,040)

Leave US 191 6 miles west of Pinedale (5 miles east of the junction of US 191 with US 189) and turn toward Cora on WY 352. The pavement ends after 25 miles; the road continues unpaved along the Green for another 19 miles, around its Big Bend, to a large parking area adjacent to Green River Lakes Campground, a large facility that offers all amenities. Be advised, though, that the campground has been favored by grizzly bears; check with the Forest Service office in Pinedale.

If you are coming from Jackson, turn from US 189/191, 2 miles after crossing the Green, onto CR 23-149. This shortcut intersects the Green River Road north of Cora, opposite the Willow Creek Road.

Jim Creek Road (8,400)

Turn off the Green River Road less than 0.5 mile past milepost 23 (that is, 23 miles from US 191), 9.3 miles from the New Fork Lakes turnoff. The Jim Creek Road climbs for a mile to a junction, where the Kendall Mountain quad shows it ending. However, the right fork continues along Jim Creek for another mile to a defunct bridge. Parking is informal, cramped, but rarely crowded. The road is passable by two-wheel-drive vehicles, but not by much.

To reach the South Fork of Gypsum Creek, follow the Jim Creek Road for a mile, then bear left onto FR 711 (shown as a trail on the Kendall Mountain quad, as a road that doesn't quite intersect the Jim Creek Road on the Earthwalk map). FR 711 is drivable by high-clearance two-wheel-drive vehicles for 2 miles, to the footbridge that crosses Gypsum Creek's South Fork (at 8,600 feet).

New Fork Lakes (7,895)

Turn off the Green River Road 15 miles from US 191, follow a dirt road 4 miles to the lower lake, and continue along the left shore to Narrows Campground (which has drinking water). The trailhead is just north of the campground.

Willow Creek (7,920)

The present road to the Willow Creek trailhead has been blocked by the owner of property it crosses.

If the original road reopens: Follow the Green River Road for 8 miles and turn right at the Box R Ranch. (If you are coming via CR 23-149, turn right onto the Green River Road, then left in 100 yards.) Follow a dirt road for 9 miles to Willow Creek Guard Station, a group of reddish buildings on the left. Park a few hundred yards beyond the buildings. The Section Corner Lake Trail begins at the far end of the turnaround/parking area, the Lowline at the left side.

Spring Creek Park (8,440)

Turn north near the west end of Pinedale onto Jackson Street, which is marked with a sign for Soda Lake Wildlife Refuge. Without turning right to Soda Lake and the refuge, continue to a T intersection, 9.5 miles from Pinedale. Turn right onto a rougher road (FR 753) that in 2.5 miles reaches a large meadow that serves as the trailhead parking area. The trails nominally begin on the road (with nearby trail variants) just right of the trailhead bulletin board. This road, though, is no rougher than what you have driven, and it is possible to continue for another mile, to a pair of ponds. Look for the Glimpse Lake Trail circling through a fine aspen grove south of the first pond.

The road that continues west of the ponds is the start of the Trapper Lake Trail. Rugged vehicles can continue on this road for another 1.5 miles, nearly to the wilderness boundary, although the final 0.5 mile is extremely rough. Park where the trail inconspicuously diverges right from the road, which climbs steeply left.

Elkhart Park (9,380)

Prominent signs near the east end of Pinedale, where US 191 bends, mark a road to Fremont and Half Moon Lakes. Follow the road 3 miles to a junction. The left fork goes to Fremont Lake; bear right for Elkhart Park. Passing turnoffs for Half Moon Lake and White Pine Ski Area, continue around a bend with a scenic viewpoint, past Elkhart Park Guard Station to an immense parking area, 14 miles of paved road from Pinedale. The Pole Creek Trail begins at the parking area. The road continues to Trail's End Campground (potable water), where the Pine Creek Canyon Trail begins.

Meadow Lake (7,920)

A mile north of Boulder, turn from US 191 onto a dirt road (FR 5106) marked with a small sign 100 feet from the highway. After 7 miles (good dirt), bear left (FR 766) as another road bears right to Boulder Lake's outlet. After another 3 miles, again bear left at a turnoff to the right for Burnt Lake, cross Fall Creek, and, after 200 feet, turn left again.

FR 766 ends at an unimproved camping area east of Meadow Lake, but turn right at a fork just before this camping area (FR 766A) and park in a meadow on the left. The road continues for a few hundred feet to a locked gate (and continues across private property). The Timico Lake Trail begins by climbing to the right just before the gate.

Boulder Lake (7,300)

At Boulder (a gas station/store/bar and a few ranches 12 miles south of Pinedale), turn east from US 191 onto a paved road, WY 353. After 2.5 miles, turn north onto a dirt road. Where it forks, bear right. In 10 miles the road reaches a backcountry parking area south of Boulder Creek. The Boulder Canyon Trail begins on this side of the creek; the Lake George Trail at the campground across the bridge, north of the creek.

Scab Creek (7,868)

Leave US 191 at Boulder, as for Boulder Lake, but continue on WY 353 for 6 miles. Just beyond a small Air Force building, near the East Fork River, turn north. Bear left at a fork and continue past Mountain Springs Ranch for a few miles to a recently expanded parking area at the base of a steep hillside. A short distance beyond is a campground, also recently improved.

Big Sandy (9,080)

There are four ways to reach this entrance. The northernmost follows WY 353 from Boulder (see Boulder Lake, above) but continues to the end of the pavement 18 miles from Boulder. The road once turned left at a junction 0.5 mile beyond the pavement's end but has been rerouted. It now continues straight for 9 miles to a junction reached after crossing the Big Sandy River. Turn left and proceed 7 miles to another junction and another left turn. Climb through aspens and pass Dutch Joe Guard Station to the meadows of Big Sandy Opening. Beyond side roads to Sedgewick Meadows and Temple Creek Summer Homes is a fork; the left road goes to Big Sandy Lodge, the right one passes through Big Sandy Campground to a wilderness parking area at the campground's far end.

The second route leaves US 191 some 15 miles south of Boulder, 30 miles north of Farson. A dirt road—the Muddy Speedway—meets the road from Boulder (WY 353) at the junction just beyond the end of WY 353's pavement.

The third route is useful for reaching Big Sandy Opening from Rock Springs and points south and east. At Farson, leave US 191, turning east onto WY 28. After 2 miles, turn left onto a dirt road; this turn should be well marked. The road leads 40 miles to the second junction mentioned above.

A fourth route is useful for getting to Big Sandy Opening from Lander and points north and east. Turn west from WY 28 onto a dirt road just south of the Sweetwater River; look for a sign indicating Sweetwater Gap Ranch. After 15 miles a road branches right to the ranch and the site of the Sweetwater Guard Station. Continue straight for another 10 miles to the third junction on the Boulder route.

Sweetwater River (8,881)

You can reach the Sweetwater River Entrance by any of the four routes to Big Sandy Opening. Take the fourth route as far as the junction 15 miles from WY 28. Alternatively, take any of the first three routes to the third junction, but rather than turning north to Big Sandy Opening, continue southeast, bearing left at a fork 5 miles beyond to reach the Sweetwater Gap Ranch junction 5 miles farther.

Turn left toward Sweetwater Gap Ranch and Guard Station; after 8 miles you reach a junction. To reach the Little Sandy and Sweetwater Gap Trails, bear left and continue for 2 miles of rough road to a small parking area in a burned forest. To reach the defunct Christina Pass Trail, turn right at the junction toward the site of the Sweetwater Guard Station. Turn left after 0.25 mile to a meadow by the Sweetwater, the site of a new campground. A sign commemorates the guard station, which burned in 1978.

Sinks Canyon–Louis Lake Road

Several trails begin along a road that crosses from Lander to WY 28 near South Pass. Follow signs in Lander to WY 131 and Sinks Canyon State Park. The road is paved as far as Sinks Canyon. Past the pavement's end, 10.5 miles from Lander, the Middle Fork Trail begins at Bruce Picnic Ground (7,139).

The road leaves the Middle Popo Agie and switchbacks up to Frye Lake. A mile beyond Frye Lake, 17.5 miles from Lander, the road to Worthen Meadow Reservoir branches west (see below).

After another 5.5 miles the road passes Fiddler's Lake (9,411); at a trailhead a few hundred feet south of the lake, the Christina Lake Trail begins. At the southeast end of Grannier Meadow (8,844), which the road passes 8 miles from Louis Lake, the Christina Lake Road begins.

Thirty-seven miles from Lander, the Sinks Canyon–Louis Lake Road reaches WY 28.

Worthen Meadow Reservoir (8,840)

Since the Cony Mountain quad was mapped in 1953, the Roaring Fork was dammed a mile below Roaring Fork Lake to create Worthen Meadow Reservoir. The Forest Service has developed the area as a campground and trailhead, and a well-graded 2-mile-long road leads to it from the Sinks Canyon–Louis Lake Road. Drive past the reservoir's south shore to the campground, to the west. Trailhead parking is beyond the campground. The Sheep Bridge Trail begins at the parking area, while the Stough Creek Lakes Trail starts 100 yards back down the road.

Dickinson Park (9,337) and Moccasin Lake (9,515)

Leave US 287 at a store and gas station at the south edge of Fort Washakie. The turn isn't marked, but the road is paved for 3 miles. Where it turns to dirt, take the right fork, which switchbacks 15 miles to a junction. Turn left for Dickinson Park and, for the Smith Lake and North Fork Trails, continue past a turnoff to Dickinson Creek Campground (no treated water). Nearly at the road's end you will see a 300-foot boardwalk to the left. Park just beyond. For the Bear's Ears Trail, turn right before reaching the campground. The trail begins at the end of this side road. Although Dickinson Park is on national forest land, the road crosses the Wind River Reservation, and a reservation permit is required.

To reach Moccasin Lake, turn right at the junction 18 miles from Fort Washakie, where the Dickinson Park road turns left. After 4 miles the lake comes into view; descend a short spur and park there, by the lake. The Gaylord Lake Trail begins by circling the lake's south end.

Washakie Park (8,960)

Washakie Park is a 2-mile-long meadow (on the reservation; you need a permit) from which you can reach Twenty Lakes Creek and Roberts Mountain in a day. The road to Washakie Park is the range's steepest access road (though it does not require four-wheel drive) and perhaps the most scenic.

At Fort Washakie, turn from US 287 onto the North Fork Road, as for Dickinson Park, but after 0.7 mile bear right onto another paved road, then after 0.6 mile bear left. Five miles from Fort Washakie, turn left onto Washakie Park Road; after another mile, turn left again onto a one-lane (though smooth for several miles) dirt road. After ascending tiny Timoco Creek's large canyon, you enter Washakie Park, 17.5 miles from Fort Washakie. Cross the meadow for 1.5 miles to its south end, where a missing culvert stops all but the boldest four-wheelers.

St. Lawrence Basin (8,561)

Turn from US 287 8.5 miles south of its junction with US 26, which is 7.5 miles from Fort Washakie and just north of Sage Creek, onto a road that is paved for 8 miles. At the only junction with another paved road, go straight rather than right. Eleven miles of dirt road lead to St. Lawrence Ranger Station. Park near the building for the Raft Lake Trail; continue to the road's end for the Paradise Basin Trail. St. Lawrence is on Indian land, so obtain a permit.

Cold Springs (9,520)

A road unmarked by a sign turns from US 26/287 a mile north of Burris (a few buildings where the highway crosses Dry Creek), 24 miles southeast of Dubois and 7 miles northwest of Crowheart. This road, labeled Gannett Peak Road on some maps, leads to Cold Springs, the closest trailhead to Gannett. However, use of this road is limited to a reservation outfitter based in Crowheart, though this monopoly is not necessarily to your detriment. The "chauffeur's" old pickup takes a beating to which you probably wouldn't want to subject your own vehicle. One section of the road is no more than a bouldery streambed that receives only sporadic maintenance, if that. The trailhead is little more than a turnaround, marked by an outhouse, where the outfitter drops you off.

In planning an itinerary, take into account that the outfitter may not drop you off early enough to allow a full day's hike.

Whiskey Basin (7,422) and Trail Lake (7,560)

Turn from US 26/287 4 miles east of Dubois onto a dirt road that immediately branches. Take the left-hand road (the right-hand road goes to a fish hatchery). After 2 miles you reach a T and an exhibit for the Whiskey Basin Wildlife Habitat, which provides winter range for bighorn sheep. For the Ross Lake Trail, beginning just north of the fenceline, park nearby.

To reach the Whiskey Creek Trail, turn left at the exhibit, then quickly turn right at the second of two dirt roads, passing a gray metal barn. After 0.7 mile, turn right again (Point 7,422 on maps); this road is the trail's beginning.

To reach Trail Lake Ranch, turn left at the T but continue on the main road past Torrey, Ring, and Trail Lakes. The road, once notoriously rugged, has been relocated and improved. The trailhead for the Whiskey Mountain, Lake Louise, and Glacier Trails is located a mile upstream from Trail Lake Ranch. While the trailhead is known officially as Trail Lake, it is actually a few miles from Trail Lake and would be more accurately called Torrey Creek. While you can sleep at the trailhead, there is no campground or treated water.

HELP US KEEP THIS GUIDE UP TO DATE

Every effort has been made by the author and editors to make this guide as accurate and useful as possible. However, many things can change after a guide is published—trails are rerouted, regulations change, techniques evolve, facilities come under new management, and so on.

We would appreciate hearing from you concerning your experiences with this guide and how you feel it could be improved and kept up to date. While we may not be able to respond to all comments and suggestions, we'll take them to heart, and we'll also make certain to share them with the author. Please send your comments and suggestions to the following address:

Globe Pequot Press
Reader Response/Editorial Department
P.O. Box 480
Guilford, CT 06437

Or you may e-mail us at: editorial@GlobePequot.com

Thanks for your input, and happy trails!

Map Legend

══287══	US Highway	▲	Campground
══353══	State Highway	🏠	Guard Station
══149══	County Road	• 3	Mileage Marker
────────	Local Road	‿	Pass
════════	Unpaved Road	▲	Peak/Summit
----------	Trail	🅰	Picnic Area
················	Off–Trail Hike	❶, ◯	Trailhead
••••••••••	Continental Divide	○	Town
〜〜〜	Small River/Creek		
⬭	Body of Water/Reservoir		
▨	Glacier		

The Ross Lakes area, seen here looking west toward the Divide from Goat Flat, is terrain of flat high surfaces and rugged canyons.

1 Ross Lakes

The Wind River block was once part of a vast flat surface, but the block rose relative to adjacent valleys, and streams over the millennia and glaciers during the ice ages whittled it into mountains. The streams and glaciers haven't finished their work, though; level areas remain, especially at the range's north end, east of the Continental Divide. Half of this area is high plateau, gently rising toward the Divide, which traverses a broad surface undulating from 11,000 feet to over 13,000 feet.

The old plateau is dissected, east of the Divide, by streams that occupy canyons: Jakey's Fork to the north, Torrey Creek's branches in the central part, and, to the south, Downs Fork, Grasshopper Creek, and Klondike Creek. These streams flow from large lakes tucked under the plateau: Simpson Lake on Jakey's Fork, the Ross Lakes on West Torrey Creek, and Downs and Klondike Lakes on their eponymous creeks.

The two Ross Lakes lie between large plateau remnants—Ram Flat to the west and Middle Mountain to the east. East Torrey Creek flows between Torrey Peak and one of the long ridges rising from the Wind River valley, Goat Flat. Near this creek's head is the area's main climbing attraction, Spider Peak. The Torrey Creeks originate in snow-filled cirques near the Divide, under the range's northernmost 13,000-foot summit, Downs Mountain.

The Divide extends northwest from Downs and Ram Flat through Three Waters Mountain and Union Peak, as the range loses its alpine character toward Union Pass. It extends several miles south from Downs past other peaks included in this chapter: Yukon, Klondike, Pedestal, and Flagstone. A long north-south trench to the east of these peaks is occupied by several snowfields, the largest of which is Grasshopper Glacier.

Most topographic maps explain the types of lines used to represent roads and trails, but on the Downs Mountain quad, instead of a legend there are the words "No roads or trails in this area." No maintained trails reach the heart of this area, and ascending the canyons by game trails, boulder-hopping, and bushwhacking can be rugged going. But whether you're approaching from the east or from Green River Lakes west of the Divide, once you get high, say via the Glacier Trail, travel on the plateaus tends to be efficient. There is occasional horrid scree, but much of the surface is easy walking, at least when the wind isn't excessive. The plateau segments offer extensive views and the possibility of seeing bighorn sheep.

Most of the peaks included in this chapter are covered by the Downs Mountain quad, though those near Klondike Lake are on the Gannett Peak quad. Ross Lakes and points north are on the Simpson Lake map, and the northwestern part of this section is on the Union Peak map. Eastern approaches are covered by the Torrey Lake, Ink Wells, and Fremont Peak North quads.

Trails

Union Peak Road

Union Pass to Granite Lake—10 miles

A road along the Continental Divide sounds exciting, but the Divide here is so gentle that you can't always tell which side you're on. This primitive road leaves the Union Pass Road about 0.5 mile north of the pass and immediately fords a fork of Warm Spring Creek, a ford that deters most vehicles. The track crosses the Divide a few times, wanders south and east, and climbs to 11,400 feet southeast of Union Peak. It ends at Granite Lake, in a cirque on the north side of Three Waters Mountain.

Simpson Lake Trail

Whiskey Mountain to Simpson Lake—7 miles

From a 10,450-foot benchmark on Whiskey Mountain's northwest shoulder, trails radiate in five directions. The Whiskey Creek and Whiskey Mountain Trails and the Ross Lake Trail northbound descend to civilization, while the Ross Lake Trail southbound descends to Lower Ross Lake, and the fifth trail descends west to Wasson Creek. The Simpson Lake quad considers this fifth trail to be a continuation of the Whiskey Mountain Trail, but signs label it the Simpson Lake Trail.

The Simpson Lake Trail levels out for an uninteresting 4 miles past Soapstone Lake, where Indians got rock from which to carve bowls, to Simpson Lake. The final 0.5 mile is incorrect on the topographic map: The trail crosses Cabin Creek and descends more to the south, reaching the lake near the large cove.

From Simpson Lake a trail goes north to Moon Lake, out of this guide's area, and the Sandra Lake Trail goes south to the headwaters of Jakey's Fork.

A trail follows Jakey's Fork and Wasson Creek upstream from the CM Ranch, but the trailhead is on private land, closed to the public, and the trail is omitted from this guide.

Sandra Lake Trail

Simpson Lake to Sandra Lake—2.5 miles

Although not shown on USGS maps, a trail leaves the Simpson Lake Trail near the cabins on the lake's east side, follows the shore south, crosses Jakey's Fork 0.75 mile above the lake, and continues upstream to Sandra and Pinto Lakes. A path continues up the valley to Pass 10,960+ at its head.

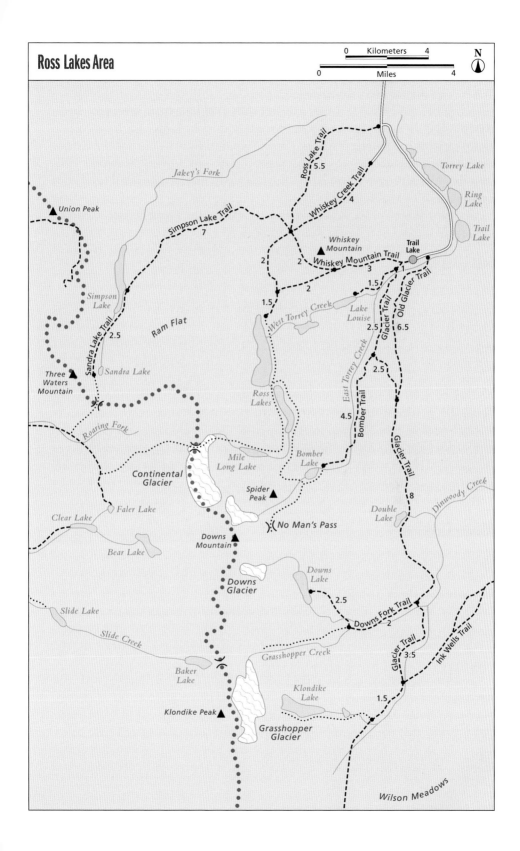

Ross Lakes Area

Kilometers

Miles

N

Ross Lake Trail

Whiskey Basin to Lower Ross Lake—9 miles

Just north of the wildlife habitat exhibit on the Trail Lake Road, a road that heads west through the sagebrush is blocked by a gate. This is the Ross Lake Trail, which is closed to vehicles to protect bighorn habitat. Turning south, it climbs above treeline on Whiskey Mountain. It meets the Whiskey Creek and Whiskey Mountain Trails, then descends into drab forest, where it inefficiently wanders up and down before descending to Lower Ross Lake.

With the closure of the Ross Lake Trail to vehicles, the Forest Service has developed the Whiskey Creek Trail, a shorter route to the same destinations.

Ross Lakes Route

Lower Ross Lake to East Torrey Creek—5 miles

Traversing the Ross Lakes' shores has long had an evil reputation; reaching Upper Ross Lake was once said to be possible only by boat. A documented trip along the shores in 1960 and occasional trips since have barely diminished the aura, and the route hasn't become a popular excursion. The Lower Lake is no problem, except that early season run-off can make crossing the lake's outlet outright dangerous; fishing trails follow the east shore. The Upper Lake's east shore, however, offers house-size boulders; the west shore is a steep, wooded slope with innumerable avalanche-felled trees. The two sides are equally time-consuming, and your choice may depend not only on the outlet but on whether your destination is Mile Long Lake, around to the west, or East Torrey Creek, across to the east; a long bog beyond Upper Ross Lake makes switching sides nasty. Making your way northeast of Spider Peak to reach West Torrey Creek above Bomber Lake isn't a problem.

Whiskey Creek Trail

Whiskey Basin to Whiskey Mountain—4 miles

Three trails climb from the Trail Lake Road to a junction on Whiskey Mountain. The Whiskey Creek Trail is a shorter route to this junction (and thus to Simpson Lake) than the Ross Lake and Whiskey Mountain Trails, though the latter offers a slightly shorter route to Ross Lakes. The Whiskey Creek Trail's virtue is its straightforward ascent by a creek, in 4 miles passing from an ecosystem of cottonwoods, wild rose, and prickly pear through forest to alpine tundra.

You can begin walking from Point 7,422 or drive 0.5 mile farther and park near the mouth of a side canyon. (The road doesn't continue as far as the wilderness boundary.) Simply follow Whiskey Creek's north bank to the 10,450-foot saddle and five-way trail junction on Whiskey Mountain's north shoulder. A mile below the saddle, at 9,800 feet, a cairn marks a side trail that switchbacks south but ends shortly. Half a mile from the saddle, at 10,100 feet, another cairn marks another trail split; both branches lead to the Whiskey Mountain and Ross Lake Trails, though the southern one is easier to follow.

Whiskey Mountain Trail

Trail Lake to Whiskey Mountain—5 miles

This trail coincides for 0.5 mile with others that begin at the Trail Lake trailhead, then leaves Torrey Creek and climbs high to the west on Whiskey Mountain. A rockslide led to a rerouting of the trail, but this should not cause confusion. After it rounds a shoulder above treeline, two lines of cairns diverge. The lower path is a shortcut to Ross Lakes; it enters a burned area, crosses a long meadow, and meets the Ross Lake Trail.

The Whiskey Mountain Trail, the upper path, climbs through bighorn pastures before descending old vehicle tracks to a junction with the Ross Lake, Whiskey Creek, and Simpson Lake Trails.

Lake Louise Trail

Glacier Trail to Lake Louise—1.5 miles

This is a useful trail to three types of mountain users: day hikers (especially in autumn, for the colors), winter ice climbers, and explorers wishing to leave the beaten path for West Torrey Creek's drainage above Lake Louise, which is too rugged for easy hiking. From Trail Lake, follow the Glacier Trail for nearly a mile. Just before the Glacier Trail's bridge across Torrey Creek's narrow gorge, the Lake Louise Trail diverges right and climbs intermittently to Lake Louise. The trail ends a short distance along the north shore. You can continue, but the terrain isn't conducive to carefree backpacking. To reach the ice climbs in winter, ski up the lake.

Bomber Trail (part unmaintained)

Glacier Trail to Bomber Lake—4.5 miles

This trail takes you between the ramparts of Goat Flat and Torrey Peak to East Torrey Creek's headwaters. From Trail Lake, follow the Glacier Trail (an obsolete version is shown on the Torrey Lake quad) for 3.5 miles to a junction where the Glacier Trail diverges, switchbacking up to the east. The Bomber Trail continues along the creek, then climbs steeply to a draw behind a dome next to the Bomber Falls.

The canyon just above the falls was the site of the only military action in the Wind Rivers during World War II. A B-17 crew, strafing either bighorn sheep or a bear, crashed west of the creek, killing the crew. You may be able to spot bits of wreckage.

The trail ends near the falls, but a path continues east of the creek, pleasant at first but progressively becoming lost in deadfall. Cross the creek somewhere before the canyon's bend to the west—to avoid a monstrous moraine and make use of a decent blazed path on the other side for the final mile to Bomber Lake. However, there seems to be no best place to cross, despite elaborate cairns advertising one crossing.

From Bomber Lake you can continue either north of Spider Peak to West Torrey Creek or south of Spider to Turquoise Lake.

Downs Fork Trail (part unmaintained)

Dinwoody Creek to Downs Lake or Grasshopper Glacier—4.5 miles

As the Glacier Trail starts up Dinwoody Creek, it circles swampy Downs Fork Meadows, turns left, and crosses Downs Fork. The Downs Fork Trail begins at the turn, going up the creek's north side, but after 2 miles crossing to the south side via a choice of logjams. The trail officially ends near the Downs Fork's junction with Grasshopper Creek, but a well-constructed and easily followed trail crosses Grasshopper Creek by another logjam and switchbacks to Lake 9,900. After crossing this lake's outlet, it climbs just west of the stream that drains the valley east of Point 11,006. Passing through the saddle north of Point 11,006, it descends to Downs Lake's east shore and acres of good campsites.

To reach Grasshopper Creek's upper valley from the creek's junction with Downs Fork, switchback to the crest south of Lake 9,900 and locate blazes leading west-southwest for 0.4 mile to a pond. Pass north of the pond and continue west-southwest, following a draw, to the stream that enters a northern bay of the 0.25-mile lake northwest of Point 10,556. Rather than crossing this stream at the lake's inlet and following the lake's irregular shore, cross a few hundred yards upstream and pass north of a knoll to the lake's west shore. Then, rather than descending the drainage through the obvious gap to the south, ascend a draw to the southwest, pass a minuscule pond, and pick your way west and south to Grasshopper Creek.

There is decent camping where you reach the creek, but if you can survive a willow jungle and a short boulder labyrinth, you'll find better campsites 0.5 mile upstream. The rest of this pleasant valley is straightforward, but you must twice ford the creek to its south side.

The final paragraphs of the Geology chapter describe a recent event that had a profound effect on this drainage.

Klondike Creek Route

Dinwoody Creek to Klondike Lake—2 miles

Klondike Creek is the most vigorous of the streams the Glacier Trail crosses between its junction with the Ink Wells Trail and Wilson Meadows. It is best to begin north of Klondike Creek, circle north of a waterfall, then cross, if possible, at Lake 10,860's outlet. Klondike Lake is most easily passed by its south shore.

According to one theory the creek got its name from an attempt to mine gold; tailings are all that remain. According to another the terrain reminded a local postmaster of Alaska.

Passes

Pass 10,960+

Sandra Lake to Roaring Fork

A high and obscure though easy Divide pass south of Sandra Lake and east of Three Waters Mountain connects Jakey's Fork and the Roaring Fork. A surprisingly well-traveled path ascends the valley from Sandra Lake to the Divide. Don't descend directly south from the pass, but bear southwest to a flat with a lake, then drop to the Roaring Fork.

Pass 12,040+

Mile Long Lake to Roaring Fork or Crescent Lake

An old rumor concerns a man crossing from Torrey Creek to Clear Creek with a pack animal. Where he crossed the Divide we don't know, but the most likely place is the low point between Ram Flat and Downs Mountain, 1.5 miles west of Mile Long Lake, at the north end of Continental Glacier. From Mile Long Lake, climb west to the glacier and ascend it to the pass. You can descend either to the Roaring Fork's headwaters or, by bearing southwest and consulting a map, to Crescent Lake or Faler Lake.

No Man's Pass (12,160+)

East Torrey Creek to Downs Fork

Most passes provide access between valleys. The narrow neck connecting Downs Mountain to Goat Flat, however, is easier as a link between two high areas. You can cross the pass from Downs Fork to East Torrey Creek, but the north side involves snow steep enough to make an ice axe advisable. It is generally easier (though still formidable backpacking) to cross the 12,200-foot saddle 0.5 mile southwest of No Man's Pass.

Baker Lake Pass (11,760+)

Grasshopper Creek to Baker Lake

Baker Lake and Iceberg Lake, separated from Baker Lake by a moraine, lie just below a low point of the Divide between Yukon and Klondike Peaks. To reach Baker Lake from the west, see the Lost Eagle and Elbow Creek routes (Green River chapter). From the east, ascend the small glacier at the head of Grasshopper Creek (ice axe and, in late summer, crampons).

Peaks

Union Peak (11,491)

The Continental Divide near Union Pass is merely a low ridge of trees and meadows. Union Peak, 5 miles east, is merely a few rocky outcrops among snowpatches and grassy slopes.

1. West Slope (I 1st class) An early survey reported that "horses can be taken to the top from the west." Now four-wheel-drive vehicles can be taken nearly to the top, though in such open country a hiker needn't follow the road.

Three Waters Mountain (11,680+)

After you round the Green River's Big Bend, heading toward Green River Lakes, you see this massive rubble-sloped mound. From Simpson Lake it appears as a steep-walled, flat-topped mountain at the head of the valley. Its distinction is that it constitutes the convergence of watersheds: Waters flow from it to the Columbia, Colorado, and Missouri Rivers. Formerly called Triple Divide Peak, its name was perhaps changed by a poetic surveyor who'd seen enough Triple Divide Peaks.

1. West Slope (I 2nd class) From the Roaring Fork, the head of Fish Creek's east fork, or the Union Pass Road.

2. Southeast Ridge (I 2nd class) From Simpson Lake by way of Pass 10,960+. A few hundred feet of scree above the pass lead to easy walking. The only problem is identifying the summit.

Ram Flat (12,242)

The range's most extensive planar surface lies near its north end, sprawling between Ross Lakes and the Divide. The western part of the plateau is called Shale Mountain, but there's scarcely a dip between it and Ram Flat. While you wouldn't go out of your way to set foot on Ram Flat's true summit, occasional visitors are attracted to the rim overlooking Ross Lakes.

1. North Slope (I 3rd class) Leave the Simpson Lake Trail in Soapstone Basin.

The easiest route onto the plateau from the Ross Lake Trail seems to be an ill-defined gully opposite Ross Lake's north end, south of Point 11,038. Steep grass and a few 3rd-class moves take you to the ridge joining Points 11,562 and 11,670.

2. Bighorn Towers (II 5.7/5.8) A stream enters the southwest corner of Ross Lake from a snow-filled cirque. The row of summits to the cirque's north are the Big-horn Towers. The south face of the tower nearest the lake has been climbed in about five good pitches. The climbers then rappelled and downclimbed to the notch to the west and climbed the next tower in several moderate, enjoyable pitches. They then ascended the rounded westernmost tower by minimal 5th-class climbing.

3. East Couloir (I Snow 3rd class) From the cirque north of the Bighorn Towers, a couloir reaches Ram Flat.

4. Crystal Lake Couloir (II 5.6) You can reach Ram Flat by a couloir west of Crystal Lake. Several short sections are class 5, but the couloir has been descended.

5. South Ridge (I 2nd class) Walk along the Divide from Continental Glacier.

The Guardian (11,256)

This steep-walled spur at Ram Flat's southeast end guards the valley above Upper Ross Lake. The first ascent team, caught by a storm on Ram Flat, was shown a descent route over the Guardian by bighorn sheep.

1. South Slope (I 2nd or 3rd class) From the east end of Mile Long Lake.

2. West Ridge (I easy 5th class) Earlier guidebook editions rated this ridge class 3 because of the report of bighorns using it to commute from Mile Long Lake to Ram Flat. However, the two-legged, while continuing to encounter the four-legged, can't figure out how they do it.

3. East Face–Machete Eddy (II 5.8) Begin this six-pitch route near the east face's south end by passing a dark dike-streaked blob 20 feet up. Continue up a thin 5.8 crack to a belay ledge below a small roof. From the ledge's right end, climb a crack that becomes a seam, face climb to a small roof, turn the roof to the left, and pass through some blocks before traversing left and climbing to a ledge with a tree. The third pitch is a 4th-class traverse left to a corner formed by a block. From the top of the block, intricate routefinding takes you up a seam, then diagonally left to a friction slab; traverse left 25 feet, 25 feet below a 2-foot roof. Finish the pitch by climbing past another dark blob. On the fifth pitch, pass a large roof to the right and then a small tree, and climb up and slightly left to a ledge. The easy sixth pitch leads to a ledge with three trees. To continue to the summit entails climbing never harder than 5.0, or you can walk off to the south.

Rundblick (12,058)

The tower 0.5 mile south of Mile Long Lake, on the eastern continuation of the Jeralee spur, was named for its view.

1. North Face (I 3rd class) From the base of the steep part of the wall, a ledge leads into a couloir that offers scrambling to the summit ridge.

2. West Ridge Traverse from Jeralee.

Jeralee Peak (12,731)

A spur juts north, then east, from Gjetetind, forming the south side of Mile Long Lake's cirque. The minor rise that constitutes the spur's high point is Jeralee Peak, which from such places as Bomber Lake appears to be a distinctive peak. (Upper Ross Lake was once Jeralee Lake.)

1. East Ridge Traverse from Rundblick.

2. Southwest Ridge (I 3rd class) From Continental Glacier a broad, gentle slope leads to a final few hundred feet of large blocks.

Ross Mountain (12,840+)

Hidden behind the Gjetetind-Jeralee ridge from viewpoints to the north and east, 1.3 miles north of Downs Mountain, is a lesser spur of Gjetetind. During their 1960 exploration of many previously unvisited high points between Ross Lakes and Downs Mountain, Chris Goetze and Brian Underhill, en route to Downs from Mile Long Lake via Continental Glacier, detoured to bag this spur's high point.

1. East Ridge Traverse from Rundblick.

2. Southwest Ridge (I 2nd class) Quickly ascended from the Ross-Gjetetind saddle.

Gjetetind (13,202)

While Gjetetind (meaning Goat Mountain), 0.8 mile north-northeast of Northwest Peak, is merely one of several scree cones on the Downs massif, it presents a bolder profile than Downs itself; this and its Gannett-like beret of snow make it conspicuous in a way that Downs' elevation does not make Downs. Moreover, the scree is granite, pleasanter walking than nearby migmatite rubble.

1. South Ridge (I 2nd class) From Continental Glacier or Downs Mountain.

2. Northeast Ridge (I 2nd or Snow 4th class) While you can climb from the Ross-Gjetetind saddle on rubble to the right, the snow makes an elegant little route of a few hundred feet.

Northwest Peak (13,246)

While its name identifies it as a satellite of Downs Mountain, Downs' northwest summit stands with enough symmetrical grace to be named on maps. While no doubt climbed only by those en route to Downs, it does offer good views of the drainages above Daphne and Bear Lakes.

1. North and West Slopes (I 2nd class) Scree. Reaching the scree is discussed under Downs Mountain.

2. East Side (I 2nd class) Cross Continental Glacier from the saddle north of Downs Mountain. Continental Glacier is unique in the Wind Rivers in that it straddles the Divide. Given a liberal definition of "body of water," meltwater ponds that form on the crest are the highest bodies of water in Wyoming.

Downs Mountain (13,349)

The range's northernmost 13,000-foot summit rises above the high plateaus as a rubble heap, a vision of the Wind Rivers before the ice ages. But standing 5 miles north of the nearest 13,000-footer, Downs dominates its surroundings and is a focal point for tundra wanderers.

Downs from Whiskey Mountain

1. East Slope (I Snow 3rd class) Downs is connected to Goat Flat by No Man's Pass, an upside-down saddle joining two heights. You can reach Downs' east flank from Goat Flat by this pass and the more benign saddle 0.5 mile southwest of it. The snow slope that rises from this saddle nearly to Downs' summit makes an enjoyable, elegant route.

You can also reach Downs' east slope from Lake 11,309 at the head of East Torrey Creek and from Downs Lake by a couloir north of Downs Glacier.

2. East Face–Cowboy Classic (II 5.9) This six-pitch route ascends the central of the buttresses rising from the glaciers above Lake 11,309; it reaches the 13,000-foot plateau north of Downs' summit. The first pitch follows a ramp up left past loose rock. On the fourth pitch, traverse right 40 feet on a gigantic detached flake, with a difficult move at the end.

3. North Couloir (II Snow 5th class WI1/2) On Downs' north face are two steep couloirs. This six-pitch route ascends the 45- to 60-degree left one.

Approach from Lake 11,309 and the glacier below the couloir. Pass the berg-schrund via snow bridges to the left. Climb near a side of the couloir, to be able to belay from rock and to minimize exposure to the rockfall to which the couloir is prone.

4. North Ridge (I 2nd class) From the west you can reach Continental Glacier, at the base of Downs' north ridge, by way of Daphne Lake or Crescent Lake; the pleasure is in the cross-country routefinding required on the approach. You can reach the ridge from West Torrey Creek by way of Ross Mountain and Gjetetind.

5. South Ridge (I 2nd class) Follow the Divide north from Baker Lake or gain it from Downs Lake via the spur south of Downs Glacier. In 1946 wanderers found their way up Downs via Lake 10,705, north of the Bear's Tooth; the only detail described was the difficulty of traversing the slabs that enclose this lake. The slope just south of Downs' summit is miserable scree, worth skirting.

Whiskey Mountain (11,157)

This rising strata between the cuts of Jakey's Fork and West Torrey Creek is separated from the Divide by the trench of Ross Lakes and Wasson Creek. The name comes from a cache once made on its slopes.

1. South Slope or **West Slope** (I 1st class) Leave the Whiskey Mountain Trail before its 10,920-foot high point or leave the Whiskey Creek Trail before the saddle where it meets the Whiskey Mountain Trail.

Middle Mountain (11,902)

Middle Mountain is the massif, sprawling onto four USGS quads, bounded by the forks of Torrey Creek and the Ross Lakes. Its upper reaches have hosted bighorn research, while waterfalls dropping from its northeast ramparts to Lake Louise are popular winter ice climbing objectives. When the Trail Lake Road is drivable, a climb can be done car-to-car in a day.

1. East Slope (I 2nd class) From Bomber Creek; used by the sheep researchers to commute to work. It seems best to cross the creek at the upstream end of the meadow where the Bomber Creek and Glacier Trails diverge. This crossing may not be feasible in early summer.

2. Lake Louise Gully (II Ice 4th class) A fall of 500 vertical feet above the lake's east end includes a few steep sections. You can add to the difficulties with variations at the top.

3. Golden Tears (II Ice 5th class) This 500-foot fall, above Lake Louise's west end, includes three vertical pitches and is well regarded by ice climbers.

4. Cony Spires From the middle of Upper Ross Lake's east shore, a ridge with five towers—the Cony Spires—rises to the Middle Mountain plateau. The route ascends the north side of the first tower, via a notch to its east, but otherwise stays mainly on the crest's south side.

Torrey Peak (12,181)

This mile-wide formation between Upper Ross Lake and East Torrey Creek can presumably be climbed in many places, though only one route has been reported.

1. Southwest Ridge (I 4th class) Approach from Lake 10,359, southeast of Mile Long Lake.

2. Point 11,428, Southwest Slope (I 3rd class) Scramble up the small formation northwest of Bomber Lake from the valley below Spider Peak.

3. Point 11,428, East Face–Bombast (II 5.9) This is the face, broken by two large ledge systems, that rises north of Bomber Lake. For the first two pitches, to the lower ledge, stay 100 feet right of a central chimney. On the route's upper section, stay left of the prominent central dihedral. The last of the route's six pitches is the hardest.

Spider Peak (12,234)

This is the one plateau fragment of the Torrey Creek cirques that is cut off from other segments on all sides. These surfaces support a surprising variety of living things: The first ascenders were impressed by the number of large spiders.

1. North Ridge (I 3rd class) Slabs rise from Lake 10,359.

2. Southwest Ridge (II 5.5) Two nice pitches after much pleasant scrambling, cleaner than the west face, less strenuous than the southeast and northeast faces. You can gain the ridge from East Torrey Creek in a number of ways. Scramble up the

Spider Peak

ridge until it abuts the south face. Climb a face for a pitch, then climb up left under an overhang to a corner, which leads to large blocks and a scramble to the summit slopes. (Or climb a 5.6 second pitch directly above the first pitch.)

3. Southeast Face (II 5.6) A system of chimneys is prominent from Turquoise Lake. Scramble to the steep upper section and follow the chimneys for four pitches.

4. East Buttress (II 5.7) Spider's southeast and northeast faces intersect at a ridge or buttress that rises from Turquoise Lake. You can reach the shoulder below the buttress unroped. Then climb three 5th-class pitches to easier terrain.

5. East Buttress Right (II 5.7/5.8) To the right of *East Buttress* is a slightly harder route. The 80-foot first pitch involves a dihedral. The 50-foot second pitch reaches a ledge right of a large roof. The third pitch involves a traverse under the roof and above a chimney, followed by a 5.7 off-width and 4th-class climbing to a belay in boulders. The fourth pitch follows a low-angle seam up right, traverses right below a roof for 20 feet, and ascends through boulders. A 4th-class pitch completes the route.

6. Northeast Buttress (III 5.8) Toward the left side of the 0.5-mile-wide northeast face is a minor buttress. The route begins on slabs and ascends first the buttress's left side, then its center. About six roped pitches.

7. Northeast Face (IV 5.9) Two crack systems converge halfway up the northeast face's slightly concave face. This route follows the left-hand crack, then the single system above the convergence (though the first ascenders exited left to a chimney one pitch from the top). They mentioned "a fair share of loose rock" on the route.

Talus Mountain (11,695)

The slag-heap shape of the formation 1.3 miles northwest of Burro Flat implies rubble to its core, but the talus—good talus—is only a veneer over bedrock. The view is up East Torrey Creek toward Downs Mountain.

1. East Slope (I 2nd class) An obvious jaunt from the Glacier Trail's Pass 10,895.

Arrow Mountain (11,588)

1. West Slope (I 2nd class) From the Glacier Trail.

Peak 11,696

The slope east of the Glacier Trail's 10,895-foot high point provides a view of Gannett and its neighbors—an opportunity for a preview or a last look.

1. West Slope (I 2nd class) Obvious; rocky only at the top.

2. East Slope (I 2nd class) From Pass 10,451.

Peak 11,016

A stone seat on the summit 2.3 miles southeast of Arrow Mountain suggests ancients contemplating the high peaks.

1. West Slope (I 2nd class) Sedimentary scree from Pass 10,451. With game trails linking Red Creek and Dinwoody Creek, this pass must have been more important centuries ago than now. Obsidian flakes are scattered around large fallen trunks, remnants of trees that presumably thrived in a more benign climate.

Peak 11,760+

From the Glacier Trail Goat Flat appears to extend three prongs into the basin of the Dinwoody Lakes—the nine lakes drained by Phillips and Double Lake Creeks. However, the apparent middle prong is separated from Goat Flat by an implausible 1,000-foot gap; this detached formation, 0.2 mile northeast of Florence Lake, is Peak 11,760+. The summit is at the southwest end of the peak's ridgeline.

1. Northeast Ridge (I 3rd class) Gained by grassy ramps above Lake 10,943's outlet.

2. Southeast Face The earliest summit register entry mentions "Diagonal Ledge on SE Face" and implies the use of a rope.

Goat Flat (12,488)

A tilted plateau rising from the Glacier Trail and ending in cliffs overlooking East Torrey Creek and Downs Lake. There are no mountain goats in the Wind Rivers, though bighorn sheep have been called goats.

1. Northeast Slope (I 1st class) A long hike from Pass 10,895, the Glacier Trail's high point above Burro Flat.

2. Wedge (I 3rd class or 5.6) Half a mile southeast of Bomber Lake, a 700-foot west-facing wedge reaches Goat Flat at about 11,700 feet. The entire climb could presumably be done unroped, but a one-pitch slab near the top makes a fun ending.

3. From Bomber Lake (I 2nd class) A draw southeast of the lake provides a route, usually on snow, to the plateau.

4. From Downs Fork (I 2nd class) The Downs Lake side of No Man's Pass is not pleasant, especially when you're burdened with a pack, but a long, gentle valley to the east is. This valley constitutes the headwaters of the creek followed by the Downs Lake Trail from Lake 9,900 to the saddle east of Point 11,006. A mile north of Point 11,006, the creek cascades down the valley's northeast side; next to these cascades is the route's only steep section, which you can negotiate by switchbacking up grass.

In an era when we find old pitons in "unclimbed" rock, when wilderness is more often an administrative jurisdiction than wildness, this valley remains free of cairns, candy wrappers, stone windbreaks, moleskin packaging, aluminum foil, and even boot prints. This guide mentions such a pristine valley because of its usefulness, but also because few will pass through it, and visitors to the environs of Downs Lake tend to savor wildness and know how to tread lightly.

5. From Golden Lake (II Snow/Ice 5th class) From the Glacier Trail you can see a snow chute that empties into the lake above the Phillips Lakes. The chute makes a ten-pitch climb.

Downs Lake Towers (12,276)

A group of fine towers rises west of Downs Lake's south end. The one reported route is on the tower nearest the lake.

1. Tower 11,680+, North Rib (II 5.4/5.5) A five- or six-pitch route ascends the rib leading to the tower's summit.

Descent: The south couloir is 3rd class.

Bear's Tooth (12,294)

In the middle of nowhere—between Downs Fork and Grasshopper Creek—stands this dark rock, visible from the Ink Wells Trail but from few other regularly visited places.

1. West Ridge (I 3rd class) The ridge connecting Bear's Tooth to the high, snowy Divide country.

2. South Face (II 5.7) Three lines of dihedrals and chimneys face Grasshopper Creek. A five- or six-pitch route ascends the largest, left-most system. Three cruxes involve getting around overhangs.

3. Southeast Aréte (II/III 5.7) The route, spoken well of by the first ascent team, follows the narrow crest.

4. Orange Wall (II 5.7) A wall of orange rock rises above Grasshopper Creek nearly a mile west of Bear's Tooth—just above the latter part of "Grasshopper" on the Downs Mountain quad. The route follows a system of dihedrals and chimneys.

Approach by following a wide, grassy ledge to a white, left-facing dihedral. Continue along the ledge another 30 feet to an orange, left-facing dihedral with a roof. Climb an easy wide crack to the roof; above the roof follow a crack to a large, grassy ledge to the right. The second pitch (4th class) passes ledges to a belay from a horn. On the third pitch, climb through a series of boulder problems, including cracks, laybacks, and a roof, ending on a ledge to the left.

Climb a right-facing dihedral for 10 feet, or a wide crack to the left, to the main chimney's blocky beginning; belay to the right after passing loose, wet blocks. Step left into the chimney system and climb over, through, and around blocks to a deep, dark chimney; follow this chimney past a blocky roof. On the sixth pitch, climb wet cracks, step right to a wet, mossy crack, then climb a blocky face to a white band and a large ledge. A 4th-class pitch completes the route.

5. First Ascent Route (4th or 5th class) Bear's Tooth's first ascent, in 1946, was reported as being by the northeast face. The climbers "overcame several difficulties," but the northeast face nevertheless appears more formidable than their sketchy account implies.

Point 11,836

Point 11,836 is 0.7 mile south-southeast of Bear's Tooth. Its north-facing wall faces Bear's Tooth across Grasshopper Creek.

1. North Face (II 5.8 A1) Right of a smooth face and left of a boulder-filled gully (farther right is a prominent gap in the skyline) are two continuous cracks. This route follows the right crack for twelve to fourteen pitches of mostly 5.3 to 5.7 climbing. Aid is required for 30 feet to pass a roof on the fourth pitch.

Peak 13,062

Between Downs Mountain and Yukon Peak the Divide undergoes several undulations, one of which, a mile east of Kevin Lake, qualifies as a peak. Most ascents have been traverses by backpackers following the Divide, though Peak 13,062 has also been reached by spring skiers.

1. North Slope (I 2nd class) Two miles from Downs Mountain (or via the Downs Glacier approaches described under Downs' South Ridge).

2. South Slope (I 2nd class) Two miles from Yukon Peak.

Yukon Peak (12,825)

1. Southeast Ridge (I 2nd class) From Baker Lake Pass.

2. Northeast Ridge (I 2nd class) The Divide between Downs and Yukon is easily traversed.

Klondike Peak (13,114)

The name Klondike was first attached to the creek, then the lake, and finally the mountain to the west. The summit, which stands 0.5 mile west of the Divide, is the source of two north-facing glaciers, J and Sourdough.

Klondike Peak, J Glacier

1. East Ridge (I Snow 4th class) Reach the main peak from the minor Divide summit due east. Approach this hump from Sourdough Glacier via Point 12,705 or from Grasshopper Glacier. The 4th-class rating indicates the prudence advised on crevassed glaciers.

2. Sourdough Glacier (I Snow 4th class) Climb Klondike directly from the glacier, which is one of the range's points of least accessibility.

Pedestal Peak (13,340)

Southwest of Klondike Lake is a small bowl occupied by the south end of Grasshopper Glacier. At the bowl's head are two broad Divide peaks. Phil Smith named the northern one for the curious rock pedestals near its summit.

1. South Ridge (I 3rd class) From Flagstone, on talus.

2. Southeast Face Scree breaks the snow slopes on Pedestal's east flank.

3. East Ridge (I 3rd class) From Grasshopper Glacier, on snow.

Flagstone Peak (13,450)

The summit of Pedestal's southern neighbor is covered with flat, frost-shattered blocks.

1. Southeast Ridge (I 3rd class) From the bowl to the east, climb to the Divide saddle just southeast of the peak, then scramble to the top.

2. East Face (II 5.5) A direct ascent from the bowl to the summit involves two 5th-class pitches on good rock.

3. Northeast Face Steep snow.

4. North Ridge (I 3rd class) You can traverse the Pedestal-Flagstone ridge in either direction.

5. South Face Dihedral A three-pitch route ascends the right side of a large triangular block. The discontinuous first pitch involves a hand crack, a finger crack, a face, and an off-width. The second pitch follows a dihedral. The third pitch, which begins from a large ledge, offers variations ranging from 4th class to 5.9.

6. South-Southeast Face (II 5.6) Approach this three-pitch route from the lakes (and recent lake—see end of Geology chapter) at Grasshopper Glacier's south end and the bowl east of Flagstone. Scramble up scree and boulders to the band of good rock below the summit. Locate the route by noting a clean 30-foot corner just below the summit ridge; begin slightly left of a point below it.

The first pitch follows a nondescript crack to a ledge 25 feet up and continues to a ledge 120 feet up. The second pitch ascends an off-width in a corner to a wide ledge and continues up nice rock to a belay at a bus-size block. On the third pitch, climb 40 feet to an easy chimney but bypass the chimney to the left, belaying near a rotten gully 20 feet below the top of the face (and left of the corner by which you located the route). Fourth-class scrambling takes you to the summit ridge 150 feet east of the summit.

Descent: You can rappel the *South-Southeast Face* rather than descend one of the easy ridges.

Peak 13,160+

A pair of unnamed summits rims the bowl above the south end of Grasshopper Glacier, 0.3 mile southeast of Flagstone Peak. The higher summit is on the Divide; the lower summit is to the east.

1. Northeast Ridge (I 3rd class) Climb to the eastern summit from the frozen lakes at its foot and continue to the main summit.

2. North Face (I 3rd class) The first ascent team traversed the peak and descended into the bowl.

Philsmith Peak (12,670)

Phil Smith spent the summer of 1946 guiding in the Wind Rivers for Floyd Wilson, but he did most of his climbing in the Tetons. With Fritiof Fryxell he made many first ascents in 1929 and 1930, including Teewinot, Symmetry Spire, and Nez Perce. The pair joined Kenneth Henderson and Robert Underhill to make the first ascent of Mount Owen. When Grand Teton National Park was established in 1929, Smith and Fryxell were the first rangers.

The peak in the Wind Rivers that bears Smith's name is the high point of the massif between Klondike and Gannett Creeks. The naming resulted from an error in an old guidebook, which mistook an ascent of Flagstone by Smith for an ascent of this summit.

1. South Slopes (I 2nd or 3rd class) Philsmith has little to attract summit seekers, but its upper slopes have been used for a high-level hike from Wilson Meadows to Klondike Lake. Climb west from Dinwoody Creek onto the broad ridge of Lake 12,156 and Point 12,540.

2. Point 12,362, North Rib (I 4th class) An ascent of the prominent rib above Klondike Lake's east end takes you to Philsmith's east shoulder; a few roped pitches are involved.

Looking south from Green River Lakes Campground and trailhead

2 Green River

Jedediah Smith learned its name as Seedskeedee Agie—Sage Hen River—when Crow Indians directed him to South Pass. Trappers also called it the Spanish River, for it flowed to Mexico, but Spaniards called it Rio Verde, because of its green banks in red canyon country.

The Green River begins flowing south to canyon country in a valley that separates the Wind Rivers from the Gros Ventre Range to the west. But if you trace the river upstream, you find it curving around a spur of the Wind Rivers; beyond, it flows from the southeast, from the two Green River Lakes, where a road that parallels the river ends and trails begin.

Above the Upper Green River Lake the scene is dominated by Squaretop Mountain's steep sides and flat summit. East of Squaretop the Green glides serenely from the heart of the northern Wind Rivers. The Green River Lakes, Squaretop, and the river as far as Three Forks Park are included in this chapter. (Above Three Forks Park the Green cascades from country covered in the Peak Lake chapter.)

The present chapter encompasses two markedly dissimilar types of terrain. At lower elevations are the much traveled, lush, moose habitat valleys of the Green River and three tributaries, the Roaring Fork to the north, Clear Creek to the east, and Porcupine Creek to the west. Several thousand feet higher are tundra-covered plateaus, habitat for bighorn sheep, with few human visitors. The valleys have trails and the plateaus are easily traveled, but the elevations between tend to be choked with deadfall and boulders.

East of the Green River, Slide, Elbow, Pixley, Tourist, and Wells Creeks cut back into the plateau toward the Continental Divide. However, ascending their steep, rocky courses—while taking you from well-traveled trails to trailless terrain that encourages you to roam freely—involves the most adventurous hiking in the Wind Rivers. This chapter's highest peaks, Solitude and Desolation, stand between Tourist and Wells Creeks. From these and the other Green tributaries you can also reach Divide peaks from Downs Mountain to Gannett Peak (covered, respectively, in the Ross Lakes and Dinwoody Glacier chapters).

However, descriptions in this chapter begin with the country reached by side roads branching from the Green River Road—country drained by Jim and Gypsum Creeks and featuring Kendall Mountain and various formations north to Big Sheep Mountain.

This chapter's trails and peaks sprawl over an area covered by several topographic maps: the Green River Lakes, Big Sheep Mountain, Squaretop Mountain, Kendall Mountain, Gannett Peak, and Downs Mountain quads.

Trails

Jim Creek Trail (not maintained)

Jim Creek Road to Porcupine Creek—8 miles

The Jim Creek Trail is mostly in good shape but isn't marked with signs and may be hard to locate in a few places.

From the bridge site at the end of the Jim Creek Road, ford the creek and continue on foot on a logging road that serves both as the Jim Creek Trail and a trail that crosses west of Kendall Mountain to Boulder Basin. After 1.5 miles the Jim Creek Trail turns left from this Boulder Basin Trail, but the junction is unmarked. Look for the junction in a meadow with scattered trees and, just southwest, a cluster of charred stumps. As a landmark, 0.25 mile before the junction you will see the pond (more logs than water) shown on maps. Descend to and cross Jim Creek (in early summer by a downstream logjam), heading toward Saltlick Mountain's lowest limestone outcrops.

The trail recrosses Jim Creek at a meadow's upper end (hop three strands separately), then crosses a third time below Jim Creek Lake's outlet. The trail is again easily lost beyond this crossing; it doesn't hug the lake's north shore, as maps indicate. Instead, 100 feet downstream from the outlet, it climbs steeply north before contouring east.

At the upper end of a meadow at the valley's head, the trail turns south, while the South Fork of Gypsum Creek Trail, marked by cairns, crosses Saltlick Mountain to Gypsum Creek. (When heading west, at the meadow's west end, look for the Jim Creek Trail higher than the meadow.)

Beyond the meadow the trail climbs through tundra before dropping to Porcupine Creek and the Porcupine Trail.

South Fork of Gypsum Creek Trail (not maintained)

South Fork of Gypsum Creek to Jim Creek—6 miles

From the end of FR 711, cross Gypsum Creek's South Fork by a footbridge and follow a conspicuous trail for 2 miles, rounding a large meadow. Beyond the meadow (near Point 9,090) the trail's identity becomes fuzzy, but by angling uphill you should locate it often enough for it to be useful. It leads, in a mile, to a crossing of Gypsum Creek's southernmost fork. After climbing to a 10,800-foot pass east of Saltlick Mountain, the trail follows cairns down an open slope to Jim Creek.

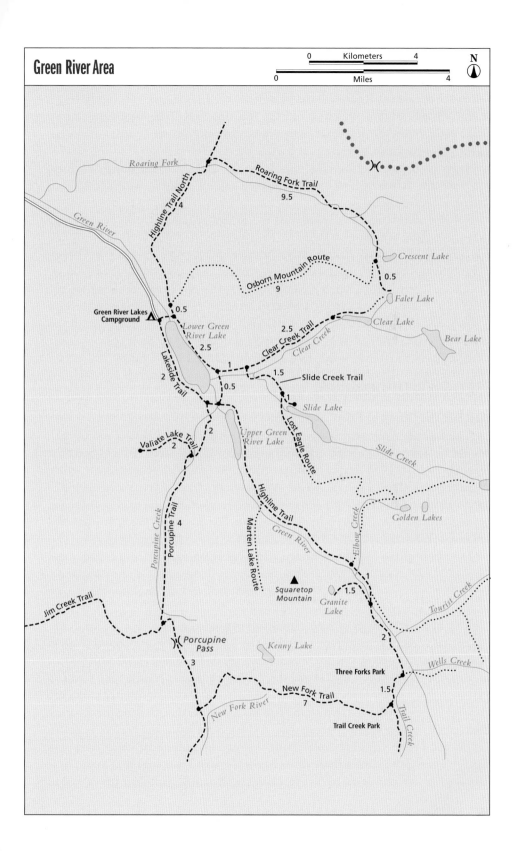

Green River Area

0 Kilometers 4

0 Miles 4

N

Roaring Fork

Highline Trail North
4

Roaring Fork Trail
9.5

Green River

Crescent Lake

Osborn Mountain Route
9

0.5

Faler Lake

Green River Lakes
Campground
0.5

Clear Lake

Bear Lake

Lower Green
River Lake
2.5

Clear Creek Trail
2.5

Clear Creek

Lakeside Trail

1

0.5

1.5 — Slide Creek Trail

2

1

Slide Lake

Valiate Lake Trail
2

2

Upper Green
River Lake

Lost Eagle Route

Slide Creek

Porcupine Creek

Porcupine Trail
4

Highline Trail

Marten Lake Route

Green River

Elbow Creek

Golden Lakes

Jim Creek Trail

Squaretop
Mountain

Granite
Lake

1.5

1

Tourist Creek

Porcupine
Pass

3

Kenny Lake

2

Three Forks Park

Wells Creek

New Fork Trail
7

1.5

New Fork River

Trail Creek Park

Trail Creek

Highline Trail North

Green River Lakes to Roaring Fork—4 miles

In previous editions this trail and the Roaring Fork Trail were considered a single entity. However, the two have met dissimilar fates: The trail north from Green River Lakes has been spiffed up as part of the Continental Divide Trail, marked with the CDT logo at absurdly close intervals, while the trail shown on maps following the Roaring Fork into the mountains has long been neglected. It is described separately, below.

For the northbound Highline, cross the bridge at Lower Green River Lake's outlet, as for the southbound Highline, but continue northeast beyond the bridge, staying right of the fence that encircles a cluster of deserted buildings (the Osborn Cabin). From here the trail doesn't closely follow the Green River, as shown on the Green River Lakes quad, but climbs and sidehills due north, as shown on the Earthwalk, Beartooth, and Bridger Wilderness maps. It eventually climbs through a notch, as shown on these maps, and descends to Roaring Fork Basin. On the far side of the creek, spanned by a bridge, it intersects the Roaring Fork Trail, while the Highline/CDT continues north, to country not covered in this book.

Roaring Fork Trail (not maintained)

Highline Trail North to Faler Lake—10 miles

The Roaring Fork, which drains the valley between Three Waters and Osborn Mountains, joins the Green several miles downstream from Green River Lakes. The Roaring Fork Trail—according to maps—is the one trail that penetrates the country between the Green and the Divide. However, this trail has long been neglected and is without signs. You need a map to locate yourself, but the map is of limited use in locating the trail, which finds its way into the mountains without regard for the map's representation.

Just north of the Highline's bridge across the Roaring Fork, you'll find a trail (though strewn with deadfall) heading upstream. At the upper end of Alexander Park, after crossing a moraine, the trail crosses the creek (though not shown on maps), only to recross it at a ruined cabin after 0.25 mile.

The Bridger Wilderness map shows the trail ending here. The Green River Lakes quad indicates the trail following Native Lake's outlet stream, but the way is blocked by cliffs rated by one party as 5.2 (though they did find an identifiable trail in places). The Beartooth map shows the 7.5-minute quad's Native Lake way. The Earthwalk map shows both the Native Lake way and a trail continuing along the Roaring Fork's north bank, which the trail indeed does. After crossing the Roaring Fork, either by thin logs or wading that can be spooky when the current is strong, you ascend beside Crescent Lake's outlet stream—the trail here being steep and loose—crossing this stream three times below the lake. From meadows near Crescent Lake, a side trail leads to Native Lake. The Roaring Fork Trail passes within sight of Crescent Lake, then climbs to an 11,000-foot saddle. Its descent to Faler Lake more or less coincides with the Earthwalk map's trail. Something of a trail follows Faler Lake's west shore.

A path follows Crescent Lake's north shore but becomes increasingly dim in the valley beyond.

Osborn Mountain Route

Green River Lakes to Crescent Lake—9 miles

Crossing Osborn Mountain makes a shorter and more scenic, but strenuous, alternative to the Roaring Fork Trail. Begin, as for the Highline Trail North, by crossing Lower Green River Lake's outlet and turning downstream. One-quarter mile downstream, beyond a fence that extends up into an aspen grove, turn right from the Highline toward a diamond-shaped boulder that sits on what appears to be a hilltop though actually is only a bump on a ridge. Horses have carried enough hunting camps up Mill Creek that a decent trail, generally easy to locate, follows this ridge.

After climbing for 2 miles, descend through a small meadow to Mill Creek and cross it; you should be able to find a well-used crossing and a path beyond. This path leads up a north-facing valley to the saddle between Osborn's main mass and Point 11,030 to its west. Turn east and gain Osborn's plateau; cross the plateau to its southeast end. Descend talus to a col overlooking Clear Lake, between Osborn and the 11,680-foot point on the southeast ridge.

Cross this point and descend northeast, toward Crescent Lake. The descent initially looks unlikely and may test your faith in guidebooks, but a convenient ridge soon appears, leading to the saddle crossed by the Roaring Fork Trail between Native and Faler Lakes.

Crescent Lake to Baker Lake

Wanderers have a reverence for a roughly 4- by 6-mile expanse of above-treeline terrain west of the Divide, in which outcrops and tundra are interspersed with Daphne, Bear, Rocking Horse, Hourglass, and Kevin Lakes and innumerable smaller lakes and tarns. Not only is this country relatively inaccessible because of difficulties encountered ascending the drainages of Clear Creek, Slide Creek, and Elbow Creek and the circuitous trajectory of the Roaring Fork Trail, but the country is convoluted enough that, while there are no dramatic barriers, neither are there trails or even obvious routes. For a guidebook to presume to describe a route would imply that its writer had tried enough possibilities to write authoritatively. It would also alienate those who seek out this country for the rare opportunity it offers for finding one's way by studying the terrain and reading a map. Real wildness is a precious enough commodity that it shouldn't be compromised with a hiking recipe.

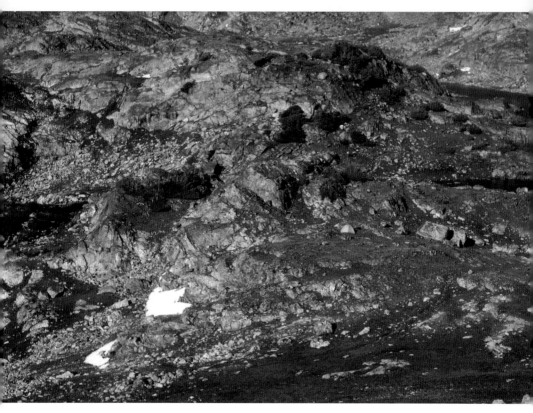

Camping at Crescent Lake

Suffice to say that it is possible to traverse between Crescent and Baker Lakes, even with a loaded backpack. One hint: It seems equally efficient (or inefficient) to ascend into this country from the upstream end of Crescent Lake or to follow the Roaring Fork Trail from Crescent Lake down to Faler Lake and ascend an improbable draw from there to Sunset Lake, the 0.25-mile-long lake north of Bear Lake. Another hint: The label "Bear Basin" on the Downs Mountain quad seems to be misplaced and would be more appropriately applied to the classic high meadow bordering the creek to the southwest.

Highline Trail

Green River Lakes to Three Forks Park—12 miles

The Highline extends along the range's west flank from Green River Lakes to Big Sandy Opening; sections are described in different chapters. The section that follows the Green River gives access to most of the peaks and other trails in this chapter. Paralleling the eastern shores of the Green River Lakes, the Highline follows the Green to Three Forks Park, where the river is joined by Wells and Trail Creeks. The net elevation gain from the trailhead to Three Forks Park is only 300 feet, though innumerable minor ups and downs mask this low relief.

From the southwest corner of the Green River Lakes trailhead parking area, descend a broad path east and follow signs to a bridge spanning the river. Walk south along the lower lake, at the head of which the Clear Creek Trail branches left and, just beyond, the Porcupine Trail branches right. The Highline continues past the upper lake, through scenic meadows for a few miles, then dull forest for a few more miles. Just beyond Elbow and Pixley Creeks, crossed by bundles of rickety poles, the trail crosses the Green in Beaver Park.

A number of bridges have been tried here, and a number have washed away. A sturdy structure was in place in 1999, but do not assume its indefinite survival. In the absence of a bridge, the best crossing is north of the bridge site. A quarter mile beyond Pixley Creek the trail passes a few feet from a loop of the meandering river; ford at the next loop. Although it isn't apparent, you are now on an island; proceed to the island's south end and wade the lesser, western channel.

When hiking north from Three Forks Park, if the bridge is defunct, continue past its site for 100 yards to a sign for Granite Lake and another few hundred yards to the crossing of the Green's western channel. Hike down the island for perhaps 300 yards to the ford of the main channel, just upstream from a river bend to the west.

Two miles above Beaver Park the Highline skirts boggy Three Forks Park, which offers camping distinctly inferior to Beaver Park below and Trail Creek Park above. From Three Forks Park you can find your way up Tourist and Wells Creeks. The Highline ascends west from here, climbing to country covered in the Peak Lake chapter.

Lakeside Trail

Green River Lakes Campground to Porcupine Trail—2 miles

This trail follows the west shore of Lower Green River Lake. It begins at the south end of Green River Lakes Campground—stay at the campground's level rather than dropping to the lake—and joins the Porcupine Trail at the upper end of the lake.

Passing through forest the Lakeside Trail is scenically inferior to the Highline, but the shade is worth considering on a hot afternoon.

Porcupine Trail

Green River Lakes to New Fork Canyon—9 miles

The Porcupine Trail begins between the two Green River Lakes. You can reach it from the Lakeside Trail, or from the Highline by crossing the Green on a bridge and traversing a swampy meadow. Crossing Porcupine Creek's channels has varied as avalanche debris has come and gone, but recently it involved a slightly spooky log across the main channel. After crossing, relocate the trail and climb 1,000 feet into the creek's hanging valley, where the Valiate Lake Trail branches right.

Continue along the valley floor, past a continuum of good campsites, to an inconspicuous junction with the Jim Creek Trail near the valley's head. The main branch of Porcupine Creek descends from the east, but the trail switchbacks south to Porcupine Pass (10,680+), which it crosses to Dodge Creek. It meets the New Fork Trail where the latter begins its steep climb above New Fork Canyon.

Valiate Lake Trail

Porcupine Creek to Valiate Lake—2 miles

Two miles from its start between the Green River Lakes, the Porcupine Trail levels out and fords Porcupine Creek by a small meadow. Here a trail diverges north and climbs to an obscure chain of lakes—Twin, Shirley, and Valiate (maps misspell the name). Although maps show the trail ending at Shirley Lake, the trail hardly diminishes as it continues to Valiate Lake; indeed, if you have reason (which this book doesn't provide) to continue to the rockbound valley above, you can follow remarkably well-maintained elk tracks.

Clear Creek Trail (part not maintained)

Green River Lakes to Clear Lake—3.5 miles

This trail branches from the Highline at the south end of Lower Green River Lake and ascends Clear Creek. The trail is maintained for 2 miles, as far as the Natural Bridge, but a fire obliterated what was once a well-used path continuing to Clear Lake. Even veteran hikers have described the charred deadfall obstacle course of the final mile as the worst traveling in the Wind Rivers.

The trail provides access not only to Clear Lake but also to Slide Lake, via the Slide Creek Trail, and Faler Lake, via steep scrambling and boulder-hopping.

Slide Creek Trail

Clear Creek to Slide Lake—2.5 miles

From Clear Creek's meadow you can see on the wall to the south what looks like a narrow snowfield—it is Slide Creek gliding down dipping strata. (In certain light Slide Creek Falls is visible from the Grand Teton.)

The trail to Slide Lake leaves the Clear Creek Trail in the meadow, crosses Clear Creek on a narrow bridge, and, without markings, traverses further meadows to Slide Creek. Either wade the creek or cross logs just upstream. The ford leads to the first of many switchbacks, the logs to a steep informal trail that bypasses the first switchback. The switchbacks end at a long meadow above the falls.

The trail ends at Slide Lake's outlet. You can continue along the east shore, but, thanks to avalanches, the going isn't the shoreline stroll associated with most Wind River lakes. Beyond the lake the going becomes extremely tough, but occasionally, determined backpackers have followed the upper creek.

Lost Eagle Route

Slide Creek to Golden Lakes—5 miles

The best route to the Elbow and Golden Lakes from the Green River isn't Elbow Creek but the valley east of White Rock and the plateau of Lost Eagle Peak. Despite lack of formal maintenance, the way is generally easy to follow, with minimal deadfall and scree. Moreover, it is easy to locate on maps.

Leave the Slide Creek Trail at the lower end of the meadow above the falls, 1.5 miles from Clear Creek, if a log makes a stream crossing feasible. If not, wade at the meadow's upper end. Head for a narrow open slope. (A trail in the trees east of the slope is hard to locate.) Take the open slope's left branch, cross the small creek that drains the valley above, and ascend just east of it to a long level section (good camping, but beware of the creeklet flowing underground in places).

Bear left at the valley's head and cross to a unique little spine that leads onto Lost Eagle. You can see about as much geologic diversity from this spine as you could want. Not only do you see the Tetons, Gros Ventres, and Absarokas in one direction and Gannett Peak in the other, but the abrupt transition underfoot from sedimentary rock to granitic rock makes the location of a major fault apparent even to a layperson.

You can cross the plateau anywhere, but descents to Elbow Lake No. 2 are limited. While you can continue to Lost Eagle's east edge, then zigzag south down ledges, it seems best to drop to the broad saddle (behind which is a steep prow) 0.25 mile west of Lake No. 2 and contour, following cairns, to the lake's theoretical outlet. From here you can work down a long grassy slope to the lake—presumably Elbow Lake No. 1—at the very northeast corner of the Squaretop Mountain quad. To reach the Golden Lakes, though, round Point 11,140 to the south and follow a convenient bench east into the bowl west of Point 11,894. After descending a few hundred feet, scramble around Point 11,894's south ridge to slopes just above Golden Lake 10,940. To continue to Baker Lake, see the *Elbow Creek Route,* below.

Elbow Creek Route

Beaver Park to Baker Lake—5 miles

Elbow Creek is the northern of two streams the Highline crosses at the north end of Beaver Park. From the Highline, follow game trails left of Elbow Creek until it is feasible to cross to open slopes on the right side. Recross above the creek's elbow and continue upstream to the lake at the Squaretop Mountain quad's northeast corner. The presence of Elbow Lake No. 2 above implies that you're at Elbow Lake No. 1. (The *Lost Eagle Route* offers another way to this lake.)

A rocky gorge leads from Elbow Lake No. 1 to the first Golden Lake (10,940). Perhaps no one knows the country beyond well enough to state confidently the best route from here to Baker Lake, but a consensus favors ascending the valley north of Lake 10,940, taking its left branch, and reaching the Slide-Elbow divide east of Point 11,894. (Continuing via the upper Golden Lakes involves shinnying up a chute near Lake 10,940's inlet.) Pass just south of the 11,520-foot tarn and continue along the ill-defined divide more or less at this elevation; hiking this part of the route is fun.

Marten Lake Route

Green River to Marten Lake—2.5 miles

Climbing into Marten Lake's cirque does not entail the mellow hiking for which the Wind Rivers are known and loved. Instead, it involves crossing the Green and ascending 2,000 vertical feet of trailless forest, talus, and boulders. However, the hillside east of the stream that drains the cirque is distinctly less unpleasant than the hillside to the west; begin east of Point 8,325. Campsites are sparse; don't be selective.

Except at high water, and with a bit of towing, you can take a canoe up the Green nearly to the mouth of the cirque's stream.

Granite Lake Trail (not maintained)

Beaver Park to Granite Lake—1.5 miles

The approach to Squaretop's easiest route begins where the Highline's bridge crosses the Green River. Leave the Highline at the bridge and follow the river downstream for 100 yards to a sign for Granite Lake. If the bridge is gone, the 100 yards become part of the Highline, the sign being a few hundred yards upstream from the ford of the Green.

From the sign, cross Beaver Park to its north end, from which the trail heads uphill. However, the park's north end is indistinct, and the trail heads uphill as several tracks, which eventually coalesce into a single trail. This trail is an old one, a relic of days when Forest Service code didn't limit switchbacks' steepness or show concern for erosion. The lower part of the steep 1,000-foot ascent uses the open slope shown on the Squaretop Mountain quad; the upper part is to the left. Above, cross a ridge to Granite Lake's south end.

Pixley Creek Route

Beaver Park to Baker Lake—5 miles

Ascending Pixley Creek is much like ascending Tourist Creek, but the difficulties are more continuous, more intense, and less likely to take you to somewhere you want to be. The lower canyon is the crux.

Three Forks Park to Scott Lake or Continental Divide

Upper Tourist Creek flows through one of the range's most charming valleys—cascades, lakes at a spectrum of elevations, profuse flowers, bighorn sheep. "Upper" explains the sparseness of humanity in this idyllic setting, for the 1,500-foot ascent from Three Forks Park to the upper valley's lip is distinctly less idyllic.

You can reach Tourist Creek in two ways: (1) You can leave the Highline where it crosses the Green in Beaver Park and parallel the river's east bank. A path for much of its 2-mile length follows a subtle ridge a few hundred feet from the river. Much of the trail is easy going; all would be were it not for deadfall. While the path may be frequently lost, it's worth relocating, for despite the deadfall it offers the best route. (2) After August 1 (typically) you can continue on the Highline from Beaver Park to the north end of Three Forks Park and cross the Green by a sandbar and waist-deep wade near Tourist Creek's mouth or by rock-hopping upstream. Unfortunately, you must hike 2 miles of the Highline before knowing whether such a crossing is feasible.

The 1,500-foot-high slope above may be divided into four zones: bog, deadfall, scree, and massive blocks. Tourist Creek reaches the Green not as the vigorous mountain stream the map implies but as a maze of channels, some doubling back, that mask the creek's identity. Minimize the confusion of this geography by being somewhat inland. Minimize deadfall encounters above by ascending well south of Tourist Creek. Likewise, above the trees (specifically, an aspen grove) you can find more stable scree well south of the creek, nearly reaching the wall that produced it. You must then, however, traverse north for hundreds of feet, nearly to the creek; there seems to be no particularly good level at which to traverse. Nor is there a recommended route through the boulders that choke the creek's narrowing gorge, as aiming for the outlet of the little lake marked 10,090 on the Gannett Peak quad or for the gap to the south also present equivalent problems. If backpacking, allow 3 hours for the climb from the Green to Lake 10,090.

Scenic Lake 10,090 offers the canyon's first pleasant campsite, and beyond here the going becomes decidedly more enjoyable. Pass north of the lake. To reach the Wells Creek drainage (e.g., Mammoth Glacier), cross Tourist Creek 0.5 mile above Lake 10,090 and ascend the valley of Lake 11,085's outlet stream. Though not shown on maps, it is a robust mountain stream, and its east bank is alternately bedrock slabs and verdant slopes. Pass Lake 11,085 on either side, cross a low divide, and descend to Scott Lake.

To reach the Divide south of Klondike Peak, continue up Tourist Creek. Stay north of the creek, occasionally climbing well above it, but cross to the south side below Pond 10,600+. Both sides of Lake 10,890 (Flagstone Lake on some maps) present inconveniences, but the north side less so. Above, ascend the valley's right side to rugged terrain for the final 0.5 mile to the Divide.

Wells Creek Route

Three Forks Park to Minor Glacier or Mammoth Glacier—4 miles

The most logical route to Gannett Peak's west side—in terms of drainage—is the Green to Three Forks Park, then Wells Creek to Mammoth Glacier. However, a disproportionate amount of the negativity that was accorded the 1981 guidebook was inspired by its depiction of Wells Creek. One unhappy soul questioned Wells' W; a Jackson Hole waitress nearly refused to serve me because Wells Creek had ruined her vacation; and a reviewer, who admitted to being one of many mountaineering greats turned back by the rugged chasm, condemned the entire book because of this passage:

> The route up Wells Creek has suffered a bad reputation, with tales of impassable cliffs and direct aid; certainly the view from below offers no encouragement. Vince Lee, though, has pioneered a route up the cleft of the creek that has proven passable to heavily laden parties ... One caution, however: The cleft is probably impassable early in summer when the creek is high.
>
> Leave the Highline near the upper end of Three Forks Park, ford the Green, and ascend the right side of Wells Creek. Enter the cleft and climb near the waterfalls, crossing the creek when necessary. Inexperienced climbers may need a rope on a few of the larger boulders.

If, while struggling up the cleft, you require less poetic prose: Expect 15-foot boulders and 5.5 moves.

An arm of Scott Lake, called Many Bug Lake, extends to the top of the cleft, with cliffs on both sides. When the lake is frozen, you can walk along an edge on snowbanks; later the lake level drops, exposing mudflats. (Scott Lake appears to have once been higher. Perhaps boulders impounding it washed away in the recent past.) You can follow either of Scott Lake's inlet streams: one to Minor Glacier, the other to Mammoth Glacier.

Unless you seek the adventure of one of the range's severest backpacks, consider Tourist Creek, which is less malignant than Wells Creek yet rugged enough to inspire curses at this guide.

Peaks

Kendall Mountain (11,091)

Conspicuous from the lowlands Kendall Mountain is the biggest of the massifs south of Jim Creek that constitute the range's western fringe. While the terrain is hardly alpine, it is hacked into pinnacles, walls, and shaggy arêtes.

1. West Slope (I 1st class) An old trail runs between Jim Creek and Lower Boulder Basin, west of Kendall Mountain. Leave the trail at its 9,800-foot high point and locate a hunters' trail near Kendall's ridge crest. Below treeline is an open forest of fine whitebark pines. Above treeline are charming alpine meadows. The crux of the ascent is relocating the trail at the far (southeast) end of a meadow just below 9,000 feet, just inside the Wilderness boundary, and at the edge of an area burned in 2007. Look for it southeast of where the map indicates.

2. East Ridge (I 1st class) Leave the Jim Creek Trail near its high point at the head of Boulder Creek and traverse several minor summits.

3. North Ridge (5.7) Long, curving ridge with several steep steps and an unprotected slab toward top.

4. Kendall Candle, South Side (I 5.10a) On Kendall Mountain's north slope, at 10,440 feet, stands this prominent spire, situated below a few less-defined crags. Begin on its south side by climbing a 5.7 chimney for 130 feet to the notch between the Candle and the adjacent formation. Rather than coping with the off-width above, which splits the Candle, climb 5.7 cracks and a chimney to the left for 80 feet to a belay above the off-width. On the 5.10a third pitch (originally aided, with a rope toss), climb an arête past two bolts to the summit.

5. Kendall Candle–Light in the Forest (II 5.10a) A worthwhile route follows the prominent crack on the Candle's west face. Begin in a small corner on the right side of the west face's toe, then ascend the main crack (5.10a) for 180 feet to a good ledge. The second pitch follows a wide crack, with a smaller crack within for protection, for 100 feet (5.9+). The third pitch coincides with the third pitch of the *South Side* route.

4,5 Descent: Rappel 75 feet to the notch between the Candle and the tower to the east, then 102 feet (31 meters) to the ground.

Point 11,120+

The formation, 1.2 miles northeast of Kendall Mountain, between Jim Creeks 3 and 4 (see Point 11,080+, below), is steep on all sides except the east.

1. East Ridge (I 2nd class) Reached from either Jim Creek fork.

2. West Ridge (I 4th class) Rugged hiking leads to the lakelet in the mouth of Jim Creek 3's canyon. Exposed scrambling up to and along the west ridge becomes easier nearer the summit.

3. South Face (II 5.6) A huge stepped system of dihedrals and slabs is located below the formation's high point. This route starts a few hundred feet right of the system, around a corner. Two pitches follow a left-leaning book; a third follows a gully/chimney onto a shoulder, and the route intersects the dihedral/slab system. A 4th-class pitch crosses the dihedral and surmounts a rib to the left. Scrambling up left a few hundred feet leads to the top. (The system itself is encumbered by loose, dirty rock.)

Point 11,080+

Squaretop is so well known that many believe they can see it from the plains west of the range. Squaretop, however, is out of sight around the Green's Big Bend; the steep-walled, flat-topped formation mistaken for it is this unnamed massif 0.8 mile south of Jim Creek Lake.

Climbers intrigued by the many craggy formations in the Jim Creek drainage have identified the forks south of the main fork, which drains Jim Creek Lake, as Jim Creeks 2, 3, and 4, from north to south. Point 11,080+ stands between Jim Creeks 2 and 3.

1. From the East (I 2nd class) A pleasant hike.

2. North Face–Client's Corner (II 5.6) The peak's north face features two large dihedrals, to the left of which is a broken corner, bordered by a rib farther left. Follow the broken corner for two pitches, then the blocky rib for three. The rock quality is disappointing.

Point 11,200+

This is the minor summit 0.6 mile southeast of Jim Creek Lake.

1. East Slope (I 2nd class) A quarter mile of grass, a few hundred feet of easy scrambling.

Saltlick Mountain (11,350)

1. Southeast Slope (I 1st class) East of Saltlick the South Fork of Gypsum Creek Trail crosses a pass from Jim Creek to Gypsum Creek. From south of this pass it is an easy stroll to Saltlick's summit, identified by a large cairn.

2. Via Point 11,218 (I 3rd class) The Saltlick massif's southwest summit (Point 11,218) is a coxcombed crest that can add zest to a trek to the main summit and the grassy west summit (Point 11,316).

Owl's Head (11,360+)

As you continue up Gypsum Creek's South Fork past Battleship Mountain, you see an incongruous element in this landscape of sedimentary reefs. A cluster of fine granite towers and buttresses rises in the angle between the South Fork and the subsidiary valley (with a tiny pond) north of Point 11,410. The main buttress, northwest-facing and crossed in its upper half by several roofs, is Owl's Head (a short-eared owl). The very steep formation to the left (east) is Nameless Tower. As you continue up the South Fork, massive, southwest-facing granite comes into view: South Wing.

1. Nameless Tower–No-Name Has-Beens (III 5.10-) This bold-looking line essentially follows the corner system on the tower's prow. Easy ledges lead to a cairn that marks the start.

Start the 5.7 first pitch by moving right to a corner. Climb this corner for 50 feet, move left and up for another 50 feet, and belay on a step below the main corner system. Reach this system by a few strenuous moves and a finger crack. Follow the corner till its crack narrows, forcing unprotected face climbing for 20 feet to a roof; pull the roof and follow a crack to a sloping ledge with a piton. Begin the third pitch by climbing the 3- to 5-inch crack left of the corner, then move left to a thinner crack, which curves back to the corner and a belay in a hole. The fourth pitch ascends an awkward groove to a semi-hanging belay below a wider crack. Climb the widening crack, which can be protected with 6-inch gear. The easy sixth pitch continues up short, wide cracks to slabs right of the summit. Third-class chimneys and slabs lead right, then left to the summit.

Descent: Hike up and east, then descend north down a wide couloir, which typically carries low-angle snow till late July.

2. Owl's Head, North Buttress (II 5.7) From the toe of the buttress, scramble up dirty cracks and ledges for a few hundred feet. The initial pitch follows easy cracks to a ramp with steep, short steps leading left. From a belay beneath an overhang, pass right of the overhang and climb a chimney and cracks. The long third lead follows cracks and chimneys to a gully just below the crest. Easy climbing leads to the summit.

3. Owl's Head–July Route (III 5.8) The left of two northwest-facing routes begins near the buttress's left side (though right of the side-canyon pond) with 160 feet of 3rd

Owl's Head

class in a low-angle, left-facing dihedral. Three mostly easy pitches ascend slabs and grassy cracks; the first begins with a traverse left. These pitches serve as an approach to the good climbing. Two steeper leads (5.7, 5.8) follow clean cracks through a break in a roof to a low-angle area below huge overhangs. On the seventh pitch, go up a 5.6 corner, traverse easily right, then downclimb a 5.4 crack to a belay. Step right (5.6) to the corner at the right edge of the overhangs and ascend the pleasant corner. Continue to the corner's top (5.6), then traverse easily left. The ninth pitch continues left, then passes through another overhang via an obvious chimney. The short tenth pitch follows a 5.6 crack to the crest. Begin the final lead with a 5.8 face, then follow 5.7 cracks and a chimney to the top.

4. Owl's Head–June Route (III 5.9) To the right of *July,* look for a beautiful, obvious crack in a dark slab and climb it for 160 feet (5.8). Traverse right on ledges and climb to a ledge (75 feet, 5.8). Begin the third pitch by climbing a clean 5.8 slab; finish via dirty 5.9 cracks. Belay at a right-rising arch; 5.8 cracks lead through the arch. The sixth lead begins with a tricky move but continues up 4th-class terrain to a notch. The seventh pitch ascends a 5.6 slab to a ramp leading right. The short final pitch reaches the crest via a thin crack.

2, 3, 4 Descent: Scramble down a gully to the south, then rappel 50 feet.

5. South Wing Left (III 5.7) The south face is characterized by vast slabs except near its left edge, which is creased by several corners. After a short scramble to a belay ledge, move left into a dihedral with a wide 5.6 crack. The second pitch continues up the dihedral, which curves right and morphs into a chimney with overhangs (5.7). The short third pitch ascends an easy slab to the base of a headwall. Pitch 4 involves a short crux corner, face climbing to the right, and easy cracks. Pitch 5 soon reaches a crest, with one 5.7 move. Traverse the 4th-class crest to a notch.

You can easily descend to the northwest from the notch, but the route continues for three pitches on the broad, not-too-steep wall above. The first of these pitches (5.6) goes up and left to a corner system and a big ledge. The second upper pitch (5.7) follows this system, eventually exiting right to a belay under an overhang. The final pitch (5.6) follows cracks right of the overhang.

6. South Wing Center (III 5.8) A prominent ramp angles up from the lower right corner of the face. Reach the ramp by a pitch in the lower wall's largest left-facing corner. Ascend the ramp for a pitch, passing one right-facing corner to a smaller one. Beginning in this corner, reach the crest in three more leads. As on *South Wing Left,* traverse the crest to the notch below the upper wall. Climb this wall to the right of *South Wing Left.*

7. South Wing Right (II 5.7) From the face's right edge, scramble a short way up the prominent ramp. The first pitch continues up the ramp, then surmounts a small overhang, then follows thin cracks to a belay in a dihedral. Exit left from the dihedral, climb an awkward step, and follow a chimney/crack to a belay on a prow. Ascend the gully above, then take the rib to the right up to the crest and join the other two routes. Follow one of them up the wall above.

5, 6, 7 Descent: Scramble west to the Owl's Head descent.

Battleship Mountain (11,607)

The summit is a limestone reef, a breaking wave of rock in a tundra sea.

1. South Slope/West Ridge (I 1st class) From the South Fork of Gypsum Creek. The pleasantest route follows the valley that heads between the main summit and Point 11,070 to the west.

2. Northeast Ridge (I 4th class) The ridge connecting Battleship's main summit with its northeast summit (Point 11,590) is an exposed knife edge.

Gypsum Mountain (11,515)

1. Northwest Ridge (I 2nd class) Leave the Moose–Gypsum Road southwest of Gypsum Park, on the trail that heads east from Benchmark 8805. Leave the trail after 0.25 mile, pass west of a pond, and gain Gypsum's northwest ridge (the ridge of Points 9,774 and 10,606).

Big Sheep Mountain (11,618)

The most vivid evidence that the Wind River block was eroded to a plain after upthrusting can be seen west of Lower Green River Lake, where Big Sheep Mountain's horizontal summit plateau bevels its tilted strata. The rocks represent the period 550 to 200 million years ago when a sea encroached from the west. The sequence of sandstones, shales, limestones, and dolomites the sea deposited reflect its increasing depth, fluctuations, and eventual retreat; fossils give further information. The 1,000-foot-thick band that forms most of the summit flat is Madison Limestone; corals, shells, and the limestone's purity indicate a warm, placid, shallow sea.

1. Northwest Slope (I 2nd class). The Moose–Gypsum Road shortcuts the Green River Road's sweep around the river's Big Bend. It is a shortcut that saves no time, but the road is scraped and graded frequently enough that it is usually tolerable for most vehicles. From its beginning, just north of The Place, follow it for 8.3 miles (stay on Gypsum Creek's east side) to where it enters Gypsum Park.

Here an unmaintained, seldom-driven road branches right, zigzagging up through clear-cuts. A passenger reading a map helps. You can drive this road for 2.3 miles, to a branch of Gypsum Creek near the Wilderness boundary. However, if you do, the drive is the climb's crux, technically as well as in terms of routefinding. The broad slopes beyond make a straightforward 2-mile hike; parking lower and hiking farther shouldn't require too long a day.

2. North Ridge (I 2nd class) From near Green River Lakes Campground you can see a valley high on the mountain, the left side exposing tilted strata. The problem is deadfall between you and the valley. A creekbed, usually dry, which descends from the valley to the campground's southwest corner, may help you keep your bearings, though the adjacent slopes present an especially thick maze.

Begin just south of the creekbed. Higher, follow that favorite of guidebook writers—if not readers—faint game trails. From the open slopes at the foot of the valley, you have two choices: Gain the ridge to the west from below the green 9,640-foot tarn or continue to the valley's head and, using ramps to bypass cliff bands, gain the rim near Point 11,403.

Osborn Mountain (11,880+)

This nominal mountain east of Lower Green River Lake is a plateau that breaks off to the north in cliffs above the Roaring Fork, and to the south toward Clear Creek.

1. From Osborn Mountain Route (I 2nd class) The route passes near the high point, which overlooks the cirque north of Clear Lake.

2. East-facing Buttress–Verloren (III 5.10)

The Osborn massif is cleft by a narrow southeast-draining cirque that separates Point 11,810 from Osborn's high point. *Verloren* ascends a handsome 1,200-foot buttress on the west side of this cirque. Although, from the perspective of Clear Lake, the buttress is just around the corner from Forlorn Pinnacle, the first ascent team approached by descending the cirque from Osborn's plateau.

Follow a splitter in the center of the face, veering slightly right to avoid a headwall toward the top.

Osborn Mountain

Twenty-Hour Tower (11,400+)

One-quarter mile west of Forlorn Pinnacle, also attached to the Osborn massif, is a slightly less conspicuous formation. The name commemorates the chronology of the first ascent (*South Face Right*), car-to-car, a longer project than the climbers had planned. Incidentally, the *You Gotta Want It* first ascent team beat that time: 22.5 hours camp-to-camp.

1. South Face Left–Alexander's Band (8 pitches, 5.10R) At least three Wind River routes have been first climbed to recover valuable stuff left on a prior climb. *Alexander's Band* was climbed because a pack filled with a thousand dollars worth of gear was left on the descent of *You Gotta Want It*. *Alexander's Band* begins left of *You Gotta Want It* and joins it at the latter's tenth pitch.

2. South Face Center–You Gotta Want It (IV 5.11) Up the center of the formation for fifteen pitches, mostly 5.8 to 5.10. The crux is a layback finger crack.

3. South Face Right (II 5.7) Scramble to timbered benches on the right side of the face. Rope up at a weakness right of a big left-facing book. Two pitches (5.6, 5.7) are followed by two 4th-class pitches that trend left to a rib. Pleasant climbing on the rib leads to a few hundred feet of 3rd class that lead to the steeper summit area. There a long 5.7 pitch ascends just right of the rib; another ascends a chimney to easier ground. The final pitch boulders up steps between ledges to the airy summit.

Descent: The *Gotta Want It* team apparently rappelled the route, at one point rappelling from a "ridiculously dangerous bush." This is from the *South Face Right* team: Descend north to the notch between the tower and Osborn Mountain by downclimbing 50 feet to ledges, then rappelling twice. From the notch, rappel into the couloir to the west and descend easy terrain (snow in early summer) for a few hundred feet to a drop-off. Three rappels down this headwall reach the drainage west of the tower. Hike down scree until cliffs beside a waterfall require two more rappels.

Forlorn Pinnacle (11,640+)

This is Osborn Mountain's spur that towers over Clear Lake, 0.5 mile northwest of the lake, conspicuous in profile from many viewpoints. While Forlorn Pinnacle itself has been climbed a few times, the splinter on its south wall—the Fickle Finger of Forlorn—attracts more attention.

1. North Ridge (II 5.5) Ascend the large couloir immediately west of Clear Lake (steep snow in early season), bypassing a number of chockstones by 4th-class scrambling, eventually reaching the notch between the pinnacle and Osborn Mountain. Follow the north ridge for five pitches to one of the Wind Rivers' airier summits.

Descent: Rappel and downclimb the north ridge, bypassing the notch by a long rappel into the ascent couloir. Descend the couloir's snow, rappelling past the chockstones as necessary.

2. Fickle Finger, South Face Left (III/IV 5.8 A2) A streambed or gully bounds the south face on the left. The better of the face's routes, ten leads long, is just right of this gully, facing Clear Lake's outlet. Climb a few pitches in the gully. Continue near the edge of the face. The most memorable move is a blind reach around an exposed corner to place an aid piece. A few hundred feet below the Finger, you reach an east-sloping slab. Round the left side of the Finger to the notch behind.

At least three cracks offer routes to the summit; they have required a bit of aid. A crack on the west side could be protected with very large pieces.

3. Fickle Finger, South Face Right (III 5.8 A2) Down-sloping holds contribute to the difficulty of this strenuous ten-pitch route. While most of the route lies near the face's right edge, eventually it crosses left to reach the notch behind the Finger. You can access a large ledge at the route's base from the stream/gully. The first pitch follows a crack in the middle of the face for 160 feet to a big ledge below a prominent left-facing corner. Climb the corner and the face to its left to a broken area. Next, climb to a pleasant face that leads to the top of a pinnacle with a chimney behind it. Work up and left for a few pitches to the east-sloping slab, where you join the left-side route.

2, 3 Descent: Rappel to the notch. Scramble down gullies to the east until you must rappel. Rappel slightly south to a chimney system, then rappel and downclimb to the cirque east of the pinnacle.

Flat Top Mountain (11,868)

On the plateau between Clear and Slide Creeks are two minor rises joined by a narrow neck, Ram Pass. You have a choice of summits—the highest point or the point named on the map—but the best views, of the canyons below, are from the plateau's edge. This plateau represents thriving bighorn habitat; the sheep, which remain year-round, are protected from humanity by Flat Top's dreadful lower slopes.

1. Southeast Slope (I 3rd class) It's not obvious how highly to recommend a route that begins with hundreds of feet of deadfall-straddling, mossy gullies; krumholz-thrashing, angle-of-repose scree; damp slab traverses; and routefinding by uninformed hunch—leading, however, to a classic, pristine high valley. Enjoyment requires selective memory. Nor is it clear how to rate a route's difficulty when the crux may involve laybacking a bush. Whether torturous or delightful, a route that below treeline is in its own way desperate, whose middle section is pleasant uphill, and whose last mile is a flat stroll, does fit the topography of the Green River's upper drainages.

Up Slide Creek 0.25 mile from Slide Lake, a creek enters from the north. The idea is to follow this creek to the lovely valley, but how best to accomplish this is hardly apparent. Significantly, most clamberers descend by a different route than they ascend. Two tactics have advocates, though not outspoken ones: (1) Leave Slide Creek only a few hundred feet past the lake, near signs of an old campsite, and head for the nearest talus, traversing east to the creek 500 feet up. (2) Continue up Slide Creek till past the side creek, then head up open slopes.

2. Northeast Arête–Trundler (III 5.8) A nine-pitch route.

Descent: Via the gully behind the wall, first west, then north.

White Rock (11,284)

Climbers entering the mountains on the Highline quickly dismiss the cliffs above Upper Green River Lake as crumbly and continue to crystalline rock beyond. A geologist, though, sees more in these sedimentary layers than in monolithic granite. White Rock's face consists of two steep bands interrupted by a broken layer. The lower cliff is Bighorn Dolomite, deposited as limestone when a sea advanced 450 to 425 million years ago and later transformed to dolomite. It was deposited in a clear sea, but the sand, mud, and lime of the broken Darby Formation above was laid in foul, turbid water. The upper cliff is Madison Limestone, deposited over 300 million years ago in quiet seas. The upper slopes are strewn with seashell fossils and obsidian chippings. Characterized as a "belvedere" in a more literate era, White Rock's summit is most notable for views of Squaretop, the Green River Lakes and the upper Green River, Gannett, and the Downs-Klondike segment of the Divide.

1. North Ridge (I 3rd class) You can reach White Rock's broad, bare north ridge by leaving the Highline a few hundred feet south of Clear Creek. Look for a path leading uphill (behind a continuum of overused campsites). However, even without a path you should encounter few obstacles in the open forest as you ascend the steep slope. There are intermittent paths; stay on the west-facing rather than north-facing slope, to minimize charred deadfall. Only a few moves on the summit cone are 3rd class.

You can also easily climb White Rock from the Slide Creek Trail and *Lost Eagle Route*.

Lost Eagle Pinnacle (11,640+)

Above Slide Lake is a striking pinnacle, visible from the Green River Road. The name Lost Eagle was apparently first applied to the pinnacle, though on the Green River Lakes quad the rim behind the pinnacle is Lost Eagle Peak.

1. From the Rim (I 3rd class) An old account reports the pinnacle to be "easily accessible" from the rim.

2. West Face (II 5.6) Ascend crummy couloirs west and south of the pinnacle until the way is blocked by walls. Rope up and traverse 200 feet onto the west face. Reach the top in about six leads.

3. Northwest Face–Jenkins-Fleming Direct (13 pitches, 5.9R) Begin in a left-leaning, left-facing dihedral and continue in another one a few pitches up. Move back right, climb an ice-choked chimney, and continue on up the middle of the face.

2,3 Descent: Three to five rappels to the south into a west-facing gully.

Lost Eagle Peak (11,840+)

1. From Lost Eagle Route (I 1st class) The plateau's summit—a rocky outcrop sporting a cairn visible from some distance—rises a few hundred yards north of your most likely route.

Peak 12,082

Although rising 0.8 mile west-southwest of Baker Lake, Peak 12,082 has been summited but not often.

1. Northwest Slope (I 2nd class) A detour from the *Elbow Creek* route.

Granite Peak (9,892)

While this knoll east of Squaretop is the lowest summit in this guide, its walls rising from the Green River draw your attention, and it offers a more distinct summit than many higher peaks.

1. Southwest Slope (I 2nd class) From the northwest end of Granite Lake, fun— first up grass, then wandering through small headwalls.

Squaretop Mountain (11,695)

Most photogenic mountains—the Matterhorn, the Grand Teton, Alpamayo, Ama Dablam, for instance—are given a focus by graceful, converging ridge lines and are lent an ethereal quality by high snow. The Wind Rivers' most photographed peak is an ancient plateau remnant, with no snow and the shape of a tree stump. It is perversely appropriate that its chunky form emblemizes the range, yet it must be said that Squaretop dominates its scene as no other Wind River peak does.

Squaretop so dominates the Green River Lakes scene that the approach looks shorter than it is; Squaretop is 8 miles from the trailhead, and its base sits 2,000 feet above the river. However, while the walls impress from afar by their steepness, a closer look reveals more lines of weakness and broken rock. You can reach the first five routes described from Granite Lake. To reach other routes, you must ford the Green—not easy unless the river is low—cross by canoe, or walk on the boulder-strewn west shore of Upper Green River Lake. Allow 2 hours for the approach from the river to the beginning of a route.

1. Southeast Ledges (I 2nd class) Squaretop's hikers' route ascends grassy ledges and broken rock above Granite Lake, gaining the plateau 0.5 mile south of the high point. Gain half the height to the rim by grassy slopes above the lake's south end, then work right and ascend a chute to a shallow saddle on the rim.

The way is less easily found when you're descending. You may need to drop down an exploratory few hundred feet in search of such reassurances as cairns and boot prints.

2. Squaretower Left Side (II 5.9) To the left of the triangular bay that faces somewhat north of Granite Lake is a long fin that culminates in a tower—Squaretower. The *AC/DC* first ascent pair climbed left-slanting gullies and headwalls to the left when weather discouraged an early attempt on the main wall; nevertheless they described their consolation as a fun way up Squaretop.

An earlier attempt that was defeated by a storm resulted in a variation involving gullies and headwalls to the left (II 5.9).

Squaretower and Squaretop Mountain

3. Squaretower Center–Marginally Orange (IV 5.10 plus rappel) To the left of *AC/DC,* at the edge of *AC/DC*'s orange rock, is a route not as highly recommended. It involves the same long, intricate approach as *AC/DC* to the big, grassy ledge where serious climbing begins, but rather than traversing right, climb the thin, 5.7 dihedral above the ledge. The second pitch features a 5.9 undercling right and layback. The third pitch ascends left of a razor flake. The fourth pitch negotiates a leaning 5.10– corner. The fifth pitch is 5.8, but the sixth pitch offers a 5.10- off-width. Begin the seventh pitch by walking right, then climb a thin 5.10 crack. The final pitch (5.5) essentially merges with *AC/DC,* 50 feet from the top.

4. Squaretower Right–AC/DC (IV 5.10 plus rappel). To spare you having to refer to first ascent information to explain the route name, the route was first climbed by Andy Carson (who characterized the climbing as "excellent, varied, and difficult") and his son Dan. The route ascends Squaretower's south face, first on the right side, then angling left to a crack and corner capped by an enormous roof, then returning right to avoid the roof. While the route begins from an obvious grassy ledge at the base of the steep upper wall, the 1,000-foot approach to this ledge is nontrivial; be prepared to uncoil the rope.

From the grassy ledge, either traverse right above a cave (4th class) or climb a 5.8 crack to meet the traverse. The second pitch offers a choice between the 5.10 cracks and flakes to the left or the outstanding 5.10 hand crack to the right, which does, however, involve a loose block that a follower should jettison. On the third pitch, follow blocky steps up right to overhanging flared chimneys (5.9). On the fourth pitch a gully/dihedral leads to another choice: a 5.9/5.10 dihedral slightly right or a short 5.9 face to the left.

Begin the fifth pitch by moving easily left, then climb an excellent though runout 5.7/5.8 face. Diagonal left on the sixth pitch to a short 5.9 squeeze chimney that leads to a ledge with a pointed flake. The first ascent topo labels the crack that begins the seventh pitch "prime"; the crack leads past three roofs (5.10, 5.10, and 5.8) to a stance below the monster roof. From here, traverse right with some downclimbing (5.7) for half a rope length to the wall's east edge. Climb cracks, 5.9 at the start but soon becoming easy, for a final pitch and a half.

From Squaretower's top, downclimb north a few feet and rappel 80 feet to a notch. Two pitches, with some 5.7 on the first, lead to Squaretop's summit plateau.

The first ascent team recommends a rack up to a 4-inch cam, with two each of hand-size cams.

In an effort to make this guidebook as useful as possible: Andy Carson lost a watch with his wedding ring attached on the third pitch.

5. Southeast Face (II 5.6) The wall above Granite Lake is bounded on the right by the steeper east face and on the left by a giant couloir that slants up left. Three broken bowls are prominent features of the face.

Ascend ledges and slabs, then traverse into the couloir (or enter the couloir below the lake's outlet). Follow the loose couloir, then climb to the first bowl. For more pleasant climbing, leave the couloir sooner and climb the rock above up and left to the bowl. Easy 5th-class climbing leads to the second bowl. Harder climbing through blocks leads to the third bowl. Up left are ramps that slant to the top of the face; they involve several enjoyable 5th-class pitches.

A major variaton, offering more sustained climbing, begins in the second bowl. Follow 4th-class ledges left for a few hundred feet to a pillar at the ledges' end. You encounter a chimney, a steep, rotten face, and a pitch with a step of aid and slab-climbing to the right around an exposed corner before you rejoin the original route near the top.

6. East Face Left (V 5.10d) The most imposing section of Squaretop's east face is flanked to the left and right by bowls, the one 0.25 mile to the north being the bowl (or huge dihedral) mentioned in the *East Face Center* description. Two teams have reported climbing this face. A 1984 pair rated their route 5.11, a 1990 party 5.10d; both found old gear.

The 1984 route climbs directly to a grassy ledge several hundred feet up, but involves a few poorly protected 5.8 and 5.9 pitches. The seventeen-pitch 1990 route, which begins a bit left of the left-hand bowl's fall line, involves scrambling up ramps to the most prominent crack system splitting the lower part of the face; it follows this crack for three 5.5 to 5.8 pitches to the grassy ledge.

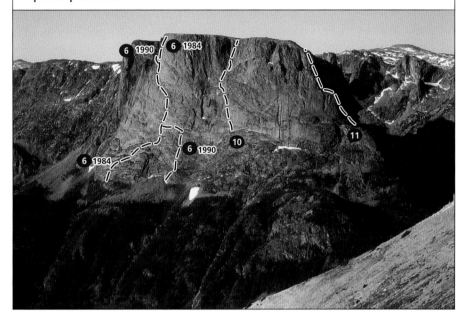

Squaretop Mountain

Both routes then traverse left for 300 feet to a right-facing dihedral. Ascend the dihedral and the nearby face for three 5.10 pitches to a left-angling ramp. Follow ramps for another three left-trending pitches. (The 1990 party bivouacked uncomfortably near the top of the first ramp.) The ramps lead to a steep seam: the 1990 route's crux. Above, move right and climb a slab to a large ledge.

The 1984 route heads up into a striking diagonal off-width bordering the upper wall's left edge. After one pitch it traverses left (crux, 5.11) into another crack system, which it follows for several more pitches to the top.

The 1990 route avoids the off-width, following a ramp left to a corner and climbing the corner past a 5.9 chimney. An easier crack leads to a belay right of a large roof. Make a thin traverse left to a big ledge and a final easy pitch.

7. East Face–Miscreant Line (V 5.10d) Two routes on the left side of the east face, *Miscreant Line* and *Conveyor Belt,* were climbed simultaneously by a group of four who split into pairs. Both routes, while predominantly independent, follow right-leaning cracks and dihedrals for eighteen pitches. The teams bivouacked together at the end of their tenth pitches.

8. East Face–Conveyor Belt (V 5.10d) See *Miscreant Line.*

9. East Face Center (IV 5th class A?) Details of the Wind Rivers' earliest long rock climb (in 1958, by Byrd, Dingman, and Wyatt on a "guides' holiday" from the Tetons) have disappeared in the mists of time. From their camp on the river, the three guides spied "a chimney in the more southerly half of the face which extends upwards through two-thirds of the wall. . . . The climbing was mostly fifth class over wonderful rock with an occasional sixth class pitch." The climb took a day and a half.

10. East Face Right (V 5.8 A2) A bowl is cut into the upper part of the 1,800-foot wall that overlooks the Green. This route ascends to the bowl, passing well right of the lower face's most prominent feature, a long dihedral that ends in an undercut ceiling. The route then continues to the top via a rib on the bowl's right side.

Ascend 500 feet of 3rd- and 4th-class rock, then move left on a narrow ledge to the start of difficulties. Mixed climbing leads past an overhang to a ledge. Move left to a corner; aid, a pendulum, free climbing, and two bolts are involved in reaching the next crack system. More mixed free and aid up the crack takes you to a big overhang. Two short pendulums, aid, and free climbing lead to the top of an overhanging chimney. Next is a corner with a wide crack. Then climb flakes and knobs on the left, rather than an ugly chimney to the right. A thin, continuous, exposed pitch—the best of the route—leads to easy climbing and the bowl.

Scramble several hundred feet to the rib that is right of the chasm in the back of the bowl. The fourth lead on the rib involves much aid and two bolts. Above this pitch, turn a corner to a wide ledge, from which you can reach the rim in two 4th-class pitches.

11. North Buttress (III 5.7/5.8 A?) A buttress facing Green River Lakes abuts the north face 300 feet below the rim. An early attempt followed the cleft on the buttress's right side, but the first successful climb was on the buttress's face. The initial 1,000 feet is easy to moderate, but difficulties increase 250 feet below the buttress's top. A pitch right of the crest ends at an overhang. Twenty feet of aid and a 5th-class section then lead to the buttress's top. The final 300 feet involve harder free climbing and an aid section near the top.

The first ascent was made from Green River Lakes Campground in a 20-hour day, a tactic the climbers retrospectively didn't recommend.

12. Northwest Chimney (II 5.7) Near Squaretop's right side, as seen from the north, is a deep chimney. Begin climbing with several pitches on slabs between two converging couloirs. Above the convergence, climb the chimney and its right wall for four leads, then continue up a steep but broken wall. The time spent in the chimney and the lack of sustained difficulties negate the appeal of a moderate route on a famous mountain.

13. West Face Dihedral (V 5.10) A giant alcove is carved into Squaretop's 1,800-foot west side (its right skyline as seen from Green River Lakes). Just right of this alcove a handsome dihedral extends most of the face's height, intersecting the arête that forms the alcove's right edge near the top. A route that has gotten mixed reviews ascends this dihedral. Scramble for several hundred feet up the buttress's toe to the dihedral. Follow the dihedral for about fifteen pitches to a short ridge that joins the buttress to the main mountain.

Two pitches are 5.10; the crux is an off-width; the route is generally well protected. It is the sort of Grade V that competent climbers complete in a single day.

Because of wet rock in the lower dihedral, the first ascent began in cracks to the left; this tactic required some aid.

14. West Face Right (III/IV 5.9 A2) From the base of the *West Face Dihedral,* climb up right for a few pitches to a black left-facing crack that is fist-width and wider. Climb it to a big terrace. Go right, then up a short corner and the next crack to the right. (Look for fixed nuts.) Follow a ramp up left, then climb to the top. The first ascenders feel you can avoid their short aid section near the top.

15. West Couloir (II 5.5) From a meadow north of the Bottle, a talus fan extends into the mouth of a large couloir. Fourth- and 5th-class climbing for eight to ten pitches leads to a bowl at the couloir's top. Pass the first waterfall on the right, the second on the left.

16. West Gully (I 3) Above Marten Lake a grassy gully cuts into the summit plateau. The gully is a useful descent route, but go far enough south from the summit before starting down.

The Bottle (11,480+)

A frequently photographed peak, this relatively difficult-to-reach summit is little known and seldom visited. The Bottle, 0.4 mile west of Marten Lake, is the most prominent of the towers above Marten Lake's cirque, west of Squaretop; its easily identified form sneaks unnoticed into many Squaretop photos.

1. South Face (I 5.5) This route begins at the notch south of the Bottle. This notch is most easily gained by circling the Bottle to the west, though it has also been reached from the east (from Marten Lake) with 4th-class scrambling. From the notch, scramble between ledges, with a few 5th-class moves, halfway to the summit—to the bottom of a chimney that extends to the summit flat. Look for a fixed nut near the chimney's base. Another chimney diagonals right, but the easiest route seems to involve climbing a slab to the left to a large ledge and a third chimney that slants right so severely that it might be described as a trough. Follow this chimney/trough to the crest, gained by a wobbly chockstone. Slabs on the crest lead to the top.

2. East Face (III 5.7/5.8) Ascend steep snow to the base of the 1,000-foot rock wall, which involves, in Fred Beckey's words, "routefinding through endless jam cracks, slabs, and short headwalls." Near the top is a narrow spine of rock; the remainder of the route is a scramble.

Tabletop (11,550)

This is the plateau west of Marten Lake's cirque. Small cirques cut into the plateau's east side are separated by pinnacled spurs that have attracted climbers.

1. South Slope (I 2nd class) For a pleasant tundra excursion, leave the Porcupine Trail near treeline north of Porcupine Pass and hike east, then north to an 11,120-foot pass. Continue at that elevation around the heads of a few north-draining valleys to Tabletop's south slope.

2. Shan Tower (II 5.7) A ridge drops east from near Tabletop's summit to Marten Lake's outlet stream; on this ridge are three spires. The splintery summit of the upper, orange spire is split by a chimney with a chockstone; also, the summit block is separated from a block to its west by a wider chimney with a larger chockstone.

Begin climbing in a rotten chimney on the east side, then work across the south face to the west ridge. Follow the ridge for a pitch to a giant chockstone, then traverse back and gain the summit by a chimney on the north side.

Descent: The 2nd-class couloir north of Shan makes a convenient descent.

3. Sail Pinnacle (II 5.7) An account of an ascent of a Sail Pinnacle locates "this alluring pinnacle" ambiguously, but it is most likely one of the lower pinnacles on Shan Tower's ridge—the formation that resembles a sail as seen from the Green River valley. Sail Pinnacle's south face is climbed by angling up left from near the east ridge's base to the summit boulder.

Scramble to a subsidiary right-trending ridge of dark rock and follow it to a grassy ledge below an obvious dihedral. Climb the dihedral and face above to a large ledge. From the ledge's left end, ascend a small face and continue to another large ledge. Traverse airily west for 50 feet, then climb to the next ledge. Traverse west on this ledge to a 5.8 layback/ramp, which leads to still another traverse left. Climb up left to the pinnacle's main ridge, just left of the summit, then traverse to easier ground west of the summit and scramble up its mushroom-shaped boulder from the southwest.

4. Cirque South of Shan Tower (I 3rd class) Reach the plateau by scrambling on rock and snow from the little valley south of Shan Tower.

5. Point 11,530, North Slope (I 3rd class) From the cirque south of Shan Tower.

Peak 11,820

The summit of the peak 0.6 mile northwest of Kenny Lake appears to be 0.25 mile south of the Squaretop Mountain quad's Point 11,820.

1. South Ridge (I 2nd class) From Kenny Lake.

2. West Slope (I 2nd class) Reached from the valley between this peak and Peak 11,850 or directly from Peak 11,850.

Peak 11,850

Porcupine Creek and the New Fork have whittled the erosion surface between them into the only peaklike architecture in the vicinity—three converging ridges flanked by steep walls, a mile east of Porcupine Pass. The ridges are immoderately broad, but this is the Wind Rivers. With no higher summits nearby, Peak 11,850 offers extensive panoramas west and north.

1. West Ridge (I 2nd class). From Porcupine Pass, skirt south of cliffs before gaining the ridge.

2. Northeast Ridge (I 2nd class). You can climb Peak 11,850 either from Peak 11,820 or presumably from the New Fork Trail by way of the valley between the two peaks.

Peak 11,246

This is a minor summit above Porcupine Creek's head, 1.1 miles northwest of Porcupine Pass.

1. West Slope (I 2nd class). From the Jim Creek Trail; grass except for the rocky summit.

Green River Pyramid (11,535)

As you proceed up the Green River, the geology to the east changes abruptly, as White Rock's sedimentary bands are truncated by towers, buttresses, and castellated gneissic ridges extending to Wells Creek. The most alluring of these formations, Green River Pyramid, rises between Elbow and Pixley Creeks (about opposite Granite Peak), 1.7 miles north-northeast of Beaver Park.

1. Southwest Face (III 5.10a) Scramble up scrubby lower slopes to a steep upper section.

Pixley-Tourist Divide (11,620)

The tableland that Pixley and Tourist Creeks (and other Green tributaries) cut into is a jungle of turrets, towers, and buttresses interspersed with ponds and snowfields. You don't climb to the tableland to peak-bag but to explore.

1. From Tourist Creek (I 3) You can reach the tableland via a couloir from Pond 10,090 on Tourist Creek. You can climb Point 11,400+ (due north of the pond) by 3rd-class rock on its south side, and from it easily attain summits to the west, including Point 11,620.

White Hat Peak (12,670)

White Hat is the peak 0.6 mile west of Klondike Peak. From Tourist Creek the name is misleading: Klondike Peak has the white hat.

1. Southwest Ridge (I 2) From the upper of the small lakes on Tourist Creek at about 10,700 feet, reach Lake 11,420 by pleasant grassy ramps and/or snow. Then gain White Hat's southwest ridge either by continuing northwest to the ridge's low point or by angling more northerly.

Mount Solitude (12,590)

Between Tourist and Wells Creeks is a high ridge, on which are two major summits, Solitude (which wasn't climbed until 1965) and Desolation. You can reach Solitude by either creek.

1. Southeast Couloir (I 3rd or 4th class) From Scott Lake, cross a low ridge into the basin between Solitude and Desolation. Climb a very loose couloir to the south ridge and continue up the summit cone's loose rock.

2. East Ridge (I 3rd class) The ridge joining Solitude and Desolation.

3. Northwest Couloir From a snowfield above Lake 11,145's outlet, pass through a cliff band by means of a snow gully, then ascend easy slopes to another gully that leads to the summit.

Desolation Peak (13,155)

In 1930 the Koven brothers made their first visit to the Wind Rivers. From Three Forks Park they found a way up the north wall of Wells Creek's gorge. They then climbed a peak with a view that Theodore Koven described thus: "The scene was one of utter chaos and desolation. On every side lay a great sprawling mass of rocky peaks, cloaked with broad glaciers and snowfields, and rent by yawning chasms." A storm was approaching, with thunder and lightning in the distance: "The sight was so grand and awesome that Desolation Peak seemed a fitting name for the mountain."

1. Northwest Ridge (I 3rd class) This qualifies as Desolation's regular route, in that it is sometimes climbed.

From Scott Lake, approach via Lake 11,510, from Tourist Creek via Lake 11,085 and the bowl to the east, which brings you to the cirque between Desolation and Solitude. On a normal summer day crampons may be helpful on the snow in this bowl. Above the snow, angle back left on bad rubble (the route's only unpleasantness) to gain Desolation's northwest ridge just east of the Solitude-Desolation col. The 0.25 mile of occasionally 3rd-class ridge is nice scrambling.

2. West Couloir (I 3rd class) From a lake "300 to 400 yards long"—presumably Lake 11,510—Theodore Koven reported turning a rocky knob on its left and climbing a steep couloir on the west face to boulder-strewn slopes and the summit snowfield.

3. Southwest Ridge (II 5.7) A buttress above Scott Lake's east end leads to pinnacles on the ridge's crest; the first spire is Broken Hand Pinnacle, named for an accident on the descent following the route's first ascent. The route ascends left of a large crack in the buttress.

Use an easy ledge to reach the start of difficulties: a traverse, then steep face climbing. Move right to a platform below an overhanging chimney. Above the chimney, continue for 300 feet on slabs and ledges. Climb a crack that passes between two prominent ceilings. Easier going then leads to the top of Broken Hand Pinnacle. Traversing the many pinnacles is fun, indeed at one point "horribly spectacular." Between the last pinnacle and Desolation is easy talus.

4. Southeast Ridge (I Snow 4th class) From the bowl between Desolation and Rampart, reach the ridge by the left-most snow gully. It is also possible to gain the ridge by ledges above the large snowfield in the bowl.

5. Three Cirque Needle, North Rib (I 5.3) The 30-foot block on the Desolation-Solitude ridge from which a rib drops north, separating the cirques of

Lakes 11,145 and 11,478 (Desolation Lake), has been named Three Cirque Needle, perhaps overly eloquently, though a third cirque faces south.

A wide snow couloir rises to the col between the needle and Desolation. This route lies on the buttress just right of the couloir. Ascend 3rd-class cracks for 300 feet, then rope up and climb up and left for three leads to the buttress's top. You can continue to Desolation by its northwest ridge.

The Bonneys mention routes on the east face, east ridge, and north face.

Peaks surrounding Dinwoody Glacier, seen looking south from Downs Mountain

3 Dinwoody Glacier

The road to Trail Lake leaves US 26/287 in country reminiscent of southern Utah. As you climb through high desert with a scent of sage and juniper, the only mountains in sight are the Absarokas in your rearview mirror. You park in sagebrush and sand. On the dry, hot, uphill Glacier Trail, the most alpine sights are snowbanks on Goat Flat's gentle tundra. You eventually drop to Dinwoody Canyon's swamps and forests, where the milky green stream gives the only hint of your purpose in being on this trail.

Then, far up the canyon, you round a bend and ahead soars a snow-crowned summit with snow slopes sweeping thousands of feet down toward the canyon. This is 13,804-foot Gannett Peak, highest in Wyoming and most backpackers' goal.

Gannett stands on the Continental Divide. Glaciers on its east slopes are sources of Dinwoody Creek; glaciers to its west start the Green on its long trek. To the east and north, Gannett Glacier laps the crest of the Divide and the protruding peaks Koven, Rampart, and Bastion. The Divide extends south from Gannett to Mount Woodrow Wilson, then turns east, separating Dinwoody Glacier from Titcomb Basin to the south. From Doublet Peak the Divide again swings south, but Dinwoody Glacier's ring of high peaks continues with Warren, Turret, Sunbeam, and Febbas, four of the range's twelve highest. Febbas is the high point of Horse Ridge, which parallels Dinwoody Creek as both descend to the Wind River.

Dinwoody Creek, beginning in Dinwoody Glacier's meltwaters, passes through a portal between East and West Sentinels and is then joined by Gannett Creek, which collects Gannett Glacier's runoff. Below this confluence is Wilson Meadows, where Floyd Wilson ran climbing camps for several summers in the 1940s.

The creek, canyon, glacier, peak, and pass, incidentally, are named for William A. Dinwiddie, who was a cavalry officer at Fort Washakie. His connection with the range seems to have been minimal; his name simply got attached to a side stream or lake in the valley, and like a spawning fish, worked upstream, though misspelled.

The glaciers' sizes have been a matter of quibbling, one claim being that they include the seven largest in the Rocky Mountains. Arguments hinge on the definition of a glacier and whether merging icefields count as a single glacier. The matter is unimportant, but it is easy to forget in this seemingly benign range that they are real glaciers, with crevasses, surrounded by alpine peaks that release rocks. Respect the glaciers and know how to minimize hazards of glacier travel.

In a range where distances from road to peak are long but climbs often short, the obvious tactic is to carry supplies for a week or more and do several climbs. A week when climbers and climbs are in shape and the weather cooperates can be a fine week. The standard was set in 1929.

Kenneth Henderson had visited the Dinwoody area in 1927, and though he didn't climb, was left with "the distinct impression that here was to be found one of the best climbing centers in the United States." He returned two years later with Henry

Taking full advantage of the campsite below Dinwoody Glacier moraine

Hall and Robert Underhill. On July 11 this trio made the first ascent of Gannett's north face, descending by the *Gooseneck Route.* On the thirteenth Henderson and Underhill went up the southwest ridge of Turret and down its north ridge, both new routes. Next day the threesome inaugurated a tradition by traversing Warren, Doublet, and Dinwoody; all terrain but the descent of Dinwoody was untrod. On the sixteenth Henderson and Underhill made the first ascent of the Sphinx, by its southeast ridge. After descending the northwest ridge, they considered doing Mount Woodrow Wilson, then thought better of it. Still, in six days they had made new routes on six peaks, including first ascents of two, and descended each by a route different from the ascent route.

In the distant past Wilson Meadows was usually reached from Cold Springs, by the Ink Wells Trail, but Cold Springs is on the reservation, and its restricted access diverts most groups to the longer Glacier Trail. You can also approach the area from Elkhart Park via Titcomb Basin and Bonney (Dinwoody) Pass, a way about equal to the Glacier Trail for length and strenuousness. You can also reach the area from Bull Lake Creek, and you can approach Gannett from the west, by routes described in the Green River and Peak Lake chapters.

This chapter's summits are on the Gannett Peak and Fremont Peak North quads. Trails also cross the Torrey Lake, Ink Wells, and Hay's Park quads.

Trails

Glacier Trail

Trail Lake Trailhead to Dinwoody Glacier—23 miles

This strenuous, picturesque trail reaches Dinwoody Creek by crossing a high divide from Torrey Creek. During the 1970s the first 6 miles were rerouted to avoid a problematic crossing of Torrey Creek and a large rockslide and to shorten a waterless section. However, while hikers prefer the new trail, horse packers have stayed with the original, which avoids the new trail's tight, rubble-sloped switchbacks.

The hikers' version, beginning at the Trail Lake trailhead, coincides with the Whiskey Mountain Trail for a few hundred feet, the Lake Louise Trail for nearly a mile, and the Bomber Trail for 3 miles (trails described in the Ross Lakes chapter).

From the trailhead, walk up Torrey Creek's north side for 0.75 mile to a junction where the Lake Louise Trail diverges right. Here the Glacier Trail crosses the creek by a bridge over a spectacular deep, narrow chasm. Beyond the bridge the trail more or less parallels Torrey Creek and its east fork through a region of sparse trees, exposed bedrock, and small domes. As the trail crosses a large meadow, 3 miles from the trailhead and a mile below Bomber Falls, the Glacier Trail turns abruptly uphill (while the Bomber Trail continues upstream).

Above interminable switchbacks the slope abates, and the trail reaches treeline, crosses a pleasant creek, and ascends a 2-mile-long valley to a 10,895-foot saddle. Halfway up this valley the old trail joins the new, after descending from slopes to the east.

To use the old Glacier Trail, descend from the trailhead parking area past horsepacker parking near the creek. If Torrey Creek is too deep and swift for pedestrians, as it typically is until late summer, drive back nearly to Trail Lake Ranch, park, and backtrack to a footbridge. An old road south of the creek soon degenerates to a trail that leaves the creek and begins a dry ascent. After crossing the rockslide and reaching treeline, it follows the strata's tilt, then descends to the new trail.

The saddle, which separates the Torrey Creek and Dinwoody Creek drainages, is unnamed but often referred to as "Burro Pass," as Burro Flat lies just beyond. On Burro Flat, a post and a cairn mark the abandoned Dinwoody Trail, which led east and descended to the Wind River valley. (This trail, while occasionally apparent and identified by sporadic cairns, is otherwise invisible and not worth trying to precisely locate.)

The first sure water beyond the saddle is below Burro Flat, nearly to Phillips Lake. You then pass Double, Star, and Honeymoon Lakes before dropping to Dinwoody Creek. All of these lakes offer feasible campsites (Star having the best), though, being conveniently located for breaking the trek to Dinwoody Glacier into two days, all are overused.

The trail ends its rugged descent to Dinwoody Creek just below Downs Fork Meadows. Except for a few patches of high ground used by horse packers minimizing their impact on Wilson Meadows, these meadows are too swampy for camping. Big Meadows, a few miles upstream, is far pleasanter.

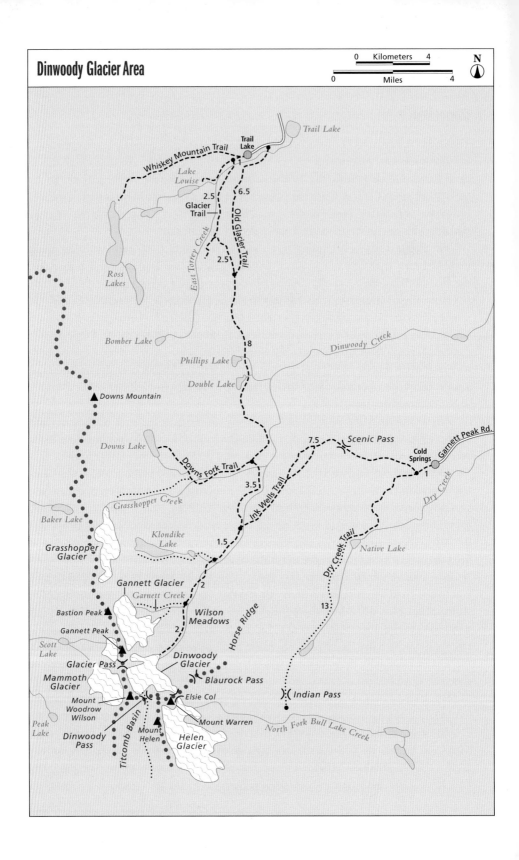

Dinwoody Glacier Area

Trail Lake

Trail Lake

Whiskey Mountain Trail

Lake Louise

1

6.5

2.5

Glacier Trail

East Torrey Creek

Old Glacier Trail

2.5

Ross Lakes

Bomber Lake

8

Dinwoody Creek

Phillips Lake

Double Lake

Downs Mountain

Downs Lake

7.5

Scenic Pass

Cold Springs

Garnett Peak Rd.

Downs Fork Trail

1

Dry Creek

Grasshopper Creek

3.5

Ink Wells Trail

Baker Lake

Klondike Lake

1.5

Native Lake

Dry Creek Trail

Grasshopper Glacier

Gannett Glacier

Garnett Creek

2

13

Bastion Peak

Wilson Meadows

Horse Ridge

Gannett Peak

Scott Lake

2

Glacier Pass

Dinwoody Glacier

Mammoth Glacier

Blaurock Pass

Peak Lake

Mount Woodrow Wilson

Elsie Col

Indian Pass

Dinwoody Pass

Titcomb Basin

Mount Helen

Mount Warren

Helen Glacier

North Fork Bull Lake Creek

0   Kilometers   4

0   Miles   4

N

Gannett Peak and Dinwoody Creek, as seen from the Glacier Trail

A bridge (replacing a famously substandard predecessor) crosses Downs Fork west of the meadows, after the Downs Fork Trail branches upstream. Above Big Meadows the Ink Wells Trail joins from across Dinwoody Creek. Soon you round a bend and are presented with one of the range's classic views; you know you are seeing Wyoming's high point. If the trail's crossing of Klondike Creek, the next formidable side stream, appears unsavory, try logs 50 feet above.

Dinwoody Creek flows through Wilson Meadows split into several channels, and the trail officially fords the westernmost of these channels. Horse parties can find far better footing by following this official trail, but backpackers generally continue on a chopped, muddy, west-bank variant, rejoining the official trail where it recrosses. Wilson Meadows is the traditional base camp site for Gannett and other high peaks.

A broken log spans Gannett Creek near its confluence with Dinwoody Creek above Wilson Meadows, but crossing the torrent is nevertheless often a problem. When the log is underwater or ice-glazed, you can wade 30 feet upstream or circle 100 feet upstream and cross the creek's several branches there by a series of logs and rock-hops.

The trail follows Dinwoody Creek for another 2 miles to Dinwoody Glacier's moraine, in the boulders of which both stream and trail vanish. Just below the moraine is an abundance of superb campsites, especially in the tundra east of Dinwoody Creek. The small lake there, hidden from the trail and unnamed on the Fremont Peak North quad, is Elk Lake. You should be able to camp apart from other groups, seeing them only from peaks, as dots crossing a glacier.

Thus ends an eventful trail that passes through most life zones of western Wyoming. Trees index the various habitats: willow, sage, juniper, aspen, Douglas fir, subalpine fir, Engelmann spruce, and lodgepole, limber, and whitebark pines.

Gannett Creek Route

Wilson Meadows to Gannett Glacier—2 miles

You can reach Gannett Glacier by following Gannett Creek from its junction with Dinwoody Creek just above Wilson Meadows. The best path seems to be on the creek's north side, but Gannett Peak is best reached by crossing to the southern of the glacier's several snouts when 0.5 mile above Dinwoody Creek.

Ink Wells Trail

Cold Springs to Dinwoody Creek—8.5 miles

Although this trail reduces the trek to Dinwoody Glacier to 14 miles from the Glacier Trail's 23, its popularity is limited by the necessity of being driven to the trailhead by a reservation outfitter, for a fee. Also, the outfitter may not deliver you to Cold Springs early enough for you to hike the 14 miles that day.

From the drop-off spot at Cold Springs, set out on the continuation of the road, which soon dwindles to a trail. Hike a mile to the meadow that is Hays Park and a junction. The left fork is the Dry Creek Trail, the right the Ink Wells Trail. It passes through a fence that is the reservation–national forest boundary and climbs onto Horse Ridge, which it crosses at Scenic Pass. Three-fourths of a mile beyond, two versions of the trail diverge, both marked by cairns as they cross tundra. The more efficient, left-hand variant stays above treeline. The lower, right-hand variant drops to a cluster of small lakes, the Ink Wells. The variants rejoin after 2 miles, and the trail passes two small lakes, the second of which, Echo Lake, offers the best camping for several miles. The trail then descends a draw and switchbacks down to Dinwoody Creek, crossing it by a cleverly placed bridge. To reach Wilson Meadows and Dinwoody Glacier, turn upstream on the Glacier Trail.

Dry Creek Trail

Cold Springs to North Fork Bull Lake Creek—14 miles

This trail begins with the Ink Wells Trail at Cold Springs, but after a mile the trails diverge. While the Ink Wells Trail branches right to some of the range's best-known scenery, the Dry Creek Trail goes left to one of the range's most obscure corners, the valley between Horse Ridge and Dry Creek Ridge. From a junction near Native Lake, a trail follows a western fork of Dry Creek into the dead-end cirque of Cub and Don Lakes; the Dry Creek Trail continues up the main stream. At the valley's head is Indian Pass, between Horse and Dry Creek Ridges. There isn't a trail beyond lakes north of the pass, but, continuing on talus and snow, you can cross the pass to the North Fork Bull Lake Creek.

Passes

Glacier Pass (12,960+)

Dinwoody Glacier to Mammoth Glacier

This crossing south of Gannett Peak links Dinwoody Glacier's north arm with Mammoth Glacier's northeast segment. It is suitable for backpacking, but the glaciers are crevassed.

Bonney Pass or Dinwoody Pass (12,800+)

Titcomb Basin to Dinwoody Glacier

This major thoroughfare across the Divide makes Dinwoody Glacier and Gannett Peak accessible from upper Titcomb Basin. The pass, between Miriam and Dinwoody Peaks, is obvious and not difficult, though from the Titcomb side the foreshortening effect of the slope's low angle masks the considerable altitude you gain. Early summer travel is mostly on snow; by late summer the south slope is largely unpleasant rubble.

Other books recommend bivouacking on Dinwoody Pass before climbing Gannett, to shorten the climbing day. However, the pass shows wear from such use, and if you're in shape to haul up the extra gear needed for a bivouac, you should be in shape to climb Gannett in a day from the meadows below Mount Helen.

Elsie Col (13,000+)

Dinwoody Glacier to Helen Glacier

You can cross this high pass between Warren and Turret with a pack, though the snow is crevassed and a bergschrund south of the col can be quite an obstacle.

Backpacker's Pass (12,840+)

Dinwoody Glacier to Helen Glacier

This is the Turret-Sunbeam col. You encounter easy snow on the east but formidable scree on the Dinwoody side.

Blaurock Pass (12,720+)

Dinwoody Creek to North Fork of Bull Lake Creek

Below Dinwoody Glacier's moraine a side valley descends from the east between the Sunbeam-East Sentinel ridge and Horse Ridge. Ascend this valley to the pass at its head, between Sunbeam and Febbas. While the pass doesn't involve glacier travel, as Elsie Col and Backpacker's Pass do, an ice axe is in order when the snow is hard.

Peaks

Bastion Peak (13,494)

The northern part of Gannett Glacier nearly reaches the Divide; a few rocky summits barely protrude through the snow. But at the glacier's north end a prominent buttress rises above the snow: Bastion's northeast peak, slightly lower than the summit back on the Divide.

1. Southwest Ridge (I Snow 4th class) From Gannett Glacier's bowl between Bastion and Rampart, climb to the Bastion-Rampart ridge and follow it to the summit.

2. Northeast Peak, Northeast Face (II 5.7) In the upper face is a big, black, wet dihedral that ends left of the summit. To its right, ending nearer the summit, is a chimney. A seven-pitch route begins in a depression halfway along the base of the wall, encounters scree in the center section, and finishes in the chimney. The crux, by the first ascent team's report, is getting onto the face from the bergschrund. The chimney, though, has interesting sections.

3. Northeast Peak, North Arête (II 5.6) Three routes have been described ascending this fine-looking prow. Start from the snow to the west, climb over two small pinnacles to the 300-foot vertical step just below the top, and climb the step in three 5th-class pitches.

The step's original line begins just right of the crest but after 20 feet regains the crest on a vein of crystals. Bear right for 20 feet until you're below an overhang, then traverse left to a belay boulder on the crest. Begin the second pitch by dropping left and traversing 10 feet onto the northeast face. The final pitch begins with a chimney leading back to the crest and ends with easy scrambling.

A second 5.6 route, whose relation to the first isn't clear, is described as following a vein that slopes up left to a crack system, following the crack to a sloping ledge, and face climbing right to a crack. Follow the crack to 4th-class terrain.

A 5.8 route follows the left-sloping vein and the crack to the sloping ledge but then veers left. Pass two roofs by wide hand cracks and belay under a V-shaped overhang. Continue up left through large blocks to a final, 4th-class pitch.

4. Northeast Peak, Northwest Slopes (I 3rd class) Snowpatches interspersed with rocks.

5. North Face Ascend the broad scree slope between the northeast summit and the Divide ridge. From the top of the scree, climb a steep and narrow but easy chimney to a broad ridge. Follow the ridge past minor buttresses to the summit slopes.

6. Northwest Ridge This ridge has been climbed.

Rampart Peak (13,435)

South of Bastion a 0.5-mile-long wall, broken at one place by a couloir, rises from Gannett Glacier to a flat-topped peak. The wall's length earns the peak the name

Rampart, though there is confusion about the summit's location. Phil Smith, who named Rampart, climbed both Point 13,370, on the Divide, and Point 13,435, to the west. Point 13,370, which appears from the east to be the summit and has a cairn and summit register, is attached to Point 13,435 by a saddle lower than the saddle joining it to nearby Bastion, yet on the Gannett Peak quad Point 13,435 is Rampart.

1. Northeast Slope (I 4th class) Ascend from the arm of Gannett Glacier between Bastion and Rampart.

2. East Face Climb from Gannett Glacier to a point just north of Point 13,370's summit.

The Bonneys describe routes on the ridge that rises from Minor Glacier west of the Divide, on the Divide ridge from the Rampart-Koven col, and in the couloir that starts from Gannett Glacier south of Point 13,370.

Mount Koven (13,265)

In 1930 Theodore Koven and his brother Gustav were the first to climb Desolation Peak; the next year the brothers and Paul Petzoldt made several first ascents in the Peak Lake cirque. In 1932 Theodore died on Denali; his body was found near a crevasse he had apparently fallen into and escaped from, only to collapse and die of exposure. In 1933 Petzoldt and others made the first ascent of the Divide summit north of Gannett and named it for Theodore Koven.

1. South Ridge (II 5.5) From Gannett Glacier you can gain the Divide ridge south of Koven in a number of places—one being the Koven-Gannett saddle, another a few hundred feet from Koven's summit.

2. East Face Climb rock left of a couloir, then the couloir's edge, meeting the south ridge a few gendarmes from the summit.

3. North Ridge (II 5th class) You can climb Koven from the Koven-Rampart col in several ways. The ridge's steep part has been turned to the east, via a few chimneys and by a long traverse across the west face.

4. Sachem Peak Sachem is the tiny 12,840-foot summit on Koven's south ridge. You can climb it from Gannett Glacier by a snow ridge and a short rock section.

The Bonneys report a route on the north-northeast face that they rate III 5.5 and a route on the west face that they rate III 5.7 A1.

West Sentinel (12,585)

Guarding Dinwoody Creek's west flank is not a noble sentinel but a stumpy mass filling the angle between Dinwoody and Glacier Creeks. Nevertheless, with moderate effort and commitment, you can surround yourself with some of the range's highest and noblest.

1. Northeast Ridge (I 3th class) About halfway between Gannett Creek and Dinwoody Glacier's moraine, an obvious slope of grass cuts into West Sentinel's flank.

From the top of this slope, ascend a rightward trajectory, passing through a bowl harboring three or four tarns, eventually reaching the right-hand end of the northeast ridge. Traverse this ridge for a mile, on its south side. It's an enjoyable excursion, with predictably good views.

2. Southwest Ridge (I easy 5th class A1) This route ascends the right-most ridge of the several that rise from the Dinwoody Glacier moraine. The one reported ascent used a shoulder-stand to surmount a short step.

3. The Bosom Anatomical names caused problems as long ago as the early 1800s, when French trappers named *Les Trois Tetons*. Two of West Sentinel's minor summits were originally called "Left Tit" and "Right Tit," but appeared in print as "Left Bosom" and "Right Bosom." This sanitized appellation is anatomically incorrect, and left and right are ambiguous. However, any of the names should enable you to recognize the formations from upper Dinwoody Creek.

The south sides of both formations have been used for easy 5th-class warm-up climbs. You can descend the cleavage between them toward Dinwoody Creek.

Gannett Peak (13,804)

Gannett is Wyoming's highest peak, topping the Grand Teton by 34 feet and Fremont Peak by 59 feet. But unlike its rivals Gannett is barely visible from the lowlands, hidden behind other high peaks. You can see its crest of snow from many points to the west, but its identity as the highest peak isn't obvious. While Fremont and the Grand were both climbed a few times before 1900, with fanfare and controversy, no ascent

Gannett Peak

of Gannett was reported until a little-publicized climb by Arthur Tate and Floyd Stahlnaker in 1922.

Yet Gannett is a noble peak, worthy of its preeminence. A snow peak in a range noted for rock, it may be the most alpine peak in the American Rockies. Not only is it crowned with snow. but it is also flanked by five glaciers: Dinwoody, Gooseneck, and Gannett Glaciers providing access from the east, Mammoth and Minor Glaciers from the west.

Henry Gannett was chief topographer of the Hayden Survey (though he didn't visit the Wind Rivers) and was later in charge of topographic surveying for the U.S. Geological Survey. As with Josiah Whitney, head of the California Geological Survey, and Sir George Everest, first Surveyor-General of India, Gannett's name has outlasted any personal fame.

1. Gooseneck Route (I Snow 4th class) Gooseneck and Dinwoody Glaciers are separated by a minor ridge that intersects Gannett's south ridge (the Divide). On the minor ridge's crest is the Gooseneck, a distinctive, conspicuous pinnacle. Gannett's regular route passes Gooseneck Pinnacle before gaining the south ridge, which it follows to the summit.

You can reach this route either from Dinwoody Creek and the Glacier Trail or from Titcomb Basin. From the Glacier Trail's end, negotiate Dinwoody Glacier's sprawling moraine—chaos not amenable to route description. From Titcomb Basin, cross Bonney Pass and traverse Dinwoody Glacier, trying to minimize elevation loss.

Gannett Peak

Gooseneck

Dinwoody Glacier

Gooseneck Glacier

Gannett Glacier

var

Gannett Peak, summit slope

From either approach, begin ascending the lobe of Dinwoody Glacier that extends (south of the Gooseneck) to Glacier Pass; this slope tends to become icy and cracked earlier than other sections of the route. At about 12,000 feet a bench that is snow covered (except in dry years) provides an easy crossing to Gooseneck Glacier. A lower crossing involves more boulders and a 30-foot downclimb. When the upper part of Dinwoody Glacier's Glacier Pass arm isn't crevassed, climbers have continued up it (45 degrees) past the Gooseneck, then gained Gooseneck Ridge.

Gooseneck Glacier's center becomes icy, but you can stay to the left, near the ridge; in early summer, climb snow on the ridge itself or, to minimize steepness and exposure, skirt the ice via snow to the right.

To Gooseneck Pinnacle's right is a 40-degree snow slope, split by a rock rib and separated from the glacier by a bergschrund. This 'schrund, the route's most notable feature, is usually bridged in one or two places, and the way is then obvious. Continue for 200 feet to the top of the rib; a few horns and blocks on the rib provide convenient sling belays. Above the rib, angle right for 100 feet to a bouldery slope that leads for 200 feet to the Divide crest.

Late in dry summers the snow bridge(s) may collapse, in which event climb 5.2 rock to the left (bring a few nuts), then continue up the 4th-class ridge to its intersection with the crest.

Having gained the crest, ascend the step above on east-facing snow, then follow the nearly horizontal but exposed ridge for 1,000 feet to the rock outcrop that forms Wyoming's high point.

2. East Face, Left End (II 5.2) The short wall below the south end of the summit snowfield has been climbed, being described as "a rotten mass of segments about fist size held in place only by frozen water."

3. East Buttress Left (II 5.5) A buttress protrudes between Gooseneck Glacier's main body and its north arm. The buttress's toe is the low point of the east face; the buttress culminates in a gendarme east of the summit. This route ascends the buttress's left side. Few details are known, except that the first few pitches above the glacier are the most difficult. From the saddle between the gendarme and the main peak, scramble to the summit snowcap and climb steep snow to the top.

4. East Buttress Right (II 5.5 A1) This route follows the wide chimney on the buttress's right side to the saddle reached by the preceding route. After crossing a bergschrund from Gooseneck Glacier's north arm, climb a pitch left of a snow couloir, then head up toward the chimney. (The first ascent used a shoulder stand at one place.) Reach the chimney by traversing up left on broken rock. About six leads on the chimney's left side take you to the saddle.

5. Northeast Ridge (II 5th class) The east face's right edge is a minor ridge that separates Gooseneck and Gannett Glaciers. At this ridge's base is a 12,920-foot col that you can reach from either glacier; the upper section of Gooseneck Glacier's arm can involve three pitches of 40- to 45-degree ice. From the col, climb straight up the ridge. Several variations have been done.

6. North Face (III Snow/Ice 5th class) Between the northeast and north ridges, Gannett Glacier reaches high toward the summit, forming a north face and providing an excellent mountaineering route when the snow is firm or icy. You can approach the face via Gannett Glacier or by the arm of Gooseneck Glacier that slants up to the col in the northeast ridge.

Pass a nunatak on the left to reach the upper north face. Four or five pitches of 45-degree snow or ice lead to a rock band, which you can pass by traversing left and through a notch to the summit snowfield. You can avoid the upper face by climbing up and right to a notch in the north ridge.

Although you can climb entirely on snow and ice, a few nuts can be useful for protection in adjacent rock.

7. North Ridge (II 5th class) Ascend Gannett Glacier to the Gannett-Koven saddle. The north ridge begins with a steep step that you can turn by traversing below it on the east for 100 feet and climbing rock for a pitch to the ridge crest. Easier rock leads to a tower near the top of the north shoulder. After surmounting the tower, reach the shoulder by 200 feet of exposed climbing. (Wet rock and verglas made this

Gannett from Squaretop

section especially tricky for the first ascent party.) It is a walk from the shoulder to the summit.

The first ascent party didn't follow the entire ridge but crossed under it on the north face, then climbed to the crest near the top of the north shoulder.

8. North Shoulder, West Face (IV 5.9 A3) In the same fantasy realm as the Fountain of Youth and the Seven Cities of Cibola is the Eiger of America. It has proved as elusive to climbers as cities of gold were to conquistadors, but inexplicably it was once said to be Gannett's west face. The face didn't fulfill its promise, but a route does ascend the 1,200-foot concave wall of the north shoulder, above Minor Glacier.

Climb slabs near the center up and right to big flakes, then continue up right for several pitches to a ledge below a dark band. Traverse left half a rope length, then climb up to easy going through the dark rock. Here difficulties increase. Climb to the right side of an alcove, cross it, and climb to a ledge. Ascend a dihedral past an overhang and continue to the top of the wall.

9. West Couloir (II 4th class) Gannett is most easily climbed from the west by ascending the couloir that extends from Minor Glacier to the col between the north shoulder and the summit, then following the upper north ridge.

10. West Face (II 5.3 to 5.6) The face right of the west couloir and below the summit is a series of ribs separated by debris-filled gullies. Several ribs provide six or seven pitches of rock climbing. The southernmost rib, which leads to a bowl in the upper face, is the best and most difficult.

Also, at least one of the couloirs has been ascended (and descended on snowboard).

11. West Face Right (III 5.7 A1) To the right of the broken rock below the summit is a steep, triangular wall. Leave Minor Glacier near the ridge between it and Mammoth Glacier and climb a snow finger up left to a series of terraces. Traverse left on rotten rock to the face's central couloir, where the rock becomes solid. A long, difficult lead up a crack system involves an aid move to exit from a recess. After two more steep pitches, climb up left into a shallow bowl, a few hundred feet below the summit ridge. Fourth-class climbing reaches the ridge a short distance south of the summit.

12. West Face-South Ridge From Mammoth Glacier the south ridge has been reached at points near its junction with Gooseneck Ridge. Several routes have been used; apparently both prominent couloirs have been ascended. One climb was by 17-year-old Yvon Chouinard, alone, on his first mountain.

13. South Ridge (II 5.5) The crest of the ridge above Glacier Pass is unpalatable, but it is possible to traverse from the pass on the ridge's west side before regaining it and continuing to the summit.

Pinnacle Ridge (13,365)

Between Gannett and Woodrow Wilson extends a ridge of many pinnacles but no outstanding summit, its high point being 0.3 mile south of Glacier Pass. This Divide segment is known as Pinnacle Ridge, or Petzoldt's Pinnacle Ridge. (Old Forest Service maps also label the crest between Tourist and Wells Creeks "Pinnacle Ridge.")

1. North Ridge (I easy 5th class) From Glacier Pass, scramble up loose rock with a few 5th-class moves. The first ascent team traversed on the ridge's west side.

2. South Ridge (I easy 5th class) This ridge involves turning some pinnacles on the west and jumping a gap.

3. East Couloir A snow climb in the obvious couloir just north of the summit, followed by a short, easy rock climb.

The Bonneys mention a route they call Central Pinnacle, Northeast Arête and rate 5.6.

Mount Woodrow Wilson (13,502)

In 1918 President Wilson listed fourteen points to be used as a basis for ending World War I. In 1924 the first ascent team of the peak that stands at the junction of Dinwoody, Mammoth, and Titcomb cirques counted about fourteen points on its ridges. They consequently named the peak for the former president, who had died earlier that year.

Although Mount Woodrow Wilson stands high above Dinwoody Glacier and Titcomb Basin, you gain most of the elevation on the approach. Dinwoody Glacier on the north and Sphinx Glacier on the south both extend above 13,000 feet.

The Sphinx and Mount Woodrow Wilson

Reach Sphinx Glacier, visible from Titcomb Basin, by scrambling up near a stream cascading from a bowl west of the glacier. Higher you must surmount a tough moraine. Approaching from either Sphinx Glacier or Dinwoody Glacier involves travel near crevasses.

1. North Couloir (I easy 5th class) The summit is slightly west of the Divide, and between the summit and the Divide a steep, icy couloir drops north to Mammoth Glacier. The couloir is best reached from the crevassed arm of Dinwoody Glacier that extends above 13,200 feet on Woodrow Wilson's north side. From high on this glacier, pass through a gap in the north ridge to the couloir. You may climb the final 300 feet either by taking the couloir's right branch or by ascending the rib on its left to a subsidiary tower. From here, traverse across the top of the right branch.

2. West Couloir (I 5.2) Reach this couloir by passing through a notch in the west ridge from the top of Sphinx Glacier. The couloir is mostly snow early in summer, ice later; it retains its ice after the south couloir melts and is then a preferable route. You can also avoid the snow and ice by climbing the steep, loose rock alongside. From the notch at the couloir's top, a pitch on rock leads north to the summit.

3. South Face (II 5.4 to 5.6 plus rappel) In the face's center a well-defined rib extends from Sphinx Glacier to a pinnacle near the summit. Begin on broken rock left of the rib and traverse right on a wide ledge to a platform on the rib. A 5th-class pitch straight up goes past one ledge to another; follow it left. Another pitch reaches a large flake. A half rope length higher, traverse around a corner, then climb to the top of the pinnacle. A 25-foot rappel leads to the notch at the top of the west and south couloirs.

The face has also been climbed by starting up the south couloir, then ascending the rib's right side.

4. South Couloir (I 5.1) A chute extends from Sphinx Glacier to the notch where the west couloir ends. When filled with snow, it is obvious from Titcomb Basin and makes a convenient, pleasant route. When the snow is gone, it is as nasty as rubble gullies can be, and you may prefer the west couloir.

5. Northeast Tower Reaching a tower northeast of the summit is an easy scramble from an arm of Dinwoody Glacier. To gain the summit from this tower, you must cross a deep notch and pass two small towers.

The Bonneys describe a Southeast Ridge *route from the Wilson-Sphinx col.*

The Sphinx (13,258)

The small, handsome peak next to Mount Woodrow Wilson was named for its appearance from Dinwoody Glacier.

1. Northwest Ridge (I 4th class) The allure of the steep ridge above the Sphinx-Wilson col is its profile, not its rock, which doesn't measure up to the profile's promise. You can reach the col easily from Sphinx Glacier, but from Dinwoody Glacier you must make a long detour around a bergschrund below the col. The ridge itself involves four rope lengths on blocks and occasional bedrock; a move here and there is 4th class.

The ridge is the Sphinx's usual descent route, but before jumping the 'schrund to Dinwoody Glacier you should be familiar with Kenneth Henderson's account of the leap: "Neither of us realized the height or we would have discussed the matter even more than we did. The take-off was easy but the landing was hard, in fact I have never felt soft snow so hard; it came right up and hit me in the face with a most impertinent smack."

2. Southeast Ridge (III 5.7+) The Divide twists up the Sphinx in colorfully serrated fashion from the Skyline col. While Henderson and Underhill, on the 1929 first ascent, avoided much of the crest and much of the color, Hans Kraus in 1945 followed the crest closely, pioneering a line of interest to modern climbers. Offering a thought-provoking crux, perhaps the range's best 5.0 pitch, and a baffling, tortuous path through a gauntlet of gendarmes, Kraus's direct line is described first.

The route is most pleasantly approached from the Dinwoody side, as the glacier reaches the Sphinx-Skyline col, while approach from the Titcomb (south) side involves a few hundred feet in a rubble-strewn gully. But descent is easier back toward Titcomb Basin (see *Northwest Ridge*).

From the Skyline col a few-hundred-foot step rises steeply. The first three pitches ascend this step's narrow face. First climb a bit left of center to a headwall with a fixed piton. From a wide crack to the left, step out right above the piton (5.7+). Proceed up to a broad, sloping ledge. Follow cracks and grooves left of the crest (5.5) and belay on a small ledge on the crest. Climb directly up the airy crest to the top of the step (5.0).

Walk along the step's flat top to the first, small gendarme; pass it high to the left (4th class). The ridge's major gendarme is split into what the first ascent account termed five "digits." Climb up right under the first digit (5.6), climb the crack that separates it from Digit 2, and then climb Digit 2. Descend to the notch between Digits 2 and 3 and pass through this notch and, a few feet farther, the Digit 3–Digit 4 notch. Descend slightly and traverse under Digit 5's right (east) side.

Continuing east of the crest, traverse under two minor gendarmes (5.4) to the last notch below the summit tower. Follow a crumbly vein up right around a corner (4th class). Two chimney systems lead toward the summit. The left is easier, but the right is solider, and its two harder sections are easily bypassed.

Henderson and Underhill climbed toward the Sphinx-Skyline col from Dinwoody Glacier. When they reached a point 150 feet below the col, they traversed up and across the east face, climbing 500 feet to meet the ridge just north of the 600-foot step.

3. Northeast Ridge (II 5.6) This is the indistinct ridge rising from the left end of Dinwoody Glacier's huge bergschrund. Start by scrambling from the glacier to a prominent black gendarme. The first pitch ascends blocks on the gendarme, then diagonals right to a ledge. For two leads, climb over more blocks, then face climb to a white dihedral right of the ridge crest. Ascend the corner for a pitch, then reach the summit by a 4th-class lead.

4. North Couloir This is the obvious couloir that splits the north face and leads to the summit. Reaching the couloir requires traversing steep snow above the bergschrund.

5. North Face (I 5.2) This route also begins above the bergschrund, to the couloir's right. Ascend steep snow to the top of the buttress that forms the face's low point. About 300 feet of 4th- and 5th-class climbing leads to the northwest ridge; follow it to the summit.

Skyline Peak (12,880+)

An insignificant summit on the Sphinx's southeast ridge.

1. North Side The party who first climbed the entire Sphinx ridge "clambered" up Skyline from Dinwoody Glacier to admire the Sphinx. Little else could motivate an ascent.

Bob's Towers (13,040+)

The cluster of four little summits at the head of Titcomb Basin is hardly a proper tribute to the man for whom they are named. Although Robert Underhill made the first ascent of these towers in 1939, he is better known as a pioneer of Northeastern climbing, for his several harder routes around Dinwoody Glacier, his first ascents in the Tetons of Mount Owen and three ridges of the Grand, his legendary introduction of "rope management" to the Sierra Club, and his first ascent of Mount Whitney's east face—all accomplished between 1928 and 1931.

1. North Faces (II 5) The towers' north sides offer the easiest routes, so the most logical start is from the north. You can reach them from Dinwoody Pass by traversing Miriam Peak. The northernmost tower is easy, and the second the most difficult.

2. West Gully From Sphinx Glacier, climb the southernmost gully, which ends just south of the Towers. The lower part is loose, but the rock improves near the top.

Miriam Peak (13,080+)

Few of the numerous feminine names sprinkled on Wind River maps commemorate women who climbed, but the little peak west of Dinwoody Pass is named for one of the best of her era. As Miriam O'Brien she had several fine seasons in the Alps during the 1920s, participating in numerous notable all-woman ascents. Manless climbing ended with marriage to Robert Underhill; in 1939 they climbed Bob's Towers, then traversed Miriam Peak.

1. Northeast Slope (I 4th class) Mostly talus from Dinwoody Pass.

2. West Ridge (I 3rd class) From Bob's Towers. Described by Robert Underhill as being "of no account, having only a few feet of climbing at the summit."

Dinwoody Peak (13,480+)

While other ranges may have two Clear Lakes or Roaring Forks, surely no other has two Dinwoody Peaks. This Dinwoody Peak stands on the Divide between Dinwoody Pass and Doublet Peak; the other, near the Ink Wells Trail, isn't of mountaineering interest.

1. West Slope (I 3rd class) Scree and boulders. Often done as a short side trip while crossing Dinwoody Pass.

2. East Chimney (I 5th class) The most difficult part of the Triple Traverse (Warren to Dinwoody) is the ascent of Dinwoody from the Doublet col; a 100-foot chimney is the major problem.

3. Northeast Couloir (Ice 5th class) A buttress separates the tiny snow-filled cirque that extends high under Doublet's north side from Dinwoody Peak's obvious north couloir. Out of sight from the north on this buttress's east flank is another couloir, which the first ascent team felt provided the best alpine ice climb they'd done in the Wind Rivers.

From the tiny cirque, surmount the bergschrund's 30-foot ice cliff, then follow the couloir for 800 feet of 50-degree ice. Above, take either the first gully up and left for easy mixed climbing or the rock rib on the left.

4. North Couloir (I Snow 4th or 5th class) A snow finger extends from Dinwoody Glacier to meet the west slopes a few hundred feet from the summit.

Doublet Peak (13,600+)

This is the splintered formation at the junction of the ridges separating the Dinwoody, Titcomb, and Bull Lake drainages.

1. South Chimney (I 4th class) Doublet was first climbed on a traverse from Warren, Les Dames Anglaises being bypassed on ice to the north. A ledge spirals up left to a short chimney, which leads to Doublet's summit.

2. Les Dames Anglaises Couloir (II Snow/Ice 5th class) You can climb Doublet without first traversing Warren or Dinwoody by ascending the couloir from Dinwoody Glacier to the Doublet-Warren col, then continuing to the summit by the *South Chimney*. The conditions of the bergschrunds and the couloir's snow vary; be prepared for ice.

3. West Face (I 5.0) Climb from the snow ridge joining Doublet to Dinwoody.

Les Dames Anglaises (13,360+)

The three pinnacles in the Doublet-Warren col reminded Hall, Henderson, and Underhill of a trio of gendarmes on Mont Blanc's Peuterey Ridge. You can approach the ladies by climbing Warren, by crossing Dinwoody Peak and traversing Doublet's south face 200 feet below the summit, or by ascending the couloir from Dinwoody Glacier to the col.

1. West Pinnacle (II 5.7 A1) The 170-foot spire nearest Doublet is the slimmest and steepest of the three. Begin at the low point on the west side and diagonal up to a platform. A thin crack on the north face requires 20 feet of aid to reach a roof; from here, traverse left around the pinnacle and climb the south face to the summit.

2. Middle Pinnacle (II 5.4) Climb this larger tower by starting on its north side and climbing up and right for a pitch. Then ascend a crack on the west face to easier rock. Climbing entirely on the west face is 5.7.

3. East Pinnacle (II 5.3) The lower half of this 120-foot tower consists of broken rock. Slabs lead around the west side to a crack, which you follow past an overhang to a short face below the top.

Mount Warren (13,722)

The range's third-highest peak is climbed far less often than the two highest. It is often climbed as the first leg of the Triple Traverse, which includes Doublet and Dinwoody.

1. East Ridge (I 4th class) Shortly above Elsie Col the ridge is blocked by an overhang, which you can turn to the left. Then climb a chimney and regain the ridge near the summit.

2. Northeast Face (II 5th class) You can also avoid the east ridge's overhang by traversing up right to a wide snow-and-ice couloir on the northeast face. On Warren's first ascent Henderson and Underhill persuaded Henry Hall to lead this couloir since, having climbed Mount Logan, he was the snow expert. Hall was soon inundated with falling slush, so they crossed the couloir, eventually working up rotten rock near the

Mount Warren, Doublet Peak, and Dinwoody Peak

right edge. Subsequent climbers, however, have found the snow pleasant climbing. A large snowpatch above leads to summit rocks.

The couloir has also been reached by leaving Dinwoody Glacier several hundred feet below Elsie Col and climbing directly up the face.

3. North Face (I Snow 4th class) Snow slopes rise from Dinwoody Glacier to a saddle just west of the summit.

4. Northwest Couloir (III Ice 5th class) A rib protrudes into Dinwoody Glacier, separating the north face's snow slopes from Les Dames Anglaises Couloir. A narrow couloir that splits this rib makes a fine late-season ice climb.

5. Northwest Buttress (II 5.5) The toe of this buttress separates the northwest couloir from Les Dames Anglaises Couloir. The first problem is a bergschrund. Rock climbing begins with a pitch that goes just left of a snow gully to the mouth of a deep, wet chimney. Avoid the chimney with a lead up and right to a drier crack. Follow this crack past an overhang. After a few easier pitches you reach a right-slanting crack. Climb the crack, then traverse right for a rope length or more to a gully that you reach below a notch between a gendarme and a ridge. Another long traverse around the gendarme leads to another gully, in a corner between a rib and the main ridge. Climb to the ridge and follow it to the summit.

The route has been rappelled to retrieve ice axes left at the start of rock climbing.

6. West Ridge (I 4th class) There is no report of Warren being ascended from the west, but steep chutes have been descended to Les Dames Anglaises Col.

7. Snow Snake Couloir (III Snow 5th class) A sinuous east-facing gully begins 300 feet up the snow slope that joins Helen Glacier to Elsie Col. The seven-pitch route that ascends this couloir, first climbed in winter, is pleasant when snow-filled, but when dry there is much loose rock.

The Bonneys mention an ascent from Helen Glacier via couloirs on the south face.

Turret Peak (13,600+)

Turret, tucked away above Dinwoody Glacier's southeastern arm and standing alone between Elsie Col and Backpacker's Pass, is a complex of ribs, couloirs, and false summits. The southern of the three summits is the highest. While usually climbed from the Dinwoody side, it can also be climbed from Helen Glacier. Some of its routes are difficult to describe, and you'll need to do some routefinding.

1. North Ridge (I 4th class) From Backpacker's Pass the chief problem is getting around and over towers and subsidiary summits near the top.

2. Northwest Face (II 5.4) The northwest face is a series of ribs rising from Dinwoody Glacier. The right-most rib, which narrows to a ridge and flattens out below the middle summit, has been climbed. You encounter steep snow on the approach. The route has a few nice pitches on the narrow ridge but is otherwise mediocre.

An easier route has been done to the left, though it isn't clear whether it reaches the north ridge near the lower towers or the flat top of the narrow ridge.

3. West Couloir (I 4th class) Turret was first climbed by the large couloir that begins just north of Elsie Col and ends at the notch between the middle and main summits. Expect both snow and rock.

4. Southwest Ridge (II 5th class) Start up the ridge from Elsie Col, but traverse left to a couloir. Ascend the couloir, then a subsidiary couloir to the right. Avoid an overhang by interesting face climbing that leads back to the ridge, which here is a knife edge. You soon reach easier rock.

5. Southeast Face (IV 5.8 A3) The wall overlooking the southern approach to Elsie Col is broken by a large corner. A route that has been characterized using the words "rotten" and "bummer" ascends the buttress left of this corner.

Climb the buttress's right side to a chimney. Follow the chimney for three leads, then climb to a dihedral that leads to a roof. Climb cracks and a squeeze chimney above the roof to a big ledge. Aid a wide crack, then a bottoming one, to the end of a ramp. Pendulum left to a large, loose flake; soon difficulties end. Traverse left and climb to the summit ridge.

6. East Ridge (II 5.6) You can climb the ridge rising from Bull Lake Creek's North Fork in its entirety, or turn the lower part to the north and gain the ridge by scrambling to a notch below the ridge's steep section. Climb the steep part in three leads: The first goes straight up; the second angles right; and the third traverses right, then heads up to a flat part of the ridge. From the top of the steep section, scramble down to another notch, then climb 4th-class rock to the east summit. The ridge between it and the main summit is exposed but easy 5th class. This is a clean, exposed route, mostly on decent rock.

Sunbeam Peak (13,440+)

A mile-long row of peaks stands between Horse Ridge and Dinwoody Glacier. The highest, Sunbeam, is at the southeast end, its flat northeast ridge and icy north face visible from upper Dinwoody Creek.

1. Northeast Ridge (I 2nd class) From Blaurock Pass the ridge begins as a broad snow slope; higher it becomes a narrower rock ridge.

2. North Face The summit register reports an ascent of the north face. It would be interesting to know more, for this could be a fine alpine route.

3. Northwest Couloir (Ice 5th class) The couloir that rises from Heap Steep Glacier to the col northwest of Sunbeam has been ascended on late-summer ice.

4. Southwest Ridge (I 4th class) This is the exposed ridge above Backpacker's Pass.

The Bonneys mention a route that ascends gullies from Dinwoody Glacier.

Heap Steep Peak (12,920+)

Illusions of guidebooks' omniscience shatter on the ridge northwest of Sunbeam. The mound at the ridge's end, overlooking Dinwoody Creek, is East Sentinel, and between East Sentinel and Sunbeam are two strikingly similar pinnacles. This much is known. Not known, though, are these pinnacles' names and climbing histories.

According to the Bonneys, the northwestern pinnacle is Heap Steep Peak and the southeastern (nearest Sunbeam) is Speck Pinnacle. According to the Fremont Peak North quad, Heap Steep is the southeastern; the other is unnamed. And the name Heap Steep seems to have originally been bestowed on East Sentinel, lending additional confusion to older accounts.

The Bonneys imply, though never quite state, that the ridge has been traversed from Sunbeam to East Sentinel. They do state that John Speck traversed his pinnacle, but don't specify how he approached or descended. An effort to resolve this enigma by actually climbing was thwarted by wind on Sunbeam.

East Sentinel (12,823)

Neither sentinel that metaphorically guards the portal below Dinwoody Glacier is at all elegant. East Sentinel is the lump of broken rock at the end of the ridge extending northwest from Sunbeam.

1. West Couloir (I 4th class) An obvious route leads up from Dinwoody Glacier's moraine.

2. Northeast Ridge (easy 5th class plus rappel) Reach the ridge by climbing out from the north gully. Follow the ridge to the northeast summit, rappel to the notch above the north gully, and continue to the main summit.

3. North Gully Snow in early summer, loose rock later, this gully leads to the notch between the northeast and main summits.

The Bonneys' guide includes a route on the southwest ridge.

Mount Febbas (13,468)

Horse Ridge is the best known of the long, gently sloped plateau relics that characterize the Wind Rivers' east flank. This ridge's microcosm includes meadows, streams, snowfields, and a lake. Horse Ridge's rise southwest toward the Divide is abruptly truncated by cirques; the ridge's high point, at its southwest end, is dignified with the name Mount Febbas. While Febbas offers no technical climbing, it gives hikers an unusual opportunity to reach one of the range's best viewpoints. And various pinnacles attached to Horse Ridge have attracted attention, the most famous—or infamous—being Chimney Rock.

1. Northeast Slope (I 2nd class) Travel on Horse Ridge is easy, and you can leave the Ink Wells Trail at Scenic Pass and walk 10 miles to the top of Febbas, though the summit cone is loose rubble. You can also reach the ridge from Wilson Meadows by Knoll Lake's outlet stream, which joins Dinwoody Creek opposite Gannett Creek.

2. Fourt's Horn (I 4th class) As seen from Wilson Meadows, this is the prominent point standing out from Horse Ridge, its buttress dropping nearly to Dinwoody Creek. It is more difficult to recognize from downstream, being one of many towers and turrets. The Fremont Peak North quad helps locate it, opposite Klondike Creek's mouth.

3. The Finger (I 5.2) On Horse Ridge's southern wall, overlooking the North Fork of Bull Lake Creek, is a pinnacle slightly more than a mile west of Indian Pass. The Finger, as it is called, has been climbed by approaching from the east and climbing a couloir to the notch between it and Horse Ridge. A short pitch on the north face leads to the top.

4. Chimney Rock Ridge (II/III 5.6) Horse Ridge's eastern arm—the section above Bull Lake Creek's North Fork—is called Chimney Rock Ridge. The south face's right edge—the ridge above Indian Pass—has been climbed in ten pitches.

5. Chimney Rock From Burris, on the Wind River, you can look up Dry Creek's valley and see a pillar that culminates in a tower standing out above Horse Ridge. That Chimney Rock is even identified on a highway map that indicates thirteen other Wind River peaks must be due to the glimpse from Burris, for it is an insignificant piece of rock, most notable for being rotten. If old reports are to be believed, the tower was once higher, and some who have ventured across the neck joining it to Horse Ridge have encountered so much rubble that they assumed no one had preceded them. It is pointless to describe a route that may crumble by next summer.

The Bonneys mention an ascent of the north face of the buttress west of Don Lake.

Dry Creek Ridge (12,720+)

East of Horse Ridge, in country as little known as any in the range, another high ridge slopes gently to the Wind River valley, dividing Dry Creek and Bob Creek. It is separated from Horse Ridge by one Indian Pass and from the Kirkland Mountains to the east by another Indian Pass. Like Horse Ridge it drops abruptly on the south to Bull Lake Creek's North Fork.

1. Point 12,562, East Slopes (I 2nd or 3rd class) In 1936 a triangulation station was established on Dry Creek Ridge's eastern summit, which overlooks Crater Lake's curious cirque. The surveyors reached the station, which they designated Bob, from the eastern Indian Pass.

The view north from Pole Creek Trail, June

4 Peak Lake

The Green River is a peaceful stream below Three Forks Park, but the forks are steep and noisy. The Highline follows the western of the three, Trail Creek, to its source high above at Green River Pass. The east fork, Wells Creek, originates in Mammoth and Minor Glaciers, under Gannett Peak. The middle fork, once known as Stroud's Creek but now considered the Green River itself, descends from Peak Lake. The little stream that drains the classic alpine valley above is thus the nominal source of the Colorado's main branch.

High peaks surround this valley on three sides, separating it from Mammoth Glacier to the north, Titcomb Basin to the east, and Jean Lakes to the south. Peaks bounding the valley to the south—Stroud, Sulphur, and Arrowhead—are of particular interest to climbers. (Many routes are more easily approached from Jean Lakes than Peak Lake.)

However, as American climbing standards have never been advanced in the Wind Rivers, Wind River standards have never been advanced at Peak Lake. Several peaks exceed 13,000 feet but are overshadowed by the higher peaks of Dinwoody Glacier and Titcomb Basin. Peak Lake's history is one of sporadic visits by climbers who have done more memorable routes elsewhere. Most of the peaks were first climbed in the 1930s, after the first ascents of most Dinwoody and Titcomb peaks. Arrowhead and Sulphur have seen difficult climbs, but only after harder routes had been done elsewhere.

While postcards and coffee-table photography ignore these environs, the valley above Peak Lake when its slopes are thick with midsummer paintbrush and bluebells, the basin of Elbow Lake with its uncountable lakes, ponds, and tarns, the many knobs and domes of Glover Peak's massif, and the vast sky beyond the Jean Lakes—these may make Peak Lake the quintessential section of the Wind Rivers, if not in grandeur, then in detail. Hikers of the Highline Trail generally proclaim the section passing Summit, Elbow, and the Jean Lakes their favorite.

Enhancing Peak Lake's obscurity is its inaccessibility. It can be reached with comparable effort from any of four trailheads—Green River Lakes, New Fork Lakes, Spring Creek Park, and Elkhart Park (plus Willow Creek, if it reopens)—but by strenuous routes that take most backpackers more than a day.

Approaches from New Fork Lakes, Willow Creek, and Spring Creek Park are redeemed by traversing high, open country with many lakes and fine views. These trails and this country, which culminates in Glover Peak, the highest summit west of the Green River and Pine Creek, are included in this chapter. Moreover, the New Fork Trail passes through New Fork Canyon, site of the range's best canyon walls, also included in this chapter. The approaches to the Peak Lake high country are both scenic and varied enough that it is worth entering the mountains by one route and departing by another.

Peak Lake's cirque and most peaks in this chapter are on the Gannett Peak quad, but Glover and others to the west are on the Squaretop Mountain map. Trails cross four other quads: New Fork Lakes, Kendall Mountain, Fremont Lake North, and Bridger Lakes.

Trails

Highline Trail

Three Forks Park to Little Seneca Lake—15 miles

The Highline's most scenic section passes through the Peak Lake area and can be used to reach the area from both north and south. The trail north of Three Forks Park is described in the Green River chapter. South of the park the Highline gains 1,000 feet by switchbacks—zigzags that are at least not overly steep, generally shady, and offer brief views of Sulphur Peak and nearby plummeting Trail Creek.

At Trail Creek Park, above the switchbacks, the New Fork Trail joins from the west. (This park, despite limited acreage, offers good camping.) A mile beyond, the Vista Pass Trail, the shortest route to Peak Lake, splits to the east. The Highline continues up the main valley, following Trail Creek, to 10,362-foot Green River Pass, then crosses an open valley to nearby Summit Lake.

At Summit Lake two trails enter from the west: the Doubletop Mountain Trail and, 100 yards south, the Pine Creek Canyon Trail. The Highline south of Summit Lake has been rerouted slightly, crossing Pine Creek higher than shown on the Gannett Peak quad before contouring southeast to a bridge over Elbow Creek. Just before you can see Pass Lake, a trail that is no longer maintained branches south to Gunsight Pass and the Sauerkraut and Bridger Lakes. The Highline beyond Pass Lake has been drastically rerouted for 0.5 mile; it now passes well south and east of the southern Twin Lake. After winding through fault-fractured, pond-strewn country west of Elbow Lake, it reaches the lake's north end, then crosses the basin above. There are good campsites, despite no trees and few boulders, in this basin north of the lake.

From near the basin's head, the Shannon Pass Trail branches north to Peak Lake; the Highline swings southeast and crosses an 11,040-foot pass to the Jean Lakes valley. Descending past Upper and Lower Jean Lakes, it reaches a marshy area where the unmaintained Lost Lake Trail heads west and the Highline crosses Fremont Creek by a bridge. Depending on your attitude, pack, and destination, the next 3 miles can be picturesque and quintessential Wind Rivers, or nondescript and against-the-grain inefficient, as you pass through conifers remarkably stout (and presumably old) for their treeline elevation and dodge numerous creeks that drop to anonymous lakes seen below.

Before the Highline reaches Little Seneca Lake, it joins the Indian Pass Trail, leading to Island Lake; near Little Seneca Lake it joins the Seneca Lake Trail, which leads to Elkhart Park. The Highline continues southeast, but this continuation is described in the Alpine Lakes chapter.

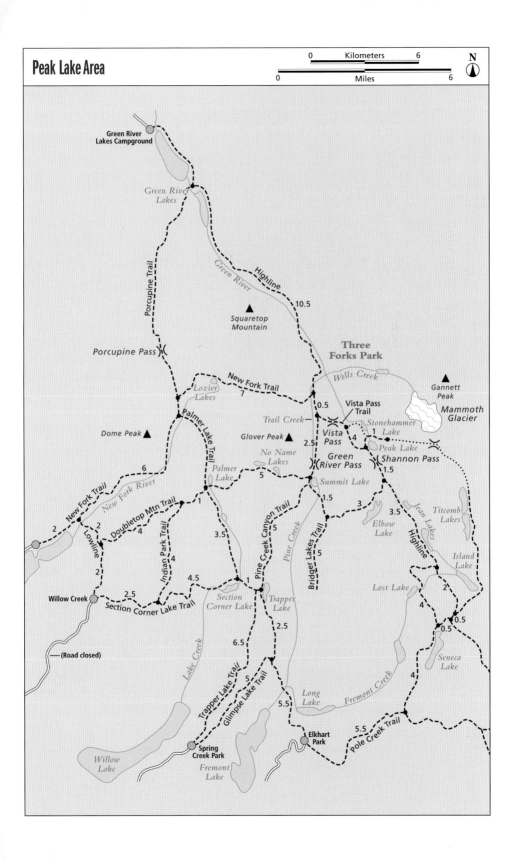

Peak Lake Area

Kilometers
0 ___ 6

Miles
0 ___ 6

N

Green River
Lakes Campground

Green River
Lakes

Porcupine Trail

Green River

Highline

10.5

Squaretop
Mountain

Porcupine Pass

Three
Forks Park

Wells Creek

New Fork Trail

Lozier
Lakes

7

Gannett
Peak

Mammoth
Glacier

0.5

Vista Pass
Trail

Palmer Lake Trail

Dome Peak

Glover Peak

Trail Creek

Stonehammer
Lake

1

No Name
Lakes

2.5

Vista
Pass

4

Peak Lake

Shannon Pass

New Fork Trail

6

Palmer
Lake

5

Green
River Pass

1.5

New Fork River

Doubletop Mtn Trail

1

Summit Lake

1.5

3

3.5

Jean Lakes

Titcomb
Lakes

2

Lowline

4

Pine Creek Canyon Trail

Pine Creek

Elbow
Lake

Highline

Island
Lake

Indian Park Trail

3.5

4

Bridger Lakes Trail

5

2

Lost Lake

4

2

4.5

1

0.5

Willow Creek

2.5

Section
Corner Lake

Trapper
Lake

0.5

Section Corner Lake Trail

2.5

Seneca
Lake

(Road closed)

6.5

Trapper Lake Trail

5

Glimpse Lake Trail

5

Lake Creek

Long
Lake

5.5

Fremont Creek

4

Willow
Lake

Spring
Creek Park

Elkhart
Park

5.5

Pole Creek Trail

Fremont
Lake

Peak Lake Detail

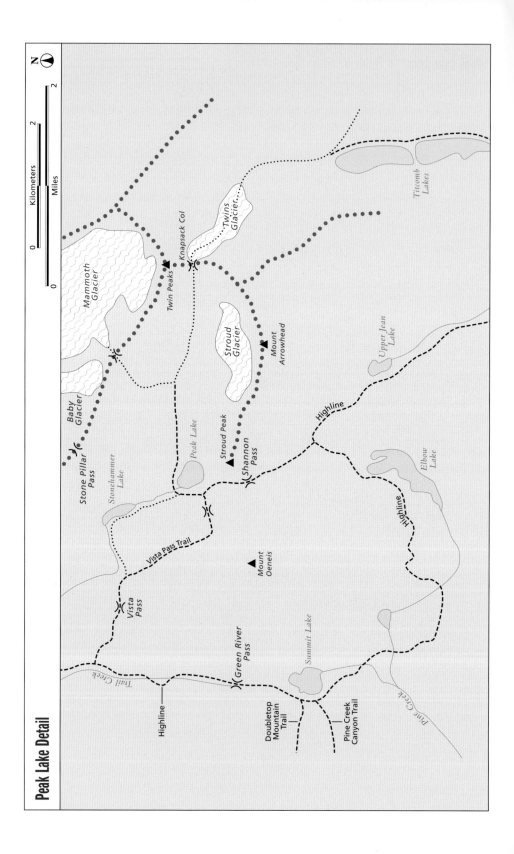

Vista Pass Trail (Glacier Trail)

Trail Creek to Peak Lake—4 miles

The trail's old name, Glacier Trail, may derive from a time when Mammoth Glacier was the main objective reached by it, or it and the east-side Glacier Trail may have been considered one, linked by Glacier Pass south of Gannett—a way for the stouthearted to cross the range. However, referring to this west-side trail as the Glacier Trail is unduly confusing; the name Vista Pass Trail more clearly identifies it.

Many years ago a rockslide in the canyon below Dale Lake obliterated a few hundred feet of the trail (thus, presumably, the gap on the Gannett Peak quad). Enough hikers, though, have worked their way through the debris that a well-defined path has evolved. While these few hundred feet may not be up to code, the slide presents only a minor obstacle, and, in conjunction with the Highline, the Vista Pass Trail makes as efficient a route to Peak Lake as any.

Leave the Highline a mile south of Trail Creek Park and climb east to Vista Pass (good camping). Descend to the Green's canyon and ascend the austere canyon (a few adequate campsites) past the rockslide to Dale Lake. Cross Cube Rock Pass and descend to Peak Lake. Above the lake the other trail to Peak Lake, that crossing Shannon Pass, joins from the south.

A water-level trail rounds Peak Lake's nearly cliffbound north shore, ending a mile east, beyond a chain of small lakes. From here you can cross the 12,440-foot pass west of Split Mountain to Mammoth Glacier or continue to the valley's head and cross Knapsack Col to Titcomb Basin.

Stonehammer Lake Route

Vista Pass Trail to Peak Lake—1 mile

Where the Vista Pass Trail drops to the Green River from Vista Pass, an improbable sign bears the words STONEHAMMER LAKE, falsely implying a trail. After fording Dale Lake's outlet stream, you encounter nasty scrambling up the Green, here the outlet stream of Stonehammer Lake. Boulders line Stonehammer Lake's east shore; slabs and steps on the west side are 3rd class. An easy path, though, follows the Green between this lake and Peak Lake.

Shannon Pass Trail

Elbow Lake to Peak Lake—1.5 miles

This southern route to Peak Lake leaves the Highline in the valley north of Elbow Lake and crosses the 11,120-foot pass west of Stroud Peak. The trail descends to Peak Lake down a steep, rocky slope that appears an unlikely site for a trail, but intelligence and hard work have made it less rugged than the Vista Pass Trail.

New Fork Trail

New Fork Lakes to Trail Creek Park—16 miles

Most Wind River trails get you from trailhead to mountain as efficiently as possible. A few, however, are best traveled with the attitude that the pleasure is in the journey. All of the routes to Summit and Peak Lakes involve uphill; the New Fork Trail, while involving more uphill than others, is continually surrounded by diverting scenery. The trail begins at the parking area north of Narrows Campground, parallels the northwest shore of Upper New Fork Lake, and crosses the Lowline Trail 0.5 mile beyond the lake. (A right turn on the Lowline reaches the Doubletop Mountain Trail in 2 miles.) The northbound Lowline, crossing New Fork Lookout Point to Boulder Basin, lies 100 feet west of where the sign implies, just east of an early summer creek.

As you climb into New Fork Canyon, you can see crystalline rock overlying younger sedimentary strata, a legacy of the thrust-faulting that formed the range. Near the canyon's major bend, the trail crosses the river twice. The fainthearted, or in early summer the prudent, can avoid these crossings by clambering through boulders on the north bank. Beyond the bend is New Fork Park, near the upper end of which the Palmer Lake Trail crosses the river and enters Palmer Canyon, while the New Fork Trail begins climbing in earnest. From New Fork Canyon's head the Porcupine Trail continues north, crossing to Green River Lakes. The New Fork Trail climbs east, to treeline and the Lozier Lakes (magical camping). Crossing a 10,920-foot divide, it descends 700 feet to Clark Lake (also good camping), then another 1,000 feet next to Clark Creek to a crossing of Trail Creek and a meeting with the Highline in Trail Creek Park.

Palmer Lake Trail

Section Corner Lake to New Fork Park—6.5 miles

Paralleling the crest in valleys at a distance from high peaks, this trail isn't a route to the mountains but can be useful as a part of various circuits from New Fork Lakes and Willow Creek. The trail begins in wet meadows where Lake Creek enters Section Corner Lake. Finding this beginning can be tricky, despite a signpost in the meadows: Beware of a well-used trail that follows Lake Creek closely, crosses it after a mile, and passes south of Lake 9,678. Noting that the Palmer Lake Trail diverges from Lake Creek and doesn't rejoin it for a few miles, start on the hillside by the west edge of the meadows and follow a lesser stream west of Lake Creek.

Round Lake is something of a hub, and wily veterans have imprinted so many shortcuts that the less experienced need a map, especially when heading north. (When heading south, don't be lured too far down Lake Creek.) One much-used shortcut angles northwest, toward Doubletop Mountain. The one signed junction is north of Round Lake, where a trail branches east to Heart Lake.

At Palmer Lake, the head of Lake Creek, the Doubletop Mountain Trail crosses, going east to Summit Lake and west to civilization. The Palmer Lake Trail continues north to a saddle, crossing it to the head of Reynolds Creek, in Palmer Canyon's south branch. (Palmer Lake doesn't drain into Palmer Canyon.) The trail switchbacks steeply down to the main canyon, crosses the river, and meets the New Fork Trail at the upper end of New Fork Park. When you are headed south from New Fork Canyon, this section is strenuous.

Lowline Trail

Willow Creek Guard Station to New Fork Trail—4 miles

The road to Willow Creek Guard Station has been blocked for several years, but let's be optimistic and imagine it reopening.

While the Highline gets the glamour, the Lowline creeps through forests and cow country below, typically intersecting popular backpacking trails near trailheads. While this guidebook ignores most of the Lowline, the section that crosses from Willow Creek Guard Station to the New Fork Trail is included because it provides access to the Doubletop Mountain Trail. No sign at the Willow Creek trailhead indicates the Lowline. The start is marked, though, by a trail register left of a PACK IT OUT sign. Descend toward Willow Creek on a road; where the road forks, follow a trail between the forks and cross the creek. Don't be surprised by mud beyond the creek. Climbing steadily, you gain 1,000 feet before meeting the Doubletop Mountain Trail near the ridge crest, just past a small meadow.

To reach the Doubletop Mountain Trail from New Fork Lakes, follow the New Fork Trail to a marked junction in the willowy meadows past the upper lake. Find your way through the creekside willows and wade across the sprawling, shallow river. (There seems to be no "official" crossing.) Switchback steeply to the ridge crest and descend a few hundred feet to where the Doubletop Mountain Trail begins. The section, already rubbly and victimized by deadfall, was severely damaged by a 2008 fire, but a 2010 trail crew did an admirable job of restoring it.

Doubletop Mountain Trail

Lowline Trail to Summit Lake—10 miles

Of the ways to the Peak Lake area, this one, though less efficient than the continuously ascending approach from Green River Lakes, offers maximum time above treeline, which you reach above Rainbow Lake, 2 miles from the Lowline. The high, open country offers frequent panoramas of Divide peaks.

You can reach the Doubletop Mountain Trail via the Lowline, either from New Fork Lakes or, when accessible, Willow Creek Guard Station. After passing Rainbow Lake and emerging above treeline, you round Doubletop Mountain. Near the trail's high point, the Indian Park Trail converges, and, as you begin descending to Palmer Lake, a well-used shortcut diverges right, toward Round Lake. Unless you're headed down the Lake Creek drainage, stay left.

At Palmer Lake, cross the Palmer Lake Trail (which sensibly follows the fractured land's grain), then immediately regain lost elevation to a vast upland that features

Cutthroat Lakes, No Name Lakes, and numerous lakes with no names. Descending to Summit Lake, you meet the Highline.

Section Corner Lake Trail

Willow Creek Guard Station to Trapper Lake—8 miles

The Section Corner Trail is described in hopes that Willow Creek Guard Station will again be accessible.

Its beginning isn't easily distinguished from various vehicle tracks; walk north from the parking area and look for a sign a few hundred feet into the woods. After unrelenting uphill to a shoulder of Big Flattop Mountain, you reach meadows at the head of Indian Park and pass a trail going south to cow country and the Indian Park Trail heading north to Doubletop Mountain.

After the monothematic drudgery of the first 5 miles, the rugged intricacy of Bluff Park Creek's drainage is welcome. The Fremont Lake North quad gives only an approximation of the trail's peregrinations; for a mile it is south of the map's trail, then north for 0.25 mile. At Section Corner Lake the trail meets the Palmer Lake Trail, theoretically at a sign back from the lake in a bog. The sign seems situated with the presumption that you don't mind wet feet (or was placed before nearby beaver dams began serving their purpose). If you do mind, and are continuing to Trapper Lake, follow the beach, as on the map. Relocate the trail, which leaves the meadow inconspicuously, on the wooded hill east of the lake and climb the charred hill. At Trapper Lake the Section Corner Lake Trail meets trails to Spring Creek Park, Elkhart Park, and Summit Lake.

Indian Park Trail

Indian Park to Doubletop Mountain—4 miles

The Section Corner Lake Trail crosses meadows at the head of Indian Park, where a trail used by packers comes in from the south. Just east of the meadow, another trail branches north and, after climbing a ridge, emerges in pretty treeline country, joining the Doubletop Mountain Trail near the top of Doubletop Mountain. (An unofficial, though better used, variation meets the Doubletop Mountain Trail 0.25 mile east of the official trail.) In conjunction with the Section Corner Lake Trail, the Indian Park Trail offers an equally attractive, though 0.5 mile longer, alternative to the Lowline–Doubletop Mountain combination.

Trapper Lake Trail

Spring Creek Park to Trapper Lake—6.5 miles

The road beyond the Spring Creek Park trailhead passes two ponds, south of which the Glimpse Lake Trail begins. To reach the Trapper Lake Trail, continue on the road west of the ponds either by foot or vehicle, depending on an outlet stream and your vehicle. The road passes a pasture and an old cabin, then climbs, too ruggedly for most vehicles, into a forest. A mile from the cabin the road curves left to an opening and ends, but the trail leaves the road before the curve and dips to the right across a stream. The trail climbs gradually but tediously to a plateau, then descends to Trapper Creek, which it follows upstream to join the Section Corner Lake Trail west of Trapper Lake. Just east is the lake's outlet and the Pine Creek Canyon Trail.

The Trapper Lake Trail is significantly less charming than the Glimpse Lake Trail, which connects the same points.

Glimpse Lake Trail

Spring Creek Park to Glimpse Lake—5 miles

Connoisseurs have declared the Glimpse Lake Trail, in conjunction with the upper Pine Creek Canyon Trail, their favorite route into the heart of the range. Much of the Glimpse Lake Trail follows a crest overlooking Fremont Lake, while the Pine Creek Canyon Trail travels through the sort of lake-filled, sparse-whitebark country that gives the Wind Rivers a special charm. After 12.5 miles you reach Summit Lake, which, considering the access it gives to a spectrum of destinations, qualifies as a heart of the range. The lack of traffic, compared to more-publicized trails, helps tilt the balance in this trail's favor.

The Glimpse Lake Trail nominally begins on the road just right of the Spring Creek trailhead bulletin board. Walk or drive this road for a mile. As you reach the first of the pair of ponds, turn right into a fine aspen grove south of the pond. The trail you turn onto isn't at first apparent, unless a sign happens to be in place, but soon evolves into an easily followed track. Ignore a trail that branches left to the cow pasture above the ponds; the Glimpse Lake Trail wanders up to the crest overlooking Fremont Lake. No further details need be given; enjoy the view before switchbacking down to Glimpse Lake from the west and joining the Pine Creek Canyon Trail just beyond.

Pine Creek Canyon Trail

Elkhart Park to Summit Lake—13 miles

On a map lacking topography this trail appears to be the best route to Summit Lake, being among the shortest and beginning at the highest trailhead. A topographic map, however, reveals a 2,000-foot drop from Elkhart Park to Pine Creek and many switchbacks regaining the lost elevation; it is actually the most strenuous route to Summit Lake.

Begin the descent at Trail's End Campground, descending past Long Lake to a bridge across Pine Creek just below its junction with Fremont Creek. Climb to the canyon's west rim, emerging near Glimpse Lake, where the Glimpse Lake Trail joins from Spring Creek Park. At Trapper Lake you meet the Trapper Lake Trail, also coming from Spring Creek Park, and the Section Corner Lake Trail, coming from Willow Creek. The Pine Creek Canyon Trail continues north (relocated somewhat east beyond Trail Lake) past Gottfried Lake, where a trail to Heart Lake diverges west, and Borum Lake, beyond which you cross a saddle and descend to Summit Lake and the Highline and Doubletop Mountain Trails.

Bridger Lakes Trail (not maintained)

Pass Lake to Bridger Lakes—5 miles

Pine Creek, Fremont Creek, and the Highline Trail between Summit Lake and Fremont Crossing bound a roughly triangular area of about 8 miles on a side. The triangle is lake-filled, mid-elevation country seen from popular trails, but canyons of the two creeks prevent it from being accessible directly from civilization. And nothing spectacular induces Highline hikers, already deep in the mountains, to turn away from the mountains to explore this country. The Forest Service has designated most of the triangle trailless, and the one trail that penetrates the area has been abandoned.

Leave the Highline at a junction by a pond northwest of Pass Lake; a gnarly stump suggests where a sign may once have been. Pass Lake sits nearly in Gunsight Pass, not the Rockies' only Gunsight Pass nor the most dramatic. After traversing somewhat above the lake and crossing the pass, descend straightforwardly past the lower Sauerkraut Lake. Continue down a small valley; the trail before crossing Cumberland Creek becomes vague, the terrain less scenic, and the descent, to 9,880 feet, may entail more elevation than you wish to lose. The descent is all the more demoralizing because, after crossing a meadow where the track disappears, you climb to 10,360 feet, following switchbacks not indicated on the map. After crossing a ridge to the Bridger Lakes drainage, you reach one of the Bridger Lakes.

Nomenclature here is unsatisfactory, there being a dozen or more lakes and ponds, none named and only one with its elevation given on a map. Calling the trail's terminus Lake 10,200+ would cause many of us to wish for reading glasses. But this guidebook doesn't give directions for commuting from one lake to another, so naming is unnecessary. Be warned, though, that despite the generic lake name suggesting a tight cluster, the rugged terrain and dense forest make for nontrivial travel.

That maps indicate the Bridger Lakes Trail but not a trail over Threlkeld Pass is not because the Bridger Lakes Trail passes through superior terrain—indeed the opposite. You wouldn't contemplate the descent to, and ascent from, Cumberland Creek without at least the remnant of a trail. The approaches to and from Threlkeld Pass are Wind River hiking at its freest. Check Threlkeld Pass, described below, for a route superior to the Bridger Lakes Trail, especially to the uppermost lakes.

Passes

Stone Pillar Pass (12,280+)

Stonehammer Lake to Baby Glacier

This useless gap between Ladd and Whitecap is reached by 2,000 feet of grass and loose talus rising east of Stonehammer Lake. From Peak Lake the pass is most easily reached by starting as for Split Mountain Pass, between G-4 and Split, then crossing the saddle between G-3 and Whitecap, though this route isn't as straightforward as it appears on a map. Even the 7.5-minute quad lacks sufficient detail to show the intricate labyrinth of fins, draws, ponds, and snowpatches between Whitecap and G-3. To the northeast of Stone Pillar Pass, below cliffs that must be skirted, are Baby Glacier's moraine and Wells Creek's south fork.

Split Mountain Pass (12,440+)

Peak Lake to Mammoth Glacier

Split Mountain Pass sits just west of Split Mountain. The trail that rounds Peak Lake's north shore becomes indistinct east of Lake 10,740. To reach Mammoth Glacier, leave the valley just beyond this lake and wander up grassy slopes to the north, staying somewhat right (east) of the stream draining the pass. Before reaching Split Mountain's ramparts, angle into the declivity below the pass, cross the stream, and zigzag up ledges that involve a few 3rd-class steps.

Knapsack Col (12,240+)

Peak Lake to Titcomb Basin

Reaching the saddle between the Twins and Winifred at the head of Peak Lake's valley involves easy grass and talus on the Peak Lake side, the snow of Twins Glacier on the Titcomb side. The glacier is steep enough that two backpackers not carrying ice axes have been seriously injured falling. Enough said, though Knapsack Col, connecting the heads of two of the Wind Rivers' premier valleys, makes possible a classic backpack loop.

Threlkeld Pass (10,840+)

Sauerkraut Lakes–Bridger Lakes

Imagine the ideal pass—gentle, grassy slopes on both sides—and you may imagine it sitting astride a much-trod thoroughfare. But while topographically Threlkeld Pass is an ideal pass, its location is so obscure that it isn't crossed by a trail. This traillessness, though, isn't due merely to its connecting two seldom-visited destinations but also to the valleys leading to it being so serendipitous that a trail is unneeded.

On both sides, however, reaching these valleys involves tactics not intuitive from map-reading. Don't ascend the drainage leading directly to the pass from Sauerkraut

Lake 10,193, but rather continue up-valley to Lake 10,432, before ascending easy slopes to the south. When approaching from the south, from the largest Bridger Lake (10,400+, just west of Guiterrez Peak), rather than trying to reach this lake's northern-most lobe by traversing its rugged northwest shore, start uphill from the lake's west end.

Peaks

New Fork Canyon Walls

The various walls, buttresses, and pinnacles that form the north and west side of New Fork Canyon culminate in minor high points and summits not worth visiting, but they are the most impressive canyon walls in the Wind Rivers. New Wind River routes often go unreported, but probably nowhere as often as in New Fork Canyon. One problem has been locating routes along the array of buttresses and turrets; another has been reluctance to report a route that may have been previously climbed.

1. Knucklebuster (II 5.12a) The first walls you encounter hiking up to New Fork Canyon are south-facing. The main one is the China Wall, but this four-pitch route is on the formation to the left. The 140-foot first pitch is a sustained finger-and-hand crack—said to be "as nice as cracks get"—just left of a left-facing dihedral. Three 5.9 to 5.10 pitches complete the climb. Descend west.

2. China Wall Left (III 5.10) Downstream from the New Fork's main bend, prominent from New Fork Lakes and US 189/191, is south-facing China Wall. The better of the wall's two routes uses left-facing corners left of the massive buttress that bisects the face. The six-pitch route leads to a minor notch left of the wall's apex.

The crux is a boulder start; nothing above exceeds 5.9, though the second pitch encounters a roof. On the fifth pitch is a crack right of red rock, left of white rock.

3. China Wall Right (III 5.10a) This route ascends corners on the right side of China Wall's prominent central buttress. Begin in right-facing corners that lead up left. The route's best section (and crux) is a one-and-a-half-pitch V halfway up. Above is excessive moss. Near the top, angle left up an easy ramp to join China Wall Left.

4. Ra Mountain, Northeast Corners (III 5.10a) The Bull's Horns are the most identifiable features on the walls above New Fork Park. Just south of the Bull's Horns is a distinctive pyramid: Ra Mountain. Near the right edge of Ra Mountain's east face are two large corner systems. This route follows the left system, the one that is continuous nearly from the bottom to the top of the face.

Approach via gullies between Ra Mountain and the Bull's Horns, then work left on the highest ledges with trees. Begin in a right-facing corner (5.8), then traverse right on a large ledge. The second and third pitches (5.9, 5.8) follow the prominent corner (except for a detour to the right at the top of the second pitch) to a small ledge beneath a small overhang. Start the fourth pitch with a detour right to avoid a grassy

New Fork Canyon and Dome Peak

crack; finish in a large V (5.8) to a hanging belay. The crux fifth pitch negotiates two overhangs. The 5.8 sixth pitch completes the route.

5. Lower Bull's Horn Two prominent pinnacles on New Fork Canyon's west wall are unmistakably a bull's horns, especially when seen from New Fork Park 0.5 mile north of the river's bend. The southern pinnacle has been climbed, but details aren't available.

6. Higher Bull's Horn–Frenzic Fang (III 5.9) The northern Bull's Horn—or Frenzic Fang, if you prefer a less hackneyed name—vaguely corkscrew-shaped, is especially impressive, as it appears to overhang on all sides. It has been climbed by a five-pitch route near the north edge of its elegant east arête. The route begins north of the edge and follows cracks near the edge. However, at least two parties have failed to locate the start.

7. Park Place Buttress (II 5.7) The wall west of New Fork Park comprises a series of buttresses. Park Place Buttress, the most conspicuous, features a steep north face and a southeast face that offers reasonable and worthwhile climbing.

The buttress is best located and approached by following the New Fork Trail to an open slope that extends from the trail to the buttress. The southeast face's most prominent feature is a dogleg chimney on its left side, but on the far right side is another large chimney that ends at a step below the top. Left of this chimney is a narrower system, its bottom marked by a black streak, below which is a 200-foot shoulder. The system splits 300 feet from the top, the right branch becoming a deep chimney featuring a huge chockstone. Both branches of the system have been climbed.

After 3rd-class scrambling on the shoulder's right side, rope up below a short right-facing corner. Step left 100 feet higher and angle right up dirty but easy grooves to the top of the shoulder. Scramble up left between ledges. From the highest block, step left, onto the steep face; after a few moves work right to a thin crack and climb it (crux) to a less steep area. Continue up the pleasant face above, eventually stepping right to the main crack system. The fifth pitch follows this system, taking the left branch where it splits. Three more pitches, on occasionally crumbly rock, reach the wall's top.

The buttress's upper section was initially climbed by the system's right fork. Aid in a dihedral (A2) leads to a ledge below a huge chockstone, passed by nubbins and laybacking.

Dome Peak (11,234)

The summit itself is of limited interest, but a few routes have been done on the walls overlooking New Fork Canyon.

1. East Slope–North Ridge (I 2nd class) A partially wooded valley ascends from New Fork Park to a saddle north of the summit; a bit of a path ascends the valley. From the saddle, follow the ridge south.

2. Bluebell Buttress (II 5.7) A steep-walled side canyon cut into the Dome Peak massif meets New Fork Canyon in New Fork Park. Bluebell Buttress, on this side canyon's west wall, stands just northeast of Dome Peak's summit. To its right is a meadow from whose apex rises a prominent ugly gully.

A six-pitch route begins left of the buttress's toe with 200 feet of scrambling up right. The 5.4 first pitch reaches a sloping ledge with a tree. The second pitch ascends a 5.6 corner. The third pitch includes a 15-foot 5.6 crack. The fourth pitch offers a choice: an easy grassy crack or an easy off-width to the left. Above a bush a crack leads to a ledge. Pitch 5 involves a 5.3 off-width and a 5.5 crack. Above are blocky flakes. The best route seems to be a 5.7 corner above these flakes, followed by a 5.5 slab. Scrambling for 200 feet leads to the buttress's top.

Descent: While you can walk off, descent has also been made by scrambling down for 150 feet to the southeast and making five 80-foot rappels, interspersed with downclimbing, in the gully left of the buttress.

3. Cruise Control (II 5.6) Near the head of Bluebell Buttress's side canyon (west-southwest of Point 11,166) is an east-facing wall ascended by this four-pitch route.

Begin just right of a low roof and a right-facing corner and below a grassy gully, traversing left to the corner. Climb it and the 5.5 face above to a ledge 120 feet up. Climb the steep face above (5.6) to a large ledge, then work up right, crossing a small stream. Belay below a left-facing dihedral to whose right is a triangular roof. Climb 100 feet to another ledge (5.6). Climb cracks in the face above to the route's end.

Descent: Walk off either north or south.

Doubletop Mountain (10,892)

The Wind Rivers offer serious climbing, but they also offer other aspects of a mountain environment. Doubletop Mountain, with a trail near the summit and a clump of small trees on top, wouldn't be included in a guidebook limited to mountaineering. But lakes, streams, meadows, and flowers—all found on the vaguely defined massif's grassy slopes—constitute an important counterpoint to rock walls, and from the Wind Rivers' easiest summit you have before you a panorama stretching from north of Gannett to Temple, 40 miles away.

1. South or East Slope (I 1st class) From the Doubletop Mountain Trail, walk a few hundred yards. This simple instruction, though, can't convey the enjoyment of a hike to Doubletop. A day hike from, in the old days, the Willow Creek trailhead, nowadays from New Fork Lakes, especially in autumn, may well be the Wind Rivers' finest stroll.

Rim Peak (10,985)

The mass filling the angle between the New Fork and Palmer and Reynolds Creeks, with its high point 0.4 mile north of Rim Lake, is separated by another fault zone from Doubletop Mountain to the south.

1. East Slope (I 2nd class) Most easily climbed by the grass above Penny Lake, though you can also ascend loose slopes farther north.

Hidden Lakes Massif (11,515)

Gathered here is not only the high point in the angle between the New Fork Trail and Palmer Canyon, 0.6 mile northwest of Hidden Lakes, but adjacent canyon walls as well.

1. Southeast Ridge (I 2nd class) Whether you begin from No Name Lakes or from the New Fork Trail between Lozier and Clark Lakes, Point 11,515's 12-foot summit pinnacle is less of an adventure than first navigating through the few sparsely timbered miles of minor domes and clefts, myriad ponds, and contorted stream drainages.

2. Palmer Creek Buttress, Southwest Face (III 5.9 plus rappel) From New Fork Park you can see this wall beyond Palmer Creek's confluence with the New Fork.

From near the confluence, scramble unroped up 1,000 feet of rubble. Ascend the crest for four pitches, the crux being a 5.9 crack. Then rappel left into a chimney; climb the chimney for four or five pitches, passing several large chockstones. Reach the rim by moderate 5th-class climbing.

Greeley Point (11,297)

1. South Slope (I 1st class) Reached by 0.5 mile of tundra from the 10,920-foot saddle crossed by the New Fork Trail between Lozier and Clark Lakes.

Pinnacle 11,400+

Between Glover Peak and Clark Creek, 0.7 mile north-northeast of Glover, is a slender 200-foot tower not apparent on the Squaretop Mountain quad but obvious from Dome Peak, Vista Pass, and from near Summit Lake. Approach from either the New Fork Trail or the Highline.

1. West Arête (I 5th class) From the notch between the pinnacle and the larger rock to its west, climb to the top in two pitches.

Descent: Rappel the route.

Glover Peak (12,068)

The only peak west of the Green River and Pine Creek over 12,000 feet, Glover dominates a country notable for numerous high lakes; by virtue of its isolation it provides an extensive panorama of high summits to the east. The summit register contains an uncommon amount of praise. The massif includes a main summit and a north summit joined to it by a pinnacled ridge.

1. East Ridge (I 2nd class) The southeast slope is broken by many cliff bands, and you need routefinding acumen to connect the magical flower- and pond-filled valleys below with the ledges that crisscross the cliffs above. To pick an easy route, use two sets of diagonal fractures, one sloping up to the north, the other to the south. Avoid loose rock on the upper southeast slopes by crossing to the cleaner east ridge.

2. Southwest Ridge (I 3rd class) From Doubletop Mountain Trail; airy scrambling.

3. North Summit, Northwest Ridge (I 2nd class) From Lake 11,192 Glover's north summit (12,045) appears at the left of two similar rubble piles. Reaching Lake 11,192 is the best part of the adventure: Either leave the New Fork Trail near the pass west of Clark Lake and wander east and south, or leave the Doubletop Mountain Trail between the No Name Lakes and head north.

Vista Peak (11,840+)

About a mile south-southeast of Vista Pass and a mile north-northwest of Mount Oeneis is a peak with views into the Peak Lake cirque and down the Green.

1. North Slopes (I 2nd class) From Vista Pass. After passing left of lower cliffs and right of upper cliffs, climb over a false summit and continue south to the true summit.

2. West Slope (I 2nd class) From Green River Pass.

Mount Oeneis (12,232)

This amorphous mass occupies an area between the Trail Creek–Pine Creek fault zone and the Green River–Elbow Creek fault zone. Alexander Klots, author of the Peterson Series' *Field Guide to the Butterflies,* participated in the first ascent. He collected specimens of the genus *Oeneis* (pronounced EE-nee-us)—drab, brown butterflies of arctic and alpine environments.

1. Southwest Ridge (I 3rd class) A pleasant excursion from Summit Lake, crossing a minor summit en route. The hardest section is the descent from this point.

2. East Face (I 3rd or 4th class) Klots and a companion descended this face by an unspecified route. The face has been ascended following an ascent of Sky Pilot by working north on ledges until just south of Oeneis's summit, then climbing straight up.

3. West Slope (I 3rd class) Oeneis's west slopes form a bowl convenient for descent; its character and attractiveness depend on the quantity and quality of snow. The easiest place to gain/leave the crest is a chute near the notch on the southwest ridge.

4. Northwest Gully (I 4th class Snow 3rd class) The middle, most prominent gully north of Point 12,093 has been ascended as an 800-foot snow climb, the maximum snow angle being 35 degrees. The route ends with a 4th-class pitch on rock.

Sky Pilot Peak (12,129)

Sky pilot, a purple flower exuding an odor unpleasant to many, is common at high elevations. It belongs to the genus *Polemonium* but is often called skunkweed by the less scholarly. Sky pilots thrive on the flat summit of the unimpressive peak betwen Oeneis and Elbow Lake.

1. Southeast Gully (I 3rd class) A prow pointing slightly west of south separates two facets of a 200-foot cliff band below Sky Pilot's summit. A complex of ill-defined gullies shatters this band just right of its prow. The approach from the 0.5-mile-long lake west of Elbow Lake passes through pleasant terrain, and the broad summit is hospitable, but the gullies are messy.

2. North Ridge (I 4th class) You can reach the Oeneis–Sky Pilot saddle from Cube Rock Pass by ascending snow to the Oeneis-G-14 col and contouring along Oeneis's east side, or from Lake 11,130, to the west at the head of a branch of Elbow Creek. Sky Pilot's narrow, enjoyable north ridge contains gendarmes, but you can pass them by descending east and traversing on exposed ledges, regaining the crest south of the gendarmes. Follow the ridge for six pitches to its steeper upper part, which you can climb in a pitch and a half.

3. Northwest Gully (I 4th class Snow 4th class) Tucked away above Twin Lakes in the Elbow Creek drainage, between Sky Pilot and Oeneis's southwest ridge, is Lake 11,130. The 300-foot-long, 3- to 10-foot-wide, 30-degree gully above this lake has been climbed in late June when it was snow-filled. Above the gully, follow the north ridge for two pitches.

4. Southwest Gully (I 3rd class) Less steep than the southeast gully but a bit loose.

G-14 (11,600+)

A minor summit, 0.4 mile west of Shannon Pass, that appears prominent from the north because it stands at the head of the upper Green River's west branch.

1. East Slope (I 2nd class) Ascend either directly from Shannon Pass or by way of a valley draining toward Elbow Lake.

Peak Lake Peak (11,175)

This is the rounded rock west of Peak Lake and north of Cube Rock Pass; its name is one of several examples of self-referential Wind River nomenclature.

1. East Slope (I 2nd class) A pleasant scramble from Peak Lake over low-angle slabs. Also easy from Cube Rock Pass.

Ladd Peak (12,957)

The Wind Rivers are Wyoming's highest range, but few peaks rise more than 3,000 feet above adjoining valleys. Otherwise unexceptional Ladd Peak, though, looms 4,500 feet above Three Forks Park—the range's greatest single rise. From most vantages Ladd is outshone by higher, steeper, and snowier neighbors, but from Three Forks Park the tiers of buttresses that constitute its northwest ridge seem to soar endlessly.

1. East Ridge (I 3rd class) From Stone Pillar Pass, with several hundred feet of distinctly 3rd-class scrambling.

2. North Couloir (II Snow/Ice 4th class) A couloir rises 2,000 feet from a pair of lakes below the north face. The ascent involves 40-degree snow and in August a few ice pitches. There is some rockfall and avalanche danger.

Whitecap (left), Ladd (right), Lake 11,085

3. South Slope-West Ridge (I 2nd or 3rd class) From Stonehammer Lake, ascend toward Stone Pillar Pass, then angle left. Looks easy but wretched.

Mount Whitecap (13,020)

The distinctive snowcap was once believed to be permanent but has vanished during recent hot, dry summers.

1. Northwest Ridge (I 3rd or 4th class) From Stone Pillar Pass.

2. Southwest Couloir (I 3rd class) The southwest ridge, the crest joining White-cap and G-3, is not well defined but does appear as the peak's left skyline when you approach from the valley above Peak Lake. To the right of this ridge, a slope of snow and talus funnels upward to a couloir that ends just left of the summit. A few hundred feet below the top, leave the couloir for rock to the right, where the route's only 3rd class is encountered.

G-3 (11,925)

Early surveyors designated unnamed Wind River peaks by a letter and numeral; G was the Peak Lake area's letter. The interesting peaks acquired names—G-9 became Arrowhead—but others didn't. G-3 is an innocuous hogback on Peak Lake's north shore, dwarfed by Whitecap behind, but its easier route involves scrambling at its pleasantest.

1. East Ridge (I 3) Bedrock slabs and knobs, joined by catenary snow crests and occasional grassy ramps, with views across Peak Lake. To reach the ridge's best 0.5 mile, leave the main valley at long, shallow Lake 10,740 and follow the bluebell-bordered outlet creek of the 11,200-foot pond that sits on the ridge. For a longer excursion, leave the valley as for Split Mountain Pass and traverse at about 11,200 feet.

2. South Buttress (I 5.6) Less than 0.5 mile east of Peak Lake a buttress rises to G-3's southeast ridge. A crack system in the middle of the buttress offers a four-pitch climb, most of which is easy 5th class. Third-class scrambling then leads to the ridge.

Descent: A 3rd-class grassy gully east of the buttress offers a handy descent route.

G-4 (12,845)

The summit on the Peak Lake–Mammoth Glacier divide between Whitecap and Split offers no reason for an ascent.

1. Southeast Ridge (I 2nd class) Rubble, from Split Mountain Pass.

Split Mountain (13,155)

The main summit is separated from the southeast summit by a great cleft.

1. West Face (I 2nd class) A pleasant excursion from Split Mountain Pass—easier, in fact, than the climb to the pass. You cross an upper finger of Mammoth Glacier,

Peak Lake's cirque, as seen from Vista Peak: Split Mountain (left), Twin Peaks (second from left), Winifred Peak (second from right), Sulphur Peak (highest peak on right)

but the snow is low-angle enough that an ice axe adds security only when the snow is particularly hard.

Continuing from the main summit to the southeast summit involves more-serious scrambling.

2. South Face (II 5.5/5.6) The main summit's south face is split by many cracks. This route follows the middle of the three most prominent cracks for two leads, then diagonals up and right on easy rock for four or five pitches to the arête on the edge of the mountain's main cleft. Easy cracks and grooves on the arête lead to the west face.

Twin Peaks (13,185)

The divides between Peak Lake, Mammoth Glacier, and Titcomb Basin converge at a pair of nearly equally high summits. The northeast Twin isn't visible from Peak Lake, but the pair could have been named from Mammoth Glacier or Titcomb Basin.

1. Southeast Couloir (I Snow 3rd class) From Titcomb Basin, ascend Twins Glacier and a finger of snow to the col between the Twins. Both summits are easily reached from the col. Mammoth Glacier extends to the col from the northwest, and an ascent from it should present no obstacles.

2. Northeast Couloir (I Snow 3rd class) A steep snow couloir that faces Titcomb Basin reaches the ridge northeast of the northeast Twin.

3. North Face (mixed) Two snow couloirs extend up from Mammoth Glacier. Climb the left one and work right onto the rock face, followed by three or four pitches of moderate mixed climbing.

4. West Ridge From the Split-Twins col, pass under a row of pinnacles on a narrow ledge. Regain the crest at the top of a couloir and follow the ridge to the southwest Twin.

5. Southwest Twin, Southwest Face A gully facing Peak Lake separates the southwest Twin from a subsidiary summit on the west ridge. Climb left of this gully; near the top, follow its left edge to the subsidiary summit.

6. Southwest Twin, Southeast Face (II 5.10) Wind River routes are often praised by characterizing their rock as "of the same quality as that in the Cirque of the Towers." The scattering of these routes in unexpected places can keep you exploring for years. The snowy Twins aren't known as a rock gym, but the quote is from the first ascent account of the Southwest Twin's Southeast Face.

Dawn light accentuates a prominent arête, which the five-pitch route ascends. The first pitch features a fingertip layback 50 feet up. On the second pitch, traverse to the arête's farthest left crack-and-dihedral system; follow it for two difficult pitches. Two easier pitches lead to the summit.

Winifred Peak (12,775)

A lesser summit at the head of Peak Lake's cirque, just south of Knapsack Col, overlooking Twins Glacier and Titcomb Basin to the east.

1. North Ridge (I 3rd class) Broken rock from Knapsack Col. You can also reach the ridge via a tongue of Twins Glacier and scree above.

2. Northeast Couloir (I Snow/Ice 4th or 5th class) A steepening finger of Twins Glacier reaches Winifred's south ridge near the summit. When late-summer snow hardens, the couloir provides an introduction to ice climbing.

G-17 (12,814)

Of the peaks still known by surveyors' designations, the summit at the end of the jagged spur of Henderson protruding toward Jean Lakes is the handsomest.

1. Southeast Slope (I 4th class) Rubble, but efficient, from the valley between G-17 and the Titcomb Needles.

2. Northwest Ridge (III 5.9) The route begins with climbing that is classic for its continuous difficulty and ends with climbing that is classic for its position, but the scrambling between keeps the overall route from classic status.

The ridge's lower half is formed of two converging spurs, approximately above Lake 11,665's outlet and separated by a deep chimney. The crux first pitch follows the prominent steep dihedral that splits the left-hand spur, for 160 feet to a small stance just below a crest. Begin the second pitch with a tricky step up left, then work up and farther left. The third and fourth pitches are 4th class. After 100 feet of unbelayed

Henderson Peak and G-17

American Legion Peak

Henderson Peak

G-17

Titcomb Needles

scrambling, diagonal to the crest to the right. Follow this narrowing feature to the summit, on the seventh and eighth pitches occasionally laybacking its edge.

3. West Face (I 4th class) Some may rappel once when descending this route.

4. South Pinnacle (I 5.4 A1) Low on G-17's south ridge is a pinnacle with a steep west face. Climb the pinnacle by circling west and north of the face and traversing around and onto an immense boulder in the notch between the pinnacle and the main peak. From the boulder, traverse left and reach the summit in one lead, using one piece of aid.

The Bonneys mention an ascent of the lower pinnacle on the south ridge.

American Legion Peak or Buchtel Peak (13,205)

Climbers have known the peak situated at the meeting of the divides between Peak Lake, Jean Lakes, and Titcomb Lakes as Buchtel, for Henry Buchtel, who made the first ascent in 1930. The name on the 1968 Gannett Peak quad, though, is American Legion. You can reach this peak from any of the surrounding valleys. The number of routes indicates broken rock rather than popularity.

1. West Ridge (I 3rd class) From the Arrowhead col.

◄ *G-17, Northwest Ridge*

2. Southwest Face (I 3rd class) Two gullies slant across the face seen from Upper Jean Lake. The right gully is easier.

3. South Ridge (II 5.4) Approach the ridge rising from Lake 11,665 from Upper Jean Lake, or from Titcomb Basin via the Henderson col. Above a prominent gendarme and a narrow crest, the ridge merges with the southeast ridge.

4. Southeast Ridge (I 3rd class) American Legion was first climbed from the Henderson col, which you can reach from Titcomb Basin by way of Summer Ice Lake and the small glacier above, or from Lake 11,665 on the Jean Lakes side. The first ascent chronicler characterized the broad ridge as a "vertical boulder field," a misleading depiction of stable and moderate-angled talus. While the talus doesn't reach the summit, the 100-foot surprise beyond and another beyond it involve minimal exposure.

5. Northeast Ridge The summit register mentions an ascent. A descent has been made with a short rappel on the ridge and a climb down a couloir to the glacier above Summer Ice Lake.

6. Other Routes The summit register also reports ascents of the north face—in September 1937—and the east face.

Mount Arrowhead (12,972)

You can't see this fine piece of rock from Peak Lake but can recognize it from Gannett or Jean Lakes—or Elkhart Park—by its symmetry: steep north and south faces flanked by uniformly angling east and west ridges. While from a distance the south face's flutings resemble certain arrowhead styles, from nearby you see them as crack systems—features that make Arrowhead the Peak Lake area's best climbing peak.

1. East Ridge (I 3rd class) You can reach the Arrowhead-Buchtel col from the north or south. The ridge doesn't require a rope, though you can find 4th-class variations on the narrow face to the left.

2. Northeast Rib (II 5.7) Toward the north face's left edge is a rib that provides a few good pitches. Reach the rib from partway up the couloir that leads to the Arrowhead-Buchtel col.

3. North Face (IV 5.9) Begin this twelve-pitch route 20 feet left of a conspicuous X formed by crossing white intrusions. Three short, easy pitches—the first up and slightly right, the second up left, and a third left to a layback, then right—lead to a good ledge. Next, step left to a broken dihedral and follow it to its top. The next three leads combine cracks, ramps, and 5.9 face climbing to bypass triangular roofs to the right and gain a set of large ledges. The final five pitches follow a curving crack: The first involves a 5.8 layback to reach an alcove, the third a 1.5-inch crack, and the fourth a 5.9 traverse left.

You should encounter three bolts; two are the anchor for the sixth pitch.

4. West Ridge (II 5.7 plus rappel) This exposed and well-spoken-of route begins at the Bow col, most easily reached from the south, though the approach may entail year-round snow. The climb goes over a large spire (the Lost Arrow, naturally), with a rappel down its east side.

Mount Arrowhead

5. Southwest Ledges (II 5.5) On the south face below the west ridge's pinnacles, a ramp of varying width angles up from the Bow col. Beyond the pinnacles easy 5th-class rock leads up to the ridge crest.

6. South Face Far Left (II 5.7) The most prominent dihedral left of the central dihedrals provides a similar and equally pleasant route. Climb the left side of the dihedral for two pitches, then cross a bowl and jog up right. The remaining leads ascend corners and ribs to the crest, which is followed for a pitch to the summit.

7. South Face Left (III 5.8) Two dihedrals extend the entire height of the face, the left one ending just west of Arrowhead's summit. Numerous cracks on this dihedral's left wall challenge your routefinding intuition but minimize difficulties. The result is one of the northern Wind Rivers' best rock climbs, even with difficulties concentrated in the first two of the six pitches. The crux second pitch is particularly good. The dihedral ends a short, easy lead from the summit.

8. South Face Center (III 5.8) Six or so pitches of climbing on excellent rock, finishing just right of Arrowhead's summit.

9. South Face Right (II 5.7) The right-hand of the two face-high dihedrals offers climbing similar to and as enjoyable as the *Left* route. Of the five pitches, the first three generally involve cracks left of the corner, while the final two stay closer to the corner. The route ends on the east ridge a few hundred feet from the summit.

Bow Mountain (13,020)

A massive, rubbly, unappealing contrast to its neighbors on the Peak Lake cirque's south wall, Bow has nevertheless provided climbers with a few worthwhile objectives.

1. Northwest Ridge (I 3rd class) From near the ill-defined saddle between Bow and Stroud (easily, pleasantly reached from the Shannon Pass Trail), ascend unstable rubble until a few hundred feet below the Bow-Brimstone col, then angle right up a 3rd-class chimneylike system to the crest. The 0.25-mile northwest ridge is generic Wind River broad talus crest.

2. Southwest Face (I 3rd class) Approach from either Elbow Lake or Upper Jean Lake, ascending much scree to a prominent Y-shaped couloir. Take the right fork. Avoid occasional snow by temporarily leaving the couloir.

3. Southeast Face Head toward a narrow couloir near the top.

4. South Face of East Ridge–Quiver Crack (II 5.8) Bow's long east ridge has a steep south face, with rock similar to Arrowhead's. Toward the face's left end, a snow-and-rubble-filled chute leads to a deep notch in the ridge. Just right of the chute, a clean crack rises to distinctive orange rock midway up the face. An enjoyable route ascends the crack (which progressively widens from hand-size to a chimney) and the face above to the crest in four or five pitches. It then follows the east ridge, with a few roped pitches and some scrambling. The crux is a thin crack in the orange wall.

5. East Ridge (II 5.7) Climbing begins at the Arrowhead col with a traverse of several gendarmes—the Quivering Pinnacles. The ridge includes several more nice pitches.

While you can most easily approach the col from the south, approaching from Stroud Glacier and ascending four or five ice pitches in the couloir below the col makes the excursion a nice mixed climb.

Brimstone Mountain (12,720+)

An interesting pinnacled ridge extends northwest from Bow Mountain. Sulphur is the imposing peak at the ridge's end, Brimstone the minuscule summit in the middle. Henderson and Underhill named the peaks for the odor accompanying falling rock.

1. West Ridge (I 4th class) Reached by a couloir on its north side.

2. North Ridge (I 5th class) Traverse from Sulphur, bypassing gendarmes.

Sulphur Peak (12,825)

The topographic map indicates a minor summit at the end of Bow's northwest ridge, but it is actually a distinctive peak, with an alpine north face and a pair of noteworthy pinnacles. The pinnacle nearer the summit is barely visible from Peak Lake's valley, but the outer one nearly eclipses Sulphur's main summit.

Sulphur Peak

1. West Gullies (I 4th class) From Peak Lake, talus and loose-rock gullies lead to the notch between the main summit and the inner pinnacle. From the notch, climb directly to the summit.

2. South Ridge (I 5th class) Sulphur was first ascended by traversing the pinnacled ridge from Brimstone.

3. Northeast Ridge (II 5.7) The ridge looks attractive, and the first ascent description includes the phrases "pleasant route," "wonderful rock," and "easily protected."

From Stroud Glacier, scramble above the lower east-face cliffs until you can see down the lower north face. Climb a long pitch to a belay on the east face, then a half rope length to a belay on the prow. The third and fourth pitches are on the north face, the crux of the route being a triangular block capping a dihedral on the fourth pitch. Two easier pitches lead to the summit.

4. North Face (III/IV 5.9 Ice 5th class) An alpine route with steep ice, difficult rock that may be ice-coated, and the possibility of falling stones—a Wind River rarity. Climb a 55- to 60-degree ice couloir for six pitches to a prominent dihedral, then follow cracks and chimneys in the dihedral for six more pitches to the summit.

The second ascent took this direct route. Icy rock forced the first ascent party to leave the dihedral 200 feet from the top and traverse to the rib on the right. They climbed the rib for a pitch, pendulumed right to a groove, and found easier going above an overhang.

5. Inner Spire The spire nearer Sulphur's summit is a 75-foot climb from the notch between it and the main summit.

6. Cutthroat Spire, North Face (IV 5.9 A4 Ice 5th class) This is Sulphur's outer, more prominent spire; the reason for the name is apparent from the north. Three easy rock pitches lead to an icefield below the spire, then five pitches on the 45-degree ice lead to the spire itself. Climb the face in six pitches, three involving difficult aid.

Descent: In addition to the *West Gullies,* the usual descent route, the east face has been descended by downclimbing interspersed with two rappels.

Stroud Peak (12,198)

Many small peaks have sharper features than higher neighbors, water and ice having had better opportunity to carve steep walls and pointed summits while reducing their height. Stroud attracts more climbers and photographers than most nearby taller summits do.

From Stroud you can see fault zones occupied by each of the Green's three forks and trace their continuations south. You can infer the two faults that give Elbow Lake its shape and follow one past a saddle on Elbow Peak to Moya Canyon. You can see White Rock's sedimentary strata, remnants of the peneplain north and east (including the best-known remnant, Squaretop), and such peaks as Gannett rising above the surface. In all directions are glacial effects: jagged crests, U-shaped valleys, and ice-carved lakes, many tinted green by glacial dust. Northwest are the sedimentary Gros Ventres, thrust southwest as the Wind Rivers were, and, beyond Jackson Hole, the classic fault-block range. Attention to the rock at your feet reveals varieties of migmatite; it also may prevent a stumble.

1. Southeast Ridge (I 2nd class) One of the range's best easy routes, distinguished by solid footing, small-scale routefinding, and perhaps improbability. Reach the ridge either by grassy slopes halfway up the Shannon Pass Trail from the Highline junction or, far less pleasantly, from Peak Lake by way of the talus slope leading to the saddle east of the peak. The summit itself is arguably 3rd class.

2. Northwest Face Left (III 5.9) A twelve-pitch route begins on the prominent buttress in the center of the face and ascends cracks and flakes near the crest. Where the buttress joins the face are three parallel right-facing corners; the route ascends the left-most. The upper quarter of the face offers several moderate options.

3. Northwest Face Right (III 5.7 A1) In what appears from Cube Rock Pass to be the face's center is a large corner system, which occupies a concavity that is obvious in certain light. Begin in a gully that slants up from above Peak Lake to the base of the corners. Ascend the corners to a prominent ledge three-fourths of the way up the face, traverse left 200 feet, and follow a gully to the top. The first ascent used two points of aid.

4. West Face (I 5.0) Gullies and slabs from Shannon Pass.

5. West Rib (II 5.7) This route ascends a minor rib that constitutes the southern-most clean rock on the west face. Begin from the top left corner of a grassy slope with half a pitch of 5.5 face climbing, followed by scrambling to the first belay, at the base of a clean, white crack. Climb this superb 5.6/5.7 crack for a pitch. Continue in the same system to an airy belay atop a buttress. After another pitch, traverse right across two loose gullies to the southeast ridge.

Elbow Peak (11,948)

A sprawling formation, as elbow-shaped as the lake to its northwest, this peak doesn't offer technical rock, but its height and isolation attract hikers from all sides.

1. Southwest Slope (I 2nd class) From Sauerkraut Lakes, with routefinding at the top.

2. South Ridge From Moya Canyon, by way of the 11,770-foot south summit.

3. Northeast Ridge (I 2nd class) You can gain the ridge most easily from the subtle height-of-land between Upper Jean Lake and the head of Moya Canyon, passing Lake 10,855. Also, the 2 miles of ridge between Elbow Lake and Jean Lakes has been followed from the Highline's high point at the ridge's end.

Guiterrez Peak (11,362)

A somewhat elegant peak, as walk-up peaks go. If you happen to be at Bridger Lakes, Guiterrez is the peak to climb.

1. North Ridge (I 2nd class) Gained from north of Lake 10,541.

2. South Ridge (I 2nd class) Fun scrambling to gain the ridge from the southeast corner of the largest Bridger Lake, which lies below Guiterrez's west face.

Into Titcomb Basin from south side of Island Lake

5 Titcomb Basin

West of Pinedale a roadside hill called Trappers' Point makes a good place for viewing the Wind Rivers. Several Rendezvous took place on the nearby Green River during the 1830s, and we can envision a trapper, climbing the hill for a respite from the revelry, surveying the panorama. The trapper's attention would have been drawn to a row of steep-faced skyline peaks, and we may imagine an occasional mountain man wondering how high these peaks were compared to others he'd seen. Apparently trapper consensus believed the peak that appears highest from Trappers' Point to be the high point of their realm, for Fremont's trapper-guides persuaded him that it was.

The escarpment seen from Trappers' Point borders Titcomb Basin on the east (named for Charles and Harold Titcomb, who visited it in 1901). Fremont called it "a nearly perpendicular wall of granite, terminating 2,000 to 3,000 feet above our heads in a serrated line of broken, jagged cones." The northern of three summits that cap this wall is Mount Helen, the middle Mount Sacagawea, and the southern that according to Fremont, "from long consultation as we approached the mountain, we had decided to be the highest in the range."

Less impressive are the summits on the basin's west side, on the ridge dividing Titcomb Basin from Jean Lakes and Peak Lake. (Those on the Peak Lake divide are described in the Peak Lake chapter.) Mount Woodrow Wilson and other peaks at the valley's north end are on the main Continental Divide, which here separates Titcomb Basin from Dinwoody Glacier. (They are included in the Dinwoody Glacier chapter.)

A minor ridge of Fremont Peak separates Titcomb Basin from Indian Basin to the east. Jackson and Ellingwood Peaks flank Indian Basin, and an old Indian trail wanders past its many quiet lakes, crossing the Divide at Indian Pass. Across Indian Pass is a vast glacier system drained by the North Fork Bull Lake Creek (covered in the Alpine Lakes chapter).

In 1924 Colorado climbers Carl Blaurock, Herman Buhl, and Albert Ellingwood first climbed Helen, from the east; in 1926 Ellingwood climbed Helen from Titcomb Basin and made first ascents of Sacagawea, Ellingwood, and Knife Point. Titcomb Basin continues to attract climbers; it is the section of the Wind Rivers that offers the greatest variety: walk-ups, easy and difficult rock climbs, ice climbs, and mixed mountaineering routes.

Most climbers and hikers reach Titcomb Basin from the Elkhart Park trailhead, by combining the Pole Creek, Seneca Lake, and Indian Pass Trails.

Titcomb Basin's popularity has caused changes since Fremont reported that "a stillness the most profound and a terrible solitude forced themselves constantly on the mind." Island Lake can be crowded. One reason was stated by Fremont: "We found ourselves all exceedingly fatigued, and much to the satisfaction of the whole party, we encamped." A less valid motivation is the treelessness of the terrain beyond. Fremont's "trunks of fallen pines [that] afforded us bright fires" are long gone, as is every dead branch within reach.

The tundra above the Upper Titcomb Lake also becomes dotted with tents, of hardier folk braving the windy desolation for access to Sacagawea, Helen, and Dinwoody Glacier. Yet the basin is sprinkled with lakes and meadows, shielded by domes and low ridges, and campsites are abundant that are private, sheltered, and scenic.

Murphy's Law states that important places are located on quad's edges and corners. Thus the Gannett Peak, Fremont Peak North, Fremont Peak South, and Bridger Lakes quads converge in Titcomb Basin; you need all four to cover the surrounding peaks. The Pole Creek Trail briefly traverses the Fremont Lake North and Fayette Lake maps, though the short sections don't justify carrying them.

Trails

Pole Creek Trail

Elkhart Park to Pole Creek Lakes—9 miles

This major artery heads east from Elkhart Park to Pole Creek, but its first half sees far more use, as part of the route to Titcomb Basin, than the half beyond Eklund Lake.

Begin at the northwest corner of the Elkhart Park parking area. After 3 boring miles you reach Miller Park, where a side trail diverges right to Miller Lake. The Pole Creek Trail eventually rounds an outcrop to a fine view, known as Photographers' Point. Shortly after descending to a saddle with a pond and a trail going right to Sweeney Lakes (and a junction with the Miller Lake Trail), you reach Eklund Lake and a junction with the Seneca Lake Trail; turn left on it to go to Island Lake and Titcomb Basin.

The Pole Creek Trail, though, goes south along Eklund Lake's east shore and switchbacks to pretty country, at about 10,400 feet, with numerous small lakes. After crossing Monument Creek the trail descends below 9,800 feet to Pole Creek Lakes, meeting the Highline near its crossing of Pole Creek. The area beyond is described in the Alpine Lakes chapter.

Seneca Lake Trail

Eklund Lake to Little Seneca Lake—4.5 miles

As the middle part of the route from Elkhart Park to Titcomb Basin, this trail leads north from Eklund Lake and the Pole Creek Trail. After rounding Barbara Lake you spend a frustrating few miles descending 300 feet to a pond, climbing over a saddle to Hobbs Lake, and, after crossing its outlet and Seneca Lake's outlet stream (during high water cross 100 yards upstream from the trail), wandering up and down through fault-shattered country west of Seneca Lake, finally strenuously climbing 300 feet to the lake.

Titcomb Basin Area

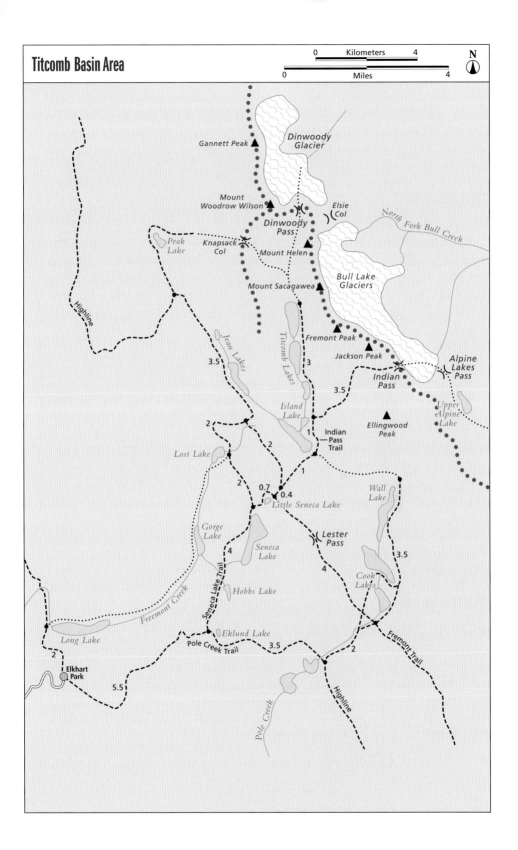

0 Kilometers 4

0 Miles 4

N

Gannett Peak ▲

Dinwoody Glacier

Mount Woodrow Wilson ▲

Elsie Col

Dinwoody Pass

North Fork Bull Creek

Peak Lake

Knapsack Col

Mount Helen ▲

Highline

Mount Sacagawea ▲

Bull Lake Glaciers

Jean Lakes

3.5

Titcomb Lakes

Fremont Peak ▲

3

Jackson Peak ▲

Alpine Lakes Pass

Indian Pass

3.5

Island Lake

2

1

Indian Pass Trail

Ellingwood Peak ▲

Upper Alpine Lake

Lost Lake

2

2

0.7 0.4

Little Seneca Lake

1

Wall Lake

Gorge Lake

Seneca Lake

Lester Pass

Seneca Lake Trail

Freemont Creek

4

Hobbs Lake

4

3.5

Cook Lakes

Long Lake

2

Elkhart Park

Eklund Lake

Pole Creek Trail

3.5

Fremont Trail

2

5.5

Highline

Pole Creek

Follow the bedrock ledges of Seneca Lake's west shore north. At the lake's head are the first good campsites for a few miles, and the Lost Lake Trail turns inconspicuously left. The Seneca Lake Trail continues upstream to Little Seneca Lake and rounds its west and north shores (though you can save 0.25 mile by boulder-hopping on the southeast shore), intersecting the Highline just beyond the lake. Turn right on the southbound Highline to cross Lester Pass to Cook Lakes, or continue up a small creek to follow the northbound Highline to Jean Lakes or intersect the Indian Pass Trail.

Indian Pass Trail

Highline Trail to Indian Pass—5.5 miles

The Seneca Lake Trail intersects the Highline just east of Little Seneca Lake. The Indian Pass Trail, the last leg of the route from Elkhart Park to Island Lake, Titcomb Basin, and the Bull Lake Glaciers, leaves the Highline less than 0.5 mile north of this intersection. Heading north, it reaches Island Lake after crossing two ridges that look insignificant on maps. (This is where Fremont complained of climbing 500 feet "but to make an equal descent on the other side . . . always expecting, with every ridge . . . to reach the foot of the peaks, and always disappointed.")

Circling Island Lake's east shore, the trail climbs to a junction overlooking Lake 10,467, where the Titcomb Basin and Indian Basin drainages converge. The more heavily used fork, the Titcomb Basin Trail, continues north; the Indian Pass Trail turns east, soon crosses the creek, and climbs into beautiful, desolate Indian Basin. Wandering past many lakes, it climbs to 12,120-foot Indian Pass (the southernmost of three Indian Passes in the vicinity) on the Divide at the basin's head. Indians built a path near the pass, but avalanches have destroyed most of their work, and when early summer snow covers bits of trail, your instincts may be more useful than sparse cairns. From the pass you can travel north across the Bull Lake Glaciers or south to Alpine Lakes Pass (see the Alpine Lakes chapter).

When descending into Indian Basin from the pass, note that the trail doesn't drop south, into Harrower Glacier's drainage, but instead crosses into Indian Basin's northerly drainage.

Titcomb Basin Trail

Island Lake to Upper Titcomb Lake—3 miles

From a junction above Island Lake the Indian Pass Trail turns east into Indian Basin, while the Titcomb Basin Trail continues north, crossing the stream that drains Indian Basin surprisingly easily and passing several small lakes before reaching the Titcomb Lakes. The trail more or less ends at the upper lake's north end (15 miles from Elkhart Park), but the valley beyond is open and travel is easy. You can reach Knapsack Col and Dinwoody Pass from upper Titcomb Basin.

Lost Lake Trail (not maintained)

Seneca Lake to Fremont Crossing—4 miles

An obscure trail leaves the Seneca Lake Trail at a signed junction just beyond Seneca Lake's upper end and heads northwest up a draw. From a height-of-land it passes several ponds, then descends to Lost Lake. At the lake's inlet it crosses Fremont Creek's three channels, requiring wading that can be impossible in early season.

The trail continues indirectly to Fremont Crossing, first heading up lower Moya Canyon, then, where the canyon forks in a meadow, turning sharply and climbing east. Crossing a saddle, it rejoins Fremont Creek at what the map shows as a swamp, though it's actually a healthy pond. A side path leads to noisy Big Water Slide at the pond's outlet. The main trail rounds the pond to the north and crosses wet ground to meet the Highline a few hundred feet north of the Highline's Fremont Crossing bridge.

The trail is easily followed, except at Lost Lake's three-channel inlet and in Moya Canyon, where cairns are helpful in locating its divergences, in both directions, from the streamside meadow. However, in terms of ups and downs, as well as distance, the Lost Lake Trail makes an inefficient route from Seneca Lake to the northern Highline, and Lost Lake, lost in a hole, offers little of the usual Wind River scenery.

Fremont Creek Canyon Route

Long Lake to Lost Lake—8 miles

Brush, cliffs, deadfall, and ubiquitous boulders large and small make the canyon of Fremont Creek less an adventure than a punishment. The gorge's rugged grandeur goes unappreciated, as obstacles at hand require full attention.

To follow the creek's northwest side, you must either cross Long Lake's outlet or descend the Pine Creek Canyon Trail to the bridge below the confluence of Fremont and Pine Creeks, then cross Pine Creek. On the creek's southeast side, cliffs next to Long Lake and the stream entering Gorge Lake from Seneca and Hobbs Lakes are obstacles. Occasionally you pass a lost campsite in an infrequent clearing, marking the day's end of some wretch's humbling efforts. The worst section is near the outlet of Suicide Lake (named not for an event but for the temptation), where you can progress less than a mile in a day of knee-straining toil.

At high water the only creek crossing seems to be at Upper Long Lake's outlet. You can, though, escape from Gorge Lake to Hobbs Lake and the amenities of a trail. Eventually you reach Lost Lake; since the Lost Lake Trail crosses Fremont Creek at the inlet, you can reach it by following either shore.

Passes

Pass 11,120+

Island Lake to Wall Lake

Wall Lake, a long body of water in a rockbound basin north of Cook Lakes, is a justly popular hiking destination from Island Lake. Follow the stream that drains the valley between Elephant Head and Mount Lester to its head, cross Pass 11,120+ northeast of Lester, and descend into Pole Creek's upper valley. The Cook Lakes Trail also reaches Wall Lake, from downstream.

Peaks

The Buttress (12,205)

Between Summer Ice Lake and Twins Glacier is this spur of Winifred Peak that ends in bluffs above Upper Titcomb Lake. No one hikes to upper Titcomb Basin to do short climbs to minor summits, but low cliffs are handy for days when you don't want to commit to bolder ventures. Four routes are mentioned; several others can't be located well enough.

1. Northwest Ridge (I 3rd class) Easily gained from Summer Ice Lake, the ridge can also be reached by steep snow from Twins Glacier.

2. East Face (II 5.7) This seven-pitch route ascends cleaner rock north of the east face's prominent gullies and just right of black water streaks. A 5.10 finger crack at the top is optional.

3. Northeast Ridge (I 5.2) Climb the east face's right edge by scrambling up right on slabs to a steep wall, traversing right to a chimney that splits the wall, ascending the chimney in one lead, and continuing up easy slabs.

4. North Gully (WI 2) An easy three-pitch ice route ascends a finger of Twins Glacier. Rock can be used for protection and anchors.

Henderson Peak (13,115)

Three converging ridges separating three glaciated faces is classic alpine architecture, but Henderson's broken rock has resulted in its being ignored in favor of its taller cohorts across the way. Kenneth Henderson, who led the first ascent, pioneered a dozen other routes in the Peak Lake, Dinwoody, and Titcomb areas and wrote the first Wind River guidebook.

1. Southeast Ridge (II 4th class) You cross much scree en route, but parts of the ridge are spectacular. From Summer Ice Lake, hidden northwest of Upper Titcomb Lake, gain the glacier to the southwest and diagonal to the southeast ridge's low point. Beyond a knife-edged section of the ridge, traverse left to a chimney. Above the chimney, traverse left again to a gully and follow it to a false summit. Easy scrambling then leads to the true summit.

The ridge has also been traversed from Garnick's Needle.

2. East Couloirs (I easy 5th class) This route's history isn't the usual saga of triumph and jubilation. After the peak's first ascent, the climbers descended the north ridge for 100 feet, dropped east down a couloir until it ended, traversed south and descended another couloir, then continued to traverse and descend couloirs. The party was large and the hour late, so they rappelled the final section in the dark. A rope stuck, so the pitch was climbed the next day to retrieve the rope.

3. North Ridge (II 4th class) A classic, despite its out-of-the-way location. Beginning from the American Legion col (reached from either Summer Ice Lake or Upper Jean Lake), Henderson's *North Ridge* route offers 0.5 mile of solid rock, exposure, routefinding challenges, and frequent 3rd-class moves (defined as "requires use of handholds and footholds; the consequences of a fall are such that an unsteady climber will feel more secure if he or she uses a rope.") The occasional moves that might qualify as 5th class are situated just above big ledges.

4. West Face (I 3rd or 4th class) Ascend the rubble-strewn face to meet the north ridge near the most prominent gendarme.

5. South Face (II 5.5) Eight pitches.

Garnicks' Needle or Great Needle (12,710)

Rising 0.4 mile southeast of Henderson Peak, between it and the Titcomb Needles, is a summit more significant than the Needles yet not a full-fledged peak. Approach all five routes by circling south of Summer Ice Lake.

1. West Face (I 3rd or 4th class) From the col south of the needle, traverse across the west face at the level of the col until past the summit, then climb to the north ridge.

2. South Ridge (I 3rd class) Climb a gully to the col south of the needle. Ascend the ridge to a huge fin that is turned to the west.

3. Southeast Face (I 5.1) The first ascent of the peak was by this route. Zigzag up 3rd-class ledges until they end and the face steepens. A few roped pitches lead to the summit.

4. East Ridge (II 5.8) Approach from south of the ridge and ascend obvious ramps and cracks.

5. Northeast Face (II 5.6 A1) Begin this twelve-pitch route by angling right up a ramp that leads to the face's center.

Titcomb Needles (12,520+)

The highest of the Needles is located 0.7 mile south-southeast of Henderson Peak. Spire, aiguille, needle—words that quicken a climber's heart. Climbers have been attracted to Titcomb Basin solely by the name Titcomb Needles. Drawn by visions of slender pinnacles in an alpine setting, they find that the Needles are simply a jagged ridge west of Titcomb Basin. Robert Underhill wrote after climbing several of them in 1939, "The most that can be said for them is that they offer a very pleasant bit of exercise under mildly exposed conditions."

The southern Needles are aligned southwest-northeast, the northern ones southeast-northwest; the spire at the angle is Vertex Point. The small point north of Vertex is the Thimble; the next one north, with three prongs, is the Trident. Underhill called the first pinnacle south of Vertex "Point 1" and the others "Minor Needles."

Approach the Titcomb Needles from Upper Titcomb Basin by way of Summer Ice Lake; cross Garnicks' Needle's east ridge to a bench from which you can reach the cols separating the various spires.

1. Trident, South Ridge (I 4th class) The three prongs can be climbed in succession from the col to the south. After climbing the southern prong, descend to the south, then turn west before regaining the ridge. Climb the north prong by ledges on its east side.

2. Trident, East Face (II 5th class) This route follows the northern of two couloirs on the east face. A pitch on slabs below the couloir and three up the couloir's steep, loose rock lead to the crest south of the Trident. Climb the central prong's northeast face; one pitch on good rock and scrambling lead to the top.

3. The Thimble (I 3rd class) Climb this spire from either its north or south col, by way of the east face.

4. Vertex Point (I 3rd class) From the southwest.

5. Point 1 (I 3rd class) From the north and east.

6. Minor Needles An ascent of the northern one was reported.

Point 12,560+

Point 12,560+ stands west of Upper Titcomb Lake. The ridge continuing south from the Titcomb Needles comprises several undistinguished summits and a number of small domes, before ending in cliffs above Island Lake. The term *minor Titcomb Needle* has roamed up and down this ridge and made climbing accounts hard to interpret. Since the summits and domes are even less needle-like than the Titcomb Needles, the term is restricted here to the cluster due west of Upper Titcomb Lake.

1. Southwest Slope (I 2nd class) Approach from Lower Titcomb Lake by the admirable draw also used to approach Point 12,450.

2. Northeast Face (I 2nd/3rd class) From Upper Titcomb Lake.

Point 12,450

The next of the nondescript summits on the ridge between the Titcomb Lakes and Jean Lakes, due west of the outlet of Upper Titcomb Lake.

1. Southeast Slope (I 2nd class) The long southeast-facing draw, conspicuous from lower Titcomb Basin, that extends from the basin floor to the saddle between

Points 12,450 and 12,560+ makes a most pleasant way to gain 2,000 feet, mixing grass, bedrock, boulders, and perhaps snow. The main Titcomb Basin stream is usually most easily crossed by the peninsula that splits Lake 10,548.

You can also approach the draw from Lower Jean Lake, passing through the col between Points 12,450 and 12,161.

Point 12,161

The peaklet west of Lower Titcomb Lake can be reached from Island Lake or Lower Jean Lake by a pleasant hike past meadows, domes, and ponds at the ridge's south end, or by a long slope above Lower Titcomb Lake.

1. South Gully (I 3rd class) The chute facing Lake 11,092 is direct, unexposed, and easy, but is a good example of a bad scree gully.

2. South Face (II 5.7) Climb a big dihedral to a belay spot below a prominent roof. Turn the roof to the left. Finish with two easy 5th-class pitches.

3. North Ridge (I 3rd class) Reach this pleasantly exposed ridge from the bowl facing Titcomb Basin.

Spearhead Pinnacle (13,200+)

On the Divide between Doublet and Helen are two easily overlooked pinnacles. Spearhead is the northern one, Forked Tongue the southern.

1. North Ridge (I 5.3) Reach the Doublet-Spearhead col from Helen Glacier. Spearhead is a short climb from the col.

Forked Tongue Pinnacle (13,200+)

1. North Ridge (II 5.3) Climb this pinnacle from the Spearhead-Forked Tongue col, reached from Spearhead by rappel.

Descent: You can descend by three long, complicated rappels to the west, but rappelling east to Helen Glacier would probably be easier.

Mount Helen (13,620)

One of the range's most interesting peaks has something for everyone: easy snow, an old classic, a big wall, and difficult ice. Much of the interest focuses on the three towers west of the summit. Tower 1 rises from Titcomb Basin in a sheer 1,500-foot face flanked by pleasing arêtes; it is separated from Tower 2 by a couloir that provides the range's premier ice route. Several routes ascend Tower 1. From Tower 1 you can continue to the main summit by the *Tower Ridge* route or descend (see below).

1. Southeast Couloir-East Ridge (I 4th class) A tongue of Sacagawea Glacier fills a high bowl between Helen's east and south ridges. Reach the glacier from Titcomb Basin by ascending talus or snow to the col south of Helen. From high on the glacier, several couloirs extend toward the east ridge. Unless late-summer bergschrunds limit

Mount Helen

Jackson Peak

Fremont Peak

Mt. Sacagawea

Tower 1

4
5
6
7
8
9

your options, the least unpleasant couloir is the one that nearly reaches the ridge just left of the two largest (reddish) towers. The east ridge is jagged and exposed.

2. East Ridge The first ascent of Helen was made from Helen Glacier, northeast of the peak, by climbing rock to the east ridge and following the ridge.

3. Northwest Face, Left Gully (II 3rd or 4th class) Two snow gullies facing Titcomb Basin break the northwest face. The left one ends on the north ridge; follow the ridge to the summit.

4. Northwest Face, Right Gully (II 3rd or 4th class) This gully, slightly harder than the left one, ends nearer the summit.

5. Northwest Face–La Mirada de la Gitana *(The Look of the Gypsy;* III M6 5.8 AI 3) This 2,500-foot route ascends the center of the face between the *Right Gully* and *Tower 1 Gully.* The lower terrain features M4 mixed steps interspersed with snow. The upper face is steeper, with an M6 chimney system to the left and a rock pitch above that takes you right to a black dike and back left on golden rock with excellent cracks (5.8). A gully to the left then leads to an intersection with the top of Tower Ridge.

6. Tower 1 Gully (IV AI 3+). The north-facing couloir between Towers 1 and 2 appears especially fearsome when viewed from Dinwoody Pass. With ten pitches and steepness up to 60 degrees, Tower 1 Gully is the Wind Rivers' classic ice route. It is comparable in length and difficulty to the Grand Teton's *Black Ice Couloir,* though never as hard as the *Black Ice's* crux. You can anchor belays in adjacent rock.

Mount Helen

Tower 1

Tower 2

11

8

9

7. Tower 1, Northwest Ridge (III 5.8 A1) A nice eleven-pitch route follows the ridge between *Tower 1 Gully* and Tower 1's west face. The last two pitches are the steepest and hardest, requiring some aid.

8. Tower 1, West Face Left (V 5.11a) Titcomb Basin's premier wall is a 1,500-foot triangular face unblemished by large ledges or gullies. An excellent eleven-pitch route begins from the main ramp that slants up left from the center of the wall's base. The first pitch is medium 5th class, the second pitch 5.8. The third pitch passes a ceiling, above which are loose blocks, and the fourth also passes a ceiling. The seventh pitch angles right, and the eighth back left to a ledge where the first ascent team bivouacked. The pitch above the bivouac ledge is the crux—a right-facing fingertip crack. The climb ends near the left edge of Tower 1's flat top.

9. Tower 1, West Face Center (V 5.10 A2) This route follows the continuous crack system, the upper part of which is a left-facing dihedral that reaches a step to the right of the face's high point.

The first four pitches are free; the first follows a corner to the top of a small pedestal. Halfway up the wall is a series of ledges. A steep pitch above the ledges leads to three possibilities. The right-hand alternative, directly above, leads to a bolt, hidden from the belay ledge, that protects a difficult traverse left. Aid leads to fine free climbing; higher, the steepening dihedral reaches overhangs near the top. The pitch through the overhangs, the route's crux, begins with an overhanging crack that reaches an alcove and continues above it in the same system. Near the top, traverse right to the face's right edge and climb two pitches to the top of Tower 1.

The first ascent team took over two days. They used nuts up to 3 inches, with extras in mid-range, and pitons that included a knifeblade.

10. Tower 1, West Face Right (III 5.6) A long system of chimneys near the face's right edge surprised the first ascenders with its lack of difficulties.

11. Tower Ridge (III 5.7) An elegant classic that has stood the test of time—first climbed in 1946 and still admired. It reaches the main summit by way of the three towers on Helen's west ridge.

The route ascends Tower 1 by its 1,000-foot south ridge. Reach the ridge by crossing the snow gully that separates Tower 1 from the other towers. A detailed recipe for the clean, enjoyable ridge is not feasible for two reasons: Much of the climbing is of a difficulty near a typical climber's threshold for wanting a rope, and many ledges cross the ridge, making variations frequently possible between ledges; no one could presume to have worked out the best route. Suffice to say that the first several hundred feet are 3rd and 4th class, and that the first distinctly 5th-class pitch involves slabs. Two pitches farther is the route's nicest pitch, with a 5.6 crack.

In general, work right up the ridge, aiming not for Tower 1 but Tower 2. While you can traverse high under gendarme-crowned Tower 2 (or climb it by a fine 5.7 crack), traversing lower and arriving directly at the Tower 2–Tower 3 notch avoids 300 feet of messy downclimbing to this notch. Scramble left around Tower 3 to the base of the 400-foot summit tower. Many routes have been tried on the summit tower, including following the loose chute to the left nearly to its top, but all seem to entail a hard move—the route's crux—near the top.

12. South Ridge Gain the south ridge from the west by a couloir that reaches the ridge three pinnacles from the top. Bypass the upper two pinnacles and reach the summit by a gully east of the ridge.

Descent: While the *Southeast Couloir-East Ridge* is the usual descent route, you can glissade both northwest gullies until late summer, when they become icy. Beware of rockfall, though.

From Tower 1 you can descend southwest, near *Tower Ridge*'s lower section, by a combination of downclimbing and rappelling. The south-facing gully between Towers 1 and 2 has also been descended.

Mount Sacagawea (13,569)

While Lewis and Clark were spending the winter of 1804–05 in North Dakota, learning what they could about the land and people to the west, they hired a trader named Charbonneau as an interpreter. He had a young woman, perhaps seventeen years old, who had been captured from the Shoshones five years before by raiding Minnetarees. The explorers learned that an overland journey would be required to reach the Columbia from the Missouri, and that the country to be crossed was inhabited by Shoshones, who had an ample supply of horses. So Sacagawea accompanied the expedition, with her newborn son Baptiste strapped to a packboard on her back. The first Shoshones encountered were her band, and the chief was her brother. While Sacagawea is usually pictured as a guide, her main contribution was teaching the men how to adapt to the country.

The peak named for the Shoshone girl is the central summit of the triumvirate on Titcomb Basin's east wall, but from the basin it isn't obvious which of the points along the skyline it is. Sacagawea's summit lies just behind the northernmost point, which is the apex of a triangular face. Several routes reach the south summit, the west face of which is characterized by a wishbone-shaped arête.

1. East Side (I 4) Between the northeast spur and the long east ridge, Sacagawea Glacier is separated from the summit by just a few hundred feet of 4th-class rock. Reach the glacier from Titcomb Basin and a Helen-Sacagawea col by skirting the northeast spur.

2. Northeast Spur (I 5.0) This is the short ridge that protrudes from Sacagawea Glacier. Gain the spur by steep snow and scramble to a minor summit. Cross a col and pass a few gendarmes en route to the summit.

3. North Ridge (II 5.2) Approach from Titcomb Basin by the southern of the cols between Sacagawea and Helen. You can climb the ridge in several ways. The section of the crest just above the col has been climbed, but you can find pleasanter rock by traversing several hundred feet east on the glacier, then climbing three easy 5th class pitches. You meet the crest halfway between the ridge's major pinnacle and the summit. (There is a more difficult variation to the right of the three pitches; it reaches the crest just south of the pinnacle.) The crest's upper part is an enjoyable pinnacled ridge.

Farther left is a rubble-filled bowl that provides the easiest, though ugliest, ascent. You meet the northeast spur a few hundred feet from the summit.

4. West Face Left (V 5.7 A2) Three routes ascend the main west face—an old one left of center, a new one between the other two, and the third near the right edge. The left side of the upper wall is very steep, but ledges and flakes lead up right. From a big ledge below an overhang, traverse right to a corner, which for 20 feet requires the climb's only aid. Follow cracks to the chimney that separates the summit from a tower to its right. Rather than climb the chimney, though, cross to the tower's right edge and reach the summit via the notch between it and the tower.

5. West Face–Indian Paintbrush (IV 5.10) Starting dead center, ascend flakes for nine pitches: 5.7, 5.8, 5.9, 5.9, 5.8 chimney, 5.10 traverse with fixed nut, 5.10 off-width, 5.10 face, 5.6 gully. The left-facing dihedral turns to an overhanging off-width/chimney for which the first ascenders had no gear, so they ramped right onto the face (5.6) and finished with two 5.7 pitches on the south ridge and a scramble west to the summit.

6. West Face Right (III 5.9) This good route, marred only by occasional loose rock, contains much 5.5 to 5.8 and a short section of 5.9, all easily protected. Reach

Mount Sacagawea

the large left-facing dihedral near the face's right edge by hundreds of feet of devious scrambling. Climb the dihedral for four leads, then step around the edge of the face. The final four pitches, which include a few pleasant surprises, ascend south-facing rock just right of the edge.

7. South Summit, Northwest Face–Dixie Chickens (1,500 feet, 5.9R) Begin many hundred feet left of the *South Summit, West Face* route. While details are not available, the climbing is said to include classic hand cracks and finger cracks, loose rock, and runouts.

8. South Summit, West Face (III 5.5) The most notable feature of the face below the south summit is an arête branched like a wishbone. The route begins in the cleft between the main peak and the south summit, then angles up and right to the wishbone's left branch, reached a few hundred feet above a snow-bearing pocket. The route then crosses to the right branch and ascends two pitches, before working back left and ending with a few leads on a ramp north of the arête.

You can also ascend the face by unroped climbing left of the wishbone, followed by three 5.6 to 5.7 leads near the top. Another variation (route 8a on map, 5.6) follows the wishbone's right branch from the bottom.

9. South Couloir (I 4th class) A steep, narrow, left-slanting gully cuts into the wall south of the south summit and promises a quick ascent of Sacagawea from Titcomb Basin. However, the gully is a horrid place, filled with unstable boulders and pulverized dust indicative of large rocks in motion. The gully's difficulty is 4th class,

Sacagawea, West Face Right

but the possibility of a rope being severed tends to limit its use. From the couloir's top, follow the crest north or traverse Fremont Glacier to the east ridge.

Fremont Peak (13,745)

The Wind Rivers' second-highest peak is so prominent from the west that it is often mistaken for the highest. This error was made as early as 1842, when John C. Fremont climbed what he believed to be the highest mountain not only in the Wind Rivers but in the Rocky Mountains.

Not only does Fremont's height attract climbers; its intricate west face does also. The peak offers both an easy opportunity to visit a high, rugged summit and several difficult rock routes. Fremont's west side is a bewildering series of walls, gullies, and towers, and orientation is necessary. The row of walls facing Upper Titcomb Lake and aligned with Sacagawea's walls is the west face. The less-steep, broken rock seen from Island Lake is the southwest face. The two faces meet at the prominent crest of the west buttress.

1. Southwest Slope (I 3rd class) A long, low ridge, rising from near Island Lake, separates Indian Basin from Titcomb Basin. You can reach the grassy saddle where this ridge abuts the main peak either from Mistake Lake, linking ledges and gullies, or— far easier and pleasanter—from Indian Basin by a long slope of snow and/or grass.

Leave the Indian Pass Trail either just before crossing the outlet stream of the lake whose elevation is slightly under 11,000 feet (north of Point 11,218) and follow the lake's west shore, or continue on the trail for another mile, leaving it where it turns east above Lake 11,008.

You can wander up the final 1,500 feet in many places, but cross a gully to its north side about halfway up. The route's popularity has caused a rubble-free path or two to evolve. The number of cairns—many not near a path worth following—is a blight on the mountainside; use a less obtrusive means to commemorate your passage.

2. Thin Red Line (II 5.7/5.8 or 5.10a) A shallow bowl separates the southwest slope from the orange spur to its right. The most prominent feature in this bowl is a crack, right of center, that intersects the spur at a minor notch. This crack makes a good climb in an unlikely place: high on Fremont's otherwise gentle side.

Following a 4th-class approach pitch, climb the crack in four pitches (5.7, 5.10a, 5.8, 5.8). You can avoid the 5.10a by climbing to its right. Small stoppers are especially useful.

3. Orange Spur (III 5.7) Several hundred feet right of the *Southwest Slope* route, forming the south face's left edge, is a prominent spur; part of it, when properly lit, appears orange. Climb the wall just left of the spur's crest by two 4th-class leads, three 5th-class pitches in a flared crack, and a few more 4th-class leads.

4. South Face (II 4th or 5th class) This route ascends a minor gully right of the orange spur but left of Five-Finger Couloir. Where the gully ends, 500 feet below the summit, cross Five-Finger and climb loose rock to the southeast ridge, which you reach two gendarmes from the summit. You can also continue up Five-Finger's left side.

Fremont Peak

5. Five-Finger Couloir (II Snow 4) From the southern Wind Rivers, Fremont is identifiable by a snow couloir, with several branches immediately below the summit suggesting the couloir's name. However, while Five-Finger Couloir may be conspicuous from 30 miles away, it is invisible from Island Lake and even much of Indian Basin, deeply inset and hidden behind ribs and buttresses. Nevertheless, until late summer its 1,500 feet offer as good a snow route as is accessible from Island Lake. Being south-facing, though, in late summer its lower half melts rather than turning icy. While a distant view suggests a slope of constant angle, the slope varies considerably, the steepest being perhaps 45 degrees.

Approach by leaving the Indian Pass Trail above Lake 11,008 and scrambling into the bowl between Fremont and Jackson, passing a few lesser couloirs that cut into the buttresses left of Five-Finger Couloir. At the couloir's top the left-most finger ends just left of the summit; the next finger, just right.

While a small selection of nuts enables you to belay on adjacent rock, with a few pickets (or good snow for axe belays) you can avoid detours to the wide couloir's walls. However, with the couloir continually slanting left, you can minimize what little rockfall danger there may be by climbing near its right side.

6. Southeast Ridge (II 5th class) Bull Lake Glacier almost reaches the crest and offers easy access to the ridge. (You can reach the glacier from Indian Basin by gullies leading to notches in the Fremont-Jackson ridge.) Gendarmes on the ridge are more easily climbed than circled. You can reach the ridge closer to the summit by 4th-class rock above the glacier.

7. Northwest Ridge (I Snow/Ice 4th or 5th class) Upper Fremont Glacier rises nearly to the ridge. You can reach the ridge from the glacier by any of several snow couloirs, the most commonly climbed couloir being the second north from the summit. The route's principal problem is usually the bergschrund, though the 45-degree slope above becomes ice in late summer.

8. West Face, Northern Buttress (III 5.9) This route ascends a buttress with large gullies on either side, near the north end of Fremont's west face; between the buttress and the west spire is another buttress. Begin in a flared chimney and after four pitches leave the dihedral and traverse left to ledges on the crest. After twelve pitches, traverse to the gully on the left. Carry protection for a 4.5-inch crack.

9. West Face Spire (IV 5.10 plus rappels) South of the Fremont-Sacagawea col are two or three buttresses, then a buttress with a slim, wedge-shaped face that narrows to a skyline spire. This face is set slightly behind the curving edge of the face to its left. Halfway up the face a ramp slants up from right to left. An eleven-pitch route ascends this face to the top of the spire, then continues to the summit.

Several hundred feet of scrambling lead to the beginning of difficulties, near the face's right edge. Reach an alcove, below and right of the ramp, after several pitches. A pitch described as "spectacular, exposed, and difficult" leads out to a prow. Next, climb up and work left to the ramp. Follow the ramp, then climb to the top of the spire.

Fremont Peak

Jackson Peak

After a short rappel to the notch behind the spire, climb the route's hardest pitch, which reaches the crest. Descend to Fremont Glacier and reach the summit by the northwest ridge.

10. West Face Dihedral (IV 5.9 A1) The next wall to the right of the spire has as its right edge the west buttress. The center of the wall is split by a very straight corner. Reach the dihedral by traversing right and face climbing; follow it for about nine pitches. A roof and thin crack low on the route require a bit of aid. Beware of a 5.8 move on the approach.

11. West Face–Dark Side of the Moon (IV 5.10 plus rappel) Starting in a seeping black cave, climb three easy pitches to vertical flakes. Two 5.9 pitches lead to an unusable seam, which can be avoided by a 5.10 traverse right to an arcing left-facing dihedral. Four lovely pitches of crack climbing (5.7, 5.9, 5.8, and as exposed a 5.10 traverse as you could hope for) get you to where the dihedral pinches off. Rappel 40 feet into the next dihedral north. Two more pitches, 5.8 and 5.7, take you to a summit scramble.

As the name suggests, this is a shady climb, except for the last two pitches.

12. West Buttress (IV 5.10) The west buttress is the narrow rib at the right edge of the west face; to its right are a deep cleft and broken, more southerly facing rock. You can avoid the buttress's lower section by starting to the left and ascending slabs and gullies up right toward the buttress.

On the first pitch, make a difficult downward traverse to the right. On the second pitch, climb to a lone dihedral. The crux is two-thirds of the way up the route—an off-width on the ridge's north side, which the first ascent party may have bypassed by a ramp to the left and a pendulum. As the buttress narrows and leans back, routefinding becomes simpler, and climbing becomes easier.

13. Southwest Face, Red Tower (II 5.6) A deep couloir separates the west buttress from the southwest face. Right of the couloir, near the southwest face's left edge and about halfway up, is a reddish tower. Approach either by traversing across from the saddle below the southwest slopes or by climbing up from Mistake Lake. Several 4th- and 5th-class pitches in the chimneys and cracks of the couloir's right fork lead up the tower's north side to the notch between the tower and the ridge that curves up to the main peak. Cross to the ridge's right side and either regain the ridge and ascend it or follow the couloir south of the ridge.

14. Southwest Face, Red Tower Arête (6 pitches, 5.10) A dangerously loose grunge pitch, several gorgeous 5.8 crack pitches, a difficult off-width, and a knife-point summit.

Jackson Peak (13,517)

Most people see Jackson from the south, as merely the peak to the right of Fremont in the postcard view. Summiteers on Dinwoody Glacier peaks or Mount Helen, however, see Jackson's north side and possibilities for ice climbing.

Jackson Peak, North Face, Central Couloir

Two Jacksons were prominent in local history. David Jackson, for whom Jackson Hole is named, was one of the first trappers and a partner of Smith and Sublette. William Henry Jackson, for whom this peak is named, was one of the West's first great photographers. He worked for the Hayden Survey and in 1878 took part in the second ascent of Fremont Peak.

1. Southeast Ridge (I 2nd class) Leave the Indian Pass Trail a mile west of the pass, at the highest lake, and ascend a left-rising broken ramp to the main saddle in the ridge. The joy of the ridge, mostly snow, should compensate for the brokenness of the ramp.

2. North Face, Left Couloir (III Ice 5th class) Rising from Bull Lake Glacier are two wide, moderately angled couloirs and a narrow one. The left one, perhaps too wide to be called a couloir, reaches the southeast ridge 0.25 mile east of the summit. A nice seven-pitch ice climb ascends the couloir. Its width and position minimize the risk of rockfall that adds zest to many ice routes, though its width precludes the pleasures of rock belays.

3. North Face, Central Couloir (III Ice 5th class) To the left of the right couloir is this narrower one, which should be accessible even when bergschrunds block the main couloirs.

4. North Face, Right Couloir (III Ice 5th class) Another wide couloir reaches the southeast ridge near the summit. It offers an ice climb of much the same length, difficulty, and character as the left couloir.

Jackson Peak

5. South Buttress (III 5.8) The south face can appear flat, but a closer look reveals a distinct buttress, which offers a long, complex climb. Its dozen pitches involve scrambling, difficult climbing, loose rock, sound rock, and opportunity for creative routefinding. A dihedral in the lower part has been climbed past a rotten overhang to a notch, and above, nice face climbing has been done near the buttress's right edge. From the buttress's top, scramble along a ridge and work up a gully to the summit snowfield.

6. South Gullies (I 3rd class) The first definite ascent of Jackson was made by the rubble gully on the right side of the south buttress. From the col between the buttress and the main peak, follow another gully to the summit snowfield.

Knife Point Mountain (13,001)

Southeast of Indian Pass runs a serrated ridge, the Divide's last glory before settling into a broad plateau. The ridge resembles a saw blade more than a knife point; a pinnacle near Indian Pass may have inspired the name. (It has also been imagined to be the Indian's feather.) The summit's location has mystified an occasional party; it is at the junction of the southwest ridge and the Divide ridge.

1. South Slope (I 3rd class) The slope at the head of Pole Creek can be easily ascended in a number of places. You can approach from Indian Basin by crossing the saddle in the Knife Point–Ellingwood ridge at the head of Ellingwood (Harrower) Glacier.

The slope leads to the Divide ridge a few hundred feet east of the summit. The summit tower is the only part of the ascent as difficult as 3rd class. When descending, begin by circling east to avoid a rubble gully.

2. Northwest Ridge (II 5.4) The mountain was first climbed by this ridge, though the ridge was gained from Knife Point Glacier some distance from Indian Pass. In making the entire 0.5-mile traverse from Indian Pass, stay right of the stiletto-like point. Most of the ridge involves unroped scrambling; most difficulties occur while downclimbing the east sides of towers. Bypass the ridge's most formidable tower, about halfway along, by ledges on the south side.

3. Southwest Ridge This ridge can be ascended from the saddle crossed by the Indian Basin approach to the south gully. Pass a large, rotten gendarme on its southeast.

Nebraska Point (12,935)

Knife Point's east ridge extends for 0.5 mile of small pinnacles, culminating in the knob of Nebraska Point, where the Divide bends south. Looming over Upper Alpine Lake, Nebraska Point's virtue is the overview of the Alpine Lakes drainage.

1. West Ridge (I 4th class) The array of pinnacles appears formidable from the Pole Creek side, but to the north is a curiously gentle basin, which allows you to stroll a few hundred feet below the crest. Where to regain the crest depends on routefinding intuition, on the amount of snow, and on whether you have an ice-axe. While an axe seems essential only in early summer, the pinnacles are distinctly thrilling.

Peak 12,480+

Peak 12,480+ is located 0.5 mile south-southeast of Knife Point Mountain. A minor spur extends south from the Knife Point–Nebraska Point ridge, splitting the head of Pole Creek valley. A hogback on the spur rises over 300 feet from the saddle between it and the ridge.

1. North Ridge (I 4th class) Eight easy leads.

Not Notch Pinnacle (12,760+)

At the Ellingwood massif's northeast end, situated 0.3 mile northeast of Ellingwood's summit, stands this serrated, double-summited formation. The southwestern summit is the higher.

1. North Face (III 5.7) Each of the seven pitches has character in some pleasant way or another, and each is 5.6 or 5.7.

Avoid a slab traverse on the approach by scrambling over a broken knob. Begin climbing near the face's left edge, where two cracks split a roof 15 feet up. Pass the roof, angle left using discontinuous cracks, and belay 100 feet up behind a mini-pinnacle. Climb to the most prominent right-facing dihedral; belay above the dihedral in a broken area to the left. Regain the face's center using black knobs and follow a crack amid the knobs. Continue up thin cracks and knobs. Climb a crack near an arête and left of a left-facing corner to a belay on a large block under an overhang, just left of a deep chimney.

Climb a thin crack near the crest to the left, step right across the chimney, and ascend 4th-class rock to a spacious ledge. Scramble up right to a double off-width. Above, connect splendid thin cracks to reach a ledge in a niche in the narrowing prow. Step left to fist cracks or climb the face straight up; after 20 feet the going is easy to the top.

A variation begins 100 feet right. After a 5.8 start, climb 100 feet of seams and hand cracks, step right to a left-facing corner, and face climb to a small ledge. Turn a triangular roof to the right, followed by nice face climbing to dirty ledges. A large left-facing corner leads to a merger with the previously described route.

Descent: From just east of the summit, rappel 150 feet into the main north-facing dihedral/gully. Downclimb for several hundred feet, wandering on exposed ledges and being vigilant for loose rock, until you can traverse 50 feet north to a rectangular pinnacle and rappel 160 feet to the ground. The ascent route deserves a better descent route.

Notch Pinnacle (12,720+)

This is the elegant tower on Ellingwood's northeast ridge, 0.2 mile northeast of Ellingwood and separated by sharp notches from Ellingwood and from Not Notch Pinnacle to its northeast.

1. South Gully, West Ridge Climb a gully on the Pole Creek side to the Ellingwood-Notch gap, then follow the west ridge.

2. North Gully, East Ridge (II/III 5.2/5.4 Ice 5th class) Two parallel gullies lead from Indian Basin to the notch northeast of the pinnacle. The left gully makes a good six-pitch ice climb. The average angle is perhaps 45 degrees, though the final pitch is much steeper. From the notch, ascend rock to the summit.

Ellingwood Peak or Harrower Peak (13,052)

Albert Ellingwood was an eminent Colorado mountaineer who first climbed Warren, Turret, Helen, Sacagawea, and Knife Point, as well as Middle and South Tetons. In 1926 he made the first ascent, alone, of this handsome peak 2 miles northeast of Island Lake. Since the 1930s the peak has been known to climbers and guidebooks as Ellingwood but appeared on the 1968 Fremont Peak South quad as Harrower, the name of a ranger and mayor of Pinedale who died in 1967. According to the Board on Geographic Names, the Sublette County Historical Society, in their proposal of the name Harrower, knew of no existing name. Climbers, feeling strongly about this renaming—because of fondness both for Ellingwood's historical importance and for the peak's north arête—persist in defying officialdom and using the name Ellingwood.

1. Northwest Couloir (I 3rd or 4th class) Ellingwood's account of climbing "the great couloir" rising from a "large talus fan" to the southwest ridge has caused climbers to assess

Ellingwood Peak, North Arête

Ellingwood Peak

Not Notch Pinnacle

Notch Pinnacle

Ellingwood Peak

Southwest Ridge

1

2

5

the relative greatness of a few couloirs, especially when descending from the summit. While the 1980 guide was vague regarding Ellingwood's route, the book served its noblest purpose in one of the couloirs: Benighted descending alpinists warmed themselves by burning the book (five pages at a time, as a technical detail). The moral is that the southwest ridge is a better descent route. Although longer, it is clean and easy to find.

Meanwhile, climbers give conflicting reports of triumphs and misadventures in northwest couloirs without identifying the specific couloir.

2. Southwest Ridge (I 4th class) Reach the ridge by rounding Elephant Head on either side, or from Wall Lake. Although it is the standard descent route, it is long and sometimes tricky, and you must search both sides of the crest for the easiest way.

3. Southeast Slope (I 4th class) Descending climbers have picked their way down to the bowl north of Faler Tower.

4. Northeast Ridge (II 5.1/5.3) From Notch Pinnacle.

5. North Arête (III 5.6) At times Ellingwood appears to have a single face extending from its northeast ridge to its southwest ridge, but morning and late-afternoon light reveal a north face and a west face, the line between sun and shade being an arête that isn't steep but rises from talus to summit in an unbroken 1,500-foot sweep. On the arête's left side, on the north face's right edge, is a route with a deserved reputation as Titcomb Basin's most enjoyable rock climb. The climbing, only moderately difficult, is nearly continuous 5th class; an indication of the route's character is that you seldom untie from your anchors before being put on belay.

Approach by way of Lake 10,813. Begin climbing up and left from a pair of dark buttresses that dip low into the talus, just left of a recess with a snowpatch. After a few pitches, slant left to reach the arête left of the crest. You don't need a detailed description: You can do most pitches in several ways, and once you pass the lower section, the route's upper part is in sight. Follow the narrowing arête; where it ends 200 feet from the top, either climb straight up or traverse left, climb cracks below the summit overhangs, and step left around the overhangs.

Faler Tower (12,607)

Extending south-southeast from Ellingwood and jutting into upper Pole Creek's gorge is an ugly coxcomb of unfriendly appearance and limited popularity. From Island Lake you can just see the summit behind Elephant Head. A point on the southeast ridge has been climbed as an end in itself.

1. Northwest Ridge (II 5th class) Reach the col between Faler and Ellingwood from the Ellingwood–Elephant Head col. From the Faler col, climb the rib left of an obvious chute. The climb ends with a few more-strenuous, exposed leads.

2. Southwest Face (II 5.4) From a left-leaning ramp that ends at a small waterfall, scramble on rotten rock into an amphitheater. Climb two pitches on fractured but secure rock. Above, ascend steep snow to the crest. Follow the crest until forced by gendarmes onto snow on the southwest side; continue on snow to the summit pinnacle.

3. Point 12,456, West Face (I 5.3/5.4) The subsidiary summit on the southeast ridge has been climbed by a six-pitch route that begins with a rotten couloir. The fifth pitch has been described as "a touchy, broken, overhanging face."

Elephant Head (12,160+)

The flat-topped formation a mile east of Island Lake has also been known as Cairn Peak, but the cairn that was once visible from Island Lake is gone, and maps designate it Elephant Head. Since it isn't one of the higher or handsomer peaks, its popularity must be attributed to accessibility and short routes.

1. South Gully (I 3rd class) The peak's south side is split by a Y-shaped gully that may contain snow. Climb the snow or rubble in either fork. The gully makes a quick descent route, especially when snow-filled.

2. East Ridge (I 4th class) Reach this pleasant ridge from either north or south.

3. Northeast Couloir (I 4th class) Broken rock between the east and north ridges.

4. North Ridge (I 5.2 to 5.6) You can climb the indistinct ridge rising from Lake 10,813's east end in various ways. There are nice patches of rock, but the broken terrain makes the search for worthwhile rock the main routefinding challenge.

5. Northwest Couloir (II Snow/Ice 5th class) The obvious couloir facing Titcomb Lakes involves mostly snow and ice, but you can pass a short waterfall

Titcomb Basin, Sphinx Glacier

midway by 4th-class rock to the right. Much of the couloir can be protected using adjacent rock.

6. Northwest Buttress (II 5.4 to 5.6) The buttress right of the northwest couloir forms Elephant Head's most elegant line, and the route involves seven or eight pitches of frequently interesting climbing. The route would be unequivocally recommended were your holds more obviously on bedrock. People who have climbed the buttress are certain either that the route is 5.4 or that it is 5.6. This disagreement probably reflects choices halfway up, the attractive prow being harder than east-facing ledges to the left.

7. Northwest Face–Packrat (III 5.9) Begin right of the *Northwest Buttress* route, just right of a white dike. Work right in several places, reaching the top slightly left of the upper face's most prominent left-facing dihedral.

On the first ascent, at a belay partway up, the belayer was distressed to see a packrat emerge from a crack and begin gnawing on the sling holding the anchors together.

8. West Face (II 5.8) A three-pitch route can't be located more precisely than being on the west face. The first pitch follows a sustained 5.6 crack. The second pitch ascends a 5.8 right-facing, right-leaning dihedral. The final pitch follows an easy left-trending ramp.

9. Southwest Face The summit register reports several short rock climbs. One route follows a big dihedral and is 5.6.

Mount Lester (12,342)

Southeast of Island Lake are clustered the three summits of Lester, which, though 1,000 feet lower than Divide peaks, stands out because of its bulk and isolation. The western is the highest. The view up Titcomb Basin illustrates the dictum that the best views are from peaks off main divides. Its position and size also attract storms; a disproportionate amount of lightning strikes Lester.

1. Main Peak, North Face (I Snow/Ice 3rd class) In early summer you can climb entirely on snow, passing a cliff band by a wide couloir. Later in summer the couloir turns icy.

2. Main Peak, South Ridge (I 3rd class) Wander up the pleasant slopes above Lester Pass to the jagged upper ridge. A number of pinnacles are most easily passed on the left.

3. Middle Peak, North Face (II 5.6) There are several ways to climb the face, all apparently wet and loose in places—i.e., alpine rock climbing. One mediocre variant involves climbing slabs left of center for a few pitches, then moving up a gully, also on the face's left side.

4. East Peak (Point 12,275), North Face (II 5.5 Snow 4th class) A worthwhile route starts at the face's left side, works up a line of weakness for several pitches, and finishes in a snow gully.

5. East Peak (Point 12,275), Northeast Ridge (I 3rd class) Gain the col between the East Peak and Point 11,740 from the north, via moderately steep snow or wretched rubble. The ridge above the col is pleasant scrambling.

From the same col, Point 11,740 is an especially enjoyable 3rd-class scramble on bedrock ledges and slabs.

6. East Peak (Point 12,275), South Slope (I 3rd class) From Cook Lakes via Lake 10,905.

7. Traverse of Three Peaks (I 3rd class) Originally done from west to east.

Brown Cliffs ridge, as seen from northeast

6 Alpine Lakes

Preeminent on the Wind River skyline, viewed from the west, are the Titcomb Basin peaks. Least interesting is the crest just to the south—plateau remnants that rise above 12,000 feet but lack distinctive summits. Yet behind these eroded surfaces is hidden one of the range's ruggedest areas. The peaks aren't sharp, but the valleys are cut deep and narrow by Bull Lake Creek and its Middle Fork, rimmed by massive red-brown rock, separated by steep cols. Everywhere you hear tumbling water.

Before the 1960s these valleys were known to few but the sheepherders who cajoled their wooly locusts across Hay Pass by the area's only trail. In a corner of the 1906 30-minute Fremont Peak quad—until 1968 the only topographic map—three lakes, connected incorrectly, were labeled Alpine Lakes. Closely spaced contour lines northeast of the lakes were designated Brown Cliffs. This was the only nomenclature in that corner of the map, but it described all that was known. Kipling's "something lost behind the ranges" could well be the Alpine Lakes. One of the area's salient characteristics, which you may find appealing, is its invisibility.

This obscurity attracted John Woodworth, who led groups that pioneered approaches from Elkhart Park and explored the Alpine Lakes area in 1961 and 1967. In 1961 he and his comrades pitched tents at the small lake they named Camp Lake; in 1967 they camped below Middle Alpine Lake's outlet. They made first ascents of and named the Fortress, Douglas Peak, Mount Quintet, and several points on the Brown Cliffs ridge.

The region, which includes Camp Lake and the Golden Lakes in addition to the Alpine Lakes, remains one of the Wind Rivers' least visited areas. The current map still doesn't have drainages quite right. While these lakes aren't easily reached, they are accessible from the west by six Continental Divide crossings, one about equidistant from two trailheads—with none standing out as the most convenient:

- From Elkhart Park to Middle Alpine Lake via 12,120-foot Indian Pass and 12,120-foot Alpine Lakes Pass is 18 miles, 3.5 of the miles trailless.
- From Elkhart Park to Camp Lake (which is 3 trailless miles from Middle Alpine Lake) via Wall Lake and Pass 11,960 is 19 miles, 4.5 trailless.
- From Elkhart Park to Camp Lake via Bald Mountain Basin and Pass 11,663 is 17.5 miles, with 5 trailless miles.
- From Elkhart Park to Camp Lake via 11,600-foot Angel Pass is 19 miles, 5 of them trailless.
- From Elkhart Park to Camp Lake via Bell Lakes, Timico Lake, and 11,320-foot Timico Pass is 21 miles, but the 4 trailless miles are mostly as easy as trail miles.
- From Meadow Lake (nearly 1,500 feet lower than Elkhart Park) to Camp Lake via Timico Pass is 18.5 miles, including the 4 benign trailless miles.
- From Boulder Lake (2,000 feet lower than Elkhart Park) to Camp Lake via 10,960-foot Hay Pass is 23 miles, all on trail.

This chapter includes minor summits, also remote and obscure, that rise among glaciers at the head of Bull Lake Creek's North Fork. No trails reach these glaciers, or the Alpine Lakes, from the east, though with a map and sense of adventure you can work out a route.

Also included is the area west of the Divide crossed by the Elkhart Park, Meadow Lake, and Boulder Lake approaches and drained by Pole Creek, Fall Creek, and the North Fork of Boulder Creek—a land of only a few gentle-sloped summits but many lakes, and charred trees. In 1988 a fire that began near Fayette Lake and spread east to Boulder Canyon and northeast to treeline burned some 40,000 acres. Some places are invigorating for the quick regeneration, spearheaded by fireweed, some places made morbidly fascinating by countless charred trunks, and some simply depressing. When choosing a campsite, bear in mind that burned trees are more vulnerable to wind than live trees are.

Most peaks described in this chapter, and the Alpine Lakes that lent their name to this chapter, are found on the Fremont Peak South quad. Much of the Bull Lake Glacier area is on the Fremont Peak North map. The country west of the Divide is located on the Bridger Lakes, Fayette Lake, Horseshoe Lake, Boulder Lake, Scab Creek, and Hall's Mountain quads. Another Alpine Lake lends its name to a topographic map, but you need this map only to explore eastern approaches, which may also require the Hay's Park, Bob's Lake, and Paradise Basin maps.

Trails

Highline Trail

Little Seneca Lake to North Fork Lake—19 miles

The Highline meets two trails in quick succession northeast of Little Seneca Lake: the Indian Pass Trail, heading in to Island Lake, and the Seneca Lake Trail, leading out to Elkhart Park. The Highline climbs southeast from the latter junction to the high point of its journey, 11,080-foot Lester Pass, then descends to the wooded valley of Cook Lakes, where two Highline variants diverge.

The Highline, including both variants, crosses Pole Creek four times; all these crossings can be formidable, or worse, at high water. Plan your trek to minimize crossings.

To continue on the Highline, turn right before reaching Pole Creek on a lesser trail and follow it down a small stream to a ford of Pole Creek. To reach the Fremont Trail, don't turn right but continue southeast to a different ford of Pole Creek. A few hundred yards beyond the crossing is a junction. The trail that continues southeast is the Fremont Trail, the more direct route to North Fork Lake; the trail that turns southwest, paralleling Pole Creek, is the Highline's southern variant. The variants meet near the northern variant's creek crossing.

When following the Highline upstream, the northern variant is the more obvious, leading you to the crossing, which is at the end of a level stretch, just below a steep

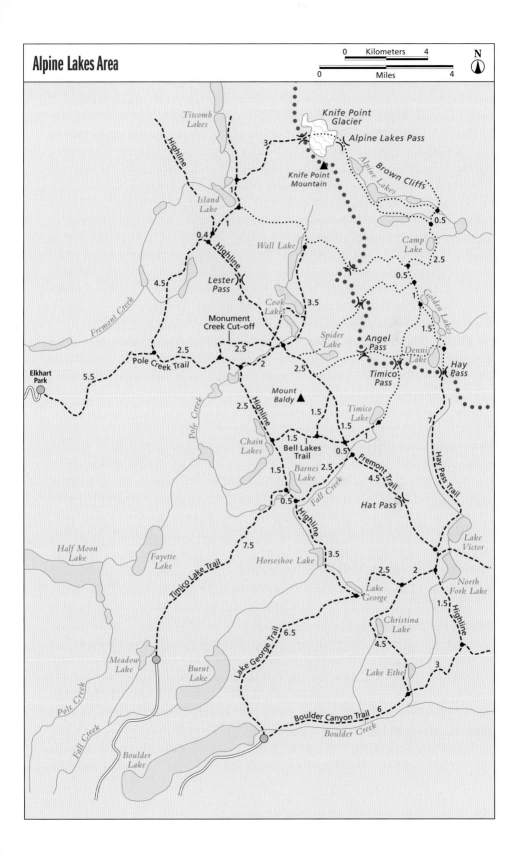

Alpine Lakes Area

0 Kilometers 4

0 Miles 4

N

Titcomb Lakes

Highline

Knife Point Glacier

Alpine Lakes Pass

3

Knife Point Mountain

Brown Cliffs

Alpine Lakes

Island Lake

1

0.4

1

Highline

Wall Lake

0.5

Camp Lake

2.5

4.5

Lester Pass

4

Cook Lakes

3.5

0.5

1

Golden Lakes

1.5

Fremont Creek

Monument Creek Cut-off

Spider Lake

Angel Pass

Dennis Lake

Hay Pass

Elkhart Park

2.5

Pole Creek Trail

2.5

1

2

2.5

Timico Pass

5.5

Pole Creek

Mount Baldy

2.5

Highline

1.5

Timico Lake

1.5

7

Chain Lakes

1.5

Bell Lakes Trail

0.5

1

Fremont Trail

Hay Pass Trail

Half Moon Lake

Fayette Lake

1.5

Barnes Lake

2.5

Fall Creek

4.5

Hat Pass

Lake Victor

0.5

Highline

7.5

Timico Lake Trail

Horseshoe Lake

3.5

Lake George

2.5

2

North Fork Lake

1.5

Highline

Meadow Lake

Lake George Trail

6.5

Christina Lake

4.5

Lake Ethel

3

Burnt Lake

Pole Creek

Fall Creek

Boulder Canyon Trail

6

Boulder Creek

Boulder Lake

slope. If heading to Cook Lakes or Bald Mountain Basin, look for the unsigned and relatively lightly trod southern trail just beyond a pond 200 feet south of the creek crossing. A sign marks this alternative's northeastern terminus, but the sign only points to destinations on other trails.

The descent by Pole Creek is enhanced by splendid mountain water, flowing and standing. However, just above Pole Creek Lakes the trail makes another wet crossing (of the wide, shallow genre), meets the Pole Creek Trail coming from the west and Elkhart Park, then again crosses Pole Creek (wide and shallow again).

Swinging southeast again, for 8 miles (to its junction with the North Fork Trail at Lake George), the Highline traverses country below 10,000 feet in which lakes are in sight more often than not (as are trees burned in 1988). Numerous side trails lead to other lakes. The Bell Lakes Trail begins at the Chain Lakes. Near Barnes Lake's outlet is a junction with the eastern, uphill section of the Timico Lake Trail and, 0.5 mile farther, with the Timico Lake Trail coming from the Meadow Lake trailhead to the west. Between this junction and Horseshoe Lake, equally used Highline versions follow both sides of Fall Creek; their creek crossings are comparable.

The Highline no longer circles the west shore of Horseshoe Lake, as some maps indicate; it has been rerouted along the east shore. South of the lake (and several hundred feet south of the junction shown on maps), the Horseshoe Lake Trail joins, offering a direct route to Boulder Lake.

The Highline has also been relocated slightly uphill (west) between Horseshoe Lake and Lake George and on the latter's west shore. The circuitous leg from a junction with the North Fork Trail south of Lake George to North Fork Lake also begins with a relocation: The trail doesn't circle north, as on the Horseshoe Lake quad, but south. A further relocation occurs north of Mac's Lake: The Highline no longer turns abruptly south toward the lake but continues east, meeting the Lake Ethel Trail well north of Mac's Lake and remaining north of Mac's Creek.

West of North Fork Lake is an unsigned junction from which the Hay Pass Trail diverges north and the Highline southeast. This continuation of the Highline is described in the Middle Fork Lake chapter.

Monument Creek Route

Monument Creek to Pole Creek—2.5 miles

While the identity of the peak climbed by Fremont in 1842 has provoked debate, his route from Boulder Lake to Island Lake has avoided scrutiny. The numerous hills, streams, and lakes he passed the first day may resist identification—especially after the 1988 fire—but evening found him in a small valley "smoothly carpeted with a soft grass, and scattered over with groups of flowers," and the next morning he reached a pass at the valley's head, where "a gigantic disorder of enormous masses, and a savage sublimity of naked rock" suddenly came into view. The only features that fit Fremont's descriptions are Monument Creek's valley and the 11,120-foot saddle at its head.

Although modern maps don't indicate it, a well-beaten path leads from the Pole Creek Trail, near Monument Creek, up the valley to the pass, and another path leads cross-country from Monument Creek to Pole Creek. The pass—from which you can descend to Little Seneca Lake, as Fremont apparently did—may be of interest only to those seeking an alternative to the Seneca Lake Trail. However, the route from Monument Creek to Pole Creek is a more efficient way to Cook Lakes and Bald Mountain Basin than descending the Pole Creek Trail to Pole Creek Lakes and following the Highline up Pole Creek. Although the Forest Service may classify this cutoff as a "bootleg trail," it is represented on the Fremont Peak quadrangle of 1906, making it at least as old as the U.S. Forest Service.

Leave the Pole Creek Trail at the west side of a pond 0.25 mile west of Monument Creek. Cross Monument Creek 0.5 mile upstream and head east, passing just south of a Y-shaped pond and staying in open country where possible, passing north of two other large ponds and reaching Pole Creek slightly north of the Fremont Peak South quad's "Pole." Follow Pole Creek upstream to the Highline's western variant.

Cook Lakes Trail

Highline Trail to Wall Lake—3.5 miles

Slightly east of the divergence of the Fremont and Highline Trails at the upper Pole Creek crossing, a trail turns upstream, rounds the south end of the lower Cook Lake, passes the upper Cook Lake on the east, and ascends a small valley to the north. The trail peters out, as shown on the topographic map, though not because hikers turn back but because so much travel is on bare rock that you neither need nor wear a trail. By following the valley's west branch to a minor divide (featuring a tarn), you reach Wall Lake near its south end, or you can continue up the main valley, pass north of a 10,800-foot knoll, and reach Wall Lake 0.5 mile from its south end. Much of the east shore is glacier-polished bedrock that provides pleasant traveling to the lake's upper end.

Northwest of Wall Lake's upper end is an 11,120-foot pass from which a creek descends between Elephant Head and Mount Lester to Island Lake. This excellent terrain is well worth incorporating into an excursion or loop.

Another Cook Lakes Trail leaves the Highline northwest of the upper Pole Creek crossing, passes west of the lower Cook Lake, reaches the main lake near its midsection, and follows, as best it can, the lake's rocky southwest shore to join the main Cook Lakes Trail.

Fremont Trail

Pole Creek to North Fork Lake—9 miles

The Highline crosses Pole Creek just below Cook Lakes, turns downstream, and takes a low, circuitous route to North Fork Lake. The Fremont Trail, continuing southeast where the Highline turns down Pole Creek, offers a rugged, direct line between the same points.

The sign at the Highline-Fremont Trail junction gives Cook Lakes as the destination in the Fremont Trail's direction, but the Cook Lakes Trail soon diverges inconspicuously. The better-used Fremont Trail climbs into wide, treeless Bald Mountain Basin, then to a 10,840-foot pass northeast of Mount Baldy, descends, and ascends a 10,800-foot shoulder. Cagy hikers can circumvent this climb by a trail that passes the Baldy Lakes and meets the Bell Lakes Trail, which then leads back to the Fremont Trail near Fall Creek. From this same junction the Timico Lake Trail heads toward the mountains; beyond Fall Creek the Timico Lake Trail heads southwest toward low country.

Halfway between Fall Creek and 10,848-foot Hat Pass, near treeline, the trail was obliterated by charred 1988 deadfall, but it is now far easier to locate than it was. However, south of Hat Pass are trail-finding problems, especially for northbound hikers, who more often than not lose the trail north of Rambaud Lake. In meadows and on exposed bedrock, keep your eyes open and map in hand, and don't get too far east.

From the first junction near the northwest corner of North Fork Lake, the Hay Pass Trail heads left, toward Lake Victor, and a 0.5-mile connector crosses meadows to the south to the Highline. The Fremont Trail follows North Fork Lake's north shore, as described in the Middle Fork Lake chapter.

Bell Lakes Trail

Chain Lakes to Fremont Trail—2.5 miles

One of several connectors between the Highline and Fremont Trails, the Bell Lakes Trail has two particular uses: making Timico Lake accessible from Elkhart Park and, in conjunction with the Baldy Lakes Trail, enabling you to detour the Fremont Trail's climb over a 10,840-foot pass. The Bell Lakes Trail involves minor ups and downs, on a track that hasn't been in great shape, through pleasant if unspectacular country past several ponds, some of which presumably qualify as Bell Lakes.

Timico Lake Trail (theoretically maintained)

Meadow Lake to Timico Lake—12 miles

Beginning at an obscure trailhead and ending at a little-known lake, this trail enables you to reach the center of the Wind Rivers seeing few other visitors, and to observe the land's resilience in recovering from the 1988 Fayette Lake Fire. Much of the trail passes through acreage burned then, but the land has rebounded with an abundance of fireweed, raspberry, paintbrush, arnica, and lodgepole saplings. Indeed, charred remnants from 1988 are less an obstacle to travel and an aesthetic blight than is the unconscionable trashing of the landscape by ATVs, as far as the Wilderness boundary, where deadfall discourages vehicular traffic. This trail is not maintained as diligently as more popular trails are.

From the locked gate on the Meadow Lake Road, head east for 0.25 mile, then turn north and parallel a fence east of the road, rejoining the road after a mile (as shown on Earthwalk, Beartooth, and Forest Service maps but not the Fayette Lake quad). After following ATV ruts up through aspen groves, cross terrain interesting only for its recovery from fire. Beyond Belford Lake, though, you ascend to a series of lakes in opener country. If the creek crossing below the lake downstream from Lake Jacqueline is unsavory, find a trail that skirts this lake to the south, ascends the north side of a draw with four ponds, and descends to meet the Highline near Barnes Lake's south end.

At Barnes Lake the Timico Lake Trail meets the Highline and turns southeast, coinciding with the Highline for 0.5 mile. It then turns northeast again; a sign marks the junction, though it only points to destinations on the Highline. Locate the Timico Lake Trail by cairns in a small meadow north of Fall Creek. The trail doesn't cross and recross Fall Creek, as the Horseshoe Lake quad indicates, but follows its northwest side nearly to the Fremont Trail (met at another signboard that ignores the Timico Lake Trail). If Fall Creek isn't crossable, stay on the northwest side; 200 feet of talus is the only impediment. Follow the Fremont Trail north out of Fall Creek's main valley, then turn east in open country near a small lake and ascend a draw to Timico Lake.

From Timico Lake you can continue up the valley on well-used nontrails to Timico Pass or cross the saddle south of Roundtop Mountain via a nearly vanished former trail. Above treeline the former trail is unneeded, but at its southeastern end its disappearance is inconvenient. The Horseshoe Lake quad shows the trail descending toward the North Fork of Boulder Creek and the Hay Pass Trail but ending 0.5 mile from the creek and the trail. This seems to be a realistic portrayal. We can offer no insight on locating the trail when going from the North Fork to Timico Lake.

Lake George Trail (North Fork Trail)

Boulder Lake to Lake George—6.5 miles

Topographic maps call it the North Fork Trail, though it's far from the North Fork. (Combined with the Highline, it does offer a way to North Fork Lake, about as long as either way via Boulder Canyon.) Signboards more logically refer to it as the Lake George Trail.

From Boulder Lake's Wilderness parking area, cross Boulder Creek by a footbridge. Walk through the campground and locate a trail beyond the farthest campsites; follow it northwest (left) for a few hundred feet to a sign. (The trail here coincides with the Lowline.) After a steep mile an alternate trail that passes Blueberry Lake branches right. (A sign says RUFF LAKE TRAIL; Ruff Lake is Blueberry Lake.) The Lake George Trail soon turns north from the Lowline, which continues west to Burnt Lake. You encounter two junctions near Coyote Lake. At the first, unsigned, the Ruff Lake Trail rejoins from the south. From the second, just north of the lake, the Horseshoe Lake Trail heads north to meet the Highline, while the Lake George Trail turns east to also meet the Highline, south of Lake George.

Lake Ethel Trail

North Fork Falls to Mac's Lake—4.5 miles

Since the 1988 fire the Forest Service has resurrected and partially relocated this once-neglected trail. For reaching North Fork Lake from Boulder Canyon, it offers an alternative of comparable length to the Lake George Trail and the trail combination via Lake Vera.

The Lake Ethel Trail branches from the Boulder Canyon Trail, not below North Fork Falls as indicated on the Scab Creek quad, but above the falls (and switchbacks), just below Lake Ethel. It climbs straightforwardly from Lake Ethel past Ed's Lake, Lake Christina (passing this lake on the west, not the east as old maps indicate), Perry Lake (which it passes to the east, not the Horseshoe Lake quad's west), and Mac's Lake. Perry and Mac's Lakes don't offer decent campsites. With the Highline being relocated to the north, the Lake Ethel Trail's intersection with the Highline is several hundred feet north of its former location.

Old maps show a trail following Mac's Creek from Boulder Canyon up to Lake Christina, but it long ago left the trail system, and the 1988 fire's devastation might make relocating it no fun.

Hay Pass Trail (not maintained)

North Fork Lake to Bull Lake Creek—13 miles

When sheep were grazed more extensively than they are now (in Titcomb Basin even), sheepmen built this trail from west of the Divide to vast high grasslands northeast of the Alpine Lakes. While the trail's lower stretches are partly obscured by encroaching willows, the herders' rockwork above treeline still facilitates hiking, as do their bridges over several larger streams. When lost, the trail is generally worth relocating.

Leave the Fremont Trail at North Fork Lake's northwest corner, pass west of Lake Victor, and follow the North Fork up a long canyon to cross Hay Pass and the Divide at 10,960+ feet. Descend past Dennis Lake (just out of sight behind a minor ridge) to the chain of three Golden Lakes—Golden, Louise, and Upper Golden (golden trout were planted in them)—on Bull Lake Creek's Middle Fork. Climb to a 10,920-foot pass at the head of the defile to the north, turn east between Douglas and Quintet, and descend to Camp Lake. Campsites near the lake are mediocre, but the benches in the valley to the south abound in nice sites.

The Fremont Peak South quad shows the trail ending at a pond to the east, but actually it crosses Camp Lake's outlet by a somewhat hidden, collapsed but usable bridge and vigorously climbs the slope to the north (though camouflaged by a few large fallen trees). It then traverses 120 feet above Camp Lake, before crossing a minor pass to a valley with a pair of small, pretty lakes. The southern of these lakes offers pleasanter camping than Camp Lake. The northern is Lake 10,239, through which, contrary to maps, Lower Alpine Lake drains.

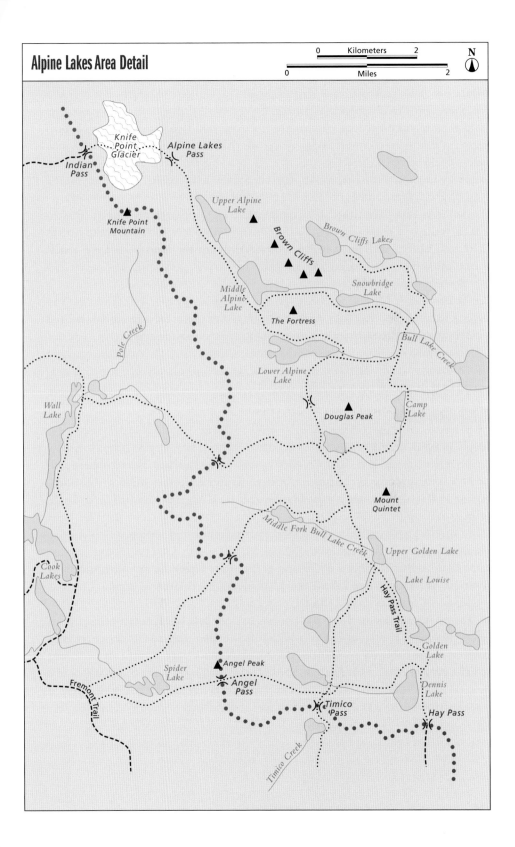

Alpine Lakes Area Detail

0   Kilometers   2

0   Miles   2

N

Knife Point Glacier

Alpine Lakes Pass

Indian Pass

Knife Point Mountain

Upper Alpine Lake

Brown Cliffs

Brown Cliffs Lakes

Snowbridge Lake

Pole Creek

Middle Alpine Lake

The Fortress

Bull Lake Creek

Lower Alpine Lake

Wall Lake

Douglas Peak

Camp Lake

Mount Quintet

Middle Fork Bull Lake Creek

Upper Golden Lake

Lake Louise

Cook Lakes

Hay Pass Trail

Golden Lake

Spider Lake

Angel Peak

Angel Pass

Dennis Lake

Fremont Trail

Timico Pass

Hay Pass

Timico Creek

After passing a little over 100 feet east of these lakes, the trail enters woods northeast of Lake 10,239 and descends steeply until it crosses the Lower Alpine Lake outlet stream just below a boomerang-shaped pond. The bridge is unusable, but logs and rocks just downstream provide a crossing.

The next section of trail, climbing to the main Bull Lake Creek, is important to locate, as it leads to a crucial bridge that spans Bull Lake Creek in a gorge 0.5 mile below Snowbridge Lake. Unfortunately, it's also the trail section most easily lost. Begin by heading northeast, but be alert, after a few hundred feet, for a long northwest diagonal. Reasonably new blazes are helpful.

North of Bull Lake Creek, bear northeast; if, 200 feet downstream and 100 feet inland, you pass a huge rusty saw blade and a small meadow, you're on route. Cairns mark switchbacks with an overall northeasterly trend that bring you to the outlet stream of the bearpaw-shaped lake northeast of Point 11,138. Cross this stream 200 feet downstream from the lake's outlet.

To continue northeast, for whatever reason, round this lake well to its east. You enter a sparsely timbered country that is a mosaic of ponds, swamps, meadows, and small outcrops; it is easy to travel through, though complex to navigate.

To ascend the valley northeast of the Brown Cliffs, cut northwest before reaching the bearpaw-shaped lake. Lake 10,590 is known as 10-Fish Lake (a generous estimate); Lake 10,980 is Brown Cliffs Lake.

Alpine Lakes Route

Hay Pass Trail to Alpine Lakes Pass—4.5 miles

To reach Lower Alpine Lake (10,895) from the Hay Pass Trail, ascend slopes south of its incorrectly mapped outlet stream from Lake 10,239. To continue to Middle Alpine Lake (10,988), either cross the Fortress's east ridge to Snowbridge Lake or, from Lower Alpine Lake's east end, pass between the lake and the Fortress. The north shore of Lower Alpine Lake, though, is not straightforward terrain, and you must climb to a bench a few hundred feet above. Middle Alpine Lake can also be reached from the Hay Pass Trail from its crossing of Bull Lake Creek, by following the creek upstream past Snowbridge Lake. Round Middle Alpine Lake to the south.

Middle Alpine Lake's west shore is easy going.

Passing Upper Alpine Lake (11,335) on its west side involves 0.5 mile of sidehilling through large boulders and tedious rubble a few hundred feet above the lake. If you're comfortable on exposed 3rd class, you can pass Upper Alpine Lake on its east side, where an elegant route has been marked with cairns past a few cruxes where ribs descend from the Brown Cliffs to the lake. (Sure-footed, liftable dogs can be portaged past the hardest part 30 feet above the lake.)

Bull Lake Glaciers from Nebraska Point

Bull Lake Glaciers Route

Indian Pass to Elsie Col or Backpacker's Pass—7 miles

The North Fork of Bull Lake Creek gathers water from several glaciers that extend nearly to the Divide east of Titcomb Basin. On the Fremont Peak North quad, these glaciers—Helen, Sacagawea, Upper Fremont, Lower Fremont, Bull Lake, and Knife Point—are collectively labeled Fremont Glaciers, but an older name—Bull Lake Glaciers—is more logical.

You can traverse these glaciers by descending Knife Point Glacier from Indian Pass, crossing Bull Lake Glacier, and continuing north. You can reach Dinwoody Glacier by either Elsie Col or Backpacker's Pass. This old-fashioned alpine excursion typically takes two days from Island Lake to Floyd Wilson Meadows. Carry ice axe, crampons, and rope.

Passes

Alpine Lakes Pass (12,120+)

Knife Point Glacier to Upper Alpine Lake

Alpine Lakes Pass is the high saddle between Knife Point Mountain and the 13,198–foot summit (Bête Noire) to its northeast. You can use this pass, in combination with Indian Pass (Titcomb Basin chapter) to reach the Alpine Lakes from Island Lake. From Indian Pass, cross Knife Point Glacier—or the site of Knife Point Glacier. Knife Point Glacier has become the poster child for glacial shrinkage. Where ten years ago you put on crampons, took ice axe in hand, and traversed glacial névé, you now negotiate recently exposed—and therefore unstable—rubble, quicksand-like mud, and gravel-embedded ice remnants furrowed with numerous rivulets several feet deep. After climbing to Alpine Lakes Pass, you once descended steep snow to Upper Alpine Lake. Now, after midsummer, the descent may be snowless. There is a pretty little campsite, as secluded as any in the range, at the upstream end of Upper Alpine Lake. To continue beyond Upper Alpine Lake, see the Alpine Lakes Route description, above.

Pass 11,960+

Wall Lake to Hay Pass Trail

You can cross the Divide from Wall Lake by an obscure saddle east of Lake 10,842 (and 0.6 mile northeast of Tiny Glacier). On the Wall Lake side, paralleling the creek flowing from Lake 10,842 and climbing to the Divide is straightforward. From the Divide you can descend to Lake 11,065, traverse its rocky north shore (see Pass 11,663), and continue to the Upper Golden Lake drainage. Or you can stay high, circling northeast (with snow varying from all to none and the plateaus's east slope intricately fractured into miniature valleys, there is no particular route), descending to Lake 10,787, and circling its south shore (unless inauspicious snow forces you to the rougher north shore) to the Hay Pass Trail.

Pass 11,663 (1.3 N Angel Peak)

Bald Mountain Basin to Middle Fork Bull Lake Creek

This pass 1.3 miles north of Angel Peak is the less obvious of two Divide crossings from Bald Mountain Basin (you can see Angel Pass from beyond Pinedale), but is nevertheless gentler than Angel Pass. However, descending the Middle Fork of Bull Lake Creek drainage is decidedly more rugged than the descent from the base of Angel Pass to Upper Golden Lake, making the routes roughly comparable.

Coming from Pole Creek, leave the Fremont Trail just before it passes a number of tiny lakes, head north of Spider Lake, and enter the canyon to the north. Turn east below Lake 10,950 and ascend steep slopes to the Divide. Descend northeast to Lake 11,065's inlet and traverse the lake's bouldery north shore. Rather than following the Middle Fork to the 0.25-mile-long lake below, cross a saddle to the north and descend a subsidiary valley. And don't try to descend the Middle Fork's cleft below this lake; follow its southeast shore and, from a pond just east of the lake, drop east to meet the Hay Pass Trail 0.5 mile above Upper Golden Lake.

Angel Pass (11,600+)

Bald Mountain Basin to Upper Golden Lake or Dennis Lake

This U-shaped gap is visible from far to the west. From the Fremont Trail, pass either north or south of Spider Lake. To avoid cliffs below the pass, zigzag between ledges, only with luck not encountering a 3rd-class move or two. The pass's east side is encumbered with several hundred feet of large blocks. (Timico Pass is far easier for backpacking.)

In the barren, silent valley east of the pass, traverse south of Lake 11,125. To reach Upper Golden Lake, turn north, descend past Lake 10,885's east shore, and continue down the east side of the lovely valley below. In the lower part of this valley, a path east of the stream facilitates travel through willows and sparse timber. To reach Dennis Lake, continue east from Lake 11,125. A path follows the northwest shore of Dennis Lake and crosses the lake's outlet. The Hay Pass Trail is just over the ridge to the east.

Timico Pass or Fall Creek Pass (11,280+)

Timico Lake to Upper Golden Lake or Dennis Lake

Above Timico Lake at the head of Fall Creek is one of the range's lower and gentler Divide crossings, yet so obscurely situated that no map has named it or implied it as a route. However, rearranged rock near Lake 11,045, an obvious path above, and Leone G. Campbell's ashes suggest a certain history. This guidebook suggests the obvious names for the pass.

While you can reach Lake 11,045, just south of the pass, by following Fall Creek upstream from Timico Lake, it is easier, if less intuitive, to reach Lake 11,045 via Lake 10,873. Lake 11,125, in the tundra between Angel Pass and Dennis Lake, lies just north of the pass. From Lake 11,125 you can descend to either Upper Golden Lake or Dennis Lake, as described under Angel Pass.

Col 11,560+

Lake 10,787 to Lower Alpine Lake

The steep scree that separates Burch and Douglas Peaks can be used as a shortcut between the Golden Lakes and Lower Alpine Lake, though not for aesthetic reasons nor, presumably, by backpackers who know what they are getting into.

Peaks

Three Brothers (12,960+)

A ridge separates Helen Glacier from Sacagawea Glacier. The ridge's high point (1.3 miles north of Mount Sacagawea) and two minor points on the ridge to the west are the Three Brothers.

1. West Ridge (I easy 5th class) The minor summits are scrambles. Climb the main summit by the buttress right of a gully on the summit's south side.

2. Northwest Ridge (II 5.6) Ascend the couloir between the west and northwest ridges, then traverse onto the northwest ridge and follow it for five or six pitches.

Mount Zebadia (12,495)

The Bonneys report ascents of this summit (2 miles northeast of Mount Sacagawea) overlooking the North Fork of Bull Lake Creek by its northwest ridge and its west ridge, with the northeast ridge party naming the peak.

Peak 13,040+

The Bonneys' guide mentions an unroped ascent of the minor summit between Upper and Lower Fremont Glaciers, a mile northeast of Fremont Peak, calling the peak Meier's Crag, after one of those making the ascent.

Peak 12,431

A vast plateau covers the northeast corner of the Fremont Peak South quad and much of the northwest quadrant of the Alpine Lakes quad. Its high point is Peak 12,431, 2.3 miles northeast of the Brown Cliffs.

1. Southeast Slope (I 1st class) Gain the plateau via the valley east of Point 11,404. Much of the final 0.5 mile is an inexplicably obvious trail.

Peak 12,730

Northeast of the Brown Cliffs rises an isolated massif with a long southeast ridge. Although gently sloping overall, this ridge presents expanses of bad rubble and is cut by a few notches. While the peak attracts few climbers, the Bonneys report an ascent of its northwest ridge.

Bête Noire (13,198)

Defining a summit, as opposed to a shoulder of a higher neighbor, is often arbitrary, never more so than with the high points of the Wind Rivers' peneplain remnants.

The objective criterion is how far it rises above its connection to higher summits. The remnant at the Brown Cliff's north end, 1.4 miles east-northeast of Knife Point Mountain, stands over 1,000 feet above Alpine Lakes Pass, its connection to a higher summit, so the highest of the rises sprinkled on the plateau qualifies as one of the range's distinct 13,000-footers. However, the massif's obscure location east of the Divide and lack of climbing objectives keep it from the list of any but the most compulsive peak bagger or curious explorer. Nevertheless, Bête Noire is feasible as a long day's excursion from Island Lake.

1. Southwest Ridge (I 2nd class) From Alpine Lakes Pass, ascend unstable scree toward Point 12,680, but before attaining this eminence, angle right to the snowfield to the east. The slope leading to Point 13,198 itself is solider than the rubble below.

Firecracker Pinnacles (12,520+)

At the north end of the Brown Cliffs ridge are two small pinnacles at a low point in the ridge. From the Brown Cliff Lakes to the east, they are visible on the horizon. The northwest pinnacle's cylindrical shape inspired the name. Approach by ascending snow gullies from the Brown Cliff Lakes valley.

1. Northwest Pinnacle (I 5.7 A1) Climb the southeast face to a chimney halfway up; follow the chimney to the top.

2. Southeast Pinnacle (I 4th class) Start on the north side and pass through a rotten chimney that splits the pinnacle. Climb to the top on the south side.

Windy Pinnacle (12,891)

This is the small pinnacle on the Brown Cliffs ridge above Upper Alpine Lake's outlet.

1. Southeast Slope (I 3rd class) Climb to the col between Windy and Tuveehant on slopes that may require ice axe and crampons. From the col, scramble easily up loose rock.

2. North Face Windy has been climbed from Lake 11,495, via the snowfield under the pinnacle.

Tuveehant Peak (12,854)

The first ascent party planned to name the broad, snow-covered summit above Middle Alpine Lake the Shoshone equivalent of Middle Alpine Peak. When they learned it would be Tuveehant Teeveeseevant Kweezooweekant, they settled for Tuveehant.

1. West Face (I 3rd class) Climb from the Windy-Tuveehant col. Short cliff bands are broken by easy chimneys.

North Wind Peak (12,440+)

Where the Brown Cliffs crest turns from southeast to east is a summit with a steep south face that towers over Middle Alpine Lake's outlet. This is North Wind Peak.

Brown Cliffs from the Fortress

1. Northwest Side (I easy 5th class) From Middle Alpine Lake, climb to the col northwest of the peak. Reach the summit in one lead.

Eagle Pinnacle (12,120+)

East of North Wind, but separated from it by an unnamed tower, is this impressive, steep-faced peak; from the east it resembles Machu Picchu. A golden eagle watched the first ascent.

1. East Ridge (I 4th class) Reach the Eagle-Hoowagant col from Snowbridge Lake by 3rd- and 4th-class slabs and chimneys. The ridge involves several leads on solid, exposed rock.

Hoowagant Pinnacle (11,845)

The name of the last major summit at the east end of the Brown Cliffs (0.4 mile north-northwest of Snowbridge Lake) is Shoshone and means "ridge's end."

1. West Side (I 4th class) A quick climb from the Eagle-Hoowagant col. A short chimney and chockstone are 3rd class, easier than the climbing below the col.

The Fortress (11,927)

The most striking formation in the area is this narrow, flat ridge standing between Middle and Lower Alpine Lakes.

1. North Slope (I 2nd class) From Middle Alpine Lake or Snowbridge Lake, ascend by way of pleasant slabs and ledges. From Lower Alpine Lake, cross a shoulder on the east ridge to reach these ledges.

2. South Face, Left Edge (I 5.5) Reach the Fortress's north ridge by climbing a face and a crack for a bit more than a rope length, then traversing off left on prominent ledges.

3. South Face Left (II 5.7) Beginning just left of the prominent system in the face's center (next route), this route diagonals up the face to the left, reaching the summit flat toward its left edge. The first pitch (4th class) angles up left. Begin the second pitch by traversing left 50 feet, then climb a steep crack, which is the route's crux. After also beginning the third pitch by working left, climb sustained 5.7 to a 3rd-class system that angles up left. After moving the belay up left, wander up 4th-class and easy 5th-class terrain.

4. South Face Center (I 5.4) Follow the obvious system in the face's center for four mostly 4th-class pitches.

5. East Face, Left Edge (I 5.8) Approach by a right-angling ramp and a left-angling 3rd/4th-class gully. Fifth-class climbing begins below an orange block, with a 10-foot crack that leads to a groove with a fixed nut. Face climb right, then pass left of the orange block. Follow a left-leaning crack to a corner and climb to a large ledge. Begin the second pitch by climbing a corner and crack to a right-leaning corner. Go left through two small roofs and climb a left-leaning crack to the top.

6. East Face–5.6 My Ass (I 5.7) Begin from the same large platform as *Left Edge,* but from behind a curved flake to the right, follow a ramp up right, then use cracks and small dihedrals to work up left to a large ledge 130 feet up. Climb cracks that lead up left to a triangular notch below black water stains, a right-leaning crack, and finally a vertical crack left of overhanging blocks.

7. East Face (III 5.9) The hardest route in the Alpine Lakes area ascends the thin wedge of a face seen from such places as Camp Lake. Of the six to eight pitches, an early one is the crux, with a layback over a roof (look for fixed pitons). The climbing above is 5.7/5.8, with a 4-foot visor looming at the very top to keep you from relaxing.

A less direct, 5.8+ variation has also been done.

Point 12,818

Knife Point Mountain is the southernmost of the high peaks rising above the erosion surface; to the south the Divide comprises long plateaus. Occasional heights-of-land are hardly summits, but provide objectives to wanderers in search of out-of-the-way destinations. Point 12,818 is 0.9 mile southeast of Knife Point.

1. South Ridge (I 4th class) Reaching the Divide from the valley above Wall Lake involves steep scrambling, but once on top it is easy walking.

Point 12,846

Another plateau high point, this one 2 miles northeast of Wall Lake, gives an overview of the Alpine Lakes area. To the north is a notch, but to the south you can traverse the Divide for miles.

1. South Ridge (I 2nd class) From Pass 11,960+.

2. West Gully (I 3rd class) A direct route from Wall Lake, but not to be chosen for aesthetics.

Burch Peak (12,314)

Though actually a mere spur of the Divide plateau, this formation south of Lower Alpine Lake and west of Douglas Peak appears from the south and east to be a prominent summit.

1. West Slope (I 2nd class) You can reach the plateau west of Burch from Pass 11,960+, Lake 11,065, or Lake 10,787. While the walk from the plateau to the summit is trivial, gaining the plateau involves minor routefinding puzzles in pleasant terrain.

Douglas Peak (12,192)

The broad-summited formation rising north of the Golden Lakes, west of Camp Lake, and south of Lower Alpine Lake was named for Supreme Court Justice William Douglas.

1. West Face (I 3rd class) Narrow grassy ledges above Col 11,560+.

2. Southeast Ridge (I easy 5th class) Gain the ridge from Camp Lake. Four roped pitches lead up slabs, a chimney, and steep flakes just west of two 60-foot gendarmes.

Mount Quintet (11,922)

The sprawling, gentle massif northeast of the Golden Lakes was first climbed by a party of five, who visited all five of the summits.

1. West Slope (I 2nd class) The grassiest route leaves the Hay Pass Trail midway between Upper Golden Lake and Lake 10,787, traverses south on a bench halfway up, and approaches the summit from the south.

2. Northeast Ridge (I 4th class) Begin from Camp Lake by ascending Point 11,691, roping for a few pitches on high-angle flakes near its top. From this subsidiary summit, continue easily south and west to other summits.

Peak 12,529

Wall Lake presumably owes its name to the 2-mile-long wall facing it and Cook Lakes. The wall culminates in erosion-surface summits, of which the highest is at the formation's north end, 0.5 mile west-northwest of Tiny Glacier.

1. Via Lake 10,950 (I 2nd class) From Spider Lake, ascend the lonely valley to its north (as for Pass 11,663).

2. Wall Lake Wall–38 Special (II 5.8) To the left of a zone of arches, a grassy ledge angles up left. This route begins farther left, in a blocky corner that leads up right to a large ledge. The second pitch follows a thin crack up left for 30 feet, then a more vertical corner to a small ledge. The third pitch follows a thin crack, then angles right on a slab to two small ledges. The fourth pitch begins easily, up right, gaining a 50-foot corner (with water streaks to the right) and ending with a 5.8 move to a ledge right of an ear-shaped flake. The short fifth and final pitch involves a balance move around to the right.

Angel Peak (12,402)

The summit overlooking Angel Pass is the closest thing to a Divide peak for many miles.

1. North Ridge (I 3rd class) From Spider Lake by way of Pass 11,663 or, more directly, the rib rising from Bald Mountain Basin.

Peak 12,367

Peak 12,367 is 0.4 mile south of Angel Pass.

1. West Slope-South Ridge (I 2nd class) Gain the ridge joining Peak 12,367 and Point 11,899 from Spider Lake.

2. East Rib (I 4th class) Begin from the snow southeast of Angel Pass. After a loose start, either of two ribs offers pleasant, easy climbing.

Mount Baldy (11,857)

Members of the Hayden Survey, approaching from the south, climbed this peak thinking it was Fremont's. From the summit their mistake was obvious, in fact embarrassing. Baldy, standing alone in mid-range, may offer the range's most comprehensive views—of seventy-something of this guidebook's peaks, from White Rock to Shark's Nose and Warbonnet.

Because an early survey determined the elevation of both this peak and a spur south of Angel Pass to be 11,850, Baldy's identity varied from one old map to another, confusion compounded by the Hayden Survey name New Fork Peak for their faux-Fremont.

The 1968 Horseshoe Lake quad chose the summit with the classic look of a Mount Baldy over the alternative, Point 11,899 on Peak 12,367's south ridge.

1. North Slope (I 1st class) Easy from Bald Mountain Basin, no doubt also from the south.

Timico Peak (12,236)

The saddle-shaped peak west of Lake 11,045, below Timico Pass.

1. South Slope (I 3rd class) From the bench west of Timico Lake, ascend the rubbly chute (the only unpleasantness) that points toward the saddle between the main peak and the east shoulder, then angle left to talus.

Round Top Mountain (12,048)

1. South Ridge (I 3rd class) From the 10,920-foot pass crossed by the abandoned trail from Timico Lake to North Fork Canyon, gain Round Top's crest west of Point 11,868.

North Fork Peak (11,747)

From the vicinity of North Fork Lake, the northwest skyline is dominated by an 11,747-foot peak. However, like angle-of-repose scree, the name North Fork Peak has crept downhill, from one map to another, coming to rest on a barely noticeable 11,175-foot shoulder. The name surely belongs on the main peak.

1. Southwest Slope (I 2nd class). From Hat Pass, one of the range's gentlest ascents.

Mount Victor (12,254)

The scenery around North Fork Lake is less spectacular than to the north and south. Yet this area's less alpine, less craggy heights, Victor for example, with gentle ridges and rounded slopes, evoke their own emotional responses—serenity in sunshine, brooding in storms.

1. Southwest Slope (I 2nd class) Leave the Hay Pass Trail a mile above Lake Victor and ascend grass.

2. South Ridge (I 5.0) Reported to be fun.

3. East Ridge (I 4th class) It's 3rd class to gain the ridge from the glacier to the north; 4th class on the ridge itself near the summit.

Europe Peak (12,259)

From Hay Pass the Divide runs southeast for several miles over a series of minor summits to a tiny cliffbound cirque overlooking Europe Canyon. Europe Peak, the high point of this ridge, sits atop this cirque, just west of the pass at Europe Canyon's head.

1. West Slope (I 2nd class) Finis Mitchell first climbed Europe Peak by following the Divide from Hay Pass, but lesser mortals can make a shorter ascent, from the north end of Long Lake. If approaching from Europe Canyon, avoid a long traverse of the crest by noting the summit's location.

Point 11,245

This is the prominent formation, 1.1 miles southeast of Mount Victor, seen as you hike up Europe Canyon.

1. South Face (I 5.7+) The reporter of this route didn't locate the start, but the first pitch ascends a 5.4/5.5 slab left of blocky overhangs. The short second pitch reaches a rock-strewn ledge left of trees. On the third pitch, climb between facing corners, traverse left under a small overhang, make a crux mantle, and climb to a ledge 20 feet above the overhang. Climbing ends with a short 4th-class slab.

Descent: From the saddle north of Point 11,245, walk off to the west.

From northwest of Middle Fork Lake

7 Middle Fork Lake

The peaks here aren't as high as peaks to the north, and though signs of past glaciers are abundant, only small snowpatches remain. The valleys aren't as intimately walled by steep granite as the cirques to the south are, though an occasional face looms as large as any in the range. It isn't an area for alpinism, and a rock climber can find denser clusters of rock routes farther south. Yet the range's central part offers routes of assorted lengths and difficulties to climbers willing to walk and explore, and provides hikers with vast open spaces and numerous lakes.

This chapter includes the headwaters of the Middle Fork Boulder Creek west of the Continental Divide and the upper reaches of the North Fork of the Little Wind River to the east. The Middle Fork begins in an alpine valley that opens north toward Middle Fork Lake. The valley is bounded on the east by nondescript Divide peaks, but near its head stands a group of jagged horns—Nylon and the Twin Lions—and to its west rise the 1,200-foot walls of Dragon Head and Pronghorn. The ridge at the valley's head separates the Middle Fork from Boulder Creek's South Fork. Beyond the Bonneville Lakes at the head of the South Fork stands the region's centerpiece, Mount Bonneville, which is included in the East Fork Valley chapter but is a common objective of climbers camped within the present chapter's area. Northwest of Middle Fork Lake is a treeline land of ponds, meadows, low ridges, and domes, in the midst of which Hall's Lake sits below Hall's Mountain.

You can combine the Boulder Canyon, Highline, and Middle Fork Trails to reach Middle Fork Lake from Boulder Lake, or the Scab Creek and Rainbow Lake Trails to reach it from Scab Creek Entrance.

Kagevah Pass, northeast of Middle Fork Lake, crosses the Divide to the drainage of the North Fork of the Little Wind River. The North Fork originates on Indian land in a complex basin occupied by many lakes; the Roberts Mountain quad gives names for thirteen and elevations for twelve others. Raft Lake, the lowest, is below treeline; the highest are tucked in treeless cirques separated from one another by spurs extending north from the Divide. The basin is enclosed on two sides by long mountains with broad summits but steep walls: Wolverine Peak on the west, Roberts Mountain on the east. Roberts and the ridge running south from it are covered in the Baptiste Lake chapter.

George Bell, Denny Fox, and Joe Sargent pulled off a notably imaginative and successful trip in 1949 when they traveled most of the length of the range and in a three-week period climbed peaks from Dinwoody Creek to the Cirque of the Towers. Their odyssey took them to such little-known places as Middle Fork Lake, where they paused long enough to make first ascents of Pipe Organ, Hall's Mountain, Odyssey Peak, South Cleft, Nylon Peak, and Renegade Peak.

This chapter's peaks are located on the Hall's Mountain and Roberts Mountain quads, but its extensive trail network also requires the Horseshoe Lake, Scab Creek, and Raid Lake maps to the west and St. Lawrence Basin and Paradise Basin maps to the east.

Trails

Boulder Canyon Trail

Boulder Lake to Lake Vera—10 miles

From the Boulder Lake trailhead, follow what begins as an old road that leads upstream, adjacent to Boulder Lake Ranch. After a mile the trail reaches a bridge, crosses to the creek's north side, and enters Stillwater Meadows, a subvalley that is separated from the creek by a moraine and in which beavers have created a 0.5-mile-long pond.

The Boulder Canyon Trail is one of the range's steeper, rockier entries but also among the most interesting. The arduous ascent of the canyon allows time to contemplate the trailhead's low elevation, but also offers the Wind Rivers' best opportunity to pass through a plant community of aspen, juniper, rose, thimbleberry, and raspberry. In addition the trail provides frequent views of a classic mountain stream. High in the canyon you encounter country burned in the 1988 fire.

The Boulder Canyon Trail no longer crosses the North Fork below the mile-long cascades known as North Fork Falls, as the Scab Creek quad indicates. Rather it follows switchbacks, west of the falls, that were formerly the start of the Lake Ethel Trail; these trails now diverge just below Lake Ethel (the very edge of the map), the Boulder Canyon Trail crossing the North Fork by a bridge. The new trail rejoins the old trail before Dugway Lake (which, lying in a hollow especially desolated by the fire, offers no campsites), then climbs to Lake Vera. Wind River entrance trails typically pass a lake that makes the first night's obvious campsite; the shores of such lakes inevitably show overuse—dirt denuded of pine needles, numerous fire rings, elaborately built benches or tables. Lake Vera, with the first decent campsites for miles, is a prototype.

Reaching Lake Vera, you also reach a junction with the Highline. Bear left for North Fork Lake, right for Middle Fork Lake, crossing the outlet creek and looking for the trail beyond the scarred camping area. Also turn right on the Highline for the Howard Lake Trail.

Highline Trail

Cross Lake to North Fork Lake—11 miles

Previous chapters describe the Highline from north to south, but, to consistently lead you into the mountains, the southern part of the Highline is described from south to north.

As discussed in the introduction, the Highline's southern identity is more a matter of semantics than of backpacking. For our purposes the trail begins west of Cross Lake; the section to the south isn't of interest to mountain travelers. The Highline, in current usage, is the trail that crosses the outlets of Raid and Dream Lakes and reaches

Middle Fork Lake Area, West of Divide

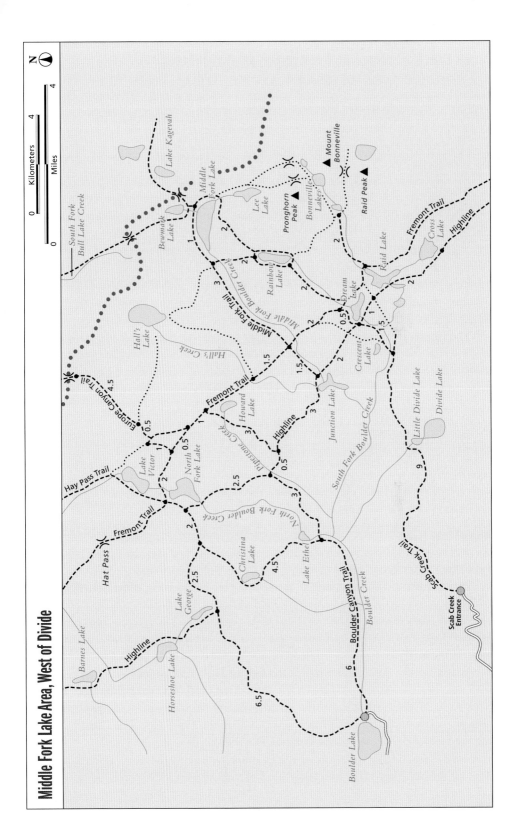

N

Kilometers
0   4

Miles
0   4

South Fork
Bull Lake Creek

Lake Kagevah

Beumark
Lake

Middle
Fork Lake

Lee
Lake

Pronghorn
Peak ▲

Bonneville
Lakes

Mount
Bonneville ▲

Raid Peak ▲

Rainbow
Lake

Middle Fork Boulder Creek

Middle Fork Trail

Hall's
Lake

Hall's Creek

Europe Canyon Trail   4.5

1

2

2

2

2

2

3

Raid Lake

Cross
Lake

Fremont Trail

Highline

Dream
Lake

0.5

1

1.5

Crescent
Lake

2

Fremont Trail   1.5

1.5

Howard
Lake

Pipestone Creek

Highline

Junction Lake

South Fork Boulder Creek

Little Divide Lake

Divide
Lake

Scab Creek Trail

9

0.5

3

2

3

0.5

3

North   0.5

0.5

1

Lake Victor

Hay Pass Trail

Fremont Trail   2

North Fork Boulder Creek

2

2.5

3

Christina
Lake

4.5

Lake Ethel

Boulder Creek

Boulder Canyon Trail

Scab Creek
Entrance

Hat Pass

Fremont Trail

Highline

Barnes Lake

Lake
George

Horseshoe Lake

2.5

6

6.5

Boulder Lake

North Fork Lake via Junction, Full Moon, and the Fire Hole Lakes and Lakes Vera and Winona. (Old maps, for example the 15-minute Mount Bonneville quad, and a few relic signposts attach High Line to the trail now known as the Fremont Trail.) Despite being the trail that extends the length of the Wind Rivers, the Highline isn't as direct or scenic a way between Cross and North Fork Lakes as the Fremont Trail. Certain sections, though, are useful, in conjunction with cross trails, for getting into the mountains.

For its first few miles, the trail's identity is additionally theoretical because of South Fork Meadow's several-square-mile treeless expanse, extending from south of Cross Lake north past Dream Lake. Tracks are trampled into the meadow in few places, and while occasional cairns mark the Highline, cairns also represent unknown byways, sheepherders' urge for self-portraiture, or simply monuments to boredom. Aim at distant landmarks and keep a map handy. (The lakes' distinctive shapes help.) Coming from the south, aim for Raid Lake's ambiguous outlet, then Dream Lake's. West of Dream Lake, climb toward the meadow's rim, where you should find the trail descending a swampy draw to Junction Lake.

The Highline swings north of Junction Lake (the junction of the Middle Fork and Hall's Creek); the Middle Fork Trail heads upstream north of the Middle Fork. One switchback before Lake Vera, another connector with the Fremont Trail begins—the Howard Lake Trail (which postdates the Hall's Mountain quad). Also at Lake Vera the Boulder Canyon Trail joins, from the Boulder Lake trailhead. The Highline continues north to North Fork Lake's outlet, which you must ford.

The trail that the Horseshoe Lake quad shows following North Fork Lake's west shore no longer exists; the only trail wanders away from the lake for 0.25 mile to an unmarked junction near ponds. To continue on the Highline, turn southwest and refer to the Alpine Lakes chapter. To reach the Fremont Trail or Hay Pass Trail, turn north, toward wide meadows and a signed junction.

Howard Lake Trail

Lake Vera to Pipestone Lakes—3 miles

Several maps, the Hall's Mountain quad being one, indicate one version or another of a trail connecting the Highline, near the Firehole Lakes, with the Fremont Trail. However, some of these versions are obsolete, others nonexistent. The recently constructed Howard Lake Trail diverges from the Highline at the switchback just above Lake Vera; look for the unsigned and easily missed junction after the Highline bends south.

After a notably indirect 0.5 mile, the Howard Lake Trail passes south of a pond 0.25 mile north of Fire Hole Lake 9,584, then turns northwest, paralleling Lake Isabella but 0.25 mile east. It meets the older (Hall's Mountain quad) trail just beyond Howard Lake's outlet, then continues for 0.5 mile to the lower Pipestone Lake, meeting the Fremont Trail on this lake's marshy east shore.

You can reach Lake Isabella from the Highline by leaving the new Howard Lake Trail for the old where they cross at the head of a draw (with a few ponds) that drains to the lake's east bay. You can also reach Lake Isabella by following the old trail from the junction at Howard Lake's outlet; indeed, it is not obvious which is the maintained trail.

Fremont Trail

Raid Lake to North Fork Lake—9 miles

According to present terminology, the northeasterly of the trails from Raid Lake to North Fork Lake is the Fremont Trail; the southwesterly is the Highline. The Fremont Trail crosses these lakes' inlet streams, the Highline their outlets. (Old maps, though, refer to the Fremont as the Highline; don't be confused by signs using the old terminology.)

For a description of the Fremont Trail south of Raid Lake, see the East Fork Valley chapter.

Circling north of Raid Lake, the trail traverses the northwest fringe of the vast South Fork Meadows, past Dream, Bob's, and Sandpoint Lakes, then fords the Middle Fork and Hall's Creek. You can follow these creeks upstream to Middle Fork Lake and Hall's Lake, respectively. (While the Fremont Trail regularly crosses major streams at right angles, it does follow a ghost of a valley—a fracture zone that predates present drainages.)

Just south of the lower Pipestone Lake, the Howard Lake Trail joins from the west. From west of the upper Pipestone Lake, the Europe Canyon Trail goes north, while the Fremont Trail turns west, away from the fracture zone, and crosses wooded country to North Fork Lake's north shore. In meadows west of this lake is a junction, from which the Hay Pass Trail heads north, a connector to the Highline heads south, and the Fremont Trail continues west, up a draw (see Alpine Lakes chapter).

Europe Canyon Trail

Pipestone Lakes to Milky Lakes—6 miles

Europe Canyon is a broad-floored, lake-speckled, elongated basin situated above treeline, with craggy walls that evoke such adjectives as austere and stark. The trail is generally poorly marked, but at least for its upper section you should need little guidance through the creekside tundra.

Leave the Fremont Trail either at a signed junction just west of the upper Pipestone Lake, passing east of Valley Lake, or, if coming from North Fork Lake, at cairns leading north across a meadow west of Valley Lake. These variants converge near Valley Lake's north end, though only a distant cairn indicates the trail's continuation into Europe Canyon.

After curving left toward the canyon's creek, the trail becomes more obvious as it climbs for 0.5 mile to a small unnamed lake. Maps show the trail into Europe Canyon crossing this lake's outlet, but the trail shown going south of the lake, crossing the inlet stream, and ending at Lake 10,542 is far more conspicuous. It doesn't end at

Lake 10,542 but follows the lake's west shore, joining the map's trail north of the lake. At the canyon's head the trail crosses the 11,459-foot Divide pass that hikers but not maps name Europe Pass, then descends to the Milky Lakes. Maps indicate the trail's end at the upper lake, but, as the entire trail north of the pass is little but occasional cairns and common sense, the end is arbitrary. You can travel easily through the flat, grassy country and continue down the valley into Terra Incognita.

When climbing to the Divide from the Milky Lakes, note that Europe Pass is to the right of the valley's apparent head.

From Valley Lake's north end you can reach Lake Victor's north end by an unmaintained trail (shown on the Hall's Mountain quad) that was historically part of the Hay Pass Trail.

Hall's Lake Routes

Europe Canyon to Hall's Lake—2.5 miles
Fremont Trail to Hall's Lake—4 miles
Middle Fork Lake to Hall's Lake—2 miles

Hall's Lake sits at 10,602 feet in the midst of a large area decreed trailless by the Forest Service. It is the best kind of trailless terrain, for you are above treeline, can locate topographic features, and get a sense of solitude in country you are probably visiting for solitude. It is fine country to wander through. Drainages are intricate and minor obstacles abound, but by paying attention and consulting a map you can get where you're going without difficulty.

To reach Hall's Lake from Europe Canyon, leave the trail near Lake 10,542 and follow vague paths north of Medina Mountain. From the Fremont Trail you can find your way up Hall's Creek. The best route seems to diverge from the creek at Lake 9,987 and pass east of the ponds east of Points 10,460 and 10,532. (The dead-end trail the Hall's Mountain quad shows following the creek to Lake 9,987 isn't maintained.)

You can also reach Hall's Lake from the Fremont Trail by following the Middle Fork Trail for 2 miles, to Lake 10,100, then heading northwest toward the pond northeast of Point 10,532. From Middle Fork Lake, descend the Middle Fork for 0.25 mile, then head northwest. To go directly to Hall's Lake, cross the 11,040-foot pass north of Point 11,164. The descent is steep but not unreasonable for a backpacker. Alternatively, follow a more southerly drainage and round Point 11,506 to the thin, 0.25-mile-long lake south of Hall's Lake.

Middle Fork Trail

Junction Lake to Middle Fork Lake—5.5 miles

Reach Middle Fork Lake from Boulder Lake by way of the Boulder Canyon and Highline Trails as far as Junction Lake, where Hall's Creek joins the Middle Fork. Be sure not to turn up Hall's Creek; cross it and turn up the Middle Fork. You don't have to follow the creek around its jog to Sandpoint Lake; cross the Fremont Trail and rejoin the Middle Fork a mile to the northeast. Continue upstream to Middle Fork Lake's north shore. (A vague trail follows the south shore, but the outlet is difficult to cross in early summer.)

The higher trail shown on maps, bypassing Middle Fork Lake and going directly to Bewmark Lake, doesn't receive enough traffic to be readily located.

Photo Pass Trail

Bewmark Lake to Deadman Lake—9 miles

Photo Pass (11,400+), a Divide crossing just west of South Cleft Peak, enables you to reach Bull Lake Creek's South Fork from Middle Fork Lake. Reach Bewmark Lake by steep slopes just east of the cascades falling to Middle Fork Lake. The Kagevah Pass Trail circles south of Bewmark Lake and climbs east, while the Photo Pass Trail follows the lake's west shore and intersects the Divide at the pass to the northwest. North of the pass the trail descends to the South Fork, with occasional crossings. After meeting the Paradise Basin Trail, which drops from Windy Gap to the east, the Photo Pass Trail continues downstream to its end in the swamps of Deadman Lake. You can continue down the South Fork but without guidebook assistance.

Scab Creek Trail

Scab Creek Entrance to Dream Lake and Raid Lake—11 miles

This is the easiest way to Raid Lake and Mount Bonneville's west side; combined with the Rainbow Lake Trail, it offers a less strenuous backpack to Middle Fork Lake than the Boulder Canyon Trail. Since the USGS quads were mapped, the Forest Service has improved the trail, in places relocating it and adding switchbacks.

Immediately above the parking area is the trail's steepest section, working up a sagebrush hillside, though the first few miles feature further steepness. The Scab Creek and Raid Lake quads consider the first 5 miles to be the Lowline Trail, but at Little Divide Lake the Lowline diverges along the lake's southeast shore, to Divide Lake, while the Scab Creek Trail follows the west shore. (Little Divide Lake offers the trail's first decent campsites—in addition to multiple outlets, one assisted by a diversion ditch.)

Switchbacks now moderate the ascent toward Lightning Lakes. At a height-of-land past the lake, the mountains come into view, and then the vast meadow of Boulder Creek's South Fork. Many trails cross this meadow, marked by few signboards but frequent cairns. You may find it easier to walk toward a landmark than to stay on a trail.

After you enter the meadow, two official trails diverge. The left, more heavily used, crosses the South Fork and follows Dream Creek to Dream Lake, crossing the signed but trackless Highline at the lake's west lobe and meeting the Fremont Trail at a pond north of the lake. The trail actually circles south of this pond (the pond just west of Benchmark 9908), not west, as indicated on maps. This version of the Scab Creek Trail leads to Middle Fork Lake by way of Rainbow Lake.

The other trail, staying right of the South Fork and curving east to join the Highline south of Raid Lake, doesn't lead to alpine terrain. However, you can reach the Bonneville Lakes by leaving this trail and heading northeast across the meadow (aim toward Mount Bonneville), meeting the Fremont Trail between Raid and Dream Lakes. The Raid Lake quad shows this route as a trail, and, while the Forest Service hasn't marked it, you don't need a trail.

When leaving the mountains, whether via Dream Lake or Raid Lake, locate the Scab Creek Trail on the meadow's west edge by aiming toward the small canyon by which the South Fork leaves the meadow. The Scab Creek Trail ascends this canyon's south bank into trees.

Crescent Lake Cutoff (not maintained)

South Fork Boulder Creek to Sandpoint Lake—2 miles

When you enter the South Fork meadow on the Scab Creek Trail, the bench just to your north appears an unlikely site for a lake. However, Crescent Lake provides good views and secluded campsites. A well-used path passes Crescent Lake.

The path leaves the Scab Creek Trail's Dream Lake branch, just after it crosses the South Fork, and climbs a small draw to Crescent Lake. It follows the lake's east shore and the meadow's west edge to Bob's Lake, passes west of Bob's Lake, descends toward Sandpoint Lake, and crosses this lake's inlet to meet the Fremont Trail.

Rainbow Lake Trail

Dream Lake to Middle Fork Lake—4 miles

You can reach Middle Fork Lake from the Scab Creek Trail by a trail that passes Rainbow Lake. Leave the Fremont Trail near the thin inlet bay at Dream Lake's east end. (You can also follow Dream Creek from the lake's west end.) Leave the creek's main branch at a notable little falls and enter, to the west, one of the range's pretty, broad, grassy draws, rejoining Dream Creek near Rainbow Lake's outlet. Trails traverse both sides of the lake, though gaining the east-side trail entails a detour to the south.

To reach Middle Fork Lake's east end, ascend the valley northeast of Rainbow Lake to a 10,800-foot pass. North of the pass is an open slope with no path worn into it. To reach the Middle Fork downstream of Middle Fork Lake from Rainbow Lake, rather than entering the valley northeast of the lake, climb a bit west to a 10,520-foot saddle.

Sunrise Lake Cutoff (not maintained)

Little Bonneville Lake to Rainbow Lake—2 miles

This is a lowland alternative to Passes 11,360+ and 11,560+ for commuting between Middle Fork Lake and the Bonneville Lakes. From Little Bonneville Lake (10,521), follow a faint path past the small pond just to its west, descend its outlet stream for 0.25 mile, and head northwest, up the valley east of Point 10,725, to Sunrise Lake's south shore; this is the one section of the cutoff not easy to follow. Cross Sunrise Lake's outlet and again head northwest, passing a smaller lake and reaching Rainbow Lake at the head of its southeast arm.

When traveling south, the turn east to Lake 10,521 is unobvious. Read the map carefully and look for a prominent split boulder and cairn (admittedly ambiguous landmarks).

Bonneville Lakes Trail (not maintained)

Raid Lake to Lake 10,521—2 miles

There are three Bonneville Lakes: 11,015-foot Sheila Lake, high under Nylon, South Twin Lion, and Mount Bonneville; Lake 10,828 (Middle Bonneville Lake), the most convenient base camp for climbing; and Lake 10,521 (Little Bonneville Lake), the pleasantest for camping. An unmaintained though easily followed trail leads from Raid Lake up the South Fork to Lake 10,521.

Leave the Fremont Trail where it crosses the South Fork, pass through meadows northwest of the creek, cross the creek, and cross back at the outlet of a tiny lake. Follow the northwest bank to Little Bonneville Lake. A trail leads along the lake's northwest shore but all but disappears beyond. You can reach Middle Bonneville Lake by either ascending a draw somewhat west of the cascading stream or crossing the inlet and zigzagging up a steep slope.

Paradise Basin Trail

St. Lawrence Basin to South Fork Bull Lake Creek—16 miles

The road that continues west past St. Lawrence Ranger Station shortly becomes a trail that follows St. Lawrence Creek to an 11,000-foot saddle on Windy Ridge, a northeastern extension of Wolverine Peak. Across the saddle is Paradise Basin, through which the trail passes, crossing Paradise Creek. After passing Lydle, Steamboat, and Hatchet Lakes and crossing Windy Gap (11,600+), the trail drops 2,000 feet to Bull Lake Creek's South Fork and the Photo Pass Trail.

Raft Lake Trail

St. Lawrence Basin to Moraine Lake—16 miles

Raft Lake is a gateway to the dozens of lakes on the headwaters of the Little Wind River's North Fork, and the Raft Lake Trail provides access to these lakes, as well as the cirques at the head of Wilson Creek.

The trail begins 100 yards west of St. Lawrence Ranger Station as a rough road. It continues as a road for a mile, to where it crosses a ridge to the South Fork of St. Lawrence Creek. (The road can be driven, but overnight parking isn't allowed beyond the ranger station.) After crossing the creek, the trail parallels it in a steep ascent to a nearly 10,800-foot saddle that overlooks the meadows of Entigo Creek. The trail

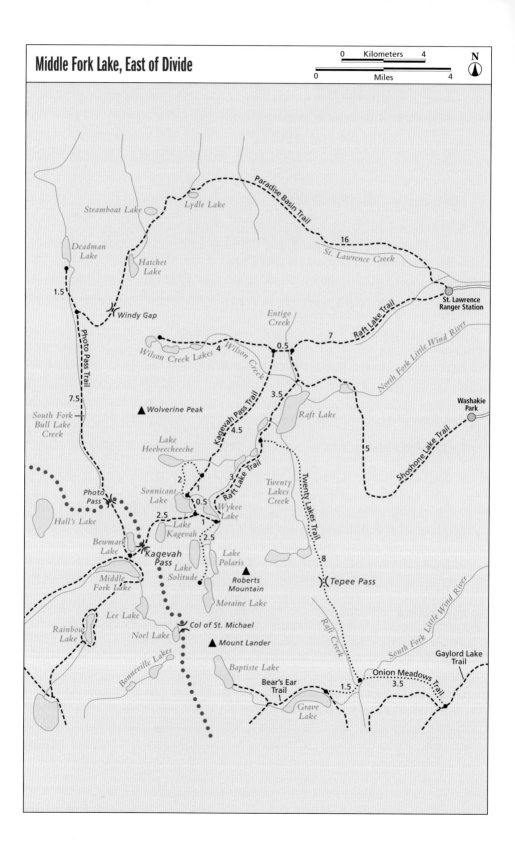

Middle Fork Lake, East of Divide

0 Kilometers 4

0 Miles 4

N

Paradise Basin Trail

Steamboat Lake

Lydle Lake

Deadman Lake

Hatchet Lake

16

St. Lawrence Creek

1.5

Windy Gap

Entigo Creek

St. Lawrence Ranger Station

Wilson Creek Lakes 4 Wilson Creek

0.5

7

Raft Lake Trail

Photo Pass Trail

7.5

South Fork Bull Lake Creek

Wolverine Peak

Kagevah Pass Trail

3.5

Raft Lake

North Fork Little Wind River

Washakie Park

Lake Heebeecheeche

4.5

Photo Pass

Sonnicant Lake

2

1

3

Raft Lake Trail

Twenty Lakes Creek

Twenty Lakes Trail

5

Shoshone Lake Trail

Hall's Lake

0.5

Wykee Lake

Bewmark Lake

2.5

1

Lake Kagevah

2.5

Kagevah Pass

Lake Solitude

Lake Polaris

8

Tepee Pass

Middle Fork Lake

Lee Lake

Roberts Mountain

Moraine Lake

Rainbow Lake

Noel Lake

Col of St. Michael

Mount Lander

Raft Creek

South Fork Little Wind River

Gaylord Lake Trail

Bonneville Lakes

Baptiste Lake

Bear's Ear Trail

Onion Meadows Trail

3.5

1.5

Grave Lake

continues west and descends to Entigo Creek, but not where the Paradise Basin quad indicates. The ground-truth trail is north of the map's, and it crosses Entigo Creek near the 10,000-foot contour.

From a junction on the creek's west bank (7 miles from St. Lawrence Ranger Station), the Wilson Creek Trail continues west, while the Raft Lake Trail heads downstream, through a well-used (misused) campsite, recrosses Entigo Creek, and descends the slope east of the creek. This section of trail isn't shown on the Paradise Basin quad, though its continuation on the Roberts' Mountain quad is. The trail makes yet another crossing (wade or rock-hop) near a beaver dam in a small meadow below the meeting of Wilson and Entigo Creeks. A trail not covered in this guide follows Wilson Creek downstream.

A half mile beyond, a side trail drops to Raft Lake, while the main trail contours above the lake's west shore to Movo Lake's outlet, where it crosses the North Fork on an elegant old bridge. Packers take horses as far as Movo Lake and thus maintain the trail, but the trail beyond has suffered from neglect. Expect slow going. The divergence of the Twenty Lakes Trail is a mystery. Traversing slopes to the east of the North Fork, the Raft Lake Trail eventually crosses the North Fork by a series of logs above Wykee Lake. From this crossing a mile-long trail follows the lake's southwest shore, then climbs to Sonnicant Lake and the Kagevah Pass Trail.

The Raft Lake Trail soon turns from the North Fork and switchbacks to Lake Solitude's bench. You can easily miss the abrupt turn, especially if you're admiring the plunge of Lake Solitude's outlet stream from the bench or an exquisite 8-foot drop of the North Fork nearby. The trail passes Lake Solitude above its east shore; a line of cairns continues south to Moraine Lake.

The given mileage of 16 miles doesn't take into account the considerable distance traveled detouring deadfall.

Wilson Creek Trail

Entigo Creek to Elk Lake—4.5 miles

The Wilson Creek Lakes lie in an out-of-the-way cirque between Windy Ridge, Wolverine Peak, and Saddle Mountain. Thanks to fisherfolk and horse packers, the trail to these lakes has evolved into the most-used trail in the area. However, the well-used trail doesn't coincide with the trail shown on the Paradise Basin quad.

On the west side of where the Raft Lake Trail crosses Entigo Creek is a junction. The trail to Wilson Creek Lakes heads west for a mile to Wilson Creek, rejoining the map's virtual trail. Packers avoid the soggy meadow west of Lake 10,081's creek by crossing Wilson Creek, and their beaten path is the obvious way. However, this trail quickly recrosses Wilson Creek, which requires either wading or nontrivial rock-hopping. You can avoid these crossings by skirting the soggy meadow to the north.

The trail crosses Wilson Creek downstream of Lake 10,207's creek, not upstream as the map indicates. It climbs to Enos Lake south of Wilson Creek, but with switchbacks the map doesn't show. Good campsites abound at Enos and nearby lakes. The trail from Tigee Lake to Elk Lake is approximately as shown on the map, but so overgrown as to be hardly useful.

Kagevah Pass Trail

Wilson Creek to Middle Fork Lake—8.5 miles

This trail parallels the Raft Lake Trail but traverses higher to the west. You can start by leaving the more heavily used Wilson Creek Trail between Entigo and Wilson Creeks, as shown on the Paradise Basin quad, or by turning from the Wilson Creek Trail onto the Raft Lake Trail, crossing Entigo Creek, and continuing west where the Raft Lake Trail turns south. Neither of the junctions is marked or obvious. Farther along the Kagevah Pass Trail, a difficult-to-locate, difficult-to-follow side trail loops west to Lake Heebeecheeche and rejoins the main trail at Sonnicant Lake. Also at Sonnicant Lake a trail drops to Wykee Lake and the Raft Lake Trail. The Kagevah Pass Trail rounds Sonnicant Lake and climbs past Lake Kagevah to 11,290-foot Kagevah Pass.

A rocky descent takes you to Bewmark Lake. From Bewmark Lake you can drop to Middle Fork Lake by a bushy slope just east of Bewmark's outlet stream, descend west and south to the Middle Fork Trail by a trail more distinct on topographic maps than on land, or round Bewmark Lake's south and west shores and climb toward Photo Pass.

Shoshone Lake Trail (reservation)

Washakie Park to Shoshone Lake—5 miles

The shortest route to Roberts Mountain involves ascending this neglected trail onto the 11,000-foot tundra uplands east of Roberts, then finding a way down nearly 1,000 feet into Twenty Lakes Creek's valley.

At Washakie Park's south end, cross the creek and follow a marginal road for 0.25 mile to its end at a line shack. Ascend the trail beyond a ROADLESS AREA sign for nearly 2 miles, following a crest distinguished by a curious 100-foot-wide treeless swath. Where this swath dwindles, angle left to avoid talus; the trail is intermittently identifiable but hardly needed as you pass through scattered trees and willow clusters. Above treeline occasional cairns lead to the 11,325-foot pass south of Mount Shoshone.

The trail descends nearly invisibly west, then north to Shoshone Lake and eventually Twin Lakes and the Raft Lake Trail, but to reach the Twenty Lakes drainage, either contour west to Pass 11,135 or cross higher on Mount Baldy and descend farther south.

Passes

Locust Pass (11,640+)

Hall's Lake to Europe Canyon

The gap between Horseshoe Ridge and the Divide (just under Point 11,871 and 0.6 mile northwest of Shoestring Lake) was found inhabited by a throng of locusts. It is suitable for backpacking.

Col of St. Michel (11,600+)

Middle Fork Lake–Moraine Lake

This strange notch in the Divide is a few hundred feet east of Noel Lake. Bell, Fox, and Sargent, who gave the name Mont St. Michel to Nylon Peak, crossed it en route to Renegade Peak from Middle Fork Lake and named it. Noel Lake evidently once drained to the Atlantic Ocean through the notch, with the Divide traversing Nylon Peak; the Middle Fork then captured Noel Lake's drainage.

Pass 11,360+

Bonneville Lake 10,828 to Lee Lake

Two passes link the Middle Fork Lake and Bonneville Lakes drainages, the lower one on the western (Pronghorn) side of Sentry Peak, the higher one on Sentry's northeast (Nylon) side. From Middle Fork Lake, reach the lower, western pass by working up rubble into a bowl south of Lee Lake. From Lake 10,828, zigzag up grassy ramps.

Pass 11,560+

Sheila Lake to Lee Lake

While the pass between Sentry and Nylon Peaks is the higher of the passes linking Middle Fork Lake and the Bonneville Lakes, it is nearly as efficient as Pass 11,360+. Grass to its northwest makes easier going than the rubble north of the lower pass, though you do encounter rubble on its southeast slope, above Sheila Lake.

Peaks

Medina Mountain (11,541)

Although but one of several isolated, low-angled peaks in the range's midsection, with little potential for technical climbing, Medina once achieved its 15 minutes of fame by being composed of the earth's oldest rock then known. Less transiently, it is the site of one of the range's better cairns.

    1. West Slope (I 2nd class) From the Pipestone Lakes or Lake Prue.

    2. East Slope (I 2nd class) A beautiful alpine valley with several lakes is easily reached from Hall's Lake. Follow grassy slopes from the valley to the summit.

Horseshoe Ridge (12,128)

A curving ridge, with no distinct summit, between Hall's Lake and Europe Canyon, enclosing a cirque to the north and east, but falling in a low-angle slope to the south and west.

    1. West Slope (I 2nd class) The ascent from Europe Canyon, passing Lake 10,542's north end, can be made nearly entirely on grass and pleasantly angled bedrock slabs. However, the summit is well southeast of where you might hope it to be.

    2. North-South Traverse (I 4th class) Mostly easy scrambling from Locust Pass, but you may want a rope in two or three places.

Milky Ridge (12,230)

1. Southwest Slope (I 2nd class) Leave the Europe Canyon Trail at Lake 10,813 and cross the Divide just east or just west of Point 11,630.

Peak 12,230

This unnamed peak stands on the Divide 0.75 mile west-northwest of Hall's Mountain.

    1. Southeast Ridge (I 3rd class) From Col 11,714.

Hall's Mountain (12,475)

This rugged Divide summit is the highest and most interesting peak near Hall's Lake. Its distinguishing characteristic is the contrast between its serrated southeast ridge, bristling with gendarmes, and its smooth, gentle, west slope—as the alpine terrain to the southeast contrasts with the rolling country to the northwest. The large gendarme on the southeast ridge is Hall's Spire.

    1. West Slope (I 2nd class) The Hall's Mountain quad appears to mislocate the high point, which is not the top of the broad 1st-class slope rising from Col 11,714 but the first pinnacle to the east. However, passing the intervening gap is not difficult. Reaching the Divide from Shoestring Lake is also easy.

2. Southeast Ridge (I 5th class plus rappels) Hall's Mountain was first climbed by passing northeast of Hall's Spire, regaining the ridge, and following it easily to the southeast summit. Getting to the main summit, though, required rappels and tricky downclimbing to reach the notch between summits. The climbers then ascended chimneys from the notch to the main summit.

3. Hall's Spire, Southeast Side (I 5th class) Use a shallow chimney and a thin rib to reach the summit ridge, then overcome a short step on the ridge.

Pipe Organ (12,225)

The most impressive skyline profile seen from US 191 is Pipe Organ's, southeast of Hall's Mountain. The formation undeservedly acquired a reputation for loose rock; while it is unlikely to become a popular objective because of the shortness of potential routes vis-à-vis its inconvenient location, the rock—though fractured—is solid. The south pipe sports a rappel sling.

1. Northwest Face (I 4th class) Scramble from the Pipe Organ–Hall's Mountain col to the rubbly gully that separates the south pipe from the summit. Leave the gully 200 to 300 feet below the top and wander up the steep but broken face left of the gully.

Peak 12,160+

This is the Divide summit 0.5 mile south of Pipe Organ.

1. North Ridge (I 2nd class) From Pipe Organ.

2. Southwest Ridge (I 2nd class) From the 11,040-foot pass southeast of Hall's Lake. An easy chute breaks the only steep section.

Peak 12,162

Another obscure Divide high point, this one a mile southeast of Pipe Organ.

1. West Slope (I 3rd class) From Lake 11,393. The only 3rd class is in the final 300 feet.

Wolverine Peak (12,631)

1. West Slope (I 2nd or 3rd class) During the 1930s surveyors established a network of triangulation stations across Wyoming. Locating these stations took the men to out-of-the-way places and resulted in Wolverine's first reported ascent. The Coast and Geodetic Survey published directions so that markers could be relocated. The instructions for climbing Wolverine tell the traveler: "Leave trail at Windy Gap, pick circuitous route southerly through rocks on west slope of ridge as far as horses can be taken. This will be about 3 or 4 miles of actual travel, and horses will be left at point about ⅜ mile north of high rocky point on crossridge at east end of which azimuth mark is located. Continue southerly on foot, keeping below crest on west slope for about ¾ mile; bear left and climb east through rocks about 0.25 mile to top."

2. Point 12,338, East Couloir (I 3rd class) Only the last few hundred feet of the obvious chute are steep and loose.

3. Point 12,338, Glacier (I Snow 3rd class) What seems to be the pleasantest way up Wolverine from Lake 10,927 is hidden from the lake by moraines and a ridge. It's the tiny glacier tucked in a cirque north of Point 12,338. The glacier isn't steep, but an ice axe is advisable unless the snow is particularly soft.

4. East Couloir (I Snow 3rd class) A snow couloir west of Lake 10,927 reaches the rim south of the summit. It's nasty and dangerous when dry.

5. East Face (IV 5.9 A2) This route rises above Lake 10,927. Begin at the highest ledges by climbing a steep face, then moving right to a crack slanting right. Ascend this and climb to a pointed flake, then traverse left to a belay behind flakes. Begin pitch 2 by climbing a corner to cracks in a steep face; use a bit of aid to reach a large ledge. Cracks and chimneys lead to a ledge below an overhanging block. A crack reaches a ledge below a ceiling, which the first ascenders passed using a 4-inch bong for aid. Pitch 6 follows a crack to the summit. Large pieces are useful.

6. Point 12,612, East Face–The Illness (V 5.10 A3) A notably straight crack system that rises from the snow of the Wilson Creek Lakes cirque to Wolverine's north summit has been climbed in nine 200-foot pitches. Pitch 1 is a splendid 5.9 crack. Other pitches require thin nailing and a few copperheads. A bolt was placed above pitch 8 to enable retreat on an early attempt. (The "illness" was attributed to Fred Beckey, the first ascent's base camp manager and spiritual advisor, for over several years visiting the obscure cirque three times.)

Thunderbolt Pinncle (12,320+)

In the notch between Wolverine and Saddle is a pair of pinnacles that received the ultimate compliment from the surveyors who climbed Wolverine: "unscalable crags." Thunderbolt is the western of the pair.

1. East Chimney (II 5.7) A three-pitch route begins from the Thunderbolt–Lightning Rod notch, which you can reach from Saddle via Lightning Rod.

Descent: Rappel the route, then drop down the couloir to the south.

Lightning Rod Pinnacle (12,280+)

Lightning Rod is the eastern of the two pinnacles in the Wolverine-Saddle col.

1. East Chimney (II 5.4) Reach the pinnacle from Saddle Mountain and climb it by a short route on that side.

Saddle Mountain (12,551)

This satellite of Wolverine is more a mesa than a peak.

1. Northeast Ridge (I 4th class) From Lake Heebeecheeche, Lake 10,465, or Glacier Creek downstream, circle east of Point 11,887 and gain the ridge at the notch closest to the peak. The steep 200-foot buttress above involves genuine 4th-class climbing.

2. North Buttress (III 5.8) This route ascends the prominent spur that projects from the west part of Saddle Mountain's north face. It is apparent on the Roberts Mountain quad north of the first "d" in "Saddle." Follow the buttress's crest for perhaps four pitches to where the crest flattens, then ascend a spur right of the crest.

3. South Face, Ess Ridge (II 5.7) Near the middle of Saddle Mountain's wide south face, a sinuous ridge rises above Lake 10,927. To its right is a bowl, farther right an impressive prow. On the Roberts Mountain quad it is the rib that reaches the rim near the "M" in "Mountain." Reach the ridge by scrambling up the drainage below the bowl. Follow the ridge's crest for a few easy pitches to the foot of two prominent pinnacles. In two pitches, climb over the first and bypass the second to the west. The long crux pitch then ascends cracks and faces near the crest. Another nice pitch follows cracks and a chimney to the end of technical ground.

4. Pinnacle 12,040, South Face (I 5.6) On Saddle's southeast ridge are two pinnacles. Climb the one closest to Saddle by traversing onto the south face from the notch between it and Hailstorm Pinnacle. Reach the top in two pitches.

5. Hailstorm Pinnacle, Southwest Ridge (I 5.5) Hailstorm is the outer, 11,887-foot pinnacle on Saddle's southeast ridge. Its southwest ridge affords a quick two-pitch route.

6. Hailstorm Pinnacle, North Face (II 5.7) No description is available.

Windy Ridge, Point 12,156

Windy Ridge extends northeast from Wolverine for more than 8 miles. Its 12,156-foot high point is 2 miles north of the Wilson Creek Lakes.

1. South Slope (I 2nd class) From the strait connecting the two small lakes northeast of and downstream from Enos Lake, climb into the valley between Points 11,533 and 11,258.

Mount Heebeecheeche (11,755)

A minor prominence just northwest of Spider Lake.

1. South Ridge (I 3rd class) A pleasant scramble from the col above Lake 11,015 or via ramps below the east face that intersect the ridge partway up.

2. Northeast Ridge (I 3rd or 4th class) Scramble to the ridge from Glacier Creek. The first ascent, made through a foot of snow, required a rope that you may not need when the route is dry.

North Cleft Peak (12,548)

Two miles north of Middle Fork Lake and just northeast of Photo Pass is a pair of summits separated by a notch (the Cleft). The flat-topped summit north of the Cleft sits on the ridge joining Wolverine to the Divide.

1. West Gully (I 3rd or 4th class) Ascend the west gully until 300 feet below the Cleft, then climb a gully leading north to North Cleft's top.

2. Giant's Tooth (I 5.7) On North Cleft's east ridge is a small pinnacle that can provide an afternoon's diversion. Climb it in a short pitch from the notch to its west.

South Cleft Peak (12,480+)

The southern of the peaks sundered by the Cleft is a high Divide summit conspicuous from Middle Fork Lake.

1. West Ridge (I 4th class) A variation of the "because it is there" theme motivated this ridge's first ascent: "it" was a camera. The climbers who first climbed South Cleft—by its southeast ridge—descended west to Photo Pass before realizing they'd left a camera on top. They made a quick return trip up this ridge.

2. West Gully (I 3rd or 4th class) From Photo Pass, climb a gully right of the west ridge.

3. Southeast Ridge (I 5.3) South Cleft was first climbed by traversing Odyssey and climbing this exposed ridge over its many gendarmes. Only a small section requires a rope, but the rock is good and the climbing enjoyable. You can approach the ridge directly, without traversing Odyssey, from the valley leading to Photo Pass.

Odyssey Peak (12,062)

George Bell's account of his epic 1949 journey with Denny Fox and Joe Sargent was titled "Wind River Odyssey." He gave the name "Pyramid" to the Divide peak they traversed between Kagevah Pass and South Cleft, but, the range being overrun with Pyramids, the Bonneys changed the name to Odyssey.

1. Southeast Ridge (I 3rd class) Pleasant scrambling for nearly a mile from Kagevah Pass.

2. Northwest Ridge (I 3rd class) The col between Odyssey and South Cleft is easily reached from the Photo Pass Trail. The northwest ridge offers more 3rd-class climbing and less hiking than the southeast ridge, which you may consider when planning to traverse Odyssey.

Prairie Falcon Peak (11,475)

West of Sonnicant Lake is a spur that extends northeast from Odyssey and ends in steep cliffs above the lake. Although it is barely a peak, the cliffs are a worthy rock climbing objective.

Prairie Falcon Peak

South Cleft Peak

North Cleft Peak   Prairie Falcon Peak   Wolverine Peak

Prairie falcons nest in high, rocky places, and a nest found near the crag's summit inspired the name.

1. Northeast Couloir (I 3rd class) The couloir is visible from Sonnicant Lake. Much of the route is near a cascading stream so is often messy but never difficult.

2. Southeast Face Left (III 5.8) Climbers following a chimney system a few hundred feet left of the *Southeast Face* route, believing they were making a first ascent, encountered several 5.8 sections and also found a piton on the last pitch.

3. Southeast Face (III 5.8) The wall above Sonnicant Lake is cut by a wide gully that slants up left. One of the better rock routes in the central Wind Rivers begins in an easy, block-filled chimney 100 feet up the gully and follows a series of chimneys for ten pitches, most of which are 5th class. You can climb most of the route using cracks and faces outside the chimneys. About halfway up, climb a beautiful, knobby wall for a pitch, and above it a classic crack in a steep wall. The last difficult pitch follows a chimney past a chockstone to an intimidating overhang; climbing becomes easier above the overhang.

4. Northeast Face (III 5.9 A3) This unappealing climb attacks an overhang, just northwest of Sonnicant Lake, that is rather large considering the shortness of the route. Reach a big ledge under the overhang by easy climbing; a short lead above leads to the summit.

Kagevah Peak (12,127)

From the south the long, flat northwest ridge, rising from Kagevah Pass, distinguishes the peak while concealing a small alpine cirque to its north.

1. Northwest Ridge (I 2nd class) A walk from Kagevah Pass.

2. Northeast Ridge (III 5.4 plus rappels) Lake Kagevah occupies a tiny cirque ringed with steep walls. A traverse of the cirque's rim, in which Kagevah's summit is hardly the objective, makes a pleasant excursion. Start northeast of the lake, ascend the ridge to the east, and climb or bypass the many pinnacles according to whim. You can continue the traverse from the summit around the lake's west side.

3. North Face (II easy 5th class) An easy though loose route ascends the center of the imposing-looking face above Kagevah Lake. Although the route begins from a residual glacier and crosses snow on the face, you need no more ice gear than an axe and perhaps crampons.

Bailey Peak (12,170)

Walt Bailey, who initiated climbing classes at Casper College and climbed in the Wind Rivers, died of pulmonary edema in Peru in 1958. The Roberts Mountain quad attaches his name to Point 12,166, though another Divide point 0.25 mile northwest is 4 feet higher and appears from Middle Fork Lake to be the peak.

1. South Slope (I 2nd class) From the vicinity of Noel Lake.

Petroleum Peak (11,915)

The name Petroleum Peak, erroneously applied to Musembeah on old maps, has been restored to the multi-summited ridge west of Moraine Lake.

1. East Couloirs (I 3rd class) Several disagreeable chutes break the face above Moraine Lake. Once you gain the ridge, you must locate the summit.

The Bonneys report routes on the northeast ridge and in a west-facing couloir.

Nylon Peak (12,392)

Southeast of Lee Lake is a massif whose sharp ridges, concave faces, and pointed summits make it a distinctive formation. A team who may have reached the top in 1946 but left their record on a ledge 30 feet below, at the base of the enigmatic summit block, named it Nylon Peak, to commemorate the virtues of nylon rope, which had just become available. A 1949 group, unaware of the prior ascent, or near-ascent, named it Mont St. Michel, its shape from the north reminding them of the abbey off the French coast. The first name isn't as euphonious as it may have been in 1946, but it is the name the USGS uses on the Roberts Mountain quad.

Nylon Peak consists of three summits, separated by sharp enough spines that none is reached trivially from another (a Wind River rarity). The northern summit is the highest.

1. West Slope (I 4th class) A bowl of broken rock south of the northwest ridge offers the easiest route to the main summit. Only the summit block is 4th class, though you must search to find a way up it that isn't desperate 5th class.

Nylon Peak

Mt. Lander · Southwest Summit · South Twin Lion

2. East Buttress A reputedly terrible route, beginning from Noel Lake, ascends the buttress that rises just right of the gully separating the north and southeast peaks.

3. East Face (II 5.7) An indistinct rib forms the north edge of a section of steep, white rock in the center of the east face. This pleasant route ascends the rib in five long pitches that lead directly to the summit block.

4. Northeast Ridge (II 5.7) This route ascends, in four pitches, the elegant left skyline ridge seen from Middle Fork Lake. Each pitch offers variations. By ascending dihedrals left of the crest, you can keep difficulties to 5.7. The first ascent party, however, used a tension-traverse to pass an overhang low on the route. One party that followed the crest found it to be 5.8; another, though capable of 5.8, required aid for a move.

5. Northwest Ridge (I 5.3) This pleasant little route begins with 3rd-class wanderings up the north face, eventually crossing to the northwest ridge. Two pitches on the ridge constitute the roped climbing; the crux is a short crack above a large ledge. For a longer climb, ascend the entire ridge.

6. West Rib–Pearl Jammed (III 5.8) A seven-pitch route follows a rib, right of an area of water streaks, to a subsidiary summit on the north summit's southwest ridge. The 5.4 first pitch reaches the top of a triangular pedestal (though the pedestal's top can also be reached from the right by 4th-class scrambling). Soon 5.7 climbing is encountered. Much of the rib's upper part is broken, and many easy ways are possible. However, the final 60 feet to the subsummit, from a sloping ledge, involve a 5.8 crack. The knife edge from this summit to the main summit is 3rd/4th class.

7. Southeast Summit, South Face (I 5.6) Begin either from the broken area below the south face, which you can gain from Sheila Lake, or from the foot of the southeast ridge (the Nylon–North Twin Lion col), accessible from Noel Lake by 4th-class slabs. Traverse the south face to a small notch 30 feet west of the summit.

8. Southeast Summit, Northwest Face (I 5.7) From the bowl high on the massif's west side, climb a long and enjoyable, though loose, pitch to meet the ridge connecting the southeast and southwest summits. Then follow the ridge for 30 feet.

7, 8 Descent: With two ropes you can rappel directly north from this summit or downclimb to the notch between the southeast and southwest summits, then rappel into the west bowl from somewhat below the notch. With one rope, downclimb the *South Face* route (the difficulties of which involve traversing).

9. Southwest Summit, Northeast Ridge (I 5.4) Reach the col between the southeast and southwest summits by circling the former from the ridge joining it to North Twin Lion. The southwest summit is a short climb from the col.

10. Southwest Summit, Southwest Face All that is known of the attractive wall above Pass 11,560+ is that it has been climbed.

The Bonneys describe a route up the southwest ridge, involving a rappel from the prominent tower.

North Twin Lion (12,326)

Noel, Sheila, Moraine, and Baptiste Lakes occupy glacier-carved cirques—steep-walled bowls separated by sharp ridges. Where these cirques meet is a pair of horns, seen as twins from the northeast. The northern Twin Lion overlooks the cirques of Noel Lake to the north, Sheila Lake to the southwest, and Moraine Lake to the northeast.

1. West Ridge (I 3rd class) From Sheila Lake.

2. South Ridge (I 4th class) The col between the Twin Lions can be reached from either side of the Divide by nasty scrambling. Follow the ridge from the col.

3. East Face (III 5.8/5.9). A route, said to be excellent but not otherwise described, ascends this steep, clean face.

South Twin Lion or Hitching Post (12,305)

Another example of a horn at the apex of three cirques. From Moraine Lake you see it as one of a pair of similar horns at the cirque's head. It is the sharpest peak beyond the head of Baptiste Lake, from which it was named Hitching Post, 0.5 mile west of Mount Lander. And it is the handsome summit rising east of Sheila Lake.

1. North Face (I easy 5th class) A face so broken that a description is neither needed nor possible.

2. South Ridge (II 5.7) You can reach the level south shoulder from a basin above Baptiste Lake, via slabby couloirs that slant left across the shoulder's east face. You can also reach the shoulder from Sheila Lake, by a slanting ramp that takes you to a gap in the ridge well south of the summit tower. From the shoulder, climb straight up for a few 4th-class pitches. Then follow the narrow crest for a pitch or two to the base of the 250-foot summit tower. Climb to a slanting ledge and follow it left for 80 feet, then make a spectacular traverse back to the ridge. Reach the summit in another long, enjoyable pitch.

You can also climb the summit tower by a 5.6/5.7 crystal-studded crack near its south side's right edge. Reach this obvious crack by way of either of two short cracks.

Descent: Two ropes are needed. Rappel twice down the west side of the summit tower. If descending to Sheila Lake, rappel twice more. Climbers camped at Baptiste Lake have climbed down the east ridge, rappelled into the notch between South Twin Lion and Lander, and traversed Lander and Cusp.

Sentry Peak (11,925)

Between the two passes (11,360+ and 11,560+) that connect the Middle Fork head-waters to the Bonneville Lakes is a minor no-account summit. The climbing isn't great, but the view is.

1. Northwest Ridge (I 4th class) From Pass 11,360+.

2. North Face (I 4th class) A mixed route requiring ice axe and crampons, snow anchors, and a small rock rack.

Descent: The east couloir has been used for descent. Hard snow may necessitate a few rappels.

Pronghorn Peak (12,388)

From the plains to the west, Mount Bonneville's distinctive shape catches your eye. The crests to either side, with low-angle west slopes, appear to be of no interest. Pronghorn, for instance, is seen, slightly left of Bonneville, as a pair of round sum-mits, the right one higher. However, the east sides of these ridges include some of the Wind Rivers' biggest faces. Two buttresses drop from Pronghorn to Lake Donna. The southern one features a 1,000-foot vertical wall that has repelled at least four attempts by veteran wall climbers, none of whom got more than a few pitches up and all of whom felt lucky to escape the flaky rock. The northern buttress features a crest that is one of the range's most eye-catching pieces of architecture.

1. West Slope (I 3rd class) From the vicinity of Sunrise Lake, which you can reach from Rainbow Lake or Bonneville Lake 10,521.

2. East Couloir (II 5.8) The east face can be climbed by ribs just left of the couloir that separates Pronghorn's main, southern buttress from Antelope Arête. One memorable pitch involves a chimney full of chockstones, sand, and mud; the route improves higher.

3. Antelope Arête (III 5.8) The arête north of the east couloir isn't as steep as the southern buttress but becomes sensationally narrow toward the top. While the route's situation is superb, difficult climbing is overly concentrated in the first two pitches.

A narrow ridge that begins north of Lake Donna abuts the arête. Follow this ridge to its top, where roped climbing begins. Climb a steep face on the arête's right side until you can move left around a corner onto the crest. Climb the face on the crest for 175 feet to a large, sloping ledge; routefinding is intricate. From the sloping ledge, climb to a broken area that makes a prominent step on the arête. Four or five more pitches lead up the crest; routefinding becomes easier as the arête narrows to a width of only a few feet.

4. Monkeyflower Dome, South Gully (I 5.5) The southeast end of the Pronghorn massif is a formation that overlooks Pass 11,360+, its south face prominent from Middle Bonneville Lake: Monkeyflower Dome. One route climbs the gully to the left of the south face in three pitches, staying on orange rock, to the saddle west of the dome. Climb two 4th-class pitches on the dome's west ridge to its summit.

5. Monkeyflower Dome, South Face (III 5.8+) After scrambling right up a 3rd-class ledge system, rope up at the base of a left-slanting orange band and climb a loose dihedral for 30 feet, traverse right, and climb past ledges. Continue up the 5.5 face to a dihedral with an overhang near its base and black knobs to its right. Ascend the dihedral for a lead (5.8+ near its top), then climb a 50-foot pitch up right (5.4) to a good belay ledge.

Either climb an incipient crack that begins at the ledge's center, then traverse left and climb a 5.8 corner to a small stance, or reach the corner via a corner that blanks out below it. The exposed sixth pitch traverses left under roofs (5.7) to a belay in a small alcove. Climb up for 100 feet (one 5.7 move), then unrope and scramble 200 feet to the top.

6. Monkeyflower Dome, Southeast Ridge (I 5.8) Approach this unsustained four-pitch route via a right-slanting grassy ramp. Two low-angle pitches end at large terraces. Continue up the ridge that separates the south face from a gully to the north, at some point exiting left from the gully, then gaining a chimney system.

Dragon Head Peak (12,205)

Middle Fork Lake's valley curves south at the upper end of the lake and is bounded on the west by a long ridge's east-facing walls. The ridge's south end is Pronghorn; the north end, with an indistinct summit, is Dragon Head.

1. West Slope (I 2nd class) Begin at Rainbow Lake.

2. East Face (V 5.8 A4) You can discern four buttresses on Dragon Head's east face, the southern two separated by a deep cleft. This route, ascending the second buttress from the right, ends north of Dragon Head's summit. It follows a right-facing dihedral for eight pitches to an overhang high on the face; right of this overhang is a large, light-colored, triangular slab. The dihedral is free climbing, except for three overhangs. The overhang at the corner's top involves spectacular aid to reach a buttress out to the left. A few pleasant leads on the buttress finish the climb.

3. North Shoulder–Kooshasha Woosha (I 5.8) Three pitches of crack climbing between large ledges, effort being required to avoid easier rock.

Skull Lake, en route to East Fork Valley

8 East Fork Valley

Climbers on Cirque of the Towers summits have long been intrigued by walls of a deep valley to the northwest—intrigue perhaps heightened by their wondering why they'd been unaware of this valley.

It is the source of the East Fork River. Early climbers visiting the valley tried various names—Desolation Valley, the Valley of the Walls, Bonneville Basin (the real Bonneville Basin is to the west)—but none stuck. The name East Fork Valley is merely the blandest. The east-facing walls seen from the Cirque, a dark row in afternoon, belong to Raid Peak, Ambush Peak, and Mount Geikie. Across the valley's head extends a serrated ridge that is a Wind River landmark, Mount Bonneville.

Until the 7.5-minute topographic maps appeared in 1981, this area, Middle Fork Lake, and Baptiste Lake were covered by the 15-minute Mount Bonneville quad. The area is such classic glacial terrain that the USGS included the map in a set assembled to illustrate geologic forms. Among the features typical of glacial topography apparent on the map are a chain of lakes on the East Fork Valley's floor, roche moutonnées at its lower end, and Mount Bonneville's narrow crest separating this cirque from the Bonneville Lakes cirque to the north.

The map also indicates U-shaped valleys, but the East Fork Valley's U is asymmetrical. The Continental Divide peaks that form the valley's east side present far less impressive faces than its west side—an asymmetry attributable to the position of faults. One of the Divide peaks, Mount Hooker, possesses the range's premier wall, but it faces the other way, toward Baptiste Lake, and for that reason is included in the Baptiste Lake chapter. Except for Hooker, this chapter includes Divide peaks—of which Mount Washakie is the highest—south to the Cirque of the Towers, though they are also accessible from the Baptiste Lake area, east of the Divide.

While the density of rock routes is greater in the Cirque of the Towers and at Deep Lake, the East Fork Valley offers enough routes of various lengths and difficulties to keep climbers happily busy. The tendency is to aspire to the longer routes on Raid and Ambush but to turn to Midsummer Dome, a low formation with excellent rock at the foot of the valley, when a full day's commitment isn't appropriate.

There are good campsites near Mae's Lake and Pyramid Lake, below Midsummer Dome, and by the slender lakes in the upper valley.

Most hikers reach the valley from Big Sandy Opening, by either the Fremont and Pyramid Lake Trails or the East Fork Trail. Bonneville's northwest side can be approached from Scab Creek, by trails described in the Middle Fork Lake chapter. Peaks toward the section's southern end are easily reached from Shadow Lake, covered in the Cirque of the Towers chapter.

Except for two of these southern peaks, which are on the Lizard Head Peak quad, this chapter's peaks are on the Mount Bonneville quad. The beginnings of the Fremont and East Fork Trails are on the Big Sandy Opening quad.

Trails

Fremont Trail

Big Sandy Opening to Raid Lake—15.5 miles

Big Sandy Opening is the Fremont Trail's southern terminus. The Fremont Trail provides access to the western side of the Cirque of the Towers, the East Fork Valley, areas to the north, and Washakie, Grave, and Baptiste Lakes by way of Washakie and Hailey Passes.

(While you may know this trail as the Highline, the USGS Mount Bonneville quad and the Earthwalk, Beartooth, and Bridger Wilderness maps label it the Fremont Trail. With Forest Service signs being inconsistent, this guide is trying to minimize confusion by adopting the maps' terminology.)

In terms of signpost nomenclature, the Fremont/Highline Trail begins at Big Sandy Lodge. However, the trailhead is at Big Sandy Opening, and you use the Meek's Lake Trail to reach the Fremont Trail from the trailhead, terminology that makes sense only as history. The Meek's Lake Trail coincides with the Big Sandy Trail for 0.5 mile; locate the beginning over a rise at the campground's upstream end. Departing from the Big Sandy Trail and the river, the trail climbs to Meek's Lake, beyond which is a meadow. A trail to Diamond Lake, V Lake, and the Big Sandy Trail heads northeast, while the Meek's Lake turns left and crosses a small creek, intersecting a trail coming from Big Sandy Lodge west of the meadow.

Turn right (north) on the Fremont Trail. After only a few dull miles, you reach Fish Creek Park's spacious meadows, with views of the East Fork peaks. The trail has been rerouted to the west (and lengthened by 0.5 mile), presumably to eliminate boots' damage to a few soggy patches. However, the larger-scale erosion gullies and bare dunes are effects of overgrazing, and if sheep continue trashing the meadow, your detouring will serve little environmental purpose. North of the park pass Mirror Lake to the west, Dad's Lake to the east, and Marm's Lake to the west. At Marm's Lake's north end is a junction. To go to Shadow Lake, Washakie Pass, Hailey Pass, or Pyramid Lake, turn right from the Fremont Trail.

The Fremont Trail continues to the junction of Washakie Creek and the East Fork. Crossing the East Fork and the East Fork Trail, it ascends to meadows west of the Raid-Geikie ridge. Many nebulous trails cross the meadows near Raid Lake, and the more ostentatious cairns are Basque objets d'art, not trail markers. The Fremont Trail north of Raid Lake is described in the Middle Fork Lake chapter.

Pyramid Lake Trail

Marm's Lake to Pyramid Lake—4.5 miles

North of Marm's Lake this trail branches east from the Fremont Trail, bends back toward the lake, then ascends a draw to open country. Before the trail reaches Washakie Creek, the Shadow Lake Trail diverges right. If Washakie Creek is overly

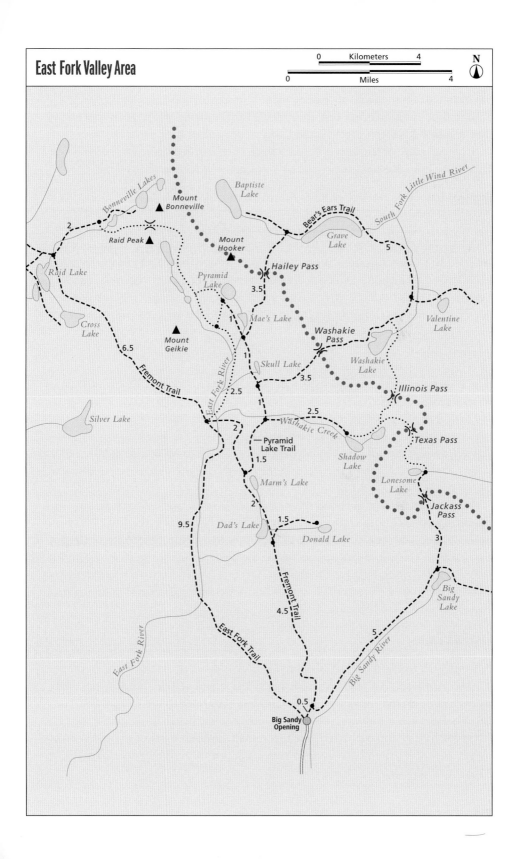

East Fork Valley Area

Kilometers
0   4
Miles
0   4

N

Bonneville Lakes

Mount Bonneville ▲

Baptiste Lake

Bear's Ears Trail

South Fork Little Wind River

Raid Peak ▲

2

Mount Hooker ▲

Hailey Pass

Grave Lake

5

Pyramid Lake

3.5

Raid Lake

Cross Lake

1

Mae's Lake

Washakie Pass

Valentine Lake

Mount Geikie ▲

6.5

1

Skull Lake

Washakie Lake

Illinois Pass

East Fork River

3.5

Fremont Trail

2.5

Silver Lake

1

2.5

Texas Pass

2

Washakie Creek

Shadow Lake

Lonesome Lake

Pyramid Lake Trail

Jackass Pass

1.5

Marm's Lake

2

9.5

Dad's Lake

1.5

Donald Lake

3

Fremont Trail

4.5

Big Sandy Lake

East Fork Trail

5

East Fork River

Big Sandy River

0.5

Big Sandy Opening

intimidating, try wading where it is wider and slower, 0.5 mile upstream. The next junction is on a hill north of the creek; the trail to Washakie Pass turns east, while the main trail continues north, passing Skull Lake, then Mae's Lake. Just before Mae's Lake, another trail branches east, to Hailey Pass. Go along Mae's Lake's west shore, then climb beside a creek to Pyramid Lake.

The trail more or less ends at Pyramid Lake, but you can easily reach the main East Fork Valley from the lake's upper end by a gap north of Midsummer Dome.

East Fork Trail

Big Sandy Opening to East Fork River–Washakie Creek Confluence—9.5 miles

This trail offers an alternative to the Fremont Trail for reaching the East Fork Valley from Big Sandy Opening. While it is slightly longer than the Fremont–Pyramid Lake Trail combination, it offers a certain charm, especially to someone jaded by Dad's and Marm's Lakes. The East Fork is a fine river, and the lusher vegetation below 10,000 feet creates a different quality of light than in the higher, open country we more often travel through.

Note that on the Mount Bonneville quad and other maps, this trail is labeled as the Highline. However, with the Highline's southern end being open to interpretation, it seems clearer to consider the trail described here to be the East Fork Trail, as on older maps.

As you drive in, before reaching Big Sandy Opening's parking area, a short side road goes west to corrals; the East Fork Trail begins here. Finding your way past several junctions in the first mile can be tricky: Don't go left to Mud Lake and Big Sandy Lodge or right to Meek's Lake. Beyond these junctions the trail crosses Iron Creek Meadow and passes Twin Lakes.

At Boulter Lake you encounter three trail junctions in quick succession, not necessarily signed. Follow the lake's southwest shore, then descend to the East Fork, slosh through a bog, and ford. An obscure trail continues west, climbing to Poston Lake, but the East Fork Trail turns upstream, following the west side of the river for a few miles, before crossing (rock-hop) back to the east. The trail crosses the river a third time, by a bridge, just before it meets the Fremont Trail, where Washakie Creek joins the East Fork. The northbound Fremont Trail diverges left, up a side valley.

East Fork Route

Fremont Trail to East Fork Lakes—4 miles

The East Fork Trail ends where it meets the Fremont Trail, but you can easily follow a path up the river's west bank. Continue upstream to the narrow East Fork Lakes below Geikie, Ambush, and Raid, climbing to the bench to the east at the first lake. Reach Mae's Lake by a well-used path that climbs just east of the lake's outlet stream. Reach Pyramid Lake by following a side stream to the grassy slopes below Midsummer Dome.

Passes

Col 11,960+

East Fork Valley to Sheila Lake

Col 11,960+ is the sharp notch 0.3 mile northeast of Mount Bonneville, between Bonneville and Peak 12,229, on the Divide to its northeast. Because Dad's and Marm's Lakes, and Middle Fork and Lee Lakes, lie in the same linear zone, the notch is highly visible and appears to be the way from the East Fork Valley to Bonneville's northwest side. However, loose scree and steep snow make this pass decidedly inferior to Pass 11,640+.

Pass 11,640+

East Fork Valley to Bonneville Lake 10,521

The saddle north of Raid Peak is high and trailless but useful for commuting between the East Fork and the lakes west of Mount Bonneville. The east side of the pass is talus and usually some snow, but the west side is gentle, with much grass. Don't follow the stream down the steep part of its descent to Bonneville Basin; leave it where it turns northwest, cross a minor saddle just east of a knoll with dwarf conifers, and descend a draw south of the stream to Bonneville Lake 10,521's south shore.

When you're ascending from the west, this draw and the reason for using it are obvious.

Illinois Pass (11,400+)

Shadow Lake to Washakie Lake

Illinois Pass could be either of two Divide crossings north of Barren Lake connecting the Shadow Lake drainage to the Washakie Lake drainage—one the obvious pass from the south, the other obvious from the north. The eastern of the two is overall the easier; reach it from Barren Lake by zigzagging up grassy ramps to the col, just west of August 16th Peak's minor west summit, that overlooks Tarn 11,140. From this tarn to Washakie Lake is a stroll. Avoid boulders that litter the lake's southwest shore by circling the lake to the east.

The original Illinois Pass (11,660+) sits at the head of gentle slopes northwest of Barren Lake, below Bair Peak. However, what appears on maps to be a quick descent to Pass Lake involves formidably large blocks and steep scree.

Peaks

Mount Bonneville (12,585)

Until 1981 this chapter, as well as the Middle Fork Lake and Baptiste Lake chapters, was covered by the 15-minute Mount Bonneville quad. Why the map was named for its fourth-highest peak wasn't obvious. You had to note that Bonneville stands across a fault zone that extends from the South Fork of Bull Lake Creek, through Middle Fork Lake, down the East Fork, and past Marm's and Dad's Lakes, making it highly visible. Compare the close contour lines on Bonneville's west side with those of such neighbors as Raid and Pronghorn. Their slopes hold snow, while Bonneville's west face, being too steep, stands out darkly after a storm. Its noticeability from the west is enhanced by the fact that US 191 approaching Pinedale from Jackson and Pinedale's main street point toward it.

Also not obvious on the map is the pinnacled ridge's symmetry; the profile is distinctive and similar from east and west. A complexity of ridges, buttresses, and gendarmes gives the triple-summited peak more architectural character than is usual in the Wind Rivers. The sum of these effects is an aura that attracts mountaineers to the suitably vertiginous summit.

1. East Face (II 5.2) A minor ridge or buttress extends southeast from the main south ridge and shelters a snowpatch on its north side. Approach the snow from the East Fork Valley's highest lake. You can climb the face above the snow in several places, but it is easiest just left of the couloir that ends in the notch north of the main summit. From the notch, climb just east of the summit pyramid's north ridge.

Mount Bonneville

Peak 12,000+ · South Summit · North Summit

2. Northeast Ridge (III 5.8 plus rappels) Bonneville's northeast ridge includes a prominent shoulder, the north summit, and two gendarmes. Reaching the north summit from Col 11,960+ at the foot of the ridge requires up to ten leads. All but a 20-foot 5.8 section near the north summit is 5.4 or easier. Continuing to the main summit involves ascents of the gendarmes (the first being the owl-eared one referred to in the next route description) and 140-foot rappels down their south sides. Join the *East Face* route near the notch between the second gendarme and the main summit.

3. North Summit, Northwest Face (III 5.9) From the west you see two sky-line gendarmes between Bonneville's main and north summits. Two small ears give the northern one an owl's profile. Below this gendarme is a concave wall, to the left of which a gully slants up to a shoulder of the north summit. A route ascends this wall and ends—with a presumably unnecessary flourish—on the gendarme's steep face, just left of a prominent chute.

From the lower gully, scramble for hundreds of feet to a series of left-facing corners that rise stepwise to the right. After nearly three pitches in the corners, traverse up left to a ledge below a wide crack. Ascend loose blocks to the crack, climb it for a short distance, then make a desperate traverse right to a ledge. Follow steep cracks for a pitch and a half to the gendarme's top, where you join the *Northeast Ridge* route. You could probably do an easier pitch by climbing left of the wide crack and reaching the ridge north of the gendarme.

4. West Face, Straight Chimney-Pinnacle (III 5.7 plus rappel) A straight chimney extends through orange rock to an inconspicuous pinnacle that, seen from

Mount Bonneville

the west, stands below the notch between the owl-eared gendarme and the skyline gendarme nearer the summit.

Hundreds of feet of scrambling, interspersed perhaps by short roped sections, lead to steeper rock and the chimney. Short escapes from the chimney are often feasible, but don't stray too far. At the end of the third pitch or start of the fourth (pitch length is affected by rope drag and the location of occasional loose rock), pass behind a prominent chockstone and climb a slab to the right. Above a short overhanging crack is a junction. Bear right up a ramp to reach a scree gully that you can follow all the way to the notch north of the main summit.

Alternatively (the first ascent route), bear left at the junction; a long, interesting pitch leads to a scree gully that intersects the above-mentioned gully behind the pinnacle. Climb the pinnacle by wandering up ledges on its north side (though the first ascent account implies a more elegant climb of the pinnacle). A two-rope rappel from near the pinnacle's tiny top returns you to the intersection of scree gullies.

At the notch above the scree, join the *East Face* route.

5. West Face, Curving Chimney (III 5.8) This route follows the west face's chimney that curves left, then ascends the face of the summit pyramid. The chimney is ugly, the face beautiful.

From Bonneville Lake 10,828, several hundred feet of pleasant slabs lead to the chimney. More scrambling in the chimney and a 5th-class pitch that is likely to be wet lead to the gully between the preceding route's pinnacle and the summit pyramid. While the gully continues to the notch north of the summit, the route ascends the right wall. There are many possibilities; apparently difficulties increase the farther right you go. Three or four pitches end at the summit.

6. West Face, Right Edge (III 5.7) To the left of the gully leading to the col between the main and south summits is a rib that offers pleasant climbing—if you ignore the gully. Begin scrambling as for the *Curving Chimney,* but continue up to the gully. Climb to the right side of the rib and ascend it for several pitches. Eventually you reach a few hundred feet of easy slabs. Above rises a buttress, left of which is a right-facing corner. Gain the buttress's crest and climb it for two leads, then follow a ramp up right to the south ridge.

7. South Summit, West Arête (III 5.7) Climb the first pitch of the *South Summit, West Face* route, but then angle left, just right of a prominent slanting chimney. Follow an easy gully around a corner and past a notch to the arête. Ascend the arête's right side, passing roofs to the right. Cracks to the right lead to a long dihedral, which ends an easy pitch from the top of the face and the 500-foot serrated ridge connecting the top to the south summit.

8. South Summit, West Face (III 5.7) Local aficionados of the ethereal (or absurd) have long sought the grail of "another Wolf's Head." Those camped at the Bonneville Lakes might be surprised to know that a candidate is nearby: Behind what appears to be Bonneville's south summit, a 500-foot coxcombed ridge continues to the real south summit. Although perhaps lacking the character of the more memorable sections of Wolf's Head's *East Ridge,* this replica comes close for exposure and routefinding puzzles, while letting you find your way free of folklore and climbers ahead of you.

Imposing from afar but broken-looking from nearby, the concave west face can be climbed by a crease in its center. Depending on where you begin belaying, about eight leads reach the top of the face. While no pitch is continuous, each offers at least a 5.6 or 5.7 move. Routefinding puzzles, however, are continuous (though the crease is apparent from a mile away, details aren't); this, combined with a need to beware of loose rock, give the face a mountaineering flavor.

9. South Summit, South Ridge (II 5.7) Beginning from the notch between Bonneville's south summit and Peak 12,000+, climb a 4th-class pitch east of the crest to the first step. Then follow the crest for two pitches. Next, climb an overhang by a finger crack. Traverse onto the west face, but use a chimney to regain the ridge on the fifth pitch.

This route joins the *West Face* route for the exposed ridge traverse to the south summit.

10. South Summit, South Gully (I 5.1) A 1927 attempt on Bonneville got as far as the south summit, presumably by climbing from the high talus on the southeast side up a gully to the notch between the south summit and a gendarme to its east. A few gymnastic moves are required below the notch, and a short 4th-class section above leads to the top.

11. South Summit, East Arête (I 5.6) Climb the gendarme east of the south summit by a crack in the minor arête that rises from the high talus slope's north end. A short section can challenge someone inexperienced in cracks. From the gendarme's top, climb down or rappel to the notch below the south summit.

12. Traverse, South Summit–North Summit (III 5.8 plus rappel) The climbers who reached the south summit in 1927 declared the pinnacled ridge leading to the main summit to be impossible. This assessment held until 1970, when Tony Qamar and Charlie Raymond reached the south summit by its west face, traversed to the main summit, and continued to the north summit. The crux of this inspired traverse is a short crack on the first tower beyond the principal notch between the south and main summits. Pass a few pinnacles on the east. From the main summit, cross gendarmes (5.7, with a rappel) to the north summit.

Descent: The *East Face* is Bonneville's usual descent route. You can downclimb it, though multiple series of anchors tempt you to rappel. If you're camped west of Bonneville, cross at about the snowpatch's level to Pass 11,640+.

You can descend from the north summit—perhaps completing a south-to-north traverse—by downclimbing and rappelling the northeast ridge or by descending the ridge to the north shoulder, then returning to the Bonneville Lakes by the loose gully to the north of the *Northwest Face* route.

Peak 12,000+

This minor summit on Bonneville's southwest ridge, 0.4 mile southwest of Bonneville's summit, offers one attraction—good rock on its short west face. While the approach from Middle Bonneville Lake is a bit much, considering the routes' lengths, you can quickly descend and climb several lines.

1. Southwest Ridge (I 2nd class) A short excursion from Pass 11,640+.

2. West Face Dihedral (I 5.7) Two of the west face's left-facing dihedrals are more prominent than the others. This route ascends the right-hand of the two, in two long pitches.

3. West Face (I 5.5) Just right of the above-mentioned dihedral is a nubbly face, split by several discontinuous cracks that allow impeccable protection. Three enjoyable pitches lead to scrambling near the summit.

Raid Peak (12,532)

Sheep have never been popular in the Wind Rivers, but complaining hikers have never resorted to the extreme measures taken in 1903 by cattlemen, who killed 1,200 sheep in a raid on the South Fork of Boulder Creek. The lake near the massacre site became Raid Lake, and the summit to the east, Raid Peak.

The 1877 Hayden Survey map places the name "Mount Bonneville" on the peak we now call Raid. William Owen reported climbing Mount Bonneville in 1890, but we may suspect that he actually climbed our Raid.

1. North Slope (I 3rd class) From Pass 11,640+, dodge some steep slabs.

2. Southwest Slope (I 2nd or 3rd class) Begin at the head of Raid Creek.

3. South Buttress, South Face (II 5.6) A pleasant route reportedly begins on the snow ramp that slants up left under the buttress, leaving the snow where it turns north and steepens and following the crest. However, while you will find good rock, you may not find a route that doesn't stay on the snow too long or isn't significantly harder than 5.6.

4. South Buttress, East Face (IV/V 5.8) On the 1,700-foot buttress that rises from Lake 10,566 to Raid's south summit is a free climb nearly as long as the range's longest, on Hooker. Begin 100 feet right of the buttress's toe with three leads up an obvious ramp. Continue up past several overhangs, reaching a large ledge after ten pitches. Gain another prominent ledge after five more pitches, one pitch from the top.

The first ascent team required over a day and used nuts up to 3 inches. Their account mentions an excessive distance between protection on several pitches. However, subsequent parties, who completed the climb in a day, found the protection adequate but the routefinding challenging.

5. South Buttress Right (V 5.10) An eighteen-pitch route that combines exposed face climbing and fine crack climbing may share the start of the original *South Buttress* route. In any event it continues angling slightly right, gaining a

Ambush Peak North

The Apostle

Raid Peak

Mt. Bonneville

5

7

4

prominent corner system that splits the east face. Follow this system to the top. The crux is a sustained crack midway up the corner.

6. East Face (III 5.7/5.8) This route follows a groove or chimney to the right of the giant dihedral between the south buttress and the main peak; the groove slants up left to the notch between the peak and the buttress. Climbing begins left of a grassy area. Several easy pitches on loose rock lead to the crux, a 130-foot dihedral with several overhangs. Two easier pitches then reach the notch.

7. Son of Raid (III 5.10c/d) Between Raid and Ambush is fine-looking rock, even if the three buttresses are dwarfed by Raid and Ambush. The seven pitches of *Son of Raid* ascend the middle of the three—second to the left of Raid, second to the right of Ambush's M Buttress. A few pitches are 70 meters long.

Begin at the low point of the slab at the toe of the buttress, near two brown dots. Pitch 1: Climb to the right of the dots and left of a pair of prominent water streaks (5.5). Pitch 2: Climb to a left-leaning seam with a bolt and continue up and slightly left past six more bolts to a right-facing dihedral and a ledge with belay bolts (5.10a). Pitch 3: Move up left, then trend right, passing two bolts protecting tricky moves, to a thin left-facing corner. Pass another bolt before laybacking right out a roof, eventually reaching a right-facing corner (5.10c/d). Pitch 4: Climb right of a suspicious flake under a roof to a crack. In darker rock, climb a slab until faced with a steep, technical, and improbable traverse left. Pass a bolt and a fixed nut to a great ledge (5.10a/b). Pitch 5: Pass three bolts (5.9) to a left-sloping ramp/ledge. Follow the ledge to the left (5.5) and belay in an alcove near a spike of rock. Pitch 6: Climb a ramp/crack right-facing dihedral system past the spike to a ledge (5.7). Pitch 7: Straight up (5.6), then out right up a 3rd-class gully.

The first ascent team placed bolts for descending by rappel, but the slanting gully between Son of Raid and the Apostle makes a quick descent without rappelling.

Ambush Peak North (12,187)

An array of minor summits punctuates the ridge joining Raid and Geikie. They would be ignored and unnamed were it not for walls, sweeping down to the East Fork, that are among the range's tallest. In 1969 Beckey, Callis, and McFeters completed the first rock route on any of these formations, which took them to Point 12,173, and they bestowed upon it the name Ambush. It was unclear how inclusive Ambush was meant to be, and climbers attached the name to everything in the vicinity, including the higher Point 12,187. Point 12,187 is nevertheless a separate summit, and with the abundance of routes now leading to 12,187 and 12,173, it may reduce confusion by distinguishing Point 12,187 as Ambush North. From the East Fork Valley floor this summit topography isn't apparent, but Ambush North stands above the head of the lake between Lakes 10,331 and 10,566.

1. West Slope (I 3rd class) Reaching the crest from Sheep Creek is easy hiking; it may have you wondering at the 3rd-class rating. From the crest, assessing the route to the summit may also have you wondering about the 3rd-class rating, for the opposite reason. Standing on the summit you may wonder about the identity of the actual high point.

2. East Face (III 5.7) The wall right of the gully between the *Golden Dihedral* and M Buttress has been climbed, though much of the rock is "alarmingly unstable." Snow and lightning sent the first ascent pair scurrying for the notch at the top of the gully, thus bypassing the face's final few hundred feet.

3. M Buttress–McMuffin (II 5.8R) Climbers in the East Fork Valley don't need a guidebook to identify M Buttress: A folded black dike labels it. A six-pitch route has been climbed beginning on the M's left side, ending in a large white dihedral.

4. M Buttress–Triple Shot (IV 5.7 plus rappel) Begin at the left side of the M, climb a beautiful left-facing dihedral and then the arête that leads to the top of the first tower. Continue past two more towers. One tower requires a rappel to descend.

5. The Apostle–Great Grey Book (III 5.9) The formation between *Son of Raid* and M Buttress may topographically be little more than a shoulder of Ambush North, but its appearance from the valley is distinct enough to earn it a name: the Apostle.

Approach by ascending the right-leaning gully to the Apostle's right for 150 feet, to below a large roof with gray rock to its left. Climb flakes to a chimney, climb the chimney (5.8), and climb up right into the gray dihedral. The spectacular second pitch follows the dihedral (5.8). Finish the dihedral (5.8) on the third pitch and climb (4th class) up right to the far side of a ledge. On the 5.9 fourth pitch, ascend discontinuous flakes and cracks through several roofs. The 5.7 final pitch is more flakes, cracks, and roofs.

Descent: After completing a route from the East Fork Valley, you will probably want to circle west around Ambush Peak to the Ambush-Geikie col. However, climbers (good climbers) have descended the gully between the *Golden Dihedral* and M Buttress. Also, the slanting 3rd-class gully right of the Apostle makes a convenient descent route from the *Great Grey Book*.

Ambush Peak (12,173)

Having separated Ambush North from Ambush, we can also separate two facets of Ambush's east face, distinguishing the main face from the nearly as impressive face to its right, the two being separated by a black dike, by calling the latter the North Buttress.

With the range's most impressive wall after Hooker and the Cathedral towers, Ambush has, since the last guidebook edition, received much attention from good climbers. Many of their efforts, while among the Wind Rivers' proudest, have been vaguely documented or undocumented. As a result there has been more intersecting of routes and redundant naming than on other formations. This edition should at least provide a clearer context for future endeavors.

1. West Slope (I 3rd class) From East Fork Valley, ascend a long scree slope to the Ambush-Geikie col, traverse north to a black dike, and climb near the dike. This is the obvious descent route after completing a route from the valley.

2. South Ridge (II 5.7) From above the Ambush-Geikie saddle, traverse grassy ledges to the right (east) of the crest. After roping up, angle up right below the crest for three pitches, then gain the crest in two more pitches.

3. East Chimney-South Face (II 5.6) A prominent chimney/gully, the remnant of a dike, cuts up left through the east face. About 1,000 feet of 3rd and 4th class in the gully lead to the crux, a surprisingly enjoyable steep chimney. Above, climb left onto the south face, where hundreds of feet of scrambling lead to the top.

The amount of scrambling may discourage climbers, and the chimney may discourage scramblers, which is too bad, for this is an enjoyable route.

4. East Face–Runnel Out (IV 5.10aR A1) *Runnel Out* is scarier and more committing than it would be were the cracks not bottoming water runnels that don't necessarily take nonchalant protection.

Ascend the *East Chimney* for 1,000 feet, past its crux chimney. Above is a roof with double cracks splitting its left end. This is *Runnel Out*'s first pitch. Pitch 1: Reach the double cracks via a flake. Above the cracks (5.9), face climb up left to a small ledge. Pitch 2: A scary, poorly protected pitch links disconnected runnels (5.10aR), reaching an open book that ends at a small roof and a white dike. Pitch 3: Traverse left on the dike past a left-facing corner to a right-facing corner topped with a small roof. Follow the corner past the roof until the crack widens (5.8). Pitch 4: Climb the widening crack (5.9+) to a small stance below an overhang. Pitch 5: Move left to a flake and left again to a thin crack used to pass a bulge. As often the case on Wind River first ascents, grass and dirt choking the crack forced the climbers to use aid (5.9 A1).

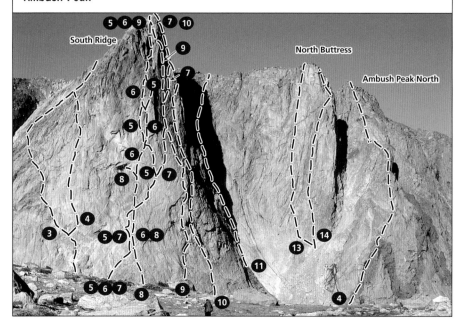

Ambush Peak

South Ridge

North Buttress

Ambush Peak North

Belay in a large red corner. Pitch 6: Climb the red corner (5.9+) to the roof that caps it. Climb a left-leaning crack through the roof and belay in an alcove. The first ascent pair finished with a 120-foot pitch involving a 5.7 left-leaning crack, rappelled from a sloping ledge 150 feet to a lower ledge, and escaped farther left up a 3rd-class gully. However, they were disappointed to not have time to explore cracks and corners above the sloping ledge.

5. East Face–California! (IV 5.11) The upper part of the central east face long remained a blank on the map, thanks to a labyrinth of roofs that scared off most prospective climbers and baffled the few who did attempt it. Now, however, the face features two routes, the first boltless (and previously unreported) and a second that apparently closely follows the original.

A California-shaped flake, obvious from afar two-thirds of the way up the east face, gives the route its name. The first ascent pair thought highly enough of their creation that with a few more ascents it may well take its place as one of the hard classics.

Begin by ascending the *East Chimney* for 300 feet. Exit right via 4th-class corners and climb 600 feet (5.8R) to rounded gray ledges. Two 5.6 pitches follow low-angle cracks and corners to the base of a faint gray V that is seen from the ground but not when you're there. The route follows the right side of this V for two pitches (5.9), passing a large right-facing corner. Just beyond this corner you reach the start of the Inverted Staircase—stepped overhangs located on the vague edge separating the east and northeast faces. *Wish You Were Here* negotiates these overhangs.

From the beginning of the Staircase, *California!* heads straight up to a fine S crack, which begins easily but on the second pitch fades to a 5.10 seam and ends at a semi-hanging belay below a prominent water-streaked overhang. A hard move leads over the overhang to a slab that is followed tortuously on dikes and flakes (5.8) up and left to the overhang at the base of the California flake. Climb the overhang easily and up the moderate crack that forms the flake's Pacific coast. From the top of California, a faint crack in a shallow corner shoots up right and offers some of the hardest climbing on the route, two 5.10+ sections. About 100 feet up this crack, features lead back left to a belay below another roof. Above this roof is easy, low-angle rock that leads up right. You could probably continue up it easily to the summit, but *California!* veers left to a huge left-facing corner, which includes an overlap you undercling around (5.11). Above, you can either escape left on a ledge to easy ground or continue up another corner, easier than the previous one.

6. East Face–I Think, Therefore I Ambush (V 5.12-) In 2011 technical face climbing linking minor crack systems resulted in a second, somewhat independent, line up the formidable upper wall. The hardest sections are well protected, often by bolts—more bolts than are customary in the Wind Rivers—but mere 5.9 sections may not be.

To reach the upper wall, you have a choice of beginning from the *East Chimney* or by climbing *Plaisir*. To start from the *East Chimney,* scramble 300 feet to a large patch of grass and follow a 4th-class ramp right to a large ledge system. Begin climbing as far right as you can walk without scrambling over exposed blocks. Trend right, from one short crack to another, aiming for the bolt on *Plaisir's* seventh pitch. Follow *Plaisir* for a few pitches, to a bolt belay below a single bolt 12 feet higher. Climb to the bolt but then diverge from *Plaisir,* using a flake system (spicy 5.8 on hollow flakes) to reach a bolt belay near a large left-facing corner. This is the first pitch of *I Think.*

Begin the 20-meter, 5.11- second pitch by climbing over hollow flakes and crossing the main left-facing corner to the base of a shallow left-facing corner. Climb it for 20 feet, then climb right around a dark block, passing two bolts, to a stance below a flake. Begin the 35-meter, 5.12- third pitch by laybacking to and around large detached blocks. Climb through the double roofs and face above (three bolts). Undercling right to a double, thin, right-facing corner, ascend it to a roof, and undercling right. Belay at a cramped stance above and right. The first 30 feet of the 35-meter, 5.11- fourth pitch is 5.9R. Climb a shallow left-facing corner with a large plate. Climb right around a rounded arête to a thin crack/flake arching right and climb it (solid protection, challenging to place). Layback around a small, loose flake to a semi-hanging stance, with a large right-leaning corner/roof up right.

Begin pitch 5 (5.10+) by reaching left to a crack and ascending the crack to its end 10 feet up. Face climb left to a crack that passes through a roof. Continue up a right-facing corner. Where the corner splits, move left to a flare and follow it to a flake and a traverse left, to belay in a nook between a chockstone and a roof. On pitch 6 (5.9), climb around the roof and move right along a right-leaning ramp past a bolt. Pull onto the second part of the ramp, climb it to its end, and ascend a flake up, then left, to a right-facing corner. Climb the corner, then step left to a sloping alcove. Begin pitch 7 by climbing out of the alcove around a chockstone. After 40 feet, traverse right on easy ledges, then climb dirty rock.

The 60-meter eighth pitch (5.9) offers options in the form of cracks reaching the summit ridge. The apparently easiest option involves loose, dirty terrain to the right and a right-facing corner. Above, scramble over large blocks to the top.

The first ascent required 22 hours, camp-to-camp. The climbers suggest RPs, stoppers, a double set of cams up to a #3 Camalot, with three .5 and .75 Camalots if you want more pro on 5.9 and 5.10- climbing.

7. East Face–Wish You Were Here (IV 5.9) This route coincides with *California!* as far as the Inverted Staircase. The first ascent pair completed *Wish You Were Here* over two years, being stormed off on their first try after climbing to the gray ledges. When they returned, they traversed to the ledges from the *East Chimney* before completing the twelve-pitch route.

Diverging to the right from *California!*, *Wish You Were Here* negotiates the Inverted Staircase's overhangs, which, thanks to chickenheads, proved to be less fearsome (5.9) than the first ascenders expected. After turning the vague edge separating the east face from the northeast face, the route crosses the *Northeast Face Left* to the *Northeast Face Right,* which it joins at a prominent tower; this crossing involves a 3rd-class traverse, a vegetated diagonal, a 5.8 dihedral, and a chimney.

8. East Face–Plaisir (III 5.9) *Plaisir* is essentially a 1,300-foot variation of *I Think* or of *California!* The upper part of the east face features roofs—a large, trapezoidal roof being the most prominent. *Plaisir* reaches this roof directly from below, but its creators, not wanting to risk the pleasurable nature of their outing, rappelled from their high point, installing bolt anchors.

Pitches 1–2: From the wall's low point, climb up an easy slab for 200 to 250 feet toward a right-facing corner system (5.3). Pitch 3: Continue for 100 feet up the corner system (5.5). Pitch 4: Up the slabby crack system (5.6). Pitch 5: Climb a small roof, followed by a dike out right, passing two bolts, to a series of overlaps, then back left to a ledge (5.9). Fun! Pitch 6: Work up into a right-facing corner, then a left-facing corner to another ledge (5.8). More fun! Pitch 7: Up broken corners and a slab (5.7). Pitch 8: Follow a finger crack up left to grass humps—the only dirt on the route (5.7). Pitch 9: Casual climbing to a finger crack intersecting a black band (5.9). Pitch 10: Pass a steep step with a bolt; trend right to a fine finger crack in black rock, belaying below the right side of the big roof (200 feet, 5.9).

9. Northeast Face Left (IV 5.8 A4) The overhangs above the lower *East Chimney* discouraged the first wall climbers, to whom the face around to the right appeared more reasonable. This is their route. Start below the overhangs and angle up right on 3rd-class slabs for several hundred feet to a large ledge below right-facing flakes. Climb to a dike, follow it right, and surmount a small overhang. Continue up and slightly right until you reach a large overhang. (A yellow hole, visible from the ground, is to the right.) Climb a left-leaning groove, then gain a ledge below another overhang. Use aid to pass this overhang.

The first ascent team bivouacked at a large flake 400 feet higher. From the flake, traverse up left under a yellow wall, then negotiate a series of loose flakes with aid. Several pitches, left of a large corner, lead to summit overhangs; turn them to easier going.

Carry gear for a 4-inch crack.

This route—or an approximation of it—has been climbed free at 5.10+ R/X.

10. Northeast Face Right–Hole in the Wall (IV 5.10+) Begin this sixteen-pitch route 150 feet right of the previous route by scrambling right up slabs to a ledge. Climb up and right, below overlaps, to a right-facing corner (5.7), then up to a large ledge. Delicate face climbing (5.9) above the ledge's right end leads to another ledge. The large yellow hole mentioned in the previous route description (which should help locate the route's start) is now to your right. Pitch 4 continues straight up to bolt anchors.

Traverse right, climb a 5.9 corner, then move back left to a belay. Climb a 5.9 pitch, then a pitch beginning with 5.7 and ending with an easy chimney, to a large ledge on the left behind a flake (ideal bivouac site). Climb a face and a thin crack (5.10+) to the base of a 200-foot dihedral that is one of the face's most prominent features. Climb the dihedral for a pitch (5.8), but rather than continuing up a yellow corner, step around to the right. Continue up and right (pitch 10).

On pitch 11, climb a 5.10b corner, then move right, skirting bulges. Pitch 12 is 5.9, pitch 13 easy to a big ledge. On pitch 14, 5.9 climbing is followed by a traverse left to 5.10a cracks and flakes. Pitch 15 also involves cracks and flakes (5.9) and leads to a final pitch.

A few pitons may be useful.

11. Dike Route (IV 5.8) The facets of Ambush that we are terming Point 12,173's northeast face and its north buttress are separated by a black dike. This twelve-pitch route ascends granite just right of the dike—at first adjacent to the dike, then for the final 400 feet following a crack system to the right.

12. North Buttress Left–Attack of the Killer Clowns (IV 5.11+ R) *Killer Clowns* ascends the wall between the dike and the more precisely documented North Buttress routes, *Center* and *Right*. The lower part of the route follows cracks to an "elevator shaft" 400 feet up. Higher, climbing involves a large roof and an off-width. A thousand feet up, the first ascent team had to choose between an overhanging flake leading left and a less-steep flake leading right. They initially went right and had to resort to aid, but, after reaching the top, rappelled and free climbed the left flake.

13. North Buttress Center–No Picnic for Old Men (IV 5.10d) The impos-ing wall just north of the northeast face of Ambush proper and separated from it by a black dike is the site of the three routes on the north buttress. The center route begins on broken rock on the face's right side, traverses to the center, and ascends the left-most of the corner systems that reach the top. Three pitches are at least 5.9. The route

Ambush Peak

was named forty years after its first ascent, when Steve Arsenault returned to find it had gotten no easier.

Climb the broken buttress on the right side of the face for 200 feet, then traverse 150 feet left to a large platform. Ascend grassy cracks above the platform for a pitch. The next pitch is the most difficult, involving strenuous climbing past large left-facing flakes and an overhang. Continue up cracks, then a short chimney and a difficult corner. Next, ascend a crack past a chockstone, avoiding the crack's least appealing section by delicate face climbing; finally step left to a small ledge. The broken chimney above leads to a more strenuous chimney. The next pitch ascends the easy, enjoyable face on the right to a broken area below a vegetated crack; bypass it by stepping right to a beautiful ledge 200 feet from the top. Climb the difficult crack above this ledge, then work into a crumbly chimney. The final lead wanders through summit blocks.

14. North Buttress Right–Golden Dihedral (IV 5.9+) Near the face's right edge is an orange left-facing dihedral that intersects the edge somewhat below the top. Begin in a left-facing corner just right of arches and directly below the orange dihedral, and climb to the dihedral in four leads. The next five pitches follow the dihedral. From the tower at the dihedral's top, go up left, then right on a ramp leading around to the north. Work up and left to a ledge at the end of the eleventh pitch, then move farther left to a difficult crack that leads to the top.

The climbing toward the top is difficult, and you may be tempted to move out right, but the rock quality out there is not good.

Mount Geikie (12,378)

American scientists working in the West during the nineteenth century were proud to be visited by eminent European colleagues and often returned the honor by attaching their guests' names to the land. The Hayden Survey named the southern peak of the East Fork Valley's western wall for Sir Archibald Geikie, a Scottish geologist who visited this country at the time of the survey. Mount Geikie's complex east face, with snow, gullies, headwalls, and grassy ledges, receives far less attention than Ambush and Raid's cleaner, steeper walls.

1. West Slope (I 2nd class) Geikie is easily climbed from the Fremont Trail via Sheep Creek's quiet little valley. You also can reach this slope from the east via the Ambush col.

2. Southeast Ridge (I 2nd class) From the Fremont Trail northwest of the East Fork–Washakie Creek confluence, avoiding the ridge's jagged section by the pretty valley to its west.

3. East Slope, Southeast Ridge (I Snow 4th class) Ascend snow below the east face to reach the col on the left skyline. The snow just below the col is steep and offers one of the valley's few opportunities to wield an ice axe.

4. East Rib (II 5.4/5.5) A rib rises from Geikie's snowfield directly to the summit. The crux is getting onto the rib; two parties climbed a couloir from the top of the snowfield for a rope length to avoid rotten rock lower on the rib. The remainder of the route closely follows the rib's crest.

Midsummer Dome (11,172)

Many Wind River cirques contain formations that are lower than surrounding peaks on the rim of the cirque but made for rock climbing. The quality of their rock isn't coincidental. Standing in the paths of ice-age glaciers, these crags and domes owe their survival to resistant rock. Formations overridden and rounded into domes are called roche moutonnées.

At East Fork Valley's lower end are three roche moutonnées. The south face of the upper one—Midsummer Dome, 0.5 mile west of Pyramid Lake—is conspicuous from the Fremont Trail and Cirque of the Towers summits. An obvious magnet for rock climbers, the dome is less committing on quasi-rest days than the higher peaks, and the downhill approach from Pyramid Lake is irresistible.

1. North Side (I 3rd class) A short scramble from Pyramid Lake or the East Fork.

2. Southwest Face (III 5.7) Good rock, easy to reach, a popular objective. However, the many large ledges that break the face, with a variety of cracks, corners, and chimneys connecting one ledge to another, mean that a precise line isn't well defined; you have leeway for improvisation. The ledges also break the climb into six to eight pitches, some much less than a rope length. A first ascender found the face "invigorating though not committing."

Midsummer Dome

Begin by scrambling up an obvious 4th-class right-facing corner for perhaps 150 feet, until it fades below a ceiling. Either traverse left below the ceiling or work left lower, then climb past one large ledge to another. Either climb up right to a curving, flared, grassy crack or work up left again to a long ledge. Walk left nearly to a clump of dwarf evergreens, then ascend a left-facing corner until you can step right to a ledge.

Climb a steep right-facing corner (which begins just about above the flared grassy crack) past a large block to another ledge. A steep layback leads to yet another large ledge, below a long right-facing corner and, to its right, a pair of difficult-looking cracks. You can avoid these cracks and the corner by a right-facing corner to the right, reached either by stepping down and around or via a few steps from the double cracks. An enjoyable flaky corner leads to a series of ledges and many ways to the top.

3. South Face Left (III 5.10a) Toward the south face's left side, a slabby apron sweeps up 200 feet to black-streaked arches. Rising from the left end of the arches are right-facing corners, which this route follows. Were the upper pitches as continuous as the first few, the route would be among the finest. Given its broken upper section, it can only be characterized as clean, enjoyable, and worth doing.

Wander up the apron to the base of the corner system, then use a trio of parallel corners to reach a single, steeper dihedral. The dihedral, which begins wide but narrows, is the route's distinct crux. As a toprope the pitch wouldn't merit a 5.10 rating, but to place protection you must pause in strenuous postures, making it a difficult lead. The pitch reaches a ledge with a large flake at its left end.

Midsummer Dome

3rd

bushes **5**

4 5.7

5.9
layback

5.7

3

5.6

2

5.9
layback

5.8

1

5.7

3rd

ROUTE 5

Climb up, then right, to a steep corner capped by a jagged overhang, which you can turn to the right. Continue more or less straight up for a few more pitches, encountering moderate moves between large ledges.

Climbing directly up from the top of the crux pitch involves enjoyable 5.7 to 5.8 climbing and may make a better route than the original line.

4. South Face Diagonal (III 5.9) Just right of the *South Face Left* route, a less likely one begins on slabs below a ceiling, then passes through the ceiling. Above the ceiling, use a corner to reach a large ledge 60 feet above. A long, spectacular pitch then goes up and right, involving hand traverses on flakes and finally passing under a 30-foot-high flake to ledges. Climb to a steep crack and follow it to the base of a large corner. The corner leads to a dead end, but enjoyable, improbable climbing to its left reaches the end of difficulties.

5. South Face Center (III 5.9+) Near the south face's center is a series of left-facing dihedrals. This excellent route follows corners just right of the main dihedrals for three pitches, then traverses into the system for the final two pitches. The first three ascents were made in the early 1970s by Gunks climbers whose standard of 5.9 was the Gunks' *M.F.,* and so this route was rated 5.9. A modern climber says the only harder 5.9 he's done is *M.F.* We'd better give the route 5.9 with a "+."

A 3rd-class ramp slants up to the right under the dihedrals. Begin roped climbing near the top of the ramp, where two cracks converge 10 feet above the ramp and just left of an overhanging corner. Climb these cracks, then follow a left-facing corner past an overhang to a belay below another steep part of the corner. Climb the corner or the face on the left to a strenuous layback. The third pitch ascends corners and ends by traversing 50 feet left to the main left-facing system. The next pitch begins with an overhang, followed by difficult, strenuous corner climbing. A final lead is 5.7, followed by 3rd-class scrambling.

6. South Face Right (II 5.9) At the south face's extreme right side, a steep ramp slants up left, crossing a black band. The ramp's 5.8 upper section leads to the crux, an overhanging, right-facing corner. Half a pitch above the corner, climbing degenerates to 3rd class.

7. Southeast Face (II 5.5) The identifying feature of this route is a right-facing chimney/corner above the black band that crosses the dome's southeast face up and right. Begin by climbing either of two steep left-slanting ramps. Above, work back right (5.5) to the chimney's base. A long pitch ascends rock right of the chimney.

The wall above is broken by numerous ledges and ramps, though 5th-class moves are often required to connect these breaks. After a few such pitches, minimize difficulties by trending left, unroping at a large field a few hundred feet below the summit.

Peak 12,229

A Divide peak with a flat summit but splintered ridges, 0.5 mile east-northeast of Mount Bonneville, is joined to Bonneville on the west and overlooks Baptiste Lake to the east.

The Bonneys mention an ascent from Sheila Lake.

Peak 12,120+

Walls west of the East Fork Valley and east of Baptiste Lake are among the range's more interesting, but several Divide peaks between are nondescript, including this one 0.8 mile northwest of Tower Peak.

1. East Slope (I 3rd class) A strangely gentle slope extends from Baptiste Lake nearly to the Divide.

2. West Slope (I 3rd class) Gain the northwest ridge from the 11,080-foot lake under Mount Bonneville. The ridge offers interesting, mildly exposed scrambling.

Glissade Peak (12,360+)

From the East Fork the location of the summit of the Divide peak 0.3 mile northwest of Tower Peak is unobvious and its broken face uninspiring. In early summer, though, you can glissade from near the summit to Baptiste Lake, an incentive for reaching the summit from that side.

1. East Ridge (I 3rd class) The only 3rd class is near the top.

2. South Ridge (I 3rd class) Glissade has been climbed by following the Divide north from Tower Peak. No ascent directly to the Glissade-Tower col has been reported, though climbers descended to the west from the col, rappelling once in the rain.

Tower Peak (12,330)

The peak just northwest of Hooker is distinguished by several towers among its gentle slopes. The south tower (12,117), particularly noticeable from Pyramid lake, has been described as a "squashed Pingora."

1. South Slope (I 2nd class) From Pyramid Lake, up unmitigated scree.

2. North Couloir (I 3rd class) Scree from Baptiste Lake.

3. Northwest Ridge (I 3rd class) Follow the Divide from Glissade Peak.

4. South Tower, West Face (I 5.5) You can climb several pitches on the low-angle wall just right of a black dike. The climbing is pleasant, but difficulties too easily bypassed. From the tower to the main summit is 3rd class. The summit block requires some thinking.

5. South Tower, Southwest Slope (I 3rd class) Connect ledges and gullies.

6. South Tower, Southeast Ridge (I 5.5) A long ridge extends from the South Tower toward Pyramid Lake. The ridge is largely scrambling, but the crest offers enough moves to make it interesting.

4, 5, 6 Descent: It's 5.2 or so toward the col to the north, but can be rappelled.

Pyramid Peak (12,030)

An aptly named formation whose one flaw is having nothing to challenge a rock climber.

1. Southwest Ridge (I 2nd class) During midsummer the slopes just north of the ridge offer an exceptional display of alpine flowers over an elevation range of 1,500 feet.

2. South Face (I 5.8) With routefinding acumen, four or five pitches can be linked between the face's large ledges. The one reported route involves a 5.8 corner on the first pitch and frequently trends right.

3. North Slope (I 2nd class) From the draw that slants from Pyramid Lake to Hailey Pass.

Dike Mountain (12,468)

Diabase dikes cross many peaks in the vicinity. Several have at one time been named for these intrusions, but the Divide summit south of Hailey Pass is now the only Dike Mountain. Its west slope is unimpressive, but walls hover over a seldom-visited valley to the east.

1. Northwest Ridge (I 2nd class) From Hailey Pass via a subsidiary summit. Grass and talus east of the crest give easy access to the upper slopes.

2. West Slope (I 2nd class) From Mae's Lake the possibilities are obvious.

3. South Ridge (I 3rd class) Traverse the Divide from Washakie Pass via Bernard Peak.

Bernard Peak (12,193)

Here is a rare summit crossed by a black dike. Most diabase dikes, weaker than the surrounding light-colored rock, erode to notches and gullies. Bernard's dike, though, is composed of a tougher rock, peridotite, which includes the green-black mineral olivine. The exposed rock's brown coloring is caused by iron. Among the scree may be found fibrous crystals of serpentine, a mineral formed by metamorphosis.

1. South Slope (I 2nd class) During the quick scramble from Washakie Pass, note the dark rubble's musical quality.

2. Northwest Ridge (I 3rd class) From Dike Mountain; easy except for one short section.

3. North Face An ascent of this fine-looking wall was noted in the summit register and has been corroborated, but details are not available.

Mount Washakie (12,524)

The peak named for the great Shoshone chief presents a noble face toward the valley he chose for his people; it dominates the scene above the Little Wind River's South Fork. Unfortunately, most climbers see Mount Washakie from the west, as another rounded hulk. Nevertheless, because of its height and location, it is one of the more popular walk-ups.

1. Northwest Ridge (I 3rd class) From southwest of Washakie Pass, ascend talus, tundra, or snow below the crest. Locating the summit is a bit of a problem; the summit block is the only section more difficult than 2nd class.

2. South Slope (I 3rd class) Mostly grassy ledges from Shadow Lake.

3. Southeast Ridge (I 3rd class) Follow the Divide from Bair Peak.

Bair Peak (12,335)

To Finis Mitchell—whose advice on Wind River nomenclature the USGS generally followed—the massive Divide peak southeast of Mount Washakie, its southwest slopes rising from Shadow Lake, was Big Chief Mountain. However, in this case the USGS did not follow Mitchell, whose Bair Peak is the point on the Divide, 0.5 mile east, between the two Illinois Passes. However, to minimize confusion this guidebook follows the USGS.

1. Southwest Slope (I 2nd class) From Shadow Lake, climb into the bowl between Bair and Washakie, then continue up.

2. East Slope (I 2nd class) From the western Illinois Pass on easy snow or talus.

3. Northwest Ridge (I 2nd or 3rd class) Traverse from Mount Washakie.

August 16th Peak (12,220)

The Divide continues southeast from Washakie and Bair to Camel's Hump. On the Divide 0.4 mile northwest of Camel's Hump is a drastically asymmetric summit with rubbly west slopes and a vertical northeast face. When Bonney and the Garnicks climbed it in 1940, they found a note left by J. I. Hoffman, who had climbed it on August 16, 1931, while trying to find a way up Lizard Head. Hoffman may have traversed the frightful-looking August 16th–Camel's Hump ridge.

1. West Slope (I 2nd class) From Washakie Lake the way is obvious. From Shadow Lake, approach via Barren Lake and Illinois Pass. From Lonesome Lake, cross Texas Pass to Barren Lake.

2. From South Fork Lakes The summit register mentions an ascent via the col north of the peak.

From Bear's Ears Trail, early summer: Grave Lake in middle distance, snow-covered Baptiste Lake farther away

9 Baptiste Lake

Unimpressive when seen as you drive up the Wind River valley, the range may remind you of long, wooded Appalachian ridges. If you look more attentively, you catch ephemeral glimpses of alpine fragments beyond the ridges, but their snow seems more incongruous than the red desert sandstone in the foreground. The road that climbs to Dickinson Park reveals scenery only slightly more encouraging—crags and outcrops. You begin the trek up the Bear's Ears Trail on faith, but after you round Mount Chauvenet, a view opens to the north.

In the middle distance is the crescent of Grave Lake. Beyond is a cirque dominated by two peaks: Mount Hooker on the west, with a smooth vertical wall rising to a wide plateau, and Musembeah to the east, an intricate mass of towers and arêtes culminating in a small flat summit. Between Hooker and Musembeah, unseen on the floor of a barren, dead-end basin, sits Baptiste Lake.

This chapter covers an area sprawled east of the Continental Divide, the country traversed by the Bear's Ears Trail in its against-the-grain journey from the North Popo Agie River to the valley of the Little Wind River's South Fork—where lie Valentine, Washakie, and South Fork Lakes—to Grave Lake, and up to Baptiste Lake. A saw-blade ridge that extends north from Baptiste Lake's cirque and culminates in the plateau of Roberts Mountain, this section's highest summit, is also included here. Numerous Divide peaks are accessible from the Bear's Ears Trail, though with the exception of Hooker they are arbitrarily included in the East Fork Valley chapter. Hooker is in Baptiste Lake's chapter because when you are at Baptiste Lake, you couldn't imagine it not being.

While the Bear's Ears Trail is the main east-side approach, you can also reach this section of the range from the west, via Washakie Pass or Hailey Pass.

This rugged land can lift your spirits when the peaks are mantled in snow and bright with sun, but when the snow melts and the wind blows dark clouds over, the bare summits' brown rock can be especially bleak and mournful. These aren't cirques for newcomers who seek easy access and popular routes. Rather, the area is for connoisseurs who have learned to appreciate desolation and the stark beauty of the steep walls and truncated summits. The rock climbs—many pioneered by Fred Beckey—are scattered in out-of-the-way places.

This chapter's peaks are located on the Roberts Mountain, Mount Bonneville, and Lizard Head Peak quads. Trails reach these mountains through country covered by the Moccasin Lake, Washakie Park, and Dickinson Park maps.

Trails

Bear's Ears Trail

Dickinson Park to Baptiste Lake—15.5 miles

This trail, climbing from Dickinson Park to the plateau that features the formation for which the trail is named, traversing high on Mount Chauvenet, descending to the South Fork of the Little Wind River, crossing to Grave Lake, and climbing from Grave Lake to Baptiste Lake, passes through much of the country covered in this chapter. The ascent to nearly 12,000 feet on Chauvenet may irritate a heavily laden climber hurrying to a great wall, but a person disposed to enjoy the hike will discover this to be as scenic as any Wind River trail.

Near Dickinson Park's north end, a road branches right from the main road. The trail doesn't begin quite as shown on the Dickinson Park quad but at the end of the mile-long branch. It ascends to treeline by interminable switchbacks, many gaining so little elevation as to seem senseless. Staying high for several miles, the trail rounds the Bear's Ears and Chauvenet. (An older version of the trail, to the south and higher, is still marked with cairns.) After intersecting the Lizard Head Trail, which also crosses terrain above 11,000 feet, the Bear's Ears Trail descends Valentine Creek to a junction with the Gaylord Lake Trail, rounds Valentine Lake, and resumes its drop, to 10,000 feet and the Little Wind River's South Fork (which you may have to wade).

From this crossing's west side, the Washakie Trail heads upstream toward Washakie Pass, while the Bear's Ears Trail heads down the stream's west bank as far as a meeting with the Valentine Mountain Trail, then climbs west and descends to Grave Lake, the outlet of which it crosses on a bridge. Rounding the lake's north shore, where it meets the defunct Onion Meadows Trail, the Bear's Ears Trail continues past Grave Lake to a final junction, from which you can continue up Baptiste Creek to Baptiste Lake or climb south to Hailey Pass. (The Mount Bonneville quad considers this Hailey Pass Trail to be the final leg of the Bear's Ears Trail.)

Hailey Pass Trail

Mae's Lake to Grave Lake or Baptiste Lake—3.5 miles

To reach Baptiste Lake or Grave Lake from Big Sandy Opening, take the Fremont Trail to Marm's Lake, then the Pyramid Lake Trail to a junction where Mae's Lake comes into view. Here a trail branches right to climb to 11,160-foot Hailey Pass. The trail's one sketchy section is where it descends to cross the stream connecting the Twin Lakes. You can also reach Hailey Pass from Pyramid Lake, by a grass slope between Mount Hooker and Pyramid Peak.

The trail north of the pass is less idyllic, as it switchbacks down a steep, barren slope, often through snowpatches, but is easily followed to the valley floor, where it curves east, crosses Baptiste Creek, and meets the Bear's Ears Trail.

Baptiste Lake Area

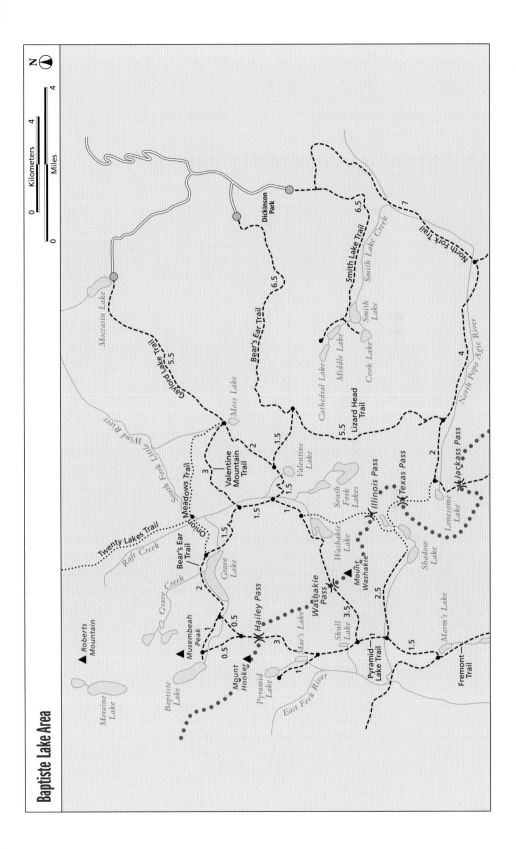

Once, you could reach Baptiste Lake more directly by following paths. These paths seem to have vanished, but it's still feasible to cut cross-country. Leave the trail where it reaches the valley floor, cross the stream that drains Lake 10,526 (under Hooker's northeast face) at a pond not shown on maps, and reach Baptiste Creek near the oval pond at 10,560 feet.

Gaylord Lake Trail (Moss Lake Trail) (part reservation, not maintained)

Moccasin Lake to Valentine Lake—7.5 miles

Trail nomenclature is convoluted in the vicinity of Moss Lake, Valentine Lake, and the Little Wind River's South Fork. The Moss Lake Trail, as defined by maps and the Forest Service, comprises two sections that more or less double back on one another. However, since signs that might identify these segments are nonexistent—indeed the trails have been abandoned—it is more logical to consider the trail from Moccasin Lake to Gaylord Lake and its continuation to Valentine Lake as one entity, here called the Gaylord Lake Trail.

This trail enables you to reach Valentine Lake—or Grave and Baptiste Lakes via the Valentine Mountain Trail—by a shorter route than the Bear's Ears Trail and eliminates that trail's climb to 12,000 feet. However, lack of maintenance, occasional uncertainty about the trail's location, and inferior scenery explain why the Gaylord Lake Trail is less popular than the Bear's Ears Trail.

Its high trailhead is another of the Gaylord Lake Trail's apparent advantages, but after circling the south shore of Moccasin Lake it immediately climbs to a 9,880-foot notch, drops to a 9,425-foot pond, and continues down to 9,335-foot Mary's Lake. In the valley of the East Fork of Mary's Creek, you will do better finding your way reading the map than by searching for the trail on the land. Eventually, near Benchmark 9607, you meet a more-used trail, coming from the southeast, from Mosquito Park and Hobbs Park. This seems to be the preferred route of horse packers, though it is longer and crosses a 10,527-foot pass by Mount Cross.

Here the Gaylord Lake Trail becomes straightforward, as it unambiguously follows a classic Wind River fault zone southwest past a few small lakes, Gaylord Lake, Moss Lake, and Dutch Oven Lake to a junction with the Bear's Ears Trail near Valentine Lake.

The trail crosses Moss Lake's outlet, Moss Creek, by a bridge; just past this bridge the Valentine Mountain Trail diverges northwest.

Valentine Mountain Trail (Moss Lake Trail) (not maintained)

Moss Lake to South Fork of Little Wind River—3 miles

The east-west leg of what maps consider the Moss Lake Trail is more descriptively called the Valentine Mountain Trail, as it was called by older maps and the 1981 guidebook. For half its length it climbs high on Valentine Mountain; for the other half it descends Valentine Mountain. It splits from the Gaylord Lake Trail just west of the bridge over Moss Creek. The trail joins the Bear's Ears Trail just beyond a crossing of the South Fork of the Little Wind River (wading or athletic rock-hopping), from where you can continue to Grave Lake. While the footing is unstable in places, and the trail could use grooming, it is otherwise efficient, climbing steadily and descending steadily. Moreover, the views from Valentine Mountain's flanks are exceptional.

Onion Meadows Trail (reservation)

Moss Lake to Grave Lake—5 miles

Earlier guidebooks described this trail as little-used. It has now regressed to the next stage in disappearance: unused. The trail left the Gaylord Lake Trail a few hundred yards east of the Moss Creek bridge and ended by a beach on Grave Lake, but neither of these termini are now marked. The Onion Meadows Trail appears on the map to have the advantage over the Valentine Mountain Trail of avoiding the climb high on Valentine Mountain. However, its many ups and downs, including a descent to 9,400 feet and a wet crossing of the South Fork of the Little Wind River, made it less efficient, even when it could be followed without excessive scouting.

Just west of the South Fork is Onion Meadows itself. According to the map, here a trail turns up Raft Creek to Twenty Lakes Creek. The Onion Meadows Trail disappears crossing the meadow; look for it at the southwest end near a national forest–reservation boundary sign. The final section climbs through timber to a beach on Grave Lake.

Twenty Lakes Trail (reservation)

Movo Lake to Onion Meadows—8 miles

This, as obscure as any trail in the range, connects—or once connected—the Raft Lake and Grave Lake drainages. While neither end of the trail is easy to locate in thick forests, you shouldn't need a well-defined track to cross the high country the trail mainly traverses. There you will undoubtedly traverse scenic terrain and are likely to find as much solitude as you wish.

The Roberts Mountain quad shows the Twenty Lakes Trail splitting from the Raft Lake Trail 0.5 mile south and east of Movo Lake. An outfitter says the trail is there, if you know where to look, but *where* doesn't seem to be where the map suggests. One problem is that the location of the Raft Lake Trail itself is ambiguous in that vicinity. The Twenty Lakes Trail, wherever it begins, intersects Twenty Lakes Creek, passes under Roberts Mountain's massive east face, and crosses Tepee Pass to Raft Creek. This stream flows not to Raft Lake, but the other way, into the Little Wind River's South Fork at Onion Meadows. Here the Twenty Lakes Trail ends by meeting the Onion Meadows Trail. This junction is also unobvious, in part because the Onion Meadows Trail disappears crossing the meadow. If beginning the Twenty Lakes Trail from this end, start optimistically up the east side of Raft Creek.

Washakie Trail

Skull Lake to South Fork of Little Wind River—4.5 miles

An ancient, important Indian route across the range ascended Trout Creek, as the present Moccasin Lake Road does, crossed to Moccasin Lake, followed the course of the present Gaylord Lake Trail to Valentine Lake, and crossed the Divide by the 11,611-foot saddle we call Washakie Pass. Washakie's Shoshones used the trail, and it was noted in the 1878 Hayden Survey report.

While the entire route was once the Washakie Trail, the term is now restricted to the section that crosses the Divide—that connects Skull Lake and the Pyramid Lake Trail to the South Fork of the Little Wind River and the Bear's Ears Trail, making Washakie and Valentine Lakes accessible from Big Sandy Opening.

A sign marks the Washakie Trail's junction with the Pyramid Lake Trail in a clearing 0.25 mile south of Skull Lake. The open country through which the trail climbs is as pretty as it gets. (You can also easily ascend the valley of the creek that flows from near the pass to Washakie Creek.) East of the pass, though, the descent to Macon and Washakie Lakes is too steep and rocky (and possibly snowy) to be as enjoyable.

Lizard Head Trail

Lizard Head Meadows to Bear's Ears Trail—5.5 miles

Lizard Head Meadows are an opening along the North Popo Agie 2 miles below Lonesome Lake. The strenuous Lizard Head Trail leaves the North Fork Trail in these meadows and climbs nearly 2,000 feet to the bare upper slopes of Windy Mountain. Partway up, a short trail branches left to Bear Lakes. Above treeline no trail has been worn, but you can follow cairns across the windswept plateau. After rounding Cathedral Peak, this trail joins the Bear's Ears Trail, just before the latter's descent to Valentine Lake.

Smith Lake Trail

Dickinson Park to Middle Lake—6.5 miles

Smith Lake and lakes upstream from it are accessible from Dickinson Park by this trail. From the parking area at Dickinson Park's south end, cross a meadow. On the far side the Smith Lake Trail turns right from the North Fork Trail and climbs over a ridge to the Smith Lake Creek drainage. Where the trail reaches the valley floor, it meets the no-longer-maintained High Meadow Trail, which connects this area to Sanford Park. The Smith Lake Trail follows the creek upstream to Smith Lake and continues to Middle Lake's north shore. Here the trail ends, but you can continue to Cathedral Lake.

East of Middle Lake the Cook Lake Trail branches south past Cloverleaf Lake to Cook Lake.

Peaks

Wykee Peak (12,055)

A nebulous massif north of Roberts Mountain, in the angle between the Little Wind Rivers' North Fork and Twenty Lakes Creek.

    1. East Slope (I 2nd class) Hiking from about anywhere. Scramble to the highest of several broken towers in the summit area from the northeast.

    2. South Summit (Point 11,793), Southeast Face (II 5.7/5.8) The face above Twenty Lakes Creek can be climbed in three or four pitches of short walls and ramps, finishing with a steep crack. The view of nearby Roberts' walls detracts from a sense of accomplishment.

Roberts Mountain (12,767)

John Roberts was a Welsh Episcopalian who asked to be sent to the wildest Indians in America. He arrived at Fort Washakie in 1883, after an eight-day trip from Green River in severe winter conditions, and served for forty years as a missionary and

Roberts Mountain, Twenty Lakes Basin

teacher. He made few converts until a tragedy gave him a chance to show his mettle. A son of Washakie was killed in a bar by a white man, provoking the chief to vow to kill the first white man he saw. The Reverend Roberts presented himself at Washakie's lodge; the chief was baptized the next day.

Roberts Mountain is the highest peak between Knife Point and Lizard Head and perhaps the largest as well. It is visible from the Wind River valley, its east face one of the few indications that the range has anything to interest a climber.

1. North Ridge (I 2nd class) Reach the Roberts-Wykee saddle from either Wykee Lake or Twenty Lakes Creek. From Wykee Lake's inlet, ascend a pleasant slope of trees, shrubs, grass, and flowers. From the saddle, follow the broad ridge, turning a few false summits to the west.

2. East Slope-South Ridge (I 2nd or 3rd class) Reach the summit plateau from the head of Twenty Lakes' basin, by way of talus on the Twenty Lakes–Grave Creek divide.

3. East Face (IV 5.9 A2/A3) This is one of the great walls of the range, in width as well as height and steepness; it is also one of the more obscure and seldom-visited. The route begins on a buttress right of which is a small waterfall, farther right a blank wall, and right of the blank wall a yellow pillar below the summit. The buttress's base is a low-angle pillar that separates two faces. To the pillar's left is a big drop-off, to the right a snowpatch. High on the face the route crosses right to another buttress, the bottom of which isn't far below the traverse, but which extends up to the rim. The route ends left of Roberts' summit.

Climbing begins with easy cracks between ledges. The second pitch ascends a chimney to a difficult crack. The third pitch starts with free climbing but ends with a thin aid crack. The fourth lead also involves aid. Next, climb a flake and work up left, then follow a ledge to the buttress's left edge. After a lead near the edge and another on blocky rock, make a long grassy traverse right across a watercourse to the second buttress. Climb up, then left, to a ledge. Finally, climb a steep face.

4. East Couloir The couloir between the main summit and Point 12,508 has been done as an early season snow climb.

5. Undistinguished Tower (I 5.9 A1) and **Point 12,508, East Ridge** (I 4th class) Northwest of Roberts Lake a tower (barely discernible on the Roberts Mountain quad) protrudes from Point 12,508's east ridge. The tower has been climbed in three disappointing pitches (5.7, 5.8, 5.9 plus aid because of a loose block). After the ascent one climber continued to Roberts' summit via Point 12,508, while his disgusted partner went fishing.

Mount Baldy (12,085)

A ridge of rocky outcrops opposite Roberts' east face.

1. East Slope (I 2nd class) From Pass 11,325 on the Shoshone Lake Trail, traverse Peak 11,765's west slopes to Pass 11,425 and cross a minor ridge that parallels Baldy's crest.

Point 12,175

The high point of the massif east of Twenty Lakes Creek isn't a named peak, but rather a point 2 miles south of Mount Baldy.

1. North Slope (I 2nd class) From the Shoshone Lake Trail cross Passes 11,325 and 11,425, then traverse Baldy's east slopes.

Peak 12,255

This remote summit rises at the intersection of the Roberts-Lander ridge with the ridge that separates Grave Creek's upper branches. Note that a mile to the southeast is another Peak 12,255 (Grave Peak). With the 1938 Mount Bonneville quad also giving Grave Peak's elevation as 12,255, but the unnamed peak's as 12,301, we may suspect an error on the 1981 Roberts Mountain quad.

1. Southeast Ridge (I 3rd class) Traverse from Peak 12,143.

2. West Slope (I 2nd class) From the head of Grave Creek's west branch.

Renegade Peak (12,470)

The ridge that runs southwest from Roberts to Lander, separating the Moraine Lake cirque from Grave Creek's headwaters, is a row of sharp summits of various sizes. Renegade, 0.5 mile southeast of Moraine Lake, is the ridge's highest point.

1. North Ridge (I 5th class) From Moraine Lake, ascend broken rock to the Roberts-Renegade col. Traverse ledges on the east face below a large gendarme (Teapot Pinnacle) and continue on these ledges past two small gendarmes. Regain the ridge by an easy chimney and follow the ridge to a short overhang. Here the first ascent team used a shoulder stand, but the overhang has also been climbed free. It is then a scramble to the top.

Descent: You can descend by climbing down the south ridge to the first col, rappelling east down a rotten chimney to a snowfield, and traversing back north to the Roberts-Renegade col.

Saber Tooth (12,280+)

This is the conical peak between Renegade and Cusp, 0.7 mile northeast of Mount Lander.

The Bonneys report a 5.6 route on its west face.

Mount Lander (12,623)

A high summit at the head of two cirques: Moraine Lake's to the north, Baptiste Lake's to the south.

1. East Ridge (II 5.5) Reach the base of the ridge from Baptiste Lake on talus or from Moraine Lake via a snowfield. High on the ridge are spiky gendarmes, which, though only 20 feet high, cannot be circumvented and require 5th-class moves.

Old accounts rate the ridge 3rd or 4th class, but a route this easy must involve following the ridge to the first gendarmes, then angling down a ledge that intersects the south couloir.

2. North Face This face was climbed in a long day, but the difficulties apparently weren't great.

3. West Ridge (I 4th class) The west ridge is most easily reached from Moraine Lake by way of a small glacier; it also has been climbed after traversing South Twin Lion. You can also reach the glacier from Sheila Lake by crossing the nasty col between the Twin Lions or by a notch south of South Twin Lion.

4. South Buttress–Wobbly Hand-Crack Buttress (II 5.5) The south face left of the south couloir is formed of two cliff bands, one above the other. Of the lower band's two gully/corner systems, this route takes the left one, then ascends the crest of the 400-foot left buttress in the upper band.

Climb 4th-class terrain for 600 feet to the lower band's left gully/corner, which leads to a large ramp/slab split by cracks and with water streaks on its right side. The cracks provide 200 feet of enjoyable, easy 5th class. Above the ramp is the upper band's left-hand buttress, with a prominent brownish face and a 100-foot zigzagging hand crack up its center. Climb the crack (5.5) on knobby rock to the top of the formation dividing two couloirs. Downclimb a cleft and continue to the summit (4th class).

5. South Couloir The snow gully that meets the ridge west of the summit has been climbed.

Cusp Peak (12,265)

This is the summit, north of Baptiste Lake, at the intersection of the Roberts-Lander and Musembeah ridges.

1. East Slope (I 2nd class) From the west fork of Grave Creek.

2. West Ridge (I 3rd class) This steep but broken ridge has been followed from Mount Lander.

3. South Face (III 5.8) Begin on loose rock just right of a prominent arête. The rock improves higher on the face.

4. Southeast Ridge–Rainy Day Ridge (II 5.4) Gain the buttress left of the gully between Cusp and the minor peak to the southeast. Begin climbing 10 feet left of a jagged off-width, ascending overlaps up and slightly left through a steeper bulge on questionable rock (5.4). Climb near the crest of the ridge for 700 feet on good rock (5.4) to the obvious notch. Scramble down and right around the notch and up to the summit (3rd class).

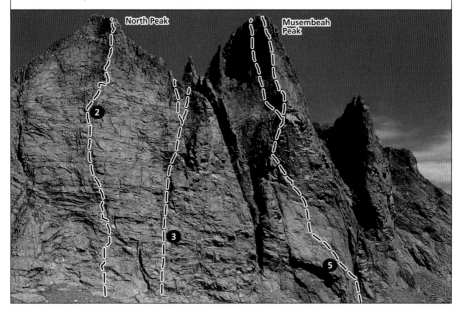

Musembeah, North Peak and Musembeah Peak

North Peak

Musembeah Peak

Musembeah, North Peak (12,320+)

A worthy peak, though remote and overshadowed by Musembeah, overlooking the
north end of Baptiste Lake and separated from Musembeah by a deep notch.

1. North Ridge (I 3rd class) Reach the ridge via moraines above Lake 10,911,
one of the many unnamed lakes in the pristine valley of Grave Creek's west fork. The
ridge itself is an enjoyable short scramble, a bit tricky toward the top.

2. West Face Direct–Wallflowers (IV 5.9) The upper part of the west face
features an orange buttress, capped by steep, dark rock, more or less in the fall line
below the summit. The face's lower part, below the buttress, features water-streaked
overhangs. This route follows dihedrals at the right edge of the overhangs, then follows the crest of the buttress to the summit.

Pitch 1: Left of a large left-facing dihedral is a crack, below the right side of the
lowest downward-sloping roofs. Climb the crack to a left-facing corner. At the top
of the corner, step right and belay (5.6). Pitch 2: Climb a slab up right to an alcove.
Climb out of the alcove (5.7) and continue up right to a 10-foot detached flake.
Climb the left side by a 5.8 crack, then continue up left to a belay below a left-facing
ramp/dihedral. Pitch 3: Step right and climb cracks and flakes until you can step left
into the dihedral. Climb to its top and follow grassy ledges up left. Then climb up
right through steep, black rock to a belay below and right of the main black roof (5.7).
Pitch 4: Trend left, passing a small roof by using a guillotine flake. Work up an open
chimney for 40 feet and traverse 15 feet left to a gully system (5.7). Pitches 5–7: Up

the gully system to the base of the orange face at the foot of the buttress (easy 5th). Pitch 8: Climb flakes on the buttress's left margin. Traverse right, using two black knobs and making a tricky step down right to a shallow left-facing corner. Climb the corner, work up left to the left-most crack splitting the top of the orange face, and climb it to a ledge (5.8). Pitch 9: Continue up the crest to a ledge below a black roof. Near the end of the pitch is an orange face with tricky thin cracks (5.9). Pitch 10: Up and right, then left on a ledge below the roof. Flakes and knobs take you through the left side of the roof. Easier rock gets you to the southeast ridge 100 feet from the summit (5.8).

3. West Face (II 5.6/5.7) This 1,200-foot wall offers a rarity for this part of the range: a long, moderate climb. It follows a groove that diagonals slightly right and eventually meets the southwest ridge. By leaving the groove before reaching the ridge, you can climb a few nice face pitches, reaching the ridge a few hundred feet from the summit.

Musembeah Peak (12,593)

A Teton climber could be disappointed by the simplicity of Wind River peaks, which may be single spires, high points of long ridges, or more often, intersections of steep faces with low-angle slopes. Seldom do you encounter the complex of turrets, gullies, snowfields, and buttresses that form Teton peaks. Musembeah, though, is an exception and with its subsidiary peaks presents a mass of towers, narrow arêtes, dark couloirs, a black dike, and, characteristic of the Wind Rivers, a plateau remnant for a summit. The rock, too, is complex: massive granodiorite, banded gneiss, the dike's diabase, and fantastically swirled layers, lenses, and chunks of migmatite.

The first party to report an ascent found a bighorn sheep skeleton near the summit, so they gave the peak the Shoshone name for bighorn. The name Petroleum Peak found on older maps was a mistake that has been corrected.

1. Southwest Ridge Musembeah was first climbed by way of Baptiste Lake Tower and the tower nearer Musembeah, with rappels from both towers. The route was described as "interesting, but not difficult."

2. South Bowl (I 3rd class) Pleasant grass on the lower slopes, messy scree higher, excellent flagstones toward the summit.

3. Southeast Ridge (I 4th class) You can follow this narrow, curving ridge for its entire length or gain it from the southwest, near the black dike. Exposed scrambling leads over a subsidiary east summit. Climbers who descended the ridge at noon after climbing the *Southwest Face* enjoyed it, while climbers descending it after getting up the *West Buttress* at dusk found it a loose, scary hassle.

4. Northeast Buttress (II 5.5) From the lake-filled basin of Grave Creek's west fork, a buttress rises, right of the black dike, to the east summit. This buttress involves three 5th-class pitches.

5. West Buttress (IV 5.8) Two beautiful buttresses, separated by a deep cleft, rise from Baptiste Lake. The left one, the West Buttress, which ends at the summit itself,

Musembeah Peak

consists of a steep lower part, a gradual rise in the middle, and an upper section that is a steep, narrow arête.

The route on the buttress isn't a classic by standards that have evolved in pure rock climbing areas. In places of mild weather and easy access, a classic must be continuously difficult. Nor is the buttress an alpine classic: The southern Wind Rivers aren't alpine, and you can spend the day in rock shoes. Nor is it remote, considering the climbing being done in the earth's farthest corners. Yet the *West Buttress* is a classic, of a genre of mountain rock climbs that give a fine feeling of accomplishment. There are hard pitches, routefinding problems, exposure, and commitment.

The route begins in the cleft between the two buttresses and ascends the left-hand buttress's southwest wall for six pitches. Wet scrambling leads to the rope-up point, below a giant chockstone. Climb a tricky corner left of the cleft to easier going near the center of the face. Intricate but not difficult face climbing reaches a broken area, just below the crest's low-angle midsection. The crest is easy for a few hundred feet, but where it steepens, work left onto the north face. The face has many cracks, corners, and overhangs; look ahead to avoid impasses and aid. Five pitches on the face, most with 5.8 moves, lead to the summit.

Since the first ascent—the upper section on the north face elegant enough to make the route a classic—an even more elegant direct finish has been added. Continue from the low-angle midsection up the crest—a variation involving four pitches: three 5.9 and one with a touch of 5.10a. The belay ledges, on steps above overhangs, are notably exposed.

6. Southwest Buttress (IV 5.10) This newer route begins as the *Southwest Face* route does, but before reaching the top of the gully, it angles left, across the face of the lower rib used to locate that route, on easy 5th-class ledges, and ascends the major dihedral near the deep cleft that defines the rib's left side. The route continues to the summit on the buttress that defines the upper southwest face's left edge.

After traversing the ledges that cross the lower rib to the big dihedral, continue left for 30 feet and belay below a ramp. Pitch 1: Climb to the ramp and continue to the main corner (5.7). Pitch 2: Climb the dihedral (5.8). Pitch 3: Climb the crack above to the top of the rib (5.9). Follow the rib's crest (easy 5th) for a pitch to its intersection with the upper southwest face, and in two pitches traverse and climb up left (5.6) to the upper buttress.

The first pitch on the buttress, the route's seventh, begins with a short, hard left-facing corner (5.10), 30 feet right of the buttress's crest. Continue up just right of the crest for this pitch and the 5.7 eighth, to a ledge below a smooth face. The ninth pitch begins with thin face climbing to a thin crack. Past a 5.10- layback step right to easier going, then a bulge split by a 5.9 crack. A short, easy lead then takes you to within 100 feet of scrambling to the summit.

Musembeah, Southwest Face

7. Southwest Face (II 5.6) The rib with a flat crest that intersects Musembeah's main wall at two-thirds height is the best way to locate this route. Begin right of the rib, ascending clean 3rd-class slabs, with a touch of 4th, until pinched into a gully a few hundred feet below the rib's crest. Climb 5th-class rock to the junction of the crest and Musembeah's upper wall. Scramble up right on the ramp that is a continuation of the crest. Three 5th-class pitches then lead to the top—the first angling up left, the second up right, and the third straight up, following a broken corner system. The climb ends a few hundred feet right (south) of the summit.

Baptiste Lake Tower (11,880+)

Musembeah's south ridge includes a pair of towers that were traversed on the first ascent of Musembeah. Although hardly a separate peak, the southern tower is so prominent that climbers have named it Baptiste Lake Tower and treated it as an objective.

1. South Ridge (I 4th class) Reach the ridge from the south end of Baptiste Lake. You can avoid 5th-class climbing by exploring.

2. Northwest Corner (II 5.5) The west face's left edge offers pleasant climbing, though scarcely of a high standard in terms of commitment or alpine mystique. The route's length can be three to five pitches, depending on how much of the couloir north of the tower you ascend before climbing out onto the face.

3. West Chimney (II 5.5) The summit register mentions an ascent of this obvious feature.

Peak 12,285

A massive, isolated, obscurely situated hulk a mile southwest of Tepee Pass.

1. North Slope (I 2nd class) Via Point 12,252.

2. West Ridge (I 3rd class) A pleasant scramble approached by the valley of Lake 11,035, south of Roberts Lake.

3. Southeast Slope (I 2nd class) Nice hiking from the east fork of Grave Creek, via the saddle just west of Point 11,701.

Peak 12,143

This summit of no distinction, 1.3 miles northeast of Musembeah, stands on the ridge between the nameless Peak 12,255 and 12,255-foot Grave Peak.

1. Southeast Ridge (I 3rd class) From Grave Peak.

2. Northwest Ridge (I 2nd or 3rd class) From Peak 12,255.

Grave Peak (12,255)

The 2-mile ridge that divides Grave Creek's branches was traversed in 1961 by Bill Buckingham and Whitney Robinson. This peak (the Peak 12,255 just northeast of

Lake 10,885, not the peak of the same map elevation a mile northwest) is the traverse's crux.

1. Southeast Ridge (I 5.2) A 100-foot wall near the summit requires a rope.

2. Northwest Ridge (I 3rd class) From Peak 12,143.

Buttressed Mountain (12,207)

East of Lakes 10,885 and 10,911 is this peak whose two summits are separated by the diabase dike that crosses Ambush, Tower, and Musembeah.

1. Southeast Ridge (I 3rd class) Follow this ridge from Redwall. The ridge's lower part is broad and gentle, but it narrows and is pinnacled toward the top.

2. Northwest Couloir (I 3rd class) From Grave Peak.

Redwall Peak (11,760+)

The ridge between Grave Creek's east and west forks ends in a pair of steep, east-facing buttresses, 1.4 miles east-northeast of Musembeah, composed of rock as red as any in the range. These red walls are conspicuous from many points to the south.

1. Southwest Couloir (I 3rd class) From the small lake below Lake 10,885 on Grave Creek's west fork, slabs lead to this obvious break in the cliffs.

2. East Face (IV 5.8 A3) This route is as easy to locate as any in the range—a dihedral from bottom to top, the face's one obvious line. The free climbing is sustained and mostly in cracks, with several pitches of 5.7 and 5.8. The roof has required aid.

Mount Hooker (12,504)

Few ranges contain peaks as strange as Hooker. One side not only has the steepest wall that high in Wyoming—with the state's hardest routes—but also a ledge that allowed a surveyor to reach the summit in 1890. The other side is comparatively low-angle, but the onion-skin slabs have turned back good climbers. The vertical walls of the north and east don't meet the southwest-facing slabs in a ridge; but are separated by a 0.5-mile-wide field of boulders, flowers, snow, streams, and even a small lake.

At least five routes were reported by their creators as being on the north face. However, the face bends around a prow and, not to diminish the achievements but rather for clarity, all but a few are described here as northeast face routes.

Those who have climbed Hooker's north and northeast face like the idea of wilderness Grade VIs and recommend preserving the flavor by giving an overview of the routes, not civilizing them through pitch-by-pitch recipes.

Two ledges slant up right across the northeast and north faces. The original route's first ascent team named the lower ledge Der Minor and the upper ledge Der Main; these names appear in the route descriptions of several routes.

1. East Ledge (I 3rd class) Sometimes a fortuitous nubbin in an unlikely place makes possible a move that would otherwise be unthinkable, and climbers suspect a benign spirit designed the route. The same spirit could have been thinking of nontechnical

Mount Hooker

climbers or weary wall climbers in need of an easy descent, and created this improbable ledge. No route less needs a guidebook description; suffice to say it is north of Hailey Pass. Its unique location makes it more invigorating that most walk-ups.

2. Northeast Face–Red Light District (IV 5.12a) This route ascends the largest, most obvious left-facing dihedral toward the broad northeast face's left side. The red light is the sun, which shines on this route, in contrast to the more northerly facing routes, until early afternoon.

Reach the dihedral by following a right-leaning ramp for two pitches, though you may want to avoid loose rock on the first pitch by climbing nearby cracks (5.8). The next six pitches follow this dihedral, with detours to the left, to Der Minor Ledge. Pitch 3 reaches the dihedral, passing a scary loose block (5.10) to a ledge. Move your belay left and climb pitch 4 in a subsidiary dihedral. On pitch 5, leave this dihedral and follow an arête (5.12a) to a ledge that takes you back to the main dihedral. Pitch 6 follows the dihedral (wide, 5.11a) to a loose, lichenous stance. On pitch 7, leave the dihedral again, traversing to another left-facing dihedral. On pitch 8, ascend this dihedral (5.11) to Der Minor Ledge and on pitch 9 traverse back (5.12a) to the main dihedral. A 5.10+ pitch above Der Minor Ledge follows the dihedral, then detours left at an overhang near the top, to Der Main Ledge.

Red Light District doesn't claim to be direct. Because of blocky roofs above, it traverses right for 0.5 mile on Der Main Ledge, a few feet wide at first but increasingly widening; despite the exposure, only 15 feet require a rope.

The first ascent team recommends two sets of cams, a few larger items, smaller camming devices, and a complete set of stoppers. They placed pitons but no bolts.

3. Northeast Face–Pay to Play (VI 5.11 A3) In nine free and four aid pitches, *Pay to Play* ascends the face between *Red Light District* and *Brain Larceny*, continuing straight up from Der Main Ledge to the top. It was first climbed over five days. Its most conspicuous features are a roof crack and a line of corners and cracks interrupted by a blank section.

Pitches 1 through 3 climb moderate cracks to an awkward 5.9 squeeze/off-width. Pitch 4, the free climbing crux, passes through the off-width roof crack and continues up a lower-angle squeeze to the blank section. The next pitch involves slabby face climbing protected by two buttonheads. The sixth pitch, the aid crux, follows a seam to a string of bat-hook holes, protected by a rivet, that leads up and right. The seventh pitch's left-facing dihedral arches left to become a roof. Two crack pitches then gain Der Main Ledge. The eleventh pitch traverses up and left, gaining a left-facing corner that leads to the top in two pitches.

4. Northeast Face–Brain Larceny (V 5.12R) To the right of *Red Light District*, low on the face, are three pointy alcoves. *Brain Larceny* ascends the right side of the upper-right alcove, with pitches fairly consistently 5.11 and 5.12. It follows Der Main Ledge for several hundred feet before finding its way to the top. The second ascent was accomplished in one day, the team finding their way with no information beyond a "matchbook-size" photocopy of a *Rock & Ice* photo.

A significant variation (4a, *Year of the Horse*, VI 5.10 A3) diverges to the right above Der Minor Ledge and attacks the wall above Der Main Ledge more directly than *Brain Larceny*'s original line does.

5. Northeast Face–Third Eye (VI 5.10 A4) The most obvious feature toward the northeast face's right side is an alcove capped by a large roof below Der Minor Ledge. The first 400 feet of this route ascend discontinuous cracks, with some A4 and rivets, toward a more obvious left-facing corner. This corner takes you, in three pitches, to the Third Eye; nail a crack in its roof. Above Der Minor Ledge, ascend a right-facing corner and finish the route in the left-most of several large right-facing corners.

The first ascent team especially suggests a #4 Camalot.

A significant—to say the least—free variation has been established (5f, V 5.12+ R). The climbers worked on its thirteen pitches over eight days; five pitches were 5.12, seven 5.11, and one 5.10. One of the climbers, considering the sustained commitment, characterized the route as "a 5.12 route for the 5.14 climber." The top half may coincide with the *Boissonneault-Larson*.

6. Northeast Face–Boissonneault-Larson (VI 5.10+ A4) The first ascent pair not only didn't publish an account of their route, other than a topo for friends, but they didn't even name it.

The key to the route is several discontinuous right-facing corners beginning a few hundred feet up and continuing to the height of, but somewhat right of, the

Third Eye. Begin by climbing to a right-rising ramp, then ascend this ramp to a hanging belay. The second pitch follows a right-arching corner to ledges; the first ascenders, having used widely spaced anchors, invite you to place bolts. The third, fourth, and sixth pitches all involve pendulums or tension traverses left to right-facing, right-arching corners. On the 5.10+ fifth pitch, bring all your large pieces.

The seventh and eighth pitches work back right, with thin nailing and a tension traverse on the eighth pitch. The ninth and tenth pitches (5.8, 5.9) follow a dihedral to Der Minor Ledge. Reach Der Main Ledge with three free pitches (5.9+, 5.10+, 5.8) in an S-shaped right-facing dihedral. Two pitches (5.8, 5.5) in the right-facing dihedral above complete the route.

The rack used on the 1979 first ascent is no doubt dated, but it included five rurps, many knifeblades, pitons up to 4 inches, copperheads, two sets of hooks, many wired stoppers, and two sets of hexes.

7. North Prow–Sendero Luminoso (VI 5.10 A4) After coinciding with *Shady Lady* for five or six pitches, *Sendero Luminoso* diagonals up left to a long, straight crack, just about on Hooker's prow, that reaches Der Minor Ledge. Directly above the crack's end at Der Minor Ledge is a right-facing dihedral that leads to Der Main Ledge. Slightly right of the dihedral's end at Der Main Ledge is a large, broken dihedral leading to the top.

The name isn't a political statement. Steve Quinlan, scouting possibilities for a route (which he soloed), had his attention drawn to the long, straight crack by a shining water streak.

8. North Face–Shady Lady (VI 5.11 A4) In 1978 Bradshaw and Dockery, not knowing where the *Original Route* went, worked out a route of their own. They finally intersected the original line high on the face.

The 1980 guide, with a draconian attitude toward Shawangunk/Joshua Tree–like irreverent route names, included the sour speculation that "other routes will be forced up . . . the wall, and the opportunity for risqué, double-entendre names so loved by climbers may be irresistable." However, while the book was at the printer's, an account of this route appeared, including such naming at its best, a doubly appropriate name that this edition is proud to include.

Like other Hooker routes *Shady Lady* reaches well-defined systems—in this case left-facing dihedrals halfway up, just right of the prow—after a nebulous start. The first pitch involves a 5.10 face climbing crux, the second mixed free and aid and a pendulum, and the third thirteen bolt and hook holes. The fourth begins with three hook moves, continuing past a thin, A4 crack to another hanging belay.

The sixth pitch follows an easy crack. However, the next several pitches involve wide fist cracks, off-widths, and chimneys, with occasional aid, tension traverses, and bolts, until the route joins the Original Route for more enjoyable climbing up cracks and dihedrals to Der Minor Ledge. Traverse 40 feet right to a dihedral and climb fine orange rock for three pitches. Reach Der Main Ledge with a few pitches on poorer rock and an A3 overhang.

Mount Hooker

Der Main Ledge

Der Minor Ledge

7

8

9

10

8

9f

9

9f

9f

9

10

9

7 8

9. North Face–Original Route (VI 5.12a). Wind River ascents rarely attract attention beyond Jackson Hole and Lander bars and a brief report in the *American Alpine Journal*. Two exceptions have been the first ascent of this route in 1964—hailed as the greatest application to date of Yosemite techniques outside the Valley and America's first wilderness Grade VI—and the first free ascent, in 1990—achieved eventually by the efforts of two competing groups, some of whose members managed to invest the experience with two qualities even rarer to the Wind Rivers than national attention: hoopla and acrimony.

While the 1964 first ascent and the 1990 free efforts qualify as climbing history, you can read between the lines of the accounts suspicions (or worse) about rock quality. For this reason, and because of the lack of sun, the route is likely to attract only the dedicated few.

Climbing begins easily enough with broken rock leading up left to a 5.7 corner and a 100-foot traverse left on easy ledges to a steep right-facing corner. The fourth pitch follows this corner (5.11d or easy aid) to an overhang and an ominous detached flake. Here the original and free routes diverge for five pitches.

The 1964 line, passing the expanding flake with difficult aid and three bolts, continues up 300 feet of rather blank rock (delicate aid, hooks, and a horizontal row of bolts) to a crack/chimney system. Much of this system goes free, and the aid isn't difficult, but some of the rock is unsound.

The free variation (9f) begins spectacularly, passing bolts on the edge of the polished green slab to the right (5.11b). The variation's next pitch (the route's sixth) involves a difficult step to reach an arching corner, 5.11d jamming, and a 5.11b escape to the left. The seventh pitch involves 5.11c climbing in another right-facing corner and a traverse left past a tooth-like flake. Another pitch, up and left, intersects the 1964 route, but the free route continues with a three-bolt, 5.12a traverse left to *Shady Lady*. Follow *Shady Lady* up a 5.10d left-facing dihedral for a pitch and rejoin the 1964 line.

Follow dihedrals up and a bit right for two more pitches, ending the twelfth pitch by traversing right from a loose pillar. (The 1964 route tension-traversed higher.) Continue traversing right and climb up to a large block. Reach Der Minor Ledge in three more pitches. (Rain on the fourteenth pitch, a right-facing dihedral, forced the first 1990 team to resort to aid for 50 feet, ending their efforts at an all-free ascent; it proved to be 5.12a when dry.)

Traverse 180 feet left on Der Minor Ledge to a steep corner; ascend it for two leads (5.9) to Der Main Ledge. Walk right for 200 yards and from its end climb a short 5.7 pitch to the strange world of grass, flowers, streams, and lakes.

The first ascent team placed thirteen bolts; the free climbers added fifteen to their variation.

10. Northwest Face–Northwest Passage (VI 5.9 A3) From approaches to Hooker the northwest face is out of sight behind the north prow; consequently it has received less attention than the oft-photographed northeast face. However, it too is vertical, while facing westerly enough to be blessed with afternoon sun.

The twelve-pitch route on the northwest face begins 200 feet right of the prow and left of blocky slabs. The best marker is a series of three prominent roofs, several hundred feet up, arranged stepwise rising left. The first three pitches trend slightly left, ascending a conspicuous corner-and-roof system, aiming for the left side of the lowest roof. This lower climbing consists of sustained A3, interspersed with interesting free sections. The first pitch involves 5.8 climbing up right, followed by A1 nailing under an arch. The fourth pitch, which turns the middle roof, begins with a pendulum left and sports the route's only bolt (other than belay bolts), used to enhance a hook move.

While most of the route links more-obvious features than those of its neighbors to the east, the middle section appears blank from below. Nevertheless, flakes and a splitter crack make it possible to free climb the fifth (5.9) and sixth (5.8) pitches. The remaining six pitches weave through a complex of crack systems, pitch 9 ending on Der Minor Ledge and the final pitch ending on Der Main Ledge. Rather than walk off on this ledge, the first ascent team climbed the 40 feet to the summit plateau.

11. Northwest Ridge (I 3rd class) The steep, exposed ridge joining Hooker to Tower Peak can be ascended from the scree-filled bowl above Pyramid Lake.

12. Southwest Face, Right Side (I 5.5) Three snowpatches usually sit in a vertical line near this slabby face's right edge. Climb slabs just left of the snow for six pitches, crossing the ledge used to reach the southeast ridge.

13. Southeast Ridge (I 4th class) The usual route from Pyramid Lake. You can follow the ridge in its entirety from Hailey Pass or gain it by grassy ledges that slant up right under the south face to a notch in the ridge. Climb up from the notch, then go left on ledges. Again, climb up until you reach the ridge crest. Follow the crest to the summit.

14. East Face–Loaded for Bear (V 5.9 A3) Hooker offers more rock than just an 1,800-foot face. As you descend north on the Bear's Ears Trail from Hailey Pass, you see a wall, overhanging at the top. This route, which ascends that wall, begins with two pitches up a friction slab. The third and fourth pitches follow shallow grooves that can be protected using heads and bashies. End pitch 4 by traversing to an off-width. The final pitch passes through the upside-down stairs of the summit overhangs.

15. Hailey Pass Slab (II 5.9) As the steep descent from Hailey Pass flattens, 0.5 mile from the pass, a 500- to 600-foot east-facing slab, leading to a domelike shoulder, stands within a few hundred yards of the trail. This slab beckons on days when the weather is too iffy for greater projects. The route described was first climbed on a day when it rained until 11 a.m.

The route is best located in terms of a distinctive wiggly crack halfway up the slab. Begin near the slab's center in a large left-facing corner, right of big overhangs, continue up the crack above, and finish the 160-foot first pitch with the route's crux, a step up left from the crack's end to a big ledge. On the second pitch, angle left on easy ramps and ledges, then ascend a left-facing corner to the base of the wiggly crack. This crack is 5.9; above, follow corners for a few more pitches to a bench, from which you can easily scramble down left.

Pilot Knob or Grave Lake Dome (10,814)

The Bear's Ears Trail passes immediately under a 500-foot cliff near Grave Lake's west end—a formation visible but easily overlooked in the standard photo of Grave Lake and Mount Hooker. The Mount Bonneville quad identifies it as one of dozens of Pilot Knobs; climbers have been using the more distinctive Grave Lake Dome. The crag's proximity to the trail might seem to enhance its popularity, but, ironically—like not seeing the forest because of the trees—its main effect is to make routes hard to locate.

1. West Slope (I 2nd class) A short hike from the trail between Grave and Baptiste Lakes.

2. Southeast Face Left (II 5.7) A five-pitch route follows a prominent right-leaning crack near the face's left edge. Begin at a ramp 30 feet right of a grassy gully. The cruxes are a squeeze chimney on the first pitch and a few overhangs near the top.

3. Southeast Face Center (III 5.10) Although this six-pitch route is reported to begin at a high point of the Bear's Ears Trail (belaying the first pitch from the trail—a unique Wind River opportunity), you may not easily locate it. It is described as going up and right on a gray wall, ascending a curving crack in an area of orange lichen, following a ramp up left, and generally zigzagging.

The first attempt, involving aid, was turned back by rain one pitch from the top; the route was completed two years later by traversing in from the left. A free ascent involved three 5.9 pitches and a 5.10 pitch.

4. Southeast Face Right–Closer to the Grave (IV 5.11 A1) Spending a middle-age birthday (George Lowe's 49th) climbing above a lake whose name reminds you of your mortality can lead to a morbid route name, especially on a route with as many difficulties as this one.

Beginning from a large flake, climb a 5.8 left-facing corner to the highest of three ledges. On the second pitch, turn ceilings in a right-facing corner (5.11), follow the corner to an arch, then escape (5.11) to a crack on the left. On the third pitch, climb a short corner to a ledge, follow two short cracks (left of a tall flake), and continue up and left to a left-arching corner (5.10-), eventually stepping right to a ledge.

Begin the fourth pitch by working right (5.10) to another ledge, above which extends a long crack that begins as two converging cracks. The first ascent pair nailed the left crack and toproped the right one (5.11+). Higher, beyond a ceiling, the crack involves 5.11- finger and hand jamming. The fifth pitch also entails fingers and hands (5.11); climb past two ledges to a third. On the sixth pitch, ascend a 4-inch crack, a thin 5.10 crack, and a 5.10 arch, and, from its top (left of a tree), climb to a groove and a ledge right of a larger tree. Beyond a prominent flake, the going becomes easier.

Chess Ridge (12,279)

A ridge extending north from Bernard Peak toward Grave Lake separates the South Fork's valley from the valley of Spearpoint Lake, which drains to Grave Lake's west end and must see as little traffic as any valley in the range's southern half. Towers around Point 12,052 vaguely resemble chess pieces, and the name may have originally applied to this array, not to the entire rambling, walled plateau, which, however, has no other name.

1. South Ridge (I 2nd class) The valley west of Washakie Lake heads in a saddle at Chess Ridge's south end.

2. West Side–Obvious Crack (II 5.9+) From the pass between Chess Ridge and Bernard, drop north 300 to 400 feet to a clean wall. *Obvious Crack,* which has been favorably compared to Haystack routes, follows the straightest crack splitting the wall's center. Scramble 200 feet to difficulties. Pitch 1 is 5.6, Pitch 2 is 5.7, and the crux third pitch is 5.9 (layback and fingers). Pitch 4 is 5.9 (corner and roof), and Pitch 5 is 5.6.

3. Northeast Chute (I 3rd class Snow 3rd class) Above Lake 10,490 a couloir extends to the saddle 0.4 mile north of the plateau's high point. The amount of snow, of course, varies with season and year, but an ice axe is generally a good idea. Late in a dry year the upper part is unpleasant rubble.

Loch Leven Peak (11,525)

Loch Leven Lake was stocked with loch leven trout, another name for brown trout. Brown trout eat other trout and were put here because they can't migrate from it to other lakes. Above the west shore looms one of the range's least distinguished peaks.

1. Southwest Ridge (I 2nd class) Approach from the northwest corner of Washakie Lake or the south end of Loch Leven Lake. The main routefinding problem is avoiding brush on the lower slopes.

Valentine Mountain (11,147)

Between Moss Lake and the South Fork of the Little Wind River are two small peaks separated by a high saddle with a magic tarn. On earlier maps only the lower, northern peak was named—Valentine Mountain—perhaps because of its more distinctive summit or its proximity to the trail that passes high on it. Now both summits have names—Valentine Mountain and Valentine Peak—though "Mountain" and "Peak" are applied contrary to formal convention, which decrees that a sprawling massif's high point is a mountain, while a subsidiary summit, especially a jagged one, is a peak. The virtue of both is the view across Grave Lake toward Hooker, Lander, and Musembeah—what would be one of the range's classic views, were either mountain or peak climbed more than rarely.

1. South Side (I 3rd class) You can no doubt approach from Dutch Oven Lake or the South Fork, but the Valentine Mountain Trail provides the most convenient approach. From near the trail's high point, scramble to the tarn between mountain and peak. You can walk to within 50 feet of the top, reached by a move on its south side.

Valentine Peak (11,361)

1. Northwest Slope (I 2nd class) The high point of the Valentine massif is a stroll from the magic tarn.

Buffalo Head or Payson Peak (11,717)

From August 16th Peak, on the Divide, a steep-walled ridge juts north between Waskakie and South Fork Lakes, culminating in a formation that bears a striking resemblance to the shaggy beast that once flourished on the Great Plains and five-cent coins. Climbers bestowed the name Buffalo Head during the 1960s; the name Payson Peak appeared inexplicably on the 1981 Lizard Head Peak quad. You wonder if the latter name wasn't intended for the ridge's 12,033-foot high point (the bison's hump), a mile south.

1. Northeast Chimney (III 5.7 A1) At the right edge of the steep east face, a chimney slants up to the formation's north-facing prow. Ascend the chimney in three pitches; aid is needed at one point. Finish the route on the prow. This is an especially unappealing-looking route.

2. North Buttress (III 5.7) Several wide ledges cross Buffalo Head's prow—the beast's nose—allowing a choice of a line from one pitch to the next (and possibilities for escape). Beginning from the lowest ledges, you can reach a prominent west-facing, rubbly chute in four leads. Leave the chute well below its apex and climb to a wide, sloping ledge. From the ledge's left end, climb a pitch to the northeast chimney. Pass behind a battery of chockstones. From the top of the gully above, another meandering pitch reaches the summit.

3. West Face–Buffalo Rib (II 5.10) Between the buffalo's head and Illinois Pass are three ribs. Buffalo Rib follows the central rib. Begin at the toe and work right in a nice crack. The second pitch follows a 5.10 finger crack. The third pitch follows fun 5.7 cracks, and the fourth ascends a wide 5.9+ crack.

Carry cams up to 4 inches, with extras in the 1-inch range for the third pitch.

4. The Skeptic (IV 5.11) The 800- to 900-foot wall facing the lower South Fork Lake has been climbed in six pitches. Begin by gaining the major left-facing dihedral in the center of the wall. The first pitch is 5.10+. The second (5.11) ascends the dihedral to a belay just beyond a large loose block. The third pitch is a long 5.11 lead that leaves the dihedral for featured rock to the left. The fourth pitch follows a 5.9 ramp up left. Pitch 5 (5.11) is somewhat to the right. On the long final pitch, climb 100 feet (5.10+) to a roof (with an optional belay beneath); above the roof, pass a chockstone, climb a 5.10 off-width, then angle right to the top.

Descent: Buffalo Head is separated from the ridge to the south by a sharp notch. Reaching this neck of the buffalo from the head requires 4th-class downclimbing and a 75-foot rappel. Gullies drop both east and west from the notch. The east-facing gully offers a quick descent toward South Fork Lakes, though an ice axe is advisable until late summer. The west-facing gully appears, from Washakie Lake, to involve a detour south on grassy ramps to avoid a steep section.

Peak 12,120+

This is the high point on the ridge between Buffalo Head (Payson Peak) and August 16th Peak, 0.9 mile south of the map's Payson Peak. Maps give an elevation for Point 12,033 to the north but not this higher summit.

1. Southwest Slope–South Ridge (I 2nd class) Obvious and easy from the eastern Illinois Pass. The ridge connecting Peak 12,120+ with August 16th Peak is also easy.

Throne Peak (12,490)

Throne Peak is the summit 0.6 mile south-southeast of Cathedral Peak.

1. West Slope (I 2nd class) From the Lizard Head Trail.

2. East Ridge (I 2nd class) From downstream of Upper Cathedral Lake, it should be obvious how to gain the ridge.

3. Northeast Face–The Scimitar (V 5.10c A3) An obvious crack system splits the diamond-shaped wall above Upper Cathedral Lake. Six pitches take you to a ledge 200 feet from the top. Two pitches of mostly aid (at least just after a snowstorm) reach the top.

Cathedral Peak (12,326)

The presence in the Wind Rivers of a Cathedral Peak isn't surprising; few ranges are without one. But hikers on the Bear's Ears and Lizard Head Trails may wonder why an undistinguished outcrop was given a name usually applied to more inspiring features. The reason is evident at Cathedral Lake, 2 miles east. Rising in its out-of-the-way cirque is a proud buttress that is split by a cleft, so that from the lake the formation has the appearance of a pair of gothic spires. The name must have migrated westward across the plateau. The spires are identified as South Tower and North Tower.

1. West Slope (I 3rd class) From the north and south, roped climbing appears to be involved, but a chute splits the west side and leads to a few steeper moves under the summit. Reach the chute easily from north or west.

2. South Tower, South Buttress (III 5.10) Begin on 5.10a slabs seen in profile from Cathedral Lake. Toward the top, angle left.

3. South Tower Direct (V 5.11b A2) This imposing route begins directly below the center of the top of the South Tower but trends left, ending south of the tower's high point. The second pitch, an overhanging crack, is the crux but still requires aid at its top. Despite several tries to push the free climbing, the first ascent team resorted to considerable aid on four pitches. A few pitches from the top, they used aid in an overhanging dihedral to pass left of a ceiling. They then veered farther left to avoid further overhangs.

4. North Tower–Orion's Reflection (V 5.9/5.10 A3) This very steep 1,200-foot route begins on the big ledge to which you can scramble from the right. Start with a difficult stem behind a large block, then follow a slanting layback crack to a spacious ledge. The next pitch, involving aid, ascends a right-facing corner and a vertical wall beneath an arch. Most of the third pitch, also mixed, is in another right-facing dihedral. Continue up a series of cracks for a pitch. Next, negotiate a dirty crack and use a bolt to bypass a detached block.

Cathedral Peak

From a ledge below a concave wall, traverse left (some aid) to bypass a large orange pillar. Steep climbing with good holds leads to a recess on the pillar's edge. Climb a left-facing corner past several overhanging sections to a sloping ledge. Move left of a blind corner, then connect discontinous cracks, trending right. Climb toward an overhanging slot, but bypass it via an aid crack to the right. Negotiate a difficult squeeze chimney to the top of the orange wall and encounter the first terrain in some time with routefinding latitude. The last problem is a flaring crack; above are a block and ledges leading to the large leaning block atop the wall.

On the first ascent Beckey and Kanzler, bivouacking high on the face, saw the constellation Orion mirrored in Cathedral Lake.

5. North Tower, Northeast Face–Flight of the Golden Camalot (IV 5.11) This recommended 1,200-foot route lies around to the right of the wall that faces Cathedral Lake. Begin with a ramp, then step left and on pitch 2 ascend steep cracks. Hand traverse left (5.10+) to avoid an off-width. Ascend a 5.11 finger crack in a corner. Above is occasional 5.10 and much high-quality 5.8.

Descent: To descend from the towers, walk west, then drop to the cirque to the north.

Cathedral Cirque

The cirque south of Mount Chauvenet, drained by Cathedral Lake's northwest inlet stream, has been intensively developed by NOLS as a rock climbing venue. While cragging elsewhere in the range isn't included in this guidebook, routes here are as long as six pitches and worth mentioning. (The cirque's many one-pitch routes are omitted, and the descriptions here give only a sampling of possibilities.)

The Geology Wall is the northeast face of the dome just east of Point 12,030, rising from Cathedral Lake's northwest inlet stream.

1. Geology Wall, Main Dihedral–Papa Splitter (II 5.10c) Begin below the left side of a 30-foot-high flake 75 feet up by climbing a 5.9+ crack to the ledge at the base of the flake. Jam the flake's left side (also 5.9+). Ascend the main dihedral (5.10c) for 150 feet to a ledge. Climb a crack for 80 feet to a larger ledge. Complete the route by a 40-foot, 5.8 crack slightly right of the end of the previous pitch. (A dihedral farther right is 5.9+.)

2. Geology Wall, Right Side–Heavy Mettle (II 5.8) This route follows the most obvious crack-and-corner system near the wall's right edge for three 150-foot pitches. Approach from the right. The 5.6 first pitch begins with easy rock that leads to a right-facing corner, which leads to a ledge below a left-angling crack. Begin the second pitch either by climbing this 5.8 crack for 30 feet to a ledge or by a 5.6 face to its left. Walk left a few feet and climb a flake that leads farther left, then move back right and climb a 5.8 crack to a large ledge. Begin the third pitch to the right of a freestanding flake by following easy cracks to another large ledge, then traverse right behind a giant boulder.

1, 2 Descent: Walk off to the south.

3. Arts and Sciences (II 5.6) This route ascends the east rib of Point 12,040+, east-northeast of the junction of the Bear's Ears and Lizard Head Trails, 0.5 mile northwest of Geology Wall. The first three of the six pitches are 5.5 to 5.6, but the angle eases above, and the upper pitches are mostly 4th class.

4. Chemistry Department–Burning Ring of Fire (II 5.7) The southeast-facing wall at the head of the cirque is the Chemistry Department. A recommended route begins from the top of a slab by following a 5.6 corner to the right end of a ledge with a tree. The 5.7 second pitch follows a wide crack right. The 5.7 third pitch skirts a few overhangs. On the fourth pitch, climb a right-facing corner to a left-rising ramp, then climb another corner. The fifth pitch is easy but unprotected.

Descent: Walk off to the east.

The Psychology Wall is the south-facing series of pillars below Point 12,068.

5. Psychology Wall–Conditioned Response (II 5.9 A2) This four-pitch route follows a corner on the right side of the second pillar from the left. Begin left of an arch near the highest trees. After three pitches, move the belay up right and climb a final pitch involving aid.

6. Psychology Wall–Behavior Modification (II 5.8) A six-pitch route on the third pillar from the left. The first pitch is easy 5th class, the second and third are 5.6, the fourth and fifth are 5.8, and the final pitch is easy.

7. Psychology Wall–Freudian Slip (I 5.8) A two-pitch route that follows a dihedral to the right of *Behavior Modification,* on the same pillar.

8. Psychology Wall–California Block (II 5.9 or 5.10) On the face to the right of the preceding routes, 200 feet above the higher of two large ledges, is a block shaped like California. (The right edge makes an angle as the California-Nevada border does; the left edge curves more or less as California's coastline does.) Two five-pitch routes reach the California Block, but since they virtually coincide after one pitch, they are described here as variations of one another:

Gold Rush begins in a 5.7 left-facing corner. *The Democrats of California* begins to the right of *Gold Rush,* in another left-facing corner. Above the corner, friction right to a roof and traverse farther right to a ledge. Climb a straight finger crack (5.10), then a left-leaning crack, and belay in a cave below *Gold Rush*'s first belay ledge.

On the second pitch of both variants, undercling left to a finger crack (5.8), which leads to the lower of the two large ledges. The 5.7 third pitch follows a vegetated crack to the higher large ledge. On the fourth pitch, either climb a straight crack (5.7), then angle left to the base of the California Block, or climb the lower left crack (5.10) to the block's base. Pitch 5 involves an awkward move left around a roof.

The Library is Point 11,629's bookish southwest face—the first wall on the right as you enter the cirque from Cathedral Lake.

9. Library–Flasher in the Stacks (II 5.10b) The Library's left-most route follows left-trending features for five pitches to a system of ledges and ramps. Approach from the left on a tree-covered ledge until below a right-facing chimney. Climb toward the chimney for two easy pitches, then work up the 5.7 chimney for 140 feet to the top of a buttress. Climb the lower half of the 100-foot crux fourth pitch using two cracks, before hand-traversing left to a left-leaning ramp that leads to a small ledge. On the fifth pitch, follow left-leaning ramps for 40 feet, then climb to a small left-facing corner that leads to the walk-off ledge.

Descent: Unroped, to the east.

10. Library–Esther Prinn (II 5.8) Approach from the left, via the *Flasher in the Stacks* walk-off ledge. A short scramble leads to the rope-up spot, below and to the right of a left-facing corner that arches into a prominent roof. The first pitch involves 5.8 in a right-arching corner; above, avoid easy but loose terrain by climbing up right to a belay among blocks. The 5.6 second pitch follows a left-angling corner. The 5.7 third pitch also angles left. Finish the route by a 10-foot step and a 35-foot traverse right.

Descent: Downclimb to the top of the third pitch and rappel.

11. Library–Study Hall (II 5.8) Approach by angling up left to a grassy bench with the highest small trees. Begin by climbing a left-facing corner in dark rock for 150 feet to a large block on a grassy ledge (5.5). Move the belay up right 50 feet. Ascend a blocky face to a ledge below a 25-foot headwall. Climb the headwall past a loose, pointed block (5.7) to a belay in an alcove. Begin the third pitch by climbing steep 5.6 rock to a grassy shelf. Above the shelf, climb the left of two cracks (5.8), then traverse left on a ledge to a belay stance. Continue left to a 5.6 chimney, which leads to another shelf. Scramble up left for 120 feet to a sandy alcove. On the fifth pitch, climb cracks and grooves (5.7) to a sandy ledge. On the final pitch, climb cracks and a 5.8- face to a wedged boulder 25 feet below the top of the Library. Scramble to the top.

Descent: Cross meadows to the northeast to the top of a large, loose gully.

12. Library–Sweet Lady (II 5.9) The most highly recommended of the Library's routes was named in memory of Patti Saurman. It ascends the most prominent left-facing dihedral toward the wall's right side. The dihedral is right of a chimney.

Approach from the right via grassy ledges and ramps. A 5.5 pitch takes you to the dihedral's base. The continuous 5.7 second pitch ascends the dihedral to a cramped belay. The third pitch, with a 5.9 move, continues up the dihedral to ledges. Scramble to the top.

13. Library–Erodismo (II 5.10 A1) To the right of *Sweet Lady* is an arch. Climb to the arch in two pitches (5.8 squeeze chimney, 5.9), then climb two pitches left of the arch (5.10 A1, 5.8).

14. Isthmus Dome, South Face (II 5.10) A four-pitch route on the formation rising north of the isthmus between Middle and Cathedral Lakes.

Mount Chauvenet (12,250)

The maps published by the 1877–78 Hayden Survey attached the name of surveyor Louis Chauvenet to what we now call Lizard Head Peak, which may explain the old conjecture that Chauvenet was the peak Bonneville climbed in 1833. Then again, it is possible that Bonneville did climb the present Chauvenet, which is merely a dome rising a few hundred feet from a broad plateau, and the surveyors assumed that no one would mistake it for "the crest of the world."

1. West Slope (I 2nd class) From the high point of the original Bear's Ears Trail.

2. East Ridge The summit register mentions an ascent of the ridge extending from Bear's Ears Mountain.

3. Point 11,785, Moss Lake Buttress (III 5.8 A1) South of Moss Lake an embayment cuts into the plateau of the Bear's Ears Trail. On its east side is a prominent buttress split by a couloir. A good seven-pitch route, notable for its crack climbing, ascends the wall left of the couloir. The first ascent team passed one section by lassoing a chockstone, the only aid required. The route ends near the top of the couloir, which narrows to a rotten chimney.

Descent: While this is the only Wind River route that leads to a trail, you can return to Moss Lake more directly by descending somewhat east of the buttress.

Bear's Ears Mountain (11,820)

From the Moccasin Lake Road you can see interesting formations to the west. A striking point on one pinnacled ridge has been likened to ursine auricles; its identity is obvious from Dickinson Park. However, you can't see the bear from everywhere, and the formation isn't as large as you might guess from a distance. You see the twin pinnacles nearby from the Bear's Ears Trail's crossing of Sand Creek.

1. North Face (I 4th class) The easiest way up the formation ascends the north side. A 40-foot steep section gets you to either ear.

Euphoria Dome 11,242

This nice little formation southwest of Sand Lake (and 0.7 mile north-northeast of the Bear's Ears) could be approached from the Bear's Ears Trail but is probably better approached from Sand Creek.

1. North Face–Joy Ride (II 5.10c) To reach the start of this six-pitch route, traverse left on a bushy ledge until below a right-arching corner. Follow the arch (5.6) to an awkward belay. Begin the second pitch by traversing right to the end of the arch, then climb a slab up left (5.6R). The 5.7 third pitch follows a left-arching corner past blocks to a belay on a block. The short fourth pitch leads to a grassy ledge. Climb a steep crack (5.10c but easily protected) for 40 feet and continue up easier cracks to a ledge. (A crack to the right looks easier.) Complete the route with easier climbing on broken rock between grassy ledges.

2. North Face–Cruisin' (II 5.7) Beginning from the grassy base's apex, climb slabs to a finger crack (5.7). Continue up 5.4 slabs, eventually reaching a ledge below a headwall two or three pitches up. Climb the headwall by short steep steps, then make a long traverse left to a big ledge. The final pitch, which could be avoided by scrambling up right, ascends a short 5.6 crack to broken terrain.

Descent: Walk off to the west.

Hobbs Peak (11,663)

Between Hobbs Park and the Bear's Ears Trail, drained by Mary's and Sand Creeks, is a pleasant land of 200- to 500-foot crags. Three miles from a trailhead, though, and neither near nor en route to the range's crest, the area seldom lures climbers. Hobbs Peak, the high point, is too splintered, and its satellite spires, despite solid granite, involve a bit too much of a walk for their size.

1. Northeast Side (I 3rd class) An easy approach from Hobbs Park, only the final 100 feet requiring undivided attention.

2. Calvin Dome–The Transmogrifier (II 5.9) Point 11,505, on Hobbs' southeast ridge, features a 500-foot east-facing slab. Begin this route by scrambling 50 feet to the clump of trees above the slab's base. Pitch 1: Climb to the right-hand of two right-facing corners; its overhanging crack is the route's distinct crux. Above, follow a ramp up left. Pitch 2: Up and right to a long, straight 5.6 crack. Pitch 3: Nubbly and low-angle to a steeper, grassy 5.3 crack, with a belay just above. Pitch 4: More nubbly slab to 5.6 moves involving twin cracks, 20 feet below a long roof. Pass the roof where it isn't a roof. A few hundred feet of 3rd/4th-class slab-scurrying lead to the bedrock crest. Follow it south 500 feet to the dome's high point.

3. Calvin Dome–Positivity (II 5.8) Begin below the right end of the ledge with trees where *Transmogrifier* begins. Climb a crack to a left-facing dihedral, a right-facing dihedral, some friction up right, and finally parallel cracks up left to a belay. Climb up right to a funnel-shaped roof—the crux; continue up a left-facing corner to the next belay. The third pitch is easy 5th class, and the fourth pitch, 4th class.

4. Calvin Dome, East Ridge (I 4th class) Looks like fun.

2, 3, 4 Descent: A hundred feet before the summit, you can easily descend north and return to the base either on that side or by passing through the Calvin-Hobbs saddle to the south.

Mary's Tower (10,693)

As sharply profiled a peak as any in the range stands 0.3 mile south-southwest of Squaw Lake. The formation, though, happens to be minuscule.

1. South Ridge (I 5.5) Excellent, highly featured rock for two and a half pitches.

Descent: Chimneys and ramps on the southeast face.

Mount Cross (10,961)

From the upper switchbacks on the Moccasin Lake/Dickinson Park Road, Mount Cross is visible as the domelike high point on the nearest ridge above treeline. To reach it, leave the Moccasin Lake Road at Mosquito Park and follow a side road for 0.5 mile to a few buildings. Follow the trail that heads west for a mile to Hobbs Park.

1. Southeast Ridge (I 5.1) The southeast ridge forms the crest flanking Hobbs Park. A 1934 ascent was said to involve "a long morning which included a good deal of fair rock climbing." With due respect for the pioneers, the ridge—with firm, knobby rock and unexposed, uncommitting climbing—has since been described as "a great climb for kids."

From Hobbs Park narrow grass slopes lead to several of the ridge's notches. The ridge's best part is between a notch with two towers and the summit. Farther southeast the crest protrudes only a few feet from a vast lawn to the north.

2. Southwest Arête–Scorpion's Tail (I 5.7) Cross's left edge, as seen from Hobbs Park, is an arête rising from Pass 10,527, a mile from the park; it culminates in an overhanging brow. Enjoyable climbing in an obscure place.

Follow the crest closely for two pitches (moving the belay up between pitches). Begin the third pitch by continuing up the arête, but duck left below the overhang— the sting—to an overhanging but blocky crack (one block wobbles), which leads to the top.

Windy Mountain (12,539)

This is the rubble east of Lizard Head Pass; the trail traverses high on its west slopes. While not a photogenic peak, it is visible from Cirque of the Towers campsites.

1. Southwest Slopes (I 3rd class) A scramble from the Lizard Head Trail.

Peak 12,258

A narrow ridge running northeast from Lizard Head separates the Bear Lake/Popo Agie drainage from the South Fork Lakes/Little Wind River drainage.

1. Southwest Ridge (I 3th class) Gain this ridge from Bear Lake.

2. East Ridge (I 4th class) Gain this ridge from the Lizard Head Trail.

3. West Face (IV/V 5.10 A0) Few climbers visit South Fork Lakes, but a nice-looking wall rises near the head of the valley. A route starts at the low point near the center of the face and culminates in a prominent right-facing dihedral system. The first ascent involved a bivouac.

Ascend 5.5 to 5.6 corners for two pitches. After a 4th-class pitch, follow 5.8 corners and cracks (left of a large right-facing dihedral) to ledges. From the ledges' high point, climb a steep face past three bolts and pass a roof in a corner to a stance (5.10). Climb an arch, then use a bolt for aid to reach lower-angle rock (5.9). Climb past another bolt to a hand crack; traverse right 80 feet (5.11- or 5.10 A0). As on most Wind River first ascents, the first ascent party came upon a fixed stopper.

Continue working up right, using thin cracks below a large right-leaning arch (5.9). You're now directly below the upper dihedrals. Five 5.8 to 5.10 pitches complete the route.

Gilman Peak (11,265)

This is the peak 0.6 mile southeast of Smith Lake, rising as slabs from the lake's south shore. Bradley Gilman, who traveled the length of the range in 1934, was credited with the first ascent. Gilman, however, denies being near the peak: "I am flattered to have my name on any hill in the Wind Rivers however much undeserved, but don't perpetuate any such error as my having ascended it."

1. Northeast Slope (I 2nd class) From Smith Lake, descend the creek to the left end of the north face's slabs. Ascend talus to a bench, then climb up right. Finding the highest point among various pinnacles is a problem, but many of the false summits are fun. Finding the 2nd-class route to the true summit requires still more looking and isn't worth the search.

2. Northwest Slope (I 3rd class) From the middle of Smith Lake's south shore, climb through a nasty forest, then work up talus west of the northwest ridge. While the summit's identity among the towers isn't obvious, turn left up a gully before passing a subsidiary summit that is to the right.

You can also reach this route from High Meadow Lake.

Cirque of the Towers from Texas Pass

10 Cirque of the Towers

The North Popo Agie tumbles out of the mountains from an alpine fastness hidden from the east; you can't see the Continental Divide peaks at its head over the foothills. During the 1920s and 1930s, when mountaineers found their way up virtually all major peaks in the range's northern half, few knew of these southern peaks. A few accounts reported unsuccessful attempts on the area's highest peak, Lizard Head, and rumors hinted that precipitous spires surrounded the North Popo Agie's source, Lonesome Lake.

Orrin Bonney and Frank and Notsie Garnick visited Lonesome Lake in 1940. After climbing Lizard Head, where they found evidence of prior ascents, they surprised themselves by climbing the especially striking tower above the lake's west end; they named it Pingora. In 1941 Bonney climbed the southernmost of the towers, which he called Warbonnet, and gave the name Cirque of the Towers to the semicircle of peaks running from Pingora to Warbonnet.

Bonney's writing made the Cirque of the Towers known, and during the 1940s and 1950s climbers reached the remaining summits, climbing the last, Block Tower, in 1957. Climbers then shifted their attention from alpinism in the north to rock climbing in the south, and the Cirque now has an exceptional concentration of climbs and, sometimes, climbers.

Lonesome Lake's water was the range's first water found unfit to drink because of human fecal material. Camping is now forbidden within 0.25 mile of the lake, meaning you must pitch your tent well above the lake. The small meadows tucked among the boulders and clusters of wind-sculpted trees above the lake make superb campsites—sites closer to most climbs than Lonesome Lake is. Look around before selecting a campsite. Good sites are scattered through the cirque; the best aren't the most conspicuous. The Cirque needn't seem crowded.

However, the Cirque's tundra is well described as a fragile alpine environment. Environmental concerns are the same as elsewhere in the range, but the concentration of climbers intensifies them. You must keep a sharper lookout for windblown food wrappers, make more certain that your latrine isn't someone else's potential campsite. No fires—and not only because fires are against the rules.

The shortest route to Lonesome Lake begins west of the Divide, at Big Sandy Opening, and involves infamous Jackass Pass. You can also reach Lonesome Lake by the North Fork Trail, which ascends the North Popo Agie from Dickinson Park. This longer route avoids Jackass Pass but does start with a long descent and requires four river crossings.

Much early Cirque of the Towers climbing was done from Shadow Lake, west of the Divide. But while Overhanging Tower and Shark's Nose are easily approached from it, Shadow Lake sees a fraction of the visitors Lonesome Lake sees. You can reach Shadow Lake from Big Sandy Opening by the Fremont Trail.

This chapter includes formations, notably the Monolith, in small cirques down the North Popo Agie from Lonesome Lake. You can reach these cirques by the North Fork Trail.

Except for Laturio Mountain, which is on the Temple Peak quad, the peaks in this chapter are on the Lizard Head Peak map. Trails also cross the Big Sandy Opening and Mount Bonneville quads.

Trails

Jackass Pass Trail

Big Sandy Lake to Lonesome Lake—3 miles

The rocky defile north of Big Sandy Lake isn't an ideal place for a trail. Boulders force meandering; unexpected descents interrupt the ascent; and near the pass the trail climbs far above it, then drops below it, and crosses well above a lower crossing nearby.

From the Big Sandy Trail's end at Big Sandy Lake's northwest corner, switchback up the hillside to the north and cross North Creek. Ascend a short distance, then traverse north until you're above North Lake (also called Shaft Lake); be alert for minor ups and downs as the trail detours slabs and boulders. Descend all the way to North Lake, round its soggy north shore, and ascend a vague streambed to meadows below Arrowhead Lake. Here you have a choice.

The official trail, to avoid cliffs that form Arrowhead Lake's east shore, turns east, climbs toward Mitchell Peak, and traverses Mitchell's slopes. After dropping to a draw, it finally climbs to a 10,760-foot saddle, then descends straightforwardly to Lonesome Lake.

However, with camping not allowed within 0.25 mile of Lonesome Lake, climbers have created an alternate route, which passes west of Arrowhead Lake, crosses the Divide by a 10,600-foot gap 0.25 mile south of the trail's crossing, and takes you toward popular camping meadows north of Warbonnet and the Warriors, south of Pingora. Leaving the official trail where it turns east and climbs toward Mitchell, follow the meadow's east edge to Arrowhead Lake's outlet. If you follow the lake's west shore, you must negotiate large boulders before climbing grassy slopes to the pass. Instead, diagonal up talus (or snow) to an opening between an especially prominent boulder and the Plume's sheer east face. Beyond this and a few more boulders is easy going to the pass and down the grassy draw on the other side.

North Fork Trail

Dickinson Park to Lonesome Lake—13 miles

Reaching the Cirque from the east involves no passes, but the trail crosses the North Popo Agie four times; a few of the crossings are hazardous when the river is high.

Cirque of the Towers Area

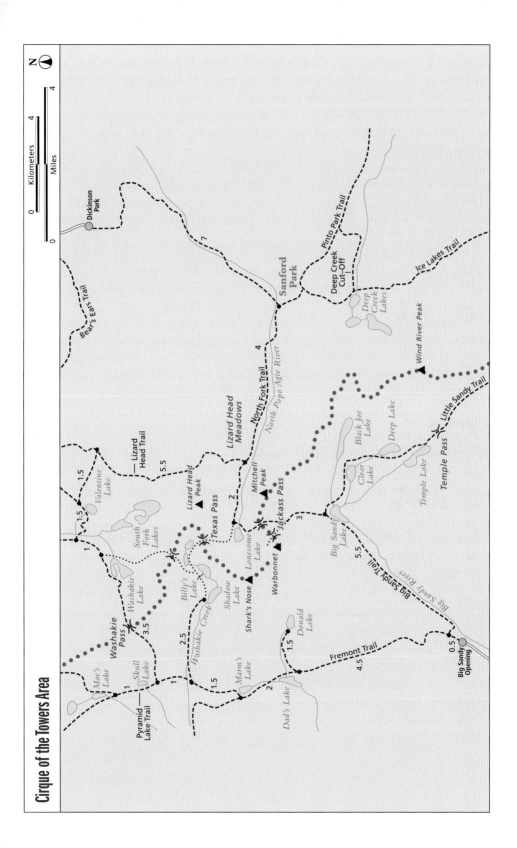

N

Kilometers

Miles

Dickinson Park

Bear's Ears Trail

Sanford Park

Pinto Park Trail

Deep Creek Cut-Off

Ice Lakes Trail

Deep Creek Lakes

Wind River Peak

North Fork Trail

North Popo Agie River

Lizard Head Meadows

Lizard Head Trail

4

5.5

Valentine Lake

1.5

1.5

South Fork Lakes

Lizard Head Peak

Texas Pass

Mitchell Peak

2

Jackass Pass

Billy's Lake

Shadow Lake

Washakie Creek

Washakie Lake

Warbonnet

Shark's Nose

Lonesome Lake

3

Black Joe Lake

Clear Lake

Deep Lake

Temple Lake

Temple Pass

Little Sandy Trail

Big Sandy Lake

5.5

Washakie Pass

Skull Lake

Mae's Lake

3.5

Pyramid Lake Trail

1

2.5

Marm's Lake

1.5

Donald Lake

1.5

Dad's Lake

2

Fremont Trail

4.5

Big Sandy Trail

Big Sandy River

0.5

Big Sandy Opening

7

1

Begin at the parking area in southern Dickinson Park. The North Fork Trail shares the boardwalk with the Smith Lake Trail, but after another 100 yards, beyond the meadow's edge, the latter veers right, while the former crosses a low ridge and drops 1,000 feet to the North Popo Agie. A trail to Shoshone Lake crosses the river, while the North Fork Trail heads upstream. The High Meadow Trail diverges northwest near High Meadow Creek, and beyond Sanford Park is a junction with the Pinto Park Trail, which leads to the Middle Popo Agie drainage. Cirque peaks finally come into view when you are nearly to Lizard Head Meadows and the junction with the Lizard Head Trail. The North Fork Trail ends near Lonesome Lake's outlet, though you can follow the lake's north shore and climb to Texas Pass or cross the outlet and climb to Jackass Pass.

A 2-mile-long use trail on Sanford Park's eastern fringe can be used to eliminate the second and third river crossings. However, enough deadfall must be surmounted and circled that, unless the river is dangerously high, you are better off wading the two crossings.

The first two crossings can be avoided by combining the Smith Lake and High Meadow Trails. However, this detour adds 1.5 miles and an indeterminate number of ups and downs, and much of the High Meadow Trail is steep, loose, and susceptible to becoming a streambed. (The junction of the Sanford Park and Smith Lake Creek legs of this trail with the leg that goes to High Meadow Lake is unmarked.)

Shadow Lake Trail

Pyramid Lake Trail to Shadow Lake—2.5 miles

To reach Shadow Lake from Big Sandy Opening, follow the Fremont Trail to Marm's Lake, then the Pyramid Lake Trail to its crossing of Washakie Creek, Shadow Lake's outlet stream. The official trail follows the creek's south side, then crosses to the north side, but you can easily follow either bank.

To continue up Washakie Creek to Billy's, Barren, and Texas Lakes, follow paths somewhat above Shadow Lake's northeast shore, just northwest of Billy's Lake and south of Barren Lake.

Donald Lake Trail

Dad's Lake to Donald Lake—1.5 miles

The trail to Donald Lake leaves the Fremont Trail, a few hundred yards south of Dad's Lake, where the Fremont Trail circles a bog before descending a draw to the lake. Be alert for the junction: The trail sees far less traffic than the Fremont Trail, and the sign may be inconspicuous. The trail angles northeast toward Donald Creek, which it then follows.

Passes

Three passes cross the Divide from Lonesome Lake to Shadow Lake and the lakes upstream from it. The longest is the easiest, the shortest the most difficult.

Texas Pass (11,400+)

Lonesome Lake to Texas Lake

The longest but easiest of the three routes crosses the Divide between Camel's Hump and Peak 11,925. From Lonesome Lake, ascend slightly east of the creek that drains into Lonesome Lake's northwest corner; the bowl above is easy going. From Barren Lake or Texas Lake, work up steep talus into which a virtual trail has been worn.

New York Pass (11,440+)

Lonesome Lake to Billy's Lake

A shorter route than the *Texas Pass* route crosses the Divide between Peak 11,840+ and Bollinger but is steeper and involves more (and looser) talus.

Wolf's Head–Overhanging Tower Col (11,720+)

Cirque Lake to Shadow Lake

The most direct route between Lonesome and Shadow Lakes crosses between Wolf's Head and Overhanging Tower. It is convenient for reaching many climbs, but steep scree on both sides—and early summer snow—make it unsuitable for backpacking.

Wisconsin Couloir

Lonesome Lake to Donald Lake

From Lonesome Lake you can see a gully slanting up right between Pylon and the Warriors. The couloir—whose floor can be hard ice, soft snow, or scree—gets most of its use as a descent from nearby peaks, but easy talus slopes descend to the southwest, to Donald Creek. (The 10,480-foot tarn below the Warriors is Hidden Lake.)

Elizabeth Col (11,400+)

Shadow Lake to Donald Lake

This col, just east of Elizabeth Peak, makes the Watch Towers and peaks to the south accessible from Shadow Lake. Nasty gullies drop north from the col, but you can bypass them by gullies that lead to ledges under Elizabeth Peak's north face; these ledges reach a snowy saddle a few hundred feet west of the col.

Fish Creek Pass (10,688)

Fish Creek Park to Big Sandy Lake

Fish Creek Park is the long meadow the Fremont Trail traverses south of Mirror Lake. This obscure pass lies between Bunion and Laturio. Leave the Fremont Trail where it crosses Fish Creek and follow the creek to its head. From Big Sandy Lake, ascend Lost Creek—the stream that enters the lake from the west—to Blue Lake and continue west to Bunion Creek's head.

Peaks

Lizard Head Peak (12,842)

A climber familiar with the Cirque of the Towers went to the East Fork Valley, where he was amazed by a high, pointed summit just northeast of the Cirque. Several hundred feet higher than nearby peaks, it featured a big north face. He was learning things about Lizard Head not apparent from Lonesome Lake. It is the area's highest peak, a distinction concealed by the flat summit ridge and the foreshortening caused by the broken south face—which also give no hint that one of the few glaciers in the range's southern half nestles under the north face.

On the map produced by the 1877–78 Hayden Survey, the peak is "Mount Chauvenet," the summit Bonneville was hypothesized to have reached in 1833. The present name is a mystery, though with imagination you can see a lizard from Bear Lakes.

1. West Ridge (I 4th class) You can have a pleasanter outing by climbing Camel's Hump and following the exposed 0.5-mile ridge to Lizard Head than by climbing a south face route.

2. South Face Left (I 4th or easy 5th class) The south face is such a jumble of broken couloirs that details would be incomprehensible and senseless. Climb from Secluded Lake (10,702) to the summit flat's west end.

3. South Face Right (I 5.0) A couloir more distinct than others meets the southeast ridge just east of the summit. Only one short section is harder than 3rd class. Low-angle slabs lead from the couloir nearly to the summit slopes.

4. Southeast Ridge (II 5.5) Much of the pleasant but rarely climbed ridge that rises from Lizard Head Meadows is easy. However, you must pass a prominent tower, accomplished most easily by traversing onto the east face, then regaining the crest.

5. Northeast Prow Left (IV 5.8 A3) The nearly vertical north and east faces meet at a steep prow broken by corners and chimneys. Much of this route follows dihedrals left of the prow.

A narrow spur conveniently sweeps down to provide access to the prow's steep part. This begins with a chimney left of the crest, requiring aid, and a traverse right to an orange nose. Next is a traverse into a dihedral and a pitch of strenuous aid. The route's middle part has some easy pitches on broken rock; look for a tunnel between large blocks. The first ascent party counted on a flared chimney to get through the final overhangs but, finding it wet, resorted to aid in a thin crack and four bolts to reach another chimney. Exposed free climbing then reaches the top.

6. Northeast Prow Right (VI 5.9+ A3) This and the preceding route both ascend the steep intersection of the nearly vertical north and east faces. While the climbers of this route began from the north face and the climbers of the other route from the east, with this route following the prow more closely, the routes may share some rock. The 1979 first ascent team rated the route a VI. With no repeat ascent being reported, the VI has not been confirmed.

From Lake 11,260, under the north face, scramble 200 feet to a small saddle. Follow the ridge nearly to the top of a pinnacle, bypass it to the left, continue to the base of the east face, and diagonal right to a ledge on the northeast prow. Climb four pitches of 5.8 to 5.9 and A2/A3 near the prow. A pitch above a wet alcove is a large ledge. Continue up on somewhat easier rock, except for a detour onto the north face on a rubbly, wet, loose, unprotected ledge. Ascend a gully to the final, 5.8 wall.

7. North Face (I 4th class Snow 4th class) Above South Fork Lakes, tucked under the Lizard Head–Camel's Hump ridge, is a small glacier. This route follows the snow-covered ramp that slants up left from the glacier to the ridge; it is one of the few Cirque routes requiring an ice axe.

Camel's Hump (12,537)

You can search in vain from Lonesome Lake for a lizard's head, a shark's nose, or a wolf's head. However, you can recognize Camel's Hump, which was named from Lonesome Lake, as twin summits to the north; you can even imagine the camel's head. The slopes facing Lonesome Lake are Camel's Hump's least impressive; steeper walls rise from Lizard Head Glacier to the northeast and Texas Lake to the northwest.

1. Southwest Slope (I 3rd class) From the south side of Texas Pass, mostly walking on conveniently slanted ledges. This route has much to recommend it as the pleasantest nontechnical route in the Cirque.

2. Southeast Ridge (I 4th class) An exposed 0.5-mile traverse from Lizard Head.

3. Northeast Face (II 5.5) Two routes of comparable difficulty ascend the wall above Lizard Head Glacier. One ends near the summit; the other begins 100 yards left of a fall line from the summit and follows a crack system, finally traversing to the southeast ridge. Ice axes are handy on the approach.

4. West Ridge (I 5.5) Beginning at Texas Pass, you can climb the slabs above for five pitches or so. While neither sustained nor committing—you can escape right to 3rd-class terrain at several points—the route is worth mentioning because it is fun.

Descent: While the *Southwest Slope* is the usual descent route, Lizard Head Glacier has been regained by four long rappels from a notch in the southeast ridge.

Skunk Knob (11,099)

This bluff overlooking the north shore of Lonesome Lake has a summit register, which delights children, and cliffs several hundred feet high, to entertain grown-ups.

1. North Slope (I 1st class) Round the cliffs on either side to the pleasant draw to the north. Lake 10,702 is Secluded Lake.

2. South Face Numerous routes have been done on this face, some as long as five pitches and as difficult as 5.9, and a few are said to be classics. Nevertheless, you are unlikely to visit the Cirque with Skunk Knob as your main objective.

Peak 11,925

On the Divide 0.2 mile west of Texas Pass is this seldom-noticed, unnamed peak, which lacks 5th-class climbing.

1. East Ridge (I 3rd class) Far pleasanter than the *West Ridge*. Start slightly south of Texas Pass.

2. West Ridge (I 3rd class) Approach from the bowl northwest of Lonesome Lake. Either climb to the col next to Peak 11,840+ and traverse a minor summit or ascend a chute more to the east to a notch in the ridge. The choice may be determined by snow conditions or your tolerance for rubble.

Peak 11,840+

This peak 0.2 mile east of Billy's Lake resists attempts to find something interesting about it. The closest it has come to a name is the Chicago Mountaineering Club's "Most Northern Peak in the Cirque." However, it is not.

1. Southwest Ridge (I 4th class) From New York Pass, scramble left of the crest. The one place someone may need a rope is above the most prominent notch.

2. North Ridge (I 5th class) Reach the col between Peaks 11,840+ and 11,925 from Lonesome Lake by slopes that can be either snow covered or scree. The ridge rises in a step climbed by a steep chimney.

3. Smoke on the Water (5.8) A seven-pitch route on the slabs rising directly from Billy's Lake.

Descent: Climbers have descended by climbing down grassy ledges on the east face, then making a short rappel.

Bollinger Peak (12,232)

The highest and broadest peak between Camel's Hump and Watch Tower (0.2 mile north of Wolf's Head) hasn't achieved the renown of its lesser, splintery neighbors. You see it from such vantages as Jackass Pass, looming behind Pingora, but climbers are more attracted to the hospitable cirque south of Wolf's Head than to the shadowy bowl below Bollinger to the north. Bollinger also towers over Shadow Lake but draws less admiration than the slender silhouettes of Overhanging Tower and Shark's Nose.

Karl Bollinger climbed this peak in 1953 and fell to his death the next day on Warbonnet.

1. Northeast Ridge (I 3rd class) From either Lonesome Lake or Shadow Lake, via New York Pass. The scrambling over large, frost-shattered slabs is rather pleasant.

2. West Face Far Left (III/IV 5.10) A few hundred feet left of the main left-arching dihedral is the west face's second-most prominent dihedral, also left-facing, extending from near the base to the summit ridge. This dihedral involves eight pitches, most about 5.9. The crux is the fourth pitch, where the first ascenders took the central of three possible lines, a hand crack.

3. West Face Left (II 5.7) Bollinger's most prominent feature facing Shadow Lake is a dark, arching, left-facing dihedral directly below the summit. An old route is described as being to the left, beginning in a corner composed of friable dark rock, just left of a long, steep gully, passing left of an overhang near the top and meeting the northwest ridge. However, the closer you approach the face, the less likely this route appears.

4. West Pillar—On the Lamb (But We Ain't No Sheep) (IV 5.10 A0) This pillar forms one of the Cirque's classic lines, and, though it is in an unexpected place, the pillar should be obvious to anyone at Shadow Lake.

After a few hundred feet of scrambling, rope up at a big ledge and climb 4th class to a short but fierce corner. Two long 5.9 crack pitches then lead to a big ledge at the base of a large left-facing corner. Climb a smaller corner (thin laybacking, 5.10) to the large corner's left and, when the crack peters out, tension traverse to the large corner, which offers an overhanging finger crack (5.10). The fifth pitch features a 5.9 crack. The seventh pitch works right to a black corner and gains a huge ledge, while the eighth pitch reaches unroping terrain, a 300-foot hike from the summit.

Bollinger Peak

5. West Face, Right—Consolation (III 5.8) The dark left-facing corner/arch forms the pillar's left side. The pillar's less obvious right side, also less hideous looking, is the site of this route. It is one of several Cirque climbs that are worthwhile but not comparable to the classics.

A major grassy ledge sweeps across the lower west face, beneath the pillar and up toward Wolf's Head. At this ledge's upper end is a shallow bowl, behind which cracks and chimneys rise toward Bollinger's south ridge. Approach via the ledge, but when past the pillar's indistinct right side, leave the main ledge and scramble up slabs near a rubble-strewn lesser ledge/gully. Rope up at a system that slants slightly right (to its right is another system). A roof capping a right-facing corner 200 feet up is a landmark.

Pitch 1: Stem up a chossy, flaky chimney and cleaner cracks to the left. Step left, amid helpful knobs, and climb to a ledge on the left. Pitch 2: Climb a right-facing corner for 30 feet to another ledge. Traverse left and climb another right-facing corner (5.8) to a roof, easily bypassed. A 5.8 mantle and a 5.7 crack in a shallow right-facing corner lead to the left end of a large, down-sloping ledge. Pitch 3: Climb the crack above the ledge's left end, then use other cracks to the left (5.7) to reach an area more broken by ledges. Pitch 4: Wander up, confronting or avoiding moderate short corners. Pitch 5: Continue up the easy right-facing system. Near the pitch's top, rock adjacent to the chimney offers pleasant 5.6 face climbing. Pitch 6: Chimney and/or stem to the end of difficulties.

6. East Face, Left Chimney (II 5.9) A chimney, beginning above the snow's high point, splits into two chimneys a few hundred feet up. This route, unlikely to become popular, ascends the left chimney and emerges on the crest left of the first gendarme south of the summit.

Unroped scrambling, followed by several easy and undistinguished pitches, leads to a pitch with a difficult move. Once on the crest, pass behind the gendarme and climb a step in the summit block by a nice pitch on its east face.

7. East Face, Right Chimney (II 5.7) This route has the same scrambling start as *Left Chimney,* but takes the chimney's more logical right branch. Two 5th-class pitches past overhangs are followed by two 4th-class leads.

8. East Face (IV 5.9 A3) The main face's major feature is a diagonal crack system. Four of this route's eight pitches follow these cracks; above, the route zigzags to the top.

From blocks directly below the summit, climb an easy slab to a right-slanting crack, which requires a bit of aid. Then climb to a higher crack; hard climbing leads to a grassy area and a long ramp, easy at first but steepening to a short aid section below a ledge. Friction left to a chimney and pass through a notch to a white V. Aid up left to a belay among blocks and flakes. A mostly free lead goes up right, passing several overhangs. Traverse right and climb ramps and overhangs to the summit ridge.

Wolf's Head (12,163)

Topographically Wolf's Head is hardly more than the junction of Bollinger's south ridge with a ridge extending west from Pingora. The gendarme at the junction presents a lupine profile toward Shadow Lake, nose skyward, though from Lonesome

Lake its identity is unobvious. But the narrow, jagged crest that extends east toward Pingora makes Wolf's Head one of the Wind Rivers' best-known formations. And with the quest for summits replaced by a quest for clean, sunny, accessible rock, Wolf's Head's broad south face has become a playground, with three 1980s and two 2000s routes ending on the east ridge far from the summit.

1. West Face (I 5.0) Only its use for descending recommends the broken side of Wolf's Head that overlooks Shadow Lake. If ascending, begin just west of the Wolf's Head–Overhanging Tower col with a short headwall. Traverse north on ledges many hundreds of feet until below Wolf's Head's summit. Climb a gully for about 300 feet until it is easy to work left. The cruxes are a 20-foot slab 100 feet below the summit and an angling crack in the summit block.

2. South Face–Canis (III 5.11c) Left of the prominent system followed by the *1966 Route,* one pitch up (discounting approach scrambling to reach the horizontal black dike) is a drastically leaning right-facing dihedral. Climb to the dihedral (5.10c) and up the dihedral (5.11c). Continue up (5.10d) to where *White Buffalo* crosses left. Rather than join the *1966 Route,* though, climb subtler, pleasanter corners to its left (5.10d, 5.10b) to the east ridge.

3. South Face–White Buffalo (III 5.12c/d) To the left of the *1966 Route,* to those with a taste for difficulty, a mouthwatering 300- to 400-foot crack splits the wall. Climb the first two pitches of the *1966 Route,* but then (protected by three bolts) traverse to the crack by "wicked nasty micro-crystal face climbing." Climb the

Wolf's Head

East Ridge

(finger) crack in two long pitches (5.11a, 5.11b/c), until you can traverse right (fixed piton) to reach the east ridge left of the Darth Vader tower.

4. South Face, 1966 Route (III 5.8) Above Cirque Lake a system of chimneys and huge flakes rises 800 feet to meet the east ridge near the Darth Vader tower. Climb the lower chimney past overhangs to the ominous flakes above. A difficult slab leads to cracks that reach the east ridge.

5. South Face Center Right (III 5.10+) The left-hand of the routes to the right of the *1966 Route,* sketchily documented, ascends the prominent right-facing dihedral that angles toward the top of the rising portion of the east ridge. Beginning just right of the *1966 Route,* easy face climbing leads to the dihedral, which is sustained in its difficulties. The route goes up right from the dihedral's top.

6. South Face Right (III 5.10b) One argument against guidebooks is that they preclude everybody's having a first ascent experience. For example, between the 1980 and 1994 guides, this route suffered three first ascent teams (all spoke highly of it). The following description reflects slight differences in the three routes.

Scramble left up ramps to a 5.6 right-facing corner, where roped climbing begins. The second pitch involves either a 5.8/5.9 layback to the right or easier climbing to the left; both ways end at a big black dike. One party continued straight up, encountering a 5.10a chimney and a long 5.8 layback; another moved right on the dike, then back left to the dihedral system by 5.4 climbing. A 5.6 crack pitch leads to one team's crux, an undercling left. Another team apparently avoided this undercling by 5.9 climbing to the right. They, however, encountered a 5.10b crack on the following (their sixth) pitch. A final crack pitch (5.8) leads to the east ridge.

7. South Face Far Right (II 5.10-) From the left end of the meadow (or snowpatch) above the ramps used on the *East Ridge* route approach, right-facing flakes extend to the top of the east ridge's rising section. The first pitch involves 5.9 face climbing to reach the flake system, the second is 5.8+, the third is the crux, and the fourth is easy.

8. East Ridge (III 5.6) The east ridge is a 1,000-foot spine, here appallingly narrow, there topped with towers passed by exposed traverses. Most climbers find this unique ridge ethereal, perhaps even surreal—or at least clean, picturesque, and surprising—but a minority complains. They cite the approach, the descent, and a lack of difficulties commensurate with their self-image. Be warned that the route requires a sense of whimsy. You must gladly be intimidated by a 30-degree slab (2 feet wide).

Much of the route is 4th class, and, if you use a rope on all of it, you'll need an early start. If you climb most of the route unroped, it goes quickly.

While Buckingham and Plummer began the first ascent by climbing from Cirque Lake to the saddle between Wolf's Head and the minor summit near Pingora (Tiger Tower), Buckingham wrote that the saddle "would most easily be reached by climbing over Tiger Tower, from the notch between it and Pingora"—that is, climbing

Wolf's Head, East Ridge ▶

the south-facing gully to the notch below Pingora's west face, crossing Tiger Tower, and descending a tricky set of steps. However, the original approach has proved to be shorter and nicer, except when early summer snow below Tiger Tower is melting profusely. Scramble to the base of the prominent chimney below the Wolf's Head–Tiger Tower saddle, but, rather than ascending the chimney, angle left up grassy ledges to the left end of a meadow (the site of the snowpatch). From its right end, follow ramps and slabs to the saddle.

Cross the ridge's narrowest portion and follow cracks for three rope lengths. A horizontal section then leads to the first tower. Pass this tower to the south, then squeeze through a chimney to a small ledge north of the second tower. (This is the largest of the towers, the one with the silhouette of Darth Vader.) Traverse a thin ledge to a crack; use it to regain the crest. Also traverse the third tower on the north, using scenic parallel cracks. Pass the next tower by descending a chimney to the south, traversing on a solitary, fortuitous horizontal crack, and stemming back to the crest. Drop north and follow broad ledges to the summit block, ascended by a chimney. (The chimney to the left is easier than the obvious one.)

9. Northeast Face (II 5.7 A2) A route ascends the concave wall at the head of the bowl between Bollinger and Pingora, reaching the crest north of Wolf's Head's summit. The first two leads follow an obvious dihedral, but above is a bewildering array of ramps and cracks. The first ascent party went too far left and had to retreat; beware of off-route bolts. Instead, the fourth lead follows a ramp up right and ascends a bolt ladder to a ledge. Use more bolts to reach another ledge, below an overhanging crack. The cracks head to a big ledge, above which two easier pitches reach the wall's top.

10. Northwest Chimneys (II 5.3/5.4) Wolf's Head was first climbed not by the *West Face* but by the more sporting gullies and chimneys that end at the notch north of the summit. Reach this system from the wide couloir leading to the Wolf's Head–Overhanging Tower col from Shadow Lake by easy ledges and gullies low on the west face.

Descent: Rappel slings make the chimney south of the summit, facing Cirque Lake, a tempting descent route, but the patience and routefinding intuition needed to descend the *West Face* are preferable to the anxiety provoked by retrieving rappel ropes in the chimney. Many have rappelled the chimney once; no one twice. A fatality occurred in the chimney when a rope dislodged a block.

Descend the *West Face* by first descending to the level of the Overhanging Tower col (despite a grid of rappel slings spread over the mountain's west side) before traversing. From the summit, rappel or downclimb toward Bollinger, then down the 20-foot slab below a large, precarious-looking boulder, to a large ledge. Walk south and work down a gully, continuing to ledges that promise to take you nearly to the Overhanging Tower col. A typical party makes about four short rappels between the summit and these ledges. Traversing the ledges involves minor ups and downs but never reaches 4th-class difficulty until the headwall overlooking the col.

Bolts enable *White Buffalo* to be rappelled with one 70-meter rope.

Pingora Peak (11,884)

The formation standing above Lonesome Lake's west end was once Popo Agie Tower, but the first ascent party renamed it Pingora, a Shoshone word meaning "high, rocky, inaccessible peak." Pingora, with its solid granite, rugged surroundings, and pleasant approach, epitomizes the southern Wind Rivers. The highest mountain, or the most conspicuous, often symbolizes a range, but Pingora, 2,000 feet lower than the highest and invisible from civilization, is what rock climbers think of as the Wind Rivers. Its presence is so integral to Cirque life that few leave without touching it. All its routes are good; some are among the range's best.

Three routes begin from the south shoulder. Gain the shoulder by zigzagging up diagonal 2nd- and 3rd-class ledges on its west side.

1. South Buttress (II 5.6) The range's most popular rock climb consists of three pitches on the steep slabs above the south shoulder. Slabs lean against one another so as to form a number of right-facing corners, which you can study from the shoulder.

Begin with two short 4th-class steps, which coincide with the *East Ledges*'s start. The classic line then ascends the right-facing corners that are second nearest the buttress's crest. The corners continue for two pitches, to ledges below a smooth slab split by cracks that form a K. (The corner system nearest the crest is 5.7. The system 60 feet right of the standard line offers continuous, pleasant 5.6 climbing, except for a slippery 5.10 move near its start.)

From the base of the K Cracks, you can descend left a few feet and climb a left-facing corner, finishing at the top of the slab. However, the K's thin left-hand crack is excellent 5.8 (protectable by many small stoppers). The right-hand crack is more serious 5.8. From the slab's top, walk left and scramble unroped for 200 feet to the summit.

2. East Ledges (I 5.2) Bonney and the Garnicks, studying Pingora from

Pingora, South Buttress

Pingora

Lonesome Lake one evening in 1940, declared it unclimbable. The next day they found this route and made the first ascent of the peak.

Where the south shoulder abuts the south buttress, climb a short, dark corner on the right to ledges that lead out onto the east face. A few upward pitches, alternating with traverses right, take you to a gully that leads to ledges below the summit.

3. East Face, Left-Side Cracks (III 5.7) Several cracks extend up the east face's left side to low-angle rock level with the south shoulder. Above and slightly right of the lower cracks, a pair of cracks splits the steeper upper face, crossing the *East Ledges*. Combining the lower and upper cracks makes a long, enjoyable route, though—because you can escape to the south shoulder or finish by the *East Ledges*—you aren't committed to a long route (or to a one-day ascent).

A snowpatch lies against the broken rock that separates the east face from the south shoulder. Right of the snow is a corner and a pair of cracks, one ending 100 feet up, the other curving left. Given the location and the lack of commitment required, it is likely that the five or six pitches ending in the low-angle midsection have been tried in every possible way. The following describes a way that keeps difficulties to 5.6.

Climb the curving crack for 130 feet (a gentle introduction to jamming), traverse right on a ledge to another crack, and belay a bit higher. (Staying in the curving crack leads to a 5.8 overhang on the second pitch.) Climb more or less up this right-hand crack for four pitches; series of ledges are interspersed with pleasant cracks and corners. Continue for three or four 4th-class pitches to the upper wall.

All four upper pitches are 5.7, the first ascending a slab to the right-hand crack of the parallel pair. Climb this crack past an overhang to a ledge shared with the *East Ledges*. (The left-hand crack is harder.) A steep corner leads to broken rock near Pingora's summit.

Of the alternate starts, the left-facing, two-pitch dihedral between the snowpatch and the cracks is 5.5. Above the dihedral, climb to a large flake, then continue up easier rock to another dihedral and a roof, bypassing it on the left to a cave. A crack above the cave leads to the low-angle area.

A major variation begins several hundred feet to the right, in a left-facing corner just left of a larger corner and a roof. Trending slightly left, it joins the other variations in the low-angle area.

4. East Face (IV 5.11–) This route ascends the center of the wall that faces Lonesome Lake, beginning from the highest talus, above a high patch of trees. (Starting farther right entails aid and bad rock.) The upper part follows straight cracks to the right of a sickle-shaped crack.

Scramble a few hundred feet to a short, steep crack and climb the crack. The first ascenders evidently continued up a corner above with aid, but you can avoid aid by dropping left, then ascending easy chimneys for a few leads to the face's low-angle midsection. Scramble up right to a left-facing corner, where serious climbing resumes. This corner is followed by two more pitches, involving cracks and intricate face climbing. Soon you reach the cracks right of the sickle-shaped crack. After a few

Pingora Peak

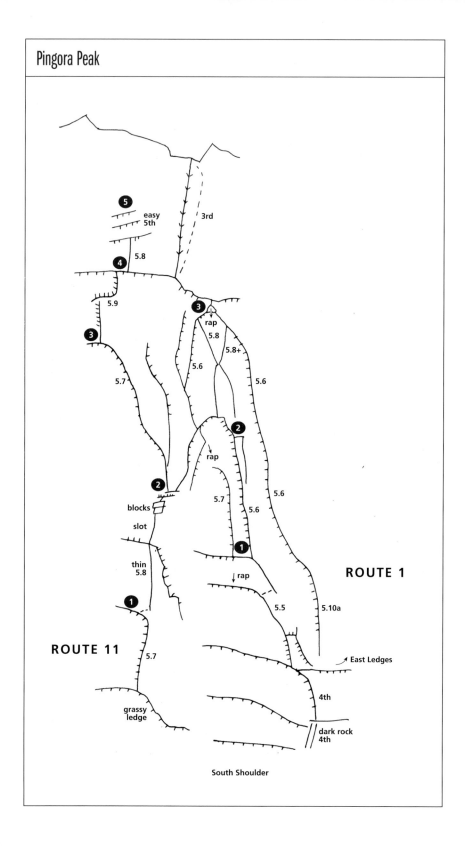

predominantly aid pitches in these cracks, step to an easier corner and follow it to large ledges near the summit.

A major variation, *The Southerners,* begins to the left and ascends discontinuous crack systems to a 5.10+ R face pitch, which gains the bottom of the sickle crack. *The Southerners* then free climbed the upper *East Face.*

5. Northeast Face (IV 5.8) Near the right skyline, as seen from Lonesome Lake, is a route that was a classic before its inclusion in *Fifty Classic Climbs of North America.* Now it can be a crowded classic. You can see the route best from north of the lake.

Pingora Peak

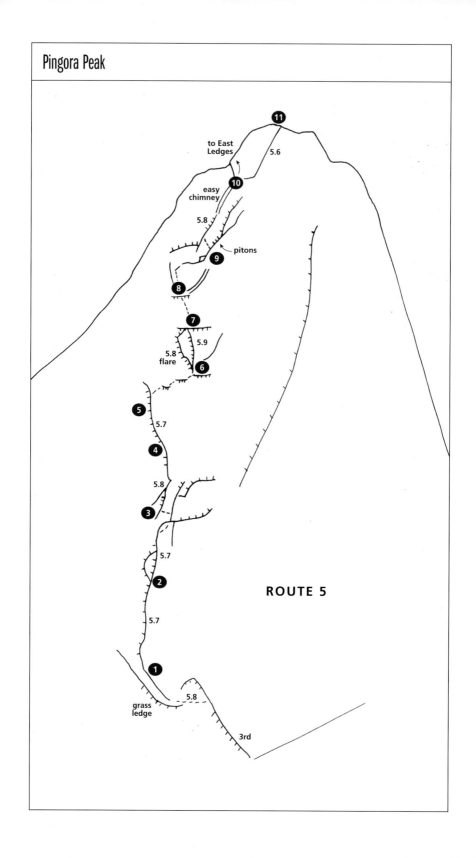

to East Ledges

5.6

easy chimney

5.8

pitons

5.9

5.8 flare

5.7

5.8

5.7

ROUTE 5

5.7

grass ledge

5.8

3rd

The most prominent feature of its lower part is a 200-foot right-facing dihedral that begins as a curving ledge and ends at a ceiling. The route then trends left, the upper part using cracks on the east face's right side. All of the first ten pitches are 5.7 or 5.8.

Reach the curving ledge by scrambling up a low-angle corner to its right, then making a delicate traverse. Ascend the dihedral, pass the ceiling above a bit to the right, and step back left to a short 5.8 crack. Work up left via ramps and short corners (once famous for grass clumps, now dwindling dirt) for 300 feet or so. Continue to ledges below the three alternatives described in the next paragraph. If you find yourself in corners taking you left of these ledges, you can easily move up right.

Of the alternatives above the ledge, the left one, a flaring crack, while still the route's crux, is the easiest; you can protect the exit from it with a 4-inch cam. The layback right of the flare is 5.9. The right-most variant involves 5.9 cracks, but neither 5.9 option requires the 4-inch piece.

Easier going then takes you up left to a ledge that is left of a pillar and 40 feet below a ceiling with blocks. Climb past a large flake; start up a crack that would lead to a chimney, then step left to another crack and follow it past the ceiling's right side into a slot. A short chimney leads to easier going.

Either walk left to the top of the *East Ledges* or step right under a ceiling to a short 5.6 corner, which leads to Pingora's northeast summit. Make a short rappel and scramble to the main summit.

6. Northeast Face Right–Stealing Thunder (IV 5.10 A2) To the classic *Northeast Face* route's right is a long, conspicuous crack system, which caught the eye of many a climber but wasn't inspected more closely because of a few hundred feet of blank rock below it. A route now reaches this system's upper part—thanks to Fred Beckey's routefinding acumen—after skirting right of the blank face and the system's lower section. Beckey descended from the first ascent because of threatening weather—thus the name.

Approach up left on ledges above the *Northeast Face*'s approach ledges (including a short 5.5 section that counts as the first pitch). Climb a 5.10 corner for 160 feet to the broad ledge that extends across the north face. Then climb a 5.10 crack and angle right to a 5.7 crack leading to a ledge right of a prominent flake. Avoid the lower part of the corner above by 5.8 face climbing to the right. Where the corner ends below a roof, make a 5.10 move and turn the roof to the right. On the fourth lead, move left past a few cracks (5.7, fixed piton) to a bulging, right-facing corner. The sixth pitch climbs this corner (5.9) to a belay on a pedestal. The corner above involves 5.10 and an A2 seam; then tension traverse left to one crack and continue to the face's main crack, ending the pitch in an alcove. Pitch 8 involves aid from a fixed piton and a 5.7 hand crack. Pitch 9 involves a 5.9 crack, face climbing between ledges, and 5.7 moves between cracks to the right. Pitch 10 is 4th-class scrambling up left, and on the final pitch, easy 5th-class climbing ends at Pingora's north summit.

The first ascenders, as is often the case, feel the route will go free with cracks cleaned out and the route's four bolts and a few fixed pitons in place.

7. North Face (III 5.8) The north face is Pingora's dark side. The peak's steepest face sees minimal sun, and Pingora's white granite is overlaid in places with darker granodiorite. The route looks unlikely from below, and routefinding is important. The ambience is further darkened by the route's upper part being far right of the start; retreat from the top half would be difficult. Moreover, a few traverses are scarier for the last climber than for the first. Its darkness may doom the *North Face* to obscurity, but it also makes it a perverse classic; here you can test yourself in a setting more ominous than the south side's sunny slabs. Difficulties are concentrated in the first five pitches, but that should be sufficient.

Climbers have been turned back by an inability to find the start. A few hundred feet right of the *Northeast Face*'s start, a ramp slants up right, above a snowpatch. Walk out the ramp, rope up, and continue right to a small overhang at the base of a short corner. Ascend the corner, step around a prow to a grassy crack, and climb to a large ledge. Above the next ledge, climb left, then move up to an overhang. Traverse right, climb over the overhang, and move right under another roof. The third pitch's crux is an overhanging corner. The fourth pitch follows steep cracks 40 feet to a bolt, from which a long, terrifying traverse leads to a ledge around a corner to the right. A short, tricky wall and a traverse right lead to a large flake's right side; climb the flake till you can make another airy traverse, to the end of hard climbing. Several mostly easy pitches and scrambling in the rotten bowl carved into the top of the face complete the route.

8. West Face (III 5.8) A series of corners rises from the notch that separates Pingora from Wolf's Head. These corners provide interesting climbing and would be more popular were they not on Pingora's "back side."

Reach the notch from the south, by the same 4th-class gully used as an approach to Wolf's Head. There are two ways to start, both 5.8. You can climb behind a block and move out right to flakes, which you follow until you can traverse left to a leaning corner. (It is possible to continue up from here and join the *Southwest Face Left* route.) Climb this corner until you can make a second traverse left, to a crack that leads to a small ledge. The alternate start follows this crack from its base left of the notch.

From the small ledge, walk left, climb to a corner that turns into a chimney, and belay in a notch at its top. Next, climb to a corner that leads to a ceiling under a protruding block; higher to the right are ledges. To avoid further difficulties, traverse left and pass through a tunnel. You can climb the chimney above or bypass it to the right.

9. Southwest Face Left (III 5.9) On the upper southwest face are several dihedrals. This route begins in the gully west of Pingora and ends in the right-facing, left-most upper dihedral.

After scrambling halfway up the gully, climb to a ledge at the top of a difficult-looking corner. The second pitch goes up left, as does the short third pitch, with thin moves between diagonal cracks. Walk left to a left-facing corner/chimney. Climb it for 60 feet, then cross right to the upper dihedral. Follow this dihedral for a pitch to a large ledge, where you intersect the *West Face* route.

10. Southwest Face Center (III 5.9) Guarding the southwest face's top is a set of overhangs. A solid, well-protected, six-pitch route begins in a cleft to the right of a line dropped from the center of the overhangs and passes through the overhangs by a corner right of their center.

Scramble unroped to the base of the cleft. Ascend a left-facing corner, a finger crack, and a layback, then move right to a ledge. Climb a left-sloping ramp, then traverse right to another ledge. Ascend a gully/crack and layback over a bulge. Begin the fourth pitch with a crack, then an arête, then a layback; finish with an off-width crack to a slot. Traverse down right on the fifth pitch, then climb easy rock to a large ledge. On the crux final pitch, follow a thin crack to an overhanging off-width, then surmount a bulge.

11. Southwest Face Right (III 5.8/5.9) This interesting, sustained, four- or five-pitch route ascends cracks and right-facing corners left of the *South Buttress*. One of the corners curves up left; the one above it ends in overhangs near the top.

Reach the route by walking left from the south shoulder on ledges or by easy climbing from the bottom of the face. Scramble to the highest ledges, below a right-facing corner; the first pitch ascends this corner. The second pitch follows a crack to the right past large blocks. The third pitch ascends the prominent left-curving corner, and the fourth continues up the steep corner above and turns a ceiling to a large ledge. Either walk right to easy going or climb the difficult crack above the ledge, then scale a few short headwalls.

Descent: You can climb down and rappel the *East Ledges,* but it's quicker to rappel the *South Buttress,* which requires a rope of at least 60 meters, two shorter ropes, or one rope and a willingness to downclimb a bit of 5th class. From the notch east of the summit, scramble down, facing Warbonnet, for 200 feet to a large ledge. Look for a rappel anchor a few feet east and below the ledge. Rappel 100 feet to the first ledge you encounter (base of K Cracks). If you have a 70-meter rope or two ropes, continue another 10 feet to a stance below the west end of this ledge; otherwise downclimb the 10 feet. There are two ways to proceed from here. One is to make two more 100-foot rappels straight down, then traverse to the south shoulder on foot-wide ledges. The other is to make a longer rappel, slanting east, to a ledge at the base of a right-facing corner, then descend 10 feet farther. The third rappel is obvious and takes you directly to the south shoulder.

Overhanging Tower (12,164)

The tower is easily identified from Cirque Lake, since the overhang is visible, but you can't see the overhang from Shadow Lake; the tower is the symmetric cone next to Shark's Nose. Despite its name, Overhanging Tower is the easiest climb of the Cirque's real towers.

1. West Face (I 4th class) Second- and 3rd-class ledges slant up across the tower's west side from the Wolf's Head–Overhanging Tower col and descend as a ramp

Overhanging Tower and Shark's Nose

Overhanging Tower

Shark's Nose

Ridge Tower

Block Tower

Symmetry Tower

toward Shark's Nose. You can climb Overhanging Tower from these ledges by numerous 4th-class and easy 5th-class two- or three-pitch routes.

2. Ridge Tower (II 5.3) On Overhanging Tower's northwest ridge is what appears from Shadow Lake to be a separate peak. Ridge Tower, though, is only a shoulder of Overhanging Tower, and an ascent of Overhanging Tower from Shadow Lake by way of Ridge Tower is as pleasant an easy rock route as the Cirque offers—as many as ten pitches on low-angle but solid rock.

Ascend the apron on the ridge's north side (approached by the chute that leads to the Wolf's Head col) for several hundred feet to the crest. Follow ramps near the crest past Ridge Tower to the small notch below Overhanging Tower's west face; finish by the *West Face* route.

The notch between Ridge Tower and Overhanging Tower can be reached (or descended from) by the grassy slopes and short 3rd-class headwalls of the couloir south of Ridge Tower.

3. Southwest Face (II 5.6?) Overhanging Tower's first ascent was made from Shadow Lake, beginning in the couloir right of Ridge Tower. North-facing rock was verglassed, so at some point the party traversed to the right from the couloir and reached the summit by the southwest face, maybe with a piton or two for aid. The route's exact location isn't known, but there are pleasant 5.6 cracks above the ramp that crosses to the Shark's Nose notch.

4. South Ridge (II 5.8) From the notch between Overhanging Tower and Shark's Nose, climb four enjoyable pitches on or near the crest. Surmount a step by steep cracks, then pass left of the summit overhang.

While most climbers reach the Overhanging Tower–Shark's Nose notch by traversing the west side of Overhanging Tower from the Wolf's Head–Overhanging Tower col, the *South Ridge*'s first ascent pair reached it from the east. They scrambled up a gully and climbed a chimney for a pitch that threads through chockstones.

Shark's Nose (12,229)

Most climbers on the Lonesome Lake side of the Cirque focus on Pingora and Wolf's Head and regard the angular towers beyond as background. Many hardly notice Shark's Nose's three pinnacles. (The northern is the summit.) However, the smooth walls and sleek profile that earned Shark's Nose its name hover over Shadow Lake, perhaps so conspicuous as to be threatening. Shark's Nose is infrequently climbed, considering that it is one of the Wind River's outstanding peaks. The rock is good, the easiest route 5.6, and the summit the kind that accommodates only one person at a time.

Shark's Nose, between middle and north summits

Shark's Nose

Overhanging Tower

Block Tower

1

2

To reach Shark's Nose from Lonesome Lake, climb to the Wolf's Head–Overhanging Tower col. Scramble up to ledges that circle behind Overhanging Tower and lead down to the notch between it and Shark's Nose. Three routes begin near this notch. To reach the southwest face, descend from this notch. To reach the notch from Shadow Lake, angle up grassy ramps on Overhanging Tower's west face.

1. Northwest Buttress (II 5.6) Shark's Nose's easiest route uses ramps and corners between the north and southwest faces. The climbing is enjoyable, the routefinding challenging, and the exposure invigorating.

Three parallel ramps slant steeply right across Shark's Nose's northwest side; your first objective is the lowest ramp. Two ledges go out right from the chute separating Shark's Nose and Overhanging Tower, the upper ledge leading from the notch to the lowest ramp. Follow the ramp for a 4th-class pitch to a small cave. Continue up harder rock to the narrowing ramp's top and a ledge; traverse right with increasing exposure to a slanting crack. This crack, the crux, leads to a long left-facing corner; ascend it until you can reach another corner, to the right. From here routefinding becomes easier.

Off-route pitons left of the cave near the top of the ramp can lure the unwary. You can complete the climb this way, via 5.9 cracks.

A four-pitch, 5.9 direct start begins 30 feet up the approach gully from the toe of the buttress.

2. Southwest Face (III 5.8) This classic nine-pitch route follows the right skyline seen from Shadow Lake. It tests your routefinding skills; study the line before

Shark's Nose

9 5.5 on east side

8

5.6

7

5.6

6

dead—end

5.8

5.8 **5**

5.8

5.7

4

block

5.6

3

2

1

ROUTE 2

rubble gully

5.5

easy chimney

100'

starting up. The first two pitches ascend unattractive rock near the face's right edge, but the third pitch takes you left to good rock. The remainder of the route follows cracks in a yellowish band that ends between the higher north summit and the middle summit. A key feature is a pair of cracks at mid-height, right of a shallow corner.

Begin just left of the crest that separates the southwest face from the hideous chute between Shark's Nose and Block Tower by scrambling up a right-leaning chimney system for 100 feet. Rope up below a bulge and continue up the system for a pitch and a half, then angle up left to a ledge below a right-facing corner. Climb this corner, follow ledges up left, and end the third pitch with a wide crack in a short right-facing corner.

Ascend the pleasant right-facing corner above past a leaning block. On the next, memorable, pitch, continue up the corner, work right to the left-hand of the parallel cracks, and climb it until you can traverse to the right-hand crack. From this crack, make a tricky step right to a corner, which leads to a belay ledge. Ascend steep cracks past the base of a block-filled chimney (which leads nowhere); step left to one crack, then make a height-dependent step to another and climb it to a ledge on the left.

The seventh pitch follows assorted cracks to a belay behind a miniature pinnacle; the eighth reaches the notch between the north and middle summits. Pass east of a tiny gendarme and reach the summit from the east.

From the end of the sixth pitch (above the long reach left) you can climb up left around a rib to a large ledge and, via a moderate, pleasant pitch, join the *Northwest Buttress* route 50 feet from the summit.

3. Southwest Face–South Ridge (III 5.7) The southwest face's right side is broken by many ledges, including a long, wide one that slopes up and right to the Shark's Nose–Block Tower notch. This route ascends the face's right side, using these ledges, to the south ridge and continues over and around several gendarmes to the main summit. Although not as good a route as the direct *Southwest Face,* the ridge is spectacularly pinnacled and airy.

Climb the direct route's first two pitches, but instead of heading up left, wander up right. Eventually you reach the wide, slanting ledge and can follow it for several hundred feet. Before reaching the Block Tower notch, though, leave the ledge and climb to the ridge. A few exciting pitches on the ridge and the east face take you past the south and middle summits. Descending from the middle summit involves either a short rappel or a tricky move.

4. North Face Left (III 5.8 A?) The north face rises only 500 feet from the Shark's Nose–Overhanging Tower notch but is an unlikely place for an old route. There is no obvious line, and the most prominent feature is a long, slanting ceiling. Only the route below the ceiling has been relocated.

Begin from the Overhanging Tower notch with a few delicate, unprotected moves. Continue to a jagged crack that passes through a ceiling near the face's left edge. Above is a ledge at the base of a dihedral that appears to go nowhere. But beyond the dihedral is a bolt, and apparently a thin crack above enables you to get through the slanting ceiling to forgotten rock. Of the mysteries above, all that we know comes from Fred Beckey's first ascent description: "We finished on a fine, difficult lead, which involved some very thin face climbing and an awkward jam-crack." This may be the crack on the last pitch of the following route.

You may need pitons for thin cracks.

5. North Face Right (III 5.8) This fine route comprises four 5.7 to 5.8 leads and the final pitch of the *Northwest Buttress.* Beginning at the Shark's Nose–Overhanging Tower notch, it passes through overhangs to the right and eventually works left to long parallel cracks that emerge right of the face's apex. Your enjoyment should be enhanced by the face's intimidating look. The wall faces just east enough that you can maximize sunlight with an early start.

Start as for the preceding route, with the same thin moves, but traverse right, climb to an overhang, and turn it to the right. Use a left-facing chimney to pass the next overhang; easier climbing then takes you to a long, sloping ledge. Walk right to a crack that passes through an overhang; above, go left to a belay at horizontal cracks. Reach the top of the face by excellent cracks that lead past blocks and through an overhang.

To prolong your sojourn on the face, don't follow the

Shark's Nose, North Face Right

Shark's Nose

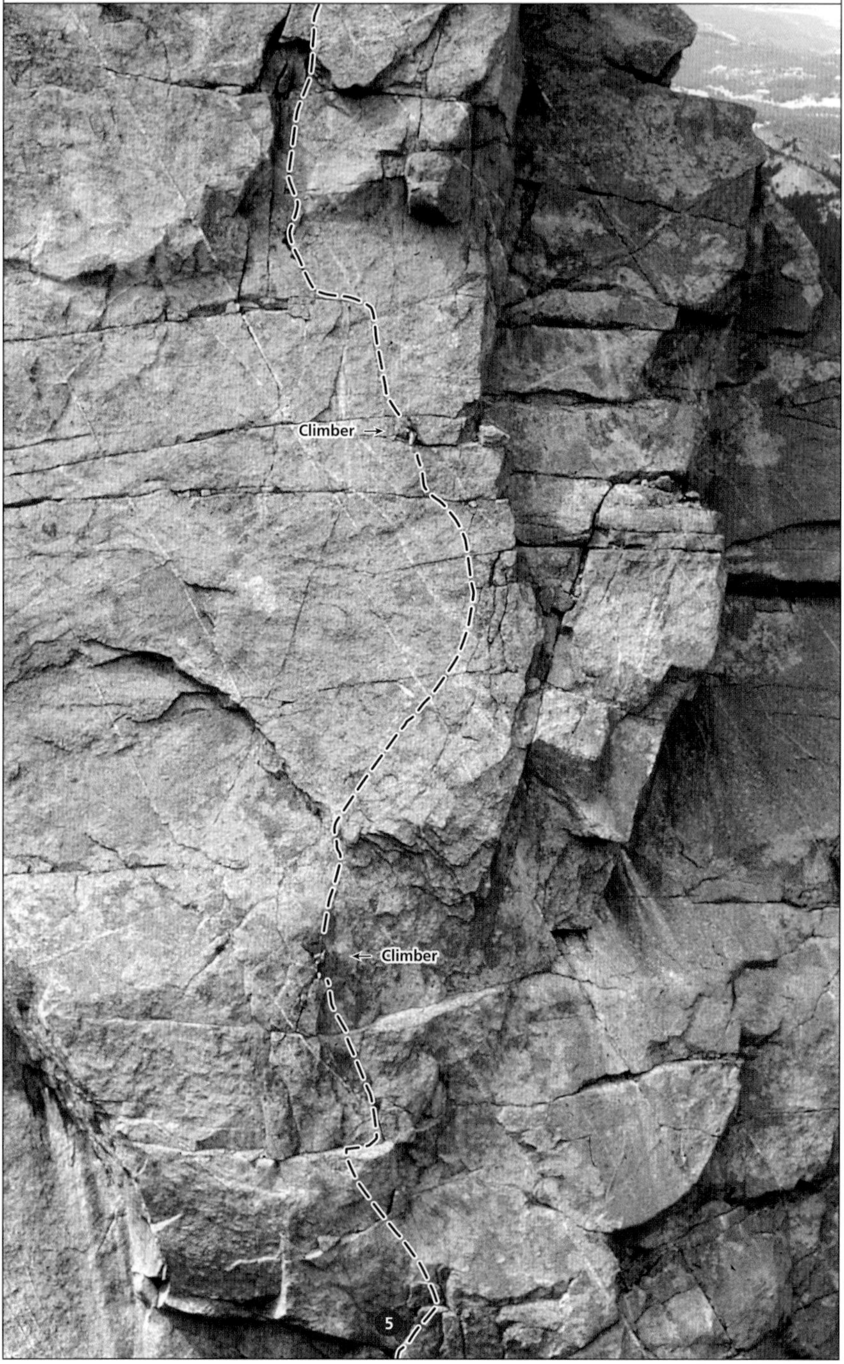

ROUTE 5

4

5.7

3

5.8

2

1

chimney

5.8

Overhanging
Tower Notch

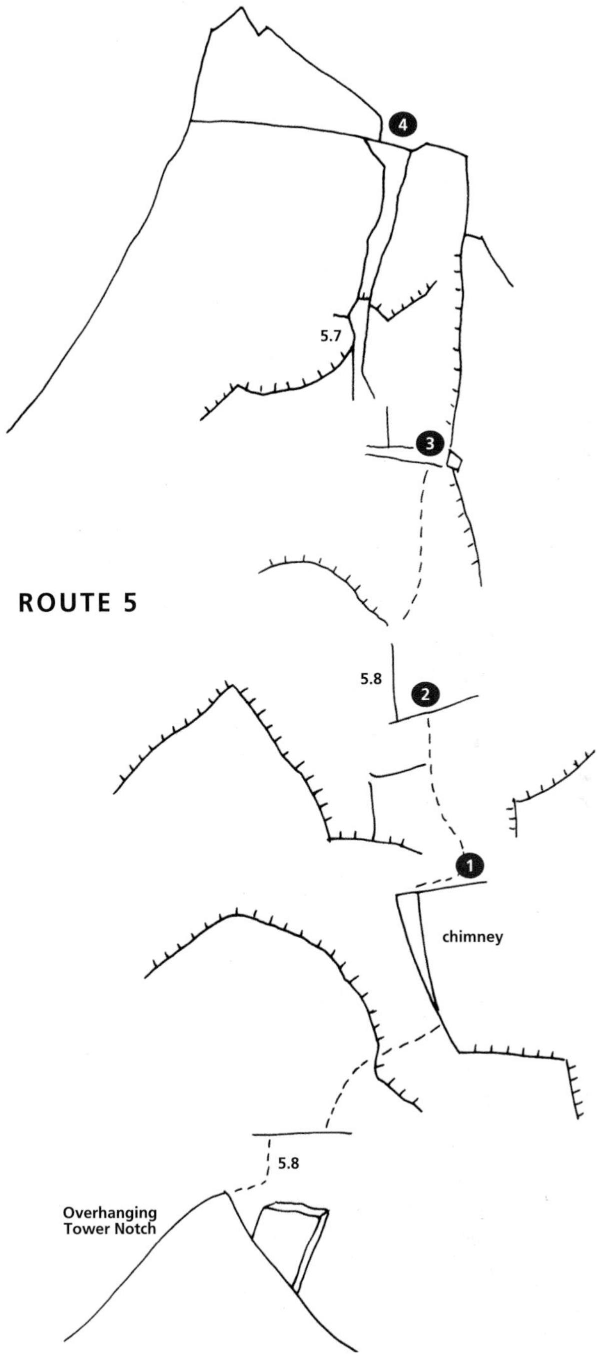

Northwest Buttress to the summit but traverse from above the cracks back onto the exposed wall and reach its apex by a 5.9 move.

Descent: The rappel route loosely follows the *Northwest Buttress* route. Two ropes aren't essential but do facilitate the nontrivial descent. With only one rope you must traverse the *Northwest Buttress*'s exposed ledge.

Rappel from just below the summit to the top of the long left–facing corner, then rappel twice down the slab north of the corner; the second of these (if you have two ropes) takes you past a headwall to anchors near the buttress's crest. From here, rappel north of the crest, either 75 feet to the cave at the top of the 4th-class ramp or 150 feet to a minor notch behind a big block.

Block Tower (12,210)

Each tower around Cirque Lake has a distinctive profile. Block Tower's is two slanting ridges converging at a square summit block. From Shadow Lake, you see Block Tower as a sliver, nearly eclipsed by Shark's Nose and barely distinguishable from Watch

Block Tower, East Face

Tower behind. Curiously, the route facing Lonesome Lake was first climbed from Shadow Lake, the route on the Shadow Lake side first climbed from Lonesome Lake.

1. East Face (II 5.5) You can easily see this route from Cirque Lake. The start lies in the chimney that diagonals left on the face's left side; the chimney is easy 5th class but a bit rotten. Leave the chimney after a pitch, for a corner to the right. The corner leads to 4th-class grassy ledges, which you follow across the face to the chimney between Block Tower and Shark's Nose. The chimney leads to the exposed north ridge, which you follow to a large platform a short lead from the summit. The lower pitches are dirty, the upper ones fun.

You can climb the face more directly, avoiding the grassy ledges, but the quality is disappointing.

2. Northwest Face (II 5.6) The rock on the upper sections of Block Tower and its neighbors is generally excellent, but much of the lower rock is vegetated and decomposed. The chutes leading to notches between Block Tower, Shark's Nose, Symmetry Tower, and Watch Tower are especially unpleasant. This route ascends the Shark's Nose–Block Tower west-side gully and the face right of the gully to the Shark's Nose–Block Tower notch, then follows the north ridge, as the preceding route does. A first ascent account states: "Steep and horribly loose rock necessitated extreme care on the entire ascent."

Descent: Descend the *East Face*. Rappel the north ridge, downclimb the grassy ledges, and rappel the chimney.

Elizabeth Peak (11,899)

A ridge, separating the Washakie and Donald Creek drainages, runs west from Watch Tower nearly to Marm's Lake. Elizabeth Peak, the ridge's high point, stands south of Shadow Lake.

1. South Slope (I 3rd class) You can reach Elizabeth Peak from Donald Lake, Marm's Lake, or Shadow Lake (via Elizabeth Col). If you anticipate a quick ascent, the view from Elizabeth Col may surprise you. However, because of the granite's quality, the puzzle is a pleasant one, with the summit's identity not revealed until the end. Perhaps you can find a 2nd-class route through the maze.

Easy Day Peak (11,660+)

No summit stands out on the long ridge paralleling Washakie Creek to the south, but the buttress opposite Shadow Lake's outlet is well situated for semi-rest days. The name is sarcastic; the first climbers on the buttress expected an easy day but instead found "hair-raising" climbing.

1. North Gully (I 3rd class) The chute west of the buttress.

2. North Face (II 5.7) The first ascent team's easy-day route isn't known, but a system of fractures goes up the face's center and curves to the right below the summit. You can find enjoyable difficult pitches between broken areas, or you can avoid them.

For example, you can avoid the lower section by traversing onto the face on higher grassy ledges. Above, you can climb a steep 5.8 crack or bypass it to the left. Chimneys continue up, and ledges lead right to a corner just below the top.

Watch Tower (12,326)

North and west of Cirque Lake are angular summits finely sculptured by glaciers on both sides of the Divide. Peaks to the south, though, were glacier-carved only on the east; these "one-sided" formations have gentle west slopes. Watch Tower is the northern of these less jagged, broader formations.

Hidden from Lonesome Lake west of the Divide, separated from Block Tower and Shark's Nose by an ugly chute, is what appears from Shadow Lake to be another freestanding tower (just below Block Tower's "w" on the Lizard Head Peak quad). However, despite the name Symmetry Tower, it is a buttress of Watch Tower, an extension of Watch Tower's talus, not a tower nor symmetrical.

1. West Slope (I 2nd class) A slope of grass and scree most easily approached from Donald Lake. From Shadow Lake, cross Elizabeth Col. From Lonesome Lake, either cross to Shadow Lake and cross Elizabeth Col or ascend Wisconsin Couloir and traverse the slopes of Pylon and South Watch Tower.

2. Watch Tower Couloir (I Snow 3rd or 4th class) You can use the couloir between Watch Tower and South Watch Tower to ascend either tower from Lonesome Lake. It is usually straightforward snow, but the top is sometimes corniced.

3. South Buttress (IV 5.11b R) This steep 800-foot buttress, Watch Tower's left edge as seen from Lonesome Lake or Jackass Pass, has the Cirque's most elegant profile. While Royal Robbins, after the first ascent, with aid, reported that the climbing "did not meet the expectations engendered by the beauty of the buttress," climbers have nevertheless been attracted by the elegant profile, especially after the route was climbed free in 1997.

Begin just inside the south couloir by following a ramp up right. From the ramp's top, diagonal right to a crack above a black dike. The third pitch goes straight up except for a detour to avoid an overhang. The fourth lead continues up a 30-foot flake. Above the flake, traverse right and climb to a ledge. A long lead ascends cracks up and a bit left to an alcove. Easier climbing leads 200 feet to the top.

4. East Face–Hay Fever (IV 5.11 A0) Beginning near the low point left of the east gully, climb nondescript rock for three pitches (5.10R). Traverse right to the left-facing dihedral that is the face's most prominent feature. Climb the dihedral for two pitches (5.11 A0, the aid being needed to get past vegetation), till it ends at a roof. Downclimb, traverse right, and climb to a ledge 30 feet above the roof. A 5.10- pitch and 400 feet of easier going then get you to the top.

5. East Gully The east face is split by a long gully, reached from south of the ridge between Cirque Lake and Hidden Lake. The gully offers a direct route but little else.

6. Right Edge of East Gully (II 5th class) This route follows the arête formed by the gully's intersection with the wall to its right. Easy climbing leads to the crux,

Watch Tower

described by a 1953 first ascender as "an overhanging jamhold affair." Above, the face lies back, and the climbing is 3rd class.

7. Northeast Face (II 5.7) A pinnacled ridge south of Cirque Lake abuts the northern of Watch Tower's two buttresses. This route ascends the buttress's face seen from Cirque Lake, beginning where the buttress meets the ridge and eventually reaching the left skyline.

From Cirque Lake, scramble toward the chimney that separates the highest pinnacle from the buttress, then up and right behind a small tower to the notch next to the face. Begin in an 8-foot chimney by climbing over a block and moving past two bulges to a ledge. Walk left and climb a right-facing corner and the face to its right to a ledge at the corner's top. Step left, then up, to a leaning right-facing corner. The fourth pitch goes up easy rock, then up a loose left-facing corner. Scramble a few hundred feet to the face's left edge. Climb toward the left of two chimneys, then traverse to the right one and climb it to a large ledge. Several hundred feet of 3rd class lead up and right to the summit.

8. Northeast Face, Route 2 A description of a second route on Watch Tower's northeast face leaves unclear the route's relation to the original line. However, the climbers did climb the pinnacled ridge below the face (rather than approaching from Cirque Lake), rappelling from the first pinnacle and turning the second pinnacle on the left.

Begin the face itself with a nice right-leaning finger crack that leads to an alcove. Step right around a corner and climb a steep wall to easier ground. Scramble and climb, trending right for 200 feet, then aiming for the left end of the summit plateau. Three final pitches involve a right-facing layback, a dirty 10-foot crack, and steep but easy face climbing.

9. Northwest Ridge (II 5.7) A nice short route begins at the Block Tower col by ascending a steep gully to the left, then diagonaling right to the ridge. The couloirs that drop from the col on both sides, however, are hideous; the only reasonable way to reach the col is by traversing Block Tower, and the route is thus of interest mainly to those making a traverse of the Cirque.

South Watch Tower (12,280+)

This is the buttress between the more distinctive Watch Tower and Pylon Peak.

1. West Slope (I 2nd class) From the west, South Watch Tower is just a high point of talus. You can climb it from Donald Lake; by traversing Watch Tower or Pylon; by ascending *Watch Tower Couloir,* between the two Watch Towers; or from Shadow Lake by way of Elizabeth Col.

2. South Face (II 5.5/5.6 A2) A six-pitch route ascends the south face's right edge near its junction with the east face. The first five leads are easy, but the first ascent team used five pitons for aid on the sixth pitch, then made a delicate traverse. The rock on the route's upper part is an improvement over the many loose flakes of the lower part.

Pylon Peak (12,378)

The peak between the Watch Towers and the Warriors, not reached pleasantly from Lonesome Lake (see Wisconsin Couloir) or Shadow Lake, is virtually ignored. Pylon is best climbed from Donald Lake, but Donald Lake isn't a climbing center. The name refers to towers on its ridges.

1. West Slope (I 2nd class) Hike up from Donald Lake or traverse from South Watch Tower.

2. Southeast Gully (I 3rd class) Flowered slopes lead from Wisconsin Couloir to outcrops near the summit. A gully splits the rock bands; near its top, cross the rib on the left to the gentle west slope.

Climbers reported a 5.5/5.6 route traversing towers right of the gully, then crossing and ending on a steep wall, but it doesn't appear worth the effort of avoiding the gully.

Bunion Mountain (11,905)

A peak of little distinction, separating Fish Creek and Donald Creek, joined to Warrior II by a high ridge.

1. South Slope-West Ridge (I 2nd class) From Fish Creek Pass a pleasant little draw leads to the west ridge. Avoid difficulties by traversing on one side or the other of the crest.

2. Northwest Slope (I 2nd class) Continue upstream from Donald Lake and turn the cliffs south of the lake to the left.

Laturio Mountain (11,342)

This is the jagged ridge with a dome at its south end as seen from the Fremont Trail. The summit is at the ridge's northeast end.

1. North Slope (I 2nd class) A slope of grass, bushes, and boulders nearly to the top. The summit outcrop involves a few moves.

Warrior II (12,406)

A mile-long ridge runs west from Warbonnet to Wisconsin Couloir. The two prominent buttresses on this ridge are the Warriors; Warrior II is the less elegant right-hand buttress.

1. Northwest Ridge (I 3rd class) From Wiscosin Couloir.

2. South and East Slopes (I 3rd class) From Donald Lake, via the Warrior-Bunion saddle; from Lost Lake's valley, between Bunion and Sundance; or from Warbonnet and Warrior I, by paralleling the rim.

3. Northeast Face (II 5.5) The northeast face is tall but broken, and this isn't one of the routes for which the Cirque is famous. Much scrambling is involved, and several ledges are large enough to be seen from afar.

Two rock ribs dip into the snow and talus at the wall's base. Ascend the right-hand rib to the first large ledge. From the ledge's right end, climb a corner, then work up an exposed arête and a chimney to the second large ledge. Corners above lead to increasingly broken rock.

4. North Face-Northwest Ridge (III 5.8?). A route, now lost, was once climbed between Warrior II and Wisconsin Couloir. It started from a snowfield, followed a straight line for six or seven pitches, and was mostly face climbing and probably 5.7/5.8.

Warrior I (12,360+)

The left-hand Warrior's walls are among the proudest in the Cirque of the Towers. Two of the routes on these walls reach what appears from the north to be the summit but is actually one of a row of gendarmes. From this gendarme there are two ways to the rim. The elegant way involves a difficult crack in the largest gendarme's east face. The expeditious way involves a rotten chimney on Warrior I's west side.

1. South Slope (I 2nd class) Talus from Warrior II, the valley to the south, or Warbonnet.

2. Northeast Face Left (IV 5.10 A1) This route ascends the large left-slanting dihedral near the face's center (150 feet left of the right-hand route). Begin left of a snowpatch by following easy right-slanting ledges to the dihedral's base. At the dihedral's top, exit right across the exposed face, then climb to a skyline notch.

The first ascent team used four points of aid to overcome grass.

3. Northeast Face Right (IV 5.9+) This was the Cirque's longest route when Beckey and Rupley climbed it in 1962, but as a free climb it goes considerably quicker than the two days taken on the first ascent. It ascends the face's right edge, near the prow that separates the northeast and northwest faces. Begin with 200 feet of grassy troughs and flakes (5.6), then climb steep cracks (5.7) for 100 feet to a step. Climb the steep face above for 30 feet, traverse delicately left across a slab to a right-leaning dihedral, and follow this strenuous dihedral (5.8+) to a small stance in a niche, 190 feet of climbing above the step. Move 50 feet up left to the left end of a ledge. (This is the original line. Parties who have taken a more direct line have found better rock.) Climb a chimney with loose rock, taking the right fork to an alcove, behind a block, with a bolt, piton, and rappel slings. Climb another, cleaner, chimney. At its Y, again climb the right branch, by unratable height-dependent stemming and a desperate step across its top, to the face's second large step.

Above rises the route's crux—a single 2- to 3-inch crack, which passes a bolt 30 to 40 feet up and another farther up, and ends at a third bolt. (Begin the pitch using the lesser system to the left.) Difficulties then ease somewhat, and you reach the top of Warrior's northern gendarme in two more leads. (The route has also been completed by working right around Warrior's prow from the top of the crux crack.)

4. Northwest Face (IV/V 5.11R) The upper face's most obvious feature is a wonderful dihedral just right of the prow. The route begins left of the *Warrior Gully*

Warrior I

Warbonnet

4 var

3

4

with a few hundred feet of 3rd class leading to the top of a pedestal. From the pedestal, climb up for a pitch to the top of a large flake. The next pitch originally involved hooks for aid to make a complicated crossing of a blank wall to a chimney to the right; it is now the route's one pitch harder than 5.9, other than two brief 5.10 sections. Wander up slightly decomposed rock to the large dihedral, then climb the dihedral.

A major five-pitch, 5.10d variation, *The Candy Shop* (4 var), ascends rock directly below the upper dihedral. Begin with parallel cracks in a steep right-facing corner (5.9) and continue up a 4- to 5-inch crack (5.10+) to a belay on top of a buttress. Follow an arête past a white band, step right to a hand crack, climb a wide crack in a right-facing corner, and move right 15 feet to a belay (5.9). On the third pitch, climb an overhanging, right-leaning crack through flakes to a roof. Above the roof (5.10d) is a dihedral. The dihedral leads to easier going, a short chimney on the left, a 5-inch crack, and a belay ledge. The fourth pitch ascends a flare up right, then back left to a right-facing corner that leads to a 5.10d undercling. Exit left to the top of a pinnacle. Begin the fifth pitch by angling up left across flakes (5.9) to a large alcove; exit left from the alcove and ascend easy ramps to the *Northwest Face*'s signature dihedral.

5. Warrior Gully (I Snow 4th or 5th class) The couloir between the Warriors makes a pleasant, moderate snow climb.

Descent: Without continuing to the actual summit, you can descend from the northern gendarme reached by the face routes by rappelling the *Northeast Face Right*.

Warbonnet Peak (12,369)

Warbonnet is the graceful spire at the Cirque of the Tower's southeast end. Its walls tower above Jackass Pass, a familiar sight to many a weary backpacker. Warbonnet's nobility is uncommon among the truncated towers, rounded humps, and angular buttresses that constitute much of the southern Wind Rivers.

The thumb on the pass side of Warbonnet is the Plume. Routes on Warbonnet's northeast face start from the notch between it and the Plume. Reaching the notch from either north or south takes a few hours. The northern approach involves, depending on the time of year, steep snow or crumbly 4th-class slabs. To the south, boulder-filled chutes connect grassy ledges. Use a high grassy ledge to reach a long diagonal chute that sweeps all the way up to the notch behind the Plume. The chute presents a few 4th-class moves, but—unlike the north approach—a rope isn't in constant danger of dislodging loose rock.

1. South Ridge (I 3rd class) From the boulder field south of Arrowhead Lake, climb to the low point between Warbonnet and Sundance Pinnacle. The ridge is unexposed; cross ribs to the right in a few places.

Two routes, *Drop of a Hat* and *War Paint,* were climbed to the left of *Weather or Not* in 2012—too late to be more than mentioned here.

2. Weather or Not (III 5.10) The first ascent team thought highly of this six-pitch endeavor to the left of the other southeast face routes, especially pitches 3 and 5.

The 5.9 first pitch follows flake systems to the prominent left-angling orange corner. The short 5.10 second pitch uses the left-angling crack to reach a double crack; follow the right-hand of the two. Begin the 5.10 third pitch by climbing to a left-facing corner. Climb the corner, which for most of its length features a wide crack, protectable with #5 Camalots. Begin the short fourth pitch (5.8) by climbing right onto a boulder and continuing up an easy corner. On the exciting fifth pitch (5.10), move out left to the double cracks that split the headwall—an excellent pitch despite suspect flakes. Pitch 6 (5.8+) ascends a groove to easier ground.

Follow the chossy ramp for 500 feet to Warbonnet's south ridge.

3. Southeast Face–The Curate's Egg (IV 5.10 A1) This route begins just left of *Black Elk* but angles left for several pitches, before heading up to the first prominent notch south of *Black Elk*. Curate's egg is a British expression meaning "good in parts."

Scramble up the same right-slanting ramp used to approach *Black Elk,* until below two left-leaning cracks. The first pitch (5.10 A1) ascends the left of the two cracks to a right-arching corner, which is followed to ledges. The second pitch (5.9) first trends left, using flakes and cracks, before angling right to a short, steep corner, then ascends past ledges to a higher ledge. On the third pitch (5.8), climb the face above, traverse left on knobs to a corner, and climb the corner to a ledge. On the short, easy fourth pitch, climb to the top of a pillar and traverse down and left on a ledge until below the left (and less steep) of two corners. On the 90-foot, 5.10 fifth pitch, climb this

Warbonnet Peak

dihedral, exiting right at its top and climbing to a ledge. On the sixth pitch (5.10), climb a corner for 50 feet, then move right to a crack and follow it to a semi-hanging belay. Continue up the crack on the short seventh pitch (5.9), but at its top move left past a small roof. Fourth-class scrambling for 300 feet up a gully takes you to the south ridge.

4. Southeast Face–Seams and Dreams (IV 5.10d R) Beginning near stacked blocks 150 feet left of *Black Elk, Seams and Dreams* goes up for an 80-foot 5.9 pitch and a 135-foot 5.10 thin-crack pitch to *Black Elk's* second belay ledge.

It then, however, breaks left with a 40-foot 5.10+ pitch to the base of a long right-facing dihedral. The dihedral is 5.8, but the fifth pitch involves a thin traverse left and a 5.10 off-width. Above, move left, pass a loose block, and continue up (5.8R). The final two pitches are more straightforward, involving a prominent crack/chimney system that reaches the upper left edge of the wall. Climbing ends at the notch where the *Curate's Egg* ends.

A later team, unaware of *Seams and Dreams,* climbed what amounts to a variation, which they called the *Neu Low.* They followed *Black Elk* as far as *Black Elk*'s crux fist crack, before going left along a ledge to *Seams and Dreams*' 5.8 dihedral.

Chris Barlow, of the *Neu Low* team, feels it is comparable in overall difficulty to *Black Elk,* is more sustained and serious, but not of as high quality and not destined to be the classic that *Black Elk* is.

5. Southeast Face–Black Elk (IV 5.11a) The first wall you see when approaching Jackass Pass has the coveted distinction of having a route considered "obligatory for hard men"—an old Yosemite guide's characterization of a certain 5.9. Jeff Lowe, describing the first ascent, compared the route favorably to routes on Long's Peak's Diamond "in length, difficulty, and beauty." While Lowe and Charlie Fowler rated *Black Elk* 5.10, the subsequent consensus rates the continuous, strenuous, rattly fist crack a bit harder. *Black Elk* is best located in terms of an immense rectangular chockstone near the top of the face. The route reaches the chockstone's left side.

Approach by angling right up 3rd-class ledges. Pitch 1: Roped climbing begins with a 200-foot face pitch (5.8R) to the intersection of a right-facing corner with a right-diagonaling crack. Pitches 2–3: Up the corner nearly to its top (5.10), belaying pitch 3 atop a pillar with a bolt to its right. Pitch 4: Traverse left to a splitter crack, the route's crux, which passes a small roof, then a larger one. Belay in an uncomfortable pod or from a crack just above. Pitch 5: More crack, making a tricky step right to another crack after 50 feet (5.10). Pitch 6: Discontinuous cracks toward the left side of the giant chockstone and behind it (5.9). Pitch 7: The right-facing corner above is tricky to protect and vegetated 5.10, but variations above the giant chockstone's right side come more highly recommended. Pitch 8: Right of another chockstone and up a chimney (5.8). Scrambling for 300 feet, with a few easy 5th-class moves, completes the route.

A 1981 pair accidentally added a major variation, known as *Elk Scat.* Rather than traversing left from the right-facing corner, they pendulumed right to other cracks, which required a certain amount of aid, before leading to the chockstone's right side.

6. Southeast Face–Lichen Never Sleeps (IV 5.11b) To the right of *Black Elk* but beginning not from *Black Elk*'s approach ledges but from the approach to the Plume col, this route generally trends right for five pitches until it meets the *East Face Center,* which it follows to the top. (Lightning discouraged a more direct finish.) The first three pitches are 5.8, 5.9, and 5.8. The fourth pitch angles back left to a 5.11b corner, while the fifth pitch is again 5.8.

7. East Face Chimney (II 5.6) An ancient summit register entry reads: "Direct E Face via largest central chockstone chimney. Rotten; much complicated work in 2-tiered chimneys."

8. East Face Center (II 5.6) The east face is the wall left of the Plume. This route isn't a classic rock climb but belongs to the genre of mountaineering routes requiring some rock climbing, routefinding, and an ability to function in steep terrain.

Approach as you would to reach the notch behind the Plume from the south. However, from the bottom of the diagonal chute, climb up left toward a 20-foot high, right-facing corner. Before reaching the corner, though, climb flakes on the face to a belay. Continue up the face (5th class) to a large ledge. Climb to a large gully and follow it for 500 feet (occasional 5th class). Where the gully branches, start up the branch that meets the south ridge after 300 feet, but after 100 feet, climb the left of two cracks and follow it as it diagonals right. Three 4th-class pitches reach the ridge a few hundred feet south of the summit.

9. East Face Right (II 5th class A?) From the chute that reaches the Plume notch from the south, traverse onto the face and climb 60 feet. Bear right up a gully; where it is blocked by a chockstone, climb left of the gully. The final pitch follows a 100-foot crack (nailed on the first ascent) to the south ridge.

10. Northeast Face Left (III 5.10+ A1) The 5.7 routes that take off from the Plume notch aim for lower-angle rock than this route, which aims for the prominent dihedral that harbors a large chockstone.

From the notch, gain a right-facing dihedral and follow it for two pitches to a large ledge. From the ledge's left end, climb a thin crack, then head up and right toward the chockstone dihedral. From a belay on the chockstone, climb a wide crack

Warbonnet Peak

in the dihedral's right wall to an overhang; here, step around right using a horizontal crack, hand traverse to a vertical crack, and climb it (crux pitch). Step left, up a bulging crack, up easier ground, right around a corner, and down to a square ledge. Climb up a dihedral to the left-most of the big chimneys near the top of the face. Then move right into another chimney, which ends on top.

Bring cams up to 4.5 inches.

11. Northeast Face Center (III 5.7) The face rising above Jackass Pass and the Plume is an obvious objective for Cirque climbers. While not classics, its two 5.7 routes offer nice climbing. To climb the left-hand route, scramble up left from the Plume notch to a sloping ledge, then up a large right-facing dihedral capped with a bombay flake. Rather than follow the dihedral, though, work out right, to a short left-facing corner (5.7). Continue working up, then right, for a few more 5.6 to 5.7 pitches, aiming for the right-most of the three 400-foot chimneys at the top of the face. Alternatively, work right lower to easier going, then climb to the right-hand chimney. The chimney is surprisingly easy (a few 5.6 moves) and ends at the summit.

12. Northeast Face Right (III 5.7) From the Plume notch, head up right toward dihedrals on a prominent pillar's left side; the rock is broken and the going easy for several hundred feet. The main left-facing dihedral is sustained but reasonable; of alternatives to the left, one appears to have been aided. Dismaying prospects above the dihedral pose a routefinding dilemma. The earliest attempts continued to the lowest notch in the feathered ridge, but were turned back by the prospect of laybacking the edge of the second feather (see *Feather Buttress,* below). On the first complete ascent, the climbers worked left below the notch, traversing to the chimney that leads to the ridge's next notch.

13. Feather Buttress (IV 5.10+) The most obvious feature of Warbonnet's thin, triangular north face is a crack-and-chimney system that curves up from left to right. The first two pitches follow a ramp to the bottom of the system; some have complained of flaky rock in this lower section. The next seven pitches follow the system, reaching the notch between the first two feathers from the west; some of these leads involve difficult chimneys. While the *Northeast Face Right* nearly reaches this notch, then traverses under the second feather, tradition dictates that *Feather Buttress* climbers layback the adrenalin-draining 40-foot feather's edge—though you can't protect this layback without vise grips.

If you've brought cams as big as 6 inches into the Cirque, they can be useful, though not essential, in the lower system.

14. Northwest Couloirs (I Snow/Ice 4th or 5th class) Right of Warbonnet, facing Lonesome Lake, is a couloir that splits halfway up, the right branch ending right of Warbonnet's southwest summit. The left branch forks again, its left fork being a wet chimney with a history, at various times, of rockfall, rescue, and death. Amid these disasters the entire gully has been climbed, but the right fork of this branch is the usual route. Conditions vary from snow to ice to dreadful loose rock. The branch that emerges right of the southwest summit may also have been climbed; the account is ambiguous.

15. West Ridge (I 3) The Warrior-Warbonnet ridge is traversed as part of a Cirque traverse, and the ridge can be gained by Wisconsin Couloir.

16. Plume, West Side (I 5.2) From the Plume-Warbonnet notch, climb past a few blocks and bumps, then ascend a short wall.

17. Plume, South Face (I 5.6) You can climb a few pleasant pitches in wide cracks by leaving the Plume notch approach chute 200 feet below the notch.

18. Plume, North Face (III 5.9) Cracks on this face were climbed so long ago that details have been forgotten.

Sundance Pinnacle (11,054)

Most backpackers need a rest or two between Big Sandy Lake and Jackass Pass, so the small peak above North Lake, joined to Warbonnet's south ridge, is much studied.

1. West Face (I 4th class) Gullies and ledges on the west side provide the quickest way to the top, but the ridges are prettier, and the *West Face* is used mainly for descent.

2. South Ridge (I 4th class) Several exquisite pitches on low-angle slabs are involved. You can lengthen the climb by ascending 5th-class corners near the east face's left edge. Aim toward the highest tree visible on the ridge.

3. East Face Left (I 5.6) A large dihedral leads to a large ledge, above which cracks diagonal to the summit ridge.

Climb the dihedral for a pitch (5.4). Continue up it and pass the large ledge to a smaller ledge. A 5.6 crack leads right to an easy ramp, which leads farther right. Climb blocks and a right-angling 5.6 crack to a belay on the face. Climb to a big ledge, walk left on the ledge, and make a few moves to the summit ridge.

4. East Face Center (II 5.9) The possibilities on this face are many, and several summit register entries report routes that can't be located. An *AAJ* note reported a dihedral just left of center being climbed in five pitches—the third, a moss-filled dihedral, being the crux.

5. East Face–Klettershoe Chimney (II 5.9) The face's most prominent line is a right-facing corner toward the right side, though off-width cracks' unpopularity has no doubt limited the number of ascents. You can reach the dihedral's base in three leads; by selecting corner systems judiciously, you can find decent 5.6 climbing. (Or you can approach the dihedral from ledges to the left.)

Carry protection for the dihedral's 4- to 6-inch crack. Above the dihedral, walk left to the south ridge.

6. East Face, Right Crack (II 5.9) This route shares *Klettershoe Chimney*'s lower nebulous corners (or approach ledges from the left), but finishes in the conspicuous left-slanting crack to the right.

The first pitch above the mid-face ledges follows intricate thin cracks to a ledge at the base of the conspicuous crack. This crack begins 3 to 4 inches wide but gradually narrows. Belay in an alcove at blocks hidden from below. Climb 15 feet from these blocks, then make an awkward, delicate 5.9 traverse left to the top of *Klettershoe Chimney*. (The overhanging continuation of the wide crack is 5.10c.)

7. Northeast Arête (II 5.10b/c) The reason for this route is the splitter crack, visible in the right light from the Jackass Pass Trail, on the face right of *Klettershoe Chimney* and the *Right Crack,* leading straight to the summit.

The approach, whether by the easy lower pitches or the ledge traverse from the left, is the same as the preceding routes. Begin climbing as for *Klettershoe Chimney,* but then angle right to a comfortable ledge (5.8). Angle farther, to a right-facing corner, and climb it. Clip an ancient bolt and traverse right, using tiny nuts, to the splitter crack. Above the splitter, traverse right to another crack (5.10-) and follow it to easier going.

8. North Face (5.11 A1). A five-pitch 2012 route near the prow.

9. Northwest Ridge (I 5.0/5.2) An enjoyable three-pitch route. Detour onto the west face where appropriate.

Mitchell Peak (12,482)

To a topographer or peak bagger, Mitchell is the 12,482-foot summit to which Finis Mitchell attached a plaque commemorating his eleven ascents over fifty years. To rock climbers Mitchell is the northwest shoulder, which rises above Lonesome Lake in a 1,000-foot wall that features three routes. The main peak's north face, less visible and looking less amenable to climbing, has been ignored.

1. South Slope (I 2nd class) Reach this long scree slope from Big Sandy Lake or from the Jackass Pass Trail near North Lake.

2. Northeast Slope (I 3rd class) Rising above Lizard Head Meadows is a steep grass slope, which in early summer features a cascading stream and a profusion of flowers that make it a magical place and an attractive nontechnical route. On the upper slope, bear right to the ridge. Avoid 3rd-class moves near the summit by a lower traverse around to the south.

3. North Ledge (I 3rd class) Two ledges diagonal up left under the main summit's north face. From Lonesome Lake the steeply rising upper ledge appears to intersect the east ridge near the summit and offer a quick, easy ascent. The intersection, though, isn't obvious, and the unwary may be surprised: Finding a 3rd-class way takes looking; most parties encounter a 5th-class pitch.

4. North Face Left (III 5.7) The wall's original route ascends its relatively broken left side to a meadow and follows ramps up right to a bowl that harbors another meadow. The final few hundred feet involve either of two chimneys. While not a classic rock climb, the route offers a good crux pitch, variety, and an opportunity that isn't overly challenging to spend a day on a large face.

Begin 150 feet uphill to the left of the larger of two shallow caves with arching roofs. After following a broken, slightly right-trending crack system for two forgettable pitches, work left to cleaner rock. A short, easy pitch leads to the crux pitch, which wanders up and left, imaginatively linking short corners and cracks. From a large sloping ledge above, step over a ceiling, angle right on grassy rock, and step left

Mitchell Peak

to a block-covered ledge. Rather than climbing ramps above, traverse easily left and ascend big ledges to the meadow.

Until you reach the meadow's right edge, the route to the second meadow appears to involve hideously vegetated flakes, but a face to the left offers a pleasanter alternative. The cracks and chimneys behind the bowl's high point can be climbed in three pitches and look like the obvious way to the top, but the deep chimney to the left offers easier going (especially for a pack), though it appears blocked by a huge ceiling.

5. North Face Center–Ecclesiastes (IV 5.9) The last of the face's three routes to be climbed, this classic follows the most obvious line: right-facing corners in the face's center. The corners lead to the bowl, where it joins the left-side route.

The name was once an enigma, but it turns out that Dick Dorworth, uncharacteristically perusing the Bible, specifically Ecclesiastes, was inspired by the phrase "It is all emptiness and chasing the wind."

The corners begin a few hundred feet from the face's bottom, but you can reach them by starting to the right, climbing up for two leads, and traversing left. Begin under an arch with black water stains—the smaller, right-hand arch of a pair. From a pointed flake, step out right around the arch and climb to a left-leaning crack that leads to ledges. Work up, then left to a thin, difficult crack; follow it to a wider crack and the top of a pillar. Don't climb a higher pillar but rather descend left, traverse

Mitchell Peak

3rd

11

11

flake

10

10

5.6

9

9

flake

ROUTE 4

upper bowl

8

easy friction

8   4th

face   thin
5.5   flakes

7

easy
chimney

grassy

meadow

6

5.9
layback

7

4th   6   blocks

5

5

5.8

5.7   4

4

3   5.9   5.8
undercling

3

ROUTE 5

2

2

grassy   1

5.8
thin crack

1

5.7

black
streaks   ramp

pointed flake

around a buttress, and climb to a stance below a precarious block and a slanting ceiling. This ceiling (the original route) provides a dramatic entry to the corner system, but you can bypass it to the right. Ascend the corners for about three pitches; above an easy chimney, exit left on flakes. The next pitch is long, complicated, and unobvious from below, but enjoyable and not too hard. A walk left and easy friction then reach the ramp of the left-side route.

6. North Face Right (IV 5.8 A2) To the right of the north face is a huge triangular recess that faces Lonesome Lake. This route follows shallow corners just left of the recess. Begin on slabs directly below the corners. The only aid has been used at an overhang near the top.

7. Northwest Face (II 5.10) This four-pitch route lies right of the north face, beginning on a slab that leads to a straight 1-inch crack in a right-facing corner. The middle section involves a left-facing corner, and the upper part ascends what the first ascent team termed Flora Corner.

8. West Slope (I 3rd class) With judicious routefinding you can gain Mitchell's northwest shoulder by scrambling over and around the talus, slabs, and cliff bands above Jackass Pass. Alternatively, a bit east and right of a minor ridge, is a gully that cuts up right, then left. Unless snow- or ice-filled, this gully offers a more straightforward route than the slope above the pass.

These slopes enable you to descend from north face routes without continuing to Mitchell's summit.

Dog Tooth Peak (12,488)

The mound midway between Mitchell and Big Sandy Mountain bears no resemblance to a canine carnassial, but a buttress to its east does. This Dog Tooth Pinnacle is the largest of a row of buttresses that overlook Papoose Lake.

1. West Slope (I 2nd class) From Big Sandy Lake, follow the seasonal stream flowing down the valley between Dog Tooth and Big Sandy Mountain. After passing the initial cliffs, the route north of the creek, ascending low-angle slabs and meadows, makes one of the Wind Rivers' most pleasant walk-ups. The hike is especially fine during early summer, when most snow is gone, the creek flows, and flowers abound.

2. North Slope (I 2nd class) From the North Popo Agie, via the steep grass between Dog Tooth and Mitchell, or traverse from Mitchell.

3. Northeast Ridge (III 5.5/5.6). A long ridge rises from Papoose Lake to meet the rim west of the Monolith. The climbing is mostly 3rd class.

4. Wisdom Tooth The Wisdom Tooth is the buttress immediately right of Dog Tooth Pinnacle. A IV 5.9 A2 route, though recommended by the 1980 first ascent party, is included here only as history. Sometime between 1983 and 1992, a slab 200 feet wide, 20 to 25 feet thick, and 300 feet high glissaded to the talus, taking with it "perfect F8 to F9 finger and hand cracks." A few recent attempts on the crisp new corner to the left were repelled by debris left in the slab's wake.

Dog Tooth Peak

For those who return when the rock becomes cleaner (to bestow an appropriate route name), the perfect cracks continued (a little aid, no ledges) through the fifth pitch. The sixth pitch, an overhanging dihedral passing through overhangs, required aid on very small nuts. The next pitch followed a long, steep, rotten crack to a large, sloping ledge. The climbers bypassed the giant triangular ceiling above by a poorly protected traverse right to a chimney. Six easier leads followed right-trending ledges, ramps, and low-angle cracks.

5. A-Frame Buttress (IV 5.9) The right-most of the formations above Papoose Lake features a pretty, slender face split by a crack system; the name should clinch its identity. The route follows the cracks for seven or eight pitches. A distinct crux pitch halfway up is long and requires careful placement of small pieces.

You can finish the climb in several ways; passing right of the gargoyles seems to be the hardest. If you work left to a ledge at the face's edge, gain the buttress's crest as soon as feasible. Traversing the tempting south-side ledges leads to unexpectedly strange maneuvers (and two of the range's most surprising trees).

Big Sandy Mountain (12,416)

This is the gentle Divide summit northeast of Big Sandy Lake. From the north it is obscured by its sensational spur, the Monolith.

1. West Slope (I 2nd class) You can climb the mountain from the Jackass Pass Trail, from Big Sandy Lake, or from Black Joe Lake. You also can traverse the Divide from Mitchell Peak. North Popo Agie approaches are included under the Monolith.

2. The Tombstone (III 5.10) This is the middle of three towers east of the Monolith. The first pitch reaches a huge chimney that splits the tower's bottom half. The chimney is easy, but above is a crux pitch that follows a thin crack. The final two leads are on the tower's left side. The first ascenders thought highly of this six-pitch route, but subsequent climbers haven't.

The Monolith (12,120+)

Hiking on the North Fork Trail between Sanford Park and Lizard Head Meadows, you see a series of small cirques cut into the Divide plateau to the south. Many formations in these cirques catch your eye; the most interesting is a buttress of Big Sandy Mountain (0.4 mile to the north-northeast) that juts into the cirque farthest upstream. This is the Monolith.

1. West Couloir (I 5th class) A couloir on the Monolith's right side provides a route between Papoose Lake and the plateau, but it is an evil place, with rotten rock, steep snow, and ice. Climbers descending from rock walls, unlikely to be equipped for snow and ice, may need to rappel several times.

2. East Side (I 2nd or 3rd class) On the east side of the cirque are alternatives to the *West Couloir*. A snow couloir and a long talus slope both reach the rim, which you can circle to the Big Sandy–Monolith saddle.

3. North Face Left To the left of the original *North Face* route is a far less obvious line. It has been climbed, but the ascent went unreported, and further information cannot be obtained.

4. North Face (V 5.9) This route follows the obvious system of chimneys and right-facing corners that slants up left, extending the entire height of the face. Climb for three pitches, using a dike with numerous horizontal holds, to a long chimney. Ascend the chimney in four leads. Then climb a short overhanging crack (5.9) and continue up a steep dihedral to an overhanging dihedral. Avoid this dihedral by easy climbing to the right, then regain the system. Here the system becomes a steep ramp; follow it for the final three pitches, at one point avoiding a squeeze chimney by 5.9 face climbing to the left.

The *North Face* is generally climbed comfortably in a day.

5. Northwest Face (IV 5.9) Describing this route in the 1967 *AAJ,* Fred Beckey wrote, "I have never seen better rock, anywhere." No one else has reported seeing such superlative rock, though a few have described epic failures. Beckey gave only these few clues: Begin by working up right, then left to steeper rock; the final 400 feet entails three exposed pitches, on the buttress's outer edge, that feature face climbing on horns and chickenheads; look for one bolt.

Point 11,165

Point 11,165 is 1.2 miles southwest of Cliff Lake, one of the nebulous formations on the north side of the North Popo Agie. The routes described are on the east side of the buttress (Point 10,640+), east of Point 11,165 and southeast of Lake 10,295.

1. Hard-Earned Money (II 5.8) Begin 30 feet right of the junction of the east and south faces and left of a prominent straight-in corner by climbing a 5.6 layback. Continue past a left-rising ramp to a dihedral, pass a loose but secure block, and climb a 5.6 off-width left of an arête to a ledge. Begin the second pitch by following an arch right (the route's only 5.8) to easier cracks. On the third and final pitch, climb an irregular crack (5.6) to a low-angle slab.

2. Fist Full of Dollars (II 5.8-) This route ascends the prominent straight-in dihedral. Begin, though, to the left, in thin right-angling cracks that lead to an off-width (crux) and a belay ledge where the off-width meets the dihedral. The second pitch ascends the dihedral. On the third pitch a grassy crack leads to a right-leaning chimney and continues past loose blocks. The short final pitch ascends a crack slightly to the right.

Descent: To the west.

South from Warbonnet after October storm; Big Sandy Lake nearest, Clear Lake in the middle, Deep Lake farthest

11 Deep Lake

The three streams that enter Big Sandy Lake from the southeast originate amid an array of walls and peaks that are distinctive landmarks to rock climbers. The northern of the three flows down a narrow defile from Black Joe Lake, a mile-long body of water jammed between Big Sandy Mountain's interminable scree and Haystack's "back side." The other streams drain prettier valleys. The middle one comes from Deep and Clear Lakes, above which rise Haystack's mile-wide slabs, sharp-peaked Steeple, East Temple's vertical northwest face, and its detached prow, the Lost Temple Spire. The southern of the three streams, Rapid Creek, comes from a glacier under Temple Peak's north side and flows from Temple Lake through Miller and Rapid Lakes below a ridge that includes A Cheval and Schiestler Peaks.

Because the walls surrounding these lakes are so accessible—all three valleys are easily reached from Big Sandy Opening—and offer so many good routes, it is surprising that before 1961 only one technical climb had been done, an anachronistic ascent of Temple's north face in 1946. In 1961, though, a group that included Fred Beckey, Yvon Chouinard, Art Gran, John Hudson, and Bruce Monroe camped at Deep Lake and made the first ascents of Haystack, Steeple, the Lost Temple Spire, East Temple's northwest face, and another ascent of Temple's north face. Climbers since have concentrated on Haystack's west face, climbing all the obvious lines, some among the range's best rock climbs.

The peaks in this chapter, which encompasses a smaller area than any of this book's other chapters, are located on the Temple Peak quad. Trails are also found on the Big Sandy Opening quad.

Trails

Big Sandy Trail

Big Sandy Opening to Big Sandy Lake—5.5 miles

The Wind Rivers' most used trail parallels the Big Sandy River. (Relocation farther from the river eliminated the older trail's wettest and most eroded stretches.) The Big Sandy Trail is used by hikers and anglers en route to popular Big Sandy Lake and by climbers going to the Cirque of the Towers and the valleys south of Big Sandy Lake.

Begin at the upstream end of the Big Sandy Campground by crossing a small rise left of an outhouse. The Big Sandy and Meeks Lake Trails both follow the river's west bank for 0.5 mile; the latter then leaves the river. Continue along the river, past a junction with the V Lake Trail, to Big Sandy Lake. At the lake's northwest corner is a junction. The Jackass Pass Trail climbs north to the Cirque of the Towers; the

Deep Lake Area

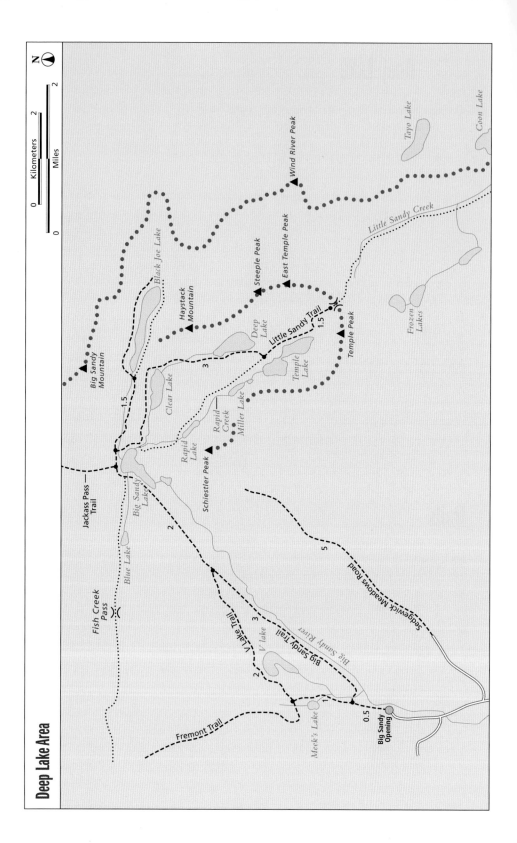

Little Sandy Trail follows the lake's north shore, providing access to valleys and peaks included in this chapter.

Little Sandy Trail

Big Sandy Lake to Temple Pass—5 miles

This trail connects Big Sandy Lake to the lakes to the south. From the end of the Big Sandy Trail (at the lake's northwest corner), follow the north shore, which not only is likely to be swampy but also involves more stream crossings than there are streams. Before you cross Black Joe Creek, the Black Joe Lake Trail splits to the left. Past the lake's east end, the Little Sandy Trail turns left and climbs; the abandoned Rapid Creek Trail continues invisibly south.

After a steep 0.5 mile, the Little Sandy Trail reaches Clear Lake's north shore; after another mile, first on slabs east of a fine stream, then west, it reaches Deep Lake. The trail then climbs west and crosses a low divide to Temple Lake, where it rejoins the Rapid Creek Trail.

From Temple Lake, work up rough slopes between East Temple and Temple Peaks to 11,480-foot Temple Pass, which overlooks Little Sandy Creek's headwaters. Indians on horse used Temple Pass, but rockslides have made it practical only for foot travel. The trail south of the pass is described in the South Pass chapter.

Black Joe Lake Trail

Big Sandy Lake to Black Joe Lake—1.5 miles

The Forest Service reconstructed the Black Joe Lake Trail, moving it slightly. Leave the Little Sandy Trail just north of Black Joe Creek, at the edge of the meadow near Big Sandy Lake's east end. Cross the creek, climb to a swamp, and cross the old trail. Eventually recross to the north of the old trail and parallel Black Joe Creek to Black Joe Lake's outlet.

To reach the lake's upper end, either cross the bridge over the lake's outlet and follow a trail that, to avoid cliffs and a waterfall, climbs high on the north side, or crawl through large boulders on the south shore.

Rapid Lake Trail (not maintained)

Big Sandy Lake to Temple Lake—3 miles

Rapid Creek's valley between Rapid and Temple Lakes is a delightful place to stroll or camp. However, the trail that the Temple Peak quad shows climbing from Big Sandy Lake to Rapid Lake has not been maintained for years, an avalanche has taken its toll, and boots have gouged the overly steep slope. If you are going to Temple Lake or beyond, go by way of Deep Lake. You can also cross a saddle from Clear Lake's outlet. If you do want to climb directly from Big Sandy Lake, try slopes west of the map's trail.

Sedgewick Meadows Road (part not maintained)

Big Sandy Opening to Head of Dutch Joe Creek—5 miles

Dutch Joe Creek drains a valley bounded by minimal alpine grandeur: 2nd-class Independent Mountain and its ridgemates on one side, Temple's "back side" on the other. Nevertheless, the valley floor is a Rocky Mountain prototype: broad meadows flanked with aspens, the creek sweeping around graceful meanders, the loops interspersed with short rapids. Beavers have thrived in the upper valley.

At the south end of Big Sandy Opening, an inconspicuous road leaves the main road at a sign reading SEDGEWICK MEADOWS. The road is closed to vehicles after a mile; if the meadow after 0.5 mile is muddy, please park at the gate before this meadow. Beyond the meadow easily followed game trails continue north and then east to the head of Dutch Joe Creek, between Temple Peak and Independent Mountain.

The pass at the valley's head has been crossed to the Little Sandy drainage and is reported to be not particularly difficult.

Peaks

Haystack Mountain (11,978)

Climbers headed to the renowned Cirque of the Towers are likely to notice a broad formation south of Big Sandy Lake. Less a mountain than a rock climbing area, Haystack presents a mile of cliffs and slabs from Clear Lake to Deep Lake. It has more routes than any other Wind River peak, but many end over 0.5 mile from the summit, and few climbers traverse the upper talus to its hard-to-identify high point. Twenty-some routes offer a variety of climbing, from scrambles to a multiday aid route, from solid granite to crumbling seams. Haystack's allure is enhanced by its accessibility: You can reach campsites under the west face in 4 hours from Big Sandy Opening.

Dividing Haystack's west face into three sections helps locate its many routes. The steep north tower, prominent from Clear Lake though lower than the rest of Haystack, is separated from the central wall by low-angle slabs cut by a diagonal ledge system, the Grassy Goat Trail. The central section is separated from the south end by comparatively broken rock and a pair of deep, intersecting chimneys.

1. North Gully (I 5.1) Haystack's north shoulder, the divide between Clear Lake and Black Joe Lake, is easily reached from either. An obvious 5-foot-wide gully diagonals from the shoulder left across the north face. Only a short section 100 feet up may be worth a rope.

You can find pleasant slab climbing, with difficulties up to 5.5, left of the gully.

The gully, however, may now be unclimbable: Climbers in 2011 found evidence of recent rockfall that led them, after climbing the 5.5 slab, to descend the Grassy Goat Trail instead.

2. North Face (II 5.6) An enjoyable route of five pitches, about equal in difficulty, begins just right of the north gully in a long left-facing corner. The first pitch
ends at a small ledge at the corner's top. A crack above leads 20 feet to a steep ramp
slanting up left. Above the ramp climb right of a large block. The third pitch ascends
a right-facing corner to a ceiling, which you can climb directly or turn to the right,
then hand traverse easily back left. The pitch ends at ledges below another right-
facing corner. This corner (5.6) leads to a triangular block; pass it to the left, using a
nubbly crack to reach a large ledge. The fifth pitch ascends easy slabs to a notch in an
overhang. Above, climbing is easy.

Note: **The next eight routes are on the north tower's west face. The wall's most obvious features
are a gigantic arch crossing the lower face and two long, right-facing, leaning dihedrals above
and right of the arch. The first route is left of the arch. The second crosses the arch's apex to
the north shoulder, the third crosses the arch near its center, the fourth begins in the left of the
two long dihedrals before heading left, the fifth and sixth climb the long dihedrals, the seventh
begins from the meadow right of the dihedrals, and the eighth begins from high grass well to the
right, aiming for a broken chimney system.**

3. Pika Illiteration (II 5.8) A four- or five-pitch route reaches the north shoulder. It is best located in terms of the face's broadest treed ledge, one-third of the way
up the face. Begin left of the left end of these trees.

Pass blocks and angle up a slab to a left-facing corner. Climb the corner past the
left end of the tree ledge, then work right up ramps, cracks, and a slab to a ledge below
a steep, blocky corner. The corner is 5.8, and above it 4th-class terrain takes you to
the shoulder.

4. Flashflood (II 5.8) Climb a system of flakes to the arch's high point below the
north shoulder. A bolt protects a continuous bit of face climbing above the arch. Two
corner pitches take you to the north shoulder. While the original route began on
flakes to the right of the main system, a direct start involves nothing harder than 5.8.

While the name was perhaps intended metaphorically/whimsically, the route
would nevertheless be worth avoiding in threatening weather.

Most climbers finish at the north shoulder, but bolts indicate that someone
climbed the exposed face above the arch pitch onto the right edge of the north face,
into a dihedral that passes some roofs, and presumably continued to the top of the
North Tower.

5. North Tower Crack (V 5.9 A4) A few hundred feet right of its high point, the
arch bulges up again; above the bulge are left-leaning corners. This unobvious route
ascends a large flake's right edge, passes over the arch at the guano-streaked bulge, and
follows the corners up left. The wall's upper part is split by two or three prominent
cracks; pass through slanting ceilings to the left-most crack.

Haystack Mountain

The first ascent required more than two days. One of the participants, Jeff Lowe, described the route as "stupid, but beautiful. Hard aid, hard free, and perfect rock." A few blank sections require exotic hardware; Lowe writes, "Take all the ticks and tacks and crackerjacks you can think of." Expect two pendulums and few ledges.

6. North Tower Center–Labor Day (IV 5.10d) This route begins to the right of the *Major Dihedral* route, joins it for two pitches, and then cuts left for six pitches that link shorter, less conspicuous (and more difficult) corners.

The first ascent began from the grassy ledge used to approach the *Minor Dihedral,* with a 100-foot 4th-class traverse down left across loose terrain to a corner. A 200-foot pitch continues the traverse (5.8) to a pair of short right-facing corners; belay above the upper one. Here this route meets the *Major Dihedral,* with which it coincides for the tricky pitch that gains the dihedral and most of one pitch in the dihedral's left-facing lower section. Before ending the pitch, though, traverse left (5.10) to a large flake and climb to a belay.

On the fifth pitch, continue to the flake's top, climb the face above to a roof, undercling down right (5.10a), and belay on a small ledge. On the sixth pitch, climb the corner above, using chickenheads, to a white, sloping face (5.10) where the route's one bolt protects face climbing up left to another small ledge. Begin the seventh pitch by climbing the corner to the left to a large right-facing corner. Thin laybacking (5.10d) leads to a finger crack, then an undercling around a roof.

On the 5.10a eighth pitch, continue up the corner past a ledge, until the corner becomes a seam slanting right to a red corner. Step left from the corner to a flake and climb it to a belay in blocks. On the ninth pitch thin laybacking and face climbing (5.10) lead to a roof under a right-facing corner. Climb this corner's crack to its end, traverse right to another roof, turn the roof to its left, and climb a left-facing corner. Here difficulties abate; traverse left and follow a corner past a roof (5.7).

7. Major Dihedral (IV 5.10d) Beckey and Fuller arrived in 1964 to try a new route, only to find Croff, Fowler, and Schori on their proposed line. "So," wrote Beckey, "we did the natural thing . . . studied out an even more direct route," using the larger right-facing dihedral that splits the upper half of the face, and climbed it in a long day.

While the Croff-Fowler-Schori route, the *Minor Dihedral,* was repeated by 1971 and has become an oft-climbed classic, the Beckey-Fuller line, described too briefly in the *AAJ* but reported to involve much aid, was ignored. A few parties traversed to the dihedral from the right (5.10a), but the lower half of the route remained an enigma. The exact path of the first ascent may remain unknown, but the free route described here is probably a good approximation and, more important, a very good route. The lower section warrants study before your climb. A key is a left-facing downward continuation of the dihedral, hidden from vantages upstream from Clear Lake.

Begin (as for the *Minor Dihedral's* original start) with an easy 50 feet to a ledge above a nebulous left-facing corner, 80 feet right of a corner topped with an orange block, 20 feet left of tiny pines. Climb into the arches above, passing the first overlap with an awkward move, and up a 20-foot corner, then turn the final overlap by a very difficult traverse to another short corner.

From a ledge 20 feet higher, traverse right and climb to a left-facing corner. Leave the corner and step left, wishing for better protection, to a long left-slanting, right-facing corner. From its top, delicate moves lead left to an unexpected and most welcome ledge. From this ledge's left end, make a 10-foot traverse via a fortuitous black knob to the major dihedral's lower left-facing continuation.

The dihedral requires little description. Suffice to say that only in a few spots (not at either ceiling) is the climbing as difficult as 5.9 and that a vegetated crack on the final few pitches forces you to do some face climbing.

8. Minor Dihedral (III/IV 5.9) This deservedly popular route passes through rock country that appears an unlikely place for 1,000 feet with only two moves as hard as 5.9. Indeed, routefinding is generally easy; you have few alternatives. The route's upper part follows the right-leaning, right-facing dihedral to the right of the previous route's longer dihedral.

Early ascents used a clever, devious, and, for one pitch, loose start to climb the wall from the ground. They began, as for the *Major Dihedral,* with a short easy pitch to a ledge above a left-facing corner, then made a long, slightly downward traverse right to a crack that splits the arch but appears from below to overhang (it doesn't), then climbed a flaky pitch upward. While this original start makes the route a Grade IV, cleverer climbers have been bypassing these three pitches and approaching from high grass right of the start of the original fourth pitch.

Haystack Mountain

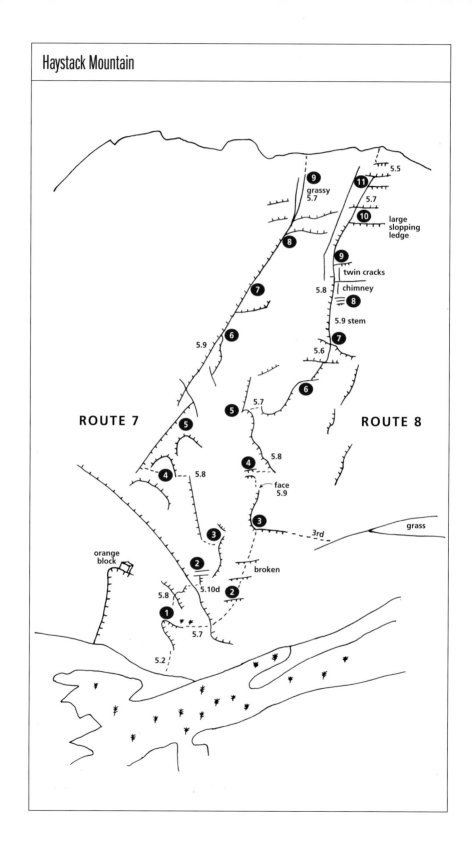

This pitch ascends a 130-foot right-facing corner, whose crux is an 8-foot discontinuity passed by delicate footwork. From the corner's top, traverse right to a ramp that slopes up left; after 160 feet you reach a big ledge above a short overhanging corner. Next a tricky traverse goes right to a scoop; cross it to broken rock. Climb a left-facing corner to a ceiling and, above the ceiling, follow a nice crack to the ledge below the upper dihedral.

The first pitch in the dihedral (5.9) ends on ledges. The next ascends a chimney (5.8) to a large ledge and continues to a ledge on the left. Continue in the system to a broad, sloping ledge. The overhang above is complicated (and the bong to its left off-route), but above is easier going for several hundred feet.

9. Seams Thin (IV 5.10d) Many climbers have admired the rock above the grassy ledge used to approach the *Minor Dihedral*. Much of the rock has consequently been climbed, usually joining the *Minor Dihedral*, typically after that route's seventh pitch, at the base of the dihedral itself. To what extent the first ascent of *Seams Thin*

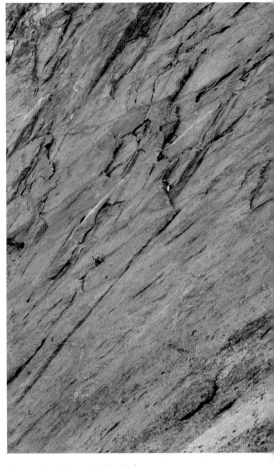

Haystack, Minor Dihedral

was pioneering is unclear; the pair reporting the route found bolts. Nevertheless, the route does remain independent of the *Minor Dihedral* (and of the *Right-Side Chimneys*) and does offer continuous climbing on a fine wall.

From the left side of the grassy approach ledge, climb a 4th-class pitch to a belay in a right-facing dihedral near a red lichen patch. Continue up the dihedral and nearby flakes and overlaps (5.8) to two old bolts, then move left to a belay in another dihedral. Rather than climb the dihedral above, step right and climb to a thin right-leaning flake system, belaying below a small roof where the system ends (5.8). The belay takes a 4-inch cam. Above the roof is a thin crack that degenerates to a seam. The seam takes tiny nuts, which protect 5.10d face climbing. Aim for a right-facing corner that leads to a ledge. This pitch is thin, runout, and considerably harder than anything else on the route.

The ledge leads left to the *Minor Dihedral,* but to continue *Seams Thin,* move the belay 50 feet right. Climb to a long right-leaning corner (white flake 15 feet up). Follow this corner (5.9) until 20 feet below the intersection of a roof with a corner to the left; move left to this larger corner. On the sixth pitch, follow this dihedral for 120 feet to its top (5.9). You are near the *Right-Side Chimneys,* in a zone of broken red overlaps, but climb out the steep wall to the left, passing left of a roof (5.9). After passing bad red rock, belay below a large left-leaning dihedral. Begin the eighth and final pitch (5.9) by climbing this corner for 20 feet, then hand traverse right to another left-leaning corner. Ascend this corner for 50 to 60 feet and again hand traverse right, this time to easy going.

10. Right-Side Chimneys (II 5.7) This route, with more loose rock than you may want to contend with, goes from the grassy slope high on the North Tower's right side up obvious right-facing flakes and chimneys, then wanders through the red rock above.

From the highest grass, scramble up a large flake's right side, walk along the flake, and work up a gully until it steepens into a chimney. Climb this chimney and the one above it for three pitches to a stance under a ceiling. Avoiding the ceiling requires a few tricky moves but leads to easy climbing on the face to the left. Next, climb a crack on the left side of a large block and another crack to the right. Three pitches of easier climbing lead to the top.

11. Grassy Goat Trail (I 4th class) Just north of the west face's central section, grassy ledges diagonal left from a triangular evergreen clump to the saddle between the North Tower and Haystack's upper slopes. Halfway up you must find your way through slabs and overhangs.

Note: **To the Grassy Goat Trail's right is the west face's central wall, the most obvious feature of which is an immense chimney formed by the erosion of a black dike. Just left of this chimney is a right-facing corner, farther left a grassy crack and a pair of parallel cracks that begin at the same evergreens as the *Grassy Goat Trail.* The next four routes follow these features. Right of the chimney is another high grass patch. Two short routes begin at this vegetation, and three other short routes ascend the broken rock farther right.**

12. Railroad Tracks (III 5.8) From near the bottom of the *Grassy Goat Trail,* scramble up low-angle rock near a single crack to the parallel cracks and climb to a small tree. Step right to a pair of facing corners and surmount an overhang. The next pitch reaches a stance in a right-facing corner. The following pitch ends above two large blocks. Twenty feet higher the parallel cracks become difficult. The right crack has been climbed with aid, the left crack free, and the cracks have been avoided by face climbing. Above the cracks' convergence climbing becomes easier.

13. Grassy Crack (II 5.6) A wide crack or chimney slants up left from the base of the *Central Corner* route. While the chimney itself is a gloomy place, the rock

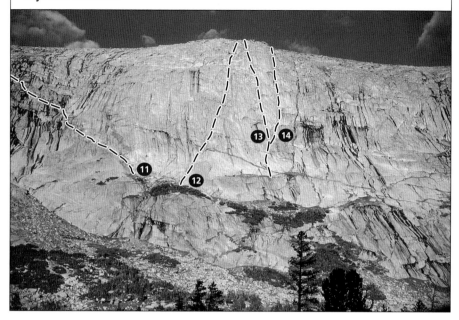

Haystack Mountain

alongside offers about six interesting pitches—albeit it with the possibility of escape into the chimney's sheltering depths always at hand. However, before the final pitch, recourse to the chimney is rarely necessary, and the overhang near the top is a pleasant surprise.

14. Central Corner (III 5.9) Left of the *Great Chimney* a right-facing dihedral extends nearly the height of the face. The route that follows this corner is among the best rock climbs in the Wind Rivers, concentrating much difficult climbing in four or five pitches.

Approach via a right-slanting, occasionally 5th-class, occasionally grassy crack in slabs below the steeper upper face, or by climbing the messy lower 200 feet of the *Great Chimney* and walking left on a big ledge.

The first pitch closely follows the crack in the corner but requires footwork (and a spectrum of hardware from small stoppers to a 3-inch cam); it ends by turning a 5-foot roof (the route's crux). The long second pitch (which can be broken into two pitches) also involves jamming, stemming, and laybacking up the continuous corner. If the main corner is wet on the third pitch, try the short corner to the right and the face above. The final pitch ascends 5.7 chimney systems.

15. Great Chimney (II 5.6) The west face's most obvious line is not its most enjoyable. The chimney's average width is perhaps 4 feet; its interior rock is weathered, occasionally loose, and often wet.

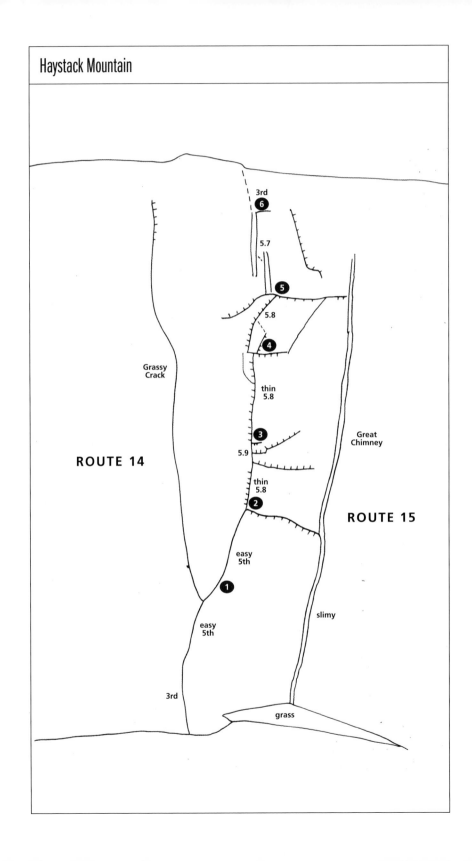

Haystack Mountain

3rd
6
5.7
5
5.8
4
Grassy
Crack
thin
5.8
3
5.9
ROUTE 14
thin
5.8
2
Great
Chimney
ROUTE 15
easy
5th
1
easy
5th
slimy
3rd
grass

The first three leads are 4th class. The fourth pitch involves stemming past overhangs. The sixth lead also requires stemming, plus a tricky move out of the chimney, where it becomes a corner for a short distance. The chimney narrows on the seventh pitch, which ends on a ledge to the left. The eighth lead is the crux, entailing a traverse under an overhang to a crack and an ascent of the crack. On the final pitch you must negotiate two chockstones.

16. Hidden Chimney (II 5.6) This short route begins at the next high grass right of the patch below the *Great Chimney* and ascends a right-facing chimney.

17. Converging Cracks (II 5.7/5.8) Right of the *Hidden Chimney,* beginning from the same high grass, is a pair of cracks that meet halfway up the face in an area of water-stained, often wet rock. A few hundred feet above the grass, a roof extends between the cracks.

The first pitch goes up right of a wide crack. The second pitch, also right of the crack, involves underclinging a flake. The next lead, the crux, goes left to the edge of a wide crack and ascends a thin crack. The fourth pitch crosses a chimney to the left through a waterfall. The fifth pitch, also wet, diagonals right. On the sixth lead, climb in and out of two black holes. Another easy pitch, ascending a corner, reaches a garden near the summit.

18. Layback (II 5.10b) With only three pitches—two easy and one hard—this route is unlikely to be Haystack's main attraction. The crux pitch ascends a right-arching corner midway up the face and midway between the west face's central section and the south gully.

Begin somewhat right of the arching corner in a broken right-facing corner (same start as *Whistlepigs*). Work left to a right-facing corner with a wide crack and end the second pitch on a ledge at its top. The third pitch offers 160 feet of laybacking, interrupted only by a step up left to pass a discontinuity. From a ledge just above the corner's top, you can walk off left.

19. Call of the Whistlepigs (II 5.10a A1) This route starts with the same nondescript corner that *Layback* does but diverges up right, toward three little parallel left-facing dihedrals, and turns into a better climb.

The second pitch ascends a ramp to the right-most of the three dihedrals and follows it (5.8) to a hanging belay. The third pitch crosses to the middle dihedral and follows it (5.10a and one aid move) to a ledge by an orange flake at the top of both dihedrals. An obvious, pleasant, 5.8 crack then leads to a ceiling, passed to the right, and a right-facing corner that leads to a detached flake and the end of 5th-class climbing.

20. Chockstone Corner (III 5.10) About 150 feet left of the south gully is a system of cracks and dihedrals marked by a large chockstone halfway up the face, below a red dihedral. This route passes the chockstone and avoids the dihedral.

Begin by following a right-facing corner to cracks on the right, below a large, lichen-covered roof. Turn the roof on the left and pass the chockstone to the right. Surmount a gray roof, right of the red dihedral, and climb cracks above to a sloping ledge. The final pitch ascends a right-facing open book left of the ledge, then cracks and bulges to easier rock.

Note: **Toward the west face's south end is a pair of chimneys or gullies that intersect halfway up to form an inverted Y. A route ascends the right-hand gully, and four attack the wall (here called the Southern Wall) between this gully and the south ridge.**

21. South Gully This gully, sometimes snow-choked, begins above Deep Lake's outlet and slants first left, then right. The route is said to be "not very noteworthy."

22. Pitch Off (III 5.10) Above the red streak used as a landmark for the *Southern Wall Center* route is a larger black area. Approach *Pitch Off* by traversing right (3rd class) from the south gully to this black rock.

Climb the S-shaped crack above the black rock to the right edge of a smaller black area, continue up cracks, and step right to a ledge (150 feet, 5.6). Climb the shallow right-facing corner above past two pointed roofs and angle up left on ledges (160 feet, 5.4). Continue up left on ledges, to a right-arching crack. Undercling left below a roof before climbing over it to a ledge in a left-leaning corner (120 feet, 5.7). Climb the corner to a right-facing flake. Climb the flake to a large ledge below two thin cracks (100 feet, 5.9). Climb the left crack, then a face, then the right side of a large roof (150 feet, 5.9).

Tiny nuts and cams are especially useful for this upper thin crack.

Haystack Mountain

Haystack, Southern Wall Center

23. Southern Wall Center (IV 5.10c) First ascent teams are notorious for over-stating their route's quality, and this route's original ascenders tried to moderate their praise. However, subsequent climbers declared it to be as good as any Wind River route they'd done. Leaving the south gully, it follows left-facing corners to a crease in the face's center, ascends the crease to the right-most of the upper wall's arching corners, and ends by traversing left above the corners.

Begin by scrambling 100 feet from the bottom of the south gully to a curving ledge below a red streak. From the ledge, traverse half a rope length right and climb to a small ledge. Climb up and traverse into the main left-facing corner; follow it and corners to its right for two or three pitches to a large, sloping ledge at the base of the crease. The pitch above the ledge is a good one; the next one, the crux, reaches a ledge below a ceiling. A crack in the ceiling leads to a ledge sloping down right. Descend this ledge, then work right past a crackless corner to a more useful one. This corner

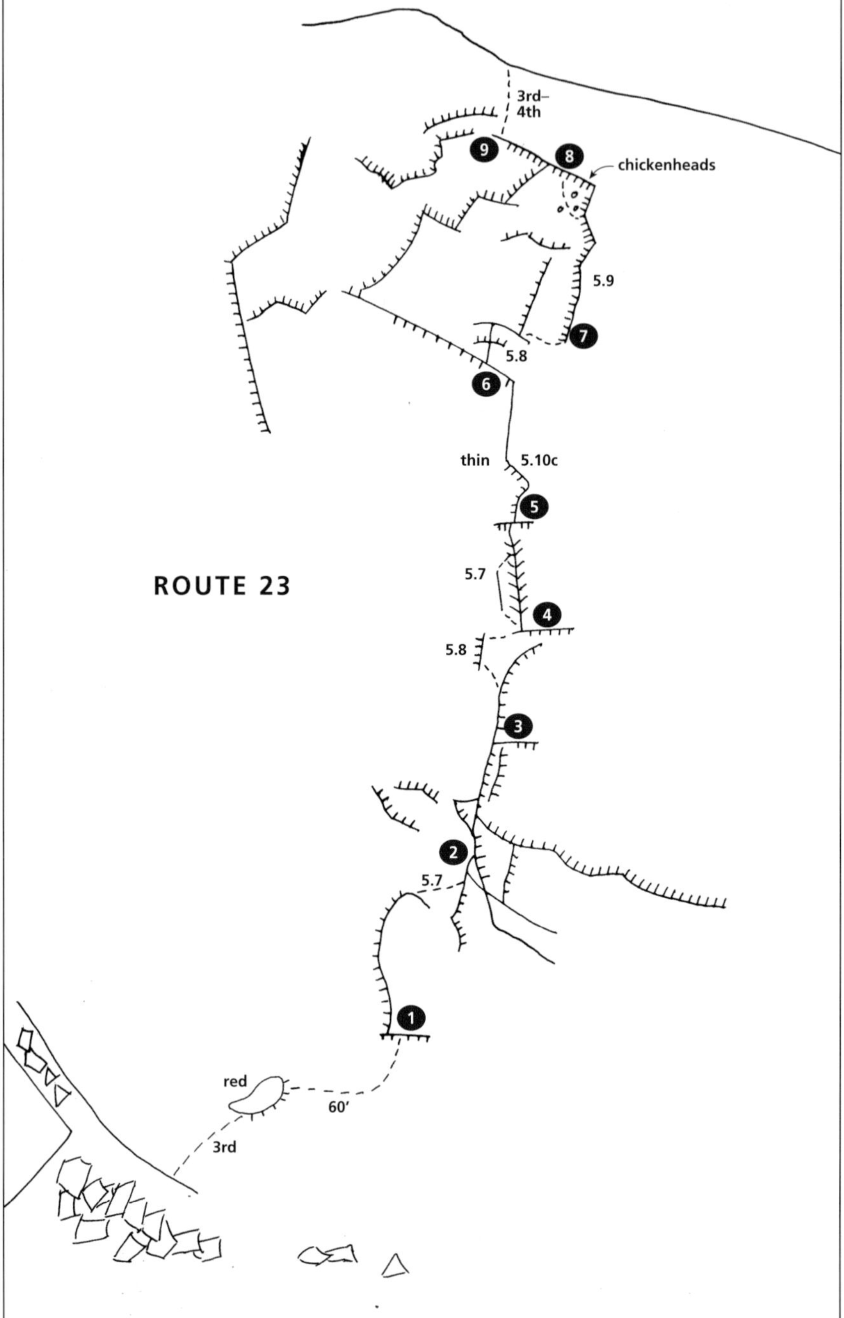

Haystack Mountain

ROUTE 23

3rd–
4th

⑨ ⑧ chickenheads

5.9

⑦

5.8

⑥

thin 5.10c

❺

5.7

❹

5.8

❸

❷

5.7

❶

red
60'

3rd

is 5.9, but eventually you can leave it, face climb to a ceiling, and traverse under the ceiling to another ledge. Follow this ledge until it is feasible to scramble to the top.

A variation goes left, rather than right, on pitch 7 and follows a 5.9 corner to a run-out slab. A final pitch crosses the original line (5.6).

24. Southern Wall Right (IV 5.10 A1) To follow this line, it may help to know that Jim Beyer couldn't complete as direct a route as he'd intended to.

Begin left of the face's low point with 300 feet of 3rd-class scrambling followed by 300 feet of 4th-class and moderate 5th-class climbing, leading to a roof formed by a series of overlaps. Ascend a ramp up left to a grassy ledge. Leaving the ramp, climb a crack to the right, overcome a difficult bulge, and pass a bolt. Climb past another bolt to a small roof; use aid to reach a crack and ascend the crack. Pendulum right, traverse right under a long roof, and surmount the roof. Follow an arch left, then tension traverse right. Climb up and right to a left-facing corner. Step right around the corner to a crack that leads to a right-facing corner. Continue up the corner to a short chimney capped by a roof. Above the chimney, traverse right under a roof. From a ledge above the roof, ascend another right-facing corner, then climb up left to a prominent corner that reaches the south ridge.

25. The Far Side (IV 5.10c A2) This nine-pitch route, the right-most on Haystack's west face, begins at the low point of the lower wall's apron. The final five pitches follow the most prominent crack above to the south ridge, though the crack is less a crack, more a seam, than it appears from afar.

Begin with 500 feet or more of 3rd, 4th, and two 5th-class pitches, aiming for an umbrella-shaped arch. (Up right from this arch is a huge overhanging corner.) Reach the arch's apex via a face and flakes below it to the right. Climb over the arch and face climb (5.9) to a belay at the top of a corner below another overhang.

On the next lead (the fifth), pass the overhang, face climb to a seam, and climb the seam (5.10 A2, difficult to protect) to a right-facing corner. Step left (to avoid dirt); undercling and layback to a belay. Climb back to the seam and follow it for 100 feet to a belay on the right. On the seventh pitch, continue up the seam but avoid a thin spot by face climbing to the right; a hand crack leads to a belay on knobs. Above, the seam again closes, requiring 5.10c climbing to gain a groove at the lip of an overhang. Belay above the lip. The final lead ascends a finger crack (5.8) in a corner.

A rack should emphasize things for thin, shallow cracks. The first ascent team found a knifeblade "comforting" on the eighth pitch. They also made one hook move. They left in place a piton and a stopper used for aid.

26. South Ridge (II 5.5) A short, pleasant route in a nice location: the long ridge joining Haystack to Steeple.

Approach from Deep Lake's upper end or from the valley above Black Joe Lake. Three easy pitches near the crest lead past one step to another. Next comes a route-finding dilemma: You can avoid an overhanging crack, but the way isn't obvious. The rock above is again easy, and roped climbing soon ends.

Haystack Mountain

Cirque of the Towers

26

28

27. Southeast Face (II 5.7) This route ascends the 400-foot face bordered by the south ridge and the east pillar. On the face's lower part, follow cracks 75 feet right of the obvious left-facing chimney system. Finish in a right-facing corner.

28. East Pillar (IV 5.9) The Clear Lake–Deep Lake valley offers more hospitable trails and campsites than Black Joe Lake's valley, and there are more good routes on Haystack's west face. Haystack's east side, above Black Joe Lake's boulder-strewn shore, could be the far side of the moon, relatively unseen and untouched. While much of the east face is unattractive, enough climbers on Steeple and East Temple admired the long pillar 0.5 mile south of Black Joe Lake that it suffered at least four "first ascents" of one route. This fine, photogenic route—which happens to end at Haystack's summit (which isn't the map's Point 11,978)—is worth the trip from Deep Lake over the saddle south of Haystack.

From the pillar's low point, climb cracks and corners for a few hundred feet toward a roof. Although you can climb the crack at the roof's left edge, a precarious block encourages a detour left. Above the roof, climb to a chimney formed by the weathering of a dike. Exit from the chimney using a slanting crack, cross the steepening face, and ascend cracks to a block near the pillar's right edge.

The headwall above offers a choice of two paths, both visible from far below and both 5.9. The pièce de résistance of the right-hand way is a bulge split by a 4-inch flaring, leaning crack, reached by a short lead in either of two lower cracks. Difficulties diminish above the short, obvious crux. The left line involves a ceiling and a long, continuous crack. The crack ends in blank rock, but somewhat lower you can traverse right to another crack. (A climber who climbed the long crack to its end, then tension traversed right, says that the quality of the crack compensates for the stigma of aid.) Above both variations two moderate pitches complete the route.

Carry a plentiful supply of tiny nuts for the shallow cracks encountered crossing right from the chimney. Carry protection that fits the wide cracks on the upper headwall—in particular, something for a 4-inch crack on the right-hand variation or several 3- to 4-inch pieces for the left-hand variation.

29. East Face (II 5.6) Haystack's east face has been ignored because its extensive lower section is broken into ledges, headwalls, slabs, and gullies; the long approach to the short upper wall has deterred aspiring adventurers. The first ascent party felt their seven-pitch endeavor near the face's center was not worth the approach.

From Lake 10,278 above Black Joe Lake, climb a 4th-class gully. Cross snow to a corner on the left. Three 5th-class leads in the corner reach a wide ledge. Walk right to a gully and follow it to the top.

30. Northeast Face Several climbs have been done above Black Joe Lake, but the climbers couldn't relate them to identifiable features. The only information about one such route is that it isn't difficult and ends several hundred yards north of the summit.

Descent: The *Grassy Goat Trail* is a convenient descent route, having the advantage over the *North Gully* (even when the *North Gully* is free of rockfall debris) of leading back toward Deep Lake, and the disadvantages of requiring your concentration for longer and being wet more often. Finding the route from the top requires some scouting and intuition, but once located it is difficult to lose.

It is possible to descend after climbing the *East Pillar* or a nearby route by climbing 50 feet down the gully just south, making a single-rope rappel to a big ledge, and traversing to the Steeple col.

Steeple Peak (12,040+)

The splendid little peak on the ridge between Haystack and East Temple is one of the rare Wind River summits attainable only by 5th-class climbing.

1. South Ridge (I 5.8) From Lake 10,602, south of Deep Lake, ascend talus, then wander up right on ledges to the col between Steeple and Lost Temple Spire. From the col, follow the 4th-class ridge to within 100 feet of the summit. The summit block has several cracks. The left-most crack is the usual route, though it begins with a difficult, exposed move. The other cracks have also been climbed.

2. East Ridge (III 5.9) Much of the ridge is unroped scrambling. Many variations are possible.

3. North Ridge (III 5.8) This colorful route ascends rock west of the crest to the north ridge's broad shoulder, disappears into the chimney above, and emerges a pitch below the summit.

Approach from Deep Lake by obvious ledges or from Black Joe Lake through the Steeple-Haystack saddle. Begin roped climbing at the base of a crack that extends 140

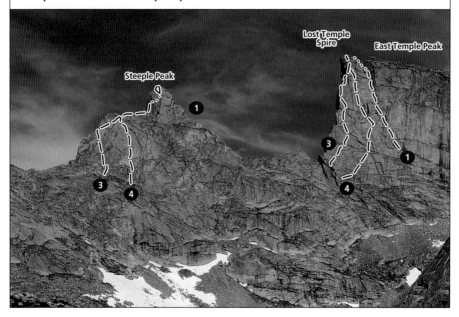

Steeple Peak and Lost Temple Spire

feet up the ridge's west side to a step below the shoulder. Avoid the overhang at the bottom of the crack by climbing the 5.8 corner to its right. (The overhang is 5.9.) From the step, ascend a trough on the ridge's west side past a detached block to a pair of diverging cracks; these lead to the shoulder.

Reach the Great North Chimney via a narrower chimney, pass between two chockstones, and belay. Tunnel southwest (toward Temple) below a pile of blocks, then climb out of the chimney. Pass around the huge block above the chimney and gain the top of a large, leaning slab, where you have two choices. You can step up left to a shallow gully that leads easily to the summit or climb the corner above you directly to the summit. This 5.8 corner is the elegant way to finish, but, as of a few years ago, an unavoidable block was questionably plastered to the ceiling just below the summit.

4. West Face, Main Dihedral (III 5.11a) Of various ascents reported on Steeple's west face, only one has been described adequately enough for a guidebook recipe. However, the report makes it significantly more difficult than other climbs; multiple routes must exist (see next description). This route follows the left-facing dihedral that is intersected, high on the wall, by a left-arching dihedral.

Approach by the grassy ramp that slants up under the west face. Climb the corner until it threatens to become more difficult and less protectable (5.9). Belay (hanging) left of a small ledge. Continue up the corner. After 30 feet the crack widens, enabling better protection and easier climbing. Belay on a 4-inch ledge left of the corner and

Steeple Peak

5

4th

leaning
slab

5.8

4

3

tunnel

Great
North
Chimney

5.6

2

5.7

flake

1

5.8
thin

3rd

ROUTE 3

below a flake (5.10R). Climb the flake, a vegetated crack, and an arching corner to an obvious ledge (5.10d). Layback to the roof above. Hand traverse left, pass the roof, and climb to the north shoulder (5.11a).

5. West Face (III 5.8) Climbers occasionally report climbing clean cracks on the west face, for six pitches or so, directly to the summit. What they apparently mean is that they climbed one of the attractive crack systems below the north shoulder, worked right below the immense block that forms the Great North Chimney's right side, and climbed to the summit from there, perhaps by the *North Ridge*'s 5.8 finish.

Descent: To descend the south ridge, drop east from the summit to a big ledge and walk south to a large block. A 75-foot rappel passes the difficult pitch; a 150-foot rappel from the block also passes the ridge's hardest scrambling.

Lost Temple Spire (12,480+)

Conspicuous in profile from the west—from the Fremont Trail, the Big Sandy Road, the Pinedale–Rock Springs Road when the shadows are right—the spire is lost against East Temple when you're looking for it from nearby Deep Lake, Big Sandy Lake, or the Cirque of the Towers. The 200-foot notch separating the spire from East Temple is out of sight from the north, making this most difficult to reach of Wind River points appear to be a stroll from its flat-topped neighbor. It is not.

1. Southwest Arête (IV 5.10a) Out of sight behind what appears, from Deep Lake, as the Spire's right edge is an abundance of crack systems. These cracks provide a route continuously difficult and occasionally picturesque, on excellent rock. With rising standards of difficulty, harder routes have become classics—this route, especially given the summit it reaches, among them.

The approach, which entails angling up grassy ledges toward East Temple, then cutting back left toward the cleft separating the Spire from East Temple, allows an overview of the route's six to eight pitches. Begin climbing at a slanting black dike, either in a difficult groove (as the first ascent party did) or by surmounting an easier overhang to the right, then climbing up left toward the crest. The next three pitches involve several left-facing corners; too many details would read redundantly and only bewilder. The first of these pitches starts with a tricky leaning dihedral, followed by a difficult move to enter a corner up right. The second pitch uses a crack to the right of a corner to reach a relatively broken area. The third begins in moderate cracks but soon reaches a difficult layback. This pitch ends on a prominent ledge atop a pillar on the crest.

To reduce rope drag you may want to break the next 150 feet into three leads. Gain a ledge 40 feet up either by traversing left to a thin crack or by a difficult corner to the right. Above are several ceilings. The first ascent reached the first ceiling directly by difficult face climbing, but you can alternatively climb a thin crack left of the ledge, then traverse right with a step around a prow. A more horrifying step, around a prow at the lip of a ceiling, and a short traverse take you to a small ledge. Pass a huge block (that appears to defy gravity) to a large ledge. A long lead in the deep chimney above ends in easier going and a scramble to the summit.

2. North Face–Separation Anxiety (IV 5.11a) To the left of the north prow is a remarkable 220-foot hand crack that caught climbers' eyes for years. The crack raised two questions: how to reach it and how to split it into two pitches.

The crack can be reached by first climbing two and a half pitches of the *North Prow,* traversing left on a big ledge, traversing another 30 feet, passing a 5.10a roof, and climbing a 5.9 fist crack. The crack itself is 5.10 hand-width; face holds are few. There are two strategies for belaying the pitch: Have a 70-meter rope and step off left where the crack narrows and the rope runs out or have enough gear to set up a safe belay in the crack. A 5.9 pitch then returns you to the *North Prow* route (below its 5.11a crux).

3. North Prow (IV 5.11a) As the spire's only route before 1980, this alluring prow saw many attempts—and many failures, before a few free ascents relatively recently. Its cold, windy location—four pitches west of the crest, before it crosses to the east—was one problem; steep cracks were another.

Begin at the notch at the spire's base by ascending a right-slanting crack, then climbing up left. Reach a large ledge after two more pitches. Climb a chimney and step left to a platform on the prow. The long pitch above—an overhanging corner leading to cracks in a vertical wall, ending at a stance on the right wall—defeated early free climbing efforts; it is now 5.10d. The next pitch involves steep flakes, and the one after, chimneying behind a giant flake. The final lead involves a narrowing chimney—and the route's crux, turning a ceiling—and a crack that ends in the summit boulders.

Take along more large cams than for most Wind River routes.

4. West Face–1986 Route (IV 5.10b A1) The face seen from Deep Lake, between the north prow and the southwest arête, was climbed at least three times between 1983 and 1993. Details of the 1983 climb aren't available, but the 1986 and 1993 lines, though they cross, differ except for the last pitch (which they also share with the *North Prow*) and are best described as separate routes. Some of the differences can be attributed to wet rock during the 1986 climb.

The 1986 team reached the gray band a few hundred feet up by beginning well to the left of a large chimney (which was wet) and angling toward the chimney's top for two long, easy pitches. Difficulties begin at the gray band.

Climb a 5.10 corner and pass right of a chimney/flake. Next, reach a grassy alcove below a left-curving overhang. Work left under the overhang, then tension traverse left to an easy corner, where you can belay. Above, the overhang curves back into a dihedral. The first ascenders found strenuous jamming here to be the route's crux, but they also found a poised flake and suggest avoiding it by jamming through the overhang to another dihedral. Above these dihedrals, head up and left on lower-angle, knobby rock. A layback leads to a large ledge near the *North Prow.* The final pitch coincides with the *North Prow*'s final pitch.

5. West Face–1993 Route (IV 5.10+) The 1993 team ascended the large chimney that leads to the gray bands for a pitch (5.8) and its left side for another pitch (5.9). They began the pitch above the gray bands in the same dihedral as the 1986 team, but soon stepped over (5.9) to a prominent ramp that angles up left, under a brown flake.

Traverse (5.9) to a left-facing corner and climb it to a ledge up right. Continue up another corner (5.10) past flakes to a wide ledge. Climb a left-facing corner for 120 feet, taking its right fork where it splits (5.10c). Begin the seventh pitch by reaching a ledge, stepping right to a white scar, ascending a hand crack, then a wide crack (5.9) that angles up left to the ledge below the *North Prow's* final pitch. Rather than attacking the ceiling above, though, the 1993 climbers made a 5.10+ hand traverse below it to 5.6 terrain.

Descent: You can descend the north prow with eight rappels of various lengths, but the southwest arête probably offers an easier descent, with fewer rappels (six) and fewer opportunities for rope-retrieval mishaps. To avoid a rappel into the chimney, the top anchors were placed north of the chimney. Continue rappelling near the ascent route.

East Temple Peak (12,600+)

Two vertical faces intersecting at a prow—the prow being the semidetached Lost Temple Spire—identify East Temple from the north. The southwest slope makes East Temple one of the most accessible of high Wind River summits, though the first big-wall ascent of Wind River rock occurred on the northwest face.

1. Southwest Slope (I 2nd class) The surface rock has been shattered by frost, but the angle is too low for erosion to remove the blocks; this felsenmeer extends nearly a mile from Temple Pass to the summit.

2. Northeast Face (VI 5.9 A3) Climbers had long noted this wall's steep profile, but the few who ventured to the head of Black Joe's valley to investigate saw little to encourage an attempt. The wall has now been climbed, but the *AAJ* account gives no more encouragement than the rock itself.

Begin not in the prominent right-leaning crack system in the center of the face ("closer observation revealed loose rock and extensive vegetation"), but in a left-leaning system 200 feet right. Intersect the prominent crack three pitches up. Continue for three more pitches ("hoping for more secure rock above") to a horizontal band and small bivouac ledge. Traverse left for a pitch and ascend a left-leaning crack (noted as "clean") directly below the wall's apex. Two more pitches lead to "a highly vegetated sloping ledge." Above is the route's only all-aid pitch. Continue up left, finishing just left of the huge finger that juts from the summit. The *AAJ* account ends with the cheeriest recommendation the team could muster: "Perhaps more ascents would lessen the rotten rock and dirt."

3. Northwest Face (V 5.8 A4) This steep wall's one obvious line is a pair of left-facing, overhanging dihedrals, one above the other. The two-day ascent of this line in 1961 was one of the earliest applications of Yosemite techniques in the high mountains. (Chouinard and Gran did about a third of the route with aid.) As for popularity, however, the route's historical value hasn't impressed climbers as much as the sunless setting and the first ascent account of awkward climbing on the overhanging right walls of the dihedrals.

After 200 feet of scrambling, climb three pitches, beginning with a flared crack, to the base of the lower dihedral. Reach its top in three more pitches, then traverse for a rope length to the upper dihedral. Climb this corner also in three pitches. On the next pitch, use aid to go left around a roof, and on the final pitch, make a long traverse right.

4. Northwest Face, Right Side (I 4th class) To the right of the sheer face a couloir diagonals up right; above it ledges slant back left. A route ascends the lower couloirs and heads up a pleasant dihedral to the southwest slopes.

5. From the Northwest (I 4th class) The ridge separating the bowl above Deep Lake from the Temple Lake cirque makes a nice way to gain the southwest slope.

Temple Peak (12,972)

The second-highest peak in the range's southern half is visible from far to the north, standing to the right of other high peaks. Views from the west show it to be another peak with contrasting sides—to the south and west, vast rubble slopes; to the north, a classic alpine face. Its routes reflect this dichotomy, varying from strenuous hikes to serious climbs.

1. Southwest Slope (I 2nd or 3rd class) Temple is climbed most easily from Dutch Joe Creek. You can link various minor bowls and ridges with talus slopes, proceeding, as William Owen did in 1890, "over a mass of granite blocks varying in size from a pumpkin to a court house."

2. South Ridge (I 3rd class) Use this grassy, boulder-strewn ridge to ascend Temple from Temple Pass or Little Sandy Creek. The ridge is most easily gained 0.5 mile from the summit; two couloirs nearer the summit are corniced early in summer and later filled with ice and loose rock. When approaching from Temple Pass, avoid descending to Lake 10,839 by a messy traverse.

3. East Couloir (I 4th class) The south ridge drops off to the east in cliffs several hundred feet high. Directly above Temple Pass a couloir cuts through these cliffs and meets the ridge near the summit. In early summer the snow-filled couloir is dangerous, as it is capped by a cornice. Later the couloir involves a few pitches of chimneys with loose rock and often ice.

The couloir has been reached not only from Temple Pass but also by ascending Temple Glacier's thin left arm to the saddle above and scrambling left to the couloir.

4. Northeast Chutes (II 5.7) To the right of the main east couloir are several other chutes. These chutes have been climbed in at least three ways. The most straightforward and easily located route ascends the first chute right of the main couloir. Separated from the couloir by a rib with a spire partway up, the chute is capped with a block forming a window. The climb begins at the foot of the rib, turns the spire to the right, and climbs the chute. Beware of ice and rotten rock near the top.

Temple Peak

Another route, rated 5.4/5.5, apparently begins in the same chute but at some point traverses across the rib to the right. A short rappel leads into the next couloir; cracks on this couloir's left side and a 30-foot chimney lead to easier going. You reach the south ridge 10 feet from the summit.

Other chimneys and chutes have been climbed but can't be identified with certainty.

5. Northeast Buttress (IV/V 5.9 A3/A4) The sheer triangular face left of and below the main north face appears an unlikely place for a route, but Wind River rock is often kinder than it looks. Jeff Lowe called the climb "an exercise in imaginative routefinding." A diagonal rappel, nuts thrown in from several feet below, pendulums, and tension traverses are all involved. Begin just right of a small toe that protrudes into the glacier. The rappel is about halfway up and slants right. The route ends near the face's apex.

6. North Face Left (III/IV 5.9) From Temple Glacier, ascend halfway up its left-slanting arm, which separates the northeast buttress from the main north face. Then follow right-angling cracks and narrow chimneys for 500 feet to a large ramp in the center of the face. Traverse 300 feet right to another system of right-angling cracks and ascend them for 300 feet of loose rock to meet the summit ridge well right of the summit.

7. North Face Right (II 5.5 A1) From a distance the face above the glacier looks overly imposing, but closer scrutiny reveals myriad ledges toward its right side.

Nevertheless, the 1946 ascent by Stewart and Willits, who reached the summit in 4 hours, was daring for the time. Their route's location has been lost to time, but Beckey and Monroe climbed the face in 1962.

From the head of Temple Glacier, two snow fingers diagonal up—one left toward the east couloir, the other right. Beckey and Monroe followed broken rock right of the right-slanting finger to a notch on the skyline. Having left crampons and axes behind, they resorted to two pins of aid on a slab they could have bypassed on snow.

8. Northwest Buttress Far Left–Last Go Round (IV 5.12) *Last Go Round* ascends a prominent splitter crack near the buttress's left side—a hand and thin-hand crack for four pitches—followed by a traverse left to an alcove and a steep dihedral to the top of the buttress. Having climbed pitches of 5.10, 5.11, 5.12, 5.12, and 5.11, the first ascent team reckoned that continuing up a rubble gully to the summit would not enhance their experience, and they rappelled from the top of the buttress.

9. Northwest Buttress (III 5.8) A thirteen-pitch route ascends the right side of the buttress located right of the main north face; this buttress culminates in a peak on the northwest ridge.

10. Northwest Ridge (II 5.3) A minor peak on the northwest ridge is separated from the main peak by a notch. From this northwest peak a ridge curves east and

Temple, Northwest Ridge

down to Temple Lake. The ridge offers a mile of delightful and frequently exposed scrambling and climbing.

Gain the ridge from the tarn enclosed by the ridge's curve or by climbing directly up from Temple Lake. After you pass a step in the ridge and a few gendarmes, easy going leads to the northwest peak. (You could reach this summit easily from North Temple Creek.) Descend to the gully between the northwest and main summits and climb the gully to the notch at its top. The next few hundred feet involve slabs, corners, and an airy ledge above the north face. Soon you reach easy talus that leads to the summit.

A Cheval Peak (11,763)

Of the several points on the ridge joining Temple to Schiestler, the peak above Temple Lake's north end is the only one distinguished with a history and a name. The name refers to a technique used on the summit block, though you can reach the top by less dramatic means.

1. Southeast Slope (I 3rd class) From the Rapid Creek Trail, walk between Temple and Miller Lakes, then south along Temple Lake, and scramble up to A Cheval's south slope. Ascend either this slope or the southeast ridge, gaining the summit ridge west of the summit. Negotiate the summit block by whatever technique you wish.

2. Cloudburst Buttress (III 5.10c) When backpackers en route from Big Sandy Lake to Jackass Pass pause, they are likely to look south and study Temple Peak. This route ascends the unnoticed buttress below Temple and slightly right.

When you are in the Rapid Creek valley, it is the buttress above the cascades between Temple and Miller Lakes. Beginning from grass at its base, climb the obvious shallow inside corner, which is awkward, dirty in a few places, and difficult to protect. After 100 feet, exit right and cross via hard friction (two bolts) to a grassy right-bearing crack. The second pitch continues up cracks nearly to a large roof, then traverses right to a belay stance. Next, climb a slab right of the roof to a short but difficult off-width; continue leftward up slabs. On the fourth pitch, climb an enjoyable orange headwall, cracks, and blocks up right to the buttress's right edge. The final roped pitch follows this edge, with one exposed, strenuous move at a short step. Scramble for a few hundred feet to the crest.

3. North Ridge (I 3rd or 4th class) From the vicinity of Miller Lake, climb a snowfield to gain a couloir leading to the north ridge, then ascend flower-studded meadows south to the top.

4. South Ridge (I 3rd class) Follow this ridge from the summit on Temple's northwest ridge.

Schiestler Peak (11,640+)

The slabs rising above Big Sandy Lake's south shore are slopes of Schiestler, the culmination of a ridge running north from Temple Peak. Schiestler is saved from obscurity by the north summit's east face. (The north summit isn't the highest, though the Temple Peak quad gives its elevation.) Although this face is far inferior to Haystack's west face, the approach is short, the descent uncomplicated, and it sports five rock routes. You can pass the face's messy lower section most easily by climbing a 4th-class gully below *Northern Pacific* and scrambling south on grassy ledges to the other routes.

Molybdenum was found on Schiestler's southwest slope around 1940; claims were staked, a crude road built, and machinery brought in. The switchbacking trail south of Schiestler was part of this operation. However, little ore was removed, despite renewed exploration around 1980—to beat the 1964 Wilderness Act's limit on mining to operations viable before 1984.

1. Southwest Slope (I 2nd class) You can reach this flank of Schiestler by crossing the Big Sandy River at Big Sandy Lake's outlet. You can also follow the mining road (closed to vehicles) from the Temple Creek Summer Homes in Big Sandy Opening.

2. East Chute (I 3rd class) Between the true summit and the north summit is a long boulder slope. The only problem is skirting immense blocks.

3. East Face, Left Edge (II 5.7) The east face's most easily recognized feature is a dihedral and chimney in the shape of a backward S. To its left, near the face's edge, is a left-facing dihedral, which this route follows. Rock quality is substandard.

Begin from the grassy approach ledge on a slab below and left of a chimney with chockstones; the chimney is part of the dihedral. Climb the corner and slabs to the left for three or four pitches. Where the corner ends at a drop-off, climb the short, steep face to the right; it leads to easier going.

4. East Face Left (II 5.7 plus rappel) This route begins right of the *Inverted S* route, crosses it, and ascends the wall to the left. The first two pitches may coincide with *Red BVD,* but this route leaves *Red BVD*'s pillar by a 75-foot rappel from a ledge on the *Inverted S*'s left edge. Obvious cracks lead up the wall on the left; pass a grassy bulge and continue to 3rd- and 4th-class rock near the top.

5. East Face–Inverted S (II 5.6) Follow the prominent curving system of corners and chimneys.

6. East Face–Red BVD (II 5.7) The inverted S forms the left side of a pillar, up which goes a route that seems to be the best on the face. Begin from the grassy approach ledge in a left-facing corner. After a few pitches of cracks and corners near the pillar's left side, you reach a dead-end corner; turn an overhanging corner to the right by delicate climbing. The going soon becomes easier, and several hundred feet of scrambling lead to the top.

7. East Face–Northern Pacific (III 5.7) The previous four routes end near Schiestler's north summit. *Northern Pacific* reaches a minor summit more to the north, though it begins somewhat left of this summit. Start from a snowpatch that remains through much of the summer, pass an overhang, then climb a corner to a grassy ledge. Friction right to another vegetated corner and climb it, then a flared chimney, a crack, and a face, to a gravel chute. Climb a slab above the chute and a little chimney, then descend right to another chimney. Slabs above lead to easy going.

You can do an easier variation by working more to the right after two pitches into 4th-class terrain, then crossing back left to even easier slabs and reaching the top of the face between the north and minor summits.

8. Big Sandy Lake Buttress–Along for the Ride (II 5.10a) The slabs rising behind Big Sandy Lake have been climbed in four pitches. Begin a bit left of the gully on the buttress's right edge by climbing a right-trending ramp to its top (5.6). On the second pitch, climb left of a tree to an overhang, pass the overhang to the left, and face climb (5.10a) to reach a crack. The third pitch ascends a grassy dihedral (5.9-). A short 5.5 pitch reaches the top.

West Temple Peak (11,930)

The peak 1.2 miles west of Temple Peak is unnamed on maps, but the name is obvious.

1. West Slope (I 2nd class) From the Temple Creek Summer Homes on the Big Sandy Road, via the old Schiestler Peak mining road. Forest Service efforts to restore wilderness by bulldozing this road have created an eyesore far more appalling than an old mining road.

Independent Mountain (11,653)

This is the mountain that from Big Sandy Opening looks prominent, southwest of Temple, though it is only the westernmost point on a ridge and not the ridge's high point. While the ridge is connected to the Little Sandy Formations ridge, Independent is approached from the Big Sandy drainage.

1. North Slope (I 2nd class) You can climb the peak in a day from Big Sandy Opening by way of Dutch Joe Creek.

12 South Pass

South Pass is a desolate, windy plain populated by pronghorn antelope, snow fences, and historical markers. Turnouts enable motorists to pause at the latter, and also offer a chance to study the southern end of the Wind Rivers, to see the range as nineteenth-century emigrants did from their covered wagons.

The gentle dome of Wind River Peak, the only 13,000-foot summit in the range's southern half, dominates the scene. It stands out especially when it is snow covered and the foreground peaks are bare. The peaks nearer South Pass are also mostly gentle sloped, and, while walls bordering Little Sandy Creek may catch your eye, bold faces are sufficiently scarce and isolated that early climbers largely ignored the range's southern end. However, with climbers now seeking new rock and not attaching importance to summits, new routes have been materializing, even if virtually none reaches a summit of consequence.

West of the Continental Divide the Little Sandy drains this section, while the area east of the crest is drained by the Middle Popo Agie and Little Popo Agie Rivers.

Northeast side of Wind River Peak

The crest and the Continental Divide coincide as far south as Mount Nystrom, a few miles south of Wind River Peak. The Divide once continued along the crest past the Atlantic Peaks, but in recent geologic times the Sweetwater River encroached from the east and captured streams west of the crest. These streams, which had been tributaries of the Green, became headwaters of the Sweetwater. The present Divide is a low ridge that wanders south from Nystrom and separates the Sweetwater from the Little Sandy.

The broad area covered by this chapter has attracted more hikers than climbers, though much of the area isn't in designated Wilderness. Many trails aren't maintained and documented as Wilderness trails are. There are valleys and lakes as peaceful as anywhere, but the area's margins have suffered from civilization, and to reach a pristine environment you may have to traverse country more noteworthy for broken bottles and monogrammed aspens.

Peaks in this chapter are spread over several topographic maps: Temple Peak, Sweetwater Gap, Sweetwater Needles, Christina Lake, and Cony Mountain. Trails are also located on the Jensen Meadows, Fossil Hill, and Louis Lake quads.

Trails

Little Sandy Trail (part maintained)

Sweetwater Guard Station to Temple Pass—11 miles

The maintained trail to Little Sandy Lake begins at the end of the road above Sweetwater Guard Station. This trail, easily lost in a few places, follows Larsen Creek to the minor (unless your pack is heavy) Continental Divide ridge. Little Sandy Lake comes into view north of the ridge, but the trail descends to the west.

The situation on the west side of Little Sandy Lake is maximally confusing. Not only does it reaffirm Murphy's Law of topographic maps—that four 7.5-minute quads meet where you most need a map—but one, sixteen years older than the others, shows no trail. You stand at the edge of the Earthwalk map. The Bridger Wilderness map labels the trail section south of the lake "Dutch Joe Larsen Creek" but doesn't show a continuation north of the lake. The Beartooth map gets it right.

All the maps, however, do indicate correctly that you must descend the lake's outlet stream to find a safe crossing, especially in early summer. North of the creek, your map may show two trails paralleling the lake's shore, but the one closest to the lake, because of cliffs, is impractical and essentially fictional. Look for a trail in a draw well west of the lake.

North of Little Sandy Lake a maintained trail follows Little Sandy Creek into its peaceful upper valley as far as treeline. Above treeline, while the Forest Service doesn't maintain the trail shown on the Temple Peak quad, you shouldn't have trouble switchbacking to Temple Pass, the 11,480-foot saddle between Temple and East

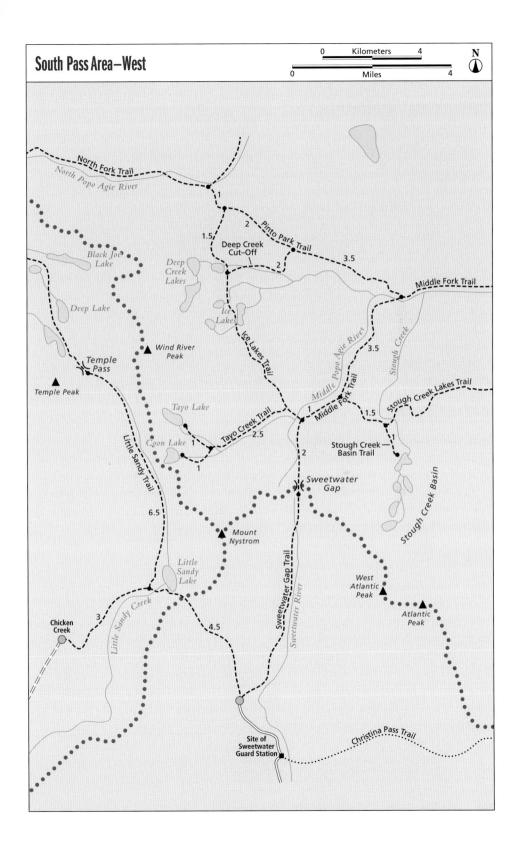

South Pass Area—West

Kilometers 0 — 4
Miles 0 — 4

N

North Fork Trail
North Popo Agie River
1
2
Pinto Park Trail
1.5
Deep Creek Cut-Off
2
3.5
Middle Fork Trail
Black Joe Lake
Deep Creek Lakes
Deep Lake
Ice Lakes
Middle Fork Trail
3.5
Stough Creek
Wind River Peak
Temple Pass
Temple Peak
Ice Lakes Trail
Middle Popo Agie River
Stough Creek Lakes Trail
Tayo Lake
Tayo Creek Trail
2.5
Middle Fork Trail
1.5
Stough Creek Lakes Trail
Coon Lake
1
1
Stough Creek Basin Trail
1
2
Little Sandy Trail
Sweetwater Gap
Stough Creek Basin
6.5
Mount Nystrom
Little Sandy Lake
Sweetwater Gap Trail
Sweetwater River
West Atlantic Peak
Atlantic Peak
Chicken Creek
3
Little Sandy Creek
4.5
Site of Sweetwater Guard Station
Christina Pass Trail

Temple Peaks. The Little Sandy Trail crosses Temple Pass to country covered in the Deep Lake chapter.

Little Sandy Lake from Downstream

Chicken Creek to Little Sandy Lake—3 miles

Little Sandy Lake can also be reached by shorter routes involving bad roads and obscure trails west of Little Sandy Creek. These routes are best followed with the Jensen Meadows quad in hand; the country crossed is south of that covered by the Earthwalk map, and the detail shown on other maps is insufficient.

One option is to leave the Lander Cutoff (the Farson-Big Sandy Road) at the second road west of its crossing of Little Sandy Creek. Follow this road (with a fence-line to your right for the first mile) for 3.25 miles and turn right (passing Benchmark 8675); after 0.5 mile turn left, before Chicken Creek. You can drive this road for 2 miles (the left variant reached immediately is likely to be less muddy than the right); park east of Point 9,030. The trail, sketchy in places, reaches the junction west of Little Sandy Lake in 3 miles, following Little Sandy Creek's west bank for the latter half of this distance.

Another option is to follow the four-wheel-drive road (FS 889) over Block and Tackle Hill to its end. A moderately used marked trail follows Little Sandy Creek.

Sweetwater Gap Trail

Sweetwater Guard Station to Sweetwater Gap—6 miles

The eastern of two trails that begin at the end of the road 2 miles past Sweetwater Guard Station drops across Larsen Creek and climbs to the Sweetwater River, which it follows up a narrowing valley to the river's head at 10,327-foot Sweetwater Gap. The Middle Fork Trail descends the gap's north side to Tayo Park, and an unmaintained trail cuts cross-country to Poison Lake.

Middle Fork Trail

Bruce Picnic Ground to Sweetwater Gap—16 miles

The classic though arduous route to Wind River Peak follows the Middle Popo Agie into the mountains, beginning where the Sinks Canyon–Louis Lake Road leaves the river. After 6.5 miles of uphill on the river's north side, the trail is joined by a shorter alternative coming from Worthen Meadow and crossing the river on Sheep Bridge. Just beyond, a trail branches right to Shoshone Lake, not covered in this guide. In Three Forks Park a trail branches right to Pinto Park, eventually reaching the North Popo Agie, while the Middle Fork Trail fords the river. You can head downstream on the south bank to Stough Creek, though not on a maintained trail as some maps indicate.

The Middle Fork Trail continues upsteam to Bill's Park, where the maintained Stough Creek Basin Trail diverges left, and to Tayo Park, a mile farther, where trails

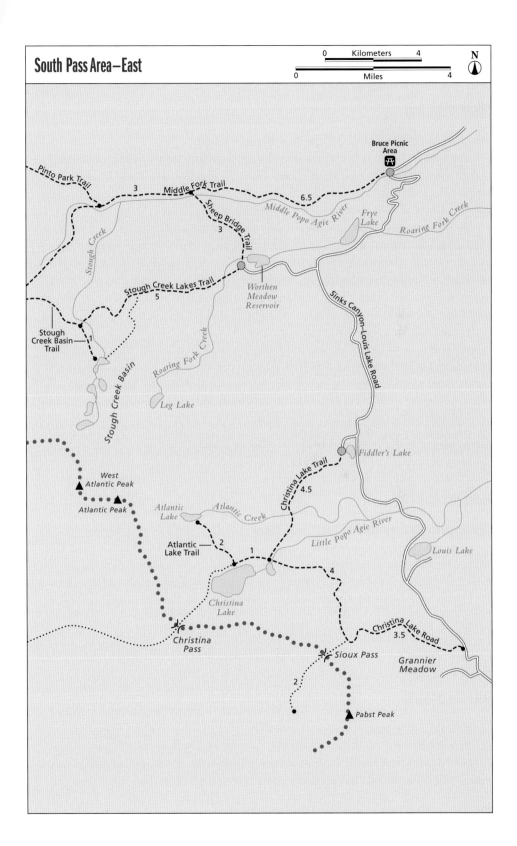

South Pass Area–East

0 Kilometers 4

0 Miles 4

N

Pinto Park Trail

3 Middle Fork Trail 6.5

Bruce Picnic Area

Stough Creek

Sheep Bridge Trail 3

Middle Popo Agie River

Frye Lake

Roaring Fork Creek

Stough Creek Lakes Trail 5

Worthen Meadow Reservoir

Sinks Canyon–Louis Lake Road

Stough Creek Basin Trail 1

Stough Creek Basin

Roaring Fork Creek

Leg Lake

West Atlantic Peak

Atlantic Peak

Christina Lake Trail 4.5

Fiddler's Lake

Atlantic Lake

Atlantic Creek

Little Popo Agie River

Louis Lake

Atlantic Lake Trail 2

1

4

Christina Lake

Christina Pass

Sioux Pass

Christina Lake Road 3.5

Grannier Meadow

2

Pabst Peak

diverge right to Tayo Creek and the Ice Lakes. The Middle Fork Trail ends at Sweetwater Gap, becoming the Sweetwater Gap Trail south of the pass.

Sheep Bridge Trail

Worthen Meadow to Middle Popo Agie River—3 miles

The Middle Popo Agie is a fine stream to walk beside, but the Middle Fork Trail makes a long, uphill route into the mountains. In the past you could shorten the hike by beginning at Frye Lake and joining the Middle Fork Trail at Sheep Bridge (approximately as shown on the Cony Mountain quad).

With the development of Worthen Meadow as a trailhead, a trail that postdates the Cony Mountain quad further shortens the hike, though without eliminating a 500-foot climb when you leave the mountains. After crossing the Roaring Fork just upstream from the reservoir, the Sheep Bridge Trail climbs the ridge to the north, where it meets the older trail. It then angles northwest and downhill to a junction, just before the Middle Fork, with the new Twin Lakes Trail.

These Twin Lakes are not those named on the Cony Mountain quad, but a pair of long ponds, southeast of Three Forks Park, that suggest an ancient alternate course for Stough Creek. The Twin Lakes Trail (see a recent Shoshone National Forest map) traverses the north shores of these ponds, crosses Stough Creek by logs downstream of its confluence with the west pond's outlet stream, and joins the Middle Fork Trail at its ford in Three Forks Park, at Benchmark 9027.

Sheep Bridge is now situated 0.5 mile east of its location on the Cony Mountain quad and most other maps. To reach it and the Middle Fork Trail from the Sheep Bridge Trail's junction with the Twin Lakes Trail, turn downstream.

Pinto Park Trail

Three Forks Park to Sanford Park—6.5 miles

This trail connects the Middle Popo Agie to the North Popo Agie, leaving the Middle Fork Trail in Three Forks Park, climbing steeply to a saddle southeast of Pinto Park, and dropping to Sanford Park and the North Fork Trail. South of Pinto Park the Deep Creek Cut-off splits left, and north of Pinto Park the trail intersects the Ice Lakes Trail.

The 3.5 miles from Three Forks Park to the Deep Creek Cut-off may be the range's dullest trail section, but Pinto Park offers an unusual perspective of the Cirque of the Towers.

Deep Creek Cut-off

Pinto Park Trail to Deep Creek Lakes—2 miles

To reach Deep Creek Lakes from the east—from Three Forks Park, e.g.—you needn't follow the Pinto Park Trail all the way to Pinto Park, then backtrack. A maintained trail, though not shown on the Sweetwater Gap quad, splits from the

Pinto Park Trail just north of inappropriately named Pinto Park Lake and heads south toward Lake 10,054, then follows Deep Creek upstream to meet the Ice Lake Trail at the northeastern Deep Creek Lake.

Ice Lakes Trail

Pinto Park to Tayo Park—7 miles

East of Wind River Peak are numerous lakes: Bear Lakes, Echo Lakes, Deep Creek Lakes, Ice Lakes. A trail that leaves the Pinto Park Trail just west of Pinto Park crosses this lake country. Although its northern end is shown on the Dickinson Park quad and its entire length on Forest Service, Earthwalk, and Beartooth maps, its major portion isn't shown on the Sweetwater Gap quad. It passes just west of the Bear Lakes (the pair a mile north of Deep Creek Lakes), between the Echo Lakes (the small pair just north of the northeastern Deep Creek Lake), just east of this Deep Creek Lake, and between various Ice Lakes. From the Ice Lakes it continues southeast through a 10,960-foot pass, crosses a second pass, and follows a creek to Tayo Park on the Middle Popo Agie, where the Middle Fork, Sweetwater Gap, and Tayo Creek Trails also converge.

Tayo Creek Trail

Tayo Park to Coon Lake—3.5 miles

Tayo Creek joins the Middle Popo Agie in Tayo Park, flowing from Wind River Peak's south slopes. By fording the Middle Popo Agie near the junction, you can reach a trail heading up Tayo Creek (as well as the Ice Lakes Trail). Above Poison Lake three forks meet. The southern comes from nearby Mountain Sheep Lake, the middle from Coon Lake, which sits on the Divide overlooking the Little Sandy valley, and the northern from Tayo Lake (10,783). The trail continues to Coon Lake; to reach Tayo Lake, ascend the west side, then the east side, of the northern fork.

Stough Creek Basin Trail

Bill's Park to Stough Creek Lakes—2.5 miles

Some maps indicate two trails from the Middle Popo Agie to Stough Creek Basin's many lakes. However, the trail shown descending the Middle Popo Agie from Three Forks Park, then following Stough Creek's west bank, isn't maintained and is hard to follow through swampy terrain. The maintained trail leaves the Middle Fork Trail at the upper end of Bill's Park and climbs east to Stough Creek. Cross Stough Creek by wading or on delicate logs, climb to a meeting with the Stough Creek Lakes Trail, entering from the east, cross a bridge, and continue upstream to the basin. The trail ends at the first large lake, but you can easily cross open country to the south to reach the higher lakes.

Stough Creek Lakes Trail

Worthen Meadow to Stough Creek—5 miles

From the Worthen Meadow trailhead parking area, backtrack down the road 100 yards to the beginning of this trail. Walk to Roaring Fork Lake on what was once a road. You must wade the lake's broad outlet (though bridges span even small creeks beyond). From the lake, head west through a pass in Roaring Fork Mountain, then descend to meet the Stough Creek Basin Trail a mile below the Stough Creek Lakes.

Stough Creek Lakes High Route

Roaring Fork Pass to Lake 10,484—2 miles

The Stough Creek Lakes Trail ascends the Roaring Fork drainage to a 10,520-foot pass at Roaring Fork Mountain East's north end, before winding down to Stough Creek. You can avoid this drop, as well as early summer snow and bogs, and gain views of Wind River Peak by leaving the trail at the pass and traversing Roaring Fork Mountain's slope. Part of the route follows the remnants of an old Indian trail.

Contour around Point 10,965's west side to the saddle to its south; a grassy bench above trees, below rubble, makes easy walking. From this saddle, angle slightly up to the tiny pass (with a huge cairn) just east of Point 11,120+; trail signs are sparse, but the pass is usually in sight. From the pass a line of cairns every 50 feet angles down for a mile to a few switchbacks north of Lake 10,484's eastern arm.

When leaving Stough Creek Basin, look for ambitious if ancient trail construction.

Christina Pass Trail (not maintained)

Sweetwater Guard Station to Christina Lake—7 miles

Shown on older maps but a victim of fire and neglect, this crossing of the range's crest doesn't afford relaxed backpacking.

Near the marker in a small meadow commemorating the Sweetwater Guard Station, wade the Sweetwater, aiming for a trail you can see angling left up the opposite bank. Follow this trail as best you can, paralleling Blair Creek on a ridge to the north, then crossing the creek and heading toward the 10,720-foot pass. Descend to Christina Lake's north shore, where you eventually meet the Atlantic Lake Trail.

Christina Lake Trail

Fiddler's Lake to Christina Lake—4.5 miles

This trail no longer begins at the campground on Fiddler's Lake's west shore, as shown on the Cony Mountain quad and some Forest Service maps, but at a newer trailhead on the Sinks Canyon–Louis Lake Road just south of the lake. The trail crosses Silas Creek (near which a trail leads to Silas Canyon) and Atlantic Creek (which can be a robust wade in early summer) before reaching the Little Popo Agie, where it joins the Christina Lake Road.

The trail that maps show reaching the Christina Lake Road from Louis Lake seems to have disappeared.

Christina Lake Road

Grannier Meadow to Christina Lake—8 miles

An old jeep road leaves the Sinks Canyon–Louis Lake Road at Grannier Meadow's southeast end, skirts the meadow, and goes to Christina Lake. The Christina Lake Trail is shorter, but the road is useful for reaching the Sioux Pass Trail, which branches south just north of Granite Peak.

The first 0.5 mile is passable for two-wheel-drive vehicles, but the road then becomes rougher. The orderly first few miles are pleasant walking through a transition from desert to mountain, but as the road enters timber, it degenerates to a multitude of braided tracks squeezing between any trees that an unconscionable driver can fit an unimaginable vehicle between, often apparently to avoid puddles in the original road. The quantity of roadside trash and ruts scarring meadows make you appreciate the Wilderness status of the mountains to the north.

Atlantic Lake Trail

Christina Lake to Atlantic Lake—2 miles

From Christina Lake's outlet, hike along the north shore, looking for a sign after 0.5 mile that identifies this trail amid sundry vehicular ruts. The trail, easier to follow than its start is to locate, leads to Atlantic Lake, which is far more pristine than Christina Lake.

You can also reach Atlantic Lake from the Christina Lake Trail by leaving the trail in the meadow north of its crossing of Atlantic Creek and following a path north of the creek.

Sioux Pass Trail (not maintained)

Christina Lake Road to East Sweetwater River—2 miles

The Christina Lake quad gives clues to the location of this trail, which is more trod by elk than boots, but shouldn't be taken literally; meadows seem to have migrated. Ancient blazes and faded pink ribbons help, but red diamonds marking a snowmobile route are sometimes misleading.

From a signpost on the Christina Lake Road, follow vehicle tracks toward a diversion ditch, parallel the ditch, then (contrary to the map) skirt a meadow's east edge, passing a ruined cabin. Near a second ruined cabin, cross the ditch, and the going is easy to Sioux Pass. This pass is less a well-defined notch than a sequence of capriciously sloping meadows; the trail crosses the west edge of the westernmost meadow.

The trail barely exists south of Sioux Pass, but it is worth locating fragments high to the east of the river. The trail theoretically joins other trails after 2 miles, but this occurs in wilderness of a different sort than Congress creates.

Peaks

Divide Plateau (12,105)

The *Dictionary of Geological Terms* defines *biscuit-board topography* as "topography characterized by a rolling upland out of which cirques have been cut like big bites, and which represents an early or partial stage in glaciation." For 4 miles from Big Sandy Mountain to Little El Capitan, such topography constitutes the Continental Divide. Geologists were inspired by numerous semicircular cirques carved into the plateau's north side by waters of the North Popo Agie, and on its east side by Deep Creek, to call it the Biscuit Board. However, they have also applied the name to upland in the Roaring Fork–Silas Canyon area, and the name has never taken with climbers.

Also according to the dictionary: "By long continued erosion a land surface may be reduced to an almost level plain, but there may still be a few hills, which, having as yet escaped final destruction, rise conspicuously above the plain These are monadnocks." A few monadnocks rise between Big Sandy Mountain and Little El Capitan, the largest of which are Points 12,036 and 12,105.

1. Point 12,036, from the northeast (I 2nd class) The northern monadnock is pleasantly gained from the North Popo Agie via the shallow drainage east of Point 11,169 and west of Long Lake.

2. Point 11,169, Northwest Face (IV 5.7/5.8) Two cirques down the North Popo Agie (that is, east) from the Monolith's cirque, just west of Long Lake, is another cirque with impressive walls. The first wall on the left as you enter the cirque has been climbed.

Climb the depressions, corners, and chimneys that form a continuous system near the wall's center. The last three pitches are in deep chimneys leading directly to the top.

It seems that this cirque was long ago named Cirque of the Moon and several routes were done but not publicized until recently. Check online.

3. Point 12,036, from the northwest (I 2nd class) You can reach the plateau from the next cirque down the North Popo Agie from the Monolith (between Points 11,320 and 11,759).

4. Point 12,105, West Ridge (I 3rd class) Talus above Black Joe Lake reaches the plateau. Point 12,105 is just jagged enough to require routefinding.

5. Point 11,524, from the east (I 2nd class) From the Deep Creek Lakes. Stunted-conifer thickets, called krummholz, develop above treeline; winter snow protects the shrublike trees, while wind-blown ice trims growth above the snow. Krummholz can be impenetrable, and extensive colonies covering the slope are the primary routefinding determinant.

Point 11,524 can be reached from the messy north shore of Deep Creek Lake 10,577, via the saddle 0.5 mile to its west.

Little El Capitan (12,825)

Homesick Californians looking east from Haystack and Steeple have seen a rounded summit with steep sides and been reminded of Yosemite's greatest rock. For those unfamiliar with Yosemite, Little El Capitan is the formation 0.5 mile north-northwest of Wind River Peak and separated from it by a sharp notch; it is a rise at the south end of the Divide Plateau.

1. Northeast Slope (I 2nd class) A ridge rises to the plateau from Deep Creek Lakes, and you can reach Little El Cap from elsewhere on the Divide Plateau.

2. West Gully (I 4th class) The gully at the left edge of the west face provides a route from the upper Black Joe Lake valley. The only difficulties occur in the first 50 feet.

3. West Face (III 5.8) The name Little El Capitan suggests an array of big-wall routes, but the rock lacks the larger El Cap's crack systems. However, a route ascends slabs at the bottom of the west face, then follows the obvious diagonal ledge, which isn't all easy walking.

4. Southeast Face (V 5.10 A2) A Yosemite-like wall also overlooks the snow-filled cirque at the head of Deep Creek. The route that ascends this wall features off-width cracks. The final lead involves bolts next to an overhanging off-width and free climbing through the three-tiered visor.

Wind River Peak (13,192)

Climbers typically see Wind River Peak during midsummer, when it is bare of snow and a scarcely noticed backdrop to more interesting peaks; that it is the highest summit in the range's southern half doesn't explain a rounded hump sharing the name of the entire range. But during spring it looms as a great snowy dome, and you can imagine how it appeared, during the cooler summers of the 1840s, to emigrants on the Oregon Trail struggling to get their wagons up the Sweetwater and across South Pass. To these pioneers, marking their progress by the approach of the mountains, it must have been *the* Wind River Peak and one of the memorable sights on an unforgettable journey.

But however magnificent Wind River Peak looked a century ago, its appeal to modern climbers is limited, and reaching its slopes is more of an adventure than most climbs of it.

1. South Slope (I 2nd class) The simplest approach to the broad summit slope is from Tayo Lake or the next valley to the east. You can also reach the slope from Bill's Park, by climbing west near a small stream, then working along a ridge, or from Little Sandy Creek, by climbing talus to Coon Lake on the Divide, then continuing to Tayo Lake.

2. Ice Lakes Wall (III 5.9) Above Ice Lake 10,760+ (the lake nearest "ICE" on the Sweetwater Gap, Earthwalk, and Beartooth maps) is a broad rhombic wall conspicuous from points southeast. Uphill to the left from this steep cliff's low point is a continuous crack-and-chimney system. The route begins in this system, but as the chimney becomes increasingly deeper, looser, and icier, pitches 2 to 5 wander up cleaner rock to the right. The sixth pitch begins with an unlikely traverse out left from the chimney, while the formidable final lead avoids the inhospitable top of another chimney with a harrowing path through the overhangs that cap the wall.

3. Northeast Ridge (I 2nd class) On Wind River Peak's north shoulder is a minor summit inexplicably called Chimney Rock. The name is a source of confusion, for a more appropriately named Chimney Rock is attached to Horse Ridge. The name is an old one, used as early as 1873 by three men who visited the Wind Rivers while surveying for a wagon road and climbed the Chimney Rock "at the head of the Middle Fork of the Popo Agie."

A broad ridge rises from the Ice Lakes Trail to Chimney Rock, separating the Ice Lakes and Deep Creek Lakes cirques. The ridge provides an easy route to Chimney Rock, with the main peak a short scramble beyond.

4. Chimney Rock, North Face–Streaked Wall (V 5.9 A3) Above the Deep Creek Lakes is a high, snow-filled, rarely visited cirque. A fourteen-pitch route follows a diagonal dike up the rounded formation north of Chimney Rock. The climb required two long days and twenty-five points of aid. With a surfeit of horizontal ledges and a shortage of cracks, you can reinvent your route from each ledge but must worry about the ledges if you fall.

5. Chimney Rock, North Face–Tempest Tower (IV 5.10a A2) A deep couloir separates *Streaked Wall* from a narrower formation to the right—*Tempest Tower*. The ten pitches on this wall involve predominantly good crack climbing, with four pitches of 5.10 and three hanging belays. The first pitch includes a shallow, grassy groove. The only aid is used on the second pitch to pass a two-tiered roof to a prominent crack that splits a golden prow. Small cams and copperheads are useful in the bottoming crack. Higher, as the crack widens, climbing becomes easier.

6. North Buttress (II 5.7) From the valley above Black Joe Lake, climb a chute to the notch between Wind River Peak and Little El Capitan. From the notch you can reach the upper slopes in three pitches. The third pitch follows a right-slanting crack just right of the buttress's crest. The rock is of mediocre quality.

7. West Gully (I 3rd class) A single gully breaks the west face. While not pretty, it makes Wind River Peak accessible from the Black Joe valley.

8. Black Joe–Little Sandy Divide (II 5.6) On the ridge between Wind River Peak and East Temple are six minor summits, which have been traversed from east to west. The summit nearest Wind River Peak is 3rd class; the others are medium 5th class. You can approach from either the Black Joe side or the Little Sandy side.

Continental Towers (12,088)

On the Divide 1.2 miles south of Wind River Peak stands a cluster of towers. From Little Sandy valley there appear to be three, but the North Tower is actually the prow of a fin—albeit impressive looking and perhaps the hardest to reach, with a garish, overhanging block as its high point. Point 12,088 is the Central Tower.

From the Little Sandy valley you can easily reach the Divide south of the South Tower by scree slopes next to a black dike. However, traversing under the towers on the east doesn't appear feasible, and there is no obviously easy approach from Lake 11,145, at the head of Tayo Creek.

1. North Tower, Southwest Buttress–North Ridge–Aristeia (III 5.9) The lower two-thirds of the west face consists of bands of gray, down-sloping slabs. These may be passed by 3rd-class scrambling to the north, to ledges below the steep, golden upper headwall. Begin serious climbing near the intersection of the west and south faces with a flake that leads to a short 5.8 dihedral, which leads to a sloping ledge. The second pitch is a long, easy traverse left, with a short 5.5 dihedral, to a large ledge that cuts across all three towers. Follow the ledge to where it peters out, then traverse easily to its reemergence farther left. Continue along the ledge to an obvious orange right-facing dihedral, which leads (5.5) to the fin's crest.

Three pitches follow the spectacular knife-edge crest, sometimes a cheval, sometimes using the crest itself for handholds. After nearly a rope length, drop down on the west side for an awkward 5.9 move onto an 18-inch ledge, which can be crawled. The next pitch ends at an exposed but comfortable ledge on the crest's east side. The final,

Continental Towers

5.7 pitch ascends the right of the two dihedrals reaching the crest from the ledge's south end and follows the crest to a stance below the summit splinters.

The first ascent team suggests a few thin pitons and a few small angles. *Aristeia,* in *The Iliad,* is one's greatest moment in battle.

North Tower Descent: Single-rope rappels from a horn and then a chockstone to the large ledge. A final rappel and tricky downclimbing take you to the ledges below the headwall.

2. Central Tower, North Ridge (II 5.8) Scramble up the gully northwest of the tower for many hundred feet of precarious rubble, occasional 4th-class moves, and one distinctly 5th-class 20-foot chimney, to the notch north of the tower. From the notch, gain the ridge's first step via blocks right (west) of the crest. Walk along a flat section of crest for 100 feet, then climb steep cracks right of the crest to a belay. Aim left to a 20-foot flared groove (the crux), then continue alternately left and up. Parallel the crest, below it to the east, then climb to the summit.

3. Central Tower, East Chimney (III 5.7 A2) Many 4th- and 5th-class pitches in a chimney system that slants up under the east face lead to the notch south of the tower. The three pitches above the notch involve sustained climbing and include a short aid section.

2, 3 Descent: Climb down the *North Ridge*'s pitch 4. Make a long rappel down pitch 3 and the top of pitch 2 to the first step. From the top of pitch 1, another long rappel takes you into the evil gully below its tricky top. Rappel the 20-foot chimney.

Alternatively, you can rappel the *East Chimney.*

4. South Tower, Northwest Arête (III 5.8) Seen from the Little Sandy, this is the tower's attractive left edge. Reach its base by scrambling up slabs for a few hundred feet. After roping up, climb the crest to a short headwall, climb the headwall, angle up right on a ramp, and work back left to a big ledge (5.6). Climb 20 feet, step left to the arête's north-facing side, and follow discontinuous cracks through blocks to an even larger ledge (5.5).

A shallow left-facing dihedral rises the height of the 120-foot wall above. To the left of its upper part is another system, which becomes a chimney behind a tiny pinnacle. Right of its upper part is another left-facing corner. Follow the main dihedral until you can avoid a difficult section by stepping to the left system, and finish the 5.8 pitch in the right corner. Wander up from ledge to ledge, using short cracks; only one move being as difficult as 5.7. A short, easy pitch reaches the boulder-strewn shoulder that forms the arête's top.

Walk to the southwest base of the summit tower. (You can avoid the arête's five pitches by scrambling to this point from the slope to the south.) Eighty feet up and left is a pair of broad ledges, visible from afar. Alternately climb up and traverse to these ledges (5.3). From the higher ledge, ascend a 30-foot wall and traverse right to a 10-foot chimney with an ancient piton at its base; from the chimney's top, move left and up, passing left around two large flake/blocks, before making final steep moves to the summit slab (5.7).

5. South Tower, West Face–Continental Drifters (IV 5.11a) *Continental Drifters* begins a few hundred feet right of the *Northwest Arête* but joins that route after five pitches. However, at the shoulder the routes diverge again, *Continental Drifters* reaching the summit from the southeast.

Pitch 1: Wander up a slab to a right-facing corner and climb it to a small ledge out right (5.8). Pitch 2: Leave the corner for a nicer crack to the left. Where the crack ends, move back right to the right-facing corner and continue to a stance beneath a downward-pointing flake (5.8). Pitch 3: Follow face holds up left, aiming for the central of three right-facing corners. Climb the corner to a roof that is turned to the right. Continue up cracks in a chimney to a ledge below a large corner (5.10a). Pitch 4: Reach to a knob, then face climb. Traverse left to a right-facing corner, eventually reaching a horizontal break. From the break's left end, follow a steep splitter crack. Continue to a ledge below a right-facing wall with parallel cracks (5.11a). Pitch 5: Continue up the double cracks to their end and climb a short crack to a talus ledge (5.8), where *Continental Drifters* meets the *Northwest Arête*.

The 240-foot, 5.10- pitch to the summit involves varied climbing up cracks and corners. With a rope less than 70 meters long, you can conveniently belay near the top.

4, 5 Descent: The summit tower can be rappelled by either route to the big shoulder. To descend the *Northwest Arête's* upper section, rappel 150 feet from the summit slabs to the ledges below the last pitch, then 80 feet to the shoulder; walk off to the south. With 70-meter ropes *Continental Drifters* can be descended to the shoulder in one rappel.

Little Sandy Formations (11,720+)

Northwest of Little Sandy Lake, a low ridge separates the Little Sandy's main valley from a parallel valley to its west, obscuring steep formations that bound the side valley. The northern formation has the biggest wall; a cluster of pinnacles stands between it and Point 11,427, the profile of which is visible from far to the south. Point 11,427 has been named Little Sandy Buttress, but the higher main formation remains unnamed.

1. Little Sandy Buttress, South Ridge (I 2nd class) Forested terrain leads up from Little Sandy Lake, the crest being easier walking than the west slope.

2. Little Sandy Buttress, East Face (III 5.8 A3) This face could be called the Wall of Forgetfulness. Fred Beckey and Bob Stevenson climbed a Little Sandy Lake Buttress, but neither's memory was stirred by photos; the buttress's identification is based largely on Beckey's comment in the *AAJ* that from the South Pass road "the profile of a sharp buttress stands out clearly." Stevenson wrote, "Beckey and I started up before sunrise and descended after sunset, and walked to Sweetwater Guard Station by moonlight. In classic Beckey style, we were in Jackson at 10 a.m. the next morning, where Beckey soon located another climbing partner and headed out for another climb somewhere. I have been back to this area several times, and I'm still not sure what we climbed."

About all that is known of the route is that several hundred feet of scrambling lead to 1,000 feet of roped climbing; that the hardest pitches are 6 and 7, which follow cracks and chimneys left of a nose; and that five bolts were placed. A dihedral two-thirds of the way toward the face's right side appears likely to be part of the route.

3. King Cone, West Face (I 5.7) The cluster of pinnacles between the two main formations has been likened to a "little Patagonia"—emphasis on *little*. King Cone is the eastern of the two 11,320+-foot towers and the most conspicuous of the cluster. Its west face has been reached by descending from the rim to the notch at the base of the face. Two crack systems rise from the notch; climb the harder right one. The first pitch (5.7) involves wide cracks and flakes. The second and final pitch is blocky and minimally 5th class.

4. King Cone, Northeast Ridge (II 5.7) Scramble for a few hundred feet on the left side of the ridge, then climb four or five fun pitches.

3, 4 Descent: Downclimb the west face's easier system to the left of the route's first pitch.

5. Western Tower 11,320+, West Ridge (I 5.3) One pitch.

6. Tower 11,440+, West Face (I 5.6) Tower 11,440+ is the highest and north-western of the cluster. The western of its two summits is the high point. Approach from the valley below by the unpleasant scree gully leading to the notch behind the tower. Begin the contrived but pleasant *West Face* route by climbing a 160-foot 5.4 pitch on the arête that from the approach gully appears to be the tower itself; there is a 30-foot pinnacle on its west edge. Downclimb from the top of the arête, walk to the main summit's west face and climb a 5.6 pitch.

Descent: Downclimb the tower's easier east side. From the tower's eastern summit, it is a walk to and from the rim.

7. East Face–Gold Dihedrals (IV 5.9) One of the range's best walls is tucked away in an unlikely place, south of alpine peaks, hidden even from most of the Little Sandy valley. Where the wall is biggest—where its base is lowest—is an assortment of corners and cracks; several nearby corners sweep up from ledges and ramps just off the ground. One corner, with a ceiling a few pitches up, ends at a ledge a few hundred feet from the top. However, the next corner right continues nearly to the top, and the route follows it to the level of the ledge atop the left corner, then heads up left.

8. East Face–Symbiosis (III/IV 5.10-) Another highly recommended route follows the gray dihedrals 100 feet right of the previous route's gold dihedrals. Begin with a 5.7 chimney to the right end of a ledge. The second pitch uses a 5.8 hand crack to reach a ledge with a leaning block. The third pitch involves 5.9+ stemming. Begin the fourth pitch in a 5.9 slot, continue to a 5.10- undercling, and finish with a 5.10- finger crack to a grassy ledge. The fifth pitch continues up the dihedral (5.10-) to a large flake. Complete the route with 300 to 400 feet of thin, shallow cracks (5.7/5.8).

7, 8 Descent: A snow slope, just north of the east face makes a handy descent route.

Mount Nystrom (12,356)

This otherwise unnoteworthy summit is the point at which the Continental Divide parts company with the Wind River crest. That is, by dividing the waters of the Little Sandy, Sweetwater, and Popo Agie, it divides the Colorado, Yellowstone, and Platte. Conspicuous from South Pass, Nystrom is also one of the more complex Wind River massifs in terms of subsidiary summits and sprawl. The multiplicity of summits and climbers' discovery of the cirque cut into the massif's east side necessitates an agreement on names: Point 12,004 is the Northeast Summit; Point 12,027, the Southeast Summit; Point 12,248, the South Summit; and Point 12,122, the North Summit.

1. Northwest Slope (I 2nd class) A walk-up from Tayo Creek's south branch, between Mountain Sheep and Coon Lakes. You can also work south and west from the head of Mountain Sheep Lake, though this is more difficult.

2. West Face of Northwest Ridge (III 5.7/5.8) Two miles north of Little Sandy Lake, just south of Coon Lake and the low point between Nystrom and Wind River Peak, are 800-foot walls facing the Little Sandy's valley. This route begins at the highest island of trees, stays near the face's center, and aims for the corner near the top. The corner, however, is loose; bypass it to the left. This is a first ascent member's assessment: "Some day this climb may be of interest to someone. I doubt it."

3. South Slope (I 2nd or 3rd class) From either the Little Sandy Trail or the Sweetwater Gap Trail.

4. Southeast Summit–Anvil Arête (III 5.8) A half mile downstream from Lake 10,624 is a tiny lake, south of which rise a number of arêtes. An eight-pitch route ascends the arête that can be recognized from the vicinity of Lake 10,624 as the right-most one crossed by a snow gully (hidden from below) and by an anvil-shaped formation high on its crest.

Approach from just upstream of the tiny lake. Begin climbing between two conspicuously orange pillars, in a crack that leads to a right-arching corner. After three pitches, which include most of the route's difficulties, reach a left-rising ridge that borders the snow gully. Cross the gully and follow the arête's prow.

5. Northeast Summit, South Face (I 5.7) Above Lake 10,624 hundreds of feet of scrambling lead to a 200-foot cliff band, which appears climbable by a number of enjoyable short routes. Fred Beckey, who called the world's attention to this cirque, didn't pinpoint a precise line, only "a fine route on cracks and steep slab." A route taken by others ascends right of a flaky orange pillar, left of a prominent left-facing corner, for a pitch and a fraction. Pleasant 3rd-class scrambling above leads to the crest, or you can rappel and climb a number of lines.

6. Northeast Summit, Southeast Buttress (III 5.9) Approach from Lake 10,624's grassy valley. Climb cracks and ramps on the reddish lower face to reach the crest. Move through a notch to the more improbable-looking upper face. Zigzag up steep rock near the buttress's airy south edge; chickenheads make the going feasible.

Roaring Fork Mountain West (12,239)

Maps show two Roaring Fork Mountains, one the ridge west of Stough Creek Basin, between the basin and Sweetwater Gap, and the other the ridge across the basin to the east, separating Stough Creek from the Roaring Fork itself. This redundancy must be a mistake, but topographic maps are considered correct by definition, so this guide uses USGS nomenclature, though the western Roaring Fork Mountain is logically a misnomer.

1. From Upper Stough Creek Basin (I 2nd class) From Stough Creek Lake 10,902, gain the main crest by scrambling up slopes west of Point 11,587. Then follow the crest west, passing a few false summits.

2. Via Stough Creek Pinnacle (II 5.4/5.5 + rappel) One of Stough Creek Basin's most notable formations is the pinnacle jutting from the wall above Lake 10,902. Climb the pinnacle in four pitches on its northeast ridge. From its summit, rappel to the notch behind and climb one pitch to Roaring Fork Mountain's upper slopes.

3. From Lower Stough Creek Basin (I 2nd or 3rd class) Begin from the lakes just north of Stough Creek Pinnacle and reach the plateau near Point 11,804.

Roaring Fork Mountain East (11,960)

This is the Cony Mountain quad's Roaring Fork Mountain.

1. West Slope (I 2nd class) From Stough Creek Lake 10,528 gain the prominent saddle under the "F" in the map's "FORK." Then identify the plateau's high point.

2. Giant's Bite–Big Red Buttress (III 5.9) That the Wind Rivers are less known than their neighbors the Tetons can be attributed in part to their being hard to see from civilization; scenic turnouts on Jackson Hole highways give even car-bound tourists an intimate view of the Tetons. Nevertheless, Lander's dump offers a good view that includes 800-foot northeast-facing cliffs that hover over the small cirque of Leg Lake. These cliffs are split by a snow couloir and bordered on the south by a jagged arête.

Big Red Buttress stands just right of a prominent snow couloir. Climb it in seven pitches by starting and finishing in cracks right of center. Pitches 3 and 4 ascend a steep, excellent 5.8 wall.

West Atlantic Peak (12,430)

This is the high rubble heap forming the east side of the upper Sweetwater's valley. Its north ridge rises from Stough Creek Basin, while its east ridge is joined to Atlantic Peak.

1. North Ridge (I 2nd class) From Stough Creek Basin, ascend the slope west of Point 11,587 to the crest between West Atlantic and Roaring Fork Mountain West, then follow the crest south for 0.5 mile.

2. South Ridge (I 2nd class) Leave the Christina Lake Trail and ascend the wooded ridge, just west of Blair Creek and its left fork, that leads to Pond 9,590. Continue up the left fork to the saddle between West Atlantic and Atlantic.

3. West Slope (I 2nd class) Hayden Survey members reported climbing the peak in 1877 from Sweetwater Gap. The easiest route involves leaving the trail 2 miles south of the pass and following a stream to its head at a saddle north of the peak.

Atlantic Peak (12,490)

As the last 12,000-foot summit at the range's south end, this peak attracted the Hayden Survey's attention; they named it apparently with reference to its being entirely in the Atlantic watershed.

1. Southeast Slope (I 2nd class) From Atlantic Lake, gaining the crest south of Point 12,261.

2. South Slope (I 2nd class) From the Christina Lake Trail, head up the forested ridge, just west of Blair Creek and its left fork, that leads to Pond 9,590. Continue up the left fork but bear right near the crest.

Silas Peak (12,248)

The windy tabletop separating Silas and Atlantic Canyons culminates in an isolated summit 1.2 miles northeast of Atlantic Peak and between the cirques at the heads of the canyons; cliffs to the west fall to Stough Creek Basin.

1. Southeast Ridge (I 2nd class) From either Atlantic Lake or lower Silas Canyon.

2. Silas Canyon Headwall–Twenty-Year Crack (II 5.8) This route ascends the most obvious dihedral in the steep 500-foot wall above the highest lake in Silas Canyon. Start up the wall 50 feet left of the main dihedral by scrambling for 120 feet. Then climb an easy roped pitch to the obvious crux pitch, a tight chimney. The final lead is the Veggie Pitch.

An ice axe may be desirable on the approach snowfield. Bring a 4-inch cam for the tight chimney.

3. Northeast Ridge (I 2nd class) From upper Silas Canyon. The mitten-shaped lake slightly below 11,000 feet is Thumb Lake.

Cony Mountain (11,109)

1. Southeast Slope (I 2nd class) A four-wheel-drive road, not shown on maps, follows the crest of Blue Ridge.

Pabst Peak (10,261)

The Wind Rivers end not with a bang but a whimper—three wooded peaks near South Pass. Granite once sported a lookout tower and Rennecker has also been climbed, but only Pabst has a history. The Titcomb brothers climbed it in 1901, and when, upon returning to South Pass City, they mentioned drinking a bottle of Pabst on top, the peak was named. The bottle was found in 1972, though we don't know whether the peak's rare visitors between 1901 and 1972 left it respecting an artifact or accepting litter as part of the scenery.

The terrain surrounding Granite, Pabst, and Rennecker is unlike the higher Wind Rivers, but the open sagebrush slopes and aspen groves make pleasant traveling. Pabst's summit is rockier than a distant view suggests.

1. East Slope (I 2nd class) There are more fences between South Pass City and Pabst Peak than in 1901, but you can drive closer. Turn from the Sinks Canyon–Louis Lake Road at Benchmark 8920, just south of Little Rock Creek, 4 miles from both Louis Lake and WY 28. Drive (or walk) on FR 309, bearing right at a junction after 1.5 miles and following red diamond markers past a big meadow. The road ends after another 0.5 mile, but a trail continues, marked by a surfeit of blazed trees, to Willow Creek. Either climb toward the Pabst-Granite col or ascend Pabst's slopes directly.

Appendix A: First Ascents

Listed here are the earliest ascents reported in journals, summit registers, or correspondence. Enough Wind River climbers are indifferent to fame, though, that this list undoubtedly misses unreported earlier ascents. Teams believing they are making a peak's first ascent often find evidence of prior visitors on top; teams thinking they are first on a route invariably, it seems, find fixed nuts. FA stands for first ascent, FFA for first free ascent, and des for descended.

Ross Lakes

Union Peak. Orestes St. John and probably Frederick Clark, Nelson Perry, and Mr. Wells, 1878.

Ram Flat. Bighorn Towers: Andy Carson and others, ca 1980. E Couloir: Finis Mitchell, 1961. Crystal Lake Couloir: Chuck Satterfield, E. Park, M. Stephens, and C. Zukowski, 1971. S Ridge: Chris Goetze and Brian Underhill, 1960.

The Guardian. S Slope: des by Chris Goetze and Brian Underhill. W Ridge: Chris Goetze and Brian Underhill, 1960. Machete Eddy: Mark Jolliff and two others.

Rundblick. N Face: Chris Goetze and Brian Underhill, 1960. W Ridge: des by Goetze and Underhill.

Jeralee Peak. E Ridge: Chris Goetze and Brian Underhill, 1960. SW Ridge: des by Goetze and Underhill.

Ross Mountain. E Ridge: Chris Goetze and Brian Underhill, 1960. SW Ridge: des by Goetze and Underhill.

Gjetetind. S Ridge: des by Chris Goetze and Brian Underhill. NE Ridge: Goetze and Underhill, 1960.

Northwest Peak. Finis Mitchell, 1961.

Downs Mountain. Surveyors, early 1900s. Cowboy Classic: Bill Daniel, Maurice Horn, and Walter Siebert, 1992. N Couloir: Pete Absolon, Dirk Kramer, Duane Mortenson, and Chris Page. N Ridge: Chris Goetze and Brian Underhill, 1960. S Ridge: Roger Beck and Gibson Reynolds, 1946.

Middle Mountain. Lake Louise Gully: George Van Sickle and Tom Walter, 1984. Golden Tears: Michael Bailey, Greg Collins, and George Van Sickle, 1984. Cony Spires: Andy Carson and others, ca 1980.

Torrey Peak. SW Ridge: Chris Goetze and Brian Underhill, 1960. Bombast: Bill Daniel, Maurice Horn, and Walter Siebert, 1992.

Spider Peak. N Ridge: Dave Dornan and Maurice Horn, 1960. SW Ridge: Vince Lee, Dennis Pierce, Terry Sawyer, and Tom Wolff, 1972. SE Face: Tom Warren and others, 1975. E Buttress: Fred Beckey, Alex Bertulis, and Jerry Fuller, 1964. NE Buttress: Beckey, Steve Jackson, and Brian Leo, 1975. NE Face: Randy Cerf, Herbie Ogden, and George Schunk, 1978.

Peak 11,760+. SE Face: Fred and Stephanie Jacquot, James Keeley, and Charles Mangus.

Goat Flat. Wedge: Fred Beckey and Cam Burns, 1997. From Bomber Lake: Vince Lee and others. From Golden Lake: Jim Halfpenny, Ed Poznanski, and David Ravert, 1970.

Down Lake Towers. N Rib: Tom Warren and others, 1975. S Couloir: des by Warren.

Bear's Tooth. W Ridge: des by Robert Parker and Don Winterbourne. S Face: Tom Warren and others, 1975. SE Arête: Fred Beckey and Reed Tindall, 1985. Orange Wall: Warren and others, 1975. First Ascent Route: Parker and Winterbourne, 1946.

Point 11,836. N Face: D. Grady and two others.

Yukon Peak. SE Ridge: des by Finis Mitchell. NE Ridge: Mitchell, 1961.

Klondike Peak. Bill Kerns and Finis Mitchell, 1961.

Pedestal Peak. S Ridge: Bob Held and Sam Streibert, 1961; des by Phil, Phil Jr., and Rodney Smith; asc by Bob Held and Sam Streibert, 1961. SE Face: Smiths, 1946. E Ridge: John Reed and others, 1960.

Flagstone Peak. SE Ridge: des by John Reed and others, 1960. E Face: Bob Held and Sam Streibert, 1961. NE Face: des By Phil, Phil Jr., and Rodney Smith. N Ridge: Smiths, 1946.

Peak 13,160+. NE Ridge: Bob Held and Sam Streibert, 1961. N Face: des by Held and Streibert.

Philsmith Peak. N Rib: Bob Held and Sam Streibert, 1961.

Green River

Kendall Mountain. Finis Mitchell, 1920. North Ridge: Dick DuMais and Chuck Schaap, 1983. Candle, South Side: Paul Horton and Norm Larson, 1994. Candle, Light in the Forest: Jack Clinton and Larson, 1998.

Peak 11,120+. W Ridge: Gary Edmunds and Paul Horton, 1985. S Face: Paul Horton and Heather Paul, 2001.

Peak 11,080+. Client's Corner: Greg Fulkerson and Paul Horton, 1997.

Owl's Head. No-Name Has-Beens: Jack Clinton and Norm Larson, 2002. N Buttress: Andy Carson and Paul Horton, 2002. July: Ryan Hokanson and Horton, 1996. June: Horton and Larson, 2000. South Wing L: Horton and Heather Paul, 2001. South Wing Center: Clinton and Larson, 2002. South Wing R: Clinton and Larson, 2001.

Osborn Mountain. Verloren: Kirk Billings and Mark Jenkins, 1998.

Twenty-Hour Tower. Alexander's Band: Oliver Deshler and Mark Jenkins, 2009. You Gotta Want It: Deshler and Jenkins, 2009. S Face R: Paul Horton and Sean O'Malley, 1997.

Forlorn Pinnacle. N Ridge: Paul Horton and Peter Thorne, 1998. Fickle Finger, S Face L: Chuck Schaap and Bob Stevenson, 1971. Fickle Finger, S Face R: Dick DuMais and Joe Kelsey, 1974.

Flat Top Mountain. Finis Mitchell, 1962. Trundler: Oliver Deshler and Mark Jenkins, 2009.

White Rock. There are obsidian chippings near the top.

Lost Eagle Pinnacle. Charles Bergenson, before 1933. W Face: Dave Eland, Maurice Horn, Joe Larson, Pat Paddon, and Bob Stevenson, 1971. NW Face: Patrick Fleming and Mark Jenkins, 2007.

Squaretop Mountain. SE Ledges: William Stroud, before 1921. Squaretower L: Andy and Dan Carson, 1998. Marginally Orange: Norm Goltra and Steve Walker: 2009. AC/DC: Carsons, 1999. SE Face: Vince Lee, E. Park, M. Stephens, and C. Zukowski, 1971. E Face L: Renato Casarotto and Jeff Lowe, 1984; Douglas Abromeit and Doug Colwell, 1990. Miscreant and Conveyor Belt: Tod Anderson, Skyler Crane, James Donnell, and Ernest Moskovics, 2001. E Face Center: Bill Byrd, Dave Dingman, and Roland Wyatt, 1958. E Face R: Fred Beckey and Jerry Fuller, 1965. N Buttress: Ed Cooper and Ron Niccoli, 1960. NW Chimney: Beckey and Layton Kor, 1961. W Face Dihedral: Kent Christensen, Greg Lowe, and Jeff Lowe, 1974. FFA Ron Matous, ca 1981. W Face R: Scott Cole and John Malken, 1992. W Couloir: Vince Lee, Bo Beckham, and Greg Smith, 1972. W Gully: H. H. Bliss, 1937.

The Bottle. S Face: Vince Lee, Polly Bennett, Gail Iler, and Dianne Riggs, 1974. E Face: Fred Beckey and Tom Nephew, 1971.

Tabletop. Shan Tower: Dave Beckstead and Bill Nicolai, 1971. Sail Pinnacle: John Gottman and Hal Gribble, 1978. Cirque S of Shan: Beckstead and Nicolai, 1971. Point 11,530: Beckstead and Nicolai.

Peak 11,820. C. L. Baker, before 1946.

Green River Pyramid. Fred Beckey, Carl Horton, and Shawn Mitchell, 1986.

Pixley-Tourist Divide. Dana Densmore, Bart DeWolf, and Beth Ruskin, 1972.

Mount Solitude. SE Couloir: Walter Hermann, Richard Judy, Gerald Marsden, Dave Sanderson, and David Spencer, 1965. E Ridge: Dana Densmore and Bart DeWolf, 1972. NW Couloir: des by Densmore and DeWolf.

Desolation Peak. NW Ridge: Dean Millsap, 1969. W Couloir: Gustav and Theodore Koven, 1930. SW Ridge: Ed Exum, Peter Koedt, and Al Read, 1963. SE Ridge: Bob Collin, Walter Hermann, Richard Judy, Dave Sanderson, and David Spencer, 1965. Three Cirque Needle, N Rib: Ed and Richard Rumelt, Paul Teplitz, and Norman Toy, 1971.

Dinwoody Glacier

Bastion Peak. FA unknown. SW Ridge: Phil Smith, 1946. NE Face: Tom Warren and others. N Arête: Bob Held and Sam Streibert, 1961. NW Slopes: des by Held and Streibert. N Face: A. H. Jackman and others, 1946.

Rampart Peak. NE Slope: Phil Smith, 1946. E Face: William Farrell, Charles Grant, and David Ragle, 1946.

Mount Koven. S Ridge: H. H. Bliss, Paul Petzoldt, and Henry Clark Smith, 1933. E Face: Frank Gaebelein and Beckett Howorth, 1942. N Ridge: Charles Grant, Jerry More, and Horace Van Valkenburgh, 1946. Sachem: Merrill McLane and Claude Vernon, 1946.

West Sentinel. Arthur Tate and a cowboy, 1920. SW Ridge: Ad Carter and seven others, 1954. Bosom Gully and Peaks: Carter and others, 1950.

Gannett Peak. Gooseneck Route: Floyd Stahlnaker and Arthur Tate, 1922. E Face L: Orrin Bonney and Frank and Notsie Garnick, 1936. E Buttress L: Millie Bennett, W. Degan, Carl Jenson, and Allen Steck, 1947. E Buttress R: Hans and Susan Kraus, Harrison Snyder, and Betsy Woolsey, 1945. NE Ridge: Bob Bates, Ad Carter, John Case, and Waldo Holcombe, 1949. N Face: Henry Hall, Kenneth Henderson, and Robert Underhill, 1929. N Ridge: Floyd Wilson and Walter Wood, 1940. N Shoulder, W Face: Martin Epp and Nels Sanddal, 1969. W Couloir: Bradley Gilman and others, 1934. W Face: Ted Coats, Vince Lee, Jim LaRue, Sam Miles, Stuart Phillips, and others, 1976. W Face R: Fred Beckey and Dan Davis, 1962. W Face-S Ridge: Ray Parks, 1928. S Ridge: G. Gambs and Floyd Wilson, 1936.

Pinnacle Ridge. N Ridge: H. H. Bliss and Paul Petzoldt, 1933. S Ridge: William Farrell, Phil, Phil Jr., and Rodney Smith, 1946. E Couloir: Beckett Howorth and Betty Woolsey, 1944.

Mount Woodrow Wilson. N Couloir: Albert Bessine, Edgar Doll, and Carol Thompson Jones, 1924. W Couloir: Henry Dobnick and Frank and Notsie Garnick, 1935. S Face: Hans Kraus, Harrison Snyder, and Roger Wolcott, 1946. S Couloir: Henry Buchtel, Jack Seerley, and Dudley Smith, 1930. NE Tower: Vince Lee and others.

The Sphinx. NW Ridge: des by Kenneth Henderson and Robert Underhill. SE Ridge: Henderson and Underhill, 1929; complete ridge: Hans and Susan Kraus and Harrison Snyder, 1945. NE Ridge: Chuck Satterfield, R. Karsten, C. Schooler, and A. Wilson, 1971. N Couloir: John Maguire and Floyd Wilson, 1940. N Face: Vince Lee, Jim Barefoot, D. Guggenheim, and G. McPherson, 1971.

Skyline Peak. Hans and Susan Kraus and Harrison Snyder, 1945.

Bob's Towers. N Faces: Robert and Miriam Underhill, 1939. W Gully: Underhills, 1939.

Miriam Peak. NE Slope: des by Robert and Miriam Underhill, 1939. W Ridge: Underhills, 1939

Dinwoody Peak. W Slope: Arthur Bent, Eric Jackson, and Jeffries Wyman, 1922. E Chimney: Henry Hall, Kenneth Henderson, and Robert Underhill, 1929. NE Couloir: Greg Collins, Rob Hess, and another. N Couloir: des by Ad Carter and six others, 1950.

Doublet Peak. S Chimney: Henry Hall, Kenneth Henderson, and Robert Underhill, 1929. Les Dames Couloir: Ad Carter, Bob Held, Sam Streibert, and eleven others, 1961. W Face: des by Hall, Henderson, and Underhill.

Les Dames Anglaises. W Pinnacle: Hans Kraus and Roger Wolcott, 1946. Middle Pinnacle: Kraus and Wolcott, 1946. E Pinnacle: Kraus, Delphine Wilde, and Wolcott, 1946.

Mount Warren. E Ridge: Carl Blaurock and Albert Ellingwood, 1924. NE Face: Allen Steck and three others, 1947. NW Couloir: Keith Goody and others. NW Buttress: Hans and Susan

Kraus and Harrison Snyder, 1943. W Ridge: des by Henry Hall, Kenneth Henderson, and Robert Underhill, 1929. Snow Snake Couloir: Ken Clanton, Walter Fish, Stacey Michael, and Will Waterman, 1976.

Turret Peak. N Ridge: des by Kenneth Henderson and Robert Underhill. NW Face: Hank Coulter, Beckett Howorth, and Charlie Webb, 1940. W Couloir: Carl Blaurock and Albert Ellingwood, 1924. SW Ridge: Henderson and Underhill, 1929. SE Face: Geof Heath and others, 1969. E Ridge: Bruce Barrus, Geoff Loftus, Craig McNamera, and Nancy Westlund, 1969.

Sunbeam Peak. NE Ridge: Pauline Clare, Donald Grant, Charles Lobeck, and Ruth Phillips, 1938. NW Couloir: Jim Donini and others, 1977. SW Ridge: John Reed and others, 1960.

East Sentinel. W Couloir: des by Ad Carter. NE Ridge: Carter and six others, 1956. N Gully: Carter, Lamont Copeland, John Hewett, and others, 1950.

Mount Febbas. NE Slope: Arthur Tate, 1920. Fourt's Horn: George Bell and Denny Fox, 1949. The Finger: A. Cannon, Ken Clanton, S. Gipe, J. Hall, and J. Lewis, 1969. Chimney Rock Ridge: Martin Epp, Jim Halfpenny, and Ernst von Allman, 1969.

Dry Creek Ridge. J. Bowie, 1936.

Peak Lake

New Fork Canyon. Knucklebuster: Tim Toula and Jacob Valdez, 1990. China Wall L: Keith Cattabriga and Lars Moeller, 1990. China Wall R: Cattabriga and Moeller, 1990. Ra Mountain: Greg Collins and three others, 1985. Frenzic Fang: Andy Carson and Mike Weis. Park Place Buttress: John Gottman and Greg Janiec (R Variation), 1979; Gottman and Bill Wallner (Free Variation), 1979.

Dome Peak. E Slope-N Ridge: Surveyors, 1905. Bluebell Buttress: Dave Klein and Reid Sanders, 1995. Cruise Control: Klein and Sanders, 1995.

Hidden Lakes Massif. Palmer Creek Buttress: Fred Beckey, Brian Litz, and David Weber, 1990.

Pinnacle 11,400+. Paul Bacon, Gus Benner, Phil Berry, Emily Hatfield, and Esther Zahniser, 1958.

Glover Peak. E Ridge: J. J. Copeland, 1939. N Summit: Finis Mitchell and two others, 1974.

Mount Oeneis. SW Ridge: David Bigelow, J. J. Copeland, Alexander Klots, and Anthony Ladd, 1939. E Face: des by Copeland and Klots. W Slope: des by Bigelow and Ladd.

Sky Pilot Peak. SE Gully: Andy Carson and P. Nichols, 1967. N Ridge: Gerald Marsden, Dave Sanderson, and David Spencer, 1965. NW Gully: Rick Rochelle and others, 1993.

G-14. Alexander Klots, 1939.

Ladd Peak. E Ridge: Evans Clark, Freida Kirchway, William Ladd, and Adolf Schultz, 1921. N Couloir: Stan Hilbert and Bill March, 1974. S Slope-W Ridge: Finis Mitchell.

Mount Whitecap: NW Ridge: Kenneth Henderson and Robert Underhill, 1930. SW Couloir: des by Henderson and Underhill.

G-3. S Buttress: Dan Robeson and three others, 1993.

G-4. Gustav and Theodore Koven and Paul Petzoldt, 1931.

Split Mountain. W Face: Gustav and Theodore Koven and Paul Petzoldt, 1931. S Face: Stan Hilbert and Bill March, 1974.

Twin Peaks. SE Couloir: Henry Buchtel and Dudley Smith, 1930. NE Couloir: Tom Warren and others. N Face: Norm Larson and others. W Ridge: Allen Drew and John Murray, 1936. SW Twin, SW Face: Gustav and Theodore Koven and Paul Petzoldt, 1931. SW Twin, SE Face: William Alexander and Jay Goodwin, 1983.

Winifred Peak. N Ridge: Arthur Tate, 1919. NE Couloir: Gerry Holdsworth and Ted Vaill, 1964.

G-17. SE Slope: Orville Crowder, Griffith Johnson, and Gordon Redmond, 1934. NW Ridge: Paul Horton and Dick Olmstead, 1890. S Pinnacle: Tom Warren and Bob Boltin, 1969.

American Legion Peak. W Ridge: Gustav and Theodore Koven and Paul Petzoldt, 1931. S Ridge: Stan Hilbert and Bill March, 1974. SE Ridge: Henry Buchtel, Jack Seerley, and Dudley Smith, 1930.

Mount Arrowhead. E Ridge: Gustav and Theodore Koven and Paul Petzoldt, 1931. NE Rib: Fred Beckey and Andy Carson, 1975. N Face: Steve Drake and Ronald Van Horssen, 1983. W Ridge: Martin Epp, D. Larson, Nels Sanddal, and B. Smith, 1969. SW Ledges: Vince Lee and others. S Face Far L: Danny and Paul Horton, Art Lang, and Bert Stolp, 2000. S Face L: Fred Beckey and Pat Callis, 1969. S Face Center: Yvon Chouinard and Mark Jenkins, 2001. S Face R: Paul Horton and Dick Olmstead, 1980.

Bow Mountain. SW Face: David Bigelow, Alexander Klots, and Anthony Ladd, 1939. SE Face: des by Bigelow, Klots, and Ladd. Quiver Crack: Paul Horton, Hal Gribble, and Bert Stolp. 2000. E Ridge: Lou Dawson and Michael Kennedy, 1975.

Brimstone Mountain. W Ridge: des by Kenneth Henderson and Robert Underhill. N Ridge: Henderson and Underhill, 1930.

Sulphur Peak. W Gullies: des by Kenneth Henderson and Robert Underhill. S Ridge: Henderson and Underhill, 1930. NE Ridge: Eric Swanson and Bruce Watson, 1982. N Face: Stan Hilbert and Bill March, 1974; Direct Finish: Lou Dawson and Michael Kennedy, 1975. Inner Spire: Henderson and Underhill, 1930. Cutthroat Spire: Dawson and Kennedy, 1975.

Stroud Peak. SE Ridge: Gaylord Hall, 1929. NW Face L: Jim and Tommie Howe, 1986. NW Face R: Fred Beckey and Dan Davis, 1962. W Face: Tom Warren and two others, 1969. W Rib: Richard Morge and two others, 1996.

Titcomb Basin

The Buttress. E Face: Nat Dyke and Mark Jenkins, 2004. NE Ridge: Ken Jern and Tom McCrumm, 1973. N Gully: Tim Wolfe and others.

Henderson Peak. SE Ridge: Kenneth Henderson and seven others, 1936. E Couloirs: Henderson and others, 1936. N Ridge: J. H. Gaines and Fred and Sue Pflughoft, 1987. W Face: Dean Millsap, 1986. S Face: John and Carol Harkness, Rod Harris, Carol Karps, and Ed Spray.

Garnicks' Needle. W Face: des by Orrin Bonney, Adolph and Rudolph Dobnick, and Frank and Notsie Garnick. S Ridge: Robert and Miriam Underhill, 1939. SE Face: Bonney, Dobnicks, and Garnicks, 1939. E Ridge: Tom McCrumm and Tinker Peters, 1973. NE Face: Ken Andrasko and George Meyers, 1968.

Titcomb Needles. Trident, S Ridge: Orrin Bonney and Frank and Notsie Garnick, 1939. Trident, E Face: Jay Orear and Bill Primak, 1967. Thimble: Bonney and Garnicks, 1939. Vertex: Robert and Miriam Underhill, 1939. Point 1: Underhills, 1939. Minor Needles: Underhills, 1939.

Point 12,560+. Finis Mitchell.

Point 12,450. Finis Mitchell.

Point 12,161. Dr. and Mrs. Beckett Howorth, 1936. S Face: Donnie Black and others.

Spearhead Pinnacle. D. McGrew and W. Witcher, 1960.

Forked Tongue Pinnacle. Ken Clanton, H. Bowron, and R. Pope, 1968.

Mount Helen. SE Couloir–E Ridge: des by Carl Blaurock, Herman Buhl, and Albert Ellingwood. E Ridge: Blaurock, Buhl, and Ellingwood, 1924. NW Face, L Gully: Bill Dougall, Mark Haun, and Jon Hisey, 1960. NW Face, R Gully: Bob Bell, Kenn Carpenter, and Monte Haun, 1960. La Mirada de la Gitana: Craig Pope and Pete Tapley, 2010. Tower 1 Gully: Ray Jacquot and Bill Lindberg, 1971. Tower 1, NW Ridge: Dean Hannibal, Dennis Turville, and Lynn Wheeler, 1974. Tower 1, W Face L: Greg Collins and Mike Kehoe, 1981. Tower 1, W Face Center: Fred Beckey, Bill Lahr, and Craig Martinson, 1976. Tower 1, W Face R: Ken Andrasko and Elwood Root, 1968. Tower Ridge: Hans Kraus and Roger Wolcott, 1946. S Ridge: Eleanor Davis, Ellingwood, Stephen Hart, and Marion Warner, 1926.

Mount Sacagawea. NE Spur: Ad Carter and seven others, 1951. N Ridge: des by Eleanor Davis, Albert Ellingwood, Stephen Hart, and Marion Warner. W Face L: Tom Warren and two others, 1975. Indian Paintbrush: Oliver Deshler and Mark Jenkins, 2011. W Face R: Michael Kennedy and Chris Landry, 1976. Dixie Chickens: Jamie and William Anderson, 1998. S Summit, W Face: Fred Beckey and Pat Callis, 1969; Left of Wishbone: Donnie Black, Guy Toombes, and Jay Wilson; Right Branch: Tom Eggen, 1975. S Couloir: Davis, Ellingwood, Hart, and Warner, 1926.

Fremont Peak. SW Slope: John C. Fremont, de Coteau (or Descoteaux), Johnny Janisse, Basil Lajeunesse, Clement Lambert, and Charles Preuss, 1842. Thin Red Line: Jim Kanzler and Al Maiuro, 1988; FFA: Lorna Corson and Norm Larson, 1996. Orange Spur: John Hooper and Steve McKinney, 1963. S Face: Robert and Miriam Underhill, 1939; Direct Finish: Jerry Hooper and Milo Prodanovich, 1963. Five-Finger Couloir: Guy Toombes, Ed Bradley, and Ron Nahser, 1973. SE Ridge: des by Thelma Bonney, Kenneth Henderson, Walter Howe, Marjorie Hurd, and Helen Spalding, 1936. NW Ridge: perhaps John Cook and Edd Pennock, 1905; Carl Blaurock, Mr. and Mrs. Herman Buhl, and Albert Ellingwood, 1924. W Face, N Buttress: Carla Firey and Jim M. McCarthy, 1977. W Face Spire: Michael Kennedy and Chris Landry, 1976. W Face Dihedral: Landry, 1977. Dark Side of the Moon: Oliver Deshler and Mark Jenkins, 2011. W Buttress: Fred Beckey, Bill Lahr, and Craig Martinson, 1976; FFA Wayne Hansen and Toombs, 1979. Red Tower: Beckey and Pat Callis, 1969. Red Tower Arête: Jenkins, 2011.

Jackson Peak. Possibly Kit Carson, 1842. SE Ridge: Orville Crowder, Grace and Griffith Johnson, James Lamb, Gordon Readmond, and Jeanette Speiden, 1934. N Face L: Bill Thompson and others, 1969. N Face Central: Jack Clinton and Joe Kelsey, 1979. N Face R: Thompson and others, 1969. S Buttress: Bill Widule, Nancy Savage, John Sellers, and Eila Weisman, 1967. S Gullies: Bradley Gilman and James Nelson, 1934.

Knife Point Mountain. S Slope: Finis Mitchell, 1949. NW Ridge: Albert Ellingwood and Stephen Hart, 1926. SW Ridge: des by Ellingwood and Hart.

Nebraska Point. Bob Bell, Kenn Carpenter, Bill Dougall, Mark and Monte Haun, and Jon Hisey, 1960.

Point 12,480+. R. N. Empson and Charles McLaughlin, 1971.

Not Notch Pinnacle. Lorna Corson, Paul Horton, Joe Kelsey, and Norm Larson, 1996.

Notch Pinnacle. S Gully: Austen Riggs, John Rowe, and Harold Sipperly, 1948. N Gully: Tom Ramer, Bill Thompson, Guy Toombes, and one other.

Ellingwood Peak. NW Couloir: Albert Ellingwood, 1926. SW Ridge: Bob Bell, Kenn Carpenter, Bill Dougall, Mark and Monte Haun, and Jon Hisey, 1960. NE Ridge: Tom Ramer, Bill Thompson, Guy Toombes and one other. N Arête: Bob Bauman, 1967.

Faler Tower. NW Ridge: Bob Bell, Kenn Carpenter, Bill Dougall, Mark and Monte Haun, and Jon Hisey, 1960. SW Face: Jim and William Petroske, 1983. Point 12,456: R. N. Empson and Charles McLaughlin, 1971.

Elephant Head. S Gully: Joe Feltner and L. W. Sprague, 1927. E Ridge: Kenn Carpenter and others, 1960. NE Couloir: des by Fred Graf, George Pokorny, and Ella and Jack Weisman. N Ridge: Graf, Pokorny, and Weismans, 1967. NW Couloir: Ann Paul, Stephanie Poland, and Bill Thomas, 1963. NW Buttress: Bill Buckingham and Art Davidson, 1962. Packrat: Ken Driese and Mark Jenkins, 2011. W Face: Dave Campbell and two others, 1990. SW Face: Maurice Horn and others.

Mount Lester. Main Peak: Lewis Perkins and seven others, 1930. Middle Peak, N Face: Larry Evans, Rich Ream, and Count Richards, 1962. E Peak, N Face: Dick Ream and Dave Wood, 1962.

Alpine Lakes

Three Brothers. W Ridge: Ad Carter and seven others, 1951. NW Ridge: Tom Warren and others.
Bête Noire. Arkel Erb, 1960.

Firecracker Pinnacles. NW Pinnacle: Ben Franklin, Chris Haig, Jim Halfpenny, and Bob Smith, 1969. SE Pinnacle: Halfpenny and seven others, 1969.

Windy Pinnacle. SE Slope: Bill Eubank, Carl Plassmann, and John Woodworth, 1967. N Face: Tom Warren and others.

Tuveehant Peak. Bill and Chris Eubank, Jim Petroske, Carl Plassmann, and John Woodworth, 1967.

North Wind Peak. Andy Carson and others, 1969.

Eagle Pinnacle. Bill and Chris Eubank, Jim Petroske, Carl Plassmann, and John Woodworth, 1967.

Hoowagant Pinnacle. Jim Petroske, Carl Plassmann, and John Woodworth, 1967.

The Fortress. N Slope: Jack Grenier, Griff June, Harold May, Roy Scharf, and John Woodworth, 1961. E Face, L Edge: Lynne Wolfe, Sean Reinhart, Richard Rosenfeld, and Matt Schoenwald, 1998. 5.6, My Ass: Laura Ordway, Jennifer Cates, and Fabio Oliveira, 1998. E Face: Brents Hawks, Keith Leonard, and others, 1985.

Point 12,818. Finis Mitchell.

Point 12,846. Finis Mitchell, 1975.

Burch Peak. Finis Mitchell and six others, 1975.

Douglas Peak. W Face: des by Harold May, Ray Scharf, and John Woodworth. SE Ridge: May, Scharf, and Woodworth, 1961.

Mount Quintet. W Slope: des by Jack Grenier, Griff June, Harold May, Ray Scharf, and John Woodworth. NE Ridge: Grenier, June, May, Scharf, and Woodworth, 1961.

Peak 12,529. 38 Special: Jim Richards and others.

Angel Peak. Finis Mitchell and three others, 1975.

Peak 12,367. E Rib. Paul Horton and Joe Kelsey, 1996.

Mount Baldy. Ernest Ingersoll, A. D. Wilson, and Harry Yount, 1877.

Mount Victor. Harry Lovatt, 1930. S Ridge: Scott Richardson and three others.

Europe Peak. Finis Mitchell, 1949.

Point 11,245. S Face: Theresa Walsh.

Middle Fork Lake

Horseshoe Ridge. Traverse: Tom Warren and others, 1969.

Hall's Mountain. W Slope: des by George Bell and Joe Sargent. SE Ridge: Bell and Sargent, 1949. Hall's Spire: Bell and Sargent, 1949.

Pipe Organ. George Bell, Denny Fox, and Joe Sargent, 1949.

Wolverine Peak. W Slope: J. Bowie, 1936. E Couloir: Tom Warren and others. E Face: Steve Arsenault and Bob Johnson, 1971. The Illness: John Chilton, James Garrett, and Ryan Hokanson, 1999.

Thunderbolt Pinnacle. Maurice Horn and others, 1966.

Lightning Rod Pinnacle. Maurice Horn and others, 1966.

Saddle Mountain. NE Ridge: Maurice Horn and others, 1966. N Buttress: Fred Beckey and Franziska and James Garrett, 1988. Ess Ridge: Andy Carson and Paul Horton, 2001. Pinnacle 12,0450+: Rod Dornan, B. Gamard, Horn, and others, 1966. Hailstorm, SW Ridge: Dornan and Bill McEnnerney, 1966. Hailstorm, N Face: Gamard and Horn, 1966.

Mount Heebeecheeche. S Ridge: des by Bill and Julie Briggs and Emily Flander. NE Ridge: Briggs and Flander, 1965.

North Cleft Peak. Barry Bishop, Dr. and Mrs. Henry Buchtel, Robert Hartsfield, Mary Hitch, David Lavender, and Sayre Rodman, 1950. Giant's Tooth: Joe Faint and Maurice Horn, 1966.

South Cleft Peak. W Ridge: George Bell and Joe Sargent, 1949. W Gully: Barry Bishop, Dr. and Mrs. Henry Buchtel, Robert Hartsfield, Mary Hitch, David Lavender, and Sayre Rodman, 1950. SE Ridge: Bell and Sargent, 1949.

Odyssey Peak. SE Ridge: George Bell and Joe Sargent, 1949. NW Ridge: des by Bell and Sargent.

Prairie Falcon Peak. FA unknown. NE Couloir: Skip Borst, Bob and L. Held, and C. Lenox, 1967. SE Face: Yvon Chouinard and Juris Krisjansons, 1970. NE Face: Steve Arsenault and Bob Johnson, 1971.

Kagevah Peak. NW Ridge: C. M. and Neal Blumenfeld and Finis Mitchell, 1949. NE Ridge: Geof Heath and Nancy Westlund, 1970. N Face: Skip Borst and Bob Held, 1967.

Bailey Peak. Gary Cole and Ray Jacquot, 1963.

Petroleum Peak. Walt Bailey, Gary Cole, Jim Kothe, Dud McReynolds, and David and Gayle Sturdevant, 1957.

Nylon Peak. W Slope: Weir Stewart and Harry Willits, 1946. E Buttress: Dave Hough and Buck Tilley, 1979. E Face: Andy Carson and Paul Horton, 2011. NE Ridge: Barry Bishop, Al Phillips, and Bill Primak, 1950; FFA Mark Robinson. NW Ridge: George Bell, Denny Fox, and Joe Sargent, 1949. Pearl Jammed: Mark Joliff, Rob Maclean, and Fabio Oliveira. SE Summit, S Face: Maurice Horn and K. Loving, 1966. SE Summit, NW Face: Robinson and others. SW Summit, NE Ridge: Horn and Loving, 1966. SW Summit, SW Face: Mike Best.

North Twin Lion. E Face: Martin Epp and others, 1970.

South Twin Lion. S Ridge: Bill Buckingham and Whitney Robinson, 1961; Summit Tower, S Face: T. M. Rawson, 1983.

Sentry Peak. N Face: Reid Sanders and three others, 1995.

Pronghorn Peak. E Couloir: Fred Beckey and Dave Beckstead, 1964. Antelope Arête: Tony Qamar and Charlie Raymond, 1970. Monkeyflower Dome, S Gully: T. Bol, R. Riman, and two others, 1994. Monkeyflower Dome, S Face: Dave Hough and Buck Tilley, 1979. Monkeyflower Dome, SE Ridge: Bol, Riman, and two others, 1994.

Dragon Head. E Face: Fred Beckey, Dave Beckstead, and Layton Kor, 1964. Kooshasha Woosha: Danny Horton, Art Lang, and Dan McCool, 1998.

East Fork Valley

Mount Bonneville. E Face: Weir Stewart and Harry Willits, 1946. NE Ridge: Ken Clanton and David Neary, 1975. N Summit, NW Face: Joe Kelsey and Buck Tilley, 1979. Straight Chimney–Pinnacle: Tony Qamar and Charlie Raymond, 1970. Curving Chimney: Fred Beckey and Dave Beckstead, 1964. W Face, R Edge: Dave Hough and Tilley, 1979. S Summit, W Arête: Tenney Cannon and Craig Cutler, 1981. S Summit, W Face: Qamar and Raymond, 1970. S Summit, S Ridge: Carol and Peter Lenz, 1990. S Summit, S Gully: W. H. Bolinger, Joe Feltner, and L.W. Sprague, 1927. S Summit, E Arête: Andy Carson and others. Summit Traverse: Qamar and Raymond, 1970.

Peak 12,000+. SW Ridge: B. Evenson, C. James, D. Kaufman, and S. Walker, 1968. W Face Dihedral: Tenney Cannon and Craig Cutler, 1981. W Face: Beverly Boynton and Joe Kelsey, 1992.

Raid Peak. Perhaps William Owen, 1890. N Slope: Weir Stewart and Harry Willits, 1946. SW Slope: J. Bowie, 1936. S Buttress, S Face: Tom Warren and others. S Buttress, E Face: Steve Arsenault and John Bouchard, 1972. S Buttress R: Charlie Fowler and Dan Stone, 1983. E Face: Fred Beckey, Pat Callis, and Gordon McFeters, 1969. Son of Raid: James Garrett and Felix Hörmann, 2009.

Ambush Peak North. E Face: Andrew Embick and Del Langbauer, 1974. McMuffin: Chuck Calef and Thomas Leitner, 1998. Triple Shot: Franziska and James Garrett, 2009. Great Grey Book: Chris Abbott and Tim Wolfe, 1998.

Ambush Peak. S Ridge: Jimmy Chin and two others, 1998. E Chimney: Fred Beckey, Pat Callis, and Gordon McFeters, 1969. Runnel Out: Chris Abbott and Tim Wolfe, 1998. California!: Rich Romano and Chuck Calef, 1990s. I Think, Therefore I Ambush: Madeleine Sorkin and Chris Barlow, 2011. Wish You Were Here: Calef and Thomas Leitner, 1998. Plaisir: Franziska and James Garrett, 2009. NE Face L: Steve Arsenault and Larry Young, 1971; FFA: Renan Ozturk and Cedar Wright, 2006. Hole in the Wall: Steve Arsenault and John Bouchard, 1994. Dike Route: Mark and Steve Arsenault, 2005. Attack of the Killer Clowns, Ozturk and Wright, 2006. No Picnic for Old Men: Steve Arsenault and Bouchard, 1972; FFA Jack Tackle. Golden Dihedral: Steve Arsenault, Charlie Fowler, and Mike Munger, 1977.

Mount Geikie. William Owen, 1890. E Slope-SEW Ridge: John Coover, Ward Wickwire, and Eberhard Zeh, 1973. E Rib: Steve Bassnett and Nigel Peacock, 1972.

Midsummer Dome. N Side: P. E. and Sue Stevenson, 1969. SW Face: Andrew Embick, David Goeddel, and Jack Norris, 1974. S Face L: Embick and Del Langbauer, 1974. S Face Diagonal: Charlie Fowler and Mike Munger, 1977. S Face Center: Dick DuMais and Dick Williams, 1971. S Face R: Dave Erickson and Roger Wiegand, 1975. SE Face: Embick and Langbauer, 1974.

Glissade Peak. E Ridge: Bill Buckingham, 1961. S Ridge: des by Buckingham.

Tower Peak. S Slope: P. E. and Sue Stevenson, 1969. N Couloir: des by Bill Buckingham. NW Ridge: Buckingham, 1961. S Tower, W Face: Buckingham, Dick DuMais, Walt Jones, Marilyn Pontius, and Lew Surdam. S Tower, SE Ridge: William Cropper and John Dietschy, 1955.

Pyramid Peak. SW Ridge: des by Bradley Gilman. N Slope: Gilman and another, 1934.

Dike Mountain. W Slope: Bill and Sheila Holmes and B. Metzger, 1946. S Ridge: Finis Mitchell, 1930.

Bernard Peak. S Slope: Finis Mitchell, 1930. NW Ridge: des by Mitchell. N Face: Jim Ratz and others.

Mount Washakie. NW Ridge: Finis Mitchell, 1930. SE Ridge: Alma and Max Eberli, Bob McMahon, and Bill and Karl Mygdal, 1953.

Bair Peak. SW Slope: Finis Mitchell, 1933. E Slope: Alma and Max Eberli, Bob McMahon, and Bill and Karl Mygdal, 1953. NW Ridge: des by Eberlis, McMahon, and Mygdals.

August 16th Peak. J. I. Hoffman, 1931. W Slope: Orrin Bonney and Frank and Notsie Garnick, 1940.

Baptiste Lake

Wykee Peak. S Summit, SE Face: Fred Beckey and Eric Bjornstad, 1974.

Roberts Mountain. E Face: Fred Beckey, Mark Meng, and Doug Randall, 1978. East Couloir: Andy Carson and others. Undistinguished Tower: Paul Horton and Norm Larson, 1998.

Peak 12,255. SE Ridge: Bill Buckingham and Whitney Robinson, 1961. W Slope: des by Buckingham and Robinson.

Renegade Peak. George Bell, Denny Fox, and Joe Sargent, 1949; FFA Gary Cole, Jim Kothe, and David Sturdevant, 1957.

Mount Lander. Walt Bailey and others, 1957. W Ridge: Bill Buckingham and Whitney Robinson, 1961. Wobbly Hand-Crack Buttress: Brian Story and brother, 2008. S Couloir: Andy Carson and others.

Cusp Peak. E Slope: des by Bill Buckingham and Whitney Robinson. W Ridge: Buckingham and Robinson, 1961. S Face: Brian and Jonathan Smoot, 1978. Rainy Day Ridge: Brian Story and brother, 2008.

Musembeah, North Peak. Wallflowers: Brian Story and brother, 2008. W Face: Fred Beckey and Layton Kor, 1963.

Musembeah Peak. FA unknown. SW Ridge: William Cropper and John Dietschy, 1955. SE Ridge: des by Bill Buckingham and John Milton. NE Buttress: Fred Beckey, Jerry Fuller, and Dick Ross, 1966. W Buttress: Beckey and Layton Kor (in a storm), 1963; FFA Richard Goldstone and Joe Kelsey (on dry rock), 1976. SW Buttress: Brian Story and brother, 2008. SW Face: Buckingham and Milton, 1961.

Baptiste Lake Tower. S Ridge: William Cropper and John Dietschy, 1955. NW Corner: Bill Buckingham and Lew Surdam.

Peak 12,143. SE Ridge: Bill Buckingham and Whitney Robinson, 1961. NW Ridge: des by Buckingham and Robinson.

Grave Peak. SE Ridge: Bill Buckingham and Whitney Robinson, 1961. NW Ridge: des by Buckingham and Robinson.

Buttressed Mountain. SE Ridge: Bill Buckingham and Whitney Robinson, 1961. NW Couloir: des by Buckingham and Robinson.

Redwall Peak. SW Couloir: Bill Buckingham and Whitney Robinson, 1961. E Face: Fred Beckey and Layton Kor, 1963.

Mount Hooker. E Ledge: William Owen, 1890. Red Light District: Craig Luebben and Tim Toula, 1992. Pay to Play: Jim Hewett and Neeld Messler, 2001. Brain Larceny: Topher Donohue and Kennan Harvey, 1994. Year of the Horse: Kevin Dunkak, Jeff Maus, and Clay Wadman, 1998. Third Eye: John Middendorf and Steve Quinlan, 1992; Free Variation: Dave Sharratt, Pat Goodman, and Taki Miyamoto, 2010. Boissonneault-Larson: Paul Boissonneault and Steve Larson, 1979. Sendero Luminoso: Steve Quinlan. Shady Lady: Rick Bradshaw and Jim Dockery: 1978. N Face, Original Route: Dick McCracken, Charlie Raymond, and Royal Robbins, 1964; Free Variation: Stuart Richie, Mark Rolofson, and Annie Whitehouse (all but 50 feet), 1990; FFA Tim Toula, 1990. NW Passage: Ryan Hokanson and Kirby Spangler, 1998. NW Ridge: des by George Pokorny, Fran Andrews, George Carrington, Bill Dietrich, Allen Drachman, and Mary O'Connor, 1973. SW Face R Side: Sue Cochran, Paul Schwartz, John Serbin, and Olle Swartling, 1973. Loaded for Bear: Brent Edelin and Jakub Gajda, 2001. Hailey Pass Slabs: Dick DuMais and Doug Snively, 1989.

Grave Lake Dome. W Slope: Finis Mitchell, 1933. SE Face L: Faith Aubin and Joe Bridges, 1984. SE Face Center: Fred Beckey and Jerry Fuller, 1966 (lower part); Beckey and Dick Ross, 1968 (upper part); FFA George Schunk, 1978. Closer to the Grave: George Lowe and Carl Tobin, 1993.

Chess Ridge. Obvious Crack: Lorna Corson and Norm Larson, 1995.

Loch Leven Peak. Finis Mitchell, 1960.

Valentine Mountain. Finis and William Mitchell, 1948.

Buffalo Head. NE Chimney: Fred Beckey and Jerry Fuller, 1966. N Buttress: Joe Kelsey and Roman Laba, 1983. Buffalo Rib: Lorna Corson and Norm Larson, 1995. Skeptic: Kath Pyke and Cameron Teague, 1999.

Throne Peak. Scimitar: Jon Allen and Doug Hall, 1994.

Cathedral Peak. W Slope: Finis Mitchell, 1948. S Tower, S Buttress: Chris McNamara and Galen Rowell, 1999. S Tower Direct: McNamara and Rowell, 1999. Orion's Reflection: Fred Beckey and Jim Kanzler, 1979. Flight of the Golden Camalot: Alan Hunt and Jason Keith, 2002.

Cathedral Cirque. Papa Splitter: Phil Powers and others, 1992. Heavy Mettle: Powers, Michael Cheek, Christine Dixon, and Mark Jolliff, 1994. Arts and Sciences: Peter Carse, Terry Hopkins, and Fil Sanna, 1995. Burning Ring of Fire: Jolliff, Jimmy Morris, and Josh Patria, 1997. Conditioned Response: Jolliff and Dixon, 1994. Behavior Modification: Dixon, Jolliff, and Cheek, 1994. Flasher in the Stacks: Jolliff and three others, 1994. Esther Prinn: Jolliff, Mike Barnhart, and Sophie Ragsdale, 1997. Study Hall: Carse and others, 1995. Sweet Lady: Dixon and two others, 1994. Isthmus Dome: Chris McNamara, Galen Rowell, and Randy Spurrier, 1999.

Mount Chauvenet: William Owen, 1890. Moss Lake Buttress: Andy Carson and two others, 1977.

Euphoria Dome. Joy Ride: Joaquin Fox and S. Robertson. Cruisin': Paul Horton and Heather Paul, 2001.

Hobbs Peak. Transmogrifier: Paul Horton and Joe Kelsey, 1996. Positivity: Joaquin Fox and Scott Smalley, 1997.

Mary's Tower. John Britton and Paul Horton, 1998.

Mount Cross. Bradley Gilman and two others, 1934. Scorpion's Trail: Paul Horton and Joe Kelsey, 1996.

Windy Mountain. Charlie Beierwalt and Joe Hawkes, 1953.

Peak 12,258. FA unknown. E Ridge: Joe Kelsey, 1972. W Face: Reid Dowdle and Chris Monz, 1993.

Cirque of the Towers

Lizard Head Peak. W Ridge: Orrin Bonney and Frank and Notsie Garnick, 1940, who found a note on top with the name Drummond and a date in 1933; an arrowhead found near the summit suggests an even earlier ascent. S Face L: des by Bonney and Garnicks. S Face R: Paul Stettner, Max Eberli, Vicki May, and Dick Skultin, 1953. SE Ridge: Chuck Loucks and Michael and Sally Westmacott, 1970. NE Prow L: Fred Beckey and Steve Marts, 1963. NE Prow R: Michael Jackson, Stephanie Petrilak, and Michael Williams, 1979. N Face: Andy Carson, Tom Warren, and ten others, 1967.

Camel's Hump. FA unknown. SW Slope: Orrin Bonney and Frank and Notsie Garnick, 1940. SE Ridge: des by Bonney and Garnicks. NE Face: Ken Clanton, Tom Warren, D. Burleigh, T. Cullen, and B. Pease, 1968.

Peak 11,925. E Ridge: Grover Hartsuch and others, 1953. W Ridge: des by Hartsuch.

Peak 11,840+. SW Ridge: David Lind and two others, 1958. N Ridge: Paul Stettner and eight others, 1953. Smoke on the Water: Tim and Susan Wolfe.

Bollinger Peak. NE Ridge: Norman Clyde, Edith and J. Holliday, and B. Pitcher, 1941. W Face Far L: Steven French and Matt Parramore, 1981. W Face L: Fred Beckey, Dan Davis, and Steve Marts, 1963. On the Lamb: Alan and Keith Cattabriga, 1994. Consolation: Ken Driese and Joe Kelsey, 1982. E Face, L Chimney: Kelsey and Chuck Pratt, 1971. E Face, R Chimney: Beckey and John Hudson, 1961. E Face: Andrew Embick and David Goeddel, 1970.

Wolf's Head. W Face: P. Calcaterra, Robert Chambers, Art Gran, and J. McLeod, 1957. Canis: Dave Anderson and Jamie Selda, 2006. White Buffalo: Greg Collins and Kent McBride, 2006. S Face, 1966 Route: Fred Beckey and Jerry Fuller, 1966; FFA Buck Tilley, 1978. S Face Center R: Rick Miller and friend, 1988. S Face R: Ken Driese and Mike Kehoe, 1981. S Face Far R: George Esson and Jim Montgomery, 1988. E Ridge: Bill Buckingham and Bill Plummer, 1959. NE Face: Fred Beckey and John Rupley, 1962. NW Chimneys: George Bell, Denny Fox, and Joe Sargent, 1949.

Pingora Peak. S Buttress: Wally Green and Bill Primak, 1951. E Ledges: Orrin Bonney and Frank and Notsie Garnick, 1940. E Face, L-Side Cracks: Elaine Mathews (lower part), 1970; Greg Donaldson and Rich Mathies (upper part), 1972. E Face: Fred Beckey, Dan Davis, and Steve Marts, 1963. Southerners and FFA: Tom McMillan and Eric Zschiesche, 1979. NE Face: Harry Daley and Jim Yensan, 1962; FFA Harry Frishman and Juris Krisjansons. Stealing Thunder: James Garrett and Dave Madera, 1994. N Face: Don Lauria, Aaron Schneider, and Ed Speth, 1964. W Face: Beckey, Rich Ream, and Court Richards, 1963;. FFA Pete Ramins, 1971. SW Face L: Joe Kelsey, Chuck Pratt, and Bill St. Jean, 1971. SW Face Center: Howard Friedman and Mike Walley, 1991. SW Face R: Kelsey and Dick Williams, 1972.

Overhanging Tower: W Face and Ridge Tower: William Cropper, John Dietschy, and Harris Tallan, 1955. SW Face: Harry King and Ralph Widrig, 1948. S Ridge: Paul Horton and Bob Myers, 1982.

Shark's Nose. NW Buttress: George Bell, Denny Fox, and Joe Sargent, 1949; FFA William Cropper and John Dietschy, 1955. SW Face: Fred Beckey, Yvon Chouinard, and Ken Weeks, 1960. SW Face-S Ridge: Louis Hock and Larry Winter. N Face L: Beckey, Chouinard, and Weeks, 1960. N Face R: Dave Loeks and Joe Kelsey, 1974.

Block Tower. E Face: Robert Chambers and Art Gran, 1957. NW Face: John Davidge, Felix Hagerman, Warren Pagel, and Olle Swartling, 1958.

Elizabeth Peak. Finis Mitchell, 1932.

Easy Day Peak. N Face: Lester Germer and John Sopka, 1955.

Watch Tower. W Slope: Finis Mitchell, 1919. S Buttress: Charlie Raymond and Royal Robbins, 1964;. FFA: Jonnie Copp and John Merriam, 1997. Hay Fever: Ben Rosenberg and Dave Stewart, 2009. E Gully: des by Karl Bollinger, Jay Orear, and Gaurang Yodh. R Edge of E Gully: Bollinger, Orear, and Yodh, 1953. NE Face: Matt Hale and Dave Roberts, 1968. NE Face, Route 2: Leslie DeMarsh and Paul Stoliker, 1988. NW Ridge: Dick McCracken, Raymond, and Robbins, 1964.

South Watch Tower. S Face: Rich Ream and Court Richards, 1963.

Pylon Peak. W Slope: Finis Mitchell, 1919. SE Gully: Paul Stettner, Grover Hartsuch, Bob McMahon, Dick Skultin, and eight others, 1953.

Bunion Mountain. Finis Mitchell, 1919.

Warrior II. NW Ridge: Bill Primak, Wally Green, Rhoda Huntley, J. Ramsey, and Genevieve Richwalshy, 1951. S Slope: Finis Mitchell, 1919. NE Face: Dan Davis and Steve Marts, 1963. N Face-NW Ridge: Todd Thompson and Doug Tompkins, 1964.

Warrior I. S Slope: Finis Mitchell, 1919. NE Face L: Brent Davis and Evelyn Lees, 1982. NE Face R: Fred Beckey and John Rupley, 1962. NW Face: George and Jeff Lowe, 1970; FFA: Brian Edmiston and Jonathan Thesenga, 2001. Candy Shop: Noah Gostout, Erik Rieger, and Drew Thayer, 2011. Warrior Gully: Jeff Lowe and Scott Etherington.

Warbonnet Peak. S Ridge: H. Johnson, 1941. Weather or Not: Nathan Brown and Jonathan Foster, 2011. Curate's Egg: Stewart Middlemiss and Kevin Smith, 2001. Seams and Dreams: Dave Anderson and Jen Goings, 2003. Neu Low: Chris Barlow and Andy Neuman, 2005. Black Elk: Charlie Fowler and Jeff Lowe, 1981. Lichen Never Sleeps: Pete Absalon and Anderson, 2007. E Face Center: Bill Buckingham and Bill Plummer, 1959. E Face R: Fritz Coester and Paul and Paul Jr. Stettner, 1953. NE Face L: Liz Donley and Cory Fleagle, 2007. NE Face Center: Eric Beck and Steve Roper, 1962. NE Face R: Jim Hagen, Barbara Larsen, Bill Primak, and Olle Swartling, 1964. Feather Buttress: Calum Hudson and Trevor Jones, 1976; FFA Fowler and Lowe, 1980. NW Couloirs: Orrin Bonney and E. Guild, 1941. Plume, W Side: Rich Ream and Court Richards, 1963. Plume, N Face: Todd Thompson and Doug Tompkins, 1964.

Sundance Pinnacle. W Face: T. Hale, B. Metzger, and John Moss, 1946. E Face Center: Anne Ketchin and Gary Ziegler, 1970. Klettershoe Chimney: Doug Robinson and John and Kurt Wehbring, 1966. E Face, R Crack: Jim Olson. NE Arête: Greg Collins, Mal Miller, and Reave Castenholtz, 1982. N Face: Matt Hartman and Jake Tipton, 2012. NW Ridge: Vince Lee, Brett Hudelson, and Andy McMillan, 1977.

Mitchell Peak. S Slope: Finis Mitchell, 1923. N Ledge: Bill Primak and others, 1951. N Face L: Fred Beckey, Yvon Chouinard, and Ken Weeks, 1960. Ecclesiastes: Dick Dorworth and Sibylle Hechtel, 1972. N Face R: Tom Bauman and Elaine Mathews, 1971. NW Face: Larry and Molly Higgins Bruce, 1983. W Slope: Fritz Coester and six others, 1953.

Dog Tooth Mountain. W Slope: Norman Clyde, Edith and J. Holliday, and B. Pitcher, 1941. NE Ridge: Peter Metcalf and Angus Thuermer, 1972. Wisdom Tooth: Ken Nichols and Al Rubin, 1980. A-Frame Buttress: Chuck Pratt and Bill St. Jean, 1970; FFA Steve Quinlan.

Big Sandy Mountain. W Slope: Finis Mitchell, 1933. Tombstone: Peter Metcalf, Glenn Randall, and Angus Theurmer, 1977.

The Monolith. W Couloir: Art Gran, John Hudson, and Doug Tompkins, 1963. N Face: Gran, Hudson, and Tompkins, 1963;. FFA: Ken Nichols and Al Rubin, 1980. NW Face: Fred Beckey and Jerry Fuller, 1966.

Deep Lake

Haystack Mountain. N Gully: des by Mike Ermarth, Rick Reese, and Ted Vaill. N Face: Jack Curtin and John Wells, 1965. Pika Illiteration: Jake Coplen, Jackson Smith, and Jared Spaulding, 2010. Flashflood: Harvey Carter and James Ebert, 1969. N Tower Crack: Geof Heath and Jeff Lowe, 1969. Labor Day: Chris Abbott and Tim Wolfe, 1996. Major Dihedral: Fred Beckey and Jerry Fuller, 1964; FFA Mike Kehoe and Joe Kelsey, 1983. Minor Dihedral: Pete Croff, Phil Fowler, and Richard Schori, 1964. Seams Thin: Abbott and Wolfe, 1995. R-Side Chimneys: Dick Compton and Charles O'Brien, 1970. Grassy Goat Trail: Jim Hagen and Bill Primak, 1964. Railroad Tracks: Kelsey and Bill St. Jean, 1973; FFA Dick Williams, 1974. Grassy Crack: Dick Olmstead and others, 1977. Central Corner: Elaine Mathews and Stuart Phillips, 1973; FFA Richard Goldstone, 1974. Great Chimney: Ermarth, Reese, and Vaill, 1964. Hidden Chimney: St. Jean and Jeannie Walter, 1973. Converging Cracks: Charles Pierce, Pat Armstrong, Gil Parker, John Sellers, Richard Stibolt, and Bill Widule, 1965. Layback: Alan and Keith Cattabriga and Lars Moeller, 1993. Whistlepigs: Cattabrigas, 1993. Chockstone Corner: Donna McBain and Steven Risse, 1985. S Gully: Barbara Larsen and Olle Swartling, 1964. Pitch Off: Abbott and Wolfe, 1995. S Wall Center: Kelsey, Dave Loeks, and Williams, 1974; FFA Charlie Fowler, 1983. S Wall R: Jim Beyer, 1979. Far Side: Norm Larson and Lorna Corson, 1996. S Ridge: John Hudson and Bruce Monroe, 1961. SE Face: McBain and Risse, 1985. E Pillar: Phil Fowler and Keith Goody, 1973. E Face: Kenny Hibbits and Skip Yates, 1976. NE Face: Gil Parker, Eila and Jack Weisman, and Widule, 1965.

Steeple Peak. S Ridge: Yvon Chouinard, Art Gran, and John Hudson, 1961. E Ridge: Alan Bartlett, David Black, and Rick Bradshaw, 1979. N Ridge: Gary Cole and Don Ryan, 1963. Main Dihedral: Chris Abbott and Susan and Tim Wolfe, 1995. W Face: Stephen Pollock and brother, 1977.

Lost Temple Spire. SW Arête: Stan Mish, Guy Toombes, and Jay Wilson, 1980. Separation Anxiety: Kirk Billings and Ty Mack, 1997. N Prow: Fred Beckey and John Hudson, 1961; FFA ?. W Face-1986 Route: Dave Anderson and James Garrett. W Face-1993 Route: Alan and Keith Cattabriga.

East Temple Peak. SW Slope: Finis Mitchell, 1933. NE Face: Alan Bartlett, David Black, and Rick Bradshaw, 1979. NW Face: Yvon Chouinard and Art Gran, 1961. NW Face, R Side: Mike Ermarth, Brad Merry, Ron Shrigley, Stu Turner, and Ted Vaill, 1964. From the NW: Al Rubin.

Temple Peak. SW Slope: George Chittenden, Edward Clymer, Frederick Endlich, and Charles Howes, 1877. S Ridge: D. Hatch, D. Koontz, J. Lander, and Jim Toler, 1961. NE Chutes: Al Brooks, Britta Lindgren, Charles and Peggy Pierce, John Sellers, and Olle Swartliing, 1965. NE Buttress: Eric Eliason and Jeff Lowe, 1988. N Face L: Fred Beckey, Paul Guaharddo, Carl Horton, and David Weber, 1988. N Face R: Weir Stewart and Harry Willits, 1946. Last Go Round: Mike Anderson, Steve Bechtel, and Ty Mack, 2009. NW Buttress: Harvey Carter and James Ebert, 1969. NW Ridge: Rod Harris, Swartling, and Charles Wiltfong, 1965.

A Cheval Peak. SE Slope: Jim Hagen, Barbara Larsen, Bill Primak, and Olle Swartling, 1964. Cloudburst Buttress: Fred Beckey, Reid Dowdle, and Jeff Niwa, 1991. N Ridge: des by Swartling and others, 1965. S Ridge: Gordon Quivey, Craig Sautter, and Bill Widule, 1965.

Schiestler Peak. SW Slope: Finis Mitchell, 1933. E Face, L Edge: Athan Pontsios, Eila and Jack Weisman, and Bill Widule, 1965. E Face L: Dave Craft, Dave Loeks, and Dick Williams, 1974. Inverted S: Harvey Carter, James Ebert, and Thomas O'Brien, 1969. Red BVD: Chuck Armstong and Nancy Savage, 1965. Northern Pacific: Armstrong, John Wells, and others, 1965. Along for the Ride: Lorna Corson, Norm Larson, and Callum Mackay, 1996.

Independent Mountain. Finis Mitchell, 1933.

South Pass

Divide Plateau. Point 11,169, NW Face: Yvon Chouinard, Juris Krisjansons, and Rick Ridgeway, 1980.

Little El Capitan. W Face: Phil Fowler and Keith Goody, 1973. SE Face: Jeff Alzner and Bob McGown, 1991.

Wind River Peak. S Slope: Ernest Ingersoll, A. D. Wilson, and Harry Yount, 1877. Ice Lakes Wall: Joe Kelsey and Mark Whiten, 1985. NE Ridge: Theodore Comstock, L. Hardy, and J. D. Putnam, 1873. Streaked Wall: Bob McGown and Jim Olson, 1984. Tempest Tower: McGown and Olson, 1984. N Buttress: Fred Beckey and Jim Stoddard, 1968. W Gully: des by Robert Cote, Dan Moore, Fritz Moyer, Athan Pantsios, and Robert Sautter, 1965. Black Joe-Little Sandy Divide: Woody Stark and Dick Webster, 1976.

Continental Towers. Aristeia: Trevor Bowman and Nick Stayner, 2001. Central Tower, N Ridge: Paul Horton and Joe Kelsey, 1994. Central Tower, E Chimney: Fred Beckey and Bob Stevenson, 1967. S Tower: FA?. NW Arête: Horton and Kelsey, 1994. Continental Drifters: Bowman and Stayner, 2007.

Little Sandy Formations. Little Sandy Buttress, E Face: Fred Beckey and Bob Stevenson, 1967. King Cone, W Face: Trevor Bowman and Nick Stayner, 2001. King Cone, NE Ridge: Norm Larson, Peter Quinlan, and Greg Sandler, 1994. Western Tower 11,320+: Bowman and Stayner, 2001. Tower 11,440+: Bowman and Stayner, 2001. Gold Dihedrals: Yvon Chouinard, TM Herbert, and Juris Krisjansons, 1971. Symbiosis: Ian Duncan, Jason Keith, and Aubin McCarthy, 1993.

Mount Nystrom. NW Slope: Finis Mitchell, 1952. W Face of NW Ridge: Ian Duncan, Jason Keith, and Aubin McCarthy, 1993. S Slope: Mitchell, 1922. Anvil Arête: Joe Kelsey and Mark Whiten, 1986. NE Summit, S Face: Fred Beckey, Tenney Cannon, and Glied Toombes, 1981. NE Summit, SE Buttress: Beckey and Kirt Cozzens, 1984.

Roaring Fork Mountain West. Stough Creek Pinnacle: Tom Warren and others.

Roaring Fork Mountain East. Big Red Buttress: Greg Collins and partner, 1993.

West Atlantic Peak. W Slope: A. D. Wilson and Harry Yount, 1877.

Atlantic Peak. George Chittenden, Edward Clymer, Frederick Endlich, and Charles Howes, 1877.

Silas Peak. Finis Mitchell. Twenty-Year Crack: Jay Miller and Gary Wise, 1999.

Appendix B: 12,000-Foot Summits

One-hundred nineteen Wind River summits are higher than 12,000 feet and rise at least 400 feet above any saddle joining them to a higher peak.

Gannett Peak	13,804
Fremont Peak	13,745
Mount Warren	13,722
Mount Helen	13,620
Turret Peak	13,600
Mount Sacagawea	13,569
Jackson Peak	13,517
Mount Woodrow Wilson	13,502
Bastion Peak	13,494
Mount Febbas	13,468
Flagstone Peak	13,450
Sunbeam Peak	13,440
Downs Mountain	13,349
Mount Koven	13,265
American Legion Peak	13,205
Bête Noire	13,198
Wind River Peak	13,192
Twin Peaks	13,185
Desolation Peak	13,155
Split Mountain	13,155
Henderson Peak	13,115
Klondike Peak	13,114
Unnamed (1.0 E Kevin Lake)	13,062
Ellingwood Peak	13,052
Mount Whitecap	13,020
Bow Mountain	13,020
Knife Point Mountain	13,001
Mount Arrowhead	12,972
Temple Peak	12,972
Three Brothers	12,960
Ladd Peak	12,957
Unnamed (2.0 NE Wall Lake)	12,846
G-4	12,845
Lizard Head Peak	12,842
Yukon Peak	12,825
Little El Capitan	12,825

Winifred Peak	12,775
Roberts Mountain	12,767
Unnamed (1.4 N Snowbridge Lake)	12,730
Dry Creek Ridge	12,720
Philsmith Peak	12,670
Wolverine Peak	12,631
Mount Lander	12,623
East Temple Peak	12,600
Musembeah Peak	12,593
West Sentinel	12,585
Mount Bonneville	12,585
Saddle Mountain	12,551
North Cleft Peak	12,548
Windy Mountain	12,539
Raid Peak	12,532
Unnamed (0.5 NW Tiny Glacier)	12,529
Mount Washakie	12,524
Unnamed (0.4 NW Klondike Lake)	12,512
Mount Hooker	12,504
Mount Zebadia	12,495
Throne Peak	12,490
Atlantic Peak	12,490
Dog Tooth Peak	12,488
Mitchell Peak	12,482
Hall's Mountain	12,475
Renegade Peak	12,470
Dike Mountain	12,468
Unnamed (2.3 NE Brown Cliffs)	12,431
Big Sandy Mountain	12,416
Warrior II	12,406
Angel Peak	12,402
Nylon Peak	12,392
Pronghorn Peak	12,388
Mount Geikie	12,378
Pylon Peak	12,378
Unnamed (0.4 SSE Angel Pass)	12,367
Glissade Peak	12,360
Mount Nystrom	12,356
Mount Lester	12,342
Bair Peak	12,335
Cathedral Peak	12,326
Musembeah North Peak	12,320

Bear's Tooth	12,294
Unnamed (1.0 SW Tepee Pass)	12,285
Chess Ridge	12,279
Mount Lester, East Summit	12,275
Europe Peak	12,259
Grave Peak	12,255
Mount Victor	12,254
Mount Chauvenet	12,250
Silas Peak	12,248
Unnamed (0.6 N Lizard Head Peak)	12,240
Timico Peak	12,236
Spider Peak	12,234
Mount Oeneis	12,232
Bollinger Peak	12,232
Milky Ridge	12,230
Unnamed (0.8 WNW Hall's Mountain)	12,230
Pipe Organ	12,225
August 16th Peak	12,220
The Buttress	12,205
Stroud Peak	12,198
Douglas Peak	12,192
Ambush Peak North	12,187
Torrey Peak	12,181
Unnamed (0.8 ESE Tepee Pass)	12,175
Bailey Peak	12,170
Unnamed (0.9 SE Pipe Organ)	12,162
Elephant Head	12,160
Windy Ridge (1.4 N Enos Lake)	12,156
Horseshoe Ridge	12,128
Kagevah Peak	12,127
Unnamed (0.8 S Payson Peak)	12,120
Divide Plateau	12,105
Unnamed (0.8 WSW Baker Lake)	12,082
Glover Peak	12,068
Unnamed (0.7 NE Klondike Lake)	12,065
Odyssey Peak	12,062
Wykee Peak	12,055
Round Top Mountain	12,048
Steeple Peak	12,040
Divide Plateau, North Summit	12,036
Pyramid Peak	12,030

Index

About the Author

Growing up in the East, Joe Kelsey began rock climbing in New York's Shawangunks in 1962. In 1969 Joe hiked into the Cirque of the Towers, to join a group of rock climbing friends, headed for Wolf's Head and Pingora and felt that he'd found his home. He has spent part of every summer since climbing and wandering in the Wind Rivers. In 2011 he backpacked to Pyramid Lake, Indian Basin, and the Bonneville Lakes and hiked a loop from Spring Creek Park to Elkhart Park via the Jean Lakes; in 2012 he spent time at Cook Lakes and Borum Lake. During his early Cirque days in the 1970s he stumbled into guidebook writing. Several friends, for one another's benefit, wrote up routes they did, collecting them in a notebook for which he became custodian. One winter he copied reports from mountaineering journals and added them to the notebook, thus unintentionally becoming an author. The first edition of the guidebook was published in 1981, the second in 1994.

Since 1972 Joe has based his Wind River excursions from a cabin in Jackson Hole, also his base when guiding for Exum for 20 years. He winters in Bishop, California, at the base of the Sierra Nevada.

PROTECTING CLIMBING **ACCESS** SINCE 1991

| JOIN US |

WWW.ACCESSFUND.ORG